THE DRAGON IN THE LAND OF SNOWS

THE DRAGON IN THE LAND OF SNOWS

A History of Modern Tibet Since 1947

TSERING SHAKYA

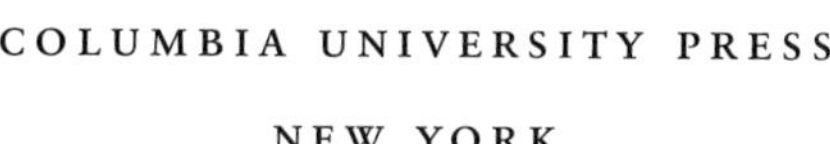

COLUMBIA UNIVERSITY PRESS

NEW YORK

Columbia University Press
Publishers Since 1893
New York

First published in Great Britain in 1999 by Pimlico

Library of Congress Cataloging-in-Publication Data
Shakya, Tsering.
The dragon in the land of snows : a history of modern Tibet / Tsering Shakya.
p. cm.
Includes bibliographical references and index.
ISBN 0-231-11814-7 (acid-free)
1. Tibet (China)—History—20th century.
I. Title. II. Title: History of modern Tibet
DS786.S49 1999
951'.505—dc21 99-14020

Casebound editions of Columbia University Press books are
printed on permanent and durable acid-free paper.
Printed in the United States of America
c 10 9 8 7 6 5 4 3

for Lhamo

CONTENTS

Illustrations

For kind permission to reproduce illustrations, the author and publishers wish to thank the following: Department of Information and International Relations, Dharamsala: 13; Roger McCarthy: 8; New World Press: 2 (from *Tibet Transformed* by Israel Epstein, 1983); The Nihon Kogyo Shimbun: 4, 9 (from *Tibet in Turmoil 1950–1959*); Potala Corporation: 1 (from *My Land and My People* by The Dalai Lama, 1985); Vladimír Sís and Josef Vaniš: 5 (© 1954); Tibet Images: 3, 6, 7, 10, 11, 12 (DIR), 15 (Stone Routes), 16 (Rajiv Mehrota), 17 (I. Greve); Tibet Information Network: 14.

Every effort has been made to trace or contact copyright holders. The publishers will be pleased to correct any mistakes or ommissions in future editions.

Acknowledgements

It has taken me a long time to finish this book and in the process I have accumulated a large number of debts to my friends and family for their support and for the inspiration they have provided.

My thanks must go to the Director of the LTWA (Dharamsala), Gyatso Tshering-la, and to the members of staff for allowing me unrestricted access to the material in their possession. While I was in Darjeeling, Mrs Norbu helped me to locate and arrange interviews with former Tibetan Government officials.

There are a great many individuals who agreed to be interviewed and have expressed a wish to remain anonymous. I wish to thank them for their encouragement and support in the course of my research. I must also thank Ather Norbu, Drungyig Lhamo Tsering and Phuntsog Tashi Takla, for readily answering many of my queries, as well as Pasang Gyalpo (alias Diwa Lang), Chatreng Tsultrim, Baba Lekshe, Ngawang Dhundup Narkyid and Dagyab Rinpoche.

I would also like to thank Hugh Richardson, Robert Ford, Professor Dawa Norbu of JNU (New Delhi), Michael Aris of St Antony's College, Oxford and Colina MacDougal who read early drafts of the manuscript and made valuable suggestions.

I would like to thank the following people for their help: Tashi Daknewa, Tenzin Gelek, Tsering Dhundup (Gyen la), Tenzin Sonam, Ritu Sarin, Dechen Pemba, Lhakpa Dolma, Jigme Pemba, and Tsewang Pemba.

I am especially indebted to James Cooper, Mary Charrington, Catriona Bass and Robert Barnett who read through the manuscript and made a great many improvements. In addition I must thank Christophe Besuchet of Atelier Golok for preparing the maps for the book. I would also like to thank the staff at the Public Records Office, Kew (London).

My deepest thanks must go to my wife, Lhamo, who has supported me throughout this project without a word of complaint. It is not too much to say that without her unwavering support and care I would have been unable to complete this book. She has sacrificed so much so that I could pursue my interest and see this in print. I would like to think that the book is as much her labour as it has been mine.

Ethnic Tibet (20th century)

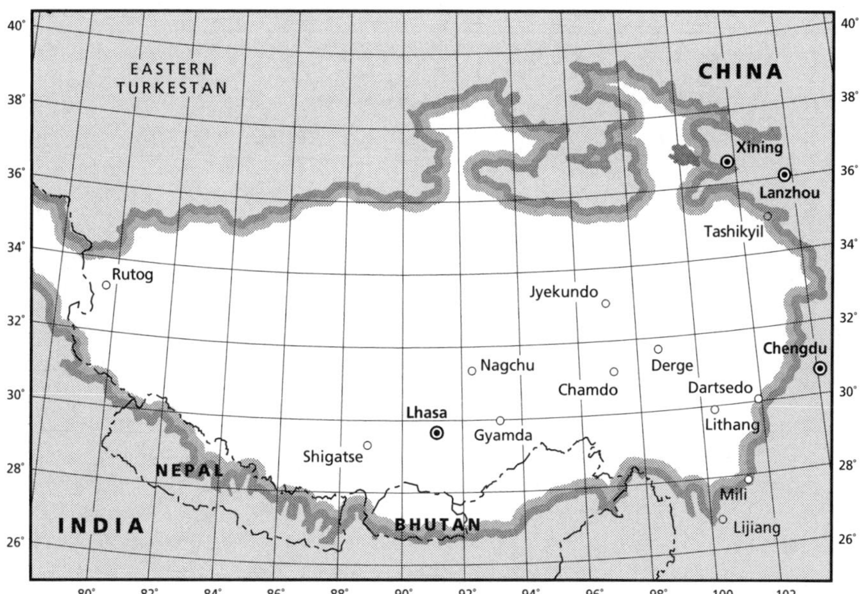

Areas with Tibetan autonomous status under regional and prefectural administration (since 1965)

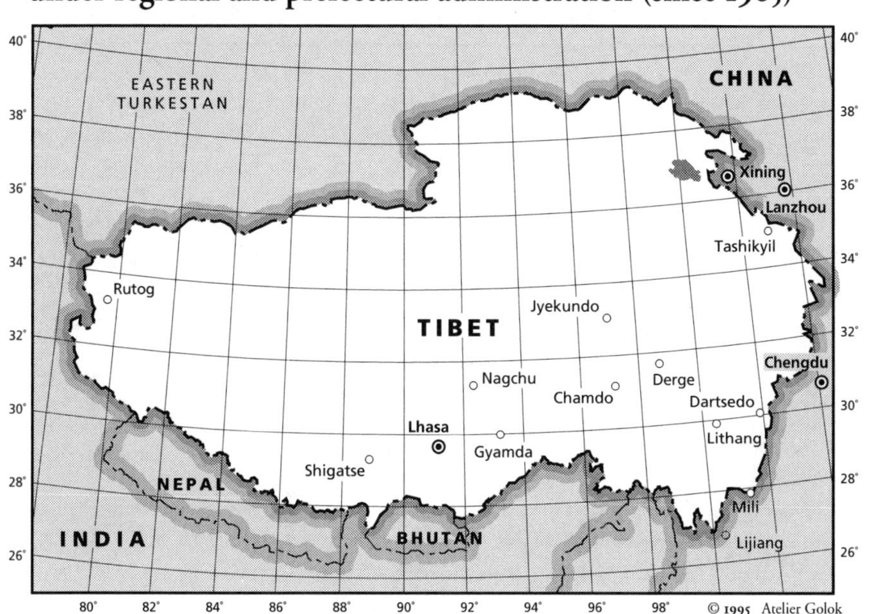

Frontier of Tibet as claimed by Tibetans in 1914

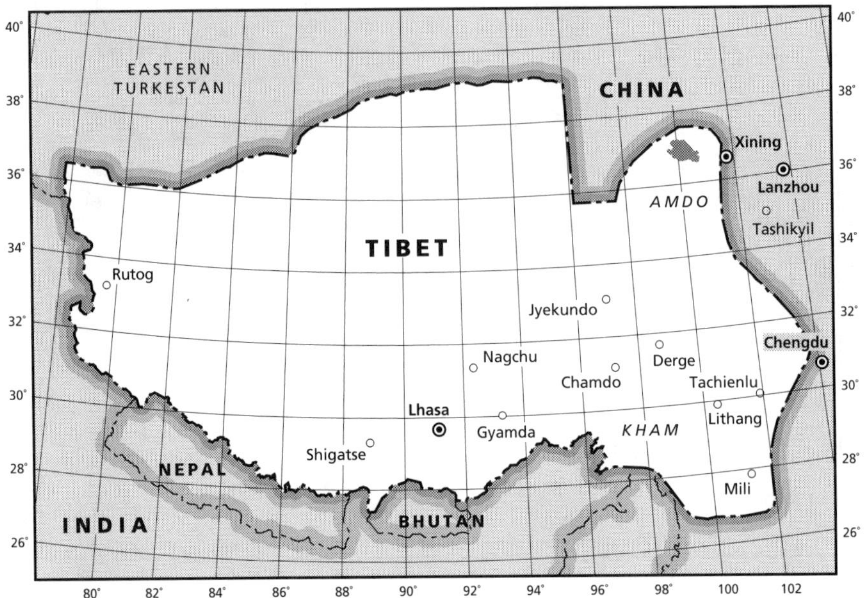

Frontier of Tibet as claimed by Nationalist Chinese in 1914

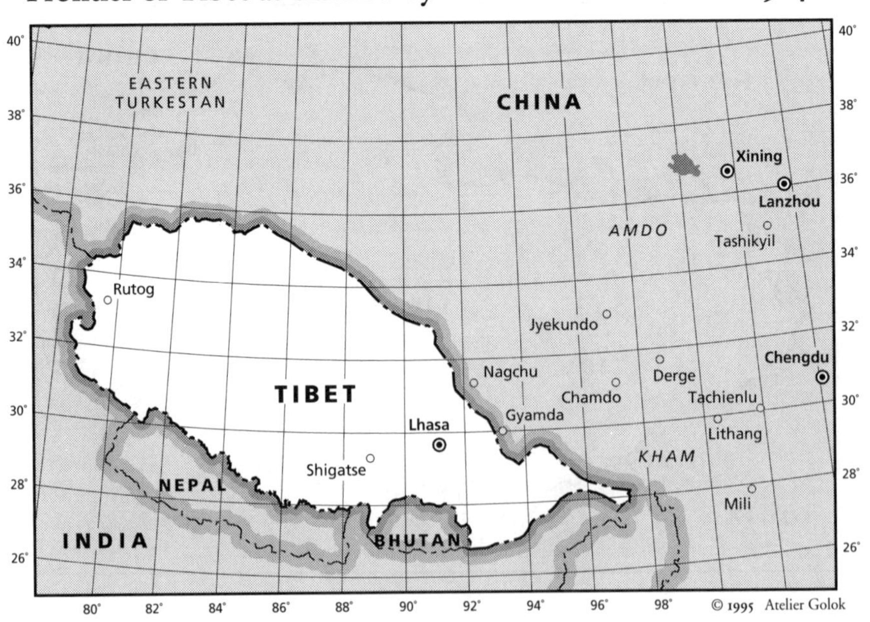

Frontier of Tibet as proposed at the Tripartite Simla Conference in 1914

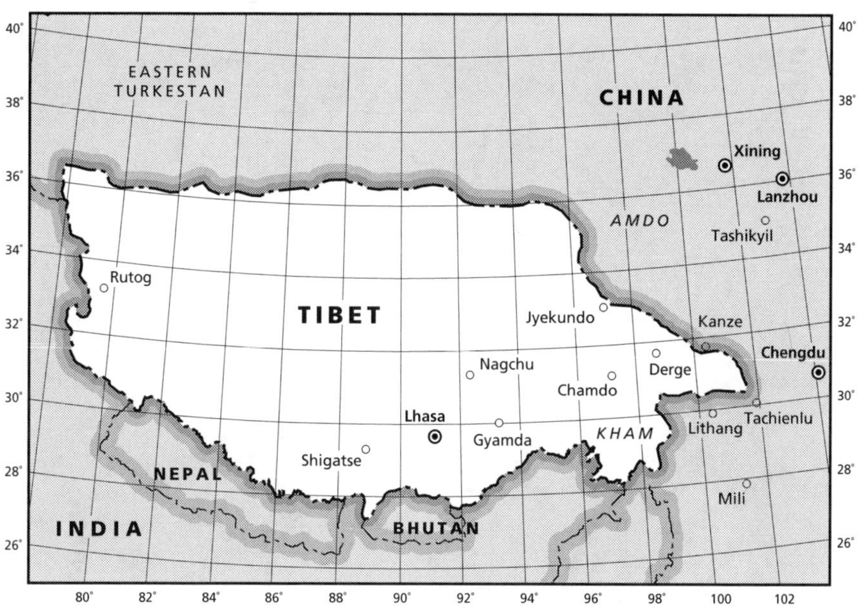

Territories under the control of the Dalai Lama's Government (1918-1950)

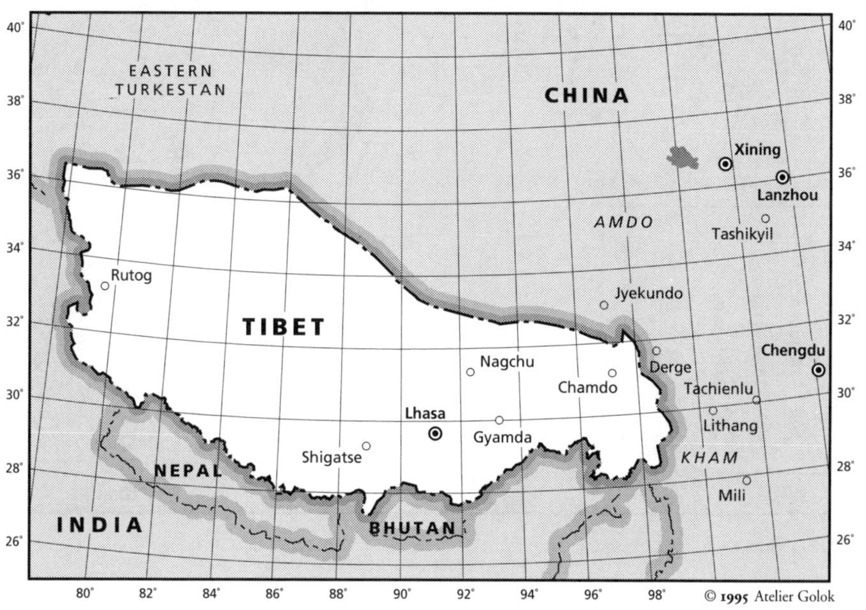

People's Liberation Army invasion of Tibet
(October 1950)

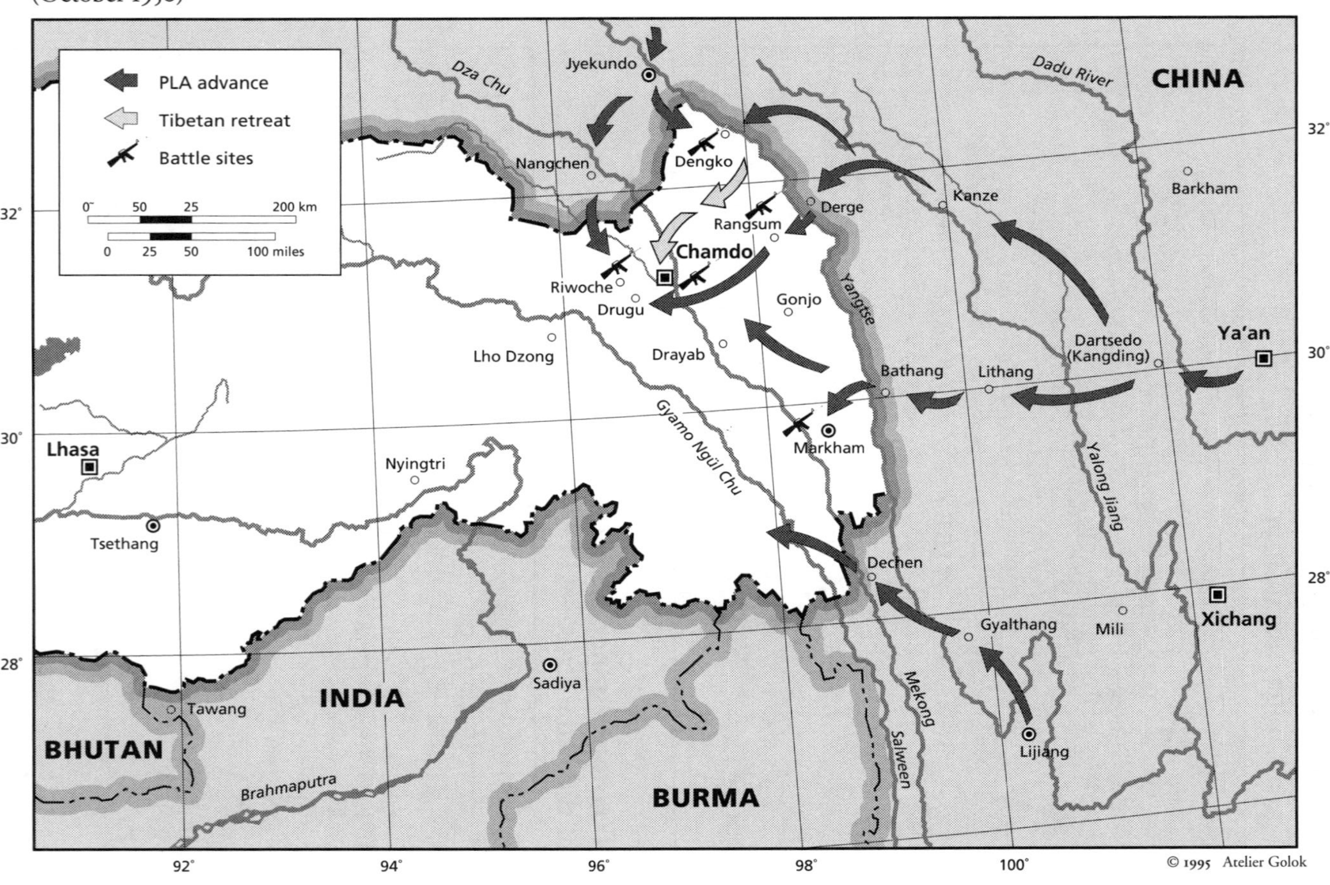

Sino-Indian Conflict: Indian Claims

(Western and Middle Sectors, under PRC's control)

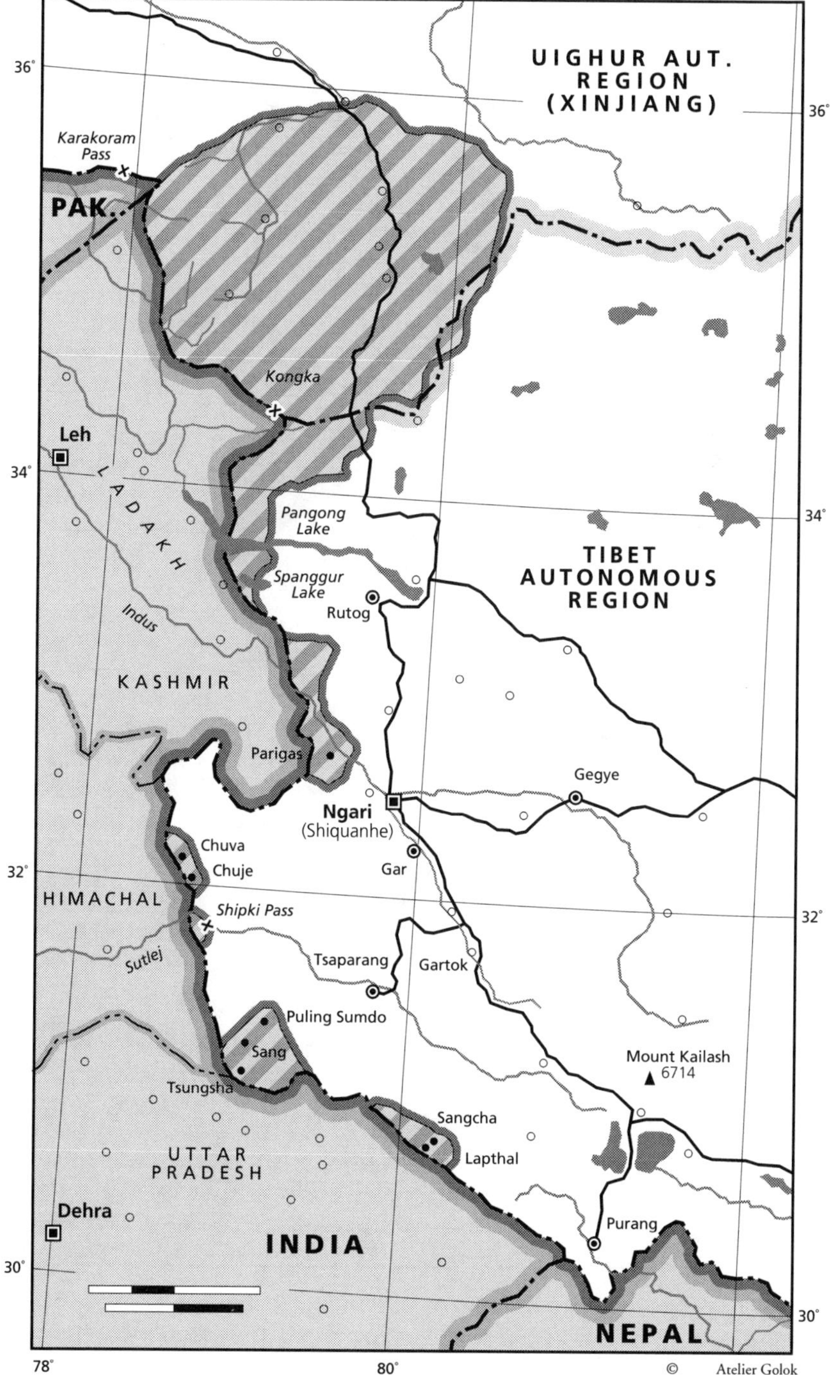

Sino-Indian Conflict: Chinese Claims

(Eastern Sector, under India's control)

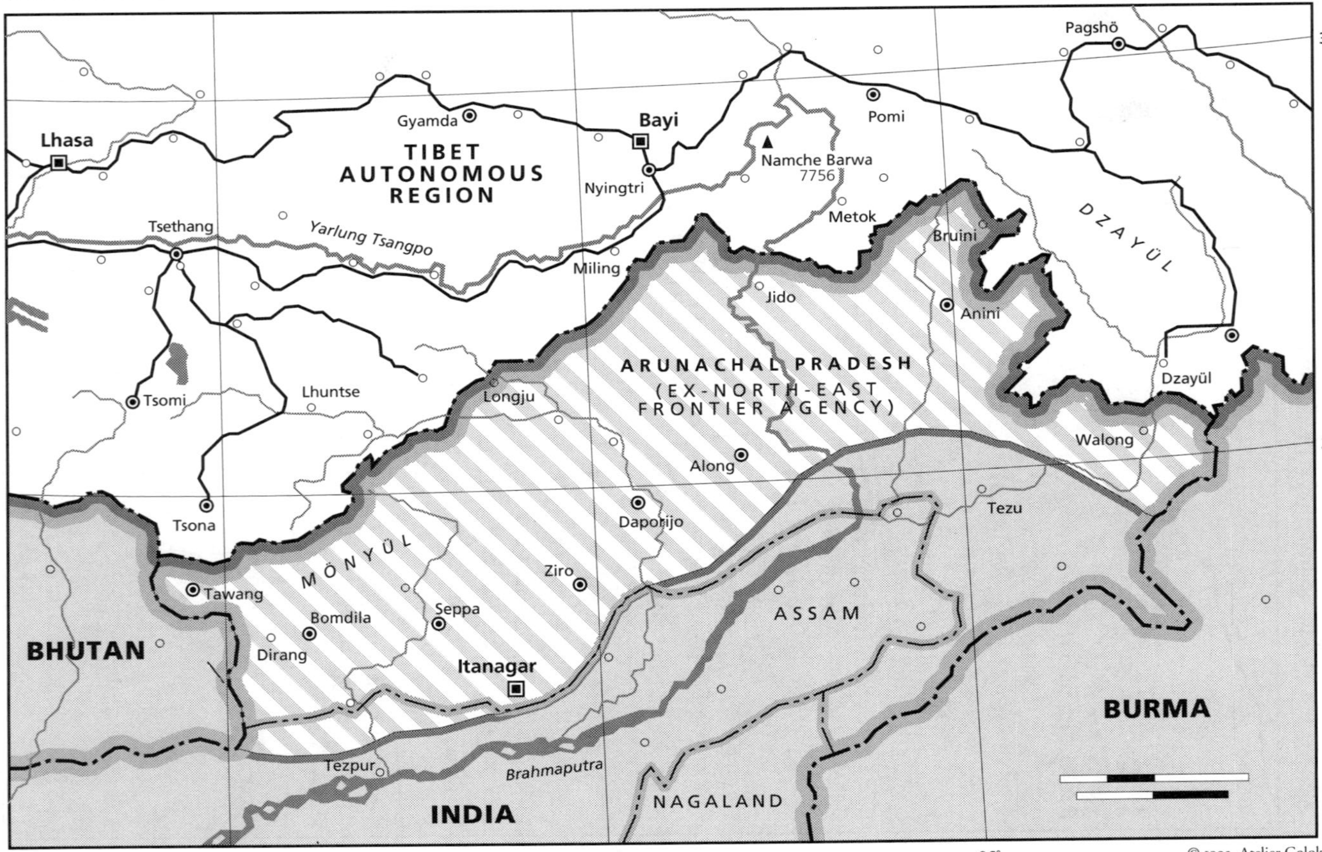

Abbreviations

Anon	anonymous
BBC	British Broadcasting Corporation
BR	*Beijing Review* (Formerly *Peking Review*)
CBA	Chinese Buddhists Association
CCP	Chinese Communist Party
CHC	*Cambridge History of China* (ed. John King Fairbank)
CLC	Chamdo Liberation Committee
CNA	*China News Analysis*
CQ	*China Quarterly*
CR	Cultural Revolution
CRO	Commonwealth Relations Office
DO	Dominion Office (London)
FBIS	Foreign Broadcast Information Service
FEER	Far Eastern Economic Review
FO	Foreign Office (British)
FRSR	Four Rivers and Six Ranges.
FRUS	Foreign Relations of the United States
FYP	Five Year Plan
GLF	Great Leap Forward
GOI	Government of India
JPRS	Joint Publications Research Service
LTWA	Library of Tibetan Works and Archives (Dharamsala)
MR	*Monthly Report* from the Indian Mission in Lhasa (PRO)
NCNA	New China News Agency
NGO	Non Government Organisation
NPC	National People's Congress
PCART	Preparatory Committee of the Autonomous Region of Tibet
PLA	People's Liberation Army
PRC	People's Republic of China
PRO	Public Records Office (London)
PTI	Press Trust of India
SCHT	Sources on the Culture and History of Tibet: Bod kyi lo-rgyus rig-gnas dpyad-gzhi'i rgyu-cha bdams-bsgrigs (Lhasa)
SCMM	Selections from China Mainland Magazines (Hong Kong)

SCMP	Survey of China Mainland Press (Hong Kong)
SEM	Socialist Education Movement
SWB	*Summary of World Broadcasts* (BBC)
TAP	Tibetan Autonomous Prefecture
TAR	Tibet Autonomous Region
TB	*Tibet Bulletins* (Dharamsala)
TIN	Tibet Information Network (London)
TJ	*Tibet Journal*
TR	*Tibetan Review*
TUCCR	Tibet Under Chinese Communist Rule
TWC	Tibet Work Committee
UN	United Nations
URI	Union Research Institute (Hong Kong)

Introduction

In recent years Tibet has attracted widespread international interest. Its political problems have been debated in parliaments around the world and occupied hundreds of column inches. Despite the unprecedented extent of press coverage given to events in Tibet between 1987 and 1994 (when there were over 50 pro-independence demonstrations in Lhasa) I was struck by the dearth of well-researched material on Tibet's recent history. As a Tibetan I was also alarmed by the generalised treatment of the issue in the international arena and the simplistic manner in which it was discussed. The political demonstrations that occurred in Tibet in the late 1980s exposed the gap that exists in research on the history of modern Tibet, and it is that gap which I hope this work may be able to fill.

There has been a long tradition of Tibetan studies in the West, but one mainly confined to the study of Buddhism, ancient history and the arts. Since the 1960s there has been a flourishing of anthropological research into Tibetan society, but these have tended to concentrate on the Tibetan-speaking populations of the southern Himalayan belt (Ladakh and Nepal), or on reconstructing a model of pre-1950 Tibetan society based primarily on interviews with refugees. These works focus on small communities and often stress the static nature of Tibetan society and its isolation from major international developments. As a subject of research, Tibet's own recent history has been much neglected, suggesting an assumption that Tibet has no recent history and leading to a tendency to portray recent events in crudely dualistic terms.

There are objective factors that prevent a meaningful and scholarly discourse on the topic. The events described in this book are to some degree still unfolding and most of the key participants who have left their mark on the contours of Tibet's history are still active. There is also a real problem of source material, on which any objective research must be based. As a result, research into the history of modern Tibet has been left to the realms of a polemical debate between those who support either the Tibetan or the Chinese claims.

Today, the issue of Tibet's recent past is hotly contested in the political arena and presented in a crude dialectic. Both the Chinese and the Tibetan authorities have vested interests in reducing the issue to simplistic terms.

For the Chinese, pre-1950 Tibet was a hell on earth ravaged by feudal exploitation. There are no redeemable features in Tibetan culture and tradition. This view is fostered by traditional Chinese prejudice against non-Chinese people. The Communists not only believe that they have succeeded in unifying China but that their rule in Tibet has constituted the liberation of the serfs and a continuous history of development and progress towards modernity.

For the Tibetans the image could not be more different. Before the Chinese invasion their country was a land of 'happy' and 'contented' people. Chinese rule has not only meant the destruction of Tibetans' independent political identity but (they maintain) four decades of near-genocide of the Tibetan people and their culture. The gulf between the two positions is as wide as heaven and earth, and it is impossible to reconcile them.

Both are part of political myth-making, in which these powerful symbols are invoked to justify and legitimise the claims of the proponents. For the Chinese it has been a political necessity to paint a dark and hellish picture of the past in order to justify their claim to have 'liberated' Tibet, a claim which is based only partly on a legal insistence that Tibet constituted an integral part of the PRC. The logic of the argument is the same as the belief held by Western colonial powers that their rule has been a civilising influence on the natives in their dominions. For the Tibetans, particularly for those who experienced firsthand the oppression of the past four decades, regaining the past has become a necessary act of political invocation, which allows them to escape from a reality which has deprived them of their future. They find meaning and identity in glorification of the past, when the land of snows was the exclusive terrain of the Tibetan people.

Neither the Tibetans nor the Chinese want to allow any complexities to intrude on their firmly held beliefs. This has resulted in what I have called 'denial of history', a process which necessarily entails negation of responsibility. The Tibetan élite claims its actions are entirely blameless, seeking to give an image of total innocence and to portray the Chinese actions as the rape of an innocent people. It is difficult for the Tibetans to admit that they were not merely a passive agent in their recent history or that there was a much more complex issue surrounding the relationship between Tibet and China. In the early 1950s there was a consensus among Tibet's secular and religious ruling classes that Buddhist Tibet and Communist China could co-exist and, accordingly, they co-operated fully with the Chinese. Moreover, there were many people in Tibet who welcomed the Chinese as a modernising influence.

Similarly the Chinese leaders refuse to see the question of Tibet in terms of the desires and wishes of the Tibetan people. For the Chinese to acknowledge that Tibet had a recent history and a personality would amount to an acceptance of Tibet's separateness from China. Chinese policy towards

Tibet stems from two ideas which have shaped modern China: first, Chinese nationalism, which attaches great importance to the humiliation of China under Western imperialism and leads the Chinese to interpret Tibet's demand for independence as an externally generated conspiracy to dismember China, a view consistently held by successive Chinese regimes from the Qing to the Guomindang and the Communists. Therefore, all Chinese leaders since the later Qing have adopted a policy of incorporating Tibet within the greater polity of China. In this scheme of things, it does not matter what the Tibetans think or want: Tibet is a part of China. The second formative view adopted by the Chinese is a narrow Marxist economic determinist view of national identity, which sees it as product of economic disparity, and argues that once economic inequality is removed, there would occur a natural withering of ethnic differences.

One of the dominant features of Tibet's recent history has been the question of its legal status and the nature of its relationship with China. It is beyond the scope of this book to delve into this subject in great detail, but suffice it to say that the historical relationship between China and Tibet is analogous to two overlapping circles. Much of the debate has been concerned with the definition or denial of this overlap. This traditional relationship between Tibet and China was set within the political culture of the Sino-Tibetan world, where the meaning of the relationship was well understood by the participants. When this socio-cultural and political environment was altered first by the arrival of Western colonial powers in Asia; and second by the transformation of the traditional Chinese Confucian-dominated polity towards a more occidental type of political system which produced a Republican China and the growth of Chinese nationalism, the traditional and established relationship became problematic. The new leaders of China sought to intrude into Tibet and transform the traditional relationship into a far more encompassing one between a central government and a local government which would have brought Tibet within the firmer jurisdiction of the Chinese government.

Today, Tibetans claim that the traditional relationship between China and Tibet has been characterised by Buddhist notions of priest and patron (*mchod-yon*). This implies that the relationship was mainly of a religious nature and did not suggest any subordination on the part of Tibet to China. However, this suggests that the Tibetans viewed the Chinese Emperor as a purely secular institution. This is far from the case. The Tibetans saw the Chinese emperor as both a religious and secular institution: in Tibetan sources the Manchu Emperor is always referred to as Jampeyang Gongma, the incarnation of Manjushri, defining him as not merely a secular patron but as occupying a space within a Buddhist pantheon exercising some measure of secular authority in Tibet. But the Manchu emperors were content with ceremonial and symbolic submission and did not attempt to integrate Tibet with China.

The arrival of the British in India and their gradual expansion into the foothills of the Himalayas brought the question of China's authority in Tibet more acutely into the foreground. Early on the British, having encountered this problem, had imposed their own terminology, referring to the relationship between sovereign and suzerain, which far from clarifying the matter had in fact made it more obscure. The Tibetans, at least from 1913 onwards, regarded themselves as independent of China and declared themselves to be an independent state, a move which was thwarted partly by internal conflicts and partly by the desire of the Tibetans to seal themselves off from the outside world. But the successive Chinese regimes never accepted this, nor was Tibet able to obtain *de jure* recognition for her independent status. Thus, the issue of the status of Tibet has been left very much in uncertainty.

In this book I have not provided a detailed exegesis of the nature of the Sino-Tibetan relationship, leaving the above points to indicate the problematic nature of the issue and the lack of any clear-cut consensus among scholars. I show that, prior to the signing of the 17-Point Agreement, the Lhasa Government did exercise complete control over its internal and external affairs; this I have used as a criterion for determining whether a state is independent or not. Until the eve of the Chinese invasion in October 1950, the Tibetan Goverment exercised internal and external freedom, which clearly demonstrated the country's independence.

Although there has been much interest in political issues concerning Tibet, at a scholarly level it has remained a much neglected subject. The few scholars who had worked on the history of Tibet in the twentieth century have dealt wholly with British policies towards the country and view Tibet as a mere 'pawn on the imperial chessboard'. There is much truth in the view that the roots of the present problem stem largely from the conflict that arose in the late nineteenth century following the creeping of British imperial interests over the Himalayas and onto the Tibetan plateau. It was a development which the Chinese could no longer ignore and they accordingly sought to bring Tibet more firmly under the control of the Chinese empire. But the subject only became an important area of scholarly enquiry with the Sino-Indian Border War of 1962, which lead to a series of writings that relied solely on the source materials preserved in British archives. Notable among these are the works of historians like Alastair Lamb, Parshotam Mehra, Premen Addy and Amar Kaur Jasbir Singh, who have traced the development of diplomatic intercourse between Tibet, China and Britain since the eighteenth century. Their works are mainly concerned with the politics of the British Empire and their effect on surrounding areas.

Therefore, their analysis finds a natural ending with the British withdrawal from India.

This changed in 1990 with the publication of Melvyn Goldstein's *History of Modern Tibet, 1913–1951*. By supplementing archive sources in the West with interviews with Tibetan personalities, Goldstein was able to bring out something of the history of Tibet in the first half of the twentieth century. This publication was a landmark in modern literature on Tibet.

Five years earlier, Heather Stoddard had published her biography of Gedun Choephel, *Le Mendiant de l'Amdo*. Stoddard's work was primarily concerned with the life of an individual, but it dealt with much of the subject-matter later covered in Goldstein's work. Both of these publications are unique in Western-language literature on Tibet in the first half of this century.

Sources

In this book I have used the withdrawal of the British in India as a starting point. This not only provides a convenient historic watershed but, as the text will show, was evidently a major transitional period in the region as a whole. In telling the story of Tibet from this point, I have used various sources to piece together the events as they unfold.

At a primary level I have used sources in Tibetan and English that are contained in various archives, including the Public Record Office (London), which contains numerous records of correspondence between the Tibetan and British governments during the period 1947 and 1951 which provide a valuable insight into the Tibetan position and policy at that time. The British records also contain a number of important accounts from the Indian Mission in Lhasa, particularly the monthly reports which give details of events in Tibet from 1950 to 1954. The wake of the Sino-Indian war led to the publication by the GOI of valuable documents which provide useful details on the question of border disputes and on the Tibetan position. The GOI's *Notes, Memoranda and Letters Exchanged and Agreements Signed Between the Governments of India and China; White Paper 1959–1963*, shows how the two countries' suspicions and apprehension escalated into a war.

Between 1950 and 1951 Tibet formed a close relationship with the USA, the resulting records of which have been published. The primary source for this is *Foreign Relations of the United States; 1949. Vol. IV: The Far East; China*. As noted in the text, there was a change in US policy in the late 1950s and they established clandestine relations with Tibet. The CIA documents concerning this episode have remained closed, and for this material I have therefore relied on two important Tibetan informants who were involved in implementing these policies.

Tibet became a subject of debate at the United Nations General Assembly in 1951, 1959 and 1962, and extensive unexplored materials on this are held in the Public Record Office in London. The United Kingdom was the only Western country to have extensive relations with Tibet in the early part of the twentieth century and was therefore consulted by the Commonwealth and Western countries. The discussions prompted by the UN debates yielded important materials on the views of other foreign governments on Tibet. I have made comprehensive use of these sources.

As mentioned before, the sensitive nature of the subject means that many valuable sources have remained restricted and it is unlikely that concerned governments would allow unhindered access to their archives. This is even the case in liberal countries such as the United Kingdom and the United States, the two Western countries that had extensive dealings with Tibet. A number of files on Tibet in the Public Record Office in London are still closed. The Americans have never officially acknowledged the CIA's clandestine involvement in Tibet and the files on this activity are still restricted. Those that have been released have been censored, rendering them of little value. India's involvement in Tibetan affairs means that its files are crucial for understanding the recent history of Tibet, but India's continuing border controversy with China has meant that the government in New Delhi remains reluctant to open up its files on this question.

The most important primary Tibetan source came in a series of recent publications in Tibet produced by the Chinese People's Political Consultative Committee (CPPCC). This is a forum to which the Communists have appointed non-Party members who are deemed to be influential in forming public opinion (in Tibet mainly high Rinpoches and former members of the aristocracy). Since 1980 the Communist Party has encouraged these men, many of them former Tibetan government officials, to write their reminiscences. In addition, some Chinese civilians and army officials have also written accounts of their experiences in Tibet which have been translated into Tibetan. These articles were published in *Sources on the Culture and History of Tibet* (*Bod rang-skyong-ljongs rig-gnas lo-rgyus dpyad-gzhi*), the first volume of which was published in 1982, under restricted circulation (*nei-bu*). At the time of writing over fifteen volumes of this collection have been published.

Although this body of publications forms an important source, a certain caution must be exercised. One of the contributors, Sampho, wrote on coming into exile that his contribution to the collected work was written by someone else and that his name was simply added to it. The articles almost always begin with a paragraph which declares that Tibet has always been a part of China and admits the writers themselves had engaged in activities aimed at splitting Tibet from the motherland. However, a judicious analysis of these articles does elicit useful facts and ideas held by certain sections of Tibetan society.

In exile some leading Tibetan officials have published their autobiographies in Tibetan (and sometimes in English). Notable among these are the two autobiographies of the Dalai Lama. These should not be taken to provide an accurate historical account; they are written for popular consumption and to entice public support for the Tibetan cause. Like all autobiographies of important historical figures, their importance lies not in what is written but in what is omitted.

Other Tibetans – Sampho, Namseling, Alo Chonzed and others – have also written autobiographies. These unfortunately provide little information of great use. This is partly due to the fact that the chief concern among Tibetan officials seems to be to avoid controversy and confrontation, with the result that very important points in history are merely glanced over. (The books written in English often provide a far better insight than those written in Tibetan.) For example, Sampho – who was one of the leading figures during the period and a member of the delegation which signed the 17-Point Agreement – remained in Tibet until the early 1980s, yet his autobiography published in India has very little information of great importance. There is in Tibet a great tradition of publishing biographies of great lamas, but these adhere to the hagiographical tradition of noting only the wondrous spiritual development of the lamas and provide no useful insights into the politics of the day. The two tutors of the Dalai Lama played an important role in the politics of the period, yet their biographies have almost nothing of significance to say on recent political history: the events of 1959, for example, are casually dismissed in a sentence.

The Library of Tibetan Works and Archives in Dharamsala, North India, contains a number of valuable oral records based on interviews with leading Tibetan personalities in the 1950s, such as Phala Thupten Woden, Liushar Thupten Tharpa, Barshi Ngawang Tenkyong, Kundeling and others. These were initially collected with a view to publication, but the Dharamsala Government later felt that some of these accounts compromised the official versions of history and as a result they remain unpublished. I have had the good fortune to be allowed access to them and I have made extensive use of them in my writing. I have found them by far the best materials for my research, often giving frank accounts of events in Tibet between 1950 and 1959. I have supplemented all the above sources with my own interviews of many of these figures.

Using official Chinese publications in Tibetan or those translated into English involves limitations and constraints. Needless to say, these serve as a vehicle for Party propaganda and for expounding current policies. Inside Tibet there has never been a tradition of independent and critical political writing or publishing, and it has lessened in recent years. The process of policy-making in China is highly secretive and often we can only find out about important events or policies long after they have taken place. This is particularly true of Tibet, which until recently had been closed to outsiders, with no one making a concerted effort to find out how things operate in the region. It is, even today, difficult to find out how important decisions are made in Tibet and how much power the regional Communist Party actually exercises. Subjects such as the question of ethnic relations in the higher echelons of the regional CCP are almost impossible to explore. In the past few years a number of important Party documents have been leaked to the outside world, several of which provide important information on the nature and functioning of the CCP in Tibet. Some of these materials have been collected by Robert Barnett of TIN.

There are also Communist Party documents relating to policy towards Tibet and other minorities which have been translated into Tibetan. After Mao's death Volume 5 of the collection of his speeches and writings was published, and this too was translated into Tibetan. The collection contains a number of documents relating to Tibet.

There are a large number of translations of Chinese publications compiled by foreign governments and research institutions. The BBC publishes the Summary of World Broadcasts (SWB) which in its Far East section contains summaries and texts of articles that have either been broadcast or appeared as news items in the Chinese language press. Similarly, the US Government publishes the Foreign Broadcast Information Services (FBIS) and the Joint Publication Research Services (JPRS). The US Consulate in Hong Kong published a Survey of the Chinese Mainland Press (SCMP) and a Selection from China Mainland Magazines (SCMM). All these materials contain articles and news reports dealing with Tibet and minority issues. The Tibetan government-in-exile also maintains Tibetan transcripts of Radio Lhasa broadcasts, but this is not readily available to the public.

These materials often provide insights into the Communist Party's official claims and raise doubts about what is believed to be happening in the Party. Some of these documents are speeches given to Party and government officials, or editorials in official journals. These are only of use in determining official policy at a particular period and in describing the various campaigns that have been carried out in Tibet. I have made much use of these materials.

Rendering of Tibetan names and Terms

I have tried to avoid the excessive use of Tibetan terms and have wherever possible used suitable English equivalents. In the text I have rendered Tibetan terms and names in more familiar Roman forms and a list of correct

Tibetan spellings is provided as an appendix. For this I have used standard written Tibetan spelling and followed the transliteration guidelines established by Wylie (1959).

Chinese names are written in the *pinyin* system except for more familiarly known names such as Chiang Kai-shek. Chinese names which appeared in the Wade-Giles system have been converted to *pinyin*, using the conversion table in Jonathan D. Spence, *The Search for Modern China* (London: Hutchinson 1990), p. xxv.

ONE

The Lull Before the Storm

On 15 August 1947, India became an independent nation and inherited the political influence and the privileges that Britain had gained in Tibet. This historic transition was marked in Lhasa with a simple ceremony: the Union Jack was lowered and the Indian national flag was raised in its place. Hugh Richardson, the last British representative in Lhasa, became the first Indian representative. Later he wrote: 'the transition was almost imperceptible. The existing staff was retained in its entirety and the only obvious change was the change of flag'.[1] But this was deceptive. The emergence of the new Republic of India changed the traditional balance of power, and Asian nationalists envisaged that the collapse of the British Empire would lead to the birth of a new order in Asia. And thus the history of modern Tibet in the second half of the twentieth century was to become a search for the maintenance of its independence and international stature in this emerging regional order.

Tibet occupied 1.2 million square kilometres of land sandwiched between the two giants of Asia. To the south, the mighty Himalayas formed a natural boundary with India. To the north and the east was China. For centuries Tibet had absorbed cultural influences from both these countries. The politics of both countries had exercised considerable influence over the historical development of Tibet. This enormous landmass had always been of strategic importance to the great powers. China had always coveted Tibet as the 'treasure house' of the western region.[2] When the British ruled India, they had always regarded Tibet as crucial to the security of India and their imperial ambitions. As a result, they sought to gain influence in Tibet such as no other Western country had ever enjoyed before. From 1913 onwards Britain achieved considerable prestige in the country, thereby bringing it within the British sphere of influence. Tibet, for her part, wanted to cultivate good relations with Britain. It was the price for keeping the Chinese at bay: as British influence increased across the Himalayas, so Chinese prestige and influence faded.

The end of the Second World War saw the collapse of the old imperial powers in Asia. The British were forced out of the Indian sub-continent and their imperial ambitions reached a convenient end. The Japanese had been defeated and expelled from the Asian mainland, which led to the eventual victory of the Communists in China. It was a shift in the balance of power that marked the beginnings of the demise of Tibet as an independent state.

When the Republic of China was founded, its authority in Tibet was virtually non-existent. One of the primary objectives of the Guomindang was to restore its influence and a number of missions were dispatched to Lhasa to re-establish relations with the Tibetans. The loss of Chinese influence was seen by the emerging Chinese nationalists as proof of Western imperialist attempts to undermine the Chinese nation. After the collapse of the Qing Dynasty in 1911, China was internally divided and militarily weak. The Chinese nationalists therefore could not put into practice their claim that China was a nation based on the 'unity of five races'.[3] Tibet remained outside the control of the Guomindang government. Moreover, Tibetans were convinced that they should have their rightful place in the world as an independent nation and were thus determined to oppose Chinese attempts to gain a foothold in Lhasa. However, we shall see later that the Guomindang regime was determined to assert its claims over Tibet.

Tibet and its Neighbours

To a large extent Tibet's ability to survive as an independent nation depended on its southern neighbour, British India. India's willingness to preserve Tibet as a natural buffer state between China and itself was crucial to the future status of Tibet. The question was: would the newly independent India have the will and the power to safeguard Tibet's inherited privileges or would these be discarded as an anachronism of the age of imperialism? At first, India appeared willing to maintain the privileges secured by its former ruler. But the question remained: would India be able to resist pressure from the newly emerging China? The new India lacked the economic and military power possessed by her former colonial ruler, whose empire had represented one of the greatest powers in the world, with naval and military power stretched across the globe. The primary tasks facing the Indian leaders were economic development of the country and cessation of the sectarian strife, which had already cost thousands of lives. Relations with the new Islamic state of Pakistan were also on the brink of collapse. Therefore, the problems that were about to unfold in the northern borders along the Himalayan range were the least of their concerns.

However, the new leaders of India should have been aware of the delicate situation they were about to inherit from the British. In March 1947, the Indian Council for World Affairs, with support from the Congress leaders, convened an Inter-Asian Relations Conference; Nehru hailed it as a landmark in the history of Asia, intended to discuss the role of Asia in the post-war and post-colonial period. Initially Tibet was represented as an independent nation. A map displayed at the conference showed Tibet as separate from China and the Tibetan delegation unveiled for the first time the newly invented national flag. These symbols of Tibet's new-found international status were rejected by the Chinese delegation, which protested to the Indian organisers.

In the end a compromise was reached: the Tibetans were allowed to participate in the conference, but the offending map and flag were removed. This benefited neither the Chinese nor the Tibetans: the Tibetan presence at the conference in no way indicated that the Chinese would concede to this temporary solution and the Tibetans were still unsure whether the international community viewed Tibet as a nation separate from China. The incident should have told the new Indian leaders that the Chinese were not prepared to accept Tibet's separate identity and that the uncertain status of Tibet at their northern border would present a major problem for them.

The Indian leaders may have felt that the civil war in China would distract the Chinese from over-extending themselves in the Tibetan plateau. But in January 1949 Chiang Kai-shek and his government surrendered to the Communists and fled to Taiwan. It was now in the hands of the new Communist government to realise the goal of unifying Tibet with China. The Communists proved to be even more determined than the Guomindang to assert China's control in Tibet. On 1 October 1949, the People's Republic of China was established and Chairman Mao proclaimed in Tiananmen Square, 'China has stood up.' For nearly two centuries China had been wrecked by civil war, economic strife and Western imperialist onslaughts. But now, for the first time, a strong central government had emerged. This Communist Government was impelled by the two important socio-political phenomena of the twentieth century: nationalism and Communism.

On coming to power, the Communists made it clear that the last remaining task for the victorious People's Liberation Army was the liberation of Tibet. The higher echelons of the Communist Party had already developed strategies for the incorporation of what they regarded as 'Chinese National Minorities' within the framework of the People's Republic of China. The Commander-in-Chief of the PLA, Zhu De, in a speech to the Chinese Peoples' Political Consultative Conference on 24 September 1949, said: 'the Common Programme demanded the waging of the revolutionary war to the very end and the liberation of all the territory of China, including Formosa, the Pescadores, Hainan Island and Tibet'.[4]

On 29 September 1949, the Common Programme was unanimously approved by the National People's Congress. Thus, as far as the new Communist government was concerned, Tibet was to be regarded as Chinese territory and Tibetan issues were to be dealt under the rubric of a 'National Minority'. Articles 50–53 dealt with national minority issues and became the basis of China's long-term policy towards the country.[5]

Nevertheless, the Communist leaders were acutely aware of their lack of influence in Tibet.

When the Communists came to power the influence regained by the Guomindang in Tibet had come to an end. The Tibetan Government decided to terminate the contacts that had been established between the Lhasa Government and the Guomindang regime. As noted earlier, the nationalists too had slowly to regain the power and influence lost by the collapse of the Qing dynasty. From 1913 onwards Tibet had, to all intents and purposes, been an independent state. It exercised full authority over its internal and external affairs, and Tibetans saw no reason why it should now succumb to the Communists' propaganda. The Tibetans' response to the Chinese claim was to declare vociferously Tibet's independence. However, Tibetans were also quick to realise that the Communists were very different from the Guomindang and other previous Chinese governments. The Tibetans had been able to dismiss all pretension that the Guomindang had any power in Tibet, but the Communists had proved their determination to win at all costs. When they declared their intention to liberate Tibet, many Tibetans realised that they meant it.

The Communists were not prepared to accept any compromises; it was anathema to them that Tibet should have an international personality beyond being a region of China. From the Chinese point of view, Tibet was an 'integral part of China' which had been encouraged by anti-Chinese and imperialist forces to break away from the 'Motherland'. From the very beginning of the anti-Japanese war, the Communists had appealed to Chinese nationalism to gain support and they developed irredentist policies. They had won mass support because of their anti-Japanese stance and militant nationalism, which promised to unify and restore dignity to China.

The Communists were clearly convinced that the territorial limits of the new China lay along the foothills of the Himalayas. Moreover, they not only believed in the incorporation of Tibet into China. They were also impelled by their revolutionary zeal to promote the socialist transformation of Tibet. The first objective of the Communists was to 're-establish [their] international prestige'.[6] The question of Tibet was bound up with China's perception of itself as a new nation, and of its international status. The Communists' victory caused immediate alarm among the Tibetan ruling élite. But because of a lack of Chinese presence in Tibet, there was still time to make a last desperate attempt to secure Tibet's independence.

The external threat to Tibet's status could not have come at a worse time. Tibet's supreme leader, the Dalai Lama, was a young boy of fourteen and had not yet established his political authority. During the Dalai Lama's minority Tibet was ruled by a regent and this transitional period had always been a strain on the Tibetan political system. The ruling élite, composed of the aristocracy and the religious institutions, was deeply divided: the whole society was recovering from the Reting conspiracy, when the ex-Regent Reting Rinpoche attempted to wrest power from the incumbent Regent, Taktra. This had nearly plunged Tibet into a civil war. The period between 1913 and 1947 was a watershed in Tibetan history: during this period there would have been real scope for Tibet to have emerged as a 'nation state', provided the ruling élite had had the foresight and willingness to adapt to the changes in the larger world. But that élite chose to remain oblivious to what was going on around them.

Resistance to change came mainly from the religious community, which was opposed to any kind of reform that appeared to diminish its power. High lamas and the monasteries used their enormous influence to obstruct reforms that were desperately needed to transform Tibetan society. By 1949, therefore, Tibet was not equipped to oppose China either militarily or socially. The immediate political reaction to the Chinese claims and to the victory of the Communists was to remove any remnant of Chinese authority in Tibet. Anyone suspected of being sympathetic to the Chinese was expelled. The highest executive body of the Tibetan Government, the Kashag, appointed the Tsipon Namseling to draw up a list of all those who were pro-Communist, including anyone who was closely associated with the Chinese Mission.

The Expulsion of the Guomindang and the Communist Victory in China

Since the eighteenth century the Chinese Government had maintained representatives in Lhasa, known as Ambans. The Amban was the symbol of Chinese authority in Tibet. But after the fall of the Qing dynasty (1644–1912) the Amban and his military escort were expelled from Lhasa and it was not until 1934 that contact between Tibet and China was renewed. On 25 April a high-ranking Nationalist delegation led by General Huang Musang, Chiang Kai-shek's Vice-Chief of the General Staff, arrived in Lhasa on the pretext of 'paying posthumous tribute to the late Dalai Lama', thus establishing the first formal relationship between Tibet and Republican China.[7] The arrival of Huang Musang in Lhasa not only marked the resumption of Tibetan and Chinese contacts but once again brought to the surface the issue of the nature of the Sino-Tibetan relationship. (This question was first raised at the tripartite Simla Conference, convened under aegis of the British, held between October 1913 and July 1914. The negotiation broke down because the Chinese and the Tibetans could not agree over the alignment of the Sino-Tibetan boundaries.) Huang's mission had in effect removed the important role played by the British as mediators between Tibet and China during the Simla conference. The real political significance of the mission was the Guomindang's attempt to woo Tibet back into the Chinese fold. Huang came to Lhasa with a specific policy objective, presenting a three-point proposal: (1) that Tibet must form a part of China, (2) that the Chinese would assume responsibility for Tibet's defence, (3) that the office of the Amban would be re-established in Lhasa.[8] According to Chinese sources, Huang's mission was successful and he obtained Tibetans' willingness to hand over the conduct of foreign affairs to China as long as Tibet was not incorporated as a province of China.[9] However, the Tibetans claim that they not only rejected Huang's proposal but demanded the return of territories east of the Drichu (Yangtze).[10] Moreover, while the Chinese were eager to discard the British as mediator, the Tibetans insisted that any negotiation must involve their southern neighbour, British India. This was clearly important for the Tibetans, for British participation would have provided a form of international guarantee, but it was in China's interest to deny any international or legal character to the meetings. This was to characterise much of Sino-Tibetan dialogue. Whatever may have transpired during Huang's visit, one thing was certain: for the Guomindang, permission to set up an office in Lhasa was a major propaganda achievement, resurrecting Chinese presence in Tibet.

The British were not prepared to acquiesce to the return of the Chinese to Tibet, and determined to counter the reassertion of Chinese influence. If the Chinese were allowed to establish a permanent mission in Lhasa, the British too wanted to set up an office in the Tibetan capital. This led to the visit of Basil Gould, the Political Officer in Sikkim, in 1936 and the eventual establishment of a British mission in Lhasa, housed at the Dekyi Lingka.

On 25 November 1939 a nine-member delegation, consisting of staff from the Mongolian and Tibetan Affairs Commission, arrived in Lhasa, and were later joined by Wu Zhongxin, the Commission's director of Tibetan Affairs. The arrival in Lhasa was carefully planned to coincide with the enthronement ceremony for the fourteenth Dalai Lama. On 22 February 1940, Wu Zhongxin and other foreign representatives attended the ceremony in the Potala, the winter palace of the Dalai Lamas. Later the Guomindang and the Communists claimed that Wu had 'presided' over the ceremony and that his involvement was essential to the recognition of the new Dalai Lama.[11]

There is no evidence to suggest that Wu Zhongxin 'presided' over the installation of the Dalai Lama. However, the delegation managed to establish a permanent office in Lhasa, and installed a direct radio communication with Nanjing. The return of the Chinese to Lhasa reflected a growing support among Tibetan officials towards the Guomindang regime. A strong faction in Lhasa felt that some kind of reconciliation could be reached with the regime, which was prepared to accept Tibet's special status within China. Later, the Guomindang was able to secure the support of influential members of the Tibetan ruling élite, most prominent among them the Dalai Lama's family.

The Tibetans never accepted that the presence of the Chinese mission in Lhasa meant that they had acknowledged Chinese sovereignty. At the same time the establishment of the British mission in Lhasa did not mean that the Tibetans were prepared to surrender to the British. The decision to allow both countries a mission was most likely meant to demonstrate Tibet's independence and maintain some kind of international visibility. The establishment of the British mission was not accompanied by *de jure* recognition of Tibet's independent status. The legal status of the mission was deliberately kept vague and it remained subordinate to the Political Officer in Sikkim. For the British the mission provided an important foothold in Tibet and its chief aim was to signal to the Chinese that the British would resist any Chinese attempt to reassert its authority in Tibet.

The Guomindang Government had not relinquished China's claim that Tibet was an integral part of China. Therefore, the Chinese saw the opening of their mission in Lhasa as an assertion of China's sovereignty in Tibet. They saw the loss of Chinese authority in Tibet as a failure of their patriotic duty to reunite Tibet with China. Therefore, the success of Wu Zhongxin's mission represented an important propaganda achievement for the Guomindang regime.

While the British were content to accept the status quo, the Chinese clearly were not. The Tibetans were painfully aware that the Chinese had never surrendered their claims over Tibet. As long as China had remained weak and beset with internal conflict, there had been very little she could do to reassert her power. However, it was be a different matter once the Communists had managed to secure victory in China. Like all previous regimes, the Communists regarded Tibet as a part of China, regardless of what the Tibetans may have thought.

Although the Chinese mission did not exercise any authority, the Tibetan Government feared that the presence of the mission would enable the Chinese Communists to establish a foothold in Lhasa. When the Kashag proposed that the mission should be expelled, this was readily approved by the Regent, Taktra. Using the secret list of suspected Communist sympathisers and spies drawn up by Namseling, the Kashag planned the expulsion. With great secrecy the Tibetan Government summoned troops from Shigatse and Dingri and placed them in strategic positions in Lhasa. The Tibetans feared some Chinese would remain in Tibet and declare their loyalty to the Communists.[12]

On 8 July 1949, the Kashag called Chen Xizhang, the acting director of the Mongolian and Tibetan Affairs Commission office in Lhasa. He was informed that the Tibetan Government had decided to expel all Chinese connected with the Guomindang Government. Fearing that the Chinese might organise protests in the streets of Lhasa, the Kashag imposed a curfew until all the Chinese had left.[13] This they did in three separate groups on 14, 17 and 20 July 1949. At the same time the Tibetan Government sent a telegram to General Chiang Kai-shek and to President Liu Zongren informing them of the decision. They stated that the action was prompted by the fear of Communist elements infiltrating the country. This fear was not without foundation; and there had been increasing discontent among members of the Chinese mission, who had been cut off from developments in China and had not received financial provisions for five months. Some staff were talking about serving the 'new government', as had happened in other parts of China, and in fact, during the early period of Communist rule (1949–54), the new government in China retained most of the Guomindang officials in the administrative structure. It was therefore likely that the Chinese mission in Lhasa would have simply switched its allegiance to the new government.

Both the Communists and the Nationalists objected strongly to the decision to expel the Chinese mission in Lhasa. On 6 August Yan Xishan, President of the Executive Yuan, said that 'all the members of the mission had been carefully selected and there were no grounds for the expulsion' and called on the Tibetan Government to 'rectify its decision'.[14] Although the Communists had not yet assumed power in China, they were quick to condemn the Tibetan action and to appeal to Chinese nationalist sentiment. The Communists accused 'imperialists' and their 'running dogs' of 'manufacturing the so-called anti-Communist incident in Tibet' and of trying 'to turn the 1.2 million sq km' into a colony. In an editorial on 2 September 1949, the *Hsin Hwa Pao* remarked:

> The affair of expelling the Han Chinese and Kuomingtang [Guomindang] officials at Lhasa was a plot undertaken by the local Tibetan authorities through the instigation of the British imperialists and their lackey the Nehru administration of India. The purpose of this 'anti-Chinese affair' is to prevent the people in Tibet from being liberated by the Chinese People's Liberation Army . . . The reactionary Kuomintang Government should be rooted out from every corner of China. But this is the business of the Chinese people in their revolutionary struggle under the leadership of the Chinese Communist Party. It has nothing to do with foreign countries.[15]

The editorial showed that the Communists saw the presence of the Chinese Mission in Lhasa as evidence of Chinese authority over Tibet, and left no doubt about the Communists' view regarding the status of Tibet, referring to the Tibetan Government as a 'local government'. The editorial went on to say:

> The Chinese People's Liberation Army must liberate the whole territory of China, including Tibet, Sinkiang [Xinjiang] and so forth. Even an inch of Chinese land will not be permitted to be left outside the jurisdiction of the People's Republic of China. We tolerate no longer the aggression of the foreign countries. This is the unchangeable policy of the Chinese Communist Party and the Chinese People's Liberation Army.

The Indian authorities were astonished at the allegations and at the unexpected display of 'militant nationalism' by the Communists. Both the Guomindang and the Communists felt that the Indian mission in Lhasa, and particularly Hugh Richardson, was responsible for the incident.[16] This is confirmed by some Tibetan officials: Lhawutara, a high-ranking monk official, writes that it was Richardson's suggestion to expel the Chinese mission.[17] Phunstog Tashi Takla, who was the main person liaising with the Chinese, also stated that the idea originated from Richardson.[18] However, Richardson does not remember that he made such a suggestion, though he concedes that he may have inadvertently commented on the danger posed by the presence of the Chinese mission in Lhasa.[19]

According to official Indian sources, the expulsions also took them by surprise. Soon after Chen Xizhang was informed of the decision, Richardson was summoned to the Tibetan Foreign Bureau and was requested to tell the GOI, and to ask them to provide a safe passage for members of the Chinese mission. The demand placed great difficulties on the GOI: if it complied the Chinese would accuse India of helping the Tibetans; if it refused the Tibetans were placed in a difficult position. Hugh Richardson recommended 'that it would have been better to allow the officials to remain and to remove only persons suspected of subversive activities'.[20] Chen Xizhang made a futile protest by refusing to provide evacuees with valid travel documents without orders from his government. Hugh Richardson noted that 'this gesture was apparently intended to provide evidence that his removal was by force'.[21]

In the end the expulsion of the Chinese mission from Lhasa was a shrewd move on the part of the Tibetans. It not only ended the influence of the Nationalists but it meant that, when the Communists came to power in China in October 1949, there was no vestige of Chinese authority in Tibet. The Communists were immediately presented with the problem of how they could assert their authority in Tibet, for it was clear that there was no scope for an internal Communist revolution there.

Along with the Chinese mission, a number of Tibetans from the eastern point of the country were expelled on suspicion of being Communist sympathisers. One of these was Baba Phuntsog Wangyal, a progressive Tibetan from Bathang in Kham who earlier had tried to organise a Progressive and Pan-Tibetan movement in Tibet. He came to Lhasa in 1946 and tried to warn the Lhasa authorities that after the civil war the Communists would invade Tibet. He argued that Tibet's survival lay in opening the country to the outside world and introducing internal reforms. When Lhasa officials did not listen to his warning, he went to Kalimpong to urge the British to arm the Tibetans. No one took him seriously, and when he was later expelled from Lhasa, he told his friend Tharchin, the editor of what was then the only Tibetan newspaper: 'If the Tibetan Government does not listen, I shall bring the Chinese Army to Tibet. Then I shall write to you'. Tharchin later recalled that in 1951, when the PLA entered Lhasa, he received a telegram which read, 'Safely arrived in Lhasa Phuntsog Wangyal.'[22] The Communists were able to recruit him to their ranks, and he was to play a leading role during the negotiations between Tibet and China in May 1951.

One of the negative aspects of this expulsion of Communist sympathisers was that the Chinese Communists became convinced that foreign powers had penetrated Tibet and had stirred up hostility towards them. Hugh Richardson in his monthly report to the GOI commented, 'At all events, they seem to have postponed the likelihood of Communist activities in Lhasa by removing suspicious persons, but who can say for how long'.[23]

But however remote the Communist threat to Tibet now seemed, the atmosphere of fear in Lhasa became palpable. When a comet appeared in 1949 it was taken as a bad omen. People were quick to point out that when Halley's comet had appeared in 1910 the Chinese had launched an invasion. The government ordered performances of religious services to avert the dangers. Yet the majority of the Tibetan peasantry, living outside the political environment of Lhasa, remained totally unaffected by the new political development. The politics of Tibet had always been the privilege of a few aristocratic families and the lamas in Lhasa. This is how Hugh Richardson summed up the situation in his monthly report for November 1949:

> Up to that time the atmosphere in Lhasa had been vague. A number of officials had [sic] personally appreciated the seriousness of their position and some are reported to be making plans for removing themselves, their families and possessions from Lhasa presumably to India. But others viewed the situation more lightly saying that Tibet is a small and poor country and that the Chinese Communists would not be likely to be attracted by it. Others again, notably minor monk officials, considered that as they were poor and had experience in governmental matters, they would be wanted by the Communists to work for them. Higher monk

officials expressed their intention of dying for religion, at the head of their retainers.[24]

One leading aristocrat later recalled that 'people started thinking of moving to India and started shifting their valuables either to India or to the monasteries' and summed up the atmosphere succinctly: 'People were like birds, ready to fly.'[25] Others thought that it would take some time before the Communists entered Tibet. Rinchen Dolma Taring, a member of a leading aristocratic family, described her reaction to Peking's broadcast of its intention of liberating Tibet: 'in the late 1940s we heard rumours that the Chinese Communists were coming, but we thought it might take them years to arrive because they has [had] said on the radio that they would first get Formosa'.[26]

The expulsion of the Chinese mission marked the beginning of a new phase in the Sino-Tibetan relationship. By severing its ties with China, Tibet had emphatically declared its desire to remain independent. On the other hand, this provocation made the Communists even more determined to gain control of Tibet. It was evident that China and Tibet had irreconcilable objectives. The question that was to dominate the first months of 1950 was whether reconciliation could be achieved through diplomacy or whether it would be by coercion.

In October 1949, the Communists assumed total control of China. A month later, the Tsongdu (Tibetan National Assembly) met to discuss the Chinese threat. It was agreed that they should take various measures to counter Chinese propaganda. First, they would make internal reforms to prepare for a possible Chinese attack. Second, they would seek to secure external support and, third, they would try to establish a dialogue with the Communists.

Up to that time Tibet had lived in isolation from the major social and political events of the world. The Second World War had passed uneventfully for the Tibetans. The Tibetan socio-economic and political system resembled that of the Middle Ages in Europe. Between 1913 and 1933 the thirteenth Dalai Lama had tried to drag Tibet into the twentieth century, but he had come up against the conservatism of the religious institutions and a few of the ruling élite. Yet Tibetan society was neither stagnating nor verging on collapse. There was a small group of Tibetans who were well informed about the international situation, and a few aristocratic families who had travelled outside Tibet and had sent their children to missionary schools in India. Through them, the centre of Indo-Tibetan trade, Kalimpong, had become a window on the outside world. It was largely these people who initiated efforts to modernise Tibet's army and administration.

Tibet Prepares to Face the PRC

The National Assembly's recommendations for major internal changes were endorsed by the Regent Taktra in 1949. The Kashag was reorganised into three separate ministries: External Affairs, Defence, and Pay and Supplies. Each *Shape*[27] was put in charge of a department; Kalon Lama Rampa was put in charge of external affairs, assisted by Lukangwa and Drungyig-chenmo Chomphel Thupten;[28] Surkhang Wangchen Gelek was given responsibility for dealing with military pay and supplies. He was assisted by the Tsipon Ngabo Ngawang Jigme[29] – who was later to play a leading role – and another of the Drungyigchenmos, Ngawang Drakpa. Ragashag was in charge of defence and the mobilisation of troops. He was assisted by Tsipon Namseling and Drungyigchenmo Ngawang Namgyal. As a matter of urgency they were given power to act without consultation with the National Assembly.[30]

The Kashag also decided they needed to monitor international news. Heinrich Harrer, an Austrian refugee who was living in Lhasa at the time, was asked to listen to the radio and provide the government with daily summaries of international news.[31] The most innovative decision was to set up a radio station in Lhasa. For a number of years the Tibetan Government had been setting up a network of wireless communication systems throughout Tibet. For this purpose the Government had employed two Britons, Robert Ford and Reginald Fox.

In January 1950, Radio Lhasa broadcast to the world for the first time, in the beginning for only half an hour a day. The news was read in Tibetan by Rimshi Rasa Gyagen, in Chinese by Phuntsog Tashi Takla, the Dalai Lama's brother-in-law, and in English by Reginald Fox. The primary purpose of the broadcasts was to counter Chinese propaganda and on 31 January 1950 Lhasa Radio rejected Beijing's claim that Tibet was part of China. The broadcast declared that Tibet had been 'independent since 1912 when the Manchu garrison had been driven out'.[32]

The National Assembly agreed to the opening of the country for motor traffic between India and Tibet. In 1949 J. E. Reid of General Electric Company visited Tibet to negotiate the Tibetan Government's purchase of electrical equipment for a small hydro-electrical station that the government planned to build in Lhasa.[33] More important, Regent Taktra gave Mr Reid a letter authorising Bharat Airways to fly the equipment to Lhasa. Tibet also expressed a desire to open an air link between Lhasa and some northern Indian cities.

Above all the Tibetans sought to strengthen their army. Since the 1930s, it had developed rapidly but was still poorly equipped and trained, despite the training of a few officers by the British. In March 1947 the Kashag asked the British Government to supply a substantial amount of arms and ammunition. This was approved by the British Cabinet and the interim Indian Government, with the exception of two anti-aircraft guns.[34] By 1949 it was clear that the stock of ammunition and arms in Tibet's possession would be wholly inadequate to counter a Chinese offensive, and so the Kashag agreed to sanction further military expenditure. For this they took silver coins (tangka) from the Potala treasury, worth four hundred thousand rupees, and minted them into 10 srang silver coins to meet the costs of military pay and supplies.[35]

In August 1949, when the Indian Political Officer in Sikkim, Mr Harishwar Dayal, made a visit to Lhasa, Tibetans saw this as an opportunity to seek support from the GOI. They hoped to establish a new relationship by drawing up a new treaty, which would supersede the 1914 Simla Convention.[36] At the first meeting between Dayal, Surkhang Lhawang Topgyal and Liushar Thupten Tharpa from the Foreign Affairs Bureau, the Tibetans asked if India could supply arms and ammunition but they were told by the Indians that the primary task was to train Tibetan troops. The GOI agreed to a small supply of arms and ammunition, and also to provide training for new troops. At the second meeting, on 8 November 1949, the Tibetans informed Dayal that the present strength of the Tibetan Army was 13,000 but they wanted to increase it to 100,000 men. They inquired whether the GOI could provide the necessary instructors, arms and ammunition.[37] In the meantime the Tibetan Government set about recruiting and training new soldiers; Heinrich Harrer describes how 'the flat pasture lands around Lhasa were transformed into training grounds for the troops'.[38]

On 25 February 1949 a meeting was held in Gyantse between Depon Kunsangtse and the representative of the GOI, Colonel Srinivasan to discuss training and weapon requirements.[39] In June 1949, the Indian Government supplied a limited amount of arms and ammunition, which included 144 Bren Guns; 1,260 rifles; 168 Sten guns; 500,000 rounds of .303 ammunition, and 100,000 rounds of Sten gun ammunition.[40] In March 1950, the GOI increased their supplies: 38 2' Mortars; 63 3' Mortars; 150 Bren guns; 14,000 2' mortar bombs; 14,000 3' mortars, and 1 million rounds of .303 ammunition.[41] The Tibetan Government provided Mr Reid with the sum of one hundred thousand rupees for the purchase of small arms.[42]

The old regiment, founded in 1931 and known as the Drongdra Magmi (Better Family Regiment), was revived to strengthen the existing groups. However, it faced such a severe shortage of ammunition that soldiers were not allowed to fire their weapons during training. The rations for soldiers were improved and an additional cash payment was agreed. Other regiments were dispatched to the border regions, in eastern Tibet and the north-east regions. The government also decided to set up four wireless stations in western and northern Tibet.[43]

On coming to power in China the Communists immediately strengthened their control in Kham (Xikang) and Amdo (Qinghai). The situation in eastern Tibet became precarious. The Tibetan Government had been observing the *de facto* boundary line agreed at the Simla Convention of 1914, which divided Tibet into outer and inner Tibet.[44] Neither the Tibetan nor the Chinese Government had ever been able to assert authority effectively in Kham. Much of the area was ruled by local chiefs, who were fiercely independent. The Debpa Zhung (Tibetan Government) ruled territories west of the Upper Yangtze. The Domed Chikyab (Governor of Kham) was responsible for both administrative and military matters in Kham. The Tibetan army guarding the eastern frontier consisted of 2,500 men,[45] who were badly equipped and had received little or no training in modern military methods. At the time the Domed Chikyab was Lhalu Tsewang Dorje, who had been in Kham for nearly three years and was due to be replaced. Lhalu was aware of the growing threat of instability in Chinese-controlled Kham where there was increasing PLA activity. The governor decided to strengthen the fortifications on the frontier and to strengthen his forces by recruiting local militia.

In the summer of 1949 Robert Ford, the Englishman employed by the Tibetan Government as a radio operator, and three trainee wireless operators were dispatched to Chamdo. Their arrival enabled Lhalu to improve the defensive measures in Chamdo and the surrounding areas. Moreover, for the first time a direct link was established between Lhasa and Chamdo. In February 1950, Lhalu asked Ford to cut short the training of the wireless operators, so that he could set up wireless stations along the frontier.[46] Rumours of the PLA advance were widespread in Chamdo. In the same month, new supplies of arms and instructors arrived and there was training in the use of Bren guns. Robert Ford wrote that 'the Tibetan Army began to look a little less like something out of the Middle Ages'.[47]

Two months later, Ngabo Ngawang Jigme was appointed as the new Governor of Kham. At the same time, he was promoted from the rank of Tsipon to Shape. The Governor of Kham had the same rank as a member of the Kashag, although he could not attend Kashag meetings in Lhasa. The position reflected the importance attached to the post, and it also meant that the governor could make immediate decisions without having to consult superiors in Lhasa. Ngabo had previously served in Kham as an official in charge of army pay and was therefore aware of the difficult position he was about to inherit. Before he left Lhasa, Ngabo discussed the situation with Yuthok Tashi Dhondup, who had also served as Governor of Kham.[48] Yuthok advised him that the best course of action was not to provoke the Chinese or antagonise the local people. Ngabo wanted to improve the conditions for the local officials and asked the government to increase their allowances.[49] Ngabo also reached the conclusion that it would be impossible to stand up to the PLA.[50]

Some saw the appointment of Ngabo as the Governor of Eastern Tibet as inauspicious. Chagtral Sonam Chophel recalls that there was a Tibetan saying that 'when the throne of Tibet is guarded by a person of lower birth, then Tibet would be invaded by China', and people soon assumed that this referred to Ngabo.[51] He was the illegitimate son of a nun from one of the leading aristocratic families of Tibet, Horkhang, who had acquired the surname of Ngabo by marrying a young widow of Ngabo Shape.

Ngabo arrived in Chamdo in September 1950 but because of the grave situation in Kham, the Kashag decided that Lhalu should also remain in power for the time being.[52] The decision to appoint two governors seems to have been a disaster. The relationship between the two was strained from the start, and Ngabo is reported to have remarked that Chamdo was too small for two governors.[53] At the end of September, Lhalu left Chamdo and set up his headquarters in Pembar Dzong, leaving Ngabo in charge of both civil and military affairs in Chamdo. The border regions on the Changthang, the high plateau of north-east Tibet, were also strengthened. On 20 June, Ragashag Shape and a lay commander made an inspection tour of the Nagchuka area. The number of men in the area was increased by the recruitment of local militia.[54]

Initially, the government wanted to raise the number of soldiers to 100,000 but it proved impractical and those who could afford to bribe recruiting officers to avoid serving.[55] The attempts to modernise Tibet's polity and the army came too late. Limited resources and the lack of a modern infrastructure hampered any military or civil defensive measures that the Tibetans adopted and there was no way that the Tibetans would have been able to resist a determined Chinese attack. The supply of arms and ammunition would not last more than six months. Nevertheless, the Tibetans did their best to show the Chinese their determination to resist invasion. The ruling élite realised that the best chance for Tibet's survival lay in outside support. The Tibetans had already opened the country to a number of outsiders; now they appealed directly to the international community. Britain had dealt with Tibet as an independent country, but she had never afforded Tibet the *de jure* recognition it sought. On the other hand, neither had the British recognised Chinese sovereignty over Tibet.

As far as the Tibetans were concerned, the status of Tibet was governed by the 1914 Simla Convention. However fragile it might be, the Convention provided some sort of definition of Tibet's status. In late 1949 and early 1950, the primary objective of Tibetan foreign policy was to maintain the status quo, whereby Tibet would have total control over its internal affairs and would maintain some kind of external personality. For many years the Tibetan Government had sought international recognition and visibility. In

1948 the Kashag dispatched a high-level trade delegation abroad in order to demonstrate Tibetan independence. The trade mission secured a major diplomatic coup when the United Kingdom and United States issued visas on Tibetan passports. This was tantamount to official recognition of Tibet's independent status.[56]

Tibet Seeks International Support

By 1949, the need for international support and recognition was more urgent than ever before. Kalon Lama Rampa[57] was given responsibility for external affairs by the Kashag. The Kashag also appointed Khenchung Lobsang Tsewang and Surkhang Lhawang Topgyal as Tibetan representatives in India who were to be based in Kalimpong. They would act as Tibetan trade agents and would also be responsible for spear-heading the Tibetan lobby in India and abroad. It seems incredible that despite the extensive political and trade relations with India, this was the first time Tibet had sought to establish a mission in India to look after Tibetan interests. India readily agreed to the setting up of a Tibetan mission. The status of the representatives was informal: they would be described as 'trade agents' and their function was described as the 'examination of trade between India and Tibet'.[58] In August 1949, the Kashag invited to Lhasa the well-known American radio broadcasters Lowell Thomas and his son. It was hoped that their broadcasts would increase public support for Tibet in the United States. When the Thomases left Lhasa they were given a letter from the Kashag to President Truman.[59]

It appeared on the surface that Tibet's attempt to gain international support might achieve some success. Britain and India had shown interest in maintaining the status quo, and the GOI had agreed to supply arms and ammunition and provide training. The British had written to the Tibetan Government stating that 'His Majesty's Government in the United Kingdom will continue to take a friendly interest in the future prosperity of the Tibetan people and in the maintenance of Tibetan autonomy' and went on to say that Britain 'hopes that the Tibetan Government will agree to a continuance of the present friendly contacts for which they would wish to provide an arrangement for visits to Lhasa to be paid from time to time by the United Kingdom's High Commissioner in New Delhi or a member of his staff.'[60]

In 1949 Britain hoped to send a special mission to Lhasa, to show that it had 'not lost interest in Central Asia as a result of handing over our power in India'.[61] But the mission was 'postponed on account of India's unenthusiastic reaction to the project'. It was considered by others that 'it would also lend weight to the Chinese Communists' allegation of imperialist plots in Tibet'.[62]

Despite the fact that the British mission to Lhasa did not take place, the Tibetans were convinced that Britain was interested in maintaining some form of relationship with Tibet and the Kashag therefore felt that with British backing they would be able to secure support from the international community. The National Assembly and the Kashag adopted a two-pronged approach. First, the Kashag sought admission to the United Nations and, second, missions were dispatched to Nepal, India, USA and UK to seek support for Tibetan independence. It was recognised that the missions' task was of great importance, for they would determine the future course of Tibet's history. Therefore, it was decided that the members of the mission should be selected by divine intervention.[63]

The most important mission was the delegation to China. It was to be headed jointly by Tsipon Shakabpa Wangchuk Deden and a monk official, Khenchung Thupten Gyalpo. Shakabpa was one of the few high-ranking Tibetan officials who had some knowledge and experience of international politics. They were assisted by Kusho Driyul, Tsetrung Lobsang Nyenda and Geshe Lodro Gyatso, who represented the monastic organisation. Two interpreters were also appointed: Phuntsog Tashi Takla, who acted as Chinese translator, and Taring Dzasa, the English translator.[64] Shakabpa was unhappy about being selected to go to China which he had visited in 1948 as the leader of the trade mission, when he had deceived the Chinese by informing them that the trade mission would not go to the United States and Britain.[65] Moreover, there were better qualified people who could have led the delegation to China. Thupten Sangye, who had been the Tibetan representative in Nanking and spoke Chinese, would have been the most suitable. The lottery selected Thupten Sangya to head the delegation to the United States.

A month after the Communists came to power in China the Tibetan Foreign Bureau wrote to the British Foreign Secretary, Ernest Bevin, seeking support. The Foreign Bureau enclosed the copy of a letter that had been sent to Chairman Mao, which declared that Tibet was an independent country and that the new government should observe the established boundary. The letter to Bevin pointed out the growing threat of Communism and stated: 'we would be most grateful if you would please consider extensive aid in respect of requirements for civil and military purposes and kindly let us have a favourable reply at your earliest possible opportunity.'[66]

On 3 December 1949, the Kashag sent a telegram to the British Government requesting support for the admission of Tibet into the UN.

As Tibet being an Independent state we have no danger from other foreign countries but in the view of the spread of Communism and their successes in China, there is now an imminent danger of Communist aggression towards Tibet.

As all the world knows that Tibet and Communist China cannot have any common sympathy by reason of religion and principles of life which are just the opposite, therefore in order to defend our country against impending threat of Communist invasion and also to preserve our future independence and freedom, we consider it most essential for Tibet to secure admission of her membership in the United Nations General Assembly.

We are sending special mission to Great Britain in this connection but, in the meantime we shall be most grateful to you and His Majesty's Govt if you would kindly help us and place our humble appeal to the United Nations immediately through your good office so that Tibet could take her place in the United Nation as a member state.

Kindly take immediate action and wire reply.

Kashag (Cabinet Ministry of Tibet Lhasa).[67]

There was general agreement in the British Foreign Office: any possibility of Tibet entering the UN was immediately ruled out. Tibet's application would have been vetoed by the Russian and Chinese Nationalist representatives. However, Britain wanted to find out the views of the United States and the GOI. The State Department told the British ambassador, Sir Oliver Frank, that the US Government had received a similar approach and the State Department had proposed to discourage the Tibetan Government from expecting any assistance. 'There was little likelihood that the administration would take a serious interest in the Tibetan request and that he thought the problem could be more properly be left in the hands of India and the United Kingdom,' Frank was told.[68]

In January 1950, the British High Commissioner in Delhi asked the GOI to forward Bevin's reply through the Indian Mission in Lhasa. It stated that 'Mr Bevin wishes to point out to the Kashag that admission to the UNO is subject to the approval not merely of the UNO Assembly but also of the Security Council where the veto is operative, and for obvious reasons it would be quite unrealistic in present circumstances to hope to secure Tibet's admission to the UNO. Mr Bevin therefore suggests that the proposed special Mission referred to in the Kashag's telegram should be suspended.'[69]

While the US thought the matter should be left to Britain and India, Britain felt that it was a matter solely for India. An official at the Foreign Office, J. L. Taylor, commented, 'It would not be possible, even if we wished to do so, to make Tibet a member of the UN. In any case we regard Tibet as primarily India's responsibility and should make it clear to both India and Tibet as soon as possible. We ought however to back India in any action we can persuade her to do.'[70] When the British approached the GOI, Bajpai, Secretary General of the Ministry of External Affairs, told the British High Commissioner, Mr Robert, that the GOI had not received a request from the Tibetan Government, and therefore it saw no reason to act. Furthermore, the GOI did not want to get 'involved in British–Tibetan dialogue' because K. P. S. Menon, the Indian Foreign Secretary, believed that this would be 'lending colour to Peking radio allegations of Anglo-Indian ganging up over Tibet by our acting together in this way'.[71] Anyway, Menon informed the British High Commissioner that there was no hope of Tibet entering the UN. He said, moreover, that some Indian officials were of the opinion that India should gracefully withdraw from Tibet. Menon particularly mentioned that Sardar Panikkar, the Indian Ambassador in China, had advised that India should 'wash her hands completely of Tibet'.[72]

As far as Britain was concerned, interest in Tibet in the past had been the result of the need to secure its position in India. Now that strategic consideration had devolved to the GOI, there were relatively few British economic interests in the country. British officials were thus quick to recognise that Tibet was redundant to their interests. A pragmatic Foreign Office staff noted: 'we therefore consider that any attempt to intervene in Tibet would be impracticable and unwise. We have no interest in the area sufficiently strong to justify the certain risks involved in our embroiling ourselves with the Chinese on this question.'[73]

The refusal of the British Government and others to provide any kind of assistance was, in the Dalai Lama's words, 'terribly disheartening'.[74] The Tibetans felt that because of past relations, Britain was in a unique position to help Tibet. By the end of January, the Tibetan mission to the UK was recalled and the project was abandoned. As far as Britain was concerned, her interest in Tibet had reached a natural end. Now the basis of British support to Tibet was 'limited to supporting Indian policy in Tibet'.[75]

By early 1950 Tibetans had begun to turn towards the United States for assistance. Tibet's relations with America had improved as a result of the visit of the 1948 Tibetan trade mission, and Shakabpa had noted an encouraging attitude among the American officials and the public. The Tibetans were also aware that the US was now the dominant power in the world. Therefore, it seemed natural for the Tibetans to foster better relations with the Americans.

At the same time, the developments on the Tibetan plateau had not gone unnoticed in America. The Communist takeover of China had meant that the US could no longer regard Tibet as an area of little concern. By the beginning of 1949, there were increasing discussions in the State Department of their policies towards Tibet.[76] After the establishment of the Communist Government in China, the relationship between the USA and the People's Republic of China deteriorated. The Americans' primary concern was the expansion of the USSR and Communism in Asia.

The Tibetan government had noted the strong anti-Communist policy of the Americans. Officials in Lhasa, on hearing a radio broadcast by Phillip Jessup, the United States representative at the UN, in which he declared US support to anti-Communist countries in Asia, immediately sent an invitation to him to visit Lhasa. Although it was most unlikely that Jessup would have come, the Kashag instructed Harrer to make preparations for the construction of an airstrip.[77]

In January 1949, the American Ambassador in India, Loy Henderson, told Shakapba that the US would 'strengthen' relations between the two countries.[78] The US Embassy in Delhi had advised the State Department that in the event of a Communist victory in China, the US 'should be prepared to treat Tibet as an independent state to all intents and purposes'.[79] The State Department was not prepared to go that far. However, there was general agreement about 'establishing some sort of contact with the government of Tibet'.[80] The rapid Communist advances in China prompted Ambassador Henderson to write to the Secretary of State, on 2 July 1949, suggesting a reconsideration of the Tibet policy. He recommended sending an American mission to Lhasa,[81] a proposal endorsed by the American Embassies in Nanking[82] and Moscow.[83] This mission, clearly intended as a signal to the Chinese that America could establish a foothold in Tibet, never happened.

On 19 November 1949, Surkhang Depon met Counsellor Howard Donovan from the US Embassy in Delhi. Surkhang handed a copy of a letter from the Tibetan Foreign Bureau to Chairman Mao and a letter to the Secretary of State, which stated, 'in the event that Mao ignores the Tibetan letter and takes an aggressive attitude by sending his troops towards Tibet, the Government of Tibet will be obliged to defend its own country by all possible means. Therefore the government of Tibet would earnestly desire to request every possible help from your government.'[84]

On 3 December 1949, the Kashag dispatched a telegram to the US Secretary of State Dean Acheson which stated that Communism and the Tibetan way of life were totally incompatible and that China was a serious danger to Tibet. Therefore, 'in order to defend our country against the impending threat of Communist invasion and also to preserve our future independence and freedom, we consider it most essential for Tibet to secure admission of her membership of [to] the United Nations General Assembly'. It went on to state that the Tibetan Government wished to send a special mission to the US.[85] The State Department wanted to ascertain Britain's views on the matter before they made any decision. However, the British refused to get involved, informing them that the 'Tibetan problem is almost exclusively of concern to India'.[86] The British showed Henderson a copy of their reply to the Kashag, and advised the State Department that the 'US reply should [take] a similar line [to the] UK draft. Visit [of] Tibetan mission [to] US would be even more undesirable than to the UK'.[87]

On 21 December, the State Department authorised Ambassador Henderson to inform the Tibetan representative in Delhi orally that the Secretary of State had 'given sympathetic consideration [to the Tibetan request] and [the] State Department was convinced that Tibet's effort [to] obtain UN membership this time would be unsuccessful in view of certain opposition [from] USSR and Chinese delegations, both of whom have veto power in Security Council. Moreover, the Tibetan plan [to] despatch a special mission [to] obtain UN membership may at this time serve to precipitate Chinese Communist action to gain control [of] Tibet.'[88]

The Tibetans were not dissuaded by the American response. The following day, the Tibetans informed the Americans that they intended to dispatch a special mission headed by Khenchung Thupten Sangye and Rimshi Dingja 'for the purpose of obtaining aid from your government'.[89] The Americans were hesitant to receive any delegation from Tibet, particularly since both India and Britain opposed any active involvement in Tibetan affairs. On 12 January 1950, Dean Acheson instructed Ambassador Henderson to 'dissuade the Tibetans from sending the proposed mission'.[90] The State Department was concerned that the presence of a Tibetan mission in Washington would raise complications regarding the status of Tibet and that it 'might hasten Chinese Communist actions'.[91] However, the State Department was in favour of meeting a Tibetan delegation in New Delhi, although, in the event the Indian Foreign Secretary ruled out New Delhi as a venue for US–Tibetan dialogue.[92]

Six months later, on 9 June, Tsipon Shakabpa, Tsechag Gyalpo and Lachag Taring met formally with Loy Henderson in Delhi. They were to make a last appeal for American assistance and sought advice as 'to whether they should negotiate with the representatives of the Chinese Government in Delhi, Hong Kong or Peiping [Beijing]'.[93] Henderson suggested that Delhi might be an advantageous place because the atmosphere of Delhi would be more friendly, and communication with Lhasa would be easier. At the same time Shakabpa also told Henderson that Tibet's attempts 'to form closer ties with the United States came too late'.[94]

On 16 June Shakabpa made another visit to the US Embassy. This time, Shakabpa asked bluntly whether the 'US Government would render assistance to Tibet in event of a Chinese communist military invasion'.[95] Henderson told Shakapba that such a request would have to be forwarded to Washington. On 7 August 1950, Shakapba was informed by Counsellor Steere that he had received a reply from Washington which gave affirmative support: 'if Tibet intended to resist communist aggression and needed help, the US government was prepared to assist in procuring material and would finance such aid'.[96] The Tibetan request couldn't have come at a more opportune time. In the summer of 1950 America was coming under increasing pressure in the Far East, there was a real possibility that the Communists would take over South Korea and Chiang Kai-shek was 'becoming a political liability of the first magnitude'.[97]

However, later the Americans evaded the question which was put to Counsellor Steere: what action would the US take in the event of a Chinese invasion? Steere merely replied that 'the US could not commit herself, in advance, on a hypothetical question'.[98] He went on to say the 'US considered it important that prompt steps be taken now as it would be extremely difficult to make aid available in time if Tibet were to wait until invasion had started'.[99] The American responses may have confused the Tibetans. On the one hand they had announced that the US was willing to provide aid and on the other they were saying that they were only willing to provide this aid in the event of a Communist attack. It was clear that the Americans wanted the Tibetans to adopt a more overt anti-Communist policy and join the anti-Communist camp. The Tibetans still hoped to divert Chinese aggression by diplomatic means and they knew that hostile anti-Communist gestures would rule out any chance of peaceful resolution of the conflict.

The British advised the State Department that no independent action should be taken without consulting the GOI and that US policies should coincide with the aims of GOI. Therefore, the Americans advised that the Tibetans 'should first ask GOI for additional aid and if refused then ask GOI [for] friendly co-operation by permitting the passage of aid it wanted to secure from abroad'. Steere further stressed that 'Tibet [should] make an approach [to] GOI without any indication of the US's assurance of aid'.[100]

Shakapba dispatched a telegram to the Kashag informing it of the American decision to provide aid. On 9 September, Shakabpa, Tsechag Khenchung and Taring visited the American Embassy and told Henderson that they had received a reply from the Tibetan Government, which had instructed them to 'express its deep appreciation of the US offer of military assistance'.[101] The Tibetan Government agreed to make a direct appeal for military assistance from the GOI. At the same time Surkhang Depon and Khenchung Lobsang Tsewang, who were acting as (*de facto*) Tibetan representatives in India, were instructed to proceed to Delhi. To lessen the chance of arousing suspicions they were again described as a 'trade mission'.[102]

The mission arrived in New Delhi on 4 October, but they did not contact the American Embassy for twelve days. Henderson suspected that the GOI might have advised the Tibetans to 'refrain from contacting Embassy'.[103] When Henderson met Krishna Menon, Secretary in the Ministry of External Affairs, he stated 'categorically [that the] Tibetan delegation had never raised [the] question of additional military aid with GOI'.[104] Although Henderson did not believe Menon, he sent a telegram to the Secretary of State on 26 October which stated 'the question of military aid for Tibet is therefore dead'.[105]

The US also recognised that the co-operation of the GOI was essential. They had approached the British to ascertain the Indian attitude and had encouraged India to develop a more active role. The British immediately informed the Americans, 'on wider political grounds the GOI were unlikely to welcome any such American intervention in Tibet.'[106] Bajpai told the British High Commissioner that US intervention in Tibetan affairs was 'impracticable and undesirable'.[107]

India was the country that would be most directly affected by any change in the status of Tibet. Tibet's relationship with the new Republic of India had started badly. In 1947, Tibet had requested the 'return of excluded Tibetan territories gradually included into India'.[108] When the request was handed to Hugh Richardson, by then the Indian representative in Lhasa, he thought it an unwise start to a new relationship with the Government of India and took the unusual step of refusing to forward it to Delhi. The Tibetan Government decided to dispatch the demand directly to Delhi. The External Ministry in Delhi was certainly bewildered by the Tibetans' demand. They were not willing to concede any territory that they had inherited from their former colonial rulers. It marked an acrimonious beginning to the Indo-Tibetan relationship. Yet two years later, when Tibet was faced with danger from the east, it was to India that she had to turn for help.

As noted before, in November 1949 Harish Dayal, who was directly responsible for Tibetan affairs, visited Lhasa. This marked a new phase in the Indo-Tibetan relationship. Now that Britain had withdrawn from the Indian sub-continent, Tibet informed the GOI that they would like to establish a new treaty.[109] Moreover, Tibet wanted to re-negotiate boundary issues, and reiterated earlier demands for the return of Tibetan territories annexed by Britain.

This marked the realisation that if Tibet had any chance of maintaining the status quo, preserving its independence, it now depended on India's perception of its role and strategic aims. In the end, it depended on Prime Minister Nehru's conflicting and ambiguous views. Soon after the Communists came to power Nehru was in Srinagar, the capital of Kashmir, addressing Indian Army Officers. He stated that the 'Chinese revolution has upset the balance of power and that the centre of gravity had shifted from Europe to Asia thereby directly affecting India'.[110] Yet Nehru had no clear ideas about how India should respond to this new challenge.

In 1948, Sardar Panikkar, the Indian Ambassador to China, who was later accused of misleading Nehru about the Chinese threat to India, wrote a long memorandum called 'When China goes Communist'. He warned that the Communists, once they assumed power, would try to assert their authority over Tibet, which in turn would bring China into direct conflict with India. He recognised that Tibet was of great strategic importance to India. Panikkar suggested that it would be advisable for India to recognise Tibetan independence as a way of 'keeping the new Chinese Communist State away from the Indian border'.[111] But later in his memoirs Panikkar wrote, 'I had, even before I started for Peking, come to the conclusion that the British Policy (which we were supposed to have inherited) of looking upon Tibet as an area in which we had special political interests could not be maintained.' He went on to write: 'The Prime Minister had also in general agreed with this view.'[112] When Panikkar handed over his diplomatic credentials as the first Indian ambassador to the new Communist government, he spoke about the common boundary between the two countries, which raised some speculative concern in the British Foreign Office, as it implied that the new GOI recognised Chinese authority over Tibet.

China for its part made it clear to the GOI that it regarded Tibet as an integral part of China, and Zhou Enlai told Panikkar that the PRC saw the 'liberation of Tibet' as a 'sacred duty'.[113] It was evident that the issue of Tibet would soon confront China and India. Nehru's primary objective was to avoid any direct conflict. He believed naïvely that there was no serious gulf between the GOI and China. As Indian ambassador, Panikkar saw his mission in China as 'nothing more than that of witnessing the development of a revolution'.[114]

Prime Minister Nehru hoped that the new Republic of India would play a significant role in international affairs. However, apart from general anti-imperialist rhetoric and slogans about Pan-Asian nationalism, he had very little idea about how these could be developed. Nehru's biographer Sarvepalli Gopal wrote, 'there was little precision and definiteness about this objective'.[115] Nehru's views on Tibet were rather unclear and confused. In a press interview on 16 November, Nehru remarked, 'In a vague sense we have accepted the fact of Chinese suzerainty [over Tibet]. How far it goes one does not know.'[116]

In November 1949, Sir G.S. Bajpai, Secretary-General in the Ministry of External Affairs, gave British High Commissioner Nye the Indian Prime Minister's view:

> The present Government of India were as anxious as any past Government of India to retain Tibet as a buffer between them and China and they certainly did not want to see any increase in Chinese and still less Chinese Communist influence there. On the other hand the present regime in Tibet was completely out of date and they did not feel that the Lamas could in the long run resist Chinese infiltration if this were

> skilfully carried out on the basis of Communist propaganda and of an attempt to improve economic and social conditions of the Tibetan population. Quite apart from whether it would be wise to attempt to bolster up the lama regime, the Government of India did not feel that they had the military resources effectively to defend Tibet against Chinese encroachment.[117]

This summed up India's view on Tibet. Nehru and some other Indian officials were antagonistic towards the social system in Tibet, but this was not a chief concern. India wanted to maintain the status quo, but did not want to antagonise China. On 27 October 1949 Krishna Menon wrote to the British Government requesting advice on what they should do to safeguard the special position of Tibet. Menon also mentioned that GOI was being advised by K. M. Panikkar, the Indian ambassador in China. The ambassador was of the opinion 'that the present lama regime was too out of date and weak to resist any real pressure from the Chinese Communists'. He said that 'even a small expedition could dispose of the present regime'.[118]

A month later, the British responded with the following eight-point memorandum:

> (1) Tibet's best chance lies in the hope that the Chinese Communists will have other matters to occupy their energies for the time being and that they may be deterred from interfering by difficulties involved, provided that Tibetans show some spirit of resistance; we agree, therefore that we must discourage a defeatist attitude on the part of GOI and we should urge them to do whatever is possible to stiffen Tibetan government determination to resist, without, if possible, provoking Chinese Communists.
>
> (2) India should do what they can . . . short of military assistance.
>
> (3) India should give reasonable diplomatic support while recognising China's new government, [and] should not raise the Tibetan issue.
>
> (4) [At a] later stage India to make a communication to Chinese regards to Tibet's status on lines of Mr Eden's memorandum to Dr T. V. Soong.[119]
>
> (5) *Recognising Tibet's independence must be ruled out.*[120]
>
> (6) Despite need for caution we think the best practical steps towards strengthening Tibetan Govt's determination to resist would be for India to be immediately forthcoming in meeting any Tibetan requests for small arms. Delay in doing so might well dishearten Tibetans. It should be possible to supply arms in an unobtrusive manner not accompanied by any other military activities which might give rise to comment.
>
> (7) Tibet is now primarily an Indian concern.

(8) India ought to be encouraged to maintain her political influence in Lhasa through her mission there.

As was noted earlier, Britain saw no practical advantage in involving herself in Tibet, but the Foreign Office felt that the GOI should take a keener interest in the developments in Tibet. India slowly began to implement some of the suggestions made by the British. While India recognised that the entry of the PLA into Tibet would have created a direct threat to India's security, the question of how India could resist a Chinese presence in Tibet was problematic. Nehru no doubt appreciated that resistance depended on some form of active Indian involvement, but this smacked of 'Western imperialism'. Therefore, his natural inclination was to avoid any physical confrontation with China, another Asian country that had suffered under imperialism. But practical considerations meant that India should at least provide some form of aid to Tibet so that she could resist the Chinese penetration.

When Tibet requested permission to set up a Tibetan mission in Kalimpong, the GOI readily agreed. Later the Tibetans asked for 10 million rounds of ammunition and 1,500 Bren guns. But India agreed to supply only 3.5 million rounds of ammunition, and to dispatch a few Indian officers to Gyantse to train Tibetan soldiers. However, it was a symbolic gesture to show that India had not lost interest in Tibet. The ammunition would not have lasted more than a few months in the event of a Chinese attack. Tibet wanted more than symbolic gestures from India. The GOI's reluctance to discuss a new treaty and its reluctance to give active support to bi-lateral relations between Tibet and the US and other countries, convinced the Tibetans that India did not have the will or the inclination to assist Tibet. Like Britain before it, India would not afford Tibet the *de jure* recognition which would give Tibet an international personality. Nehru had somehow hoped that China could be persuaded to leave Tibet alone. India believed that her support for China over other international issues would have prevented China from directly antagonising India by invading Tibet. In the end this was not to be. If Tibet could not obtain any support from the world community, its best chance of survival lay in reaching a compromise with the new government in China.

Tibet Negotiates with the Communists

The Tibetans quickly realised that the Communists would win the civil war, and that contact with the new Chinese Government must be established. The letter that the Tibetan Government wrote to Chairman Mao on 1 November 1949 not only requested that the Communists respect the independence of Tibet but furthermore confidently demanded the return of all territories annexed by the Nationalists. The letter was shown to Hugh Richardson and Harish Dayal who advised that at present the Tibetan Government should avoid 'all bellicose language and action against the newly established Peking government.'[121] Nevertheless, the letter was dispatched:

> Tibet is a peculiar [unique] country where the Buddhist religion is widely flourishing and which is predestined to be ruled by the Living Buddha of Mercy or Chenresig [the Dalai Lama]. As such, Tibet has, from the earliest times up to now, been an independent country whose political administration had never been taken over by any Foreign Country; and Tibet also defended her own territories from Foreign invasions and always remained a religious nation.
>
> In view of the fact that Chinghai [Qinghai] and Sikiang [Xikang], etc, are being situated on the borders of Tibet, we would like to have an assurance that no Chinese troops would cross the Tibetan frontier from the Sino–Tibetan border, or any such Military action. Therefore please issue strict orders to those Civil and Military Officers stationed on the Sino–Tibetan border in accordance with the above request, and kindly have an early reply so that we can be assured.
>
> As regards those Tibetan territories annexed as part of Chinese territories some years back, the government of Tibet would desire to open negotiation after the settlement of the Chinese Civil War.[122]

The British felt that the rather arrogant language of the letter might annoy the Chinese. Dayal told the Foreign Bureau that it should avoid 'controversial points' and should avoid specific mention of 'independence'.[123] We don't know how the Communists reacted to this letter. The Tibetans never received a reply.

The Tibetan delegation headed by Shakabpa left Lhasa for China on 19 February, 1950. The members of the group were issued with specially prepared Tibetan passports from the Foreign Bureau, which were signed by the Kalon Lama Rampa.

The National Assembly authorised the mission to discuss the following points:

(1) concerning the unanswered letter to Chairman Mao Tsetung from the Foreign Bureau of the Government of Tibet;

(2) concerning the (atrocious) radio announcements from Xining and Beijing;

(3) to secure an assurance that the territorial integrity of Tibet will not be violated; and

(4) to inform the Government of China that the people and Government of Tibet will not tolerate any interference in the successive rule of the Dalai Lama, and they will maintain their independence.[124]

The Tibetan Government instructed the group that the discussion with the Chinese should take place in a neutral place, either in Hong Kong or Singapore. The Tibetan Government feared that if the group proceeded to Peking, they might be intimidated by the Chinese. The Tibetans also felt that a neutral place would enable them to speak more openly with the Chinese.[125]

The Tibetan delegation applied for diplomatic visas, as they felt such visas would carry more weight and offer greater facilities, and also they felt that official status would be given to the mission. The Tibetans' decision to hold the meeting in Hong Kong or Singapore caused a fierce debate in the British FO. A number of officials felt that some support should be given to the mission, as J. L. Taylor commented: 'we should, I think, put no obstacle in Tsipon Shakabpa's way; his negotiation may help to achieve a solution which would leave a greater measure of autonomy than a military conquest by the Chinese would'.[126] There were others who disagreed. P. D. Coates wrote: 'It seems to me somewhat doubtful whether the presence of a Tibetan representative in the imperialist colonies of Singapore and Hong Kong is likely to do the Tibetan cause any good. It opens a further gate for Chinese allegations that Tibet is just a puppet state.'[127]

The FO consulted the governors of Hong Kong and Singapore about the desirability of allowing Tibetans to conduct negotiations in British territories. On 9 March 1950, the governor of Hong Kong, Sir A. Grantham, informed the FO by telegram that he was totally opposed to any negotiations taking place in Hong Kong. The governor was particularly concerned with the presence of Shakabpa, the joint leader of the mission: 'we do not wish the person named to come to Hong Kong to contact Peking, presumably through an intermediary. We have enough problems on our hands already. We were particularly impressed with the person named when he passed through Hong Kong two years ago. He is a slippery customer and obviously out to make the best deal he can with Peking. There is no reason why he should not carry on any necessary arrangement from India'.[128] The governor of Singapore was equally opposed giving visas to the members of the mission.

However, on 4 May the West Bengal Government, who handled some of the British councillory services in Calcutta, issued 'gratis official courtesy' visas for Hong Kong to the members of the mission. When the FO learned that visas had been granted, it sent a telegram to the High Commissioner in Delhi: 'we are disturbed to find that visas have already been issued for Hong Kong. As you know from our telegram, we are not at present prepared to agree to the issue of visas for Singapore or Hong Kong. We trust therefore that the issue of "gratis official courtesy" visas for Hong Kong is the result of misunderstanding on the part of the government of India and we hope that it will be possible for you to arrange for them to be withdrawn.'[129] On 6 May the visas were duly withdrawn. The Tibetan mission was told that they had been granted prematurely and that the question of whether they should be official or diplomatic was still under consideration.

On 11 May, Shakabpa and the interpreter (Taring) visited the UK High Commissioner in Calcutta to ask why the visas had been withdrawn. Shakabpa told the High Commissioner that the flight had already been booked for 4 June. The High Commissioner was clearly embarrassed by the incident and informed the FO that 'when they asked why the visas had been cancelled they were told that we were in no position to discuss the matter.' And he added, 'the position is somewhat embarrassing to us here'.[130] When the British authorities asked for the Tibetan passports so that they could cancel the visas, the Tibetans refused to surrender their passports. They said that the passports were made of parchment and could be easily damaged.[131] The British were therefore unable to cancel the visas on the Tibetan passports.

On 24 May, Tsipon Shakabpa wrote from Kalimpong to the UK High Commission in Calcutta, protesting about the British withdrawal of the visas. The Indian authorities informed Shakabpa that the Government of India had referred the matter to the British Government to obtain diplomatic visas and the official visas already issued must be cancelled in the meantime. Shakapba insisted that the official visas should be cancelled at the same time as the issue of diplomatic visas. Otherwise the mission would be compelled to travel with official visas as they already had booked their flight on 4 June.[132]

When the Tibetans asked why the visas had been withdrawn, the British failed to provide a reason. They merely stated that earlier visas had been granted prematurely and that the British were not fully aware of the purpose and the nature of the mission. On 1 June, the Deputy High Commissioner in Calcutta wrote to Shakabpa advising him to consider the 'suggestion that it would be more suitable and favourable for your mission to conduct negotiations in India with representatives of the Chinese Government when they reached India'.[133]

On 4 June, two members of the mission, Dayul and Phuntsog Tashi Takla tried to leave for Hong Kong, to make the necessary prior arrangements. They were prevented from boarding the plane at Dum Dum Airport in Calcutta.[134] Shakapba and Sechang went to see the High Commissioner the next day and informed him that the refusal of visas and travel facilities would be 'interpreted in Tibet as desertion of Tibet by India and HMG'.[135]

As the matter was not getting anywhere, the Tibetans felt they should go to Delhi to appeal directly to the GOI and the British High Commissioner. On 7 June Shakapba visited the British High Commissioner, who for the first time provided some explanation for their reluctance to grant visas. The High Commissioner explained that it was more desirable for their negotiations to take place in India than in Hong Kong, for the following reasons:

(1) The imminent arrival of the new Chinese Representative in India.

(2) The poor state of British relations with the Chinese People's Government would make Hong Kong a bad place for negotiation.

(3) Good relations between India and Chinese made Delhi a more suitable place.

(4) Peking evidently did not wish to [deal] with the Tibetan mission on equal terms.[136]

Shakabpa informed the British that it was becoming urgent that the mission should meet the Chinese because he had received reports that Chinese forces had made advances in eastern Tibet.

Both the Indian and the British authorities were dubious about the success of the mission, and in fact they placed unnecessary obstacles in its way. The British refusal to grant visas and allow the mission to negotiate in Hong Kong incensed the Chinese and, moreover, it convinced them of 'foreign interference'. On 23 June 1951, a Chinese paper, *Guang Ming Daily*, published a statement by Geshe Sherab Gyatso, the Vice-Chairman of the Qinghai Provincial Government: 'although the delegation was hindered in India they can still come overland to inland China by way of Sikang [Xikang] and Chinghai [Qinghai]. The Imperialists will not be able to thwart the resolute will of the Tibetan people to join the motherland'.[137]

From the very beginning, the Indians and the British were both convinced that 'no good would be achieved by any attempt on the part of Tibetans to contact the Beijing Government'.[138] Since Shakabpa and other members of the mission were refusing to surrender their passports, the British now informed the mission that they were not prepared to issue visas on Tibetan passports. The visas would consequently be issued on 'affidavits'. The Governor of Hong Kong agreed to allowing transit visas for fourteen days. But the group would be treated as private persons and would not be allowed to hold a press conference. This would mean that the negotiations would have to take place in Peking.

On 17 June Shakabpa once again informed the British High Commissioner that the Tibetan Government had done its best to secure Chinese agreement to holding talks in Delhi. But the Chinese had refused and had insisted that the group should proceed to Beijing via Hong Kong. Meanwhile the Chinese Consulate in Calcutta stated that the members of the mission would be issued with Chinese passports and that they would be making the necessary visa arrangements. In September, Shakabpa once again came to Delhi and met with Nehru. He informed him that the mission would seek to meet with the Chinese representative in Delhi.

After six months of fruitless discussions, Bajpai and Menon were of the opinion that the mission should go to Beijing in accordance with their earlier undertaking. The Indian Ministry of External Affairs stated that they 'felt that the present time when the Peking Government should be on their best behavior in the hope of securing admission to the UN was the most propitious moment for the Tibetans to negotiate with them'.[139] It also appears that the Indian Government had been given assurances by the Chinese that the Tibetans would enjoy full autonomy.

On 16 September the Chinese ambassador, Yuan Zhongxian, met with the Tibetan delegation in Delhi. At the meeting the Tibetan delegation stressed that the traditional relationship between Tibet and China had been one of *mchod yon* (priest and patron).[140] They also said that there were no foreign imperialist influences in Tibet. The Chinese ambassador told the Tibetans that China could never accept Tibetan independence. He gave them a copy of the 'Common Programme' telling them to study articles 50–53.[141]

The Chinese ambassador Yuan also gave them a three-point proposal:

(1) Tibet must be regarded as part of China;

(2) China will be responsible for Tibet's defence;

(3) All trade and international relations with foreign countries will be handled by the PRC.[142]

Shakapba replied that he would inform the Kashag of the proposals. On 19 September Shakabpa sent a telegram to Lhasa with the Chinese three-point proposal, recommending that the Kashag should accept the proposals. Shakapba suggested that the first point about Tibet being part of China should be accepted only in name.[143] On the second point regarding defence, Shakabpa recommended that there was no need to station a Chinese army in Tibet, since neither India nor Nepal was a threat to Tibet's security. However, in the event of danger, Tibet should request Chinese assistance. Third, Tibet should insist on the right to maintain direct trade and cultural relations with Nepal and India. Shakabpa also requested that his mission should be allowed to proceed to Peking for further negotiations.

In retrospect, it is impossible to say whether the Shakabpa mission would have achieved a peaceful and better solution to the status of Tibet.

Shakabpa's request was turned down. The Kashag was not prepared to negotiate with the Chinese since they believed the Chinese proposals would have far-reaching consequences. The strong reaction from the Kashag may have been influenced by the increasing American willingness to supply aid to Tibet. The Tibetan Government hoped that USA might provide a last chance for Tibet's survival.

But on 6 October 1950, the Chinese launched a full-scale military invasion of Tibet. The primitive Tibetan defences in Chamdo collapsed with little resistance. Shakabpa said in an interview with Reuters in Calcutta that 'Chinese forces had entered Tibet. This was because his delegation had been delayed in India due to visa difficulties.'[144]

The Chinese made it clear that the failure of the mission to proceed to Beijing and obstacles placed by Britain and India had forced them to adopt a military solution. An editorial in the *People's Daily* on 17 November stated:

> The British government deliberately delayed issuing transit visas for Hong Kong to the Lhasa delegation, making it impossible for them to come to Peking. According to reports from various sources, when the Lhasa delegation were loitering in India, the British High Commissioner Nye, and other foreign imperialist elements used every effort to persuade the delegation not to come to any agreement with the Chinese People's Government. Then on the 12th August, when the Indian Government saw that the operations of Chinese government's forces to enter Tibet were about to begin, they informed the Chinese government that the British government had withdrawn its refusal to issue visas to the Tibetan delegation and that facilities for the departure of the delegation for Peking were available. But more than two months have passed and still 'the stairs have been created but no one has come down'. It is obvious that the delay of the Lhasa delegation in coming to Peking to carry on peaceful talks is the result of instigation and obstruction from foreign states who must bear the responsibility for obstructing and sabotaging the peaceful talks. It is only necessary for the local Tibetan authorities to strive to correct their former errors and abandon the erroneous position of relying on foreign influences to resist the entry of the people's liberation army and the Tibetan question can still be settled peacefully.

TWO

China Invades

The Chinese Communists first came into contact with the Tibetans during the Long March, the period described by Zhou Enlai as the 'darkest period in the history of the party', when 90,000 Red Army troops were pushed out of Jiangxi Soviet region by the Guomindang encirclement and forced to march north-west to secure safe bases.

In April 1935, the First Front Army led by Zhu De (the commander in chief of the Red Army) and Mao Zedong crossed the upper course of the Yangtse, known to the Chinese as the Jinsha River, and to the Tibetans as Drichu. This brought them outside the confines of the Chinese cultural sphere and later into contact with Tibetans. The area known by the Nationalists as Sikang (Xikang)[1] was predominantly inhabited by Khampas, who were culturally Tibetan and were nominally under the rule of the Guomindang government, though in reality the area was ruled by *Pons* (local chiefs).

The Second and the Fourth Armies also crossed into the Tibetan areas in 1935, with the Fourth Army remaining for nearly a year. The Communist leaders were immediately struck by differences in culture and language.[2] During their time in Kham, the Red Army was desperately short of food and provisions and the Communists were forced to abandon their rules about not taking anything from the people. The army was obliged for the first time to take food and goods from villagers.[3] The Communists were not able to communicate with the local people. When they entered villages, the people had fled, having hidden their provisions. The unprecedented number of soldiers in the area caused severe shortages of food. The Khampas attacked the exhausted Red Army, causing them great hardship.[4] The Communists' experience in Kham was summed up by Edgar Snow, 'Passing into the (Mantzu and) Tibetan territories, the Reds for the first time faced a populace united in its hostility to them, and their suffering on this part of the trek exceeded anything of the past.'[5]

The Communists' encounter with Tibetan-speaking people was confined only to eastern Tibet, and they had no idea of the situation in central Tibet, the area under the jurisdiction of the Dalai Lama. They recognised, however, their lack of influence and power in Tibet. Immediately on coming into power, they divided China into six military-cum-administrative regions, but Tibet remained outside this administrative division. Instead, the Communists adopted two strategies to bring Tibet within the structure of the PRC. On the one hand the Chinese boasted of their military superiority, constantly reminding the Tibetans that they had defeated the Nationalists. On the other hand they sought to win over the ruling élite by dampening their fear of Communism. The Communists were determined that Tibet should be incorporated into the administrative and constitutional structure of China.

The Communist Party had a small Tibetan membership, which had been recruited during the Long March and included people like Sangye Yeshi (Tianbao) and Sherab Dhundup (Yang Dongsheng),[6] two of the first Tibetans to join the Communist Party. Most of the recruits were from very poor families who were genuinely attracted to the promise of an egalitarian society. Others were young boys who drifted into the ranks of the PLA. The party was quick to realise the potential of these recruits and some were sent to the Party school in Yan'an. The Communists left behind a group of pro-Communist Tibetans who founded the first *Bod-pa* (Tibetan) Soviet in Garze in 1936.[7] It is interesting to note that they identified themselves as *Bod-pa*, a choice which undoubtedly implied some kind of Pan-Tibetan movement. At this stage, it seems the Communists were willing to pander to Tibetan nationalist aspirations of a united Tibet. All the Tibetan Communists were from eastern Tibet, which traditionally had been outside the control of the Tibetan Government in Lhasa and the Lhasa authorities were therefore unconcerned by the activities of this group. At another level there were people like Geta Rinpoche of Beri Monastery in Kham who realised that the Communists would win the civil war in China.[8] Geta Rinpoche had the traditional status and authority of an incarnate Lama and so he could influence his followers, but the Tibetan Communist Party members had very little influence among Tibetans.

China Woos Tibet

The first concern of the Chinese was to prevent any foreign powers from establishing a base in Tibet. When the Kashag decided to dispatch missions to Nepal, USA and Britain, the Chinese held protest rallies and Sangye Yeshi broadcast on Peking radio urging the Tibetan Government not to send the missions.[9] The Communists met with general distrust in all Tibetan areas. Guomindang propaganda had played on the anti-religious ideology of the Communists and had publicised the fact that the Communists would destroy monasteries and that Lamas would be imprisoned.[10] Therefore, when the Communists entered Tibetan areas they had to develop a cautious policy. They could not be seen to be reinforcing any of the Guomindang propaganda and initially adopted a policy of appeasement, doing their best to stress that the existing social and cultural system would not be altered. They could not engineer an internal revolution in Tibet. Therefore, the Chinese adopted a policy of winning over the ruling élite on the principle of revolution from above.

In March 1950, the Communists allowed a major religious ceremony to take place at Labrang Tashikhyil Monastery in Amdo, for the installation of the new incarnation of the Jamyang Zhepa. The ceremony was attended by Buddhists from Mongolia and other areas, and Chinese radio reported that 20,000 Tibetans and Mongols attended the ceremony.[11] This was a major propaganda victory for the Communists, who used the occasion to publicise their religious policies and the Common Programme. At first the relationship between the monks from Labrang and the Communists was quite friendly. A number of monks were recruited to carry out translation work, translating the first Communist document into Tibetan, the 'Eight-Point Contract'.[12] This was an important manifesto outlining the policies that the Communist Party intended to pursue after its victory. It was first distributed in areas where the Communists had no control, which suggests the Communists recognised that despite their victory they had not gained influence in Tibetan areas.

The Communists decided to retain the Mongolian and Tibetan Affairs Commission[13] and recruited many members of the existing staff to work for the new government. These people were well informed about internal Tibetan political conflict. The first director of the Commission was Zhu Shiguai. He was the father-in-law of Gyalo Dhundup, the elder brother of the Dalai Lama. The Communists at first tried to exploit this family connection by encouraging Zhu Shiguai to keep in communication with Gyalo Dhundup. Dhundup had escaped from Nanjing a few months before the city had fallen to the Communists. While Dhondup was in India he had been advised by his father-in-law to urge the Tibetan Government not to send missions abroad and that a peaceful settlement should be reached.[14]

The Communists immediately sought to exploit the internal divisions within Tibetan society and recruited all those who were disaffected with the Tibetan Government. The ninth Panchen Rinpoche, the second-highest ranking incarnate lama of Tibetan Buddhism, had been exiled in Amdo since 1928.[15] He had fled from Shigatse when a conflict arose between his monastery, Tashilhunpo, and the Tibetan Government. When he passed away in Jyekundo[16] in 1937, the Nationalists saw an opportunity to gain influence in Tibet by giving political support to a child born in Amdo as the tenth incarnation of the Panchen Rinpoche.[17] When the Communists came to power the child had been installed at Kumbum Jampaling as the tenth Panchen Rinpoche. But the Tibetan Government refused to recognise the child and put forward its own candidate.[18]

On coming to power the Communists reported that the young Panchen Rinpoche had sent a telegram to Chairman Mao and Zhu De, the Commander in Chief of the PLA, on the day that the People's Republic of China was founded. It allegedly stated: 'I sincerely present to Your Excellencies *on the behalf of all the people in Tibet* our highest respects and offer our heartfelt support.'[19] The Panchen Rinpoche was aged twelve at the time.

In January 1950, Beijing Radio and Xinhua released another telegram to Chairman Mao and Zhu De in the name of Panchen Rinpoche. It expressed the Panchen Lama's support for the Communist Party and urged the PLA to liberate Tibet and to unify it with the Motherland.

> On behalf of the Tibetan people, we respectfully plead for troops to be sent to liberate Tibet, to wipe out reactionaries, expel the imperialists, consolidate the national defences in the south west and liberate the Tibetan people. This assembly vows to lead the patriotic Tibetan people to mobilise the Tibetan people in support of the liberation army and to struggle hard for the People's Motherland.[20]

At the same time the Communists held a meeting in Beijing of 'democratic personages' from Tibet to discuss the Tibetan problem and to endorse the Common Programme. The meeting was primarily held to oppose the Tibetan Government sending missions abroad.

The Tibetan Government was aware of the threat that the Panchen Rinpoche and his followers posed. They had been monitoring the activities of the Tashilhunpo monks, and immediately after the fall of Xining in 1949 the Governor of Kham was instructed by the Lhasa Government to inform the Panchen Rinpoche and his followers that, despite past differences, the government would not take any action against them.[21] The Tibetan Government was increasingly suspicious of new arrivals from Amdo in Tashilhunpo, whom they suspected of being Communist agents. In April the Government ordered a search of some monks' quarters in Tashilhunpo.[22]

While Lhasa recognised that a few Tibetan Communists would not present a serious threat to Tibet's status, the reported support by Panchen Rinpoche of the new Chinese Government was 'causing a lot of anxiety in official circles'.[23] The government attempted to counter Chinese propaganda by broadcasting its attitudes towards the Panchen Rinpoche and his officials on Lhasa Radio. But the broadcasts stated that the new incarnation of Panchen Rinpoche could only be recognised after the traditional ceremonies had been completed.[24] This seemed to imply that Lhasa was still not prepared to recognise the new Panchen Rinpoche. As a result the Panchen Rinpoche's followers might have felt that their best chance of regaining power in Shigatse lay with co-operating with the new Chinese Government. The Panchen Rinpoche's followers were also aware that the Lhasa Government had tried to impose their own candidate as the new incarnation of the Panchen Rinpoche and that automatic recognition would not be extended to a candidate enthroned in Kumbum. Since the child in Kumbum had been accepted by the Tashilhunpo monastery, the seat of all the Panchen Rinpoches, renewed confrontation between Lhasa and Tashilhunpo monastery was likely.

The Chinese were skilfully exploiting the religious sentiments of the Tibetan people. They used prominent religious figures to communicate with the Tibetan government in Lhasa and selected Geta Rinpoche to proceed to Lhasa to establish contact and explain the party's nationality policy to the government in Lhasa. With the support of the Panchen Lama, Geta Rinpoche and other important religious figures, the Communists achieved a major propaganda victory. They were able to show that they would respect religious freedom.

At the same time the Communists strengthened military control over Kham and Amdo. They stepped up military pressure on the weak Tibetan defence system. In Chamdo, Lhalu was constantly receiving news of a build-up of Chinese troops in the border regions. The Chinese were careful not to cross into territories controlled by the Tibetan Government, hoping that a negotiated settlement could be reached with Lhasa.

Negotiations between the Chinese Ambassador and the Tibetan delegation in New Delhi had reached a stalemate. Shakabpa and his delegation had been waiting for instructions from the Kashag, and were hoping that the recent change in American policy would provide some measure of international support. The Chinese were frustrated by the fact that the Tibetans seemed to be more concerned with internationalising the Tibet issue and assumed that there was a real danger of intervention in Tibet from foreign powers.

On 6th May 1950, Geshe Sherab Gyatso (a noted Tibetan scholar and former abbot of Sera Je Monastery in Lhasa, but also deputy Chairman of the newly established Qinghai Provincial Government) made an appeal to the Tibetan people and to the Dalai Lama. It was an extraordinary broadcast in that, unlike previous radio messages, it implicitly warned that the Chinese would use force if necessary to 'liberate Tibet'. In retrospect, this appears to have been the final warning to the Tibetan Government.

The broadcast promised that Tibet would be liberated, since it was part of China and the People's Liberation Army was 'strong enough to fulfil this task'.[25] It went on to urge Tibetans not to believe in 'British and American imperialist slander aimed at sowing discord between nationalities'. Tibet was by no means 'too remote from Chinghai or Sikang,' it argued. 'If anyone should doubt the ability of the PLA to overcome geographical difficulties they need only remember the Long March or the recent liberation of Hainan.' Geshe Sherab Gyatso stated that any hope of relying on British or American intervention was 'futile', as the destruction of the Guomindang had clearly shown.[26]

Finally, the broadcast assured the Tibetan people that, under the leadership of the Communist Party, all nationalities of the People's Republic of China would be treated equally and religion would be respected. In accordance with the Common Programme of the CPPCC, Tibet would be granted 'regional autonomy' after liberation.[27]

The PLA Attacks

The first military skirmish between Tibetan troops and the PLA took place at the end of May 1950, when a group of fifty PLA attacked Dengo, situated on the bank of the Drichu, ninety miles from Chamdo. The Tibetans in Chamdo first heard of the attack when the radio message from Dengo was abruptly cut off in the middle of transmission. Robert Ford was on the Chamdo end, and told one of his assistants to keep on calling Dengo.[28] He immediately went to inform Lhalu, who was still in command at Chamdo, Ngabo having not yet arrived from Lhasa. In Ford's words, 'Lhalu looked grave but gave no sign of alarm. He murmured a brief prayer and then went into action'.[29] Lhalu recalled the 500 men from Changthang, and planned the recapture of Dengo. He also sent a scout team to monitor any PLA movements.[30]

Dengo was strategically very important. It was the most likely route along which the PLA would advance and it was on the main trade route from Kanting to Chamdo, giving access to Jyekundo in the north. From Jyekundo the PLA could march southward cutting off any escape route for the main garrison in Chamdo. Lhalu therefore told Ford that Dengo must be recaptured, or it would be impossible for them to remain in Chamdo.[31]

If the PLA had decided to proceed to Chamdo, it would have taken them several days, even if they were not opposed. Lhalu informed Lhasa of the fall of Dengo and requested further military supplies. He also informed the Kashag that he had the support of Khampa leaders and the monks of Dargye monastery. He wanted to launch a direct attack on the advancing PLA and capture all territories up to Jyekundo.[32] The Kashag, fearing this might lead to a full-scale military clash with the PLA, instructed him to recapture Dengo but not proceed beyond territories controlled by the Tibetan Government.[33] The Kashag told Lhalu that although his army might be able to advance further into Chinese-controlled areas, it would not be possible to maintain control of these areas for long in the event of a concerted Chinese attack.[34] They considered it unwise to march into Chinese-controlled Kham.

Four days after the fall of Dengo, scouts arrived back in Chamdo with the news that the Chinese had confiscated all Dengo's communications equipment. They also learned that there was only a small group of PLA men in Dengo.[35] Ten days after the attack, the regiment in Changthang led by Muja Depon arrived in Chamdo. Lhalu wanted to strengthen further the number of armed men, and therefore suggested that 500 monks should be armed.[36] Since monks are not supposed to engage in the use of arms, this needed to be sanctioned by a higher spiritual authority. Lhalu and Khenchung Dawa decided to seek advice from Trijang Rinpoche, the Dalai Lama's junior tutor, who was in Lhasa. Ford describes how an elaborate radio discussion was held between Trijang Rinpoche in Lhasa and Lhalu in Chamdo. When Trijang Rinpoche was asked what advice he would give, he simply said that they should 'obey the wishes of the Governor-General [Lhalu]'.[37]

Lhalu had dispatched Muja Depon and his regiment, with an additional 200 Khampa militia men. This brought the number of men to 700. Muja Depon and his men attacked the PLA group and recaptured Dengo. This small victory provided the Tibetans with a much-needed morale boost and enabled them to push the Chinese back to the *de facto* border. It is interesting that the PLA did not try to recapture the area or launch a full-scale military invasion. It is not clear why the Chinese decided to attack Dengo in May. It was either to put pressure on Lhasa and the Shakabpa mission in Delhi who were meeting the Chinese ambassador, or to test Tibetan defensive measures. The Communists were fearful that the Tibetans might be establishing a formidable defensive wall in Chamdo.

On 29 July, Beijing Radio broadcast a speech by General Liu Bocheng, who stated that the primary task of the South-West Military Administrative Committee was to liberate Tibet and that the 'PLA must launch an attack'.[38] But no attack came until October. It gave Lhalu and his officers time to strengthen the fortifications in Chamdo. Bren guns were placed in strategic positions and everyone was kept on guard.

In the middle of 1950, the Korean issue was dominating the international situation. The Chinese feared that the Americans might use this as a pretext for their involvement in Tibet. If the international tension should degenerate into a war, there was a likelihood of the Tibetan case being entangled in the wider issues. On 16th May, Radio Beijing reported that 'Henderson, US Envoy to India, had agreed with the GOI that a large shipment of rifles, machine guns, sub-machine guns, grenades and ammunition should be sent to Calcutta for transfer to Tibet via Darjeeling. US guards were to accompany the convoy and there was to be no Indian inspection'.[39] The GOI denied the Chinese accusation as 'entirely without foundation'.[40] Although it was untrue that there was any such agreement between India and USA, the Chinese were none the less fearful of international involvement in Tibet. Generally, the Tibetans have dismissed the Chinese accusation of imperialist machination in Tibet by saying that there were no Americans or British officials in Tibet and the only two Europeans in Tibet were employed by the Tibetan Government. However, we need to understand the Chinese accusation in a much wider context. The Chinese had a legitimate fear of US determination to undermine the new Communist Government of China. At the end of May 1950, the Communists noticed that Gyalo Dhundup, brother of the Dalai Lama, had turned up in Taipei and had met Chiang Kai-shek on 21 May. Taipei Radio reported that Gyalo Dhundup had arrived to seek military aid from the Americans.[41]

The Chinese concentrated on strengthening their position in Kham (Xikang). They had not been able to win over the Tibetans in Bathang, Lithang and Markham. The largest anti-Chinese group was led by the Pomdatsang brothers, who ruled Markham. In Bathang, Phuntsog Wangyal (who had been expelled from Lhasa with the Chinese mission in 1949) and a small group of pro-Communists had taken power and were busily trying to persuade Pomdatsang and the king of the Derge Se, Ngawang Kalsang, to surrender to the Chinese.[42] The Communists knew that if they were eventually to advance into central Tibet, then they would need to win over the Khampas. It now seems incredible that the Communists were able to win over the vast majority of the Khampas and enter Kham without any resistance. In fact many Khampas were willing to assist the PLA's entry into Tibet. According to Ford, the Tibetan soldiers feared the Khampas more than the PLA.

After the Dengo incident, the Chinese must have come to the conclusion that the Tibetans were going to resist any military incursion. They were also convinced that Shakabpa's mission in India was prevented from leaving for China by foreign powers hostile to China. Even members of the mission stated to the press that they had been prevented from going to China for discussions. The Chinese decided to make contact with the Tibetan Government by sending a number of influential pro-Communist Tibetan Lamas to Lhasa via Kham.

On 10 July 1950 the Communists dispatched Geta Rinpoche to Chamdo.[43] He had been elected the Vice-Chairman of the Xikang Provincial People's Government. He arrived in Chamdo and informed Lhalu that he wished to proceed to Lhasa. There was a flurry of radio communications between Chamdo and Lhasa.[44] While he was waiting for confirmation from Lhasa, Geta Rinpoche was treated with the respect and reverence shown to all incarnate lamas.[45] It is not clear what message he brought with him. It is most probable that Geta Rinpoche brought the same three-point proposal presented to Shakabpa by the Chinese ambassador in New Delhi, or perhaps a more detailed proposal. In the end the Tibetan Government refused to allow him to proceed beyond Chamdo, and on 22 August, Geta Rinpoche fell ill and died. The Chinese believed that Geta Rinpoche had been murdered by imperialist agents. After the fall of Chamdo, Ford was arrested and accused of the murder of Geta Rinpoche. Despite four long years of imprisonment, Ford denied any involvement.

In June a group from Xining arrived in Lhasa disguised as traders. The group brought a letter addressed to the Regent Taktra and another to the Tibetan Government. The letters urged the Tibetans to seek an agreement and to send a delegation to Beijing for negotiation. The group was accompanied by a radio operator. When they reached Lhasa, the government confiscated the radio.[46] About the same time in Amdo, the Chinese recruited another of the Dalai Lama's elder brothers, Thubten Norbu, an incarnate lama at Kumbum Monastery and two other prominent lamas from Amdo, Shar Kalden Gyamtso and Shalu Rinpoche, to proceed to Lhasa with a special message.[47]

It was most probable that the proposals that Thubten Norbu brought were similar to the three-point proposals that had been presented to Shakabpa in Delhi. Thubten Norbu says that many of the proposals were similar to points covered in the 17-Point Agreement.[48] The Communists first planned to send a group of PLA soldiers to accompany the delegation but after some discussion with Geshe Sherab Gyatso, it was decided that only two Chinese officials and a radio operator would accompany them.[49] Thubten Norbu met with Geshe Sherab Gyatso, who stated that it was advisable for the Tibetans not to speak of independence.[50] The journey from Amdo to Lhasa took more than three months. The group was met at the Tibetan border in Shagchukha in the north-east by the Tibetan army, who refused to allow the Chinese official and the radio operator to proceed to Lhasa; they were detained on the outskirts of Lhasa.[51] The Chinese were furious that they were not allowed to proceed to Lhasa. The Chinese escort insisted that if that was the case, then Thubten Norbu would not be allowed to go to Lhasa.[52] The escort also boasted that he had just received a radio message that the Chinese forces had launched an attack in eastern Tibet and captured a number of prisoners.[53] By the time the group arrived in Lhasa, the Chinese had already invaded Chamdo and Lhasa was in panic. Thubten Norbu met with the Dalai Lama, and for the first time the Dalai Lama received a first-hand account of Communist rule.

While the diplomatic negotiations were going on in Delhi, it was left to Ngabo, who by now had taken over from Lhalu in Chamdo, to repel any Chinese incursions. Lhalu had adopted an offensive policy and had successfully repelled the initial Chinese attack. In contrast, Ngabo believed that it was futile to fight the Chinese. Soon after he took office Ngabo decided to dismantle some of the defensive measures taken by Lhalu. Ngabo felt that Tibetan defensive measures would be construed by the Chinese as provocation. Ford advised Ngabo to dispatch one of the portable radios to Riwoche, which would give an early warning of Chinese movements. At the time, Ngabo 'seemed to have everything under control'. Ford described him as 'cool and efficient and quietly confident'.[54] Ngabo told Ford, 'we shall not give the Chinese permission to send troops into Tibet. If they enter by force we shall resist. If necessary, of course, we shall evacuate Chamdo and retreat to Lhasa. *There will be no local surrender* as long as I am in Chamdo.'[55] In retrospect, it seems Ngabo was ingenuous in believing that the Chinese could be stopped in Chamdo.

On 17 August the Guomindang intelligence reported that the Communists were planning to advance into Tibet. The First Field Army under General Peng Dehuai was moving southwards to Tibet from its bases in Xinjiang and the Second Field Army, led by Liu Bocheng, was moving westward.[56] The Communists continued to send informal emissaries to Lhasa and the Tibetan Government adamantly refused to meet any of them. However, Shakabpa had been instructed by the Kashag to keep in touch with the Chinese ambassador in Delhi, and since July 1950 the two had met several times. By September, both Shakabpa and the Chinese in India were increasingly frustrated by the fact that the Tibetan Government had refused to give any definite replies to the three proposals put forward by the Chinese. Despite Shakabpa's recommendation that no agreement could be reached with China unless Lhasa compromised on the issue of Tibetan independence,[57] the Kashag had decided not to accept the Chinese proposal. Knowing that if they were to inform the Chinese of their refusal, the Chinese would probably adopt military means to achieve their aims, the Tibetans naïvely tried to gain time by refusing to reply. The Kashag merely told Shakabpa to delay giving any answer to the Chinese until the international situation improved.[58] Lhasa was aware of the growing tension over Korea, and therefore it was hoped that the Korean issue would either divert Chinese intention or the Americans would come to Tibet's aid. On 28 September, the Chinese ambassador asked Shakabpa what response he had received from the Kashag. Shakabpa said there was a fault on the telegraph line, and a second message had been sent by horse rider, but it would be several days before they received a reply from the Kashag.[59] It was unlikely that the Chinese would have believed Shakabpa's delaying tactic.

Shakabpa was clearly irritated by the Kashag's indecisiveness. On 30 September, he informed the Kashag it was imperative a decision be reached before the Chinese started to use military force.[60] The Kashag once again replied that, because of the 'uncompromising position' of the Chinese stand, and because it would have serious repercussions on the future status of

Tibet, they should wait until the international situation had improved before informing the Chinese of their refusal to accept the three-point proposal.[61]

There was, however, no improvement in the international situation. The Korean issue had become a major crisis. The Tibetans' refusal either to receive emissaries or reply to their proposals convinced the Chinese that their peaceful attempts had been thwarted by foreign powers, and that the Tibetans were recalcitrant. They were determined that Tibet should be, in their words, 'unified with the Motherland' without delay.

On 25 June 1950, the North Korean army had crossed the 38th parallel and marched into South Korea. The Americans were able to repel the advancing North Korean troops. Using K. M. Panikkar as intermediary, the Chinese informed the UN that if the US were to cross the 38th parallel, the Chinese would intervene on the side of the North Koreans. On 7 October, US troops under the command of General MacArthur crossed the 38th parallel. Under the aegis of the UN, the American forces recaptured Seoul on 26 November.[62]

On 7 October,[63] while the world's attention was focused on the crossing of the 38th parallel, 40,000 PLA troops from the South-West Military Region, led by Zhang Guohua, crossed the Drichu river. The Chinese caught the Tibetans by surprise. Their tactic was to overwhelm the Tibetan troops by sheer numbers and speed. According to Zhang Guohua the plan for the invasion was drawn up by the top three Communist officials in the South-West Military Region: Liu Bocheng,[64] Deng Xiaoping [65] and He Long, who 'personally planned and made preparations for the expedition' into Tibet.[66]

The success of the PLA depended on swift encirclement. 'The enemy was familiar with the terrain of this vast area and, besides, they [the Tibetans] were all expert horsemen. We were like a tiger trying to catch a fly – it was a hopeless task. Therefore the leaders of the SW Military District instructed us to carry out an outflanking movement. We were told that everything depended on our catching the enemy, that victory would be ours if we could surround the enemy.'[67]

The PLA attacked from three directions. The main aim was to capture Chamdo and prevent the Tibetan troops from retreating to Lhasa. One group assailed the small frontier post at Kamthog Drukha, east of Chamdo, capturing all the Tibetan soldiers stationed there.[68] As the PLA marched towards Chamdo, by way of Rangsum, they met resistance from the Tibetan army.

The 54th Regiment crossed the Drichu river north of Dengo and marched towards Jyekundo, which was directly north of Chamdo. From there the PLA marched southward, and encircled the Tibetan army, cutting off their escape route. The Chinese tried to cross from Dengo, but since the earlier incident it had been well guarded and Muja Depon was initially able to repel the Chinese attack.

The PLA group crossed the Drichu from Bathang and marched straight across to Markham, where Derge Se commanded a small force of 400 men. The area was seven days' march from Chamdo and was not seen by the Tibetans as an important sector and so had not been heavily guarded.[69] On 10 October Derge Se received reports that the Chinese were rapidly advancing towards Kungo Dzong, the civil and military centre in Markham. Derge Se tried to withdraw north. Geoffrey Bull, a missionary who had been living in Markham, writes: 'As soon as news of the proposed withdrawal leaked out, social order began to break down. People began to loot and soldiers to desert.'[70] They were cut off by the advancing PLA and Derge Se had no alternative but to surrender, his men 'utterly bewildered' by the sheer speed of the Chinese advance.[71] Derge Se announced to the Chinese, 'I surrendered because I consider that further bloodshed is absolutely useless.'[72]

The news of the PLA's advance did not reach Chamdo until 11 October. As soon as Ford heard the news of the invasion, he went to see Ngabo and requested that a radio should be sent to Riwoche, so that they could monitor PLA troops coming from the north to cut off their escape route to Lhasa. Ngabo told him that this route was secure and he needed a spare radio set in case the other broke down.[73] The news of advancing PLA troops caused panic in Chamdo. People engaged in a frenzied round of prayers and rituals. The monastery performed rituals to ward off evil. The rich tried to save their wealth by depositing it in the monastery.[74]

When news of the Chinese attack reached Ngabo, he immediately informed Lhasa, and requested instructions from the Kashag. In retrospect it seems incredible that the Kashag did not respond at once. In desperation Tsogo, one of Ngabo's officials contacted Dumra, a Kashag aide-de-camp, on 15 October but was told the Shapes could not be disturbed because they were at a picnic.[75] Tsogo exclaimed in exasperation, '*skyag pa'i gling kha*: Shit the picnic!'[76] This was the last communication between Lhasa and Chamdo.

There was no possibility that the Tibetan Army could stop the PLA advancing towards Chamdo. Ngabo decided to evacuate. Reports suggested that the Chinese still had not reached Riwoche and that the escape route back to Lhasa was safe. But in the middle of the night came news that the Chinese were indeed nearing Riwoche. Without warning, on the night of 16 October Ngabo and the Lhasa officials fled Chamdo. Those who remained felt betrayed, because Ngabo had commandeered most of the ponies, leaving the local people without transport.[77] Ford writes: 'panic was breaking out in the town. People were running about in all directions, carrying or dragging their personal belongings. Monks were hurrying towards the monastery, gabbling their prayers. The stalls in the main street were deserted'.[78]

The Chinese took Riwoche and encircled the retreating Tibetan troops near Drukha Monastery. There was no fighting. As Robert Ford says: 'the Tibetan Army was not designed for retreat. When troops went to the front line they took their families with them; and with Muja's men now came with as many women and children, with all their household goods and personal belongings piled up on yaks and mules. There were tents, pots and pans, carpets, butter-churns, bundles of clothes, and babies in bundles on their mothers' backs. It was a fantastic sight.'[79]

The Tibetans surrendered to the PLA. On 19 October Ngabo sent two messengers to inform the Chinese that he would surrender. Ford was simply told by Muja to make camp: 'Ngabo was brought out of the monastery, looking less frightened than I had seen him since we left Chamdo. He summoned Dimon and Muja, and gave them some orders, which they passed on to the Rupons. Then all the Tibetan troops began handing over their arms to the Chinese.'[80] Inside the monastery the Chinese filmed Ngabo signing the surrender document. The prisoners were gathered and given lectures on socialism and the unity of the Motherland. All the Tibetan soldiers were then given provisions and money and allowed to return home.[81] Ngabo and the officers were taken back to Chamdo. Later the Chinese announced that 'a total of 5,738 enemy troops had been liquidated' and 180 Tibetans troops killed or wounded.[82]

The military action was meant as a display of Chinese military strength; it showed her determination to 'integrate' Tibet within the new China. The Chinese could have marched straight on to Lhasa but the repercussions would have been far-reaching. Instead they attempted to convince the Tibetan Government that a negotiated settlement could be reached, and that they were still willing to seek 'peaceful liberation'. As the PLA were advancing into Tibet, Zhou Enlai announced at the National Committee of the CPPCC: 'The PLA is determined to march westward to liberate the Tibetan people and defend the frontiers of China. We are willing to undertake peaceful negotiations to bring about this step which is necessary for the security of our Motherland. The patriots in Tibet have expressed and welcomed this and we hope that the local authorities in Tibet will not hesitate to bring about a peaceful solution to the question.'[83]

China Imposes Terms on Tibet

On 10 November, the Chinese issued a major policy statement for the first time. It was probably written by Deng Xiaoping, who was at the time the Secretary of the South-West Bureau of the CCP Central Committee and the Political Commissar of the South-West Military Region.[84] The statement embodied the CCP's basic nationality policies and the Common Programme.

Later the document became the basis for the 17-Point Agreement. It stated that:

> All the religious bodies and people of our Tibet should immediately unite to give the PLA every possible assistance, so that the imperialist influence may be driven out and allow the national regional autonomy in Tibet to be realised; fraternal relationships of friendliness and mutual aid may be established with other nationalities in the country, so that a new Tibet within the new China may be built up with their help.
>
> Now that the PLA has entered Tibet, they will protect the lives and property of all religious bodies and people, protect the freedom of religious belief for all the people of Tibet, protect all lamaseries and temples, and help the Tibetan people to develop their education, agriculture, animal husbandry, industry, and commerce, so as to improve the livelihood of the people.
>
> The existing political system and military system in Tibet will not be changed. The existing armed forces of Tibet will become part of the national defence force of the PRC. All members of the religious bodies of all classes, government officials, and headmen will perform their duties as usual. All matters concerning reform of any kind in Tibet will be settled completely in accordance with the wishes of the Tibetan people and through consultation between the Tibetan people and the leadership personnel in Tibet. Government officials who were formerly pro-imperialist and pro-Kuomingtang [Guomindang] will remain at their posts and no action will be taken concerning their past actions, provided that subsequent facts prove that they have severed relations with imperialism and the Kuomingtang and that they do not carry out acts of sabotage and resistance.
>
> The PLA vigorously maintains its discipline and will faithfully carry out the above-mentioned policies of the Central People's Government. It will respect the religion and customs and habits of the Tibetan people, be gentle in speech, buy and sell fairly, not take a single needle or piece of thread from the people without permission, only requisition furniture with the consent of the owners and pay compensation at the market price for any damage done, pay an adequate price for the services of the men and seize animals it employs [sic].
>
> It is hoped that our Tibetan peasants, herdsmen, workers, and traders and all other people will, without exception, live in peace and follow their pursuits happily. They must not believe lightly in rumours of disturbance and frighten themselves. This is an earnest and true proclamation.'[85]

Having heard the news, the Kashag decided not to give any publicity to the Chinese invasion, for it would have caused panic in Lhasa. On 14

October, the Kashag instructed Shakabpa in India to contact the Chinese Ambassador and request that they stop any further advance into Tibetan territory.[86] Shakabpa did not receive the telegram until 17 October, when he immediately rang the Chinese Embassy and asked for a meeting with the ambassador. He was told that he should come to the embassy the next day. On the following day, he met with Yuan and informed him of the situation in Tibet. Yuan replied that he was aware of the news and that it was the Tibetans' fault for not responding to the Chinese proposal.[87] Yuan wanted to know the Kashag's reply to their proposal, but once again Shakabpa was in no position to give an answer.

Despite the fact that Tibet was militarily defeated and there was no hope of repelling the PLA forces now occupying eastern Tibet, the Kashag could not agree among themselves on how to respond either to the earlier Chinese proposal or to the invasion. It was not until 21 October that the Kashag instructed Shakabpa that the National Assembly had met and had agreed that he should proceed to China for negotiations.[88] Finally, the Kashag agreed to discuss the Chinese three-point proposal and gave Shakabpa the following guidelines;

(1) They *should accept Tibet as part of China*, as long as it does not alter the status of the Dalai Lama and the Tibetan religion. [In Tibetan it says 'accept Tibet as part of China, only in name' ('*ming tsam*')].[89]

(2) Tibet should have the right to establish external relations, particularly with Nepal and India.

(3) It was unacceptable to station Chinese troops in Tibet. It would seriously threaten its religious and political systems.

(4) They should release all prisoners captured in Chamdo.[90]

Shakabpa was disparaging about the Kashag's response. He felt such a compromise had come too late,[91] especially since he had already recommended adoption of a similar policy. He arranged to meet the Chinese Ambassador on 23 October but a few hours before the meeting Shakabpa received a telegram. It informed him that the Kashag had submitted its proposals to the Dalai Lama, who in turn had suggested that the oracle should be consulted. The oracle had pronounced that they should not accept the Chinese proposals. Shakabpa had to keep his appointment with Yuan. Upon his arrival at the Chinese Embassy, Shakabpa was asked for the Kashag's response. He simply said: 'We have not received a reply.'[92]

The news of the fall of Chamdo and the fear of the imminent arrival of PLA troops in Lhasa alarmed officials in government circles. The Regent, the Kashag and abbots of the three great monasteries held a meeting to discuss the situation. It was evident that they did not know how they should respond to the invasion. There were factions who advocated all-out war with the PLA and others who felt a negotiated settlement should be reached. One thing was clear: no one was willing to take charge. The Tibetans have always consulted State Oracles when faced with making a difficult decision, a device that ensures neither the Kashag nor individuals are held directly responsible for unpopular or dangerous decisions.

It was agreed that the two State Oracles, Gadong and Nechung, should be consulted to ascertain the best course of action. In early November (8th of the 10th Month of the Tibetan Calendar) the Regent, the Kashag, and four Drunyigchenmos from the Yigtsang (Ecclesiastic office) consulted Gadong oracle. One of the Drunyigchenmos asked:

> What course of action, violent or non-violent, should be adopted in order to protect and perpetuate the religious and political system of Tibet? And who should bear the responsibility for the political and religious system of Tibet?[93]

The oracle's pronouncement was unclear. 'If you don't offer prayers and propitiate the deities, then you cannot protect the Dharma and well-being of all sentient beings.' As the oracle was about to come out of the trance, the four Drunyigchenmos sought further clarification: 'At this critical stage in the history of Tibet, when the very survival of Tibet's religion and polity is in danger, we are hampered by our ignorance. You are the protector of Dharma and all-knowing. You must give a clear prophecy.' This time the oracle pronounced 'If the All-knowing and all-seeing Guru assumes responsibility for the religious and political system, then the Dharma, Tibet and all beings would benefit.' This was of course taken to mean that the 14th Dalai Lama should assume religious and political authority. When they consulted the second oracle, Nechung, he accorded with the Gadong's pronouncement.[94]

The 14th Dalai Lama, Tenzin Gyatso, was only sixteen years old at the time. Traditionally, the Dalai Lama ascended the throne at the age of eighteen but it was clear that internal factions and panic had placed severe strain on the Tibetan Government. This is how the Dalai Lama described the situation: 'We had reached a state in which most people were anxious to avoid responsibility, rather than accept it. Yet now, under the threat of invasion, we were more in need of unity than ever before, and I, as Dalai Lama, was the only person whom everybody in the country would unanimously follow.'[95] The Regent Taktra and the Kashag called a meeting of the Tibetan National Assembly (Tsogdu Gyenzom), the highest decision-making body of the Tibetan Government, to confirm and endorse the oracles' pronouncement.

The National Assembly agreed to request that the young Dalai Lama assume full powers. The Dalai Lama later wrote in his autobiography: 'I hesitated but then the National Assembly met, and added its plea to the Cabinet's, and I saw that at such a serious moment in our history, I could not refuse my responsibilities. I had to shoulder them, put my boyhood behind me, and immediately prepare myself to lead my country, as well as I was able, against the vast power of Communist China.' He goes on to say: 'So I accepted, with trepidation'.[96] On 17 November a ceremony was held in the Potala. It was attended by the representatives of India and Nepal, and the Chogyal of Sikkim. A message of felicitations was received from the President of India. The Regent Taktra handed over power to the young Dalai Lama. To mark the occasion an amnesty was declared for all prisoners. The Kashag instructed Surkhang Wangchen Gelek in Delhi to inform the Chinese Ambassador that the Dalai Lama had assumed full power.[97]

In Chamdo, Ngabo and his officials were ignorant of the developments taking place in Lhasa, and Ngabo feared that the Dalai Lama and the members of Kashag might have escaped to India. He later wrote that he and other officials were worried that the people in Lhasa might be panic-stricken by rumours about the PLA. He and thirty-six other officials therefore decided to write a joint report to Lhasa (it was addressed to 'whomever is in power in Lhasa'). The report gave a glowing account of the behaviour of the PLA and stressed the futility of resisting the Chinese army. They advised Lhasa that if a peaceful agreement could be reached, the people would not suffer, nor would the monastic or Khim zhi (family estates) be dismantled. Therefore, for the common welfare of the people, a peaceful agreement should be reached with the Chinese.

On 7 December, Gyaltsen Phuntsog and Samlingpa Phuntsog Dorje arrived in Lhasa with a message from Ngabo. They brought a letter addressed to the Dalai Lama and the Kashag. Surkhang and other members were anxious to hear the news from Chamdo. They questioned the two messengers about the situation and the strength of the Chinese army. Gyaltsen Phuntsog informed the Kashag that he did not know the strength of the PLA. Otherwise they gave a positive report on the behaviour of the PLA and stressed that they were very well disciplined. Kalon Rampa Thupten Kunkhyen asked why the PLA 'were strong as iron while we melt like dough'.[98]

Gyaltsen Phuntsog reported that after Ngabo met the Chinese Commander Wang Qimei, he was dispatched to Lhasa. It was most probable that Wang Qimei presented Ngabo with the eight-point proposal which was brought to Lhasa by Gyaltsen Phuntsog. It was the most comprehensive proposal made by the Chinese to date and included the three-point proposal the Chinese ambassador in Delhi, Yuan Zhongxian, had put to the Kashag two months earlier.

(1) Union of the five races of China in a manner not prejudicial to the interests of the minority races.

(2) Tibet to remain under the rule of the Dalai Lama.

(3) Tibetan religion to receive protection.

(4) China to help Tibet in reforming her army into a powerful defence against external aggression.

(5) China to provide Tibet with expert guidance in matters relating to agriculture, animal husbandry, commerce and industry.

(6) Administrative reform in Tibet to be undertaken only after mutual consultation between China and Tibet.

(7) Collaborationists with American, British and Kuomintang [Guomindang] interests not to be persecuted.

(8) Tibet to be assured that the liberation movement is not in support of anti-Tibetan elements like Tashilhunpo and Reting factions.[99]

On 12 December the National Assembly discussed the eight proposals received from Chamdo. The Kashag and the abbots of the three monasteries held a secret meeting on the security of the Dalai Lama. It was agreed that it was not safe for the Dalai Lama to remain in Lhasa. There was a passionate debate among the members. Some argued that the Chinese could not be trusted and that the Communists' offer was described as 'trying to lure a fly with honey spread on a sharp knife'.[100] In the end, due to growing fear that the Chinese would march into Lhasa, the National Assembly agreed to negotiate. Shortly after the arrival of the messengers from Chamdo, Ngabo had secretly dispatched a separate message which stated that he was no longer free to act independently and was conforming to the wishes of his captors[101] and that the Government should take any action necessary, without worrying about Ngabo himself or other officials.[102]

Although the PLA had not made moves to advance on Lhasa, the Tibetans feared that they might try to cut off their escape route to India. A message arrived from Lhalu, which warned of 800 PLA soldiers on horseback moving towards Lhasa from the north. The Tibetans dispatched a number of officers to stop any Chinese attempt to cut off their escape route to Dromo, a small town 150 miles from Lhasa and near the Indo-Tibetan border.[103] In Lhasa there were rumours that the Americans were sending a plane to pick up the Dalai Lama and an area behind the Potala was cleared for a plane to land.[104] The ruling aristocratic families began to send their wealth to India or to their estates in the country. The Tibetan Government also decided to dispatch to India substantial quantities of gold and silver which were held in the Potala Treasury.

On the night of 16 December, the Dalai Lama, dressed as a commoner, with two tutors and the members of the Kashag, left Lhasa for Dromo. This caused panic in Lhasa among the ruling élite, but the authorities were unable to prevent people from leaving, nor could they instruct anyone to stay. Therefore it was decided that important officials should consult the oracles on whether they should leave or not.[105] Heinrich Harrer writes, 'every day caravans of heavily laden mules were seen leaving the town in charge of the men of the bodyguard. Consequently, the nobles hesitated no longer and began to move their families and treasures into safer places.'[106] The Indian representative in Lhasa informed Delhi that the Tibetan spirit of resistance seemed dead and that they were merely trying to postpone the arrival of the Chinese through negotiations.[107] Before the Dalai Lama left Lhasa, Lukangwa Tsewang Rapten and a monk official Lobsang Tashi were appointed as the joint caretaker Prime Ministers (*Sitsab*).

THREE

Tibet's Appeals to the UN and the 17-Point Agreement

With 40,000 PLA soldiers on standby before marching into Lhasa, there was very little the Tibetans could do to counter the Communist advance. The Chinese knew that in terms of military force, nothing could stop them reaching Lhasa. However, they made a tactical decision to obtain some legitimacy for the entry of Chinese troops into Tibet's capital. They did so by inviting the Tibetans to send a delegation to negotiate with the Beijing authorities.

The only possible way forward for the Lhasa Government was to seek international support, even though it was all too clear that the world's attention was gripped by the Korean War. Tibet's repeated appeals to India and Britain were fruitless. The final and only diplomatic recourse for Tibetans was the United Nations. They hoped against hope that the moral weight of the UN could be brought to bear on China.

On 7 November 1950, the Kashag instructed Shakabpa to make an urgent appeal to the United Nations. The Tibetans were aware of the UN's actions in Korea, where it had taken military action to push back the North Korean invasion of South Korea. It was hoped that the UN might be urged to put pressure on China to withdraw its forces from Tibet. However, there were major obstacles facing the Tibetan appeal. First, neither Tibet nor the People's Republic of China were member states of the UN. Second, the major powers were not willing to sponsor a discussion on Tibet in the General Assembly.

Four days later, Shakabpa dispatched Tibet's appeal to the United Nations from Kalimpong. The Indian Government, in strict confidence, told the British that the appeal was written by Mr Sinha, the Indian representative in Lhasa.[1] However, authorship of the appeal did not mean that the Indians had either prompted the Tibetans or supported their appeal to the UN; it was a simple and practical issue of finding someone to write the appeal in coherent English. The appeal stressed that the past relationship between Tibet and China 'was essentially born of belief in a common faith and may correctly be described as the relationship between a spiritual guide and his lay followers: it had no political implication'. It went on to state, 'the armed invasion of Tibet for the incorporation of Tibet in Communist China through sheer physical force is a clear case of aggression. As long as the people of Tibet are compelled by force to become a part of China against their will and consent, the present invasion of Tibet will be the grossest instance of the violation of the weak by the strong. We therefore appeal through you to the United Nations of the world to intercede on our behalf and restrain Chinese aggression.'[2]

For decades Tibet had deliberately avoided contacts with the outside world and had refused to join any international organisations. It was not that the Tibetan rulers were unaware of the existence of the United Nations: in the 1920s, the 13th Dalai Lama had contemplated joining the League of Nations. But the fear of having to open the country to outsiders had prevented them from seeking membership.[3] When the Tibetan appeal reached the United Nations headquarters in New York on 13 November, the officials in the Secretary General's office were totally ignorant about Tibet's status and the situation in the country. They were prepared to dismiss the appeal as a 'communication from [a] non-governmental organisation', and no further action would have been taken.

India, the US and the UK were the only countries that were aware that Tibet had submitted an appeal to the UN. The British delegation made inquiries at the office of the Secretary General about what it intended to do concerning the Tibetan appeal. The British were told that the Secretariat would simply record the appeal on the routine list of communications from non-governmental organisations. Furthermore, they stated that since the telegram was dispatched from Indian territory, technically it could not be considered as an appeal coming from Tibet.[4] The British delegation had to explain to the Secretariat the whole situation. Technically it was not possible for Tibet to dispatch a telegraph direct from Lhasa. There was no telegraph link between Tibet and New York. The Secretariat would not take further action other than to distribute the appeal informally to delegates on the Security Council. It appeared as though this was the end of Tibet's appeal.

The UN Problem

The Tibetans requested the GOI to raise the Tibetan issue at the UN, but India was not prepared to take responsibility. They advised the Tibetans to make a direct appeal. Increasingly the Indians found themselves in a difficult position. They were seriously concerned with the developments in Tibet, but Nehru still did not wish to antagonise China. Bajpai and Nehru held a meeting to discuss the question of India sponsoring Tibet's appeal.

Nehru stated that 'if either the United Kingdom or the US sponsored it, the Chinese would inevitably talk of Anglo-American imperialist influence'. He went on to say: 'even if India sponsored it the same accusation might well be made'.[5] Bajpai told the British High Commissioner on 16 November that he personally felt that India should sponsor a resolution and raise the issue at the Security Council: it was 'important on grounds of international morality but also with regard to Tibetan morale. This would certainly drop if their appeal were merely pigeon-holed without a debate and those Tibetans who wanted to make a fight for Tibetan autonomy would be correspondingly discouraged.'[6] But there were others in the Indian external ministry who felt that India should not be involved because pro-Chinese nations might 'drag out [the] old skeleton of Hyderabad'.[7] The permanent Indian representative at the UN, Sir Benegal Rau, informed Delhi that there were no members of the Security Council interested in raising the Tibetan question, therefore he recommended that India should drop the matter.[8]

Apart from India, who for historical and geo-political reasons was most directly affected by the Chinese invasion, Britain was the only nation who had substantial knowledge and historical contact with Tibet. The Tibetan Government therefore appealed to the British Government to back its appeal to the UN. But Britain was not prepared to take the initiative. However, the British had adopted a basic policy of supporting the GOI. Britain considered what actions it should adopt in the event of Tibet being raised at the UN and on 10 November the Foreign Office informed the High Commissioner in Delhi that because of the 'preponderance of Indian interests in the matter', the 'initiative lies with her [India]'.[9] The British informed other Commonwealth partners that she would support any reasonable action India felt fit to adopt.

Privately the Foreign Office had reached the conclusion that 'since Tibet has from 1913 not only enjoyed full control over her internal affairs but also has maintained direct relations on her own account with other States, she must be regarded as a State to which Article 35(2)[10] of the UN Charter applies and that her appeal may therefore be heard by the United Nations'.[11] The Commonwealth Relations Office (CRO) telegrammed the High Commissioner in Delhi that this interpretation was not to be communicated to the GOI. Whether HMG was 'prepared to support this interpretation of Tibet's international status in the course of preliminary debate in United Nations on validity of her appeal remains for decision'. However, it went on to state that 'assuming that India takes this attitude we should probably be prepared to do so too'.[12] Similarly the British informed the Canadian Government that 'we have not, so far, used this argument publicly and whether we do so or not will depend on what arguments are advanced by the GOI.'[13]

The British Delegation at the UN recommended that the UK should not take any initiative. On 15 November Sir Gladwyn Jebb wrote to the Foreign Office: 'What we want to do is to create a situation which does not oblige us in practice to do anything about the Communist invasion of Tibet.' Therefore he advised that the best position to adopt was to argue that the legal status of Tibet was extremely obscure and that the matter could best be handled by the Security Council rather than the General Assembly.[14]

The Americans had already shifted their policy on Tibet, and the Chinese invasion was a further justification for this change. However, like the British, the Americans were prepared to accept that India was primarily responsible for Tibet. On 3 November, Loy Henderson had met with Nehru to discuss Tibet, informing him that because of 'geographic and historic factors the main burden of the Tibet problem rested on India'. He went on to say that the 'US did not want to say or do anything which would increase this burden; on the contrary we [the US] desired to do what we could to help'. Therefore, Henderson asked Nehru what actions the US should adopt. Nehru simply stated that he thought that the 'US could be most helpful by doing nothing and saying very little now'. Nehru further stressed that US support for Tibet would give 'credence to Peking's charges that great powers had been intriguing in Tibet'.[15]

The State Department was not optimistic about the UN being able to do much about Tibet. On 16 November Dean Acheson instructed the US delegation at the UN that the US did 'wish to take up the initiative' on the Tibetan appeal. Acheson stated that he doubted if the 'UN can bring effective pressure upon Chinese Commie [sic] Government to withdraw or agree to respect Tibet's autonomy.'[16]

UN Postpones Debate on Tibet

India, Britain and the US were not prepared to take the initiative in placing Tibet's appeal on the UN agenda, but all three countries were willing to support a reasonable resolution condemning the Chinese action. Since most countries looked to the US, the UK and India to raise the issue, the Tibet appeal was left without a sponsoring country. On 17 November, a meeting of the Commonwealth delegation to the UN was held to discuss their joint actions and they all naturally looked to the UK and India for a lead. The Indian representative, Mr Nambair, told the delegates that India did not wish to see the matter raised in the Security Council nor did they favour inclusion of the item in the General Assembly agenda. The delegation concluded that the deck should be kept clear for Korea. The Commonwealth delegation constituted a power block at the UN and the loss of their support practically ruled out any chance of Tibet's appeal succeeding.[17]

However, support for Tibet came from the most unlikely area. On the same day, the Chairman of the El Savadorian delegation,[18] Hector Castro, wrote to the President of the General Assembly requesting the 'invasion of Tibet by foreign forces' to be included on the agenda for the General Assembly. He also submitted a draft resolution:

> Taking note that the peaceful nation of Tibet has been invaded, without any provocation on its part, by foreign forces proceeding from the territory controlled by the government established at Peiping,
> Decides;
>
> (1) To condemn this act of unprovoked aggression against Tibet;
>
> (2) To establish a Committee composed of (names of nations) [sic] which will be entrusted with the study of the appropriate measure that could be taken by the General Assembly on this matter;
>
> (3) To instruct the Committee to undertake that study with special reference to the appeal made to the United Nations by the Government of Tibet, and to render its report to the General Assembly, as early as possible, during the present session.[19]

Hector Castro suggested that because of the urgency of the matter the draft resolution should be placed on the General Assembly agenda without referring to the General Committee.

At the time when the Tibet issue was being raised, the debates in the UN were dominated by Korea. There was a general consensus that the Tibet appeal should not be allowed to sidetrack this international concern. The El Savadorian draft resolution raised many awkward questions regarding the legal status of Tibet. Naturally the Chinese nationalists and the USSR would urge that Tibet was an internal affair of China and that the discussion was a contravention of Article 2(7) of the UN charter, which forbade intervention in the internal affairs of a State.

The General Committee, under the Chairmanship of Nasarollah Entezam of Iran, met again on 24 November to discuss whether the draft resolution should be placed on the General Assembly Agenda. Hector Castro made a passionate appeal for its inclusion and argued that the Assembly could not ignore the aggression by the Chinese. He went on to state that 'Under the terms of Article 1, paragraph 1, of the Charter, the United Nations must "maintain international peace and security".' He pointed out that although Tibet was not a member state of the UNO, the organisation had a responsibility for maintaining peace in the world. Castro quoted from a number of encyclopaedias to show that Tibet was an independent country and stated finally that the representative of the Tibetan Government who was coming to put forward their complaints should be heard by the General Assembly.

When the meeting opened for general discussion, the British representative, Mr Younger, stated: 'the Committee did not know exactly what was happening in Tibet *nor was the legal position of the country very clear.*[20] Moreover, it could still be hoped that the existing difficulties in Tibet could still [sic] be settled amicably by agreement between the parties concerned. In those circumstances, before taking a decision the members of the General Committee would be wiser to wait until a better idea could be formed of the possibilities of a peaceful settlement.' Therefore the British recommended that the decision should be deferred.

The crucial decision rested with the GOI, since everyone acknowledged that India was the country most affected by the issues and expected her to take the lead. The Indian representative, Jam Saheb, stated that in the 'latest note received by his government, the Peking Government had declared that it had not abandoned its intention of settling those difficulties by peaceful means'. He maintained that the GOI was 'certain that the Tibetan question could still be settled by peaceful means, and that such a settlement could safeguard the autonomy which Tibet had enjoyed for several decades while maintaining its historical association with China.' He then advised that his government would endorse the recommendation made by the UK.

The Russian representative, K. J. Malik, naturally supported the adjournment of the debate, arguing that the substance of the question was a simple one: 'Tibet was an inalienable part of China and its affairs were the exclusive concern of the Chinese Government.' The American representative, Gross, said that he agreed with the recommendation to postpone the discussion, particularly 'in view of the fact that the GOI, whose territory bordered on Tibet and which was therefore an interested party, had told the General Committee that it hoped that the Tibetan question would be peacefully and honourably settled'.[21] The General Committee unanimously decided to postpone *sine die* consideration of the draft resolution to the General Assembly. It was clear that there were no major powers who were willing to take up the Tibetan issue.

On 3 December the Kashag wrote to the Secretary General expressing their 'grave concern and dismay' at the decision to postpone the discussion.[22] The letter stressed that 'we do not wish the world to be convulsed into an armed conflict for our sake and we would like to know that the world has given thought and consideration to the issue that we have so humbly brought before them and advised the Chinese not to indulge in murder and intimidation of our peaceful land.' The Kashag also stated that 'should there be any doubt or hesitation on the part of any of the various delegations to the United Nations regarding our claim to be a separate Tibetan culture and existence apart from the Chinese we should be happy to welcome a United Nations fact-finding commission to carry out investigation in Tibet.'[23]

The reasons for the lack of support from India and Britain were complex.

British apprehension was summed up in a letter from W. E. Beckett, legal adviser to the FO, to the Attorney-General, Sir Hartley Shawcross, whose legal advice was sought to clarify disagreement between the Foreign Office and the UK delegation to the United Nations.

> It seems to me that it is most important from the point of view of British interests that HMG, in approaching this question of the status of Tibet, should either go clean to the right or clean to the left, that is to say, it should either say definitely that Tibet is a State enjoying *external* as well as internal autonomy or that Tibet enjoys no international personality at all and the Peking Chinese Government are right in their view that relations between China and Tibet are, because of Chinese suzerainty, a domestic matter which is of no concern of the United Nations. The United Kingdom has many protected States enjoying internal autonomy but whose foreign relations are entirely conducted by H. M. G. We certainly wish to maintain the position that questions between the UK and these States (and indeed all colonial conflict) are domestic matters in which the UN has no right under the charter to interfere. If we adopt a sort of half-way house position *we may be creating precedents which can be used against us in the future.*[24]

The Indian reasons for not raising the Tibetan issue were based primarily on the false belief that a peaceful solution could be reached and that the status quo could be maintained.[25] The Indian representative at the UN, Sir Benegal Rau, told Gross that the latest communiqué from Peking was encouraging and that Tibet and China were willing to settle the dispute peacefully. This was clearly untrue. At the time of the UN discussion, the Kashag had not yet decided to negotiate with China and had placed its hope on international pressure on China to withdraw. The Indian External Ministry was clearly aware of the situation in Tibet. They had received reports from Lhasa that the Tibetans were not prepared to negotiate. Bajpai told Henderson that GOI 'had only a faint hope' of the Tibetan question being resolved by negotiation'.[26]

India's reluctance was compounded by its belief that it would be playing a major role in the Korean problem. The External Ministry informed Rau:

> The question of timing of the handling of the Tibetan appeal needed careful consideration. Korea was obviously of first importance and it was therefore desirable that nothing should be said or done which was likely to embitter relations with China at this critical stage, and it would be preferable therefore for no action to be taken on the Tibetan appeal for the present. Little good could come out of any condemnation of Chinese

> action in Tibet and at this stage such condemnation might conceivably do a great deal of harm.[27]

There was also a general consensus that there was nothing the UN could do to help Tibet. The Americans hoped that a debate would serve as anti-Communist propaganda, but they were not prepared to take any action to place it on the agenda. Both Britain and India shared the view that any UN resolution should be limited to a statement calling on both sides to settle their differences by peaceful means because 'stronger resolution (e.g. calling upon China to withdraw her forces from Tibet and to restore the status quo) would merely be ignored by China' and therefore 'the UN would lose prestige'.[28]

On 21 December the Kashag informed the British High Commissioner in Delhi that a six-man delegation led by Shakabpa would be leaving for New York to agitate and seek support for the appeal submitted to the UN. The Kashag once again requested British support for Tibet's appeal. In a letter to the High Commissioner it was stated that the 'Government and the people of Tibet great [*sic*] hope that your Government will afford effective help in any problem of Tibet and therefore they earnestly hope that your Government will help to bring the question of Tibet under discussion in the United Nations Assembly as soon as possible'.[29]

There were differing views in the British Foreign Office, where some officials felt that the Chinese action should be condemned by the UN. Sir Pierce Dixon wrote: 'it is of course clearly impossible to enforce any UN resolution which calls upon China to withdraw her troops, and we should therefore wish to avoid any resolution of this kind. On the other hand, I do not think we can allow the Chinese resort to force to pass unnoticed by the UN; we should therefore be prepared to support a resolution condemning the Chinese action but which does not threaten or imply military action by the UN'.[30] On 16 December, the (CRO) instructed the High Commissioner in Delhi to communicate the following message to the Tibetan Government:

> Government of UK continues to maintain the friendly interest which they have taken in the maintenance of Tibetan autonomy since August 1947, when the rights and obligations arising from the existing treaty provisions devolved on the GOI. Since the Government of the Chinese People's Republic has resorted to force instead of seeking to reach agreement on the question of Sino-Tibetan relations through the peaceful methods of discussion and negotiation, the Government of *the United Kingdom are prepared to afford their general support to the Tibetan Government's appeal to the United Nations.*[31]

However, the CRO added that the communication should be shown first to the GOI, and withdrawn if they had any strong objections. The High Commissioner responded on 18 December: 'I would strongly deprecate making this communication to GOI and would also recommend against making any reply on the proposed lines to the Tibetan letter at this stage'. He went on to say that 'our suggested reply to Tibetans some five weeks after their letter to us would probably be interpreted by them as a direct encouragement to become more active at Lake Success. If it came to the ears of the Chinese they would surely regard it as further evidence of British interference.'[32]

On 21 December, the Kashag once again wrote to the Americans requesting their help and support for Tibet's appeal to the UN. The US position had not changed and they were still anxious to work with the Indians. On 27 December Henderson met with Bajpai, and asked whether the GOI had received a similar letter from Tibet. Bajpai told him that they had not. However, the GOI had met with Shakabpa and the Tibetan delegation to the UN in Kalimpong. Bajpai stressed that the GOI's position regarding the Tibetan appeal to the UN had remained unchanged and they held the view that 'if GOI should press the Tibetan case just now in the UN, Communist China would be alienated to such an extent [that] GOI would lose all ameliorating influence on Peiping [Beijing] re: Korea and related problems. Therefore the Tibetan case would remain temporarily in abeyance.'[33]

It was clear to the Americans that the GOI would not take any initiative, nor would it allow America to be involved in raising the Tibetan issue. On 30 December, Henderson informed the State Department: 'we have been giving considerable thought this end to the problem Tibetan case before UN. Thus far seemed preferable India take lead this matter UN. Representatives of GOI had repeatedly assured us it intended to do so.' Henderson recognised that Indian officials did not wish to take up the issue under the present world context. He suggested, therefore, that the US might support 'some power other than India' taking the initiative or accept the postponement of hearing Tibetan pleas until autonomous Tibet ceased to exist.[34]

For 'some power other' the Americans turned to the British. The State Department presented the British Embassy in Washington with an *aide-mémoire* which implied that the Americans were willing to change their policy, and encouraged Britain to take a more active part in supporting the Tibetan appeal.

> The United States, which was one of the early supporters of the principle of self-determination of peoples, believes that the Tibetan people has the [same] inherent right as any other to have the determining voice in its political destiny. It is believed further that, *should developments warrant,*

consideration could be given to recognition of Tibet as an independent State. The Department of State would not at this time desire to formulate a definitive legal position to be taken by the US Government relative to Tibet. It would appear adequate for present purposes to state that the US Government recognizes the *de facto* autonomy that Tibet has exercised since the fall of the Manchu Dynasty, and particularly since the Simla Conference. It is believed that, should the Tibetan case be introduced into the United Nations, there would be ample basis for international concern regarding Chinese Communist intentions towards Tibet, in either the UN Security Council or the UN General Assembly.[35]

On 9 January 1951 Ringwalt from the American Embassy in London visited the Foreign Office and said that the State Department, was 'restive at the failure of the UN to take any action over Tibet'. Ringwalt also wanted to know the view of the Foreign Office. Mr S. L. Oliver from the FO replied that, in general, the British were in favour of making some form of protest at the Chinese invasion. However, since the Chinese were determined to complete their occupation, there was nothing that could be done to stop them. Any protest would be made only on moral grounds. Even this 'was bound up with the whole question of our relations with China and was obviously a very secondary consideration compared with the mainstream of events in Korea'.[36]

Neither India nor Britain was willing to support America, who was anxious to turn to other powers to support Tibet's appeal. However, the international situation deteriorated and the Korean issue came increasingly to dominate the minds of US officials. On 24 January, Robert Strong informed the Director of Chinese Affairs in the State Department that the US delegation at the UN was opposed to raising the Tibetan issue, because they claimed that 'any move regarding Tibet might further injure our chances of getting what we need in connection with Korea'. Livingstone Merchant, the Deputy Assistant Secretary for the Far East, recommended to Dean Rusk that the matter should be dropped. Dean Rusk noted in a memo to Merchant: 'I believe we should go slow on this because of (1) our Korean imbroglio and (2) the forthcoming Kashmir flap.'[37]

Tibet and China Negotiate

In the end, there were no major powers prepared to support Tibet's appeal to the UN. India was caught up in the delusion of playing a historic role as mediator between East and West over the Korean issue, and failed to see the wood for the trees. The Chinese made it clear that the Indian views on international issues of the day did not count for much. The British felt their obligations towards India were paramount, even to the extent of alienating the Americans. Initially both Britain and India chose to mislead the UN by providing inaccurate information about Tibet's legal status and the prospects of any peaceful settlement between Tibet and China. As the Korean issue took over the United Nations' agenda, Tibet's appeal faded into obscurity. This dispelled the hopes that the Tibetans had placed in international support: there was no alternative but to seek negotiations with China.

Before leaving Lhasa the Dalai Lama and the Kashag decided to give Ngabo full power to proceed with the negotiations with the Chinese. They appointed Sampho Tenzin Dhondup and Khenchung Thupten Legmon to assist him. They reached Chamdo at the end of February (the beginning of the Tibetan New Year) where they were welcomed by the PLA and met by Ngabo and the Tibetan officials who had been captured. Sambo handed Ngabo the letter from the Kashag which authorised him to hold discussions with the Chinese. The letter also stated that he must insist on Tibetan independence and refuse the stationing of PLA troops in Tibet. Ngabo thought the points were unrealistic: there was no scope for discussion with Chinese, since it was clear that they were determined to gain control of Tibet. Sampho also gave him a five-point written statement as the starting point for discussions:

> (1) There is no imperialist influence in Tibet; the little contact Tibet had with the British was the result of the travels of the 13th Dalai Lama to India. As for the relationship with the United States, this was only commercial.
>
> (2) In the event of foreign imperial influence being exerted on Tibet, the Tibetan government would appeal to China for help.
>
> (3) Chinese troops stationed in Kham should be withdrawn.
>
> (4) The Chinese Government should not be influenced by the followers of the Panchen Lama and the Reting faction.
>
> (5) The territories taken by Manchu China, Kuomintang and the new government of China must be returned to Tibet.[38]

Ngabo knew that the five points would be unacceptable and that they might infuriate the Chinese. He asked Sampho if he had received any oral instruction from the Kashag. Sampho did not even know whether they were to negotiate with the Chinese at Chamdo or were to proceed directly to Beijing. When Ngabo gave the statement to the Chinese, they repudiated much of it point by point:

> (1) It was clear that the British and American imperialists had interfered

in the internal affairs of China. It was evident from the fact that they had prevented the negotiating team from leaving India.

(2) The defence of the motherland was the prime objective of the PLA and it was imperative that the PLA should defend the frontiers of the Motherland.

(3) The existing political system and the status of the Dalai Lama would not be altered. However, in the event of the Dalai Lama going into exile, he would lose all his powers and status.

(4) Tibet would enjoy regional autonomy.

(5) China would not interfere in internal political rivalry and factions.[39]

Ngabo met with Wang Qimei, one of the commanders of the Chinese forces in Chamdo, and suggested that the negotiations should take place in Lhasa. This was agreed. Ngabo immediately radioed Lhasa for permission for a small delegation of Chinese to proceed to Lhasa for discussions. The two Prime Ministers in Lhasa, Lhukhang and Lobsang Tashi, accepted Ngabo's suggestion.[40] At the same time Ngabo received a telegram from the Dalai Lama, via the Chinese embassy in Delhi, instructing him to proceed to Peking for discussions. Ngabo later wrote that, since the Dalai Lama's order superseded instructions from the Kalons, on 22nd March his party in Chamdo reluctantly proceeded to Peking.[41]

The Kashag recalled Shakabpa and Thupten Gyalpo from India to discuss the international situation and the possibility of foreign aid. The Tibetan political élite was increasingly divided between those who advocated negotiation and those who urged the Dalai Lama to seek political asylum in India. Shakabpa informed them of the international situation and the lack of concrete support given by any country. He told the Kashag how the British and the Indians had prevented them from leaving India. Moreover, he told the Kashag that there was a general lack of support for Tibetan independence from the GOI.

In Dromo the Dalai Lama and the Kashag heard the news that the General Committee of the UN had unanimously agreed to postpone the inclusion of Tibet on the General Assembly agenda. This was further evidence of Tibet's isolation from the international community. The news was a severe blow to the Tibetans' morale. In his autobiography the Dalai Lama wrote: 'the [next] grievous blow to us was the news that the General Assembly of the United Nations had decided not to consider the question of Tibet. This filled us with consternation. We had put our faith in the United Nations as a source of justice. We were astonished to hear that it was on the British initiative that the question had been shelved.'[42]

It was apparent that a negotiated settlement had to be reached with China. As mentioned before, it was agreed that the meeting would be held in Beijing. In Delhi, Surkhang Dzasa and Chomphel Thupten secured agreement from the Chinese Ambassador that for the duration of the meeting Chinese troops would not proceed any further into Tibet. The Kashag appointed Lhawutara Thupten Tender and Kheme Sonam Wangdu to proceed to Beijing. They were assisted by Phuntsog Tashi Takla as the Chinese interpreter and Sangdu Lobsang Rinchen as the English interpreter. The delegation was provided with a written document with the names of five representatives; Ngabo Nawang Jigme was named as the chief representative. The delegation was given instructions that it should on no account accept Chinese sovereignty over Tibet. The delegation should refer all important points back to Dromo for consultation, and for that purpose a direct wireless communication was to be established between Beijing and Dromo.[43] It was clear that although Ngabo was appointed as the chief representative, he did not have any authority to make decisions without further consultation with the Kashag and the Dalai Lama. The delegation was also given a ten-point oral proposal, which they were to raise with the Chinese.[44]

On their way to Beijing, the Tibetan delegation went to Delhi where, on 24 March, they met Nehru. Lhawutara presented a letter from the Dalai Lama and asked Nehru's advice on the forthcoming talks. The Tibetans also asked whether India could mediate between Tibet and China. Nehru made no comment on this point. According to Lhawutara, Nehru advised them that the Chinese would insist on three points. First, the Tibetans would have to accept the Chinese claim that Tibet was a part of China; according to Nehru, Chinese claims over Tibet were internationally recognised. Second, the Tibetans would have to surrender the right to conduct their own external affairs. Third, the Tibetans must not agree to the stationing of Chinese troops in Tibet, since this would have serious repercussions on India.[45] Nehru's statement was a great disappointment for the Tibetan delegation. Now the Tibetan delegation was leaving for Beijing with the knowledge that India was not prepared to support Tibetan independence.

In Delhi the Tibetan delegation also met with the Chinese Ambassador, who provided each member of the delegation with a Chinese passport. The Chinese Embassy made all the arrangements for travel and obtained transit visas for Hong Kong. Ngabo, Sampho Tenzin Dhundup and Khenchung Thupten Legmon left Chamdo and arrived in Beijing on 22 April where they were welcomed at the railway station by Zhou Enlai and Baba Phuntsog Wangyal, who became the chief interpreter during the negotiations. Four days later Zhu De, the commander of the PLA, met Lhawutara and Kheme Sonam Wangdu at the railway station.

After the Tibetan delegation had assembled, they were informed that the Panchen Rinpoche and his retinue would be arriving in Beijing and the Chinese asked if they would come to the railway station to welcome him.

Ngabo, not wanting to give any impression of formal recognition of the Panchen Rinpoche, suggested that only the junior members of the Tibetan delegation – Sampho, Takla and Sangdu Rinchen – should go to the railway station.[46] The presence of the Panchen Lama and his retinue were to become a major stumbling block during the course of the negotiations.

Lhawutara and Kheme brought further instructions from the Kashag, which stated that at first the delegation must make a claim for Tibetan independence, and argue that the past relationship between Tibet and China had been that of 'Priest and Patron'. If the discussion reached deadlock, then they could accept Tibet as part of China, on the following conditions:

(1) Tibet must enjoy full internal independence.[47]

(2) No Chinese troops would be stationed in Tibet.

(3) The Tibetan army would be responsible for defence.

(4) The Chinese representative to Lhasa, his personal staff and guards must not exceed 100 men.

(5) The Chinese representative must be a Buddhist.[48]

The Tibetan delegation discussed the proposals, and agreed that these terms would be unacceptable to the Chinese. Ngabo sent a telegram to Dromo stating that it was impossible to refuse Chinese troops in Tibet; there would otherwise be no scope for discussion. The Kashag's reply once again insisted that no Chinese troops should be deployed in Tibet, but they proposed that the existing Tibetan army could be incorporated into the Chinese army and would be responsible for defence.[49]

The Tibetan delegation met once again to discuss the Kashag's reply. Ngabo stated that the Kashag had already made a major concession in agreeing to accept Tibet as part of China, therefore all other issues were minor. He scornfully remarked, 'Who has heard of a Communist Buddhist?' implying that the Kashag was not well informed.[50] Ngabo said that there was no point in referring all the matters back to Dromo, since the Kashag had agreed on the most important point.[51] Moreover, there would be a considerable delay if every single point was referred back to Dromo, from where the Kashag and the National Assembly would take days to reply. In the event of a long delay the Chinese might resume their military actions.

On 29 April 1951, the Tibetan and Chinese delegations met at an army headquarters in Beijing. The Chinese group was headed by Li Weihan, one of the key members of the Communist Party. Li had studied in France in the early 1920s and was a co-founder of the French section of the CCP. In 1944 he became director of the Party's United Front Work Department and the Chairman of the Nationalities' Affairs Commission of the State Council. Li was assisted by a little-known veteran of the PLA, Zhang Jingwu. Zhang had served as a deputy chief-of-staff of the South-West Military Region under Ho Long, and at the time of his appointment Zhang held the position of director of the People's Armed Forces Department, which was responsible for organising the militia. It was an important position as the militia (People's Armed Forces) played a significant role in the Korean War. Zhang Jingwu was to became the key Chinese figure in Tibet for the next two decades. Zhang Guohua, the leader of the 18th Corps of the Second Field Army (which led the PLA's invasion of Tibet), was also a member of the Chinese negotiation team, along with Sun Zhiyuan from the United Front.

The appointment of Li meant that the negotiation was carried out by the United Front section of the Party. This made it clear that the Chinese regarded the Tibetan issue as essentially an internal affair: the United Front was primarily concerned with gaining control and influence over non-Communists and minority groups within China. The Tibetan delegation, however, did not grasp the significance of this; they assumed they were dealing with the Chinese Government.

On the first day, the formal meeting only lasted for half an hour. The two sides merely agreed to draw up a written statement on their respective positions and then the meeting ended. On the second day, Li Weihan presented a proposal, which was the same as the one issued by the South-West Military Command soon after the fall of Chamdo. Li suggested that the Tibetan delegation should study the proposal and then they should meet again. The meeting was resumed on 2 May, when the Chinese delegation explained each point of their proposal. According to Phuntsog Tashi Takla, the Chinese delivered their position rather like a lecture, with a mixture of Communist interpretation of recent history and of their nationalities policy.[52]

When Ngabo opened the discussion, he declared that Tibet had been an independent country and the past relationship with China had been one of priest and patron relationship and that there was no need to deploy Chinese troops in Tibet.[53] Li Weihan responded by saying that the question of the status of Tibet was not under discussion and Chinese sovereignty over Tibet was non-negotiable. He added that it was a historical fact that Tibet formed an integral part of China, and her claim over Tibet was internationally recognised. He went on to say that the purpose of the meeting was to discuss the proposal that had been submitted and no other issues should be added to the agenda. The Chinese delegation claimed that the decision to liberate Tibet had been made and that the defence of 'the Motherland' was the responsibility of the PLA.[54] For the Chinese to place the question of the status of Tibet on the agenda would be seen as recognising Tibet's separate identity. As far as the Chinese were concerned, Tibet was an integral part of the PRC and it did not matter what the Tibetans thought about their status.

The Tibetan delegation realised that the Chinese could not be moved from their position and, moreover, that they had no manoeuvring points to counter tight control by the Chinese over the agenda for discussion. It became apparent that what was expected of the Tibetan delegation was ratification of the proposal.[55]

In subsequent meetings the Chinese and Tibetan delegations discussed each of the articles of the 17-Point Agreement. The Tibetan delegation made some minor changes in the wording, and in fact much of the discussion centred on semantic issues. The newly coined Communist terminology which was used in the text was difficult to translate into Tibetan.[56] The discussion of the semantics suggested that there was a general agreement.

But by 10 May the meeting was threatening to break down. The Chinese were proposing that they would set up a Military-cum-Administrative Commission in Tibet. When Lhawutara asked what the functions of this commission would be, Li Weihan stated that the commission would be responsible for the implementation of the agreement and would 'decide' all important political and military issues. Lhawutara pressed further, saying that this would contradict the assurance that the power and status of the Dalai Lama and the existing political system would not be altered. At this point Li Weihan got irritated and said, 'Are you showing your clenched fist to the Communist Party? If you disagree then you can leave, whenever you like. It is up to you to choose whether Tibet would be liberated peacefully or by force. It is only a matter of sending a telegram to PLA group to recommence their march into Tibet.'[57]

The meeting ended abruptly, and for several days the Tibetan delegation was taken on a sightseeing tour. Lhawutara writes that he feared the Chinese might have already ordered the PLA to march into Tibet. He asked Ngabo to find out from the Chinese if they had ordered the PLA to continue their advance.[58] The Chinese insisted that it was necessary to set up the 'Military-Administrative Commission' in Tibet, that the Commission would be the representative of the Central People's Government and that it would be responsible for the implementation of the agreement. It would also be responsible for 'unifying the command of all armed forces in Tibet in order to safeguard national defence'.[59] Li Weihan also tried to reassure the Tibetans that they should observe the behaviour of the PLA for a while. In time they would see that the PLA were making a constructive contribution to Tibet. Moreover, he told the Tibetans that 'the PLA movement into Tibet is the established policy of the Central Government, since Tibet is an integral part of Chinese territory and all China must be liberated'.[60] It was evident that the key to Chinese policy in Tibet was the establishment of the Military-Administrative Commission. It was also evident that, initially, the military would play a leading role not only in the defence of the 'border regions' but in establishing the internal structure for Chinese rule. The PLA had also been seen as an essential element of the nation-building process in China itself. After the Korean War both the external defensive role and internal power of the PLA had increased. Since the Chinese lacked any power base in Tibet, it was essential that the military should play the key role in the 'integrating' of Tibet. The Military-Administrative Commission would form a parallel administrative organ and they were therefore determined not to compromise on this point.

In the end the Tibetans decided to drop their objections and the meeting was resumed. There were no other points of disagreement. The Tibetan delegation informed the Chinese they were willing to sign the agreement. Nevertheless, they were anxious that the Kashag might not approve of the agreement. Ngabo told the Chinese that there would be no problem if the Dalai Lama and the Kashag approved. But should they repudiate the agreement and the Dalai Lama escape abroad, they would need some form of guarantee that the power and the status of the Dalai Lama would be protected.[61] Therefore the Tibetan delegation proposed a new clause to the agreement, which stated in the event of the Dalai Lama going into exile, he could remain outside Tibet for up to five years and still maintain his existing status and power. The Dalai Lama could observe from outside the prevailing conditions and progress. If he chose to return to Tibet, his status would be reinstated. The Chinese made no objections, but insisted that this should not be included in the main agreement but form part of a separate clause.[62]

This was to become the first article of a seven-part secret agreement. Another important clause stated that after the establishment of the Tibet Military Commission, one or two members of the Kashag would hold positions in the Commission.[63] Other clauses dealt with the phasing out of Tibetan currency, and the right of the Tibetans to maintain a small independent police force.

On 17 May, the two delegations met to discuss the draft of the agreement. When the meeting opened Li Weihan stated that the problems concerning the central and the local Tibet government had now been resolved. However, there still remained the internal problem arising from the conflict between the 13th Dalai Lama and the 9th Panchen Lama. It was imperative that this was also solved.[64] Therefore, Li Weihan asked Ngabo what instructions he had received from the Kashag regarding the 10th Panchen Rinpoche.[65] Ngabo said he was sent to Peking with terms of reference to discuss the relationship between Tibet and China, and he did not have any power to discuss internal affairs of Tibet. If the Chinese Government wanted to discuss the issue, it should be dealt with separately.[66]

Li Weihan stated: 'this is your home business [internal affair], but at the same time in order to solve the Tibetan issue, it is impossible not to discuss the question. This question must be settled! Regarding the method for reconciliation between the Dalai Lama and Banqen [Panchen] Lama, mutual agreement must be reached through negotiation'.[67] He also stated that if this issue was not solved, there was no point in signing the agreement. The threat irritated Ngabo who announced that he was happy to return to Chamdo and he would be instructing the other Tibetan delegates to return to Lhasa. At this point the meeting again broke down and the Tibetan delegations returned to their hotel.[68]

It was interesting that Ngabo stubbornly refused to discuss the Panchen Rinpoche issue, although he knew that the Dalai Lama and the Kashag had agreed to recognise the 10th Panchen Rinpoche. When he heard that the Panchen Rinpoche had arrived in Peking, Ngabo had immediately telegrammed the Kashag and advised that they recognise the 10th Panchen Rinpoche otherwise there would be difficulties in reaching an agreement with the Chinese. The Kashag replied that they had received representations from Tashilhunpo authorities, who had appealed to the Dalai Lama to recognise the same 10th Panchen Rinpoche. The Dalai Lama and the Kashag had finally reached the decision to recognise him.[69]

Back in Beijing the deadlock continued. One morning at 9 o'clock, Sun Zhiyuan, accompanied by Baba Phuntsog Wangyal, came to Ngabo's hotel to discuss the issue of Panchen Rinpoche. Ngabo adamantly refused to be drawn into discussion. Sun Zhiyuan insisted the issue must be settled. The meeting lasted until 6 o'clock in the evening when Sun Zhiyuan finally suggested that they could agree to the phrasing, 'the relationship between the Dalai Lama and the Panchen lama should be based on the amicable relationship that existed between the 13th Dalai Lama and the 9th Panchen Lama'.[70] Ngabo raised no objection and this later became clauses five and six of the agreement (see appendix).

On 23 May, the Chinese and Tibetan delegations signed the final copy of the agreement. The document was entitled 'Agreement of the Central People's Government and the Local Government of Tibet on Measures for the Peaceful Liberation of Tibet'. The preamble to the agreement stated that Tibet had been part of China for the past 'hundred years or more' and that imperialist forces had caused disunity between the Tibetan and Han nationalities. It further stated that 'the Local Government of Tibet did not oppose imperialist deception and provocation, but adopted an unpatriotic attitude towards the great motherland'. The first article stated that 'the Tibetan people shall return to the big family of the motherland the People's Republic of China'.

Next day the Chinese held a banquet for the delegation. There was also an hour-long meeting with Mao, who opened his speech by saying that he wanted to 'welcome Tibet back into the Motherland'.[71] He went on to say that for the past century the relationship between Tibet and China had been lost because of the oppressive polices of the Manchu and Chiang Kai-shek's reactionary policies, and that moreover the imperialists had conspired to split the Motherland. Now that the imperialists had been destroyed, 'the relationship between Tibet and China would be like brothers. The oppression of one nationality by another would be eliminated. All nationalities would work for the benefit of the Motherland'.[72]

During the course of the meeting the Chinese repeatedly asked Ngabo if he was empowered with the authority to sign the agreement. This point was clearly important for the Chinese and had he given a negative answer, the negotiations would undoubtedly have been terminated. However, Ngabo replied that he had been given full authority to sign.[73] It is not clear why Ngabo gave an affirmative answer, as he later admitted not having the authorisation to sign a agreement without referring back to the Kashag and the Dalai Lama in Dromo.[74] The Chinese also asked if the delegation had brought its seals to place on the document. Ngabo told the Chinese that he did not have the seals. It was true that other members of the delegation did not have their seals with them, but Ngabo was in possession of the seal of the Governor of Kham, which, as a member of Kashag, he could have affixed to the document. Ngabo later told Phala that he refused to use the original seal because he wanted to show that he did not approve of the Agreement.[75] The Chinese proposed that new seals should be made, to which the Tibetan delegation agreed. Later, Tibetan exiles claimed that the Chinese forged seals and affixed them to the document.[76]

As far as the Chinese were concerned, the Agreement came into effect immediately after the signing. It is not clear why the Tibetans did not insist upon keeping the Agreement secret until the Kashag and the Dalai Lama had time to ratify the agreement. It may be that it was beyond the power of the Tibetan delegation to prevent the Chinese from publicising the Agreement. The extensive international publicity surrounding the signing of the Agreement gave China a major propaganda and diplomatic victory. We will see later that the international community accepted the agreement as a *fait accompli.* For the Chinese it was a political necessity that they should announce to the world the peaceful resolution of the Tibetan problem.

The Tibetan delegation dispatched a telegram to Dromo, informing the Kashag and the Dalai Lama that an agreement and a secret clause had been signed.[77] The Dalai Lama described his initial reaction to the announcement:

> We first came to know of it from a broadcast which Ngabo made on Peking Radio. It was a terrible shock when we heard the terms of it. We were appalled at the mixture of Communist clichés, vainglorious assertions which were completely false, and bold statements which were only partly true and the terms were far worse and more oppressive than anything we had imagined.[78]

The Tibetan Government was clearly shocked and alarmed by the terms of the agreement. Some officials urged the Dalai Lama to leave Dromo and seek asylum in India, others felt they should wait until members of the delegation returned to Tibet to wait for their explanation.[79] From Dromo the Kashag immediately dispatched a telegram to Ngabo requesting the full text of the agreement and the secret clause. The delegation was instructed to remain in Peking until further notice. Ngabo replied that because of the secret nature of the separate agreement, he was not willing to dispatch it on the radio. He bluntly stated that the agreement had been signed and that if the Kashag was not satisfied with the agreement then they should send a new team to Beijing.[80]

The Tibetan delegation left Beijing in two groups after the Chinese told Ngabo that he must return via Chamdo because they feared for his safety. In reality the Chinese were suspicious that Ngabo might remain in India rather than returning to Tibet.[81] Ngabo and Thupten Legmon travelled home by the land route. On 16 June, Zhang Jingwu, the new Chinese representative to Tibet, and the rest of the Tibetan delegation left Beijing for Hong Kong.

The impending arrival of the Chinese representative caused a great deal of uncertainty in Dromo. The Tibetan Government clearly felt that the agreement compromised Tibet's independent status and, moreover, they were concerned that the Tibetan delegation had agreed to the deployment of Chinese troops in Tibet. Ngabo was not empowered to sign the agreement and his decision to sign the agreement was clearly *ultra vires*. This would have been sufficient grounds for repudiating the agreement. Yet the Kashag did not want to denounce the agreement without hearing what the Tibetan delegation had to say. They were suspicious that the delegation in Beijing might have been coerced into signing. It was clear that the Chinese had not deviated from the initial document the PLA had released immediately after their victory in Chamdo in October 1950. There was a striking similarity between the content of this document and the 17-Point Agreement, supposedly reached after mutual consultation.

US Intervention in the Tibetan Issue

The Tibetans once again turned to the United States for help. The Americans had shown their willingness to provide both diplomatic and military aid.[82] Nevertheless they were hampered by India's fear that US involvement would bring the Cold War to the foothills of the Himalayas, and this prevented the US from taking any positive action. The Americans were clearly frustrated by India's and Britain's refusal either to co-operate with them or to allow the USA to do what they themselves were unwilling to contemplate. The Americans were concerned that the Chinese would gain control in Tibet without any protest from outside. In March 1951, the Americans approached the Indians and asked what their reaction would be if the Sino–Tibetan negotiation failed. US officials were amazed to discover that the Indians had not given much thought to it and merely suggested that it could be left with the UN.[83] The Tibetans had already given up hope that India would provide any political or diplomatic aid. The Tibetan delegation had not even contacted the Indian Ambassador while in Beijing.

In March, Loy Henderson met Heinrich Harrer, who had left Lhasa with the Dalai Lama and had spent some time in Dromo. Harrer was well-informed about the internal situation there. The Americans were for the first time able to get reliable information on the thinking of the Tibetan Government and more importantly on the Dalai Lama's own feelings. Harrer told Henderson that the delegation to Peking was dispatched with great reluctance and 'the Dalai Lama has doubts about returning to Lhasa. Some of the monks about him, however, insist that he should come to terms with Beijing. The Dalai Lama does not know which way to turn for advice'.[84] Loy Henderson wrote to Mathews, the Director of South Asian Affairs in the State Department, suggesting that a secret personal message to the Dalai Lama should be sent, though on plain paper and without any formal authorisation from the American Government. He also submitted a copy of the letter to the State Department:

> (1) The Peiping Communist regime is determined to obtain complete control over Tibet. No concession made to that regime by His Holiness can change this determination. The Chinese Communists prefer to gain control through trickery rather than through force. They are therefore anxious to persuade His Holiness to make an agreement which would allow them to establish a representative in Lhasa.
>
> (2) The establishment of a representative of the Peiping Communist regime in Lhasa would serve only to speed up the seizing of all of Tibet by the Chinese Communists.
>
> (3) Until changes in the world situation would make it difficult for the Chinese Communists to take over Tibet, His Holiness should in no circumstances return to Lhasa or send his treasures or those of Tibet back to Lhasa . . . Any treasures which might be returned to Lhasa would eventually be taken over by the Chinese Communists.
>
> (4) His Holiness should not return to Lhasa while the danger exists that by force or trickery the Chinese Communists might seize Lhasa. He should leave Yatung for some foreign country if it should look like the Chinese Communists might try to prevent his escape.
>
> (5) It is suggested that His Holiness send representatives at once to

> Ceylon. These representatives should try to arrange with the Government of Ceylon for the immediate transfer to Ceylon of the treasures of His Holiness. They should also try to obtain permission for His Holiness and his household to find asylum in Ceylon if His Holiness leaves Tibet. After the GOC has granted permission for asylum, His Holiness should ask the GOI for assurance that if he and his Household should leave Tibet they could pass through India to Ceylon.
>
> (6) If His Holiness and His Household could not find safe asylum in Ceylon he could be certain of finding a place of refuge in one of the friendly countries, including the United States, in the Western Hemisphere.
>
> (7) It might also be useful for His Holiness immediately to send a mission to the United States where it would be prepared to make a direct appeal to the United Nations. It is understood that His Holiness is already aware that favourable consideration will be granted to the applications made by members of a Tibetan mission to the United Nations for United States visas.[85]

Henderson's letter was given to Liushar, who took it to Dromo. On 21 May, the Dalai Lama acknowledged receipt of the letter and stated that at present negotiations were proceeding in Beijing and, if Tibet needed to, he would approach the USA, in which case he hoped the USA would do its best to help.

On 26 May, Shakabpa and Jigme Taring met with Fraser Wilkins, First Secretary from the American Embassy in Delhi, who had come to Calcutta for the meeting. Shakabpa told Wilkins that they had received a message from the Tibetan delegation that on 13 May the meeting had reached deadlock, and that therefore they would like to ask US advice on what Tibet should do in the event that talks in Beijing broke down. He went on to say that the Chinese wanted total control of defence and external affairs and that the Dalai Lama was adamant in refusing to concede to the Chinese demands.[86] If the Chinese were to assert their claims by further incursions into Tibet, then the Dalai Lama would leave Tibet. Shakabpa also stated that he had seen Henderson's letter and he put forward a number of questions to Wilkins:

> (1) Should Tibet report [to the] UN when current talks break down, and how should they do it? Was the UN still interested in Tibet and could it be of any help? What would US do? Would it be willing [to] grant visas?
>
> (2) As Tibet had no official relations with Ceylon re: asylum, would US be willing to approach Government Ceylon re asylum for the Dalai Lama and his followers?

(3) Would US be willing [to] grant asylum [for the] Dalai Lama and approximately 100 followers ? How would he be received? As head of State? Would US be willing [to] provide for their expenses?

(4) If the Dalai Lama leaves Tibet would US be willing to supply the Dalai Lama with military assistance and loans of money when the time is ripe for purpose [of] enabling Tibetan groups rise against Communist Chinese invader? Money needed to encourage groups.

(5) Would US be willing to establish some form representative at Kalimpong for Liaison between US officials and Tibetan authorities? [Shakabpa stressed necessity for representation which would be informal and covert in character.][87]

The sixth point requested asylum for Thubten Norbu,[88] who was anxious to leave Tibet. It is not clear why Thubten Norbu wanted to visit America, as the Tibetans and the Americans had already established a good relationship and there existed a proper channel of communication. It appears that his visit was primarily to gain publicity, which would appeal directly to the American public. Steere from the American Embassy in New Delhi forwarded the questions to the Secretary of State, with the following recommendations, which were approved by Loy Henderson:

(1) US believes Tibet might reiterate the contents [of] Tibet's previous appeal to UN, adding new developments such as Tibet's endeavour through talks [in] Peiping to reach agreement and substance [of] Tibetan and Communist positions. Tibet might dispatch Tibetan delegation to Lake Success with new appeal instead waiting UN invitation. US believes UN still interested and that Tibet entitled to hearing. While US was one only of many UN members it would do its best persuade other UN members consider new Tibetan appeal. US continued be willing grant visas.

(2) US considers much wiser for Dalai Lama's own representatives [to] approach Ceylon Government in Colombo in first instance. Approach would be from one Buddhist country to another. Ceylon would probably prefer direct approach rather than indirect through US. If we approached formally, US might subsequently be charged with imperialistic plot which would embarrass Ceylon Government. If Tibetan Govt requests, US would, however, be willing approach Ceylon Govt informally re matter. US would in any event be willing approach Ceylon Govt re permission for Tibetan representatives to enter and travel in Ceylon and re appointments with Ceylonese officials.

(3) US would be willing grant asylum to Dalai Lama and approximately 100 followers including members families. Dalai Lama would be received

as eminent religious dignitary and head autonomous state of Tibet. US unable promise [to] pay expenses but would be willing consider what assistance might be given. If Tibetans should come US, it would be advisable they live in modest and dignified fashion. US will do [its] utmost [to] help Tibetans solve [their] financial problem. Tibet might, for example, hold present and future gold purchased in US instead [of] shipping [it to] Tibet.

(4) US still prepared [to] provide military assistance providing practicable ship Tibet [*sic*] without violating laws or regulations of India. US unable to promise loans money in advance as would depend on situation. Although US unable now [to] state what it might be able do in financial field for purpose indicated, US prepared take action which might be effective [in] encouraging Tibetan regime and maintain autonomy.

(5) US willing send US officers [to] Darjeeling and Kalimpong for frequent queries of situation but could not establish official representation for Tibet.

(6) US would be willing [for] Takster and servant [to] visit US if unable remain in India.[89]

On 30 May, Steere asked Bajpai what the GOI's reaction was to the Beijing announcement. Bajpai merely glossed over the issue and stated that 'India was the heir to British policy which had sought [to] achieve a buffer state in Tibet against Russia and China. GOI however was not disposed [to] create or support buffer States,' and went on to say that the 'GOI recognised that throughout the centuries Chinese influence and control in Tibet had fluctuated with the strength of the regime in power. Weak Chinese governments lost nearly all influence, strong governments regained it.' In the final analysis, 'it was inevitable that the present Chinese government should gain control of Tibet, and there was nothing that the GOI could do about it.'[90] On 3 June, Henderson telegrammed Dean Acheson and summed up the Indian attitude as 'philosophic acquiescence'.[91] Therefore, once again India was willing to sit back and do nothing about the situation. The State Department informed the British that they were no longer prepared to 'appease India and were content to suffer a deterioration in relations if that were to be the result of their taking action which they thought was justified by the need to counter aggression'.[92]

The Americans began to take direct initiatives without consulting the GOI. The staff from the embassy in Delhi and consulate officers from Calcutta made frequent visits to Kalimpong to meet with Shakabpa and other Tibetan officials. The Americans kept these visits secret from the Indians; American officials visited Kalimpong as tourists.[93] On 2 June, Dean Acheson replied to the questions raised by Shakabpa. Acheson's reply did not differ substantially from the recommendation made by Steere. He stated that the US would give its support if Tibet were to make a new appeal to the UN. However, it urged Tibet to approach the UK, GOI, Pakistan, France and the USSR for their support and to mobilise world opinion before sending a delegation to Lake Success. He also stated that the Tibetans must decide whether to send a delegation or not. Acheson approved of the suggestion made by Steere regarding the second point. On the third point the US was not prepared to make a commitment to providing funds to the Dalai Lama and his retinue. On the fourth question, of military assistance, Acheson stated that the US would be prepared to supply a small quantity of light arms, depending on the political and military situation in Tibet and on the GOI's attitude and co-operation. Moreover, he stressed that the US could only give effective support if the Tibetans inside Tibet showed openly that they were willing to resist the Chinese both politically and militarily. Otherwise, 'US [was] unwilling [to] commit itself to support any such undertaking from outside, but if resistance is maintained in Tibet from beginning the US would contribute in so far as [the] attitude [of the] GOI makes it possible'. On the fifth question the USA agreed that it would be willing to maintain informal contacts in Darjeeling and Kalimpong, and such contact would be purely informal. Acheson's telegram ended with: 'US is sympathetic to Tibetan position and will assist insofar as practicable but can help only if Tibetans themselves make real effort and take firm stand'.[94]

Clearly, the Americans were aware of Beijing's claims that an agreement had been reached and that the Tibetan delegation in Beijing had full authority to sign the agreement. Therefore, Acheson stated that the US would reserve final judgement in the absence of conclusive information regarding the status of the agreement.[95]

On 11 June 1951, Wilkins met with Shakabpa to discuss Acheson's answers. He questioned Shakabpa about the claims made on Beijing Radio. Shakabpa insisted that the Tibetan Government did not recognise the agreement and had instructed the Tibetan delegation in Peking to inform the Chinese that it was unacceptable.[96] Next day Shakabpa stated that he had received an urgent message from the Dalai Lama which indicated that the Dalai Lama was not prepared to accept the 17-Point Agreement, and was willing to leave Tibet. However, the Tibetans could not successfully resist the Communists unless they were certain that the US would provide assistance. Shakabpa also stated that the public repudiation of the Sino-Tibetan agreement would not be made until the Dalai Lama had left Tibet.[97]

On 16 June, the Americans informed the British that representatives of the Dalai Lama had approached the US stating that '(a) the Dalai Lama does not accept Sino-Tibetan Agreement, which was signed under duress; (b) the agreement would be repudiated as soon as Tibetan delegates are safely out of China; (c) Tibet will resist further Chinese aggression and was considering a renewed appeal to UN.'[98] The British expressed considerable doubt regarding the authenticity of the Tibetan approach and the Foreign Office instructed the British ambassador in Washington to inform the State Department that 'any encouragement of the Tibetans to denounce the Peking agreement, though it may provide the American public with propaganda material, would not aid the Tibetans', and went on to say that it would jeopardise Indo–American relations.[99] On 27 June the British High Commissioner, Nye, met Steere to discuss the situation. Nye insisted that the USA should inform the GOI of its intentions and if at all possible should not diverge from the GOI's policies. Nye later advised the CRO that 'since India had the primary interest in Tibet I considered that the attitude of HMG should be in harmony with that of the GOI and that a divergent line should be followed by us [HMG] only if there was some important point of principle on which we differed from India.' He went on to say 'it was important [in my view] that no support should be given to the Tibetan Government or any statement made until India had taken her decision.'[100] Steere's notes of the meeting show that Nye told him that, in the event of differing attitudes between the USA and the Indians, the UK 'might find itself leaning toward India rather than the US side in this matter'.[101]

The Dalai Lama and the Kashag in Dromo were under increasing pressure to make a decision. The Chinese had already announced that they would be sending their representatives with the Tibetan delegation who were returning to Lhasa. They were due to arrive shortly in Dromo via India. The Chinese had given massive international publicity to the signing of the agreement and it appeared as though the Tibetans had fully accepted the agreement. Therefore, the Tibetans were under pressure from the US to denounce the agreement. Yet at the same time the Tibetans felt that before making any statement they should wait to hear the reports of the delegation on their return. Shakabpa kept the Dalai Lama and Kashag informed of the latest American proposals. Although the American support was encouraging, the Tibetans were uncertain about how they should react or how committed the Americans were in their support. The Americans were clearly anxious to receive an affirmative answer from the Dalai Lama that he would denounce the Agreement and leave Tibet.

In a meeting with Shakabpa, Thacher (an official at the US Consul in Calcutta) stressed that it was most important that the Dalai Lama's public refutation must come before the Chinese arrived in Calcutta and that the GOI policies were constrained by the absence of any definite statement from the Tibetans.[102]

In late June, Thubten Norbu came to Kalimpong and planned to leave for the US. On 25 June, he met Wilson from the US Consulate in Calcutta. Norbu affirmed that Shakabpa had been authorised by the Dalai Lama to maintain contact with the USA and he further declared that:

(1) Tibetan government does not approve of Sino-Tibetan agreement and Dalai Lama certainly does not approve.

(2) [It is] Likely that Dalai Lama will issue statement disavowing agreement before arrival in India of Chinese and Tibetan delegates.

(3) Dalai Lama will definitely leave Tibet although may not have time before their [the Chinese] arrival in Tibet.

(4) Dalai Lama would probably find it awkward to remain India in view of close relations between GOI and China and would prefer seek asylum in USA.[103]

Thubten Norbu's confirmation was encouraging to the Americans, who on the 27th informed the GOI of their discussions with the Tibetans. The day before Shakabpa had met Thacher in Kalimpong and stated that he had received five questions from the Tibetan Government:

(1) Whether GOI would allow Dalai Lama to [go through] India 'en route to USA'.

(2) Whether US aid would be restricted to 'assisting Dalai Lama's flight' or whether aid might also be forthcoming for resistance.

(3) Whether US aid would be given 'openly or surreptitiously'.

(4) Whether US Govt would give any assistance if Tibetan Govt should announce its acceptance of Sino-Tibetan Agreement.

(5) If Dalai Lama should go to USA, how would he be received?[104]

Shakabpa stated that he had taken the initiative and informed the Tibetan Government of his understanding of the US attitude to the question, and Thacher thought that the replies given by Shakabpa accurately reflected the American stance. But the Americans were alarmed by the fourth question and Wilson informed the State department that it was 'extremely disturbing'. However, Shakabpa stated that as far as he knew there were no plans to co-operate with the Communists. Later, when the Americans questioned Shakabpa, he hinted that there was pressure on the Dalai Lama to accept the agreement. He said that over 50 per cent of Tibetan officials had no understanding of the implications of the situation faced by the Tibetan Government. Those who urged the Dalai Lama to leave Tibet were unable to 'persuade the Dalai Lama to act'.[105]

The British were sceptical of the American initiative, and Nye even went so far as to write to the Foreign Office, requesting them to contact the State Department directly, because he believed that the State Department was not getting 'sound advice from Delhi'. He went on to say that Steere, who was handling the case, was rather confused and his 'judgement was not his strong point'.[106] The British felt that the Americans were rushing into action without giving due consideration to Indian thinking, and told the Americans that it was not a question of 'appeasing' India but realising that she carried great weight in Asia and therefore it was 'obvious common sense to try to get her on our side on this issue'.[107] The British raised two further points. First, they asked on what legal grounds the Tibetans would be denouncing the agreement: and, second, they suggested that public refutation of the 17-Point Agreement might 'affect prospects of success of Korean peace moves'.[108]

On 29 June, the Foreign Office told the American Ambassador in London that the FO's legal adviser had suggested that the Tibetans could repudiate the 17-Point Agreement on the following grounds:

> (a) If they can show that duress was applied to the individual members of their delegation in Peking.
>
> (b) If they can show that their delegation exceeded their instructions or acted at variance with them. [109]

If Tibet were to repudiate the agreement on these grounds then the agreement would be invalid. The British also told the Ambassador that they did not wish to raise the Tibetan question at the UN.[110] By the end of June, the Dalai Lama and the Kashag in Dromo were unable to make up their minds as to whether to denounce the agreement or to work with the Communists. The Tibetans were anxiously waiting for the Chinese representatives to arrive. On 1 July, the Tibetan delegation accompanied by Zhang Jingwu arrived in Calcutta. The party was met at the airport by the Chinese ambassador and after a few days, the party left for Kalimpong.

When Zhang Jingwu and the party drove up the winding road, they were given a tumultuous welcome. From the Teesta bridge in Kalimpong to the Himalayan hotel, a distance of twelve miles, thousands of Indian Communist party members and Tibetans lined both sides of the road carrying the Chinese flags. There was not the slightest hint that the Tibetans might be opposed to the agreement.

The Tibetans living in Kalimpong and the Indian Communists held a reception for the Chinese representatives at the old Chinese school maintained by the Guomindang. At the reception, Tharchin Babu, who edited the only Tibetan newspaper, *Tibet Mirror*,[111] said:

> In Tibetan, we have a proverb which says that everything changes. For example there is happiness, which can easily change into sorrow. Everything turns like a wheel. This, it seems, is quite true even today. Just the other day (pointing to the wall) there was a different kind of

> picture on the wall, but now Chiang Kai-shek's picture has disappeared and Mao's picture has taken its place.
>
> Tibet for centuries has been an independent country. The Chinese claim that it was under China. This state of affairs will not last permanently. It too will change. They (Chinese) will have to give up their claim to Tibet. Tibet will once again enjoy its original freedom and independence, free of all Chinese control.[112]

Immediately after the speech some people rushed forward and carried Tharchin on their shoulders. This was the only protest that the Chinese faced. The speech clearly irritated General Zhang, who later refused to be interviewed by Tharchin.[113]

On 2 July, Thubten Norbu informed the Americans that he had been advised by the Dalai Lama not to proceed to America. However, Norbu stated that he would leave for the USA, despite the Dalai Lama's advice. He also told them that he would send a reliable messenger to urge the Dalai Lama that he should leave Tibet at once and publicly disavow the Sino–Tibetan agreement.[114] The Americans were concerned that the Dalai Lama had not committed himself fully to denouncing the agreement and they were increasingly doubtful whether their communications were reaching the Dalai Lama. Thubten Norbu assured the Americans that it was only a matter of deciding when to make a public statement. He went on to confirm that he had a private conversation with a member of the Tibetan delegation to Beijing who had told him that the Tibetan delegation had been forced to sign the agreement on Chinese terms and had been denied the opportunity to refer to the Dalai Lama for instruction. They had been told to sign or 'there would be war'.[115] Here, Thubten Norbu was trying to keep the Americans interested and show that there were grounds for denouncing the agreement.

Although Shakabpa and Thubten Norbu told the Americans that the Dalai Lama would denounce the agreement, the Americans were slowly realising that they may not have had unrestricted access to the Dalai Lama. On 8 July, Steere sent a telegram to the State Department saying: 'Throughout the current discussions with Tibetan officials, Embassy and Consul General have been greatly hampered by the lack of secure means [of] communication with the Dalai Lama. The latter who is literally God-King is almost inaccessible except to certain traditional advisers and certain family members. Shakabpa and Taktse [Thubten Norbu] both left Yatung [Dromo] prior to Peiping [Beijing] announcement re: conclusion [of] Sino-Indian agreement. Written communications are couched in generalities lest they fall into unfriendly hands and are usually carried by runner.'[116]

At the beginning of July 1951, as the Chinese delegation was about to arrive in India, the Americans decided to dispatch with great secrecy a direct appeal to the Dalai Lama. Like the earlier letter, it was written on plain paper and was neither addressed to the Dalai Lama nor signed. However, an oral message informed him that the letter was from the US Government. The letter once again urged him to denounce the agreement and seek asylum in India.

> We sent you a letter two months ago about the danger of the Chinese Communists. Some of your advisers probably think that they understand the Chinese Communists and can make a bargain with them. We do not think they understand Communism or the record of its leaders . . . Your Holiness is the chief hope of Tibet. If the Chinese Communists seize control of Tibet, you will be of greater help to Tibet outside Tibet where you will be the recognized leader and will symbolize the hopes of the Tibetans for the recovery of Tibet's freedom.
>
> We do not know whether you received our letter about the Chinese Communists. We would like to know.
>
> Since sending the previous letter we have read in the newspapers your delegation to Peiping signed an agreement with the Chinese Communists. We do not believe they signed it with your permission but were forced to do so. However, the world is beginning to think that you do not object to the agreement because you have made no statement about it. We think you should make this statement soon because the Chinese Communists are sending a delegation to Yatung through India. If you make a statement before they reach India, it should make it difficult for the Chinese delegation to come to Tibet. If you do not make such a statement, we think that Tibetan autonomy is gone for ever.
>
> The only access we have to Tibet is through the country of India. It is therefore important that Tibet tell India what you now want to do and persuade India to help you or permit other countries to help you. We don't know for sure but we think it possible India will permit help because although India now seems friendly with the Chinese Communists we know many Indians are fearful of the Communists near India.
>
> We are willing to help Tibet now and we will do the following things at this time:
>
> 1. After you issue the statement disavowing the agreement which your delegation signed with the Chinese Communists in Peiping, we will issue a public statement of our own supporting your stand.
>
> 2. If you decide to send a new appeal to United Nations we will support your case in the United Nations.
>
> 3. If you leave Tibet, we think you should seek asylum in India, Thailand or Ceylon in that order of priority because then you will be closer to Tibet and will be able to organize its resistance to the Chinese Communists. Although we haven't consulted India, we think it would let

> you come to India because it said you could come last year. We haven't consulted Thailand or Ceylon but we will ask them if you can come if you want us to talk to them. If you are unable to remain in any of these countries you can come to our country with some of your followers.
>
> 4. If you leave Tibet and if you organize resistance to the Chinese Communists, we are prepared send you light arms through India. We think, however, that you should first ask India for arms and, if they cannot give to you ask India for permission for other countries to send them through India. If you are able to organize resistance within Tibet, we will also give consideration to supply you with loans of money to keep up the resistance, spirit and morale of the Tibetan people. This is important if Tibet's autonomy is to be maintained or regained in the event you should feel impelled to seek asylum outside of Tibet. We will discuss plans and programs of military assistance and loans of money with your representatives when you tell us who your representatives are.
>
> 5. We have already told your brother, Taktse Rinpochi, that he can go to our country and we are making arrangements for his departure.[117]
>
> We are willing to do all these things. We have sent you many messages to this effect. We do not know if you have received them. Therefore we ask you to write us when you have this letter. We ask you also to send us a personal representative or write us which Tibetan representatives in India have your confidence.[118]

It was believed that the letter reached Dromo on 6 July. Meanwhile, Thubten Norbu left Calcutta clandestinely with the help of George Patterson and arrived in New York on 8 July.[119] The Americans still hoped that he could persuade the Dalai Lama to denounce the agreement and seek asylum in India. Before leaving India, Thubten Norbu made a last appeal and wrote to the Dalai Lama. The letter was given to Patterson to take to Kalimpong where it was passed to Phuntsog Tashi Takla.[120] Shakabpa's ability to influence the Dalai Lama was limited: he did not have unrestricted access to the Dalai Lama and his views were widely known. The Americans turned to Phuntsog Tashi Takla, who had been the translator for the Tibetan delegation in Beijing and was the Dalai Lama's brother-in-law. Takla was regarded as a senior member of the Dalai Lama's family and would have unrestricted access to the Dalai Lama.

Unknown to the Americans, there was a strong faction who were adamant that the Dalai Lama should return to Lhasa and accept the agreement as the best possible solution. This group was led by the most influential section of Tibetan society: the abbots of the three great monasteries who had recently arrived from Lhasa to urged the Dalai Lama to return. They were supported by the Dalai Lama's senior tutor, Ling Rinpoche. The faction which advocated that the Dalai Lama should seek asylum and repudiate the agreement was led by Phala Thupten Woden, Surkhang Wangchen Gelek and Trijang Lobsang Yeshe. This faction was supported by Shakabpa and Thubten Norbu, who had been responsible for mustering international support.[121]

In Dromo, a meeting of thirty officials was held to decide whether the Dalai Lama should return to Lhasa or seek asylum in India. Tsipon Namseling opened the meeting by stating that the 17-Point Agreement was a mistake and that it must be repudiated. He urged that they petition the Dalai Lama to leave for India. Namseling was followed by Drungyigchenmo Chomphel Thupten, a monk who exercised considerable influence over the religious community. He was in favour of accepting the agreement and of the Dalai Lama returning to Lhasa. He stated that the agreement was correct and he did not believe that the Tibetan delegates had sold out Tibet. 'We have looked for foreign support but it has been fruitless and in the future it is unlikely that the foreign governments will support us. Therefore it is best that the Dalai Lama should return to Lhasa.'[122]

Sholkhang Dhondup Dorje supported Chomphel Thupten and said that for over a year Shakabpa had been in India seeking international support. What had been achieved? he asked. He went on to urge them to accept the agreement and to return with the Dalai Lama to Lhasa.[123] The majority of the religious and secular officials endorsed the sentiments expressed by Chomphel Thupten and Sholkhang. Later Shokhang told his son, 'no matter what happens, we have made up our mind to persuade His Holiness the Dalai Lama to return to Lhasa. On no account should he go abroad.'[124]

Tsipon Namseling was only a 4th-rank official who openly advocated that the Dalai Lama should leave for India. Although there were a number of people who were in favour of denouncing the agreement, none of them spoke at the meeting: they concentrated on influencing the Dalai Lama personally. It was thought that the Dalai Lama's family was in favour of him seeking asylum in India.

The meeting did not discuss in detail the 17-Point Agreement. Kheme and Lhawutara made a detailed report to the Kashag, and were told that the final decision would be made in Lhasa. Kheme and Lhawutara were not granted an audience with the Dalai Lama. This reflected the Dalai Lama's disapproval of the agreement. The meeting ended acrimoniously. It was finally agreed that the Dalai Lama would meet Zhang Jingwu in Dromo and then proceed to Lhasa. The Dalai Lama wrote: 'I was not looking forward to it. I had never seen a Chinese general, and it was a rather forbidding prospect. Nobody could know how he would behave, whether he would be sympathetic, or arrive as a conqueror. Some of my officials, ever since the agreement had been signed, had thought I should go to India for safety before it was too late, and it had only been after some argument that everyone agreed I should wait until the general came, and see what his attitude was before we decided.'[125]

Although it was clear that the majority were in favour of the Dalai Lama returning to Lhasa, the final endorsement came from divine intervention. Two balls of tsampa were placed in a bowl, one contained a rolled-up slip of paper on which it was written that the Dalai Lama should return to Lhasa, the other a slip stating that he should not. As the bowl was shaken in front of an image of the goddess Palden Lhamo, one of the balls fell on the ground. When the ball was opened, and the slip of paper read out, it confirmed the decision of the meeting. Surkhang Shape and Trijang were suspicious that the other ball might contain the same slip of paper, but when they opened it, their suspicion proved unfounded.[126]

On 11 July, Shakabpa in Kalimpong informed Linn and Wilson from the American Consulate in Calcutta that he had received word from the Dalai Lama that he would meet the Chinese delegation and then return to Lhasa in ten days. However, the Americans were undaunted and Wilson told the State Department that Shakabpa was still arranging the Dalai Lama's escape.[127] In New York, Thubten Norbu was met by officials from the State Department, who again stated that they would provide assistance on the condition that the Dalai Lama denounced the agreement and showed willingness to resist the Chinese. They also told Thubten Norbu, 'resistance in Tibet must be viewed as a long-range problem limited by physical political conditions in Tibet and in adjoining areas, over which the US of course had no control . . .' Moreover, the Americans stated that their assistance was conditional on the Dalai Lama making a public denouncement of the agreement and seeking asylum in India.[128]

The Tibetans told the Americans that they were unable to make a public statement because they did not know the reaction of the GOI. On 14 July Wilson informed the State department, '[Name deleted from US document] told Linn Tibetan Government has little confidence in GOI and DL's advisers now favour co-operating with Chinese Commies [sic] rather than with GOI'.[129] The Americans tried to urge India to adopt a more active part in Tibetan affairs. On 16 July the Americans approached the British and GOI. The Americans merely informed the Indians that they had received information that the Tibetans would be approaching the GOI to seek asylum for the Dalai Lama.[130] In London, Arthur Ringwalt of the US Embassy approached the FO and informed them that the Dalai Lama was hesitating before leaving Tibet because of 'fear of the implications it might have on the friendly relationship between India and Communist China'.[131] Therefore the State Department requested that the UK Government advise the GOI to invite the Dalai Lama to India.

The British Government and the GOI had earlier discussed the Tibet issue, and India had expressed its reluctance to get involved in Tibetan affairs. At this critical stage, the relationship between India and Tibet was at its lowest ebb. The Tibetans were convinced that India had lost interest in Tibet and was at pains to maintain friendly relations with China. India felt that the Tibetans had marginalised India's concerns and sought direct aid from the US, without consulting the GOI. On 4th of July, Nye had met Bajpai, who criticised the Tibetans, saying that the Tibetan delegation in Beijing had made no attempt to contact or inform the Indian Ambassador of the progress of the negotiations. Moreover, India felt slighted by the fact that the Tibetans approached the Americans first about the possibility of repudiation of the agreement by the Dalai Lama. Therefore, Bajpai said: 'in these circumstances he did not think that the Tibetans could reasonably expect a great deal of sympathy from the GOI'. He added that 'in any case there was nothing which his Government could usefully do to alter the situation and it was evident that he was disposed to wash his hands of the whole affair'.[132] Nye informed the CRO, after his discussion with the GOI, that his feeling was that the GOI would be disinclined to take a strong line on the issue.[133]

On 13 July the Chinese delegation left Sikkim and crossed the Nathu la pass into Tibetan territory, where it was received by Phala Thupten Woden. Three days later Zhang Jingwu was taken to Dongker monastery to meet the Dalai Lama. Zhang had insisted that he should meet the Dalai Lama on equal terms. However, when the actual meeting took place, Zhang Jingwu's seat was slightly lower than the Dalai Lama's which, according to Tibetan etiquette, signified the supremacy of the Dalai Lama.[134] Zhang handed the Dalai Lama a letter from Mao and a copy of the 17-Point Agreement. Zhang asked when the Dalai Lama would be returning to Lhasa. The Dalai Lama simply replied, 'Soon.'

On 8 August Zhang Jingwu and his party arrived in Lhasa. The Kashag decided that the two Prime Ministers, Lukhangwa and Lobsang Tashi, should not travel to greet the Chinese group, because the Tibetans still felt that the ultimate power in Tibet would rest with the Kashag. If the Prime Ministers were to travel outside Lhasa to greet the Chinese representative, it would imply that the Tibetans had acknowledged the supremacy of the Chinese representative. The Chinese, even more conscious of ceremony, noticed the Tibetans' symbolic gesture. It was to be the start of the strained relationship between the Prime Ministers and Zhang Jingwu. The reception committee for Zhang Jingwu was headed not by Lukhangwa and Lobsang Tashi, but by Lhalu, the former Governor of Kham. It was only a week later that Zhang Jingwu was to meet the Prime Ministers. At that meeting Lukhangwa said that Ngabo had been sent to Beijing to discuss 'peace' and he himself had no authority to discuss Tibet's military or defence affairs. Therefore, he would wait until Ngabo returned before discussing the agreement.

The Americans were convinced that if they could present the Dalai Lama with a definite plan for escape and US commitment, then the Dalai Lama could be persuaded to reverse his decision to return to Lhasa. On 17 July, Wilson reported to the State Department that they were proposing a plan of escape for the Dalai Lama, which was being taken to Dromo by an unidentified Tibetan[135] who had come to India. The US urged the Dalai Lama to adopt one of the following three courses of action:

> a) Choose small group of faithful followers and leave quietly with them. This would presumably involve leaving at night in an effort avoid deputations which have come to Yatung from principal monasteries and from the government at Lhasa to persuade the Dalai Lama return to Lhasa.
>
> b) order [name deleted] bring him surreptitiously to India . . .
>
> c) If neither (a) nor (b) are feasible, Dalai Lama should send msg to [name deleted] requesting [name deleted] to send Harrer and Patterson secretly and in disguise to meet Dalai Lama near Yatung in accordance with prearranged plan and bring Dalai Lama back. Detailed plan for this operation also being conveyed by [name deleted] but he is to make clear to the Dalai Lama that it is to be adopted only as last resort.[136]

On 20 July, the plan and a supporting letter from Thubten Norbu in Washington were taken to Dromo by the unnamed Tibetan. Meanwhile, the Americans set out to encourage the GOI to extend a formal invitation for the Dalai Lama to visit India. The British also undertook to persuade the Indians to extend an invitation to the Dalai Lama.[137] The Americans had already advised Shakabpa to approach Dayal, the Political Officer in Sikkim, to seek asylum for the Dalai Lama. At the same time the US consulate received a message from Dromo that the Dalai Lama would definitely be returning to Lhasa.

The above episode is still shrouded in secrecy and it is not clear whether the Dalai Lama received the American messages. On 23 July the Dalai Lama left Dromo and headed back to Lhasa. George Patterson writes that he and Harrer made plans to bring the Dalai Lama to India. The US records also confirm that they were involved. Patterson states that Phuntsog Tashi Takla, the Dalai Lama's brother in-law, carried the plan to Dromo. Takla returned three days later and told them that the Dalai Lama would return to Lhasa.[138]

By the end of July 1951, the Americans informed the British that they had given up hope of the Dalai Lama seeking asylum. They were changing their tactics. Until now they had been trying to influence the Dalai Lama directly; their letters were addressed to him personally. It is likely that the

American communications were known only to a select few, and that the majority of the Kashag were not privy to the information. Now the Americans decided to make separate appeals to influential members of the Kashag. They chose to appeal to Ragashag Shape, who was Commander-in-Chief of the Tibetan army. On 18 July, the Americans sent a messenger[139] to meet with Ragashag (who was returning to Lhasa with the Dalai Lama), and this took place near Phari Dzong. The Americans urged Ragashag to persuade the Dalai Lama to seek asylum in India and gave assurance of US support. Like previous letters from the Americans, the letter was unsigned and did not contain any reference to the US Government, but Ragashag was informed that the message was from them. When the messenger returned to Calcutta, he informed Wilson (the Consul General) that Ragashag would not be able to 'convince the Kashag of US Govt interest without signed letter on US letterhead'.[140]

Wilson and Linn discussed Ragashag's response with the messenger, who stated that should an opportunity arise in Lhasa to convince the Dalai Lama to leave Tibet, it would require a signed letter. Wilson remarked that it would be dangerous in the event of the letter falling into Chinese hands. The messenger pointed out that at present there were only a few Chinese in Tibet and so this was most unlikely. The messenger also told Wilson that he would be prepared to take a signed letter to Ragashag.[141]

On 13 August, Wilson sent a telegram to the State Department suggesting that the Dalai Lama was due to arrive in Lhasa soon and that there was still a chance that he would repudiate the agreement and seek asylum abroad. Therefore, he recommended that the messenger take a formal letter to the Dalai Lama, along with copies for the two tutors. The letter might become the 'deciding factor' in the Dalai Lama disavowing the agreement and seeking asylum abroad.[142]

However, Horace Holms, from the US embassy in Delhi, opposed sending a formal letter because of 'risks involved in transmitting proposed letter are far greater than advantages which may result for US and Tibet'. Moreover, there was no doubt that all previous communications had been received by the Dalai Lama and his advisers were sufficiently aware of the US offer of help. Holms thought that, instead of sending an official letter, it might be better if the US could urge the Dalai Lama to send a trusted personal representative to discuss the matter with US officials. The State Department accepted Holms' recommendations.[143]

Loy Henderson suggested that the US should adopt more practical measures to convince the Tibetans of continuing US assistance. For example, the US should increase the purchase of Tibetan wool and sanction the transfer of funds and goods as long as they were not detrimental to the US and would not benefit the Communists. This was an interesting change of policy. It was seen as an important issue by the Tibetans.

After the Communist victory, the Americans had frozen Chinese assets in the country, and since Tibet was regarded as part of China, some Tibetan assets were also frozen. In May, when Steere met with Liushar, a member of the Kashag in charge of foreign affairs, and Yamphel Pomdatsang (one of the wealthiest people in Tibet; his family had exercised a virtual monopoly over Tibet's wool trade and they were major players in Tibetan politics), the two Tibetans told Steere that the restrictions on the purchase of Tibetan wool were seen by the Tibetans as a sign that 'the US was no longer interested in Tibet'.[144] On 10 September the State Department agreed that Tibetan assets in the US would not be detained and that it would be willing to consider on an *ad hoc* basis the transfer of funds in the 'most liberal working arrangement'.[145]

It was unlikely this would have influenced the Dalai Lama or other Tibetan officials: the American gesture had come too late. However, a few Tibetan families traded internationally and the lifting of restrictions on the purchase of Tibetan wool would have a major impact on the Tibetan economy, since the restrictions had produced a glut and were causing strain on the Tibetan economy. As we shall see later, the Chinese were able to purchase the surplus wool and to secure a propaganda victory.

The issue of sending a headed letter once again surfaced, when Heinrich Harrer came up with a novel idea. He informed the Consul General in Calcutta that the messenger was willing to return to Lhasa at considerable personal risk to urge the Dalai Lama to leave Lhasa. Therefore, Harrer suggested that letters setting out US assurances to the Dalai Lama should be written and shown to the messenger but would not be delivered. Then the messenger would give his assurance to the Dalai Lama of the existence of the signed letter. Harrer explained that the Dalai Lama was personally in favour of seeking asylum but lacked sufficient support among the officials and was unable to overcome opposition from the monks. However, if the Dalai Lama was in a position to show that there was a real commitment from the US to back Tibet, and the messenger confirmed on oath the existence of the signed letter, then they would be in a position to convince a large section of the lay officials.[146]

On 12 September, Henderson requested authorisation from the State Department to draw up a signed letter. He suggested that Harrer's initiative raised less objections than sending an actual letter. Two days later, Dean Acheson agreed to the plan. The content of the letter was similar to the earlier unsigned letter and was shown to the messenger in the presence of a US official.

US records do not reveal whether the Dalai Lama received the assurance. It was unlikely that a copy of the letter was ever shown to him. The situation in Tibet had changed: the Chinese had entered Lhasa. More and more PLA troops were arriving with every day. The Chinese were urging the Dalai Lama to accept the Agreement.[147] By the end of September, the Kashag and the National Assembly were under considerable pressure to make a final public statement of acceptance of the 17-Point Agreement. The Prime Ministers, Lukhangwa and Lobsang Tashi, told Zhang Jingwu that neither the Kashag nor the Dalai Lama would be able to make a public statement without full discussion in the National Assembly.[148] Before the National Assembly met, the Prime Ministers told Ngabo the Agreement was not acceptable. They particularly objected to the deployment of Chinese troops in Lhasa.[149]

Tibetans Discuss the 17-Point Agreement

At the end of September, the National Assembly met to discuss the Agreement. The meeting was attended by over 300 officials. Normally, the Shapes were not allowed to attend the meeting but Ngabo told the Prime Ministers that he should be given the opportunity to address the meeting, along with the other members who had signed the Agreement, because as head of the delegation he should explain the terms of the Agreement and he also wished to clear his name from the allegations and rumours about his conduct.[150]

When the meeting began, the delegation who had gone to Beijing were seated in a separate area. Ngabo was the first to speak. He stated that neither he nor any member of the delegation had accepted any bribes from the Chinese. During his stay in Beijing he had only received the gift of a photo of Mao and a box of tea. Ngabo spoke for nearly an hour and a half, explaining the instructions he had received from Dromo, and arguing that the Agreement did not endanger the status and the power of the Dalai Lama, nor would it harm the religious and political system of Tibet. Finally, Ngabo urged the Assembly to accept the Agreement, but conceded that if the Assembly decided to repudiate the Agreement, and argue that he had acted without full authorisation, he was willing to accept any punishment that the Assembly imposed on him, including the death sentence.[151] After Ngabo had given his speech, the delegation to Beijing left the meeting.

The National Assembly finally advised the Dalai Lama to accept the Agreement. The memorandum from the Assembly to the Dalai Lama confirmed Ngabo's view that the Agreement did not threaten the status and power of the Dalai Lama, and that the religious and political system of Tibet would not be in danger. Once the Agreement had been accepted by the National Assembly, Zhang Jingwu urged the Dalai Lama to issue his own public acceptance. On 20 October 1951, a year and thirteen days after the Chinese invasion of Chamdo, a letter of acceptance of the 17-Point Agreement was drafted which Phuntsog Tashi Takla translated into

Chinese. When it was shown to Zhang Jingwu, he objected to the use of the term 'Gya-Bod' (China and Tibet): as far as he was concerned, the term China naturally included Tibet, whereas the use of the distinct terms Tibet and China implied separate nations. He wanted the letter to use the term *U-zhung* (Central Government) and *sanas-zhung* (Local Government).[152] On 24 October, the letter was dispatched to Mao in the form of a telegram:

> The Tibet Local Government as well as the ecclesiastic and secular people unanimously support this agreement, and under the leadership of Chairman Mao and the Central People's Government, will actively support the People's Liberation Army in Tibet to consolidate national defence, drive out imperialist influences from Tibet and safeguard the unification of the territory and the sovereignty of the Motherland.[153]

Four few days later, the Panchen Rinpoche made a similar public statement accepting the Agreement. He urged the 'people of Shigatse to give active support' to the implementation of the Agreement.[154] The independence that Tibet had enjoyed since 1911 had ended. Tibet became part of China.

The most vocal supporters of the Agreement came from the monastic community: they felt that the Agreement gave a guarantee that Tibet's traditional social system would not be altered, and that the Chinese had no interest but to secure their symbolic claim over Tibet. Tibet's traditional élite was governed by narrow self-interest: the preservation of the existing social order, which safeguarded their power and privileges, was seen as synonymous with the legal status of Tibet.

In the end, for many Tibetans, the 17-Point Agreement met in part the need to safeguard Tibet's cultural and social independence. It guaranteed that the existing political system would function as before, that the power and privileges of the ruling élite would be protected and that religious freedom would be protected. Moreover, the Agreement did not even mention the words 'socialism' or 'Communism'. It merely stated that 'various reforms' would be carried out according to the local conditions and wishes of the Tibetan people. To many Tibetans, it made very little difference if Tibet was regarded internationally as a part of China as long as their social and cultural autonomy were safeguarded.

There were strong factions in Tibet which felt that the Agreement was acceptable and that Communist China and Buddhist Tibet could co-exist peacefully. Tibetan acceptance was not based on a legal interpretation of the Agreement, which transformed Tibet's international legal status from independent state to region of China. In the Tibetans' view their independence was not a question of international legal status, but of 'our way of life and culture, which was more real to the unlettered masses than law or history, canons by which the non-Tibetans decided the fate of Tibet'.[155]

However, it must be recognised that the Chinese would not have secured the Agreement had they confined themselves to diplomatic means. It was only after the Chinese had invaded and attempts to secure international support had failed that Tibet fought a dialogue with the Chinese. Once the Chinese had shown their military might, the Tibetans had no choice but to reach a diplomatic compromise. Nehru perceptively noted that the Tibetans accepted the Agreement 'without joy and under the compulsion of circumstances'.[156] This was the first formal agreement between Tibet and Communist China. It set the legal basis and to some extent the tone of Chinese rule in Tibet.

FOUR

An Uneasy Co-existence

On 26 October 1951, Generals Zhang Guohua and Tan Guansan arrived in Lhasa. Zhang Jingwu was made the representative of the Central Government. Shortly afterwards, several thousand PLA troops arrived in Lhasa and thousands of people flocked to watch them marching into the city. They arrived with a great fanfare, carrying banners proclaiming the 'Peaceful Liberation of Tibet' and urging Tibetans to unite with the Motherland and strive to drive out 'imperialist aggressive forces'.

The arrival of the Chinese in Lhasa marked a new phase in Sino–Tibetan relations. It was the beginning of Tibet's history under Chinese Communist occupation. All previous Chinese rulers had been content to exercise territorial claims over Tibet through a symbolic presence in Tibet. The Communists had very different ideas and saw their actions in Tibet as a process of nation-building. Many writings on Tibet stress the predatory nature of the Chinese annexation of Tibet, sometimes arguing that the Chinese actions were motivated by a desire to acquire Tibet's natural resources and by a policy of *Lebensraum*.[1] I think this is a misinterpretation of the Sino–Tibetan conflict. Chinese polices must be seen within the context of the emergence of Chinese nationalism: the Chinese Communists and the Guomindang were passionately nationalistic and believed that the territorial limits of modern China lay in the foothills of the Himalayas. From the Chinese point of view, their policy towards Tibet was preoccupied with the integration of the region within the political and economic system of the new China. The Communists did recognise that Tibet constituted a distinctive region differing from other administrative regions.

The PLA and the Party cadres were not merely symbols of Chinese authority; it was they who would be instrumental in the transformation of Tibet into a socialist society. The Tibetans desperately wanted to avoid the deployment of Chinese troops in Tibet, but for the Chinese the key to their Tibet policy was the constitutional and administrative integration of Tibet into China. The stationing of Chinese representatives and PLA troops were the means of achieving this end. During the course of negotiations in Beijing, the Chinese insisted that they had inherited the right to station troops in Tibet from the Qing period.[2]

From the start, the Communists had a realistic appreciation of the situation in Tibet. Although the Chinese had achieved their main objective of establishing a claim over Tibet, and Tibet was now regarded internationally as a 'Region of China', the Communists promised that Tibet would not be compelled to carry out social reforms. It nevertheless remained the long-term objective of the Communists to promote social reforms and eventually bring Tibet within the social system of China.

The signing of the 17-Point Agreement was clear proof of China's recognition of Tibet's separate cultural and political identity. Mao warned PLA troops and Party cadres leaving for Tibet that the political and cultural milieu in Tibet was different from any situation they had faced in China. There were no indigenous revolutionaries that they could ally themselves with, as Mao pointed out: 'we have no material base in Tibet. In terms of social power they are stronger than us, which for the moment will not change'.[3] The Chinese therefore had to adopt policies whereby they would win over the 'patriotic upper strata' of Tibetan society. Mao's instructions were to:

> Make every possible effort to use all suitable means to win over the Dalai Lama and a majority of the upper strata and isolate the minority of bad elements in order to achieve long-term goals of transforming Tibetan economy and polity gradually without spilling blood.[4]

At another meeting with PLA officers and cadres, one of the cadres commented that reforms in Tibet would have to be promoted at the pace of a tortoise. Mao interjected that even this would be too fast.[5]

The first problem faced by the Chinese was not political resistance but the logistics of accommodating and supplying provisions for thousands of PLA troops. By the end of 1951 the population of Lhasa and the surrounding areas had doubled.[6] The Chinese troops came in three main groups: 2,000 men led by Wang Qimei arrived from Chamdo; and both Zhang Guohua and Tan Guansan arrived with 3,000 men. Not only were the troops to be fed; several thousand ponies, yaks and camels required grazing land and feed, causing an enormous burden on Tibet's traditional subsistence economy.

The Tibetan Government was faced with the task of feeding and accommodating the Chinese. A monk official, Phala Thupten Woden, and Kunsangtse Dzasa were appointed to take charge of finding accommodation for the PLA troops. Since there was a severe shortage of accommodation in Lhasa, the soldiers and their officers ended up in tents. One of the main problems was fuel for cooking. Phala recalled:

> We had to provide firewood for the soldiers, and because there were so many of them, we were not able to meet their needs. The soldiers were so

> well disciplined. They were camped near a field, where there were lots of trees. They did not even cut a single branch. They waited until we brought some wood. For two days the troops did not have any fuel to cook.[7]

The problem of fuel eventually led to the first resentment from the Tibetan people. In desperation, the Chinese started to burn discarded yak horns, causing a stench all over Lhasa. The Tibetans complained that this would pollute the air and anger the deities.[8]

The peasantry suffered most from the severe strain on Tibet's fragile economy. S. Sinha, the Indian representative in Lhasa, wrote: 'the introduction of large Chinese forces has brought in its wake problems that are not easily soluble. It has added a load on to the limited resources of Tibet; it has badly shaken the economic structure of the country, and has already affected the livelihood of the poor man, whose share of food and daily necessities has been ruthlessly whittled down'.[9]

The PLA troops remained at camp sites and did not venture into the city. They showed themselves to be as well disciplined as the Chinese cadres. A directive issued by the Central Committee of the CCP 'called upon the expeditionary forces to unite themselves closely with their brethren in Sikang [Xikāng] and Tibet to carry out faithfully and correctly the nationalities policy laid down in the common programme, strictly observe the three major rules of discipline and the eight points of attention, and the eight point contract, to carry out intensive investigation, research, and propaganda work, learn the local language, understand the way of life of the local people, show concern for the suffering of the local people, and help them actively to free themselves from their suffering and difficulties'.[10] But the officers and troops did not attempt to communicate with the masses. Instead they concentrated on working with the existing Tibetan infrastructure and gaining the confidence of the traditional Tibetan bureaucrats (*zhung zhub*). One way of winning over the ruling élite was to co-opt them into helping the Chinese cadres and PLA troops to build a new infrastructure.

The influx of Chinese also meant new business opportunities for Tibetan traders. As winter was approaching, it would have been impossible to keep the troops in tents indefinitely. The Chinese started to buy or build houses: Members of aristocratic families saw this as an opportunity to make quick money. They readily sold land and accommodation to the Chinese at exorbitant prices. The prices of all goods increased several-fold. There were demands for food, fuel, and construction materials, which had to be imported from India. The aristocracy and traders made enormous profits supplying Chinese needs.

As a part of their propaganda, the Communists had always stated that they would pay for everything they acquired. Chinese money was, however, not accepted by the Tibetans (since it could not be exchanged in India); with great ingenuity, the Chinese collected silver ornaments and religious objects in China which were melted down into bullion. In Chengdu a special mint was set up to produce the old Nationalist silver dollar known as Da Yuan. This was used exclusively in Tibet.[11] The circulation of the Da Yuan in Tibet served two purposes: first, it was acceptable to Tibetans because it could be melted down and resold. Second, the large-scale use of Da Yuan meant that the Chinese were able to undermine the circulation of Tibetan currency and make it virtually worthless.

There was a popular saying that the Chinese dispensed silver coins like a shower of rain. The Da Yuan were smuggled to India, where there was a great demand for silver. Sinha reported to the GOI: 'the Kutras [aristocrats] have done well by themselves as a result of the influx of Chinese into Tibet, for the Chinese desperately needed goods and services (monopolised by the Kutras), and were almost incredibly over-generous in meeting their obligations with large sums of silver dollars, squandered with the liberality of princes and the sleek abandon of rakes'.[12]

The Chinese concentrated their activities on Lhasa and Shigatse. Only specially trained propaganda units were sent out into the villages. The top cadres were mainly engaged in social activities, giving lavish banquets to the ruling élite. The masses were entertained by song and dance. Most evenings, the Chinese showed newsreel films of the Communist war against the Guomindang and Japanese. These were very popular in Lhasa and hundreds of people flocked to see them. It was a brilliant propaganda exercise. The films were deliberately chosen to show the might of the PLA, and it was the first time that the majority of Tibetans had seen modern weapons and warfare. The PLA opened a dispensary in Lhasa and gave free treatment to the people. In serious cases, the PLA doctors would visit the home of the patient. The Indian mission hospital had been the only source of modern medicine for many years and it complained that the Chinese had 'deprived our hospital of nearly half its patients'.[13]

The major problem still remained the sheer number of Chinese in Tibet; every day, new groups would arrive. Because there was no means of transporting goods from the east, the Chinese were entirely dependent on Tibetan produce. The Tibetan Government could only provide a limited amount of provisions so the Chinese started to acquire land for cultivation. Grazing land near Drepung and Tsedrung Lingka was brought under cultivation, causing a great deal of resentment from the local peasants.[14]

The Two Prime Ministers

The first real opposition to the Communists came from the two acting Prime Ministers, Lukhangwa and Lobsang Tashi, who had already made known their opposition to the 17-Point Agreement. The Chinese were faced with a desperate shortage of grain, so Zhang Guohua met with the Prime Ministers and requested that they authorise that the grain reserves of the Tibetan Government be sold to the PLA. Lukhangwa refused, insisting that there was not enough and the surplus was needed for the coming winter. He said defiantly, 'It was bad to lose a war, but it is worse to let people starve.'[15] (After the government refused to sell grain, however, many aristocratic families were cautiously selling grain from their estates.) Zhang Guohua gave a highly melodramatic account of the meeting: 'the first words Lokongwa [Lukhangwa] said when he saw us were: Commander Zhang, isn't hunger more intolerable than being defeated in battle?'[16] Zhang mistook Lukhangwa's statement as meaning that the Tibetans would starve the PLA troops. The Chinese were shocked by the defiance of the two Prime Ministers, who in turn insisted that the only solution was to reduce the number of troops and cadres.

It was clear to the Chinese that the Prime Ministers were determined to oppose any rapid changes and, moreover, that they continued to exercise absolute power. The Prime Ministers insisted that all negotiations between the Chinese and Tibetan Governments should be conducted through the Office of the Prime Minister. The Chinese therefore began to seek ways to undermine their authority. At first the Chinese insisted that they should be allowed to discuss issues directly with the Dalai Lama, but the Prime Ministers insisted on being present at any such meeting.[17]

Although in theory the Dalai Lama had assumed full power, in practice the two Prime Ministers met with the Chinese and were at the height of their authority. They remained the main obstacle to the Chinese and the relationship soon began to deteriorate. At one meeting the Chinese raised the issue of Tibetan soldiers who were staying in Lhasa without work and whose old regiments had not been reconstituted. The Chinese were anxious lest these soldiers might turn against them, and suggested that the troops should be merged with the Chinese and undergo retraining with the PLA. Lukhangwa opposed this, declaring that the soldiers had not recovered from the defeat at Chamdo and therefore could not undergo retraining.[18]

The Chinese insisted that the Prime Ministers should discuss methods of implementing the 17-Point Agreement. Lukhangwa responded by saying that before they would discuss any issue, the Chinese must hand over the occupied areas in Chamdo to the Tibetans. The Chinese claimed that the area had been liberated and an administrative organ known as the 'Chamdo Liberation Committee' had been established. The Committee was composed of officers of the advancing PLA units and a few Tibetans who had been captured. Zhang Guohua told the Prime Ministers that it was useless to discuss what had happened in Chamdo. It would be up to the people of Chamdo to decide.[19]

The Kashag was also alarmed by the growing rift between the Chinese and the two Prime Ministers. Moreover, the office of the Prime Minister was becoming more dominant than the Kashag and this caused friction between some of its members and the Prime Ministers.[20] Although the Kashag held regular meetings, they were unable to make any decisions. Katsab (acting Kalon) Shasur Gyurmed Dorje raised the issue at a Kashag meeting. He stated that members of the Kashag should support the Prime Ministers, otherwise they would be in a vulnerable position when dealing with the Chinese. The next day when the Kashag met with the two Prime Minsters, Lhalu asked them why, in an earlier meeting with the Chinese, the Prime Ministers had responded without any consultation with the Kashag. Lhalu went on to point out that if they were to discuss matters in the Kashag first they would be able to present a united front to the Chinese. The two Prime Ministers merely responded by saying 'Yes, Yes' (*La se, La se*).[21] The Prime Ministers' reluctance to discuss all the issues in the Kashag may have been due to the fact that they did not trust that the discussion would not be leaked to the Chinese.

In late September 1951 the Chinese informed the Kashag that they would celebrate Chinese National Day on 1 October. It was the first time that such a celebration had been observed in Tibet. The Chinese had hoped that the celebration would be symbolic of the final integration of Tibet into China. The Tibetans agreed to the holding of the celebration and that the Tibetan army would march with the PLA troops. The Kashag informed the Prime Ministers that the Chinese were insisting that the Tibetan troops should carry the Chinese National flag. Lukhangwa defiantly stated that the Tibetan army should only march behind their national flag. The Chinese were naturally opposed to Tibet displaying a symbol of its separate identity.[22] The Kashag decided to compromise and agreed that both the Chinese and Tibetan flag would be carried by the Tibetan army.[23]

The Chinese were clearly frustrated by the Prime Ministers' refusal to co-operate with them. Rumours about their opposition to the Chinese became widely known in Lhasa. The incident about the flag was openly talked about in the streets but, like many rumours, the story was told very differently. It was said that the Chinese wanted to hoist the Red Flag over the Potala, and that Lukhangwa had declared that, as long as he was alive, the only flag hoisted over the Potala would be the Tibetan national flag. The two Prime Minsters became folk heroes to the masses. However, in certain Tibetan political circles, including those who were in favour of reaching quick agreement with the Chinese, the Prime Ministers were regarded as conservative, and their uncompromising stance against the Chinese was viewed with alarm. Phala says that the Chinese again tried to bypass the

Prime Minsters and meet directly with the Dalai Lama. Lukhangwa replied that the Dalai Lama was young and if they did not take their responsibility seriously the people would accuse them of leaving the Dalai Lama to fend for himself.[24]

The Chinese set out to win over the masses. Groups of propaganda teams were sent out to remote areas. Yin Fatang (later First Secretary of TAR) remembers that his propaganda team travelled from village to village, showing films and performing songs and dances. There was an occasion when he went to a village and found it deserted, the villagers having fled. On another occasion found a deserted village, but with the villagers all camped nearby, tending their animals. Soon the villagers returned, one by one.[25] The team's main task at this stage was to publicise the 17-Point Agreement and to assure the people that there would not be any dramatic change. The Chinese propaganda was effective, and, for the majority of Tibetans this was the first time they had heard of the 17-Point Agreement and of the fact that Tibet had become part of China.

The Chinese tried to win over the masses by using the propaganda tactics that they had found so useful during the Long March. Yin Fatang writes that all the propaganda teams entering villages were told to observe the traditional PLA disciplines. They were also expected to observe the following rules in Tibet:

(1) Never occupy a house without the consent of the people.
(2) Never kill birds.
(3) Never catch fish.
(4) Observe and respect local customs.
(5) Respect all religious objects, e.g. prayer flags.
(6) No female cadre should visit a monastery.[26]

The PLA troops and propaganda teams went around villages without their weapons. They were more like visiting performers than a foreign army. The propaganda teams consisted of a song-and-dance group and a medical unit. In rural areas the Communists were not seen as an immediate threat to the Tibetan way of life. However, the Tibetan people remained suspicious of Chinese motives, seeing the large influx of Chinese as a desire for land. Despite their skilful propaganda, the Chinese were not able to win over the masses. In China the Communists could appeal to Chinese Nationalism and arouse anti-Japanese sentiment among Chinese people. Out in Tibet, the rhetoric of anti-imperialism and unifying the 'Motherland' made no impact.

The Communists' main task was to build an infrastructure for their long-term goal. But for the time being, the Chinese allowed the traditional political and administrative structure to function as before. At the same time the Chinese wanted to establish a parallel administrative structure, which would initiate and run new projects and reforms. Eventually, it was hoped that the traditional government structure would become redundant. The Chinese established educational committees which were responsible for setting up schools, carrying out translation work and recruiting students and teachers. This was a clever move on the Chinese part since the traditional Tibetan Government structure had no section dealing with issues such as education. The education committee did not conflict with the traditional Government structures.

In the Education Committee the majority were Tibetans. Leading officials like Surkhang, Kapshopa, Sampho, Tsarong, Pomda Yanphel, Tsatrul Rinpoche, Ngapo, Changlochen and members of the Dalai Lama's family were recruited. The committee was divided into various sub-committees, and asked to find resources for schools. For example, Tsarong was given the contract to purchase school books and Pondatsang was given the contract to supply furnishings. Since all these resources had to be imported from India, there were opportunities for the Tibetan suppliers to make a profit.

Despite this ingenious policy to win over the upper classes, the failure to recognise that the Tibetan environment and economic system could not support thousands of PLA troops and cadres made the Chinese unpopular among the masses. Furthermore the Chinese army found themselves on the very edge of starvation. Many PLA troops had been forced to forage for food by digging up roots, which later resulted in illness.[27]

Despite growing anti-Chinese feeling among the people, the Chinese were successful in achieving their goal of establishing an administrative structure in Tibet. The committee for setting up schools was functioning well. They had managed to co-opt many influential Tibetan Government officials and intellectuals like Geshe Choedrak, who had few years earlier published a new Tibetan dictionary. The Communists republished the dictionary with Chinese added to it: the first modern Tibetan–Chinese dictionary. Most importantly, on 10 February 1952, the Chinese announced the establishment of the Tibetan Military District Headquarters, which was seen as a key to establishing effective Chinese rule in Tibet. The inauguration of the Headquarters was celebrated with great pomp and fanfare for three days. The PLA groups performed songs and dances. In one of the dances, two groups of Chinese dancers, one dressed in the uniforms of the Drapchi Regiment, the other in PLA uniforms, danced in the spirit of friendship and rejoiced that from now on they were soldiers in the same army.[28]

The Tibetan Military District command was made up of ten members. Zhang Guohua was named as the Commander of the Commission. There were only two Tibetan representatives: Ngabo was appointed first Deputy Commander and Ragashag Phuntsog Rabgye was appointed Second Deputy

Commander.[29] During the celebrations, Ngabo and Ragashag appeared in the uniforms of the Chinese army for the first time. The Chinese members of the commission were divided between representatives both from the North-West Military Region and the South-West Military Region.

At that time, it had not yet been settled in Beijing whether Tibet should come under the jurisdiction of the North-West or South-West Military Region. It was the army of the South-West that had conquered Tibet and most of the soldiers in the country were from the South-West Military Region. However, PLA troops from the North-West Military Region had been entering Tibet from the north and from Xinjiang in the north-west. The North-West Military Region also held a trump card: the Panchen Rinpoche was in their hands, and they had insisted that his entry into Tibet would be made via the much longer and more arduous route across the Changtang plateau.

For the Chinese, the establishment of the Tibetan Military District Headquarters was necessary to gain control of Tibet's primitive and discontented army, which presented a threat to their goal, and it reduced the conflict between the two military regions. But the primary reason was to place Tibet within the military-administrative structure of China. Articles 15 and 16 of the 17-Point Agreement allowed the setting up of the Military Area Headquarters.

After the establishment of the Headquarters, the Chinese demanded, as stated in the 17-Point Agreement, that the Tibetan army be incorporated into the PLA. But the Prime Ministers again insisted that before they could talk about the implementation of the agreement, the number of Chinese troops must be reduced. The position of the Prime Ministers remained uncompromising. The Chinese were disturbed by their failure to bring any pressure to bear on the Prime Ministers and concerned that the increase in prices and the shortage of food were deliberately engineered by the Prime Ministers to drum up anti-Chinese feelings.[30]

The Chinese were anxious to counter the growing anti-Chinese sentiment by stressing that the PLA troops had entered Tibet to build a modern Tibet. The annual celebration of Monlam provided the Chinese with an opportunity to gain the confidence of the Tibetan people. The leading Chinese officials visited the monasteries and reassured the monks that religious freedom would be protected. In February 1951, the Chinese set up a committee to discuss policies concerning the forthcoming Monlam festival. The committee consisted of twenty-one people: four representatives from Drepung, three from Sera, two from Gaden and eight Drunyikchenmo.[31] Monlam is one of the most important festivals in the Tibetan religious calendar.[32] Thousands of monks and pilgrims from all parts of Tibet would gather in Lhasa for a month-long ceremony. This was potentially a dangerous period for the Chinese, yet if they adopted sensitive policies, they could win over the Tibetan masses. The committee was headed by Fan Ming, who met with the abbots of the three great monasteries. During the course of the meeting Fan Ming elicited detailed information on the normal procedures that were adopted and how the Chinese could contribute to the Monlam festival. Traditionally, during the Monlam the Dalai Lama and Tibetan Government distributed alms to all the monks attending the ceremony; wealthy individuals would also give alms. The Chinese decided that they too would give alms. The Committee calculated that it would cost the Chinese 33,000 yuan.[33] The Communists were quite happy to patronise monks and religious institutions (this policy did not diverge from traditional Qing policy towards Tibet, where the Chinese Emperor became one of the great patrons of Buddhism in Tibet and conferred titles on high-ranking lamas): they were quick to recognise the effectiveness of such a policy. Later, in 1952, when the Chinese Buddhists Association (CBA) was founded, many Tibetan lamas were given leading posts in the association. Although the Communists despised religion, in the early period Mao realistically believed that religion could not be abolished by coercive measures. He argued that religious idealism could only be eliminated by persuasion and education.[34]

The Chinese were seriously concerned about security during the festival. A gathering of thousands of people from all over Tibet could easily turn into an anti-Chinese demonstration. Moreover, the popularity of the two Prime Ministers was increasing because of their anti-Chinese stance.[35] The abbots of the three monasteries argued that traditionally security and discipline during the Monlam festival was organised by the monks. The Chinese countered that it was important that a good relationship between the monks and the army should be maintained. The Tibetan Government had to seek assurances from the abbots of the three monasteries that the monks would not use the occasion to agitate against the Chinese, and in return the Chinese took the precaution of keeping the troops out of Lhasa. During the Monlam ceremony, the Chinese Government served tea to all the monks.

The Chinese did not wish to lose an opportunity to use the occasion for propaganda purposes. They distributed money equally according to status: high-ranking lamas received 10 srang; middle-ranking lamas 4, and ordinary monks 1 srang and 4 zho. (The Chinese were careful not to exceed the donations given by the Dalai Lama and the Tibetan Government.)[36] The Chinese also distributed propaganda booklets and a photo of Mao to all the monks. The Indian representative present at the ceremony wrote: ‘the monks accepted the money but treated the leaflets with contempt, some blew their noses in them, others spat on them, and still others crumpled and hurled them back at the Chinese’.[37]

Opposition of the People

During the Monlam ceremony a number of anti-Chinese posters appeared in the streets of Lhasa, demanding the withdrawal of the Chinese from Tibet and a restoration of the position of the Dalai Lama. The posters described the Communists as the Tendra (enemy of faith) and said that protestors were deferring 'taking action against the Chinese until the Monlam was over'.[38] In the beginning, such anti-Chinese groups were unorganised and spontaneous, their main grievance being the influx of Chinese cadres and PLA troops. Yet the Chinese were alarmed at the growing anti-Chinese feeling in Lhasa, and they began to pressurise the Kashag to curb the activities of protesters.[39] The Kashag was asked whether the Tibetan Government would deal with the anti-Chinese activities. If they were not prepared to do so, the Chinese would take action. There were rumours of the formation of an organisation calling itself the *Mimag Thutsog* (People's Representatives) which was planning anti-Chinese demonstrations in Lhasa.[40]

The Chinese demanded an investigation into the activities of the so-called People's Representatives, and asked the Kashag for the names of the people involved. The Chinese were convinced that members of the Kashag were involved in the activities of the People's Representatives. The Chinese insisted that the Dalai Lama and the Kashag should not meet with the members of the organisation. It was believed that the People's Representatives were planning to submit a petition to the Dalai Lama and the Kashag for the immediate expulsion of the Chinese and refutation of the 17-Point Agreement. The Chinese insisted that the Dalai Lama should not accept any petition submitted to him by the People's Representatives. There was another group calling itself *Lhasa Mangtsog Ruchen* (Lhasa People's Organisation) which was planning to encircle the Yuthok and Sandutsang houses, which had been purchased by the Chinese and were now being used as residences-cum-offices by the senior Chinese cadres.

One of the main reasons for the increasing anti-Chinese movement was the implementation of article eight of the 17-Point Agreement, which made provision for the dissolution of the Tibetan army and its integration into the PLA to 'become part of the national defence forces of China'. By March 1951, only three regiments had been retained; all the others had been disbanded and a large number of ex-soldiers had remained in Lhasa rather than returning to their villages. The soldiers not only had to face the humiliation of defeat; they now had to face the prospect of returning to their villages with no promise of work. The Tibetan Government sympathised with the plight of the ex-soldiers but had deliberately disbanded the army rather than place them under the command of the People's Liberation Army.

The Chinese learned that many members of the People's Representatives were former soldiers, and there were rumours that the group had managed to get weapons from the Tibetan Government's arsenal. This was very worrying for the Chinese, who saw the disbanding of the army as a deliberate attempt to instigate a mass anti-Chinese movement. On 31 March the People's Representatives from Chushul, a village near Lhasa, came to Lhasa and presented a petition to the Kashag. The villagers complained about the soaring prices due to the influx of Chinese and urged the Kashag to persuade the Chinese to restrict Chinese troops to the number stationed in Lhasa during the period of the Amban.

The group also presented a six-point petition to the Chinese representative, Zhang Guohua. They made the following demands:

(1) The status and power of the Dalai Lama must not be changed.

(2) All religious institutions and monks should be protected.

(3) All development programmes for a prosperous Tibet must be executed by the Tibetans.

(4) The Tibetan Army should not be merged with the PLA.

(5) Tibet should be allowed to maintain its traditional relationship with India.

(6) The number of Chinese troops in Tibet should not exceed the level during the period of the Ambans.[41]

On the same day, over 1,000 people surrounded the house where Zhang Guohua was staying and demanded that Chinese troops be immediately withdrawn and that no changes be made to the existing social-political system of Tibet. The demonstrators refused to vacate the area until they had received a reply from Zhang Guohua.[42] The Chinese were terrified as there were not many Chinese guards at the houses. The guards were instructed not to open fire, unless they were attacked. Zhang Guohua had no option but to agree to meet representatives of the demonstrators and listen to their demands. That night a curfew was declared in Lhasa by the Chinese.[43]

The next day, Zhang Guohua wrote the following letter addressed jointly to the Dalai Lama and the Kashag:

> On 31st of March reactionary and criminal elements organised an illegal demonstration. A group calling itself Lhasa People's Representatives was deployed secretly to surround my residence (Sandutsang House). From my investigation and the accounts of eye witnesses, in the reactionary group there were even monks disguised in laymen's clothes. Moreover, Tibetan soldiers in uniform and vagabonds were involved.
>
> Their intention was to instigate a violent confrontation [with PLA

guards]. But due to the alertness and utmost restraint shown by the PLA troops, they prevented the situation deteriorating into a blood bath.

I must point out that the activity of this reactionary movement is not a natural political development. It was organised secretly to disrupt the relationship between the nationalities. The activities of the reactionaries are contrary to the wishes of the Dalai Lama to establish a new Tibet based on the 17 Point Agreement and the unity of the Motherland. The illegal activities pose a threat and will undermine the spirit of the Agreement. Therefore, immediate and resolute measures must be adopted to curb the illegal activities of the reactionary group. To avoid undesirable consequences for the people, you must issue the following orders without delay:

(1) All the members of Tibetan army, including your [the Dalai Lama's] body guards must return to their barracks. They should not leave the compound without permission and they must not participate in illegal activities that undermine the 17-Point Agreement.

All soldiers must be educated to respect and support unity between different nationalities. They must oppose the practice of outwardly showing support and inwardly despising.

(2) All monks must return to their monasteries. The abbots of the monasteries must undertake to ensure that no monks create disturbances and participate in demonstrations.

(3) The so called 'People's Representatives' must be disbanded and all participating members must return to their homes. Those who return to their homes immediately will be given amnesty and their activities will not be investigated.

(4) Peace and stability must be restored so that the people of Lhasa can go about their normal activities.

The Prime Ministers and the Kashag must issue an order in consultation with the Tibet Military District Command, warning that in future illegal activities that create disunity between the nationalities and violate the 17 Point Agreement will not be tolerated and the perpetrators will be dealt with firmly.[44]

On the same day the Kashag and the Chinese met at the Potala to discuss the growing anti-Chinese activities in Lhasa. The abbots of Sera, Gaden and Drepung monasteries were present at the meeting. The Chinese were nervous because the Potala was guarded by the Kusung Magmi (the Bodyguard regiment) and the Chinese reinforcements had not yet arrived in Lhasa. One of the Chinese recalls that they feared that Zhang Guohua might be killed by the Tibetans or would be held for ransom. When other Chinese officials warned Zhang, he replied that they should 'not always anticipate the worst'. He stated that 'since the Qing period there had been 78 Ambans in Lhasa, and only one had been killed; I would be happy to sacrifice my life for the cause of Peaceful Liberation of Tibet. We must do everything to achieve this end and never fire the first shot. In the event of reactionaries launching an attack, we would have truth on our side and we would have done everything to prevent bloodshed'.[45]

The Chinese raised two questions. First, whether the Kashag was willing to take action against the group and whether the Kashag was able to maintain security in Lhasa or not. If the Kashag was not able to provide security then the PLA would take on the responsibility. Second, since many of the people who were involved in anti-Chinese activities were ex-soldiers, the Chinese insisted that they must have been assisted by members of the Kashag. The Chinese stated that the Kashag must hand over the names of those individuals involved in the two anti-Chinese organisations. Moreover, the Chinese implied that the Tibetan Government had provided weapons for the group.[46]

Surkhang told the Chinese that the Kashag would give its answers after it had met with the People's Representatives. The main anti-Chinese activities were the numerous appearances of anti-Chinese posters in all parts of Lhasa. The Chinese were anxious that the Dalai Lama and the Kashag should not be seen to be supporting any anti-Chinese groups. After the meeting with the Kashag, the Chinese wrote directly to the Dalai Lama asking him not to meet with the anti-Chinese agitators.

In their increasing anxiety, the Chinese began to recall troops to Lhasa and Shigatse that had been sent to border areas. One high-ranking cadre recalled that during that period, because of the dangerous situation, he slept fully dressed. At the end of March the situation in Lhasa was tense. S. Sinha, the Indian Representative, wrote in his monthly report:

> The period under review was one of some anxiety. Rising prices, shortage of essential supplies, increased death from smallpox and influenza epidemics have all gravely stressed the underlying political imbalance in the country. While most officials live smugly in their ivory towers, leading much the same life of idle dissipation, the common people find the heavy burdens imposed on them insupportable. For them Communism in practice has fallen far short of expectations, and they have derived little comfort from the alliance which the Communists have forged with the ruling aristocracy of Tibet. In complete disenchantment, they ask whether this is 'liberation'. The market price of the poor man's food, tsampa, has shot up to 100 sang per khe, and even at that price tsampa is not easily available. Starvation has weakened resistance to disease and many have died in the last month either from the epidemics

or from throat infections, only to receive watery burial in the river Kyichu.[47]

The relationship between the Kashag and the Chinese was rapidly deteriorating. The Kashag was coming under increasing pressure from both sides. The Chinese were demanding that the Kashag should take action to stamp out growing anti-Chinese movements, while the Tibetans were becoming agitated by the failure of the Kashag to stop the influence of the Chinese.[48] The atmosphere in Lhasa was tense. All the intelligence that the Chinese had gathered suggested that the Tibetans were organising a major anti-Chinese campaign and that they might use force to achieve their ends.[49]

It is difficult to say whether the Chinese were justified in their fear of imminent revolt by the Tibetan people. If the Tibetans had succeeded in organising a revolt, the Chinese would have faced great difficulty in controlling the uprising. In the early period the Communists would not have been able to reinforce their troops rapidly. The Chinese knew that any confrontation with the Tibetans would be a disaster. On the other hand, if they were to cave in to the Tibetans' demands it would be seen as weakness and the Chinese could not afford to be seen as weak. On 1 April an incident occurred at the Ngabo house which brought the Chinese and Tibetans into open conflict.

There are two versions of what happened. Ngabo had been recently appointed as a deputy commander of the Tibet Military Area and had appeared for the first time wearing a Chinese uniform, discarding traditional dress. The Chinese claimed that on the night of the 1 April, Tibetan reactionary rebels armed with rifles attacked Ngabo's house. The Chinese guards managed to overpower them and captured three people. A few days later, the Military District Headquarters issued a notice that they were outraged by the imperialist agents' attempts to disrupt the peaceful relationship between nationalities. It warned that in future they would take serious action to deal with any anti-Chinese activities.

Another version of the incident was described in the monthly report from the Indian Mission in Lhasa, which said that the Chinese who were guarding Ngabo's house had for some time been entering the garden of the adjoining house and stealing vegetables. The Tibetan soldiers, who were occupying the house, kept watch on the night of the incident. When the Chinese entered the garden, armed Tibetan soldiers went into the garden to apprehend the intruders. The intruders escaped over the wall in the direction of Ngabo's house, and the Tibetan soldiers opened fire as a warning. Later more Chinese guards from Ngabo's house came to rescue their comrades and fighting ensued.[50]

For the Chinese, the incident was the culmination of anti-Chinese sentiments which had been developing for the past few months. Although the incident at Ngabo's house was, apparently, accidental, the Chinese made it into a major issue. Since his return to Lhasa, Ngabo had been the main advocate of co-operation with the Chinese. The Chinese were so apprehensive that they strengthened the number of guards at Ngabo's house. S. Sinha wrote to the GOI that 'the Chinese are becoming neurotic'.[51]

The day after the incident, Zhang Guohua reported the situation in Lhasa to Mao and the Central Committee in Beijing. On 6 April 1952 the Central Committee of the Communist Party issued an important directive on work in Tibet which gave general guidelines and recommended that the United Front policy should be carried out. As mentioned earlier Mao was clearly aware of the vulnerability of the Chinese position in Tibet. The opposition encountered by the Tibet Work Committee was a clear proof of this weakness. The directive made it clear that Mao and the Chinese leaders were anxious to avoid direct confrontation with Tibetans. Realising that the issue of the Tibetan army was one of the sources of contention, they made the following recommendation:

> It is our opinion that the Tibetan troops should not be reorganised at present, nor should formal sub-areas or a military and administrative commission be established. For the time being leave everything as it is, let this situation drag on, and do not take up these questions until our army is able to meet its own needs through production and wins the support of the masses a year or two from now. In the meantime there are two possibilities. One is that our united front policy towards the upper stratum, a policy of uniting with the many and isolating the few, will take effect and that the Tibetan people will gradually draw closer to us, so the bad elements and the Tibetan troops will not dare to rebel. The other possibility is that the bad element, thinking we are weak and can be bullied, may lead the Tibetan troops in rebellion and that our army will counter-attack in self-defence and deal them a telling blow. Either will be favourable for us [*sic*].
>
> As the top echelon in Tibet there is no sufficient reason now for implementing the agreement in its entirety or for reorganising the Tibetan troops. But things will be different in a few years. By then they will probably find that they have no choice but to carry out the Agreement to the full and to reorganise the Tibetan troops. If the Tibetan troops start one or even several rebellions and are repulsed by our army each time, we will be all the more justified in reorganising them.
>
> Apparently not only the two Silons [Prime Ministers] but also the Dalai Lama and most of his clique were reluctant to accept the agreement and are unwilling to carry it out. As yet we do not have a material base for this purpose in terms of support among the masses or in the upper stratum. To force its implementation will do more harm than good. Since

> they are unwilling to put the agreement into effect, well then, we can leave it for the time being and wait.[52]

It was apparent that Mao felt that the Tibet Work Committee had pursued its policy in haste, and he was not in favour of any social reforms or changes in the traditional polity. Mao clearly recognised that the Chinese administration and the PLA had to achieve self-sufficiency in production before they could launch any reforms. Mao saw advantages in postponing the reforms: the directive went on to say that 'the longer the delay, the stronger will be our position and the weaker theirs. Delay will not do us much harm; on the contrary, it may be to our advantage. Let them go on with their insensate atrocities against the people, while we on our part concentrate on good deeds of production, trade, road-building, medical services and united front work so as to win over the masses and bide our time before taking up the question of the full implementation of the agreement [the 17-Point Agreement]. If they are not in favour of the setting up of primary schools, that can stop too.'[53]

Despite Mao's recommendation, the Chinese officials in Lhasa were clearly concerned with the growing anti-Chinese activities. They had identified the two Prime Ministers as an impediment to the future development and were determined to remove them. The Chinese decided to raise the issue of the attack on Ngabo's house with the Kashag and the two Prime Ministers. They accused the Prime Ministers of being influenced by imperialists and masterminding the attack. Tan Guansan accused them of being involved in the anti-Chinese movement. The Chinese went on to identify the actions of the 'People's Representatives' and the 'Lhasa People's Brigade' as creating discord between the nationalities. They demanded that the members of the anti-Chinese organisation should be severely punished, and warned that in the event of a failure to punish, the 'liberation of Tibet would no longer be implemented by peaceful means'.[54]

One of the Prime Ministers, Lobsang Tashi, spoke for the first time in Chinese. The Chinese had been unaware of his command of the language, but Lobsang had in fact worked in Nanjing at the Tibet Bureau in the late 1930s.[55] The Chinese thought he had deceived them. Lobsang Tashi told the Chinese not to accuse him without evidence. The meeting soon developed into a fierce argument. Zhang Guohua tried to mediate and calm the meeting down.[56]

The Chinese attempted to encourage Tibetan officials to instigate charges against the Prime Ministers. Zhang Guohua approached Ragashag to lead the charge against them, but Ragashag made a fierce defence of their actions.[57]

The Chinese then decided to take the matter into their own hands and asked for the resignation of the Prime Ministers. They presented their demands to the Dalai Lama and the Kashag. The Dalai Lama wrote later: 'I received a written report soon after this meeting, in which the Chinese insisted that Lukhangwa did not want to improve relations between Tibet and China, and suggested that he should be removed from the office'.[58] The Dalai Lama goes on to say that he was 'faced with a very difficult decision. I greatly admired Lukhangwa's courage in standing up to the Chinese, but now I had to decide whether to let him continue, or whether to bow yet again to a Chinese demand.'[59] The Kashag could not readily agree to the Chinese, because they would be accused by the masses of caving in under Chinese pressure. Increasingly the Kashag was having to tread a tightrope. They had to solve the problem of growing anti-Chinese agitation but action against the Prime Ministers would be interpreted by the public as being motivated by the pursuit of personal power. The Prime Ministers were very popular among the people; they were seen as incorruptible and staunch defenders of Tibetan culture. The Prime Ministers rarely participated in Chinese banquets and celebrations, having always maintained their distance from the Chinese just as, from the very beginning, they had refused to go and meet Zhang Guohua and others when they arrived in Lhasa: the Chinese had had to come to meet them. The position taken by the Prime Ministers was seen by the Tibetans as preserving the dignity of the Tibetan Government. Despite their popularity it was a curious omission that Lukhangwa and Lobsang Tashi had never been promoted to the full status of Prime Minister, their official title having remained Sitshab, Acting-Prime Minister. There was no doubt that if they were given the full title of Silon, the Chinese would have regarded it as a act of defiance.

The more the Chinese denounced the Prime Ministers, the more popular they became in the eyes of the Tibetan masses. Sinha wrote, 'the irony of the fact is that the very reasons for which they were being accused endeared the Prime Ministers all the more to their people. The Tibetans know them for their integrity of character and devotion to duty, and will remember them long after they have departed from the political scene for the noble and courageous efforts they made to rescue the Tibetan administration from becoming a subsidiary bureau'.[60] He went on to say that 'admittedly the Prime Ministers had often enough opposed Chinese guidance out of blind respect for tradition, but as it so often happened elsewhere, the external domination of their country made them pathetic introverts'.[61]

The Chinese authorities in Tibet were determined to stamp out anti-Chinese agitation before it got beyond control. In fact Mao in his directive wrote, 'at present, in appearance, we should take the offensive and should censure the demonstration and the petition for being unjustifiable (for undermining the Agreement), but in reality we should be prepared to make concessions and to go over to the offensive in the future (i.e., put the Agreement into force) when the conditions are ripe'.[62] However, Zhang

Guohua and others in Lhasa viewed the removal of the Prime Ministers as necessary in order to get rid of the anti-Chinese group. And if concession were made at this stage, it would be seen by the Tibetans as weakness and might lead to further demands. Therefore, contrary to Mao's advice, the Prime Ministers were accused of various crimes and the Chinese stated that if the Prime Ministers had been Chinese, they would have faced a 'firing squad'.[63] As the Chinese wanted to impress upon the Tibetans that their demands must be taken seriously, they stepped up the pressure on the Dalai Lama and the Kashag. The Military Commission brought an additional 3,000 troops to Lhasa. The first batch of 800 soldiers arrived from Kongpo and Tsethang on 10 April and a further 700 soldiers arrived four days later.[64]

The Prime Ministers were supported by every section of Tibetan society. In his monthly report, Sinha wrote:

> For days the highest in the land, the Kashag, Trungtsi [*sic*] and the Abbots of the three pillars of the state (three great monasteries, Sera, Drepung and Ganden) went begging to the Chinese for compassion in dealing with the two Prime Ministers. They asked for a period of grace during which the Prime Ministers could voluntarily retire from office. Messengers and envoys from the Dalai Lama, among them Gyalo Dhodup [*sic*] and the Chikyab Kenpo [*sic*], hurried along to the Chinese, but nothing availed against the irrevocable decision reached in the Chinese camp. Indeed Tibetan emissaries from the Dalai Lama went back with the alarming news that the Chinese had summoned an additional force of 5000 men for their garrison in Lhasa.[65]

On 25 April, Zhang Guohua visited the Dalai Lama at the Potala Palace and made a final request that the Prime Ministers be dismissed. If the Dalai Lama failed to meet their demands, the Chinese would have to consider making charges against the Dalai Lama himself for aiding and abetting the Prime Ministers.[66]

In the end the Tibetans caved in. The Dalai Lama and the Kashag agreed to ask for the resignations of Lukhangwa and Lobsang Tashi. The Dalai Lama wrote: 'I sadly accepted the Cabinet's [Kashag's] recommendation and asked the Prime Ministers to resign. They came to call on me, and I gave them scarves and gifts and my photograph. I felt that they understood my position very well.'[67] On 27 April, the Kashag made a formal public announcement that the Prime Ministers had resigned.

The actions to remove the two Prime Ministers must have been approved by Mao and the Central Committee in Beijing. Mao's initial recommendation had been to adopt a policy of wait and see, rather than confrontation. It is unlikely that Zhang Jingwu and Zhang Guohua would have taken a unilateral decision without the approval of the leadership in Beijing. They may have been able to persuade the Central Committee of the absolute necessity of removing the Lukhangwa and Lobsang Tashi and the People's Representatives (*Mimang Tsongdu*).

The People's Representative was disbanded and six leaders of the group were briefly detained by the Kashag. As instructed by the Chinese, the Kashag issued a public notice in Lhasa announcing that in the future any individuals or groups organising activities to disrupt the implementation of the 17-Point Agreement would be dealt with severely.

The dismissal of the Prime Ministers and the break up of the Peoples Representatives were a severe blow for Tibetan morale. It was the final victory for the Chinese. There was a great deal of disillusionment among all sectors of Tibetan society. Lukhangwa left Tibet and sought refuge in Kalimpong.[68] Lobsang Tashi, who was a monk, returned to his religious duties.[69]

The dismissal of Lukhangwa and Lobsang Tashi dissipated the Tibetans' resolve to resist Chinese rule. Many aristocrats resigned their posts in the guise of going on a pilgrimage to India and sought refuge in Kalimpong, where there was a growing number of Tibetan nobles who had set up house to watch the events in Tibet. The Dalai Lama's elder brother Gyalo Dhundup also left Tibet and established himself in Kalimpong. He told Sinha that he had left Lhasa because the Chinese were trying to use him against the Dalai Lama. The Chinese were seriously concerned that many members of the Dalai Lama's family were leaving to live in exile. The Dalai Lama's younger sister Jetsun Pema and the children of the Dalai Lama's elder sister, Tsering Dolma, were in schools in India. The Chinese tried to persuade them to send all the children of the Dalai Lama's family to China for study.[70] This was an important issue for the Chinese, who regarded the refusal by the most important family in Tibet to send their children to study in China as an indication of their lack of faith in the new regime. As we will see later, other aristocratic families began to dispatch their children to China for education.

Tashilhunpo Factions

Mao perceptively noted that the demonstrations were taking place at a time when the Panchen Rinpoche was shortly to arrive in Lhasa for the first time. Mao warned Zhang Guohua that 'after his arrival they will probably go all out to work on him to join their clique. If on our part we do our work well and the Panchen does not fall into their trap but reaches Xigaze [Shigatse] safe and sound, the situation will then become more favourable to us'.[71] The return of the Panchen Rinpoche to Tibet was to be a major propaganda victory for the Chinese. The Chinese Military in Lhasa radioed the Panchen Rinpoche's military escort warning them of the situation in Lhasa and advising them to take precautions.[72]

In April 1952 the Panchen Rinpoche was escorted by a large group of PLA troops, and on their journey from Amdo the party was kept fully informed of the developments in Lhasa.[73] The Panchen Rinpoche's estate had already sent their representative to Lhasa, Chen Jigme,[74] who was adamant that the Panchen Rinpoche and Tashilhunpo's status should be restored to the pre-1923 level. He had come to Lhasa a few months earlier and had made himself thoroughly unpopular by demanding that the Panchen Rinpoche should be treated as of equal status with the Dalai Lama.

On 28 April the Panchen Rinpoche, escorted by over 1,000 Chinese troops, entered Lhasa. Hundreds of Tibetans lined the road to welcome him. The first problem was who should be responsible for the Panchen Rinpoche. The Chinese wanted to maintain their control over him and his court. But now that they were in Tibet, would they be able to exercise the same power over him as they had done in Beijing? The Tibetans were clearly aware of the danger that this presented. At the same time the Panchen Rinpoche's estate wanted to maximise their authority in Shigatse and Tsang. This was not an easy problem to solve. Chen Jigme, the main spokesperson for the Panchen Rinpoche's estate, was a shrewd man. He had already managed to secure major concessions from the Tibetan Government and the Chinese. While the Chinese played the Panchen's estate against the Tibetan Government, Chen Jigme played the Tibetan Government against the Chinese.

Immediately after the arrival of the Panchen Rinpoche, Zhang Guohua requested that the Panchen Lama should be allowed to dispense with the normal etiquette of prostrating himself three times in front of the Dalai Lama. For centuries, when the two great Lamas of Tibet met, the Dalai Lama was seated on a higher throne. The Chinese and Panchen Rinpoche's coterie wanted the thrones to be of equal height. When the Tibetans would not accept these demands, the Chinese tried to use Ngabo to persuade them, but Ngabo refused.[75] When the Panchen Rinpoche arrived in Lhasa, he and the Dalai Lama met for the first time. The return of the Panchen Rinpoche was a great propaganda triumph for the Chinese, who stressed that the PLA had brought not only liberation to the Tibetan masses, but the return of the Panchen Rinpoche, thus restoring 'harmony among the Tibetan people'.[76]

The Panchen Rinpoche and his court remained in Lhasa for nearly a month. There was uncertainty as to what role he would play in this most critical stage in Tibetan history. The Tibetan Government had been trying for many years to reduce the power of the Panchen Rinpoche and his estates. In 1937, the 9th Panchen Rinpoche was refused entry into Tibet because he was accompanied by a Chinese escort. Some of the people of

Lhasa were disparaging about the new Panchen Rinpoche, referring to him as 'the Chinese Lama'.[77] When the Chinese tried to explain the notion of 'regional autonomy', a Lhasa official nervously asked if this meant that Shigatse would enjoy 'regional autonomy'. In Shigatse, the seat of the Panchen Lamas for centuries, the reaction was different. They viewed it as the rightful restoration of the Panchen Lama's authority. There the Tibetan Government's past attempts to integrate the Panchen Rinpoche's domain within the ambit of the Lhasa Government had been unpopular and since 1928 the relationship between the subjects of the Panchen Rinpoche and the people of Lhasa had been uneasy at best and, at worst, openly hostile.

At Tashilhunpo itself the return from exile of the Panchen Rinpoche and his followers caused a serious rift. The people who had stayed in Shigatse felt that they should be allowed to continue to manage the affairs of Tashilhunpo.[78] But the group who had just returned after years of exile with the Panchen Rinpoche wanted to maintain their privileges and authority. This group was led by Chen Jigme, and it was he who managed to seize power. This meant that the Panchen Rinpoche and his coterie were able to act independently of Lhasa.

The Panchen Rinpoche was only fourteen years old at this time and he may not have been aware of the protracted negotiations that were taking place in his name. The Panchen Rinpoche's followers maintained that all the privileges and authority exercised by the previous Panchen Rinpoche must be restored and all the properties confiscated by the Lhasa Government must be returned. The Chinese demanded that these issues should be dealt with by a joint committee composed of Lhasa and Tashilhunpo officials. Tashilhunpo argued that the Tibetan Government must refund all the taxes levied on the Panchen Rinpoche's demesne since 1928 and provide substantial loans, so that the debts incurred by the Panchen Rinpoche's estate while he was in exile could be repaid.[79]

The Lhasa authorities were clearly unhappy about the demands made by the Panchen Rinpoche's followers, but they were not in a position to refuse. The Chinese constantly reminded them that the relationship between the Dalai Lama and the Panchen Rinpoche should be restored, as stipulated in article 6 of the 17-Point Agreement. Eventually, the Tibetan Government agreed to provide substantial compensation and loans to the Panchen Rinpoche's estate.[80] On 30 June, the Panchen Rinpoche was formerly enthroned at Tashilhunpo.

The 23rd of May 1952 marked the first anniversary of the signing of the 17-Point Agreement. The Chinese organised a massive celebration. They had managed to make considerable headway in a year. All opposition was effectively eliminated and the Tibetan Government was virtually without effective leadership. They had won over many of the ruling officials. The Chinese began to invite influential Tibetans to visit China for study and inspection tours of industrial cities in China. In the summer of 1952, the Tibetan Government dispatched to China Liushar Thupten Tharpa, who was a monk official in charge of Tibetan Foreign Affairs, and Trijang Rinpoche, the Dalai Lama's junior tutor, and there was a steady number of Tibetan dignitaries arriving in Beijing. At the same time the Lhasa Government decided to establish a three-man liaison office in Beijing. The visits of the Tibetans provided the Chinese with a great deal of international publicity. The Tibetan delegation was met by Mao and later, in a broadcast to Tibet, Liushar told Tibetan listeners that Chairman Mao had assured them among others things:

> (1) That the Chinese Communist Party has adopted the policy of protecting religion. Protection is given to all, whether one believes in religion or not, whether one believes in this religion or that religion; one's belief is respected; the policy of protection of religion is adopted today as it will be in the future.
>
> (2) The problem of the division of land is different from that of religion. Land has been divided in the Han nationality areas, but religion is still given protection. Whether the land should be divided in the minority nationality districts is a matter for the minority nationalities to decide. In the Tibet region, the problem of division of land does not exist now. Whether or not land should be redistributed in the future the Tibetans will have to decide by themselves; we cannot do it for you.
>
> (3) The establishment of a military and administrative committee and the reorganising of the Tibetan army have been stipulated in the Agreement. But since you are afraid, I have notified those comrades working in Tibet, telling them to go slowly. However, the Agreement must be implemented, although it will be postponed because you are afraid. We can put it back to next year, if you are afraid this year; we can put it back until the year after next, if you are still afraid next year.
>
> (4) Tibet covers a large area but is thinly populated. Its population should be increased from the present 2 or 3 million to 5 or 6 million, and then over 10 million. Then the economy and culture should also be developed. Culture embraces school, newspapers, cinemas and also religion. In the past, the reactionary rulers, from the Emperors of Qing dynasty to Chiang Kai-shek have oppressed and exploited you. Imperialism has done the same to you. As a result, you are weak economically, backward culturally and your population is small. The Chinese Communists, standing for national equality, do not want to oppress and exploit you, we want to help you achieve development in population, economy and culture. The entry of the PLA into Tibet is aimed at giving you such assistance. Not much assistance can be expected in the beginning but in

three years much help can be given to you; if not the Chinese Communist Party will be of no use.[81]

The Chinese also invited Tibet's leading business families, like Pomdatsang and Sandutsang, to China. At the time the Chinese were desperate to get the co-operation of the Tibetan business community, whose trade they were dependent on. The three major trading groups, the Pandatsang, Reting estate and Sandutsang, were affected by the slump in demand for Tibetan wool, which had been exported to America until stopped in 1950. Since wool export was the major source of Tibet's foreign currency, its collapse had had a powerful negative effect on Tibet's economy, and major investors, monasteries and other religious institutions had all been badly affected.

The newly established Chinese State Trading Company decided to purchase surplus wool, at a higher price than the Tibetans would have got on the international market. The wool was exported to China via Calcutta. Chinese generosity in rescuing the Tibetan wool industry was not merely a propaganda exercise:[82] the Chinese were increasingly concerned with their lack of control over Indo-Tibetan trade. Over 70 per cent of Tibet's foreign trade was with India, while China accounted for less than 20 per cent: in terms of economy, Tibet was far more integrated with the Indian subcontinent[83] and it was evident that if the Chinese were to establish effective rule in Tibet, they would have to change the balance in favour of China. By effectively buying up Tibet's most lucrative export, the Chinese managed overnight to achieve control of Tibet's economy. The business community was grateful to the Chinese for purchasing their wool: the slump in the world wool market would otherwise have had disastrous consequences on the Tibetan business community. The Chinese intervention also effectively ended the involvement in Tibet of Nepalese and Indians who for decades had exercised control over Tibet's exports.[84]

By the end of 1952, the Chinese had effectively established their own infrastructure. For the first two years the Chinese had neither forced the Tibetans to change the traditional polity nor asked them to carry out reforms. Only two Tibetan institutions came under Chinese attack, the army and the Tibetan Foreign Bureau. Article 14 of the Agreement stated that 'the Central Government will handle the external affairs of Tibet', and accordingly the Chinese demanded that the Tibetan Foreign Bureau should be merged with the Chinese Foreign Ministry. The Foreign Bureau had been established by the 13th Dalai Lama in an attempt to achieve an international personality for Tibet; its disbanding marked the end of Tibet's foreign relations. The Indian and Nepalese missions were informed that they would have to report to the newly established Foreign Office, which was staffed by Chinese and members of the Foreign Bureau. Tibet's relations with its neighbouring countries, Nepal and India, were now effectively conducted from Beijing. As far as the Nepalese and the Indians were concerned, as long as the Tibetans were happy with this state of affairs, they were not going to make any protests. For the Chinese this was an important achievement. Both Nepal and India had for many years maintained direct contact with Tibet.[85]

The traditional Tibetan Government structure was becoming redundant; its authority had been undermined. The Kashag was still nominally the highest authority in Tibet, but the increasing complexity of the work that was demanded by the Chinese meant that the Tibetan administrative system ceased to be effective. Moreover, the Chinese had managed to co-opt most of the Tibetan Government officials to work in the new governing structure that they were establishing. S. Sinha wrote: 'the present Tibetan Government resembles an army which has lost all its generals after a series of tactical defeats on the field; they are leaderless, without morale and rapidly disintegrating' and he goes on to report that the dominant tendency among members of Kashag was to 'escape responsibility and ultimately to avoid public criticism'.[86]

The Chinese were also to a certain extent beginning to gain the trust of the Tibetan masses. There was a genuine feeling that the Chinese had come to 'modernise' Tibet. The majority of Tibetans were ignorant of the technological developments in the world and began to see China as the centre of technology and modernity. For the first time there were trucks and jeeps in Lhasa. Small-scale hydro-electric plants were built. The Chinese introduced new printing plants, and newspapers were published in Tibetan; prior to the arrival of the Chinese, there had been no modern printing centre. Newspapers were published every ten days and were very popular. For the first time the people of Lhasa were able to read about international news. Many educated Tibetans were enthusiastic about all the new innovations that were taking place. Tibet's leading intellectual, Gedun Choephel, advised his students to go to China for study and learning about the modern world and the ways of the new ruler of Tibet.[87] Many young aristocrats began to volunteer to go to China for further studies. Of course they were not merely compelled by strong desire for education or modernising Tibet: most of all, for the aristocracy, sending their 'beloved' children to schools in China was meant to prove their fidelity to the Chinese. They began to recall their children from private schools in India and to dispatch them to China.

Some even went further and introduced reforms in their private estates. Ngabo was the first to take the lead, disbanding his manorial estate and freeing 2,500 *mi ser* (subjects) belonging to the estate.[88] Many of his subjects were paid compensation from his own wealth. The Dalai Lama's brother Gyalo Dhundup also disbanded the estates belonging to the Dalai Lama's family.[89] These gestures may be regarded as pragmatic in the face of the inevitability of reforms, but, given the strong opposition they faced, particularly from the monasteries, whose sources of income depended on their manorial estates, they were also an indication of a growing feeling among Tibetans that social reforms were needed. In fact the Dalai Lama set up a new office of reform, 'Legchoe Lakhung', headed by Ngabo and Surkhang Wangchen Gelek. It was supposed to introduce social and land reforms, but the Tibetans' ideas of reforms merely meant tinkering with the existing system and making minor changes. Since the majority of religious establishments and aristocratic families were totally dependent on the revenue from their estates, they could not envisage social reforms without substantial monetary compensation, which the Tibetan Government was in no position to meet. Even at this late stage the religious institutions were opposed to any reforms that threatened their position in the society. There was a suggestion that the monasteries and lamas should surrender those estates which were situated in the border areas, but this was rejected by the lamas and the monks. The strong opposition from monasteries meant that the few lay officials who would have welcomed the reforms were reluctant to demand change for fear of being accused of being Chinese sympathisers.

The Chinese established a Grain Procurement Board to solve the problem of food shortages. The board was composed mostly of Tibetan businessmen and aristocratic families with large estates. The Chinese gave them interest-free loans to import food and other goods from India. Road construction was proceeding at a remarkable pace, and so some provisions began to arrive from China. The increase in food supplies began to reduce public anger. Sinha was amazed by certain changes in the Tibetans attitude towards the Chinese:

> One is confronted with the unusual spectacle of Tibetan love and enthusiasm for things Chinese; there is everywhere a keenness to imitate the Chinese, to dress, to talk, behave and sing as the Chinese do, and this is particularly noticeable among the respectable bunch of official families in Lhasa, who first succumbed to the spell. The inroad of neo-Chinese culture into Tibetan society whether in music, ideology, dress or speech is truly remarkable for what was static in this land has become alive and dynamic. There is not a home in Lhasa where portraits of Mao and his colleagues have not found a place in the domestic shrine.[90]

It was not only in Lhasa that there was enthusiasm for China and Mao. Dawa Norbu recalls that in Sakya, after a delegation from the district had returned from China, they were 'full of admiration for the new China' and that one family had placed a figure of Mao on their family altar.[91]

For the first few years the Chinese did not attempt to create a Communist Party in Tibet. Their main task was to establish an administrative structure.

The work in Tibet was carried out by the Tibet Work Committee and the Tibet Military Commission. The Chinese established quasi-governmental organisations, like the Youth Association and the Women's Association, Tibetans were actively encouraged to join these organisations. The groups organised trips to China and film shows. In January 1953 the Chinese organised the first meeting of the Tibet Military District Party Conference, the first step towards building a Communist Party in Tibet. The conference discussed the achievements of the past two years and merely endorsed the nationalities policies that had been agreed in Beijing. The meeting was attended by Chinese cadres and the only Tibetan members were those Communists who had joined the Party in Kham and Amdo. They were employed in Tibet as interpreters. The Chinese did not at this stage urge Tibetans to join the Communist Party.

The Indo-Chinese Trade Agreement

By the end of 1953, the Chinese were confident that they had achieved considerable success. Internal opposition had been reduced and the ruling élite were beginning to look towards China. Internationally, there was acceptance at all levels that Tibet was a part of China and no one was about to challenge China's claim. As far as China was concerned the only outstanding problem was Tibet's relationship with its neighbours, India and Nepal. Both India and Nepal had missions in Lhasa. Moreover, these two countries enjoyed extra-territorial rights in Tibet.

For the Chinese, the extra-territorial rights exercised by India were anathema – a residue of imperialism and symbolic of the humiliation that China had suffered under the Western powers. Therefore, China was determined to place the Sino–Indian relationship on a more formal level. Even Nehru regarded the presence of Indian troops in Tibet as 'a symbol of British imperialism'. He saw no reason why India should follow an arrangement created by the British, which he argued 'related neither to the fact or to intelligence'.[92]

In 1953, as far as the GOI was concerned, the Tibetans, by signing the 17-Point Agreement, had surrendered their right to conduct external relations and, as we have seen, the Indian Mission in Lhasa was informed by the Chinese that they would have to deal only with the newly established branch of the Chinese Foreign Office in Tibet. But China remained concerned about the legal status of the Indian Mission in Lhasa, which even the Indian Ambassador in Beijing regarded as an 'office of dubious legality'.[93] Zhou Enlai proposed that the Indian mission should be turned into the Indian Consulate General, and China also demanded that, in return, a similar facility should be granted in Bombay.[94]

On 31 December 1953 negotiations began in Beijing between India and China which led to the signing of the 'Agreement on Trade and Intercourse in the Tibet Region of China'. The preamble proclaimed the famous 'Five Principles of Co-existence' (*Panch Sheela*)[95] and the agreement formalised the trade regulations between Tibet and India. India also agreed to withdraw its military escorts stationed in Gyantse and Dromo (Yatung), and announced, as an expression of good will, that the GOI would transfer to the Chinese Government free of cost and without compensation the postal, telegraph and telephone installations operated by India.[96]

For China, the agreement was a major achievement.[97] Despite the fact that it was concerned with trade, the wording of the treaty tacitly acknowledged India's unequivocal acceptance of China's sovereignty over Tibet. Tibet was referred to as a 'region of China'. The agreement marked a change in India's view on the legal status of Tibet. In the past India had followed the traditional policy established by the British which, while recognising China's 'suzerainty' over Tibet, never accepted China's sovereignty. This was the first international agreement which recognised Communist Chinese sovereignty over Tibet. Nehru announced that India had done 'nothing better in the field of foreign affairs' and went on to defend the agreement as 'not only good for our country but for the rest of Asia'. Nehru naïvely assumed that the agreement secured China's acceptance of the Sino–Indian frontier, and peace.[98]

Neither the Chinese nor the Indians consulted the Tibetans during the course of their discussion and the Tibetans for their part remained oblivious to the change in Indian Government policies. On 30 May Xinhua reported that the signing of the agreement was celebrated in the Norbulingka, where the Dalai Lama and the Kashag held a party to mark the occasion. The report quoted the Dalai Lama as saying that 'under the brilliant leadership of Chairman Mao, the Chinese and Indian agreement had been signed according to the principles of mutual respect for each other's territorial integrity and sovereignty'.[99] In May 1954, B. N. Mullik, chief of Indian Intelligence, visited Kalimpong, the centre of Indo–Tibetan trade which had become a gathering place for dissident Tibetans, to assess the reaction of influential Tibetan émigrés. There he found 'the Tibetans shocked and anguished'.[100]

In discussions with Mullik the Tibetans living in Kalimpong made a five-point suggestion. First, Tibetans should be allowed to enter India freely and should be exempt from any immigration control. Second, Tibetan émigrés should be exempt from Indian customs and income tax control. Third, leading Indian politicians should make a public declaration of a desire to continue traditional cultural ties with Tibet. Fourth, India should criticise China for any violation of the 17-Point Agreement. The fifth point was that the Tibetan trade mission in Kalimpong should be independent of the

Chinese trade mission and should be allowed to function as a representative of the Dalai Lama. The Indo–Chinese agreement allowed for the establishment of a Chinese trade agent in Kalimpong and the Chinese wanted the existing Tibetan trade agency in Kalimpong to be transferred to the Chinese. It was unlikely that the Chinese would have accepted the existence of a separate Tibetan agency in Kalimpong.[101] Mullik reported his conversation to Nehru, who immediately questioned him as to whether the views expressed were only those of rich Tibetans. Nehru also instructed Mullik to give assurance to the Tibetans living in India (Kalimpong) that they would not be handed over to the Chinese and that the money and gold brought out from Tibet would be exempt from taxes.[102]

The Chinese would not agree to any direct relationship between India and the Tibetans, but they were aware that they would need to reduce Tibetan opposition to the Indo–Tibetan trade agreement. The Chinese appointed Pomda Yanphel (one of the most influential Tibetan businessman, with virtually a monopoly over Indo–Tibetan trade) as the Chinese Trade Agent in Kalimpong. This to some extent helped to reduce Tibetan opposition.

Britain was the only country clearly aware of the serious repercussions of the Sino–Indian agreement. The Foreign Office officials were amazed when the Indian Government announced that the agreement does not 'depart from the view of the UK Government before 1947 of Tibet's position vis-à-vis China'.[103] R. K. Nehru from the External Ministry told the British Deputy High Commissioner that the reference to the 'Tibet region of China' was a 'concession only to realism'.[104] The question was raised in the Foreign Office regarding HMG's position on the status of Tibet. It was apparent that although the GOI had inherited the policies of the British, the subsequent changes in the GOI's policies vis-à-vis Tibet did not mean that Britain too had changed its policies regarding Tibet's status. P. Wilkinson of the FO noted that 'HMG position is still exactly the same as that at the point when British Government in India terminated, namely HMG recognises only Chinese suzerainty over Tibet, and that this position will continue unless HMG makes an act or declaration of recognition of Chinese sovereignty over Tibet.'[105] However, Britain was not willing to voice publicly its policy and oppose the Sino–Indian agreement. Tibetans were cut off from contacting the British, and it therefore made no difference whether the British continued to recognise Tibet's right to conduct direct external relationships or not.

For the Chinese the Indo–Chinese agreement was a triumph in international relations. This was the first agreement signed by the Chinese with a non-Communist country. Their propaganda projected amicable ways in which other Asian countries could settle their disputes. When China signed a trade agreement with Nepal in 1956, the agreement reaffirmed the

Panch Sheela as 'the fundamental principles guiding the relationship between the two countries', and went on to refer to Tibet as a 'region of China'.[106] Article 3 of the agreement stated that 'All treaties and documents which existed in the past between Nepal and China including those between Nepal and the Tibet Region of China are hereby abrogated.' This referred particularly to the Tibet–Nepal treaty of 1865, which gave Nepalese traders much more favourable trading rights in Tibet. The 1956 Agreement eliminated these advantages and changed the Nepalese mission into a consulate.

In the meantime, infrastructure-development was continuing inside Tibet. One of China's most remarkable achievements was the construction of two main roads connecting Tibet with China. Since 1950 thousands of PLA troops and Tibetans had been employed on road construction. By 1954 they had built over 2,000 kilometres of road. The 'Qinghai–Tibet Highway' was completed by the end of the fourth year, with the first vehicles reaching Lhasa on 15 December. Roads linking Lhasa, Shigatse and Gyangtse were also proceeding at a rapid pace. The success in road-building greatly improved internal communication and for the first time large quantities of supplies could be transported by road, relieving the strain on the Tibetan economy. Now it was possible to travel from Xining to Lhasa in about twelve days, and from Beijing to Lhasa in twenty days. The much longer route from Dartsedo to Lhasa was also nearly completed. The Chinese were rightly proud of their achievements. Fan Ming, the Deputy Secretary of the Tibet Work Committee, commented that 'these two newly-opened roads yet again indicate the concern and care which the CCP and Chairman Mao have for the Tibetan people'.[107]

The Chinese employed over 30,000 Tibetans on the road-building projects. This had a remarkable effect on Tibetan economy and society. The majority of the workers were farmers or herdsmen, who had never been incorporated into a cash economy before. The Chinese paid the Tibetan workers three or four Da Yuan, which was a considerable sum at the time. For the first time the Tibetan masses were becoming wage labourers, with many families sending one member of the family to work on the roads to supplement their income. For many farmers and nomads this was the first time they had surplus cash to spend as they wished.[108] But this was not to last. By the end of 1955, the Chinese needed to reduce their expenditure and began to urge the people to work for less money as a contribution to building a strong Motherland.

For the Chinese the road construction provided an opportunity to mobilise the Tibetan people. The PLA troops would organise political study classes and publicise the fact that the Chinese had come to modernise Tibet. One Tibetan aristocrat, Kapshopa, recalls that he was sent as representative of the Tibetan Government to Nagchuka, where a landing strip was being built. When the work was completed, the Tibetan workers and he himself were so impressed with the conduct of PLA troops that they submitted a petition to the Dalai Lama to speed up the reforms.[109]

Most importantly, the roads were strategically necessary to establish effective control over Tibet as well as to provide supplies which would, it was hoped, lessen the dependence of the Tibetan economy on India.[110] By the end of 1954, China had managed to secure all its objectives in Tibet, while internationally, India's acceptance of Chinese sovereignty over Tibet left no room for other foreign powers to raise the Tibetan issue at international forum. That year, the Chinese invited the Dalai Lama and the entire Tibetan hierarchy to Beijing. For the Dalai Lama the invitation to China meant an opportunity to meet with China's leaders. Later he wrote: 'I thought I ought to meet the highest authorities in China, and try to persuade them to carry out the promises they had made in the agreement they had forced on us. So I decided to go.'[111]

The Dalai Lama Meets Mao

The Tibetan delegation consisted of the Dalai Lama, his family, two tutors, the leaders of all the Buddhist schools and three *Shapes*. The Panchen Rinpoche and his followers were also invited, but left Tibet by a separate route. The Tibetan groups met in Xining and than proceeded to Beijing. In total there were 400 Tibetan officials and servants. The procession of Tibetan dignitaries was spectacular; never in Tibetan history had there been gathering together of so many important Tibetan officials. The delegation left Lhasa on the newly built road and, where there was no road, travelled by traditional transport.

The timing of the visit was of crucial significance. As noted by the Dalai Lama, 'At the time, a session of the Chinese National People's Congress was being prepared in Beijing to frame a constitution, and the Chinese had allotted ten seats in the assembly to Tibet. The Chinese representatives were said to have been elected, but I had been asked to nominate the Tibetan members, and the Chinese Government suggested that I should lead the Tibetan delegation myself.'[112] Not all Tibetans were happy with the Dalai Lama going to Beijing. Some thought that the Dalai Lama being a mere member of the NPC was not in keeping with the status of the sovereign of Tibet. However, the Dalai Lama personally felt that by refusing to attend the NPC, Tibet 'might lose whatever chance of autonomy' it might possess. On the other hand, he felt that by attending the NPC he might 'possibly help in persuading the Chinese to keep their promises'.[113] The new constitution adopted at the National Congress explicitly recognised China as a multi-national and unitary state with Tibetans as one of the nationalities of

China. The CCP's view on the nature of the Chinese State had gone through a number of changes. The manifesto adopted at the Second National Congress of the Party in 1922 advocated China as a federal State, with Tibet, Mongolia and Xinjiang enjoying the status of republics on the Soviet model. A decade later, the constitution agreed at the Jiangxi Soviet Republic (1931) gave the Republics the right to secede and form their own independent countries.[114] But the new constitution adopted in 1954 ruled out any possibility of minority groups seceding from China. In article 4 it made provision for the establishment of 'Regional Autonomy' in 'areas where people of minority nationalities live in concentrated communities'. It was stressed that these 'Autonomous Regions' were 'an integral part of the People's Republic of China'.

The main discussion at the NPC was to approve the new constitution, therefore Tibetan participation was important to the Chinese. Although the NPC was constitutionally the highest legislative body, in practice it merely rubber-stamped Party decisions. The Tibetan representatives sat through exhaustive rounds of meetings. The Dalai Lama later wrote that he found the meetings boring and he could not follow the discussions because everything was conducted in Chinese. The Tibetan presence at the NPC was widely publicised in the Chinese and international media. Photos of the Dalai Lama and Panchen Rinpoche voting at the Congress were distributed throughout the world as proof of Tibetan acquiescence to Chinese rule.

While in Beijing, the Dalai Lama and the Tibetan delegation met with other Chinese leaders. The Dalai Lama was also presented to foreign heads of state who were visiting China, meeting Nehru, the Indian Prime Minister, for the first time. It appears that Mao got on quite well with the Dalai Lama and there were frequent meetings between the two leaders. Mao, the elder statesman, was paternalistic, lecturing the young Dalai Lama on 'the true form of democracy' and advising him on how to become a leader.[115] The Dalai Lama recalls a meeting where Mao 'began by saying that he was glad Tibet had come back to the Motherland' and went on to say that China's aim was to 'bring progress to Tibet'. He also told the Dalai Lama that if he was unhappy with the Chinese representatives in Tibet he should communicate directly with him.[116] On 27 September, the Panchen Rinpoche was elected to membership of the 1st National People's Congress Standing Committee and the Dalai Lama was made its Vice-Chairman.

One of the purposes of the visit was to impress the Tibetans with China's progress and industrial development. They were taken to visit shipyards, factories and steel plants. A Manchurian travelling with the Tibetan delegation noted: 'Their programme had been carefully calculated to drive home some particular point which Peking was trying to impress on the people of Tibet and their leaders. All the achievements of Chinese art and industry were somehow presented as triumphs of the Communist regime, as if nothing worthwhile had existed before.'[117] The majority of the Tibetans had very little knowledge of modern developments and were undoubtedly impressed by what they saw. The Tibetan visitors were lavishly entertained by the Chinese. Rinchen Dolma Taring, a leading aristocrat, described the arrangements in Beijing:

> The Peking Government organised us very thoroughly. Each of the high Lamas and Shap-pes was given a car with a driver; all the officials from the fourth rank up had one car between four, and junior officials and servants were taken everywhere in buses. The arrangement of the three kitchens was always observed. Officials and servants were given pocket-money, according to rank. When winter approached new warm clothes were made for everyone. A daily programme was fixed and we were taken to see factories and ancient places. Only those officials with important work had to attend meetings; others spent their time shopping and resting. We Tibetans enjoyed shopping outside Tibet and taking things home for presents or for sale, and in Peking the servants wanted to take advantage of the free transport to do trade when they got back to Lhasa.[118]

In February 1955, the Tibetan visitors celebrated the Tibetan New Year in Beijing.[119] The occasion was marked with banquets, which Mao and other Chinese leaders attended. According to the Chinese press, the Dalai Lama gave a speech, saying that his visit to industrial sites had impressed him with the 'greatness and splendour of our Motherland'[120] and Panchen Rinpoche somewhat more cautiously remarked that 'we are convinced of the might and power of our Motherland'.[121]

Preparatory Committee for the TAR

One important episode during the Tibetan delegation's stay in Beijing was the setting up of a Preparatory Committee for the eventual establishment of the Autonomous Region of Tibet (PCART). It was a mark of Tibet's separateness and special situation that the Communists had from the outset avoided implementing any of the nationalities polices which were in force in other regions. The Chinese government was quick to integrate Xinjiang and Mongolia by granting autonomous region status for these areas. However, it was recognised that they would need to adopt more cautious policies to gain the confidence of the Tibetans. Mao told the Dalai Lama that originally the Chinese had wanted to establish direct administration from Beijing but because of the situation in Tibet, it was decided that for the time being a Preparatory Committee would be set up.[122] The function of the PCART was defined as 'an authoritative body for consultation and planning during the transitional period before the establishment of the Autonomous Region of Tibet.[123]

On 9 March 1955, the 7th Plenary Session of the State Council attended by the Dalai Lama, the Panchen Rinpoche, Ngabo, Surkhang, Liushar and other Tibetan leaders adopted the resolution on the establishment of the Preparatory Committee. The Chinese' decision to set up the PCART was partly a desire to speed up the reforms and to integrate the Tibetans within the administrative structure of China. Since 1951, the main work in Tibet had been carried out by the Tibet Military Commission. The Tibetans were openly hostile to the Commission and it was seen as an alien institution, often in direct confrontation with the Tibetan Government. As long as the Commission was seen as a Chinese institution, its ability to instigate reforms was severely hampered, remaining at best a parallel administrative structure having to rely on force to effect its reforms. Despite their initial success in Tibet, the Chinese were aware that, as Zhang Guohua pointed out in a report to the State Council, the 'achievement was small by comparison with the task of completing construction in Tibet'. Moreover, the Chinese were prepared to recognise their weaknesses. Zhang Guohua's report to the State Council stated:

> The officials of the Han nationality who entered Tibet developed many shortcomings and committed many mistakes in their work. Vestiges of big-nation chauvinism were present to a greater or lesser extent in many of them. For instance, they did not seriously respect the religious beliefs or customs or habits of the people of the Tibetan nationality, did not give due credit to the Tibetan nationality cadres, and failed to respect them or help them as much as they should. Secondly, some of the Han nationality cadres did not sufficiently understand the local conditions and mechanically applied the work experience which they had gained in areas inhabited by the people of Han nationality, and tended to rush things in their work.[124]

If the Chinese were to succeed in their long-term goal of fully integrating Tibet and promoting 'democratic reforms', then they would need to be seen to be promoting the reforms with the explicit co-operation of the Tibetan ruling élite. Zhang Guohua recommended that future work in Tibet must be carried out in a 'spirit of democratic consultation' and 'things should be done only after the conditions have ripened and agreement has been reached by all'.[125] It appears that the Dalai Lama and the Tibetan leaders seem to have welcomed the decision to establish PCART. This had at least postponed immediate 'democratic reforms'.

This marked the period when the relationship between the Chinese and Tibetans was at its best. It was a sign that the Communist Party was satisfied with their achievement in Tibet. Both Zhang Guohua and Zhang Jingwu were promoted and given military honours for their accomplishment. In 1955 Zhang Guohua received first-class Orders of Independence and Freedom and of Liberation, promoting him to the rank of lieutenant-general in the PLA, while Zhang Jingwu was appointed Chief of Staff of the PRC Chairman, an administrative office directly under Mao himself. However, Zhang Jingwu was not moved to Beijing but served out his post from inside Tibet.

On 29 June 1955 the Dalai Lama and the Tibetan delegation arrived in Lhasa and a month later the Panchen Lama returned to Shigatse. On his return the Dalai Lama writes that he found that the relationship between the Kashag and the Chinese was 'tolerably friendly' and that the 'hostility of the Lhasan people seemed to have died down and given way to a feeling of complacency. The city was quiet and peaceful.'[126]

It was not until almost a year later that the inauguration of PCART was held in Lhasa. The occasion was marked by the arrival of an 800-member delegation from Beijing led by Chen Yi and Wang Feng, Vice-Chairman of the Nationalities Affairs Commission. On 22 April 1956 the PCART was formally inaugurated with great pomp at a ceremony below the Potala Palace. Chen Yi remarked that the establishment of the PCART was 'a new milestone for the Tibetan nationality on the road to unity and progress'.[127]

The Dalai Lama made the usual cautious speech welcoming the founding of PCART, but he warned about the need to go slowly and added that 'Tibet is the centre of Buddhism, in which religion the whole Tibetan population has a deep belief. The Tibetan people treasure and protect their religious beliefs as they would their life'.[128] He went on to say that the Chinese constitution and Mao had stated that freedom of religion would be protected. The Dalai Lama also warned that Tibet was not ready for rapid 'democratic reforms'. He said that 'The present conditions in Tibet, are still a long way off from socialism, and we must carry out reforms step by step. When to carry out reform and the means to reform depend on the development of the work and the practical conditions in various respects. The reforms will be done through consultation by the leaders of Tibet and the broad masses of the people themselves, and not by others on their behalf.'[129]

Since 1954, there had been an increasing number of refugees arriving from Kham and Amdo with stories of Communist attacks on religion and religious institutions. The Dalai Lama's speech referred to 'some news from neighbouring provinces' which had 'aroused suspicions and anxieties among' the people.[130] Zhang Guohua reassured the Tibetan ruling élite that their position and role in the future government was secured and that they would be urged to play an active role in promoting 'democratic reforms'. He told them that 'according to the instructions of the Central People's Government, the future reforms in the Tibetan region must be carried out from the upper to the lower levels', and went on to say that 'necessary steps [to] ensure that the political position and material life of the upper class people of the Tibetan nationality (including upper class people in the religious sphere) will not be reduced, and that it will possibly be better than before'. Zhang concluded by saying that 'when the Communist Party says something, it does just that. It will never go back on its promises.'[131] The Chinese strategy for ensuring the success of the PCART was based on the exclusion from positions of authority and prestige of those who would not accept the legitimacy of Chinese rule, as shown by the removal of Lukhaṇgwa and Lobsang Tashi. They also succeeded in manipulating the divisions and different interest groups among the Tibetans.

On 9 March 1955 the State Council issued a four-point guideline, defining the role and the function of the PCART. However, it was not until September, at the 47th Meeting of the Standing Committee of the NPC, that a detailed outline of the regulations of the PCART was agreed. On 26 September, Mao issued a decree, 'Outline of Regulations Governing the Organisation of the PCART'. The most important part of the regulation was article 3, which divided the Tibet Autonomous Region into three geographic and political groups: (1) the Tibetan Government in Lhasa, represented by the Dalai Lama, (2) Panchen Rinpoche and his followers, and (3) the People's Liberation Committee of Chamdo (CLC).[132]

The division of Tibet into three political and administrative divisions was not just a Chinese attempt to divide and rule their subjects. To some extent it reflected the divisions within Tibetan society. During the visit to China, the relationship between the Lhasa group and the Panchen Rinpoche's followers had been antagonistic. The followers of Panchen Rinpoche had been arguing that Panchen Rinpoche should be given complete authority in the Tsang region. The Lhasa authorities were opposed to these demands but the Panchen Rinpoche's followers were bold and spoke publicly about their demands. Chen Jigme (the director of the office known as Panchen Kanpo Lija) said in his speech at the NPC that there still existed some problems in the relationship with the Kashag. He mentioned that there were still unsettled issues regarding the boundary between areas under Panchen Rinpoche's jurisdiction and the Dalai Lama's.[133] It was evident from his speech that Panchen Rinpoche and his followers were asking for far-reaching concessions. Chen Jigme spoke about the right to levy taxes and to maintain an army. He went on to say that with the help of the Central Government they had been able to solve many of these problems.[134] Panchen Rinpoche and his followers were thus able to lobby Beijing to put pressure on the Tibetan government. The Dalai Lama writes that Mao suggested that they should settle their differences while they were both in Beijing.[135]

The creation of PCART resolved the earlier dispute about the status of Tashilhunpo and the Lhasa Government. The new organisation gave Panchen Rinpoche the same status and power as the Dalai Lama in Lhasa. Unprecedented authority was thus conferred on Panchen Rinpoche and his estate. It gave him the right to appoint his own people to the PCART. Although the Lhasa authorities deeply resented the change, they seemed to be unable to influence the development. The worst humiliation for the Tibetan Government was that the 'Chamdo Liberation Committee' (CLC) was given the same status and power as PCART. Since October 1950, Chamdo and outlying areas had been under Chinese control and the Tibetan administration had ceased to function there despite demanding that these areas should be returned to the Tibetan administration. The Tibetan Government argued that there was no need for the CLC, since Lhasa's authority over the area was undisputed, and that the Chinese should restore the Tibetan administration that was destroyed by the invasion. Despite Tibetan claims that they had exercised full authority in the Chamdo area, the Chinese were fully aware of the precarious nature of Lhasa's power in the Chamdo and Dagyab provinces. In the traditional Tibetan political structure they were known as *Khrim gos rangwang rangtsen* and exercised a considerable degree of autonomy. These two territories were administrated by the head lamas of the two major monasteries in the regions: in Chamdo's case, Phagpa Gelek Namgyal, and in the case of Dagyab, Dagyab Rinpoche Loden Sherap. At the time of the Chinese entry the two lamas were very young and did not exercise any effective authority: in 1950, when Phagpa Gelek Namgyal was 'elected' as deputy director of CLC, he was only ten years old. Similarly, Dagyab Rinpoche was only fourteen when his name appeared as a member of the Chamdo Liberation Committee.

For the Chinese the Chamdo Liberation Committee was a necessary instrument for implementing their policies and they argued that the CLC should exist as a separate organisation, since the area had already been liberated. The committee was composed of progressive Tibetans, Lhasa officials who had been captured in October 1950, and prominent religious figures from the area. It also contained members of the PLA forces that captured Chamdo. The Chinese could now co-opt other Chinese into the PCART as members of the CLC, and they could bring into the administration of Tibet progressive Tibetans like the secretary of the CLC, Baba Phuntsog Wangyal, who was a member of the Communist Party.

In reality the Tibetan Government was increasingly isolated on the PCART issue. Not only was its ability to influence the course of events curtailed by the Chinese, but the antagonism between the Tibetan Government and the Panchen Rinpoche's followers meant that there was no possibility that they would co-operate effectively, while the third group, the CLC, was completely under the control of the Chinese. According to the regulations governing PCART, the committee would be composed of 55 members: 15 representatives from the Lhasa Government, 10 from the Panchen Kanpo Lija Committee, 10 from Chamdo Liberation Committee, 5 from the Tibet Military Commission and a number of other members to be selected from Tibetan religious sects and monasteries.[136] Although the regulations appeared to allow each group to nominate their own representatives to the committee, Article 5 of the regulations stated that 'Nomination for the appointment and dismissal of the members of the Committee, and for the succession to such appointments, shall be made by the various circles after consultation and they should be submitted to the State Council for approval. The Chairman, the Vice-Chairmen and members of the Committee shall be formally appointed by the State Council'.[137] Ultimately all decisions and policies had to be approved by the State Council, which in effect meant that any appointments and decisions had to be endorsed by the Chinese representative. Article 13 of the regulations governing PCART allowed them to apply directly to the State Council for funds. This enabled each group to establish its own budget and reform program.

The Dalai Lama noted in his autobiography:

> Twenty of the members [although] they were Tibetans, were representing the Chamdo Liberation Committee and the committee set up in the Panchen Lama's western district. These were both purely Chinese creations. Their representatives owed their position mainly to the Chinese support, and in return they had to support any Chinese propositions; though the Chamdo representatives did behave more reasonably than the Panchen Lama's. With this solid block of controlled votes, in addition to those of the five Chinese members, the committee was powerless, a mere facade of Tibetan representation behind which all the effective power was exercised by the Chinese. In fact, all basic policy was decided by another body, the Central Committee of the Chinese Communist Party in Tibet, which had no Tibetan members.[138]

The Dalai Lama was appointed Chairman of PCART, while Panchen Rinpoche and Zhang Guohua were appointed Deputy Chairmen. In practice, Zhang Guohua took charge of the day-to-day running of the affairs of the committee. The PCART was made up of fourteen separate departments,[139] each of which was headed by a director and two or three deputy directors. Ngabo was appointed General Secretary of PCART, and in addition represented the Lhasa authorities. There were two Deputy Directors: Lhamon Yeshe Tsultrim, who represented Panchen Rinpoche and Zheng Jingpo, another Chinese official who represented the Chinese Government in Beijing.

The PCART became the main governing body in Tibet. It was clear that the scope of work envisaged and the increasing apparatus of the State meant that the Tibetan Government could neither oppose the new creation nor insist that Tibetans could effectively carry out the task. Even after the establishment of the PCART, the Chinese did not demand the disbanding of the Kashag, and the Tibetan Government structure continued to function. However, the Kashag had neither the resources nor the power to launch a direct challenge to Chinese authority, which was now firmly established in Tibet.

FIVE

The Rift

The setting up of the PCART was, on the surface, an apparent triumph of Chinese diplomacy and pragmatism. The Chinese hoped that it would give legitimacy to the transition from the Dalai Lama's rule to the supremacy of the Communist Party. The Chinese were able to claim, at least on paper, that they had set up a workable administrative structure during the transitional period before they introduced fully fledged 'democratic reform' in Tibet.

The Dalai Lama's initial acceptance of the PCART threw the Tibetans into confusion. On the one hand many felt that they should oppose it; on the other, some argued that since the Dalai Lama had given approval, opposition would be going against the will of the Dalai Lama.[1]

The Chinese were confident that they could spearhead their projected reform policies within five years of setting up PCART. Their certainty was based on a number of objective factors. First, the completion of the roads linking Tibet with China enabled them to secure effective military control of Tibet. Second, they had managed to secure the support of some sections of Tibetan society, particularly those which were opposed to the Lhasa regime. Third, there existed a strong faction in Lhasa which either saw the Chinese as a modernising influence or believed that by co-operating with the Chinese it could postpone the inevitable absorption of Tibet into China.

A leading Sakya aristocrat described one way the Chinese persuaded Tibetans to co-operate. She was offered a position in the Women's Association and, when she refused, it was 'emphasized that when in the future equality among peoples of Tibet was achieved then those who had not co-operated with the Chinese would have no position in the Communist ranks.'[2] When she went to ask advice of another aristocratic woman as to whether she should take up the post, she was told to accept the Chinese offer, because 'we [the aristocracy] are no longer free'. She was advised to 'learn to live with this. If not, later you will be degraded to the level of a roadworker'.[3]

In reality, the establishment of PCART and related institutions aroused fear among Lhasa officials, particularly those who were close to the Dalai Lama. The Tibetans were concerned that PCART would eventually take over the administration of all Tibet and that the ultimate political power would rest in the hands of those who controlled PCART. Clearly, the organizational structure of PCART had reduced the traditional power and status of the Tibetan Government. More importantly, the Chinese policy of divide and rule had, intentionally or unintentionally, disturbed the traditional balance of power in Tibetan society. For many Tibetans the threat to the Dalai Lama's rule did not come only from the Chinese: it was felt that the growing prominence of Panchen Rinpoche was a challenge to Lhasa's authority. This was evident from the fact that the Lhasa regime had had to surrender the powers it had acquired over the Panchen Rinpoche's territory in the early part of this century and from the fact that since the middle of the 1950s the Panchen Rinpoche's faction was acting as an independent group and dealing directly with the Chinese.

The disunity among the Tibetans suited Chinese objectives. The Communists were guided in Tibet by their 'United Front' policy, where different power or interest groups were invited to endorse the CCP's decisions. The highest organ dealing with the so-called 'nationalities problem' was the 'Party Central Committee's United Front Work Department'. In China this had meant that intellectuals and other political parties were invited to take part in various national organisations. In Tibet, on the one hand it meant that the reforms would be promoted from the top; on the other, that the Chinese would mobilize and recruit traditional figures, 'democratic personages' who had been previously kept outside the Tibetan governmental structure.

Among these newly involved figures promoted by the Chinese were prominent leaders from other religious sects. Article 3 of PCART regulations made this possible. Since the establishment of Gelugpa rule in the seventeenth century under the 5th Dalai Lama, political power had been the monopoly of the Gelugpa school. All the monk officials in the Tibetan Government were exclusively recruited from the Gelugpa monasteries around Lhasa. For the first time since the seventeenth-century, lamas belonging to the Sakya, Kagyu and Nyingmapa schools were invited to participate in the Tibetan polity. In this way the Chinese were able to broaden their support but it aroused deep suspicion among the traditional Gelugpa hierarchy. Almost all Tibetan Government officials were given posts in the new departments established under PCART and they were paid a monthly salary. One lama recalls that, although he did not attend a single meeting of the committee to which he had been nominated, the Chinese continued to deliver his monthly salary to his home.[4]

Soon after the inauguration of PCART in Lhasa, branches were opened in other parts of Tibet. At the local level, as at the national level, officials were recruited from the traditional Tibetan bureaucracy and religious hierarchy. In Sakya in western Tibet, the Chinese 'offered good posts' to members of the Sakya aristocracy, who continued to enjoy their lifestyle, as they had in the past.[5]

At the popular level, Tibetans who had viewed the Dalai Lama as the highest authority in Tibet were alarmed by his loss of prestige and power. Many Tibetans felt that the aristocracy, whose duty was to serve the Tibetan Government, had opted to work with the Chinese, or had left the country. They therefore blamed the aristocracy for abandoning the Dalai Lama and only looking after their own interests. People like Phala, who were close to the Dalai Lama and who had from the start opposed the 17-Point Agreement, felt that the primary objective was to secure the status and authority of the Dalai Lama. But there was a growing division among the Tibetan authorities about how this could best be achieved.

Since many Tibetan Government officials had accepted positions in PCART and at the same time maintained their traditional position in the Tibetan Government, a rift developed in Tibetan ruling circles. Increasingly, the people around the Dalai Lama, led by Phala, began to distrust Tibetan officials who had accepted work with the Chinese. Some officials expressed growing concern at the number of Tibetan Government officials now working for the PCART.

Although it was clear that the traditional Tibetan Government structure had become ineffectual and that the PCART had assumed a more dominant role, the Chinese did not demand the dismantling of the Tibetan Government. The Kashag continued to meet and exercise its symbolic authority. However, its ability to exert power on both the technical and political level was seriously undermined. Many officials were faced with divided loyalties. Their time was increasingly taken up with their work in various offices of PCART, yet their traditional loyalty to the Dalai Lama demanded their service as government servants. At the same time, although the Chinese did not demand abjuration of their loyalty to the traditional government, it was clear that the Chinese would not tolerate any opposition to their policies.

This precarious situation meant that there was a breakdown in trust between Tibetan officials. Phala describes the entire system at this time as in disarray. Tibetans accused the Kashag of being unable to prevent the erosion of the Dalai Lama's authority. The Chinese accused it of failure to contend with the anti-Chinese feeling that was growing in Lhasa.

One important consequence of PCART was the growth of numerous institutions. As the Chinese set up new infrastructures, a steady influx of Chinese cadres and PLA troops arrived in Tibet. Since Tibet lacked skilled labourers and trained cadres, the Chinese had to bring many additional workers from China. The troops were sent to border areas and were mainly engaged in setting up defensive infrastructure. By the middle of 1955, every Tibetan began to feel the presence of the Chinese. In fact, as early as 1953, when the Chinese began to carry out a census in all parts of Tibet, Chinese cadres accompanied by Tibetan interpreters were visiting homes and asking questions. This was seen by Tibetans as an intrusion in their lives. A Tibetan tailor recalled that his family was asked which Buddhist sect they belonged to. The Tibetan laity was never firmly divided into different sects, and such questions were considered strange and offensive.[6]

More importantly, the Chinese cadres and researchers began to carry out surveys of land owned by monasteries and aristocratic estates. Jamyang Sakya describes how the Chinese officials visited agricultural areas 'counting yaks, horses, sheep and other animals acting under the pretence that they wanted to vaccinate and prevent disease'. She goes on to say that 'they also counted the fields and their production, particularly the estates of wealthy land owners'.[7] This was to cause great alarm among the 'upper strata' and the religious leaders.

After the establishment of the PCART, the Chinese concentrated on constructing infrastructure; they ignored the social issues and conflicts that were emerging in Tibet. Contrary to later Chinese claims, the Communists did very little to mobilise the Tibetan peasantry, nor did they overtly advocate socialism or class consciousness. To some extent they took for granted that the Tibetan peasantry would in time put class interest first and support the Communist Party. Because of the policy of 'reform from the top' the Tibetan peasantry were at best treated with 'benign neglect', and at worst exploited as a source of cheap labour.

Another consequence of this policy was the hundreds of Tibetan officials and students who were sent to China for education from 1950, the majority of whom were children of the aristocracy and wealthy traders. It was envisaged that these students would become the core of the Tibetan cadres in the future.

This education policy was undertaken because the Communists did not wish to alarm the Tibetan ruling élite and they needed to exploit it. However antiquated Tibetan polity might have been, it was a functioning system. The Communists had to rely on traditional authority to sanction their directives. Despite the rapid improvement in communications, the Chinese were very much dependent on Tibetans and the traditional mode of transport. For example, later Communist propaganda made much of the abolition of the hated *U-lag* system (corvée labour) but after 1954 the Communists made use of it to ease their transportation problems. Chinese propaganda teams and cadres visiting remote parts of Tibet requisitioned horses and provisions. This increasing demand for transportation was resented by the people. In 1955, a group of corvée labourers in Rinam Dzong petitioned the Kashag, asking to be exempt from providing corvée labour to the Chinese. They insisted that they would be willing to continue their service as long as it was for the Tibetan Government.[8] One Tibetan Government official who had to organise corvée labour between Gyantse and Phari said that the frequent arrivals of Chinese officials meant that the corvée labourers had no time to rest before they had to go on another assignment.[9]

By the mid 1950s, the Chinese were beginning to feel the economic pressure and cost of their policies in Tibet. Consequently they began to take greater control of the Tibetan economy. In the early 1950s the Chinese had established a branch of the State Bank of China, which provided interest-free loans for Tibetan traders and businessmen. They also actively encouraged imports from India. The Chinese State Trading Company purchased Tibetan wool, leather and other goods at high prices. When the roads were completed the Chinese began to expand and direct the Tibetan economy.[10] There was a dramatic increase in the volume of goods from China. This meant that Tibetans spent their money on Chinese products, rather than the money going abroad (to India). A Chinese newspaper reported that 'owing to the increasing abundance of materials shipped into Tibet from the interior [China], a great deal of money in circulation was returned to the State'.[11]

The Chinese ability to control Tibet's economy was crucial to their long-term objective. In fact, early in 1952 Mao had warned that one of the keys to winning over the Tibetans was the gaining of control of 'production'. This had meant controlling the external trade and internal economy. The 1954 Sino–Indian, and later Sino–Nepalese, trade agreements had cancelled the extra-territorial trade privileges enjoyed by these countries. Mao warned: 'if we [Chinese] cannot solve the two problems of production and trade, we shall lose the material base for our presence'. He went on to say: 'the bad elements will cash in and will not let a single day pass without inciting the backward elements among the people and the Tibetan troops to oppose us, and our policy of uniting with the many and isolating the few will *become ineffectual and fail*'.[12]

Once the Chinese realised that the Da Yuan (the silver coin that had been introduced into Tibet) was being smuggled abroad, they tried to gain control of the Tibetan economy by integrating Tibet fully within the monetary system of China. They started to urge Tibetans to use paper money, which many Tibetans refused to do. They also took control of all the Tibetan customs offices along the Indo-Tibetan trade route. Chinese cadres were sent to take over the customs offices in Phari and Gyantse. The Tibetan officials said that they would refuse to hand over the customs offices unless they received written instructions from the Kashag.[13] But the Chinese were able to present the Tibetan officials with these.

Pasang Gyalpo, a Tibetan Government official who worked at the Gyantse customs office in 1954, recalled that the Chinese began to impose taxes on goods imported from India and that Tibetan traders were told that they were not allowed to take Da Yuans to India. In an attempt to reduce their expenditure, the Chinese began to ask the people working on road construction to take a reduction in their pay. The Tibetan workers were urged that they should give their labour free as a contribution to the 'construction of the Motherland'. Barshi, a Tibetan Government official, remembered that when the people refused to accept a cut in their wages, the Chinese started to lecture them, saying that in the new Tibet everything was owned by the people, and that the wealth of the state was inseparable from the wealth of the people.

The Uprising in Kham and Amdo

The main thrust for destabilising the Chinese position in Tibet was to come from an unexpected direction. While in the first few years of their rule in central Tibet, the Chinese had done little to disturb the Tibetan way of life, this was not the case in eastern and northern Tibet. This was the area Tibetans called Kham and Amdo which was inhabited by ethnic Tibetans who had cultural ties with the rest of Tibet. The Communists adopted a very different policy in these regions. The policy in Eastern Tibet is crucial to the understanding of what later happened in Tibet proper.

The Tibetan regions of Kham and Amdo were legally under Chinese jurisdiction. Some of the people in these areas had accepted nominal Chinese rule since the Qing period and many of the local leaders had been appointed to various posts under the Nationalist Government. However, the Nationalists were never able to establish effective rule. A French doctor, André Migot, who travelled in the area just before the Communists came to power, remarked that the 'Chinese control is little more than nominal', and that 'the Tibetans completely disregard the Chinese administration and obey only their own chiefs. One very simple fact illustrates the true status of Sikang's Chinese rulers: nobody in the province will accept Chinese currency'.[14]

When the Guomindang troops capitulated to the PLA, the Communists had initially managed to gain control of Kham and Amdo without much resistance. The Guomingdang officials had either escaped to Burma or chose to work with the new Communist Government. Local Khampa leaders didn't have the resources to launch large-scale revolts against the Communists, since the Tibetan Government refused to aid the Khampas; but the Khampas had in any case little reason to fear the Communists, and so many sought to work with the new Communist Government. Although Guomindang propaganda had portrayed the Communists as murdering hordes and anti-religious, it seems to have made very little impact on the

Tibetans, who had witnessed different Chinese regimes come and go. In Gansu almost all Tibetans followed Geta Rinpoche, the abbot of Bri Monastery, who welcomed the Communists. Thubten Norbu, one of the Dalai Lama's older brothers, who was an incarnate lama at Kumbum monastery, remembered that soon after the fall of Lanzhou a delegation of monks went to meet the Communists and sought their assurance that the monastery would be allowed to function as it had done in the past. The Communists told them that freedom of religion would be safeguarded under the new government. The monks of Labrang monastery also welcomed the Communists, and Geshe Sherab Gyatso, one of the leading monks from the monastery, was to occupy an important position in the new government.

When the Communists gained control of Kham and Amdo, the main task they faced was to build up the administrative and Party structure. Here they were not bound by any agreement, unlike in central Tibet where they were to some extent constrained by the 17-Point Agreement. The Communists, like the previous Chinese Republican Government, saw the whole of Kham and Amdo as falling directly under the legal and political jurisdiction of the Chinese Central Government. The work of pacifying and integrating Kham was the responsibility of the South-West Military-cum-Administrative Committee; Amdo came under the North-West Committee.

At the beginning of the 1950s Communist policy acknowledged that these areas occupied by 'minorities' presented special problems. It was believed that such areas were less developed and socially 'backward',[15] and that they could not implement the same democratic reforms as in other parts of China. The Communists exempted 'the minorities' from various campaigns, and considered it wrong to carry out rent-reductions and land reforms in the same way in minority areas as in Han districts.

The first task was to integrate the region into the administrative structure of the new constitution, which allowed for the setting up of autonomous administrative areas. In areas where the Tibetans constituted the majority they were granted local autonomy. By 1956 the Communists had created a number of Tibetan autonomous districts in Kham and Amdo.[16] In 1955 the Communists abolished the province of Xikang (Sikang) set up by the Guomindang and integrated it into the province of Sichuan. In other parts of Amdo, the Communists kept the Guomindang province of Qinghai. But six new autonomous *zhou* were established in areas of Amdo where the Tibetans formed the majority. The principal districts were the Jyekundo (Yushu) and the Golok Tibetan Autonomous Zhou. Gansu was the cultural boundary between Tibet and China, the area which was furthest from Lhasa. Here the Communists set up Gannan Tibetan Autonomous Zhou, with Labrang as its capital – a main centre of Tibetan activity, with one of the most important Gelugpa monasteries. However, all these administrative changes existed merely on paper and most Tibetans continued to show allegiance to their traditional leaders.

There was very little open resistance to the establishment of these administrative units and, unlike in Tibet proper, the Chinese also managed to recruit a few Tibetan Communists so that the CCP was able to establish a Party structure in these areas with relative ease. The Chinese were determined that in areas where Tibetans were the majority, Tibetans should be appointed to key posts. However, since there were so few Tibetan Communists, many of them had to occupy a number of posts simultaneously. Sangye Yeshi (Tian Bao) was Chairman of the Gannan Tibetan Autonomous Zhou and the Apa [Ngaba] Tibetan Autonomous Zhou. He was also a member of Xikang and the Sichuan Provincial People's Government until it was dissolved in 1955.[17] Although theoretically autonomous districts were to be self-governing with their own non-Communist representatives, all executive power in fact rested with the Party members. Moreover, Gansu, Sichuan and Qinghai were regarded as provinces of China and the 'Autonomous Zhou' were subordinate to the provincial government.

In the early 1950s, as well as carrying out the census, the Communists made extensive surveys of the areas. They made a detailed study of the pattern of land ownership and the economy, much as they were doing in the rest of Tibet at that time. It was believed that the research findings would provide information for future work. At the beginning of 1954 the Communists made tentative plans for the redistribution of land. At first they merely took over uncultivated land which PLA soldiers would make ready for cultivation before re-distributing to the landless peasants. One Khampa from Nyarong remembered that 'the land was distributed with much ceremony and speech making, everybody was made to clap heartily when the title deeds were handed over to the poor people'.[18] In some parts of Kham, as in Gyalthang (Dechen Prefecture), the Communists started to classify and divide people into different class groups.[19]

In July 1954, the Dalai Lama passed through Kham on his way to Beijing. Phala recalled that some of the local leaders warned the Dalai Lama of the growing danger from the Communists.[20] These conversations prompted the Dalai Lama to make a reference to the situation in eastern Tibet in his speech at the inaugural meeting of the PCART in Beijing, where he warned the Chinese to adopt more cautious measures in implementing the reforms. The first confrontation over Chinese reforms in Kham and Amdo took place towards the end of 1954. The Chinese were aware that there would be some resistance to reforms. They were also anxious about the ready availability of weapons and the fact that every man carried a gun or a sword. The people of eastern Tibet were fond of guns, and after the Second World War and the Civil War in China there had been an influx of cheap guns into Kham and

Amdo. It seems that the Chinese felt that the level of conflict could be reduced by confiscating arms.

An amnesty was declared for all arms handed in to the authorities. But there was no possibility of the Khampas surrendering their weapons. A Khampa from Lithang told me that after the Chinese failed to persuade the people to hand over their weapons voluntarily, they tried to urge local leaders to encourage people to relinquish their weapons. At one meeting a Khampa leader told the Communists, 'Guns are like ornaments,' and so they could not surrender them.[21] The Chinese were forced to take more aggressive measures to disarm the Khampas. As Geshe Sherab Gyatso (a member of the Qinghai Provincial Government and Chairman of the All China Association of Buddhists) complained to the National People's Congress: 'in some cases when the people were requested to surrender their arms, even the fire arms on the altars of the Buddhas were removed'.[22]

Between 1955 and 1956, China reached what Mao was calling 'the high tide of collectivisation' when over 80 per cent of China's peasants were involved in 'the advanced stages of agricultural co-operatives'. Mao believed that the 'national minorities' should now undergo socialist reform, otherwise they would lag further behind the Hans in socialist progress. This meant that, like the rest of China, minority areas were forced to undergo collectivization. In 1955 the Communists launched full-scale 'democratic reforms', which consisted of the establishment of 'mutual aid groups' and the redistribution of land. In Amdo and Kham, the Communists made tentative measures to settle the nomads. This led to sporadic uprisings and by late 1955 more serious fighting had erupted between Tibetans and Chinese in some parts of Tibetan-populated areas in Gansu, Sichuan and Yunnan.

While the inauguration of PCART was taking place in Lhasa, in eastern Tibet there was a major revolt, which led eventually to the nationwide Tibetan revolt against the Chinese. The Communists called it 'the Kanding Rebellion', after the main Tibetan town in eastern Tibet (known in Tibetan as Dartsedo). The town marked the frontier between Tibetan and Chinese culture and had been from ancient times a major trade centre between China and Tibet. Under the Guomindang, it had been the capital of Xikang province.

The fiercest fighting took place in Lithang, Changtreng and Gyalthang in the Yunnan area. The Kanding Rebellion was not organised nor was there any cohesive leadership. The revolt of the people of eastern Tibet was characterized by spontaneous and localised attacks on Chinese cadres and work places. When cadres came to villages to enforce collectivisation and other measures, they were attacked and, in many instances, killed by the villagers. Anna L. Strong, an American journalist and Communist sympathiser, described the revolt:

> The Kanting [Kanding] rebellion broke in the winter of 1955–56 and took the form of murdering central Government officials and Han [Chinese] citizens, there being no PLA in the area. As soon as the PLA arrived, they easily put down the rebels, but these fled into deeper hills and eventually into Chando [Chamdo]. Arms were easy to get, for at least fifty thousand muskets and rifles had been left in the area from the warlords' battles between Tibetans and Szechwan warlords. The few air drops from Chiang Kai-shek of American weapons and radio transmitters were hardly needed except for the sense of 'foreign support' they gave the rebels. The Szechwan-Chamdo rebellion was basically repressed by the end of 1956, though isolated groups would remain as bandits as long as any monastery fed them or until 'local people's control' was organized. The bulk of the defeated rebels moved into Tibet. They were the Khampas, Sikang troops, [Guomindang troops], cavalry, wild and undisciplined, accustomed to living by loot.[23]

A monk from Changtreng Sampheling monastery (one of the largest monasteries in Kham, whose head lama was Trijiang Rinpoche, the junior tutor to the Dalai Lama) remembers that the initial conflict with the Chinese occurred when they attempted to introduce land reforms in February 1954. Most people in the surrounding villages refused to co-operate and insisted that there was no need for land reform. When cadres accompanied by PLA escorts entered villages, they were either attacked or people simply refused to co-operate with them.[24] Later, the people in Changtreng blocked the brook which took water to the Chinese camp, which was situated less then a mile from the monastery. The Tibetans managed to cut off the water for nearly fifteen days.[25]

The ensuing fighting in surrounding areas forced many people to seek refuge in the monastery. By the end of February 1956, the 3,000 monks in Changtreng Sampheling had taken in thousands of villagers. Some were refugees from other parts of Kham; others had come to defend the monastery. At first the PLA troops laid siege to the monastery and an aeroplane dropped leaflets urging the monks and people to surrender. Although the monastery was well fortified, the Tibetans did not have any defence against Chinese mortar attacks. The PLA troops did not storm the monastery, which would have caused heavy casualties on the Chinese side, but called in a single plane which bombed the monastery. The Khampas had no choice but to surrender. The monastery was in ruins and hundreds of monks and laymen were killed. Those who survived either surrendered to the PLA or fled further west to central Tibet.[26]

News of the destruction of Changtreng Sampheling monastery spread like wild fire throughout eastern Tibet. Within a week of its destruction, the people of Lithang had organised a militia and came to defend the Lithang monastery. The charismatic young leader of Lithang, Yonru-Pon Sonam Wangyal, had organised hundreds of militia to defend the monastery. On the second day of Tibetan New Year (the end of February) 1956, as Yonru-Pon rode towards the monastery, his group was ambushed by the PLA troops and Yonru-Pon was killed. When news of his death reached the villages, the people of Lithang rose in revolt.[27] All the surrounding Chinese encampments were attacked and many Chinese cadres were killed. For over a month the PLA troops laid siege to the Lithang monastery until finally they were reduced again to calling a single plane to bomb the monastery.

Following this fighting, hundreds of Khampas crossed the Drichu river into central Tibet. The refugees brought news of the destruction of monasteries and the deaths of hundreds of monks. Previously, the people and the monasteries in eastern Tibet had dispatched petitions to the Dalai Lama, the Tibetan Government and the three great monasteries of Lhasa asking for their support. In his memoirs the Dalai Lama later wrote:

> Slowly, from the reports of refugees, we began to receive a clearer impression of the terrible things that were happening in the east and northeast . . . The Chinese were using artillery and bomber aircraft, not only against the guerrillas when they could find them, but also against the villages and monasteries whose people they suspected, rightly or wrongly, of having helped them. Thus villages and monasteries were being totally destroyed. Lamas and the lay leaders of the people were being humiliated, imprisoned, killed, and even tortured. Land was confiscated. Sacred images, books of scriptures, and things of holy significance to us, were broken up, derided, or simply stolen. Blasphemous proclamations were made on posters, in newspapers and preached in schools, saying that religion was only a means of exploiting the people, and the Lord Buddha was a reactionary.[28]

To the amazement of the Khampas, their appeals landed on deaf ears in Lhasa.[29] Phala Thupten Woden, a monk official, remembered that he was constantly approached by Khampa traders in Lhasa and messengers from all parts of Tibet. It was Phala who controlled all access to the Dalai Lama and he refused to allow Khampas to meet him. Phala feared that if the Dalai Lama were to meet with the Khampas, the Chinese would implicate him in the Khampa uprising.[30] The best consolation Phala could offer was to urge the Khampas to be patient. He told them, 'We would need to take the egg, without frightening the hen.' Phala and other Tibetan officials were worried that the revolt in eastern Tibet would spread to central Tibet and the Chinese would take action to suppress it.[31] The Chinese, equally worried that the revolt would spread to central Tibet, restricted Tibetan language newspapers published in Kham and Amdo to prevent information spreading. These papers carried propaganda campaigns against religion advocating its eradication and describing religious figures as 'reactionary and exploitative'.[32]

As the fighting in eastern Tibet wore on, the number of refugees grew dramatically, with hundreds pouring into central Tibet. Once the Khampas had crossed into areas under the jurisdiction of the Tibetan Government, the Communists took no action to detain them. Tenzin Tsultrim, a young man from Changtreng who fled to Lhasa, recalled that 'once we crossed the Drichu river, the Chinese were very different. They were polite and we felt safe'.

In central Tibet the Khampas were able to remain as pilgrims, but they did not find immediate sympathy or welcome. Many people refused to believe their reports. A Khampa who witnessed the destruction of the Changtreng Sampheling remembered that when he arrived in Lhasa even his relatives would not believe him. The Khampas faced widespread prejudice amongst the Lhasa people, who tended to stereotype them as 'unruly and troublesome'. Their only support came from the traders from eastern Tibet living in Lhasa. Resentment against the Khampas was caused in part by the fact that the Tibetans had already experienced a large influx of PLA troops, and now the number of refugees was causing further strain on the Tibetan economy.

Many Khampas were forced to flee to India. Athar Norbu, a young trader from Lithang, and other young men from Kham living in Lhasa, were sent to seek help in India by an influential Lithangpa trader, Andrug Gonbo Tashi, who was later to play an important role. Athar remembers that they set off without any knowledge of whom to contact. When they reached Kalimpong they found other people from Kham had already made contacts with the Guomindang agents in Kalimpong and Calcutta, where there was a sizeable Chinese community. Lekseh, a young Khampa from Bathang, also remembered that while in Kalimpong they were contacted by Guomindang agents.

The arrival of Khampa refugees in India alerted the international media to the revolt in eastern Tibet. By then it had spread through all the Tibetan-inhabited areas. At first the Communists denied the reports of revolt as Guomindang propaganda, but on 6 August, the Chairman of the Nationalities Affairs Committee of NPC admitted that, at the end of February 1956, a revolt had occurred. He claimed that it had been organised by feudal landlords at the instigation of Guomindang agents. The quote from Anna L. Strong (see note 23) was also an admission from the Chinese that the revolt had occurred and that the reforms were not welcomed by the people. However, by the middle of 1956, the Communists had secured a firm base in the whole of eastern Tibet. Their good military infrastructure and completion of the roads made it easier for them to control the rebellion.

The Communists' claim that the revolt was organised by Guomindang agents and a few reactionary landlords cannot account for the popularity of the uprising. It is true the leaders of the revolt were all drawn from the traditional élite, but it none the less cannot be explained purely in terms of vested interests nor by the class composition of the leaders. It was rather a consequence of a clash between two world views. When the Communists tried to introduce 'democratic reforms', they did more than change traditional patterns of land ownership. Tibetans who were sympathetic to the Chinese warned them that the reforms must be carried out with due consideration for Tibetan religious sentiments. Geshe Sherab Gyatso told the 1st session of the National People's Congress on 30 June 1956 that he believed reforms were inevitable and that socialism could not be achieved without collectivisation of agriculture and animal husbandry. However, he said, 'Owing to differences in standards, the methods to be adopted should be different. A vital point in this connection is to pay keen attention to the religions of the minority nationalities.'[33] A monk himself, Geshe Sherab Gyatso was painfully aware of the consequences of the reforms on the religious institutions and on the monk population. This was evident from Chinese research in Eastern Tibet which showed that in Ganzi Tibetan Autonomous Prefecture (in Sichuan) there were 50,000 monks, representing 11 per cent of the population, and in some areas like Ngaba the number of monks increased to 20 per cent of the population.[34] Moreover, the monasteries were the largest landowners in all Tibetan areas.

The Tibetans saw the reforms first and foremost as an attack on their value system; whether rich or poor, they were united in their belief in Buddhism and in their support for the religious institutions and could not envisage any reform that would mark the end of these religious institutions, which formed the centre of their world view. As noted earlier, despite the inequality and exploitation that existed in Tibetan society, there was no peasant uprising against the injustice that prevailed in the traditional system. Geshe Sherab Gyatso was clearly aware of the Tibetans' attachment to the existing system. He advised the National People's Congress on a four-point strategy for implementing the reforms:

(1) After collectivization of monastic property and animals, the monks and monasteries should be given an income so that they could continue their activities.

(2) After the reforms appropriate methods should be adopted to deal with funding of religious activities. Traditionally, individual families or a village would meet the expenses for a particular ceremony at a monastery.

(3) Freedom of religion must be fully guaranteed. Individuals or entire villages should be allowed to practice such merit-earning religious activities as alms-giving and praying.

(4) Those people who choose not to join collectives should not be discriminated against and the 'principle of free choice should be allowed'.[35]

The Tibetans 'are very conservative and hold fast to their native customs', Geshe Sherab Gyatso observed. He added that 'seeking rapid development of anything else should not be permitted'.[36] Criticism of the reforms was also made by Tibetan members of the Nationalities Committee of the NPC. Ngawang Gyatso told the Committee that 'shortcomings had been observed in the socialist transformation due to insufficient attention being given to the characteristics and demands of the minority nationalities'.[37]

However, despite these appeals from Tibetan leaders, the Communists proceeded with reforms regardless of popular opposition. Once the revolt became widespread, the question was no longer whether they should postpone reforms; now the issue was how they could 'eliminate counter revolutionaries'. But in central Tibet the Chinese did not immediately take action against Khampa refugees, as it would have meant adopting coercive measures in an area where their position was not entirely secure. In Kham and Amdo the Communists found they could no longer achieve their objective by normal means of control, and so they adopted more coercive methods. As they sought to suppress the revolt, the theatre of conflict shifted to central Tibet.

Growing Opposition in Central Tibet

The setting up of PCART had already caused serious anxiety among the Tibetan people and now the influx of refugees from eastern Tibet was further exacerbating the situation. During the Monlam ceremony of 1956, wall posters appeared denouncing the Chinese and saying that they should return to China.[38] The posters and pamphlets were distributed by a group called 'Mimang Tsongdu'. The name is similar to that of the group that was suppressed by the Chinese in 1952. The group was created in 1954, on the eve of the Dalai Lama's visit to China, in order to persuade him not to go. Many officials did not want the visit to take place and it appears that Phala and others thought that the only way they could stop the Dalai Lama going to China was by mobilising the people to request the Dalai Lama personally not to accept the invitation.[39]

The Mimang Tsongdu to some extent represented the culmination of

Tibetans' resentment against what they saw to be the erosion of the authority of the Dalai Lama. The name 'Mimang Tsongdu' was deliberately defiant. The Tibetan term 'Mimang' had been coined by the Communists who had created it from Tibetan to mean 'people' as understood in Western political terminology.

The Mimang Tsongdu came into being for several reasons. Not only was there a feeling that the Dalai Lama's position was being undermined, there was at the same time strong resentment against the traditional ruling élite who, it was believed, had left the young Dalai Lama to fend for himself. The Mimang Tsongdu handed a petition to Zhang Guohua, saying that there was no need for PCART and that Tibet must be ruled by the Dalai Lama. The organisers of the Mimang Tsongdu were traders and lower-ranking Tibetan officials. The main initiator was a shrewd Lithangpa trader named Alo Chonzed Tsering Dorje. Alo Chonzed had made his fortune from trading between India and Tibet. He was well known in Lhasa as the man who had revolutionised Tibetan house construction: in the 1940s, he had imported iron beams from India, thus doing away with the need for large numbers of supporting pillars in Tibetan houses. While in Lhasa, he had received many reports of the revolt in Kham and the destruction of Lithang monastery. More importantly, in India he had witnessed the nationalists' agitation for Indian independence.

Other leaders of the Mimang Tsongdu were Lhabchug Dhargpa Trinley and Bumthang Gyaltsen Lobsang. Both were minor Tibetan Government officials. Like other junior officials they had joined the Mimang Tsongdu because they believed that many senior Government officials were either weak or actively collaborating with the Chinese. At first the activities of Mimang Tsongdu were centred on Lhasa and their protest was characterised by putting up wall posters and submitting petitions to the Kashag. On another level the Mimang Tsongdu's actions reflected a Tibetan cultural response to Chinese pressure. The group sponsored rituals to propitiate wrathful deities and long-life prayers for the Dalai Lama.[40] The Mimang Tsongdu also campaigned for Tibet to be allowed to maintain its army and separate currency.

The Mimang Tsongdu achieved considerable popularity and was able to extend its activities beyond the vicinity of Lhasa. It also managed to secure the support of influential officials like Phala and Kalon Surkhang Wangchen Gelek, who was a member of the Kashag. These two believed that the protest movement would enable the Tibetan Government to put pressure on the Chinese. They therefore actively encouraged the Mimang Tsongdu to intensify its activities. In fact, Kalon Surkhang arranged for financial assistance to be given to the group.[41] Prominent religious leaders also gave their support, among them Tsatrul Rinpoche, who became a sort of spiritual adviser to the group and wrote the petitions that were submitted to the Chinese or to the Kashag.

The Mimang Tsongdu managed to establish branches in other major towns, such as Shigatse and Gyantse. In Gyantse, posters were put up demanding the reinstatement of the Dalai Lama as the supreme head of Tibet and the withdrawal of Chinese troops.[42] In Shigatse, however, the activities of the Mimang Tsongdu were not entirely welcome; in fact it was accused of endangering the peace. One Tashilhunpo official even tried to arrest the organisers.[43]

The Mimang Tsongdu also had more ambitious objectives: it wanted to be recognised as a legitimate political group by the Chinese and Tibetan Governments.[44] Of course there was no possibility that the Chinese would tolerate its activities. On the other hand, the response from the Kashag and people close to the Dalai Lama was complex. They actively supported and encouraged the group to agitate against the Chinese but the Kashag was only prepared to maintain covert links with the group. By 1956 the Mimang Tsongdu had begun to develop more imaginative activities. They set up another organisation called 'the Welfare of the Poor' which attempted to meet not only the needs of the increasing number of refugees from eastern Tibet but also the poor people in Lhasa who were badly affected by the increase in prices. The group organised distribution of relief for the poor and medical provisions. The Mimang Tsongdu urged the Tibetan Government to provide free use of the water mills for the poor, so that they could mill their barley.[45]

Despite all these activities, the economic and political impact that they could make was limited. By the time the group had become prominent and developed a more coherent political agenda, the Chinese position in Tibet was firmly established. Had the Dalai Lama and the Kashag given open support to the movement then the group might have been able to mobilise the people in a popular uprising. Since the group never received overt support from the Dalai Lama and the Kashag, many people had an ambivalent attitude towards its activities. Nevertheless, the group was able to some extent to unite Tibetan people in common sentiment and shared values.

Although the group was causing a great many problems for the Chinese, Mao himself seemed unconcerned. He told a Tibetan delegation led by Lhalu that the activities of the Mimang Tsongdu were simply caused by the temporary economic hardship and once the economy had been improved the resentment would wither away.[46] Nevertheless, the Chinese in Tibet were not prepared to allow its activities to go unchecked. Soon after the Monlam festival in 1956 the Chinese asked the Kashag to stop the activities of the Mimang Tsongdu; if not, the PLA would be forced to take action. The Chinese also stated that if the Kashag failed to take action, it would be assumed that members of the Kashag were involved in and sympathised with the reactionary activities of the group.

By the end of March 1956, the atmosphere in Lhasa was tense. The revolt in eastern Tibet was spreading into central Tibet and the activities of the Mimang Tsongdu had reached their height. Alo Chonzed was informed by a Tibetan official, Tsipon Namseling, that the Chinese had instructed the Kashag to arrest the ringleaders of the group.[47] The Kashag summoned Alo Chonzed, Bumthang and Lhabchug to the Norbulingka, the summer palace of the Dalai Lama, where Kalon Sholkhang spoke to them. As Alo Chonzed recalls, Sholkhang seemed irritated. He spoke harshly, telling them that the 'activities of the Mimang Tsongdu were damaging the relationship between China and Tibet', and that 'in the past, whatever difficulties Tibet had had with Nepal or China, it had been the responsibility of Government officials and the people should not concern themselves with the affairs of the State'.[48] What may appear to us as a strange statement, in fact reflects the prevailing idea that matters politic were the exclusive concern of the aristocracy and Tibetan Government officials.

Mimang Tsongdu became the first popular movement in Tibetan history. Support for the group came from all sections of Tibetan society. They not only challenged the Chinese but also the political monopoly of the traditional ruling élite. On the 19th of the first Tibetan month, the Tibetan police surrounded Alo Chonzed's house and arrested him. Bumthang and Lhabchug were also arrested and brought to Lhasa for questioning.

A joint committee composed of Chinese and Tibetan officials was set up to investigate the activities of the Mimang Tsongdu. Alo Chonzed remembers that the main thrust of Chinese questioning was whether the group was supported by the Guomindang or the Americans. Alo Chonzed replied that if the Chinese had any evidence of external support then it was up to them to prove it.[49] The investigation could not prove that the Mimang Tsongdu was supported by external groups. Nevertheless, its three leaders were detained for several months and while in prison Lhabchug, who represented the Tsang region, died.[50]

Immediately people started petitioning for their release. The abbots of the three great monasteries also appealed on their behalf. There was a danger of them becoming a rallying point for the Tibetans. The last thing the Chinese wanted was to create martyrs out of the leaders. Therefore they decided to release Alo Chonzed and Bumthang on condition that they would not try to revive the organisation and that they would not take part in any further political agitation. The abbots of the three monasteries gave guarantees that they would refrain from politics. On 25 August 1956, Alo Chonzed and Bumthang were released. A few weeks later they went into exile in India and settled in Kalimpong, where Bumthang died in the late 1950s. Alo Chonzed has remained active and is a controversial figure in Tibetan *émigré* politics.[51]

The Dalai Lama Visits India

By the middle of 1956, the Chinese found themselves under attack from all sections of Tibetan society. There was muttering among some officials that the Dalai Lama should leave Tibet until the situation in Lhasa calmed down. In 1954, the Crown Prince of Sikkim, Dhondup Namgyal, had come to Lhasa and presented the Dalai Lama with an invitation to visit India for the celebration of the 2,500th anniversary of Buddha's Birth (Buddha Jayanti). With increasing tension in Lhasa, the invitation provided an opportunity for the Dalai Lama to get away.

The visit would have serious political implications for Tibet and other countries. The Government of India had itself previously sent an invitation to the Dalai Lama via the Chinese Government. But the Chinese Government had neither passed on the invitation to the Dalai Lama nor given an answer to the Indians. The direct invitation from the Chogyal of Sikkim removed the awkward diplomatic position in which China and India found themselves. The Chogyal's decision to invite the Dalai Lama arose from complex circumstances. It was possible that the Tibetan *émigré* community in India, which was close to the Sikkimese royal family, may have prompted the Chogyal to invite the Dalai Lama. On one hand the invitation and his visit to Tibet provided the Chogyal with the opportunity 'to feel the pulse of the Chinese and assess their attitude to Sikkim and Sikkim's relationship with India'.[52] On the other hand there were Tibetan and foreign powers who were of the opinion that the Dalai Lama was surrounded by pro-Chinese officials and that he was not in a position to speak freely while in Tibet, and that the only way they could influence the Dalai Lama and ascertain his personal view would be for him to come to India.

The deteriorating situation in Tibet encouraged the *émigré* community to revive the Dedon Tsogpa (Committee for Tibetan Social Welfare), an organisation that had originally been set up in 1954, with Gyalo Dhundup and Khenchung Lobsang Gyaltsen as a joint President. Lobsang Gyaltsen was a influential monk official in charge of the now defunct Tibetan trade mission in Kalimpong. Shakabpa was selected as the secretary of the group. From the start the group had political ambitions and sought to spearhead the anti-Chinese movement from Kalimpong. Dedon Tsogpa had been established to meet the emergency needs caused by the Gyantse flood in August 1954. This also enabled the *émigré* group to disguise their political activities. It was clear that the GOI would not tolerate any overt political agitation based in Kalimpong. Since 1954, the GOI had began to restrict the activities of Tibetan *émigré* groups in India. The resurgence of the Khampa resistance movement in central Tibet encouraged the *émigré* group to intensify its anti-Chinese campaign. The Chinese were worried by the vigorous campaign coming across the border. They requested that the Indian Government 'repress' the activities of the *émigré* group.[53] The Indians reassured the Chinese that the Tibetans would not be allowed to engage in political activities. However, Mullik, the chief of the Indian Intelligence Bureau, has said that Nehru told him 'no Chinese protests would be entertained' and that no notice would be taken of the activities of Tibetans in Kalimpong.[54]

At the same time the Americans were adopting an increasingly hostile policy towards China. Earlier the United States had held the view that if they could talk directly with the Dalai Lama, they would be able to make a definite policy. This view was shared by the Tibetan *émigré* community in India: if the Dalai Lama came to India there would be a good opportunity for the *émigré* group to talk with him. His brothers, Gyalo Dhundup and Thubten Norbu, would have unrestricted access to him.

The invitation put the Chinese in a difficult position. If they were to prevent the visit, they would be accused of imprisoning the Dalai Lama, but if he was allowed to leave he might come into contact with people who would encourage him not to return. At first the Chinese told the Indians that the Dalai Lama would not be able to undertake the visit as PCART had just been set up and there were many tasks that required the Dalai Lama's presence. When the Dalai Lama asked the political commissar for the PLA, Fan Ming, whether he should accept the invitation, the commission tried to dissuade him and suggested that since it was not an official invitation from the Government of India, it would be appropriate to send a suitable deputy.[55]

The Chinese were aware that the Dalai Lama was keen to visit India and that since the Chogyal had given the invitation directly to the Dalai Lama it was difficult for them to intervene. The Chogyal wrote to his friend Nari Rustomji that the Dalai Lama 'seemed keen to come but much depends on the Chinese and how they move. The general opinion here is "how can the Chinese refuse?" and none but the pro-Chinese younger officials seem reluctant to let him go to India.'[56] The Chinese knew that they could not command the Dalai Lama not to accept the invitation without arousing the Tibetans' anger. Mao later commented that 'the Central government recognised that it is better to let him go than to prevent him from going'.[57] In October 1956, the Indian Government sent another official invitation for both the Dalai Lama and the Panchen Rinpoche. The inclusion of the Panchen Rinpoche seemed to have allayed Chinese fears. They were confident that he would represent a pro-Chinese faction within the Tibetan group.

For the Dalai Lama the invitation to visit India came at a most opportune time, like a 'ray of sympathy and sanity from the outside world'.[58] The

Buddha Jayanti would provide him with an opportunity to go on pilgrimage to Buddhist holy sites, and more important:

> from the secular point view, a visit to India seemed to offer me the very opportunity I wanted to withdraw from my close contact and fruitless arguments with the Chinese, at least for a time. Not only that, I hoped it would also give me a chance to ask Mr Nehru and other democratic leaders and followers of Mahatma Gandhi for advice. I cannot exaggerate our feeling of political solitude in Tibet. I knew I was still inexperienced in international politics, but so was everyone in our country, We knew other countries had faced situations like ours, and that a great fund of political wisdom and experience existed in the democratic world; but so far none of it had been available for us, and we had to act by a kind of untrained instinct. We desperately wanted sympathetic wise advice.[59]

The visit certainly provided an opportunity for the Dalai Lama and for Tibet once more to renew its contact with the outside world. And, the Tibetan émigré community (which included former Prime Minister Lhukhangwa, Tsipon Shakabpa, and Gyalo Dhundup and Thubten Norbu, who had been resident in US) saw it as a chance to encourage the Dalai Lama to repudiate the 17-Point Agreement. The Chinese were clearly worried about a meeting with the *émigrés* in Kamlimpong. They advised the Dalai Lama to travel by air,[60] which would have meant bypassing Kalimpong and other areas with a heavy concentration of Tibetan émigrés.

The Chinese were particularly concerned with the activities of Thubten Norbu, who maintained close contact with the US State Department. In October 1956 he had conducted meetings with Foreign Office officials in London.[61] The Chinese made a formal protest to the British Government. They clearly saw, especially in the aftermath of the Hungarian revolt, that there was growing anti-Communist sentiment in the Western press, which had equated revolts in Eastern Tibet with events in Hungary.

Before the Dalai Lama left Lhasa, he was briefed by Zhang Jingwu. Zhang mentioned the events in Hungary and said that there were reactionaries who were seeking to 'create trouble' but China would not allow any country to interfere in Tibet. Zhang added that in the event of Indian officials asking the Dalai Lama about the boundary, he was to say that such matters are best discussed with the Central Government.[62] At the same time, on the 15 November 1956, Mao made a lengthy speech in Beijing at the Second Plenum of the Eighth Central Committee in which he dealt with the worsening international and domestic situation confronting China. He warned that there was a possibility the Tibetans would use the absence of the Dalai Lama from Lhasa to create disturbances, and that the Dalai Lama might declare Tibetan independence in India.[63] It appears that the Chinese had expected some kind of showdown between the Tibetans and PLA. Mao said that the troops should prepare themselves by 'building fortifications' and storing 'food and water'.[64]

Five days later the Dalai Lama and members of the Kashag left Lhasa for Sikkim. The Tibetan delegation included Ngabo, Surkhang and Ragshar, the uncle of the Chogyal of Sikkim. A second Tibetan delegation made up of the Panchen Rinpoche and his entourage left Shigatse. Once again there was tense rivalry between the two Tibetan groups throughout the visit. While the Dalai Lama and the Lhasa delegation were received with a great deal of ceremony and attention, by both the Tibetan *émigré* community and Indian Government officials, the Panchen Rinpoche and his officials were treated like minor officials. In fact Tibetan *émigrés* were hostile to the Panchen Rinpoche's delegation, regarding it as pro-Chinese.

When the Dalai Lama and the Tibetan delegation crossed the Tibetan boundary, they were welcomed by the Chogyal of Sikkim, Sir Tashi Namgyal and Apa Pant, the Indian Political Officer. In Sikkim, the Dalai Lama was also met by the Chinese ambassador to India. From there they were driven to Bagdogra Airport. On 25 November, the Dalai Lama arrived in New Delhi, to be welcomed at the airport by the Indian Vice-President Radhakrishnan and Nehru. The Chinese Ambassador made the point of introducing the Dalai Lama to the diplomatic corps, but when the American ambassador was introduced, the Chinese left. The Dalai Lama was treated like a head of state, which annoyed the Chinese.

The euphoric atmosphere of the visit was summed up by the slogan '*Hindi Chini Bhai Bhai*' (Indo-Chinese Brotherhood). The Tibetans saw the visit as an opportunity to develop some form of external relations. But since the Sino–Indian agreement of 1954, India had explicitly recognised Tibet as a region of China and the GOI had not insisted on the rights inherited under the British, which would have allowed them to maintain a direct relationship with Tibet. The Chinese were aware that there would be enormous pressure on the Dalai Lama either to remain in India or to denounce the Chinese presence in Tibet. On 28 November the Chinese Premier, Zhou Enlai, made a visit to India. He was accompanied by He Long, who had recently been elected as a member of the Central Committee and the Politburo. He Long had been one of the PLA generals in charge of the invasion of Tibet; and as a high ranking member of the South-West Military Region he was responsible for the administration of Tibet. Zhou's visit aimed to prevent any embarrassing diplomatic entanglements, and to keep an eye on the attempts by Tibetans to gain sympathy for their cause.

Not wanting to damage its ties with China, India made assurances that the activities of the Tibetan *émigrés* would be curbed. The Chinese tried to make it appear that the visit was a delegation from China by arranging for the Dalai Lama to present a gift from the Chinese Government. When the

Dalai Lama and Panchen Rinpoche visited the famous Buddhist university city of Nalanda, the Dalai Lama gave Nehru the relics of the Chinese monk Xuan Zang who had visited India more than a thousand years earlier, and announced that the Chinese Government would donate 300, 000 yuan for the construction of a memorial hall.[65]

This ceremony could hardly conceal the serious diplomatic and political problems that had emerged. It was common knowledge among Tibetan officials that the Dalai Lama was considering remaining in India. Gyalo Dhundup had already told B. N. Mullik that the Dalai Lama would not be returning to Tibet. Mullik immediately told Nehru, who said that Mullik should advise the Dalai Lama to return to Tibet, as he was the only leader capable of uniting the people. Were the Dalai Lama to remain in India, the people would be demoralized and easily fall under Chinese domination. Nehru said that he would give the same advice to the Dalai Lama when he approached him.[66]

In late December, the Dalai Lama met Nehru and 'explained how desperate things had become in eastern Tibet and how we all feared that worse troubles would spread through the rest of the country'.[67] He said he feared the Chinese would destroy Tibet's religion and customs – Tibet now 'pinned their last remaining hopes on the government and people of India'.[68] The Dalai Lama told Nehru that he wished to remain in India until the situation improved. However, the Tibetans did not have any specific suggestion as to how India might be able to help, nor did they come up with any particular initiative. Nehru listened patiently and told the Dalai Lama that there was nothing the Government of India could do. Tibet had never been recognised as an independent country. The best hope for Tibet was to try to work within the 17-Point Agreement.[69] Nehru also said that it would be futile to fight against the Chinese, but assured the Dalai Lama that he would speak to Zhou Enlai. He also recommended that the Dalai Lama meet with Zhou in Delhi.[70] The Dalai Lama took the opportunity to invite Nehru to Tibet: the Tibetans wanted to keep some form of contact with India, as their right.

Nehru's advice to the Dalai Lama should not be dismissed as either naïve or misleading. As a leader who had fought the British and been to jail for his country's independence, he knew what was meant by fighting for one's rights. Nehru was convinced that the best chance still lay in making the Chinese honour the 17-Point Agreement. To this end he came to see the Dalai Lama in his room in the Presidential guest house, bringing with him a copy of the 17-Point Agreement, and proceeded to tell the Dalai Lama the points on which he could challenge the Chinese.[71] In Nehru's view, remaining in India would be 'the height of folly'. The Dalai Lama's place was in his country, leading the people during a difficult period.[72]

Nehru firmly believed that there should be peace between India and

China. Therefore, he did not relish the diplomatic problems that might result from the Dalai Lama's decision to remain in India. Nor had he lost any of his early enthusiasm for China. However, a tension was developing between the two countries. India was concerned about growing ties between China and Nepal, which were interpreted as a sign of the latter's desire to prevent Indian encroachment. India and China also disagreed over events in Hungary: in his speech to the Indian Parliament, Zhou stated that the two countries did not share common views on some international issues. If the Dalai Lama had been allowed to remain in India, there is no doubt that the Chinese would have accused India of being directly involved, or of failing to prevent groups hostile to China from operating on Indian soil.

When Nehru met Zhou Enlai, he told him that the Dalai Lama had expressed a wish to stay in India. With characteristic diplomatic charm, Zhou was able to conceal his irritation and say that the Dalai Lama could stay in India as long as he abided by Indian regulations.[73] When Nehru mentioned that the reforms were causing difficulties, Zhou told him that 'the idea that they could introduce communism into Tibet was rather fantastic, because Tibet was very backward and as far removed from communism as any country could be.'[74] Zhou managed to assure Nehru that the troubles in Tibet were a temporary aberration and that the Party would rectify any mistakes.

The news that the Dalai Lama was intending to stay in India was not wholly unexpected. At the Second Plenum of the 8th Central Committee, Mao had said: 'you can't have a husband and wife [relationship] simply by tying two people together. If a person no longer likes your place and wants to run away, let him go'.[75] He added, 'I will not be sad if we lost Dalai'.[76] While Mao appeared to be unconcerned and disinterested at the prospect of the Dalai Lama remaining in India, the efforts being made by Zhou Enlai in Delhi to persuade the Dalai Lama to return to Lhasa showed that the Chinese were worried about the situation.

The Chinese must also have been aware of the pressure on the Dalai Lama to remain. His entire family was now in India and would without doubt have stayed with him. The members of the Kashag accompanying him, including Ngabo, would also be inclined to remain with him.

Zhou Enlai Urges the Dalai Lama to Return to Tibet

The Chinese knew that the Dalai Lama's brothers, Gyalo Dhundup and Thubten Norbu (who had come to India from the United States), were in favour of him staying in India.[77] In fact Norbu was developing plans with the Central Intelligence Agency for covert action in Tibet. The US were beginning to shift their policy from attempting to influence the Dalai Lama directly to a clandestine policy of destablising the Chinese hold in the country. When Zhou met the brothers at an official reception given by the Indian President on 30 November 1956, he told Thubten Norbu that he should return to Tibet. Zhou Enlai also invited them for discussions at the Chinese Embassy. Both brothers went to the Chinese Embassy the next day, where they met Zhou and He Long.

> Chou Enlai wanted to know the reasons for our refusal to return, and so we gave them to him, one by one. We pointed out that Communist China had not honoured the terms of the agreement which had been signed five years previously between Lhasa and Peking [Beijing]: and we quoted examples of Chinese behaviour directed towards bringing about the final desolation of Tibet as an independent state. We blamed the Chinese invaders for the shortage of foodstuffs, rising prices, and the expropriation without compensation of land to build strategic roads. We also complained that the powers of the Dalai Lama had been restricted and our religion had been persecuted.[78]

The brothers also accused the Chinese of supporting the Panchen Rinpoche in order to undermine the authority of the Dalai Lama.[79] Thubten Norbu and Gyalo Dhundup exercised considerable influence over the Dalai Lama, but they did not occupy any formal position in the Tibetan Government. In fact Gyalo Dhundup's relations with Lhasa officials were at best uneasy. The final decision as to whether or not the Dalai Lama would remain in India could only be made in consultation with the Kashag.

Zhou firmly told Gyalo Dhundup and Thubten Norbu that the present problems in Tibet were 'unavoidable at the beginning of any new undertaking'.[80] If they wished to they could stay abroad and observe the changes and they could return when things improved.[81] Zhou said he had learned that the Dalai Lama was planning to remain in India and he urged them to encourage the Dalai Lama to return to Tibet.

When Zhou Enlai sent a message that he wished to meet the Dalai Lama, the members of the Kashag accompanying the Dalai Lama advised against it. The Kashag felt that the Chinese premier should be met by them rather than the Dalai Lama personally. Zhou first met with the members of the Kashag, who told him that the Dalai Lama was unable to come to the meeting because he was not well. Zhou told the Tibetans that he had learned that the Dalai Lama was planning to go to Kalimpong and that he would advise the Dalai Lama not to proceed to Kalimpong as the place was a centre for reactionary groups. Zhou said this was the only reason why he wished to meet with the Dalai Lama. Ngabo said the Dalai Lama had been invited to Kalimpong by Tibetans who had been resident in the area for many years and that the Dalai Lama had already accepted the invitation. If he were to postpone the visit, it would disappoint many people. Ngabo further stressed that since it was in Indian territory, the GOI would guarantee security.[82] Zhou knew perfectly well that this was not truc and insisted that the Dalai Lama should meet him.

On 1 December 1956 the Dalai Lama met Zhou Enlai at the Chinese Embassy in Delhi. He raised the subject of the revolt in eastern Tibet, and the fact that the Chinese were enforcing reforms without proper consultation with the people. Zhou once again assured the Dalai Lama that he had communicated his concerns to Chairman Mao, and that the problems were caused by mistakes made by local officials.[83]

Zhou received consistent protests from all the Tibetans he met. After meeting with the Dalai Lama, Zhou met with members of the Kashag: Ngabo, Surkhang Wangchen Gelek and Ragashag Phuntsog Rabgye. It was Ngabo who made the most vocal criticism of the Chinese. He stressed the need to reduce the number of Chinese troops and cadres and declared that the Chinese had failed to appreciate the 'feelings of the Tibetan people'. The Tibetans also demanded that the former Prime Ministers, Lukhangwa and Lobsang Tashi, be reinstated.[84]

Zhou listened to the Tibetans' protests and admitted that many mistakes had been made by both sides and these should be rectified. He suggested the problems could be best discussed when they returned to Tibet, as could the reinstatement of the former Prime Ministers.[85] The Chinese were in no position to coerce the Tibetans to return to Lhasa. They could only stop the Tibetans from carrying out their plans by appeasement and an agreement to further discussion in Tibet. On 10 December Zhou left India for Rangoon.

It was clear to the Chinese that they would either have to make substantial concessions or they would have to work in Tibet without the Dalai Lama. By the beginning of 1957, the Khampa revolt in the east had moved into central Tibet and there were thousands of refugees camping around Lhasa. There were rumours in Lhasa that the Dalai Lama would not be returning. While the Dalai Lama was on pilgrimage to Sarnath, where the Buddha gave his first sermon, he received a telegram from Zhang Guohua in Lhasa urging him to return immediately.[86] Yet in Beijing, Mao still continued to appear unmoved, telling a meeting of Provincial and Municipal Party Secretaries that 'even if the Dalai Lama doesn't return, China will not sink into the sea'.[87] The Tibetan problem was becoming more complex and there were no signs that the Dalai Lama was prepared to return to Lhasa. On 24 January 1957, Zhou was back in Delhi. He told the press that he had returned to Delhi for private talks with Nehru. It was clear that he had come to make a final appeal to the Dalai Lama to return to Lhasa.

A day later the Dalai Lama met Zhou Enlai for the second time at the Chinese Embassy in Delhi. It appeared that since their last meeting Zhou

Enlai had been in consultation with Mao and he brought a message from him. Zhou told the Dalai Lama that he had been assured by Mao that the reforms would be postponed for the next five years and if necessary they would be put back a further five years until the time was right for the local Tibetan Government.[88] But Zhou also warned that if the situation in Tibet did not calm down, the Central Government would be obliged to put down the revolt by force. The Dalai Lama wrote that Zhou: 'told me again that the situation in Tibet was worse, and that I ought to go back. He left me in no doubt that if there really was a popular uprising he was ready to use force to put it down'.[89] Zhou went on to tell the Dalai Lama that he should not be swayed by the Tibetan *émigré* community in India, and he should not meet with the former Prime Minister Lukhangwa, who was living in Kalimpong. Next day the Dalai Lama was visited by He Long who also urged the Dalai Lama to return to Tibet. (As one of the architects of the 1950 invasion of Tibet, He Long must have been a forbidding reminder of Chinese force.) He Long made a cryptic remark: 'The snow lion looks dignified if he stays in his mountain abode, but if he comes down to the valleys he is treated like a dog.'[90]

The small Tibetan *émigré* community in India presented petitions to Nehru and demonstrated outside his residence urging him to support Tibet. The Tibetans must have been aware that although the GOI would not force the Dalai Lama to return to Tibet, it would not accord any special privileges or assistance to him. In fact Nehru was still convinced the Dalai Lama's place was with his people. The Dalai Lama was disappointed and found it difficult to accept Nehru's advice, telling Apa Pant, the Political Officer in Sikkim: 'I am a very young man. I do not know which way to look. The medicine that the doctor [Nehru] is proposing for my weakness seems to be bitter and unpalatable. I do not know whether I would really get well with that medicine.'[91]

When the Dalai Lama arrived in Kalimpong on 22 January, he had some doubts as to whether he should return or not. Most of the Tibetan officials, and all the members of the Dalai Lama's family, were in favour of the Dalai Lama staying in India. Lukhangwa was adamant that the Dalai Lama should seek asylum. Ngabo asked, more realistically, what could be achieved by remaining in India and what assistance foreign governments were going to provide. He argued that there was no sign that either the GOI or any other foreign government was willing to aid Tibet and that the Dalai Lama would be treated as a private citizen, and that it was therefore not advisable for the Dalai Lama to remain in India.[92] No one could dispute Ngabo's arguments or come up with an alternative solution apart from Thubten Norbu, who told the Kashag that he had obtained 'foreign support'. As Ngabo was present Thubten Norbu did not want to mention the name of the country, but everyone knew that it could only mean the Americans. Ngabo once again stressed that before committing themselves they needed to know more definitely the nature of this 'foreign support'.[93] Takla recalls that the US offer of support was not considered to make much difference and it was not mentioned again. As we will see later, however, the US was beginning to develop very different strategies.

The Panchen Rinpoche and his entourage were faced with a different set of problems. His officials felt that they were being treated dismissively, and international attention was focused on the Dalai Lama. The Panchen Rinpoche met the Indian leader only at public ceremonies, while the Dalai Lama had private meetings with Nehru. The Panchen Rinpoche later said that some Indian officials had 'discriminated' against him, and his 'entourage had to sleep on the trains sometimes because they were not provided with housing'.[94] This may appear to have been a minor indiscretion on the part of the Indian Government and an overreaction from the Panchen Rinpoche, but there were indeed a deliberate attempts on the part of Lhasa officials to denigrate the Panchen Rinpoche. They resented the fact that when the Dalai Lama and the Panchen Rinpoche had visited China in 1954, the Chinese had tried to promote the two lamas as equals. Among the Tibetan *émigrés* in India there was talk of bringing down the Panchen Rinpoche from his high horse.[95]

The Panchen Rinpoche's group also learned that the brothers of the Dalai Lama had raised the issue of the status of the Panchen Rinpoche with Zhou Enlai. It would appear that the Chinese did not want to antagonise the Lhasa officials further either by actively promoting the Panchen Rinpoche abroad or by seeming to favour him. Zhou made two visits to India but he did not have any private meetings with the Panchen Rinpoche. The group felt slighted from all quarters and realised it was better to return to Shigatse as quickly as possible. By 29 February the Panchen Rinpoche and his group had returned to Tibet while the Dalai Lama and some members of the Kashag remained in India, without having come to a decision.

It appeared to the Dalai Lama that no help was forthcoming from the Americans. It is most likely that they did not favour the Dalai Lama staying in India either. For, although the Dalai Lama's refutation of the 17-Point Agreement in 1951 would have been a major propaganda victory for America, in 1957 the Dalai Lama's propaganda value had diminished. American interests were best served if the Dalai Lama stayed in Tibet and resisted the Chinese. Therefore, like Nehru, the Americans might have felt that it would be the 'height of folly' for the Dalai Lama to remain in India. In any case, America saw the revolt in eastern Tibet as a major setback for the Chinese which would provide an opportunity for their involvement.

On 27 February, while the Dalai Lama was still in Kalimpong, Mao delivered his famous speech. 'On the correct handling of contradictions among the people, in front of a specially invited audience of Party and non-

Party members attending an enlarged session of China's State Council. He admitted that a conflict of interest could exist in a socialist society, and identified twelve types of contradictions. The abridged version of the speech was published by Xinhua and later included in the collected works of Chairman Mao,[96] but only when the original text was published did it show that the whole section on the minorities dealt with the situation in Tibet. The speech clearly reveals how vexed the Chinese leader was at the time.[97]

> The eleventh problem [is], the problem of national minorities and great Han chauvinism and *the problem of Tibet*. China has several tens of millions of national minorities; the land that the national minorities occupy is a some 50 or 60 % [of all China]; their population is about 6% of China's. That's why I had a section in my ten great relationships saying that the relations between Han and national minorities should be conducted well. This is principally the resolution of the Han chauvinism. Has it been resolved? It still has not been resolved well. The Communist Party is preparing to hold a high level meeting this year, at the plenum of the Central Committee [which will] specifically [discuss the question of] United Front and the national minority problem. We must certainly change this great Han chauvinist work style, ideas, sentiments, monopolising matters that ought to be done by others (the National minorities themselves), the disrespect for minorities.
>
> There is a group in Tibet who wants to set up an independent Kingdom. Currently this organisation is bit shaky; this time India asked us to let them return. We permitted the Dalai Lama to go to India; he has already gone to India. Now [the Dalai Lama] has already returned to Tibet. America does [its anti-communist] work. There is a place in India called Kalimpong where they specialise in sabotaging Tibet. Nehru himself told the premier [Zhou Enlai], that this place is a centre of espionage, primarily American and British.
>
> If Tibet wants to be independent our position is this: [if] you want to agitate for independence, then agitate; you want independence, I don't want [you to have] independence. We have the 17 Point Agreement. We advised the Dalai Lama that he'd be better off coming back: if you stay in India [and] then go to America it might not be advantageous [to you or Tibet]. Premier [Zhou] has spoken with him several times. Also with other independence movement people, a group of [whom are] residing in Kalimpong, [the Premier] has also talked with them, [saying] they do better to return. As for reform, the 17 Point [Agreement] stipulates that reforms be made; but the reforms need your agreement. [If] you don't want reform, then we won't have any. If in the next few years you don't [want] reform, then we won't have any. This is way we have spoken to them just now. There will be no reform under the second Five Year Plan,

> in the third Five Year Plan we will see what you [the Tibetans] think; if you say [there should be] reform, then [we'll introduce] reform; if you say no reform, then we will continue not to reform. Why [do we have to be in] such a hurry?[98]

The speech confirmed the assurance given by Zhou Enlai to the Dalai Lama that the reforms in Tibet would be postponed for five years. Mao's speech also reveals the extent to which the Tibetan issue irritated the Chinese leadership. While in the earlier speeches Mao seemed to have been unruffled by the Dalai Lama's refusal to return to Lhasa,[99] here he moved towards admitting that they had made mistakes and had been forced to alter their policies because of the Dalai Lama's threat to remain in exile. Mao blamed the problems of Tibet on 'Han Chauvinism'.

Although Mao said that the Dalai Lama had returned to Tibetan territory, he was still in India when the speech was made.[100] It was Zhou's renowned charm and persuasiveness which convinced him that the Chinese would keep their promise.[101] In the Dalai Lama's talks with Nehru, the Indian leader had made it clear that no help would be forthcoming from his country. In these circumstances it was evident that little positive advantage could be gained by staying in India. The decision to return to Tibet was endorsed by the Nechung and Gadong oracles, who pronounced in favour of the Dalai Lama returning to Tibet.

To the great relief of the Chinese, the Dalai Lama returned to Tibet at the beginning of March 1957. The only people who stayed behind were those who had decided to remain in India in 1951. The Dalai Lama's party arrived at Gyantse in time to celebrate the Tibetan new year, when thousands of people flocked to welcome him. On 6 March, the Dalai Lama arrived in Shigatse where he was also welcomed by an enthusiastic crowd.

The Dalai Lama found that the situation in Tibet had deteriorated. Hundreds of refugees from Kham had arrived in Lhasa and were camping in the vicinity. They brought more news of the destruction of monasteries. On the surface, however, the Dalai Lama's relationship with the Chinese improved. Chinese officials in Tibet told the Kashag that 'they understood that the people were getting anxious about the proposals for reform' and insisted that they 'did not want to disregard the people's wishes'.[102] This conciliatory attitude was noticeable when Zhang Guohua announced, in a speech at the celebration of the first anniversary of the establishment of PCART: 'the Tibetan people, like other fraternal nationalities, must take the road to socialism. Only by doing this can the Tibetan people achieve a high degree of political, economic and cultural development. Only by doing this can the Tibetan people forever shake off poverty and the state of backwardness.'[103]

But he went on to admit that 'certain conditions are necessary to carry out peaceful reforms in the Tibetan area, such as the demand of the masses of people for reforms, and the support of personages of the upper strata.'[104] Zhang stated that since the 'democratic reforms' would not be carried out, various departments set up to carry out the reforms would be reorganised and that 'Han [Chinese] nationality who came to help to prepare for democratic reforms in Tibet must also be transferred to other areas of the Fatherland to take part in socialist construction'.[105] The Communists' admission that the social conditions in Tibet were not ripe for socialist reforms meant that they had to develop new strategies for the long-term integration of Tibet into China.

The Communists' reluctance to proceed with reforms was to a certain extent a product of internal Party conflicts and difficulties which were emerging in China. In August 1957, the reorganisation of PCART was declared. Many of the original departments were abolished and a simplified administrative structure was introduced. It was announced that 90 per cent of cadres working for PCART would be Tibetans and that only a small number of Chinese cadres would be retained.[106] The postponement of the reforms was not only the result of popular resentment that the Communists faced in Tibet: by 1957 China had lost some of its initial revolutionary fervour and had to face the hard reality of a failing economy. In April 1956 the first air link between Tibet and China was inaugurated; by this time, considerable progress had been made in road building. However, the soaring cost of building basic infrastructure in Tibet was impinging on the Chinese economy and there was great pressure on the Tibet Work Committee to economise. The Party Committee on communication systems announced that various work units must cut expenditure and told some work units to reduce telegram traffic by 50 per cent.[107]

The Dalai Lama began to make cautious criticisms of the Chinese policy. 'The decisions made by the PCART were found to be unfeasible because they were at variance with the concrete conditions in Tibet; mistakes of various categories had been due to the unsound organisation of organs concerned', he said, adding that 'some newly arrived cadres of Han nationality, who were ignorant of conditions in Tibet, paid no respect to local customs and usage'.[108] It was a criticism shared by most Tibetans: a popular protest sung in the streets of Lhasa reflected the mood of the people:

> We would rather have the Dalai Lama than Mao Tse-tung
> We would rather have the Kashag than the *Uyon Lhen Khang* [PCART]
> We would rather have Buddhism than Communism
> We would rather have *Ten sung Mag mi*[109] than the PLA
> We would rather use our own wooden bowls than Chinese mugs.

However, the Chinese promise to halt reform did help to prevent unrest for a time. The Chinese encouraged leading Tibetan officials to visit areas containing resistance groups and encourage them to surrender to the PLA. After returning from India, Ngabo was asked to go to Chamdo and help the Chinese stop unrest spreading into central Tibet. Other leading Tibetans like Gyalwa Karmapa, the head of the Karma Kargyu school of Tibetan Buddhism, were encouraged to tour eastern Tibet and urge the resistance groups to stop fighting. A Khampa resistance fighter, Gyakhar Gonpo Namgyal from Derge, remembers that they received numerous appeals from Tibetan leaders to surrender to the Chinese and eventually received a letter from the Dalai Lama urging them to meet with the Chinese to reach a peaceful agreement. Such letters were sent to all areas where Khampas had not surrendered, and they had the intended effect. Since the letter was a command from the Dalai Lama, many fighters agreed to surrender to the Chinese.

> The tone of the letter was very desperate and, while we were discussing what to do, the people told us that we could never reach an arrangement with the Chinese and pleaded with us not to go. In the end, however, it was decided that 23 leaders (including myself and assistants) should go. Thus, accompanied by 100 armed men on horse we came to Jomda Dzong. The Chinese welcomed us with a big banquet.[110]

The group was met by Wang Qinmei, the head of the Chamdo Liberation Committee. He told the resistance fighters that 'the Central Government had decided to forgive and forget [these] past mistakes'.[111]

Primarily because of the revolt, the Chinese were forced to rethink their policies towards 'minority nationalities' not only in Tibet, but also in all areas occupied by the 'minorities'. It was recognised that the reforms would only succeed 'if minorities genuinely desired reforms and were able to implement these reforms themselves'.[112] The Chinese blamed 'Great Han Chauvinism' for the failure of the reforms. They were forced to postpone the introduction of reforms,

The Chinese promise of 'no reform' only applied to areas under the control of the Tibetan Government, but they were willing to slow down the pace of the reforms in eastern Tibet, because they were worried about the growing number of refugees from Kham and Amdo arriving in central Tibet. The Communists, who could no longer believe that the revolt was caused by a small minority of 'reactionaries', now had to divert people's fears and win them over. Andrug Gonbo Tashi, a wealthy trader from Lithang living in Lhasa, wrote that the Tibetan Communist Baba Phuntsog Wangyal called a meeting in Lhasa to persuade Khampas to return to their homes. He told the Khampas that they had misunderstood the motives of the reforms.[113]

While the Chinese were to some extent able to win the support of the local leaders in areas under the jurisdiction of the Dalai Lama, they were faced with a very different situation in Kham and Amdo. Once the destruction of monasteries had taken place in various parts of eastern Tibet, there was very little the Chinese could do to win back the support, nor could the traditional leaders continue to acquiesce in Chinese actions. Therefore, the Chinese could no longer prevent the revolt spreading into central Tibet.

SIX

The Revolt

By the middle of 1957, the Khampas were desperate for arms and were faced with pressure from the PLA forces. They had no alternative but to leave Kham and seek safety in central Tibet. Thousands of Khampas poured in disguised as pilgrims. Neither the Dalai Lama nor the Tibetan Government was willing to support the Khampa revolt because they feared the Chinese would adopt more forceful measures in central Tibet.

Many Khampas felt that the failure of the Dalai Lama and the Tibetan Government to aid the Khampas was a great setback. Although Tibet was not in any position to provide effective military or political support, the Dalai Lama and other religious leaders could have given moral support to the revolt. Michel Peissel, a French writer sympathetic to the Khampas' cause, wrote: 'a word from the Dalai Lama, one single proclamation, and all Tibet would undoubtedly have stood up and faced the Chinese'.[1] However, it would have been misleading of the Dalai Lama to have encouraged the people to revolt, when the Tibetan Government was not in a position to provide any realistic aid. Moreover, despite cultural and religious affinity, the Lhasa regime clearly regarded the events in eastern Tibet as outside their jurisdiction. Some Khampas were aware of the Tibetan Government's predicament. Andrug Gonbo Tashi, who later organised the main Khampa resistance group, writes 'the Tibetan Government was in an awkward position. Although they sympathised with us, as did the people, no doubt, they were hamstrung and unable to help us. To do so would have been an unequivocal invitation to the Chinese to introduce the intolerable measures that central Tibet had been so far spared, but which then existed in eastern Tibet. The Kashag fully realised the gravity of the situation and so did we.'[2] It was left to the Khampa and Amdo traders living in Lhasa to gather support for their compatriots who were fighting the Chinese.

But the resistance did not fade. While the PLA were able to secure a hold in most parts of Kham and Amdo, the resistance fighters fled to the mountains. Once in central Tibet, the Khampas were faced with enormous hardship, besides the loss of family and friends back home. And at first they were met with, at best, indifference and, at worst, hostility from the people in central Tibet.

The Chinese also faced protests from a very different group of people. In

May 1957 the Chinese told the many Tibetan students studying in China that they could return home.[3] It had been planned that the Tibetan students would undergo rapid training in China and then return to form the bulk of the cadres, but once the reforms were postponed indefinitely, there was no urgent need for trained Tibetan cadres. These students were to become one of the centres of protest against the Chinese.

Mao had just launched his Hundred Flowers Campaign. For five weeks (from 1 May to 7 June 1957) the Chinese intellectuals and cadres were authorised by Mao to voice their grievances against the CCP. Although the campaign was not officially launched in Tibet, members of minority areas were actively encouraged to participate, including many Tibetan students in Beijing and other parts of China. Ngawang Dhondup, then a Tibetan student at the Minority Institute in Beijing, recalls that the students were encouraged to speak freely. Under the guise of the Hundred Flowers Campaign, and drawing their inspiration from Mao's speech 'On the Correct Handling of Contradictions Among the People', Tibetan students put up posters denouncing the 17 Point Agreement, with some arguing that the setting up of PCART had undermined the authority of the Dalai Lama. The students at the Minority Institute were drawn from members of the Tibetan aristocracy. When the Chinese lecturers taught that Tibet was a part of China, the students argued that the Chinese had distorted the historical relationship between the two countries. At one meeting Tibetan students criticised Zhou Enlai, who had said that Tibetans should follow the Manchus and adopt Chinese culture.[4]

At the institute, a clandestine group calling itself Tsen gol (*bstan-rgol*)[5] was set up by some students. The group put up posters demanding the restoration of the Dalai Lama. Although the group was confined mainly to the Beijing Minority Institute, the Chinese suspected that Tibetan students in other colleges or institutions were involved. Yet for most other Tibetan students the first they heard of the group was when the Chinese called a meeting and told them that there were reactionary separatist groups who did not want reform to take place and opposed socialism. When the Hundred Flowers movement was crushed, the Tibetan students had shifted their campaign to Tibet. This was a serious concern for the Chinese, who had envisaged that the returning students would become the vanguard of the reforms and the first batch of indigenous cadres.

Despite the universal resentment against the Chinese, there was an absence of violent confrontation in central Tibet. The Khampas were exhausted and bewildered by their own predicament. The Chinese were prepared for the time being to watch and not to take any action against the Khampa refugees. The lull in the fighting provided the Khampas with time to rethink their strategies and regroup themselves. Although the revolt had the support of all sections of the Khampa community, it lacked a single leadership and cohesive organisation.

The Founding of 'Four Rivers, Six Ranges'

By May 1957, Tibetans were psychologically and politically disturbed by the worsening situation. There was a belief that Tibet was going through a period of 'degeneration', and in the eyes of many Tibetans this was confirmed by a number of natural calamities that struck at the time. On the eve of the Chinese invasion of Chamdo, there was an earthquake; in 1954 there was a flood in Gyantse causing hundreds of deaths and destruction of property. Many people reported incidents which were considered bad omens. These signs were interpreted as a warning that the teaching of Buddha would be vanquished in Tibet. It was believed that the status of the Dalai Lama and the fortunes of the Tibetan people could be safeguarded by performing the appropriate rituals. A group of wealthy Khampa traders living in Lhasa initiated a performance of rituals for the long life of the Dalai Lama.[6] It involved an offering of a golden throne. Angdrug Gonbo Tashi organised a group of people to travel to all parts of Tibet to collect contributions from the people.[7]

Although one may dismiss this as a futile gesture, and anachronistic in the twentieth century, it goes to the heart of the Tibetan belief system and to the way in which they saw the political developments around them. As mentioned earlier, the general population was excluded from higher politics and there was no forum for the masses to express their political grievances. Any popular grassroots movement was looked on with suspicion and distrust by the Tibetan Government and, of course, by the Chinese. But the Chinese could not prevent the masses assembling for religious purposes, and the Tibetan Government naturally had no alternative but to support them. In his memoirs, Andrug implies that the idea of offering the golden throne was motivated primarily by the desire to organise a clandestine resistance movement, but this may have been a consequence rather than a motivation. It is more likely that religious conviction initially prompted the action.

The ceremony had serious political and social implications. For the first time all Tibetan people were united in common purpose and shared values, which helped to identify the common enemy. The Chinese were labelled Tendra (*brtan dgra*) 'the enemy of the faith', and the Khampa resistance groups were seen as the '*fidei defensor*'. On 4th July 1957 a ceremony was held in the Norbulingka, the summer palace of the Dalai Lama, to offer him the golden throne.[8] It was an affirmation of the Tibetan people's faith in the Dalai Lama and, more significantly, a symbolic defiance of the alternative system and reforms instigated by the Chinese. This was understood by the people themselves: 'It expressed the people's loyalty and confidence in the Dalai Lama's leadership and confirmed his earthly sovereign powers.'[9]

The organisation which was set up to collect donations and supervise the construction of the throne became the focus of the resistance movement. The main instigator, Gonbo Tashi, was to become the leader: he had wealth and commanded the loyalty of many Khampas, particularly people from Lithang. His attempts to organise resistance groups attracted little interest from Lhasa officials, however. Phala remembers Gonbo Tashi coming to see him riding one of the few motor bikes in Lhasa, and often in an intoxicated state, to discuss his plans. Phala gave some words of encouragement and then dismissed him.[10] He knew that he was not in a position to provide any effective support.

Since the Chinese were not able to control the ever increasing number of Khampa refugees coming into central Tibet, the Tibetan Government could pretend the revolt was a purely local affair. At first both the Chinese and the Tibetan Governments were apprehensive about the consequences of the influx of refugees. It presented political and social problems. Later the Chinese would claim that there was a co-ordinated conspiracy between Lhasa officials and the Khampas to launch a rebellion.[11] In fact, as noted earlier, the Tibetan Government had encouraged the Khampas to co-operate with the Chinese reforms. All the evidence suggests that the Khampa revolt was not instigated by either the Lhasa officials or external agents (Guomindang or the Americans), but purely a reaction against the reforms.

By late 1957, Khampa resistance could not be regarded merely as an uprising by a few reactionary landlords – it had become a nationwide rebellion. Different groups had discarded their traditional feuds and enmities and were united in their opposition to the Chinese. The Communists, no longer able to win over the people by appeasement, waged a full scale war against the Khampas: Tibet was seen as a crucial test for the policy of integrating 'national minorities' within the framework of the new China. By the beginning of 1958, more than 15,000 families had sought refuge in Lhasa and the surrounding areas.[12]

The Chinese were faced with a dilemma as to whether to extend military actions into central Tibet to expunge the Khampa rebels. They feared that such action might ignite an uprising in central Tibet, while not taking steps to curtail the activities of the Khampas might encourage the rest of Tibet to join the rebellion. The Chinese had to restrain their policies in central Tibet because of the 17-Point Agreement, and they had also recently assured the Dalai Lama that no reforms would take place. The Khampa issue was beginning to dominate the relationship between the Lhasa Government and the Chinese. As we have seen already, Lhasa officials showed very little sympathy for the plight of the Khampas and were keen to avoid any confrontation with the Chinese over the issue. The Tibetan Government agreed to deport a few hundred Chinese nationalists and Khampas who had sought refuge in Lhasa.[13] This caused great alarm among the Khampas, who believed that sooner or later the Tibetan Government would be forced to expel them. Many Khampas began to move south-east towards Lhokha. There were also practical reasons for the exodus. Inevitably Lhasa could not support the influx of refugees and, as it became ever more difficult to obtain provisions, friction arose between the Lhasa people and the Khampas. Moreover, the Khampa leaders were under strict surveillance, making it impossible to meet freely. Lhokha would provide easy access to India for escape and supply routes.

The gathering in Lhokha marked the birth of a pan-Khampa resistance movement called *Chu-zhi Gang-drung* (Four Rivers, Six Ranges).[14] It was symbolic that the group adopted the ancient name for Kham, which encompassed all the ethnic groups in the area.[15] With the imminent threat of expulsion, it was agreed that the main discussions would take place in a safe area.

The growing opposition to the reforms in eastern Tibet and other areas forced the CCP to review its policy towards minority areas. In May 1957 the CCP held a special meeting of the Nationalities Affairs Commission,[16] where Liu Chu, the Vice-Chairman, announced the formal launch of a Rectification Campaign among Chinese cadres working in minority areas.[17] The Rectification and Hundred Flowers campaigns brought to the fore debate among the CCP members over the reason for the failure of the reforms in Tibet and other minority areas.

Speeches of leading cadres in Tibet and other areas made it clear that there were those who blamed 'Great Hanism'. They argued that Chinese cadres working in Tibet (and other minority areas) had failed to win over the masses because they held the view that the 'Han [Chinese] nationality is superior in everything and that the minority nationalities are backward in all things'.[18] Fan Ming, the Deputy Secretary of the CCP Tibet Work Committee, told a meeting that 'Great Han Chauvinism in Tibet is manifested in the feeling of superiority of the Han race, repugnance towards the backwardness of Tibet, discrimination against Tibet, distortion of Tibet, failure to respect the freedom of religious belief and the traditional customs of the Tibetans'.[19] Such views, he said, had become prevalent among the PLA and other officials who had become 'conceited and arrogant, and cherished the thought of having special privileges'.[20]

Although Fan Ming also criticised 'local nationalism', he placed greater blame on Han chauvinism. He likened Han chauvinism to a spear and local nationalism to a shield. It was necessary that 'the one who held the spear must lay it down before the one who carried the shield was required to lay down his weapon,' he observed.[21] Fan Ming was one of the few cadres belonging to North-West Military Region. All other senior Chinese officials were from the South-West Military Region, and they interpreted the criticism as a politically motivated attack on them. (Ever since the PLA's entry into Tibet there had been rivalry between the two groups.)

As Tibetan opposition continued, those who emphasised 'Han chauvinism' became the victims of the Anti-Rightist Rectification Campaign. It was announced in Beijing that Rightists had allowed local nationalism to flourish unimpeded by claiming that overcoming Great Hanism would lead to local nationalism naturally fading away.[22] One of the Tibetan officials who became the victim of the anti-rightist purges was Baba Phuntsog Wangyal, who had been an interpreter during the 17-Point Agreement negotiations in Beijing. Phuntsog Wangyal was the only Tibetan who had a measure of status in the Communist Party. Not only did he have a competent knowledge of Chinese language but his ideological commitment to Communism enabled him to compete for positions with other Chinese cadres. Since his arrival in Tibet he had held the position of Director of the Propaganda Department of the 18th PLA Corps, stationed in Tibet. His removal lost Tibet the only Tibetan Communist who could have influenced the inner circles of the Communist Party. While in Tibet he occupied the unenviable position of trying to explain the Chinese position to the Tibetans and the Tibetan stance to the Communists. Although he was distrusted by many Tibetans, he became a close friend of the Dalai Lama, who requested that Mao appoint Phuntsog Wangyal local Party Secretary.[23] In the wake of the Khampa revolt Phuntsog Wangyal made a realistic suggestion to the Chinese, arguing that the Khampas could be placated if the Communists were to extend their 'no reforms' policy to eastern Tibet. Later, he suggested that all Tibetan areas should form a single autonomous region, which would require major constitutional and administrative changes.[24]

The Chinese officials working in Tibet were not prepared to accept any criticism of their work, arguing that they had achieved considerable success in bringing Tibet back into the 'bosom of the motherland'. Zhang Guohua and Zhang Jingwu felt that the criticisms were unjustifiable attacks on them. As the anti-Rightist campaign progressed and the Chinese were unable to quell the rebellion in eastern Tibet, the campaign against 'Great Han Chauvinism' was replaced by an attack on 'Local Nationalism', defined as an 'anti-socialist tendency undermining the unity of the motherland and opposing the socialist transformation'.[25] It was argued that the current problems were the result of allowing local nationalism to grow by saying that 'if there were no Great Hanism there would be no local nationalism'.[26]

In Tibet the anti-Rightist campaign was confined to CCP members and it did not alter the promise made by Mao that Tibet would not be forced to undergo reforms. However, it confirmed that the Communists were not willing to compromise their stance in eastern Tibet. They were not prepared to abandon their attempts to integrate and communise the Khampas. The CCP never took up Phuntsog Wangyal's suggestion. He was recalled to Beijing and became one of the few minority cadres who was purged.[27]

The Chinese decision not to make any concessions to the Khampas meant there was no possibility of reconciliation.[28] In March 1958, sixty prominent Khampa leaders and traders met clandestinely at Andrung's house in Lhasa to discuss the situation. Their first decision concerned whether to continue to reside in Lhasa. All the Khampas expressed a fear that the Tibetan Government would be forced to expel them. The leaders of different Khampa groups were receiving daily reports of the worsening situation in Kham. They felt helpless and frustrated by their inability to do anything. Some prominent lamas from Kham had already fled and settled in India and many Khampas were feeling dejected. It was crucial for morale that they should come up with a decisive plan.

The founding of the 'Four Rivers, Six Ranges' meant that the Chinese could no longer ignore the activities of the Khampas. They were alarmed by the gathering in Lhokha, where there were well over 15,000 men who looked a formidable challenge to the Chinese. The Khampas were organised into different regiments based on different regions, such as Lithang, Bathang, Gyalthang and Changtrengpa.[29] Andrug Gonbo Tashi was formally recognised as the leader of the organisation. It was a considerable achievement to unite the different factions. Despite overwhelming support from the people, the Khampas were badly equipped and there was no way that they could lead a sustained fight against the PLA. Volunteers had to bring their own weapons and provisions, and therefore most of the Khampas were unarmed. Loden, a young Khampa who joined the resistance movement, remembered that out of eighty people in his group only twenty possessed arms.[30] Even those who had arms had only a limited supply of ammunition. Therefore the success of the Khampas would depend on their capturing Chinese weapons.

The activities of the 'Four Rivers, Six Ranges' attracted the attention of the Tibetan *émigré* groups in Kalimpong, which was now the main centre for Tibetan opposition. By 1958, Gyalo Dhundup, Shakabpa, former Prime Minister Lukhangwa and Alo Chonzed (leader of Mimang Tsongdu) were joined by large groups of Khampas and a number of influential lamas from Kham. The news of the formation of the resistance group caused elation among the *émigrés*, who were to play a leading role in obtaining external support for the Four Rivers, Six Ranges.

The Chinese had always been concerned about the activities of the *émigrés*. They were also aware of the fact that some members of the group, particularly Shakabpa and Gyalo Dhundup, had developed contacts with the Americans. In the early fifties the Chinese instructed the Kashag to issue a notice that all Tibetan officials residing in India must return to Lhasa, but this was ignored by most people. From 1950 to 1954, the *émigrés* were prepared to accept the situation in Tibet as a *fait accompli* and there was no attempt to organise into any effective opposition group. But the revolt in eastern Tibet changed the situation. A number of the refugees arriving from Kham were recruited by Guomindang agents in Kalimpong. It appeared that the Guomindang was gaining a foothold in eastern Tibet and some of the Khampas went to Taiwan for training.[31] The Guomindang began to claim credit for the revolt in eastern Tibet.

Clandestine Support from America

The news of the Khampa revolt spurred American interest in Tibet. There were no signs of improvement in the relationship between the United States and China. In 1956 John Foster Dulles, the Secretary of State, announced that Communism in China was a 'passing phase' and that the Americans would 'do all that we can to contribute to that passing'. America's China policy was directed towards maintaining the Guomindang regime in Taiwan. Between 1954 and 1958 the USA was engaged in what was described as a 'pinprick war' against China using Nationalist forces. It had no serious impact on China other than to enrage the Communists.[32] The Chinese counter-attacked with the bombing of Quemoy Island and the tension between the Americans and the PRC was further increased with the US deployment of the 7th Fleet in the Taiwan Straits.

This period also saw America's adoption of covert methods to realise its foreign (and diplomatic) objectives. In December 1955 President Eisenhower authorised the CIA to develop secret activities to undermine 'international communism', which resulted in the establishment of underground, resistance and guerrilla groups.[33] Under the tutelage of Allen Dulles, the fifties were 'glory years' for the CIA. While John Foster Dulles led the diplomatic initiatives to contain China, his brother was planning clandestine operations in Tibet.[34]

News of the Khampa revolt came at an opportune time for the US. The Tibetan issue had propaganda appeal in the era of the Cold War: the Chinese actions were seen as evidence of the Communists' desire for world domination. Tibet was presented as a small nation fighting for the survival of its culture and way of life. It is unlikely that the US regarded Tibet as strategically important. However, if the Khampa revolt was successful, it would cause immense difficulties for the Chinese. The US objective was to destabilise the country, and it was for this reason that it abandoned diplomatic initiatives in favour of covert activities.

Accounts of CIA involvement in Tibet are often sensational and exaggerate the role of the CIA in the flight of the Dalai Lama from Lhasa.[35]

CIA activities remained on the periphery of Tibetan political concern. Although Chinese fear of US intervention was an important factor in the Chinese perception of the situation, it must be seen in the light of the bipolar division of the world and the rhetoric of the time. It does not matter whether the CIA parachuted in a few agents or sent an entire regiment: from the Chinese point of view the American involvement in Tibet transformed the entire situation. It was no longer a question of revolt by some troublesome Tibetans but an international conspiracy to undermine the victory of the Communist Party in China. Moreover, it presented a direct threat to China's security. This may explain the ferocity of Chinese suppression of the Tibetan revolt.

Since 1951 the Americans had maintained close contact with the Dalai Lama's brothers. Thubten Norbu had been in America for nearly five years and his younger brother, Gyalo Dhundup, had been organising the Tibetan *émigrés* in India. The Americans were not certain how much support the *émigré* group had from the Dalai Lama, and experience had shown that the *émigrés* did not have much influence over him: in 1956 they had been unable to persuade the Dalai Lama to remain in India. It appears that the brothers, in order to disguise their lack of influence, may have told the CIA that they were prevented from meeting him by the Indian authorities.[36] However, the Americans had shifted their position and now sought to establish covert activities, with or without the Dalai Lama's blessing. It was therefore unimportant whether the Dalai Lama's brothers and other *émigrés* had influence over the Tibetan Government. What they needed was a small group of dedicated people who were willing to work inside Tibet.

The arrival of Thubten Norbu in India in 1956 marked the first phase of CIA involvement. It appears that he came to India with a proposal from the CIA to establish a clandestine network of activists inside Tibet.[37] Takla, a senior member of the Dalai Lama's family, does not recall these plans being revealed to members of the Kashag or to the Dalai Lama. It is likely that the Americans did not want them to be known, as their experience had shown that the Tibetans tended to choose the side of caution rather than incur the wrath of the Chinese. But Takla thinks that the plan may have been revealed to Phala, who later became the main contact inside Tibet. The promise of American support appealed to the Tibetan *émigré* group, known as the Dedon Tsogpa, since their credibility inside Tibet depended on being able to obtain external material support. While Thubten Norbu liaised with the CIA, it was left to his brother Gyalo Dhundup and to the Dedon Tsogpa to recruit volunteers to work inside Tibet.

Athar, one of the first Khampas to be recruited for training by the CIA, remembers that just before the Dalai Lama came to India for the Buddha Jayanti celebration, a group of twenty-six young Khampas had been contacted by Guomindang agents with the offer of guerrilla training in

Taiwan. They had readily accepted and were preparing to leave India. When Dedon Tsogpa learned of the plan it sent Gyalo Dhundup to visit the recruits. He told them that he had managed to secure US backing and advised them that it would be better to go to America than to Taiwan which, he said, was not in any position to provide assistance. Athar recalls that the Khampas were elated by the news that the US was prepared to provide aid. They all knew that America was 'the most powerful nation' in the world. To the dismay of the Guomindang agents, the Taiwan plan was aborted. The Khampa recruits travelled to Bodh Gaya, where the Dalai Lama was on a pilgrimage. They were met by Thubten Norbu, who took photos and details of each member of the group.[38] In March 1957 Thubten Norbu returned to the US. Shortly afterwards, Athar remembers that six of them were selected for training. The first six recruits were (1) Lithang Athar Norbu himself, (2) Lotse, (3) Gyathotsang Wangdu, (4) Dharlo, (5) Tsewang Dorji and (6) Baba Changtra Tashi. They were called to a house in Kalimpong, where Gyalo Dhundup and Khenchung Lobsang Gyaltsen gave them advice (*slob gso*) and told them that they should keep their mission secret and not even tell their families.

On the night of 21 March 1957 the Khampas slipped out of Kalimpong. Gyalo Dhundup drove them to the Indo–Pakistan border. The Khampas crossed the Siliguri river into East Pakistan (present-day Bangladesh), where they were met by Dhondup Gyaltsen, the personal servant of Thubten Norbu. He had been in America since 1951 and had acquired enough English to act as a translator. The Khampas were officially met by Pakistani army officers and were then flown to a secret American military base on the Pacific island of Saipan (the Khampas had no idea where they were). During the training Thubten Norbu also acted as a translator. They were taught English, and their military training consisted mainly of learning how to use a wireless, to map read and how to organise guerrilla groups.[39] During the training Athar remembers that they were told by the Americans that they regarded the Khampas as no more than a rebel group. The signing of the 17-Point Agreement and the subsequent participation of the Dalai Lama and Tibetan Government officials in the Chinese National People's Congress had, according to the Americans, effectively ended Tibetan independence. Furthermore, until the Dalai Lama made a personal appeal to the United States Government for formal assistance they would not be able to aid them officially. The Khampa recruits retorted that they were separate from the Tibetan Government in Lhasa, and that they had not signed any agreement with the Chinese. When the time came for them to be parachuted back into Tibet, the Khampas learned that they were going to be dropped into central Tibet and insisted that they should be dropped in their home country, adding that they did not know anyone in Lhasa who would be willing to help them. Later, Thubten Norbu had to intervene and persuade them of the need to obtain the co-operation and blessing of the Dalai Lama.[40] Only then did the Khampas agree to go to Lhasa.

The attitude of the Khampas is crucial to the understanding of subsequent developments. The Khampas were primarily concerned about the reforms carried out in their homeland. They felt that the problems of the Lhasa Government were nothing to do with them. Their separatist viewpoint was shared by the Tibetan Government, which did not concern itself with the events in eastern Tibet. Although the Khampas were united in their opposition to the reforms, they lacked coherent organisation or leadership. A great many people expressed their readiness to fight the Chinese, but they were doing it for the defence of their locality, their monasteries, and their lamas. The Khampas did not have a shared concept of fighting for a country. It was only after the establishment of 'Four Rivers, Six Ranges' that the Khampas began to form a united and effective opposition to the Chinese. Not only was it a military challenge, it also marked an important stage in the formation of pan-Khampa identity.

The Chinese knew that the Khampas were gathering force and organising guerrilla groups. The rebels' original plan was to organise themselves in central Tibet and later move towards their homeland to wage guerrilla war against the Communists. However unrealistic it may have been, the nationwide revolt in Kham and Amdo had an enormous de-stabilising effect in the region and by the late fifties the Communists had lost any social base for their rule in the area, so that the guerrillas could have gained universal support from the local people. But they were never able to extend their activities beyond central Tibet.

While the activities of the 'Four Rivers, Six Ranges' were confined to central Tibet the Chinese observed caution and did not use the PLA in putting down the revolt. Instead, the Chinese put the onus on the Kashag to control the activities of the Khampas. This placed an enormous burden on the Kashag. Khatsab (Acting Kalon) Shasur, a senior member of the Kashag, likened the Kashag to a *dar-ma-ru*, a small double-sided hand-held drum used by monks for ritual, which is beaten from both sides. The Chinese proposed that either the Tibetan Government should expel the Khampas or the PLA would be used to eliminate the Khampa insurgency.[41]

The Kashag had a major problem on its hands. There was a faction which felt that the activities of the Khampas were putting the Tibetan polity in danger and that the Tibetan Government should use force to expel them. This faction believed that, in the past, the Tibetan Government had not exercised any authority over Kham and that the Khampas should be handed over to the Chinese. There was also some resentment towards the Khampas from the local population; many Tibetan villagers felt intimidated by them. The relationship between Khampas and local people had begun to deteriorate. This was fuelled by the traditional prejudice against the

Khampas. For many people in *U-tsang* (central Tibet), the Khampas were considered to be bandits (*jag-pa*) and were more of problem than the Chinese, especially since a severe shortage of provisions had forced the Khampas to take food from villagers. Some villages in Lhokha sent a petition to the Kashag complaining that they had been harassed by the Khampas[42]

The Chinese encouraged the Dalai Lama to issue orders to the Khampas to disband. They accused 'reactionary elements' in the Tibetan Government of instigating the Khampa revolt. The Tibetans retorted that the revolt had started in areas under Chinese control and it was their responsibility to prevent it from spreading into central Tibet. They argued that the area of Chamdo affected by the revolt had been under the direct administration of the Chamdo Liberation Committee, and demanded that the CLC be disbanded and placed under the control of the Lhasa government.

By late 1957, the Khampas started to attack Chinese garrisons and cadres working on road construction sites. The Chinese started to arm their cadres and brought a small number of PLA troops in to guard the major roads. The Chinese had to decide whether to launch a full-scale military operation to eliminate the Khampas, which they could easily have done. For the Chinese the priority remained the winning-over of the Dalai Lama and the Tibetan Government. Despite considerable progress in establishing their rule, they were still faced with opposition and on no account could claim the support of the vast majority of the Tibetans, who saw themselves as a separate group and looked towards the traditional leadership as the legitimate government of the land.

The Chinese worried that if the Khampa revolt spread further and managed to achieve some success, it would provide an opportunity for third-party intervention. This fear was to become a reality in December 1957,[43] when a plane took off from East Pakistan with the six Khampas on board. The first flight had to be aborted because of the weather, but finally, on 7 December 1957, two Khampas, Athar and Lotse, were dropped near Samye, Tibet's oldest monastery. The plane then flew towards Kham to drop another four Khampas, but once again the drop had to be aborted because of the weather. A few days later the plane again flew over Lithang, but this time, disaster struck. Changtra Tashi, who was specially trained as a radio operator, lost his nerve and refused to jump. Later, Tashi had to enter Tibet overland, and he was never able to make contact with the others. In the end only three people were parachuted into Lithang, where fighting was taking place.

Wangdu and others found that most of Kham was in revolt and a large Khampa militia force had gathered in the Lithang region. He immediately radioed the Americans, informing them that there was an open revolt against the Chinese and that the majority of the Khampas were actively engaged in fighting the PLA. More than 50,000 men were involved in the fighting, Wangdu reported, requesting that the CIA make an arms drop. To Wangdu's dismay, the CIA refused to believe his report – apparently dismissing it as an exaggeration. Wangdu's trainers did not think highly of him: during training sessions he had not performed well and was regarded as a bit of maverick. More important, they could not envisage simple Tibetan tribesmen challenging the PLA in such a great numbers. The request for arms was refused. The Khampas were left to their own devices.

Later, one of the CIA-trained Khampas was captured by the PLA. It was most likely that the Chinese were able to extract a confession from him and learn of the American project. It appears that the Chinese also learned about the Dalai Lama's brothers' involvement. About this time the Chinese instructed the Dalai Lama and the Tibetan Government to issue a public notice denouncing the activities of Tibetan *émigré* groups in India.[44]

Athar and Lotse's drop was more successful. They had been instructed not to make any contact or to proceed to Lhasa. They had to hide for nearly two months in case the Chinese had monitored the plane's flight over Tibet, and were on the lookout for new arrivals in Lhasa. Their first task was to make a detailed study of the conditions of the airport at Damshung (the first airport in Tibet), sixty miles north-west of Lhasa. Athar and Lotse camped some distance from the airport disguised as pilgrims and observed activity there for several days. They made daily reports to the CIA. While they were watching the airport no planes landed, and they were able to report that the airport did not have any complex radar systems. Later on Athar and Lotse were instructed to proceed to Lhasa.[45]

Athar and Lotse's mission was to meet with the Dalai Lama and the Tibetan Government to ascertain their plans for the future. They were also to report on the conditions and military needs of the main Khampa resistance groups. At the end of February 1958, Lhasa was in a festive mood for the celebration of the Tibetan new year, with many pilgrims flocking into Lhasa. Disguised as monks, Atha and Lotse entered the city and made contact with Gonbo Tashi (the leader of Four Rivers, Six Ranges) whom they knew well. He was fully informed about the CIA involvement. Athar remembers that, while they were in training, they received a message of encouragement from Gonbo Tashi. It was most likely that he had been kept informed by Gyalo Dhundup and others from Kalimpong.

Athar and Lotse were dispatched to convince the Tibetan Government that the US was once again willing to provide aid and establish direct contact with Lhasa. The Americans found they were hampered by their lack of access to the Dalai Lama and people in power in Lhasa. It was clear that the Americans did not trust the ability of Shakabpa, Gyalo Dhundup and Thubten Norbu to influence events inside Tibet.

Earlier Phala remembers that he received a message from Shakabpa in

Kalimpong in 1957, which requested that the Tibetan Government send to India 'a person of the highest rank' so that they could negotiate with foreign governments. Since Shakabpa and other *émigrés* in India were acting purely in an individual capacity, the foreign governments (the Americans) did not have faith in them.[46]

It was clear by then that the Kashag was not in a position to meet such a request and still held to the belief that it could avoid confrontation with the Chinese. Phala found himself in a difficult position: on the one hand he knew that the Kashag would not dare to expose itself to the accusation of colluding with foreign powers, and that it was anyhow unlikely that any senior member of the Kashag would agree to go to Kalimpong. On the other hand, the Americans would not deal with anyone other than a senior member of the Kashag. Phala took the matter into his own hands and did not forward Shakabpa's request to the Kashag. Nevertheless, Phala knew that there were some junior officials in the Tibetan Government who were keen to work outside Tibet. In late 1957, Phala asked two officials, Thubten Nyinche and Jampa Wangdu to go to Kalimpong to work with Shakabpa. But both Thubten Nyinche and Jampa Wangdu were low-ranking officials: they were hardly what Shakabpa was expecting. They did not have the power nor the status that would convince the Americans of the seriousness of the Tibetan Government's desire to oppose the Chinese. It may even have confirmed the Americans' suspicion that opposition to the Chinese was confined to a small group of Tibetan officials. The failure of Tibetans to send any high-ranking official to Kalimpong may have been one of the reasons for dispatching Athar and Lotse to Lhasa.

For the Chinese, the matter was becoming urgent. Khatsab Liushar recalls that, in March 1958, the Chinese asked for a meeting with the Kashag. Zhang Guohua and Tan Guansan attended the meeting and angrily accused the Kashag of making a serious mistake by relying on the Americans for help. The Communists had already defeated the Guomindang, they warned them. The Chinese mentioned that they knew of the secret radio communications based in Gamphel Utse, a small mountain peak near Lhasa. It was most likely that the Chinese had monitored Athar and Lotse's communications. The Kashag had not known of any radio contacts with foreign governments until that moment.

Soon after the Tibetan new year in 1958, Gonbo Tashi took Athar and Lotse to meet Phala, who was staying in the summer palace of the Dalai Lama. They requested a personal meeting with the Dalai Lama. Athar had been instructed by the CIA to meet with the Dalai Lama personally and establish whether he was prepared to make a direct appeal for assistance. Athar remembers that as soon as they mentioned that they had been sent by the Americans, Phala looked worried and said that it was too dangerous for them to be meeting, and certainly impossible to meet the Dalai Lama. He feared that such a meeting could not be kept secret because there were many Tibetans who were sympathetic to the Chinese. When Athar asked whether the Tibetan Government would make an appeal to the Americans, Phala said that the Kashag was terrified of the Chinese and would not take any action.[47]

Athar and Lotse met Phala again, but he still refused to allow them to meet the Dalai Lama. Later Phala refused to see them himself. It was dangerous for him to associate with them and he warned that the Chinese were aware of their radio communications. Their specific objective was to keep in close touch with Phala, but since he was unwilling to meet with them or provide information, he effectively ended the CIA's attempts to make direct contact with the Dalai Lama. Athar and Lotse were bewildered and frustrated. They could not reveal themselves, as they did not know, or could not trust, any other high-ranking Lhasa officials. They sent a message to Phala asking for instructions as to whether they should remain in Lhasa or join the 'Four Rivers, Six Ranges'. Phala advised them to join the Khampa resistance group, as there was nothing they could do in Lhasa. Athar and Lotse radioed the CIA and sought permission to leave Lhasa, but they got no reply.

At the end of May, Athar and Lotse set out for Lhokha with Gonbo Tashi. Their departure marked the end of the Americans' attempts to establish some form of legitimacy for their clandestine activities: their hope of obtaining the Dalai Lama's approval had come to nothing. Athar was indignant at Phala's refusal to make contact with the Americans and, like other Khampas, he was quick to condemn Lhasa officials of cowardice. Athar believes that, if the Tibetan Government had made a formal appeal for help, the Americans would have provided a great deal of aid.[48] The Khampas were faced with a shortage of arms and were desperately looking for extra provisions. The arms drops came only much later, when the Khampas were already retreating to India.

In Driguthang, Lhokha, on 16 June, the inaugural meeting of Four Rivers, Six Ranges, was held with pomp and ceremony. A new yellow flag with two crossed swords was unveiled as the standard of the resistance movement. Athar radioed the Americans about the inaugural meeting and strength of the resistance movement. This seems have encouraged the Americans in a belief that the resistance movement was beginning to organise itself into an effective anti-Chinese force inside Tibet.

Phala never told the Dalai Lama or the Kashag of the arrival of Athar and Lotse. Nor did he inform the Dalai Lama of American willingness to provide aid if he were to make a direct appeal. Phala says that he did not trust the Kashag. He feared that if the information was leaked, he would be in serious trouble with the Chinese. The Tibetans' refusal to meet the American request meant that the CIA had to change its policy. If the Dalai

Lama's government was unwilling to seek American aid, the Americans now were prepared to establish links to the Khampas.

The Americans were clearly aware of the revolt in eastern Tibet and they had welcomed the establishment of Four Rivers, Six Ranges. Now they turned to building up the group. Athar received a radio instruction recalling either himself or Lotse to Calcutta for a meeting. Athar decided to go because he spoke better English. In May, Athar, disguised as a vagabond, travelled to Darjeeling, where he made contact with Gyalo Dhundup and delivered letters he had brought from Gonbo Tashi, along with an appeal addressed to the Americans.[49]

Athar was accompanied to Calcutta by Lhamo Tsering, who had studied together with Gyalo Dhundup at an institution set up by the Guomindang to educate the élite members of minority groups. When the Communists captured Nanjing, the two had escaped to Hong Kong and made their way to India.[50] This was the first time Lhamo Tsering had come into contact with the CIA and led to him managing the entire CIA operation in Tibet until 1973. In Calcutta, Lhamo Tsering and Athar saw a high-ranking CIA agent. The meeting was arranged in classic spy story style, with dead letter drops and hidden messages for rendezvous. The American agent brought the radio messages that Athar had sent, which the Americans had been unable to decipher. Lhamo Tsering identified the agent as Mr Frank and noted that he spoke very good Chinese.[51] Athar and Lhamo remember that the meeting was dominated by three main subjects. First, the CIA agent bluntly told them that the Khampas would not be able to expel the Chinese and that the best plan would be for the Khampas to form underground guerrilla groups. Since the Four Rivers, Six Ranges organisation had already been established, the CIA had abandoned their attempts to contact the Tibetan Government and decided, at the highest level, to support the Khampa groups. Second, although the decision had been made to support them, the agent told them that they had reservations about the ability of the Khampas to wage a war against the PLA. Therefore, Mr Frank asked about the intentions of the Four Rivers, Six Ranges organisation, and what type of weapons they possessed. Third, he enquired about Gonbo Tashi's ability to lead the group. Athar gave a glowing account of him as a leader. It was most likely that Athar would have given an exaggerated account of Gonbo Tashi's accomplishment and ability: although Gonbo Tashi had the loyalty of the Khampas from Lithang – the largest group – many others' first loyalty was to their traditional leaders. The Americans must have had some doubts about Gonbo Tashi's knowledge of modern warfare when Athar handed to Mr Frank an appeal from Gonbo Tashi requesting a weapon which he had heard they had invented: a lethal mirror which could be shone onto the enemy, who would instantly burst into flames. Such fanciful requests did not increase America's confidence in the Khampas' ability to fight the PLA.

The CIA agent asked Athar to draft a detailed list of the arms needed by the Khampas. Athar's training meant he had sufficient knowledge of modern weaponry and was able to provide a realistic plan. He asked for more radio operators and trained personnel.[52]

The meeting in Calcutta was a turning point in American involvement in Tibetan affairs. According to Athar and Lhamo Tsering, the CIA had at that point made no commitment to supply arms to the Tibetans. Athar made his way back to Tibet at the end of July and joined Gonbo Tashi in Lhokha. In India, more Khampas were selected for training. By then Gonbo Tashi had based himself in Lhokha and reorganised Four Rivers, Six Ranges into a disciplined army, although 'a group of bandits went about robbing people of their animals and other property and often inflicted severe injuries on them.'[53] Gonbo Tashi realised that if the Khampas were to have any success, they needed a good relationship with the local population. The growing activities of the Khampas had placed the countryside in chaos, with the Chinese coming under constant attack. News of the success of Khampa attacks on Chinese garrisons shifted people's sympathies towards the Khampas and, by the beginning of 1959, a sizeable number of people from central Tibet had joined the Four Rivers, Six Ranges. Diwa Lang, a Tibetan official, remembers that a group of soldiers set out from Gyantse to join the Khampa group. At the same time there was an extensive anti-Chinese campaign being carried out all over Tibet. The last testament of the 13th Dalai Lama, which warned of the Communist threat to the Buddhist faith, was printed by Alo Chonzed in Kalimpong and widely distributed. Other anti-Communist literature was also printed. One of the most eminent Rinpoches from eastern Tibet, Zongzer Kyentse (then in exile in Sikkim) wrote a pamphlet on the destruction of Buddhism in Mongolia. This was smuggled into Tibet.[54]

Another success for the Khampas came soon after Athar returned from his meeting with the CIA officer in Calcutta. The Americans were sufficiently encouraged by Athar's reports to make small-scale arms drops to the Khampas. Athar and Lotse were instructed to find secure dropping zones and were able to report a number of successes over the PLA: in August 1958, Gonbo Tashi and his men had attacked PLA troops in Nyemo, an area south-east of Lhasa, killing 700 Chinese soldiers. Gonbo Tashi led his men further north and attacked the Chinese garrison based at Damshung airport and ransacked store houses. The Chinese were under great pressure from the Khampas, who moved freely by keeping to the mountains and moving rapidly on horseback.[55] Most of the remote areas, stretching from Chamdo in the east to the borders of India in the south, were under the control of Khampa resistance groups. The CIA were able to make two arms drops in this area, which shows the extent of the Khampas' control. The CIA's first arms drop into Tibet in July 1958 consisted mainly of ammunition and automatic rifles. Athar and Lotse took charge of these weapons and began distributing them to Khampa resistance fighters.[56]

The relationship between the Panchen Rinpoche and the Chinese began to come under strain. Many Khampas and Amdo people were followers of the Panchen Rinpoche, and Dongke Rinpoche, one of the most respected Rinpoches from Amdo, had sought refuge in Tashilhunpo; other followers had brought news of Communist repression in their homeland. Although the Panchen Rinpoche's entourage could not openly declare its support as its own position still very much depended on Chinese patronage, increasing numbers of his followers were joining the Khampa resistance groups. In fact, the Khampas and Amdowas had a closer relationship with Tashilhunpo than with the Lhasa Government. Chagtrag Sonam Choephel, a Tibetan government official, remembers that most Lhasa officials did not know many of the Khampa leaders and when they wanted to make contact with them they had to rely on Tashilhunpo officials to provide introductions.[57]

Appeasing the Chinese and Quelling the Khampa Revolt

The issue of the Khampas became a major obstacle between the Chinese and the Tibetans. In the past the Chinese had done their best to undermine the traditional Tibetan Government structure, yet now they wanted to place responsibility for quelling the Khampa revolt on the Tibetan Government, which had neither the confidence nor the resources to deal with the large groups of Khampas roaming the country. In August 1958 the Chinese presented an ultimatum demanding that the Tibetan Government find ways of getting rid of the Khampas. The government called a meeting of the National Assembly. It was the first time since the founding of PCART that such a meeting had been convened. In the past the Chinese had tried to stop such meetings, as they had been seen as an alternative to PCART and might become a forum for opposition groups. The agenda placed before the National Assembly was titled: 'The ways of quelling the Khampa revolt and calming the Central Government's mind'.[58]

The Chinese decision to allow the meeting to take place reflected the urgency of the situation. The meeting was unusual in many ways. It marked to some extent the revival of the traditional Tibetan polity. Normally the Kashag members did not attend the National Assembly but this time they were asked to attend. Ngabo refused, saying that since all the Khampas regarded him as pro-Chinese, there was not much point in him attending the meeting. He recommended therefore that Kalon Surkhang Wangchen Gelek should lead it.[59] More than seventy officials were present and everyone knew that they were faced with the crucial task of deciding whether to expel the Khampas, who had the admiration and support of many of them. Some were afraid that the Chinese would accuse them of being reactionaries and might exclude them from the various opportunities provided in the new system. Phala said that it was dangerous to speak freely at the meeting, since whatever one said would be reported outside. Later it was agreed that the discussions would remain secret.[60]

The Assembly was divided into a number of sub-committees and each group was asked to discuss how to deal with the Khampa situation and report back. Barshi, a junior official who attended the meeting, remembers that there was a clear divide between the more senior and the junior officials. He himself made a passionate appeal for the Khampas but was rebuked by Tsipon Tsechog who said that it was easy for a junior official to make such a statement since he did not have to confront the Kashag or the Chinese.[61] Lhawutara, a high-ranking monk official and one of the signatories to the 17-Point Agreement, claims he suggested that since the Chinese wanted the Tibetan Government to expel the Khampas, the Chinese should allow the Tibetans to increase their army and should provide them with arms. Later, this was taken up by the National Assembly.[62] It was a clever move on the part of the Tibetans. The Chinese knew very well that the Tibetan army was not in any position to confront the Khampas but were aware that if the Tibetans were allowed to increase their army, there was a danger that it might be used to challenge the PLA. A decision not to allow the Tibetans to increase their army would justify the Tibetans' refusal to expel the Khampas. Both the Chinese and the Tibetans were conscious that whoever used force to crush the Khampas would be unpopular. The Tibetans feared that the Chinese insistence that the Tibetan army should be used to expel the Khampas was a ploy to instigate civil war (*nang-khrugs)* between the Khampas and the people in central Tibet.[63]

The Tibetans hoped that the Khampa revolt might persuade the Chinese to withdraw and allow Tibetans to reassert some authority. The Chinese, on the other hand, knew that any compromise would be seen as a sign of weakness which might intensify the Khampa revolt. Thus, from the middle of 1958 until the Lhasa uprising in March 1959, there existed a peculiar situation, in which neither the traditional Tibetan Government nor the Chinese had much control over the course of events in Tibet. The Chinese were under increasing pressure from the Khampas. The main body of the 'Four Rivers, Six Ranges' had moved further east, into areas under the control of the Chamdo Liberation Committee. Here the Khampas scored many successes and the Chinese work units came under constant attack; large numbers of PLA were deployed to protect the main supply routes. The Chinese were unable to contain the fighting within the area under CLC jurisdiction and the Khampa resistance fighters were now able to cover territory stretching from the eastern and south-eastern routes leading into India. The Chinese were desperate to eliminate the Khampas.

In early 1959 the Tibetan Government had another reason for wishing to achieve some stability in the country. After many years of studying Buddhist philosophy, the Dalai Lama was to undergo his final public examination at Drepung monastery, an event which would coincide with the great Monlam Chenmo, the festival which in the past had been a focal point for anti-Chinese agitation. Earlier, the abbots of the three great monasteries had expressed fears that the Dalai Lama might be invited to attend the National People's Congress, forcing a postponement of the examination. The abbots had made it clear that the Dalai Lama's examination must pass without incident. If the Khampa revolt was to spread unchecked the Chinese might demand it be cancelled.

The Chinese also wanted to prevent the Khampas from using the Monlam ceremony to stage a revolt. They had already told the Kashag that the PLA would take responsibility for guarding the Chinese centres and insisted that the Tibetan Government should disarm the Khampas when they entered Lhasa for the ceremony. The Kashag dispatched emissaries to Lhokha. In August 1958 the Khashag appointed Tsipon Namseling Paljor Jigme (much to his surprise) to head a delegation to negotiate the disarming of the Khampas.[64] It was common knowledge that he was sympathetic to the Khampa cause and had been present during the first meeting held at Gonbo Tashi's house in Lhasa to discuss the formation of the Four Rivers, Six Ranges. It was likely that the Chinese felt the Khampas would listen to someone they trusted. Accompanied by a junior official called Thubten Samcho and three ecclesiastic representatives, Namseling left Lhasa on 4 August with a letter from the Kashag which Namseling claims was written by the Chinese.[65] The Kashag had instructed Namseling to persuade the Khampas to surrender their arms and abandon their attacks on Chinese garrisons.

When the delegation arrived in Driguthang, Namseling found that the Khampas were hostile. Gonbo Tashi refused to meet them because he feared that it might be a trap to arrest him. The Lhasa delegation, meanwhile, insisted that they would only discuss the mission with Gonbo Tashi. The meeting between Namseling and Gonbo never took place. In the end the Lhasa delegation had to conduct discussion with representatives sent by Gonbo Tashi. Although Namseling was sympathetic to the Khampas, he faithfully put forward the Kashag's demands and insisted that the Khampas should stop fighting. He also warned that there should not be any disturbances during the forthcoming ceremony to mark the Dalai Lama's examination.[66] Gonbo Tashi dispatched a written appeal to the Kashag stating that they were not lawless criminals and that their 'objective was to resist and to oust the Chinese who were oppressing our people'. He felt that 'our national institutions and way of life were being extinguished'. Instead of returning to Lhasa, Namseling and other members joined the

Khampa group, but they were not received enthusiastically because the Khampas saw Four Rivers, Six Ranges as essentially a pan-Khampa movement. The issue of whether people from *U-tsang* (central Tibet) were members of the Four Rivers, Six Ranges remains a controversial debate among Tibetan refugees. In exile the organisation continues to insist that it is a purely pan-Khampa movement that does not accept as members people from *U-tsang*.

The Khampas knew that if they were to launch a direct attack on the vicinity of Lhasa they would force a counter attack from the PLA and, besides: 'they could not assault the enemy in or near Lhasa as that would endanger the safety of the Dalai Lama and the holy places and relics in the city'.[67] The Khampas' intention was to drive east towards their homeland and liberate it from the PLA. However the PLA already had launched a full-scale operation to put down the revolt in Kham and, by late 1958, they had managed to gain some control in the area.

The Khampas continued to face problems with provisions. In September 1958 a group of Khampas attacked the government granaries in Lhokha and large quantities of grain were pillaged. The grain had been intended to supply the rations for the small Tibetan army. This meant that for several months no rations were given to the soldiers.[68] Phala says he and others feared that there might be a mutiny among the soldiers who would demand compensation for the loss of their rations. According to Phala, there was also the danger of fights breaking out between Tibetan Government soldiers and the Khampas.

Despite the fear caused by some Khampas, many Tibetan officials remained sympathetic to them. Since 1957 Gonbo Tashi had been trying to persuade Phala to hand over some of the Tibetan Government's weapons to the Khampas. Phala knew that the Tibetan Government could not officially give any arms to the Khampas, but he told Gonbo Tashi where the government had hidden arms.[69]

After the signing of the 17-Point Agreement, the Tibetan regiment from Changthang had been withdrawn and disbanded. But their weapons were hidden at the Shang Gaden Chokhor monastery near Shigatse where the Dalai Lama and the members of the Kashag had stayed on their return from India. The monks requested the Kashag to remove the weapons as they feared that the Chinese might find out about them. By 1958 the Kashag was under considerable pressure from the monastery to dispose of them.[70] Phala suggested that the Four Rivers, Six Ranges should rob the monastery. Gonbo Tashi immediately realised the risk and insisted that he would only take the weapons if he had written authorisation from the Kashag. Naturally Phala refused and restated that if the Chinese were to find out that the government had released the weapons to the Khampas there would be no knowing what the Chinese would demand.[71] In September 1958 Gonbo

Tashi led 600 Khampas to the monastery and laid siege to it. The monks refused to hand over the weapons without authorisation from the Kashag, fearing that if they did so, the Kashag might confiscate monastic assets. The monks resisted for three days before surrendering the weapons.[72] A monk from the monastery later wrote that robbery was elaborately staged to make it appear that the Khampas had forcefully taken the weapons. In reality the monks were collaborating with the Khampas,[73] who were able to obtain a sizeable number of weapons. With these Gonbo Tashi led his group north-west towards the Changthang Plateau. It was envisaged that they would cross the Drichu river towards Kham to liberate their homeland. They were joined by Athar who informed them that the Americans were going to supply weapons. At the end of February 1958, the CIA made a second arms drop for the Khampas.

At the end of 1958, despite the intensification of fighting between the Khampas and the PLA, the Chinese could claim some measure of success and had not been deterred by the Khampa revolt from planning ambitious projects. The major roads linking Tibet with the rest of China had been completed, greatly improving communication and bringing Tibet within the economic structure of China. At a meeting of the PCART on 26 December, Tan Guansan, the deputy secretary of the Tibet Work Committee, announced that one of the main tasks for the following years was the construction of a railway line between Tibet and China. Tan went on to say that the year 1959 was going to have a 'decisive significance for changing the appearance of our fatherland'.[74]

SEVEN

The Flight of the Dalai Lama

By the beginning of 1959, the Dalai Lama was 'very near despair'.[1] The Khampa revolt had spread throughout Tibet and the PLA were on full alert. The Tibetan Government found themselves fragmented and unable to make decisions. The officials continued to meet but the lack of trust among them meant that they were too frightened to express their views.[2] The Kashag and a few other high officials continued to advocate caution but many of the junior officials felt this had left them without any leadership. There were rumours that, once the Dalai Lama had finished his examination, the Chinese would invite him to Beijing and that this time there would be no grounds for rejecting the invitation. Many officials felt that once the Dalai Lama was in China, he would not be allowed to return to Lhasa. It was feared that the Chinese would use the Dalai Lama as a means of putting pressure on the Khampas and others to end the uprising.

As the anti-Chinese rebellion gathered strength, the Communists began to intensify their campaign against 'Rightists', blaming them for the success of the uprising. The cadres were urged to raise their ideological consciousness and to 'mingle' and 'hear the views of the great masses of the people, so that all the problems encountered by the latter would be solved quickly'.[3] If these were attempts to appease the Tibetan peasantry, they came too late: there was now well entrenched anti-Chinese feeling among all sections of the Tibetan population. Nevertheless most Tibetan officials continued to attend meetings convened by PCART and, more importantly, officials were diligently taking part in study sessions organised by the CCP to persuade the Tibetans of the superiority of socialism. The fact that many high-ranking lamas also dutifully attended these classes may have encouraged the Chinese to believe that the 'upper strata' of Tibetan society had accepted the reforms. In January 1959 the Communists announced that Tibetan cadres were to be dispatched to China to study the peoples' communes, apparently in the hope that changes in China would further encourage the Tibetans to support the reforms.

At this critical juncture the Chinese seemed to have misjudged the situation. In March the Party's Central Committee recalled to Beijing the two highest-ranking officials in Tibet, Zhang Jingwu, the Chinese Government's representative in Lhasa, and Zhang Guohua, the head of the

Military Commission in Tibet. They may have been recalled to discuss the deteriorating situation, but the absence of two leaders from Lhasa at such a time shows that the Chinese were unprepared for a major crisis. After nearly a decade in Tibet the Chinese leadership should have known that during Monlam anti-Chinese activities would be at their peak.

As noted before, the Monlam ceremony of 1959 was particularly important because the Dalai Lama was to take his final Geshe examination. This meant that Tibetan officials had to meet regularly to make arrangements for various religious ceremonies, giving them opportunities to discuss the increasingly strained situation in Lhasa. Barshi remembers that many government officials were worried that the fighting in the countryside might spill over into Lhasa. He also recalls unofficial meetings of officials below the 4th rank in the Norbulingka to discuss the dangers presented by the forthcoming Monlam festival. The meetings were attended by representatives from the monasteries and army as well as lay officials. Everyone shared the same concern that the Monlam festival would be a dangerous period; Barshi told one meeting that he had noticed that the Chinese were preparing for it by piling sand bags on the roofs of their offices. At another meeting it was agreed to take an oath to defend the Dalai Lama and the political and religious system of Tibet.

The Tibetan Government's immediate aim was to see that the Monlam ceremony was not marred by any confrontation with the Chinese. When Kashag members learned of the meetings, they realised that the Chinese would be angry. The next day those who had attended were summoned to their respective offices. The monk officials and the representatives of the monasteries were called to the Yigtsang (Ecclesiastical Office) where Drumyigchenmo Chogtag warned them that they should not engage in activities which would provoke the Chinese. Similar warnings were also given to the lay and military officials. However, this did not prevent them from meeting further. That same day, the monks and Tibetan army officials convened at the Tsuglakhang; this time no lay officials attended. Once again they expressed concerns that the Monlam period would expose the Dalai Lama to danger and proposed forming their own unofficial guard during the ceremony by mingling with the crowd.[4]

The Spark of the Uprising

Tibetan officials feared that if fighting broke out the Chinese would claim that they were in the best position to safeguard the security of the Dalai Lama and would make him leave Lhasa, so they could use him to quell the uprising. On the morning of the 24th day of the first Tibetan month (3 March 1959), two days before the end of Monlam, Barshi and the abbot of the Gyume monastery, Ngawang Lekden, went to consult the Nechung Oracle. Barshi invoked the oracle, saying, 'In this turbulent time, you, the omniscient deity, should provide guidance on what is the best course of action that should be adopted to protect the Dalai Lama and the religious and political system of Tibet.' At first, the oracle announced that certain *zhabten* (rituals and prayers) should be performed for the well-being of the Dalai Lama. Barshi was not satisfied with this general pronouncement and, when the oracle got up to leave, pressed him further. 'Why are you reticent about giving a clear pronouncement? You, the *lha* [deity] who possesses power beyond human capability, must give us guidance. We are prepared to undertake any instruction that you may give.' The oracle showed signs of irritation but when he sat down, he made the pronouncement. 'It is time to tell the all-knowing Guru not to venture outside'.[5] This prophecy was first written down on a *sam-tra* (slate)[6] and then copied onto thick Tibetan paper, to which the seal of the Nechung oracle was affixed.[7]

Barshi then went to the Tsuglakhang and gave Phala the written pronouncement from the oracle and asked him to show it to the Dalai Lama.[8] It is difficult to say whether this prophecy had much influence on later decisions. Phala told Barshi that he had shown the pronouncement to the Dalai Lama but Phala's account of subsequent events does not make any reference to the oracle. It is clear, however, that later on, the oracle's pronouncement influenced the actions taken by Barshi and made Tibetan officials very apprehensive.

On the 29th day of the 12th Tibetan month (7 February 1959) a religious dance by monks from the Namgyal monastery was held at the Potala Palace, to mark the end of the Male Earth Dog year. It was attended by the Dalai Lama and the Kashag. Tan Guansan, then the acting representative in Tibet, and Deng Shaodong, the deputy commander of the Tibet Military Command, were also present. During the show Tan and Deng mentioned to the Dalai Lama that a newly established dance group, which had been training in China, had returned to Lhasa, to which the Dalai Lama politely replied that he would like to see them.[9] Tan suggested that he could arrange a performance at the Norbulingka. The Dalai Lama is reported to have said that there were no facilities to stage the show there and that the newly built auditorium in the PLA headquarters would be more suitable.[10] At the time nothing more was thought about this casual conversation, but in the event it was to become the final spark which led to the Lhasa uprising. It appears that most Tibetan officials were not aware that the Dalai Lama had expressed a wish to see the dance group.

The Chinese wanted to use this performance as a celebration to mark the Dalai Lama's graduation ceremony. In his memoirs the Dalai Lama describes how the date for the performance was agreed.[11] The Chinese pressed him to set a date for the show. At first he stalled, saying he was too busy but would set a date as soon as the Monlam ceremony was over. On 5 March the Monlam ended and the Dalai Lama moved with his court to the Norbulingka. This annual event involved a spectacular procession with hundreds of people lining the route along which the Dalai Lama was carried on a golden palanquin, led by Tibetan soldiers dressed in ancient costumes.

Two days later Tan Guansan again requested that the Dalai Lama set a date when he could come to the show. Finally, on 7 March, the Dalai Lama agreed to attend the show three days later.[12] This fact was known to only a very few people in Norbulingka. Strangely enough, it appears both from the published sources and oral accounts that no discussion took place between the Tibetan and Chinese officials about the arrangements until the day before the visit. Furthermore, members of the Kashag were not informed of the visit.

The announcement on the 9 March that the Dalai Lama would visit the military headquarters for a show on the following day therefore came as a surprise to many Tibetan officials. Barshi, who was to play an instrumental role in mobilising public opposition to the visit, remembers that on the morning of 9 March he was in the Norbulingka attending the morning tea ceremony (*drung-ja*). This was an important ritual, during which monk officials would be allocated tasks for the day by a Dronyerchenmo. That morning, two *tse drung* (monk officials) were told that they would be accompanying the Dalai Lama to the military camp for the show. This was the first the monk officials knew of the forthcoming visit. Barshi recalls that when he heard this, he said, 'It's all over'.[13] He immediately remembered the prophecy warning the Dalai Lama not to venture out. When others asked Barshi what he had meant, he told them of his suspicion that the Chinese might detain the Dalai Lama. Once he entered the military camp, there was nothing the Tibetan army would be able to do.

Even Ngabo, one of the highest-ranking Tibetan officials and a member of the Kashag, says that he only found out about the date of the visit on the evening of 9 March.[14] Depon Takla, who was not only the general of the Dalai Lama's bodyguard regiment, but also married to the Dalai Lama's eldest sister, was not informed of the visit until the morning of 9 March, when he was called to a meeting by the Chinese to discuss the visit.[15]

What was the source of the rumour that the Dalai Lama would be abducted? Did it stem from remarks made by Barshi or did Tibetan officials have other channels of information? In any event, by the next day all Lhasa knew of the Dalai Lama's plan to visit the Chinese military camp. The news was spread deliberately. Barshi's belief that the Dalai Lama would be abducted was supported by two other monk officials, Tsedron Yeshi Lhundrup and Khenchung Tara. They immediately phoned Takla's residence, but were told that he had left for a meeting with the Chinese. They left a message asking Takla to come to Phala's house in the

Norbulingka.[16] When they reached Phala's house he was in a meeting with Drunyigchenmo Chogtag, another high-ranking monk official. Yeshi Lhundrup and Tara went inside to talk to Phala, while Barshi, according to his own account, waited in the ante-room. Without any consultation, he decided to write a letter addressed to *Lachi*, the head monk of the Drepung and Sera monasteries.[17] He said that the Dalai Lama would be going to the Chinese military camp the next day and that all the monks should come to Norbulingka to pay their respects (*phyag-'tshal zhu-ba)*.[18]

Barshi knew that he did not have the authority to summon the monks and that an anonymous letter would not persuade them to come to the summer palace the next day. To legitimise his letter he stamped it with the seal of the Yigtshang, which was in a pouch hanging from a pillar in the ante-room. Anyone who received such a letter would think that it was from the highest office and would not dare to disobey the instructions. Barshi knew his action was *ultra vires* but he wanted to spread a *krog-ta* (rumour) that would galvanise people into action.[19]

Barshi did not intend to incite a major revolt: his main motive was to prevent the Dalai Lama from going to the military camp. The letter merely informed the monks that they were required to come and pay their respects to the Dalai Lama. Barshi does not say whether the letter was received at the monasteries but one monk from Sera says that he was told late in the afternoon of 9 March that the Dalai Lama would be going to the military camp, and that the monks agreed to go early the next morning to wait near the Norbulingka. This suggests that a message was received, but it is also likely that monks knew about it independently, as the Chinese had begun to invite high-ranking lamas to the show on that same day.

In Lhasa the Chinese were busy issuing invitations to officials; in the Norbulingka concern about the visit was growing. When Takla arrived at the Norbulingka, he confirmed the Tibetan officials' worst fears. To his astonishment, the Chinese had told him that the Dalai Lama should dispense with the usual ceremony and that he should not be accompanied by his personal bodyguards. Takla claims that the Chinese further demanded that Tibetan guards should be stationed at a bridge known as the *Do zham* (Stone bridge), which was two miles from the military camp. The Chinese added that they would be responsible for security. Takla says that he told the Chinese that he would need to discuss this with Phala, who was the chief of protocol.

The Chinese had not even informed the Kashag or other Tibetan dignitaries of the visit until the day before the show. Liushar received a phone call from a Chinese official inviting him to attend and telling him to go to the military camp directly. This contravened normal protocol, which would have requested members of the Kashag to accompany the Dalai Lama from Norbulingka. Liushar phoned Norbulingka and was told that he should proceed to the show directly; later he was told that Kashag members were supposed to accompany the Dalai Lama from the palace.[20] This confusion shows how badly the whole thing was organised.

Takla found Phala and the other officials in an anxious state. His conversation with the Chinese seemed to confirm their suspicions that the Dalai Lama would be abducted. There were reports in Lhasa that a number of Chinese planes had landed at Damshung airport, and trucks had also congregated at the military camp.[21] Suspicions were fuelled by the fact that the Chinese had been pressing the Dalai Lama to attend the National People's Congress in Beijing, which was scheduled for April 1959.[22] At a time when the Khampa revolt had reached its peak and had drawn international attention to the Communists' failure to win over the 'minority people', the Chinese would have regarded the presence of the Dalai Lama at the NPC meeting as of crucial propaganda value.

In the Norbulingka, Phala, Takla, Khenchung Tara, Tsedron Yeshe Lhundrup and Barshi decided to persuade the Dalai Lama not to attend the show next day. They approached the Chyikhab Khenpo (Lord Chamberlain), who was a monk called Gadrang Lobsang Rigzin, through whom meetings with the Dalai Lama were arranged. When they passed on their request that Dalai Lama stay away from the show, Gadrang became irritated and told them it was unprecedented to make demands of the Dalai Lama. He told them that he was not prepared to put such a request to the Dalai Lama alone but he would take them to see the Dalai Lama so that they should put their request directly.[23] That afternoon, Gadrang took Phala and Takla to see the Dalai Lama, and they informed him that the Chinese had imposed conditions and that they felt that it would be dangerous for him to attend the show.[24] The Dalai Lama did not take their warning seriously and insisted that he would attend the show.[25] The news that the officials had been unable to persuade the Dalai Lama to cancel his visit immediately caused alarm among the officials in the Norbulingka.[26]

The key to understanding how the revolt started is the question of how the rumour was spread among the public. At the time the Tibetans did not have control of radio or newspapers and the public was not at first aware of the issues surrounding the visit to the military camp. The rumour was, in fact, deliberately disseminated by a small group of junior officials in order to mobilise the punblic. After failing to persuade the Dalai Lama, they were determined to prevent him leaving the Norbulingka, and this seemed the only way to muster public support. Two monk officials, Yeshi Lhundrup and Barshi, volunteered to go to Lhasa and spread the news. At first they contacted officials who had earlier participated in a meeting at the Potala and taken an oath to defend the Dalai Lama.

Barshi recalls that he left the Norbulinkga on a bicycle and Yeshe Lhundrup rode off on a horse. Each visited different parts of Lhasa. Barshi went to the Potala palace, where the Trapchi regiment (one of the few remaining traditional Tibetan regiments) was stationed. He told the commander of the regiment, Gyapon Kalsang Damdul, that the soldiers should be armed and positioned outside the Norbulingka next day. To emphasise the danger, he showed the commander the oracle's pronouncement. Many of the soldiers were staying in Shol, a village just below the Potala. It was most likely that the news spread by word of mouth among the people. Later, Barshi informed other government officials that they were required to come to Norbulingka next morning. Similarly, Yeshe Lhundrup went around Lhasa telling people that they should gather outside the summer palace.[27] A Chinese source claims that 'on the evening of 9th March, the Miboin [*sic*: mayor, *mi-dpon*] of Lhasa provoked citizens by saying: Tomorrow the Dalai Lama will go to the Military Area Command for a banquet and performance; Hans have prepared a plane to kidnap the Dalai Lama to Beijing; every household should send people to Norbulingka, the residence of the Dalai Lama, to petition him not to attend the performance.'[28]

Throughout the day, news of the Dalai Lama's visit to the Chinese military camp spread. The atmosphere in Lhasa at the time ensured that dissemination of the rumour was quick, and widely believed. There was a shared fear that something awful was about to happen. When one group of officials received the news they asked Khatshab Shasur and Kalon Surkhang's opinion. They immediately realised that a demonstration would be dangerous and warned some officials not to proceed with the plan to encourage the public to gather outside the summer palace.[29] By next morning, one leading Lhasa aristocrat said that 'rumours were falling like hailstones'[30] and that it was now too late to abort the plan.

In 1959, the Dalai Lama was twenty-five years old, an 'obstructive year' (*skag*)[31] according to Tibetan belief. It was believed that not only would the Dalai Lama experience hardship, but also the whole Tibetan nation. With such convictions prevalent, it was not difficult for the public to convince themselves that the Dalai Lama was in danger. On the morning of 10 March, as the inhabitants of Lhasa woke up, they saw a stream of people heading towards the Norbulingka. This was the beginning of what the Dalai Lama was later to call a 'most momentous' day.[32] Like most rumours, it spread like wild fire. Some people claimed that they had heard that the Dalai Lama had been abducted by the Chinese in the middle of the night, others that the Chinese had attacked the palace. Some were told that they should rush to the Norbulingka to prevent the Dalai Lama from being kidnapped by the Chinese.[33]

Siege of the Summer Palace

The revolt was not pre-arranged in the sense that the instigator wanted to spark off a nationwide uprising. Those who spread the rumour of the Dalai Lama's imminent abduction did not envisage that outcome. Phala and others felt that a request from the people would be sufficient to cancel the show, which they genuinely believed was staged to abduct the Dalai Lama, although there is no evidence that the Chinese were intending to kidnap him: the idea was born out of the Tibetans' fear and supported by circumstantial evidence. In the Tibetans' mind the demands imposed by the Chinese confirmed their suspicion. But what would the Chinese have gained by such an act? Any actions taken against the Dalai Lama would certainly have provoked the Tibetan masses, whose faith in him as their spiritual and political leader was unquestionable.

The thousands of people who turned up outside the Norbulingka were not only expressing their anger against the Chinese but their resentment against the Tibetan ruling élite who, they believed, had betrayed their leader. By 10 a.m. the numbers outside the summer palace had swelled to several thousand demanding to see the Dalai Lama.[34] As government officials arrived, they found the road leading to the palace blocked. The huge crowd outside the gates vented its anger on the Tibetan officials believed to be pro-Chinese. One of the first to suffer from the mob's violence was Sampho, a member of the delegation that had signed the 17-Point Agreement. Since the founding of the PCART, Sambo had become one of the highest-ranking Tibetan officials in the Tibet Military Commission. His jeep was driven by a Chinese chauffeur[35] and he was wearing a PLA uniform, which the crowd took as a symbol of betrayal. People started to throw stones, hitting Sampho on the head as he got out of the jeep. Later he was rushed to the Indian Mission hospital.[36]

Another influential official who was attacked was Khunchung Sonam Gyamtso,[37] a member of the Chamdo Liberation Committee and the Religious Affairs Committee of the PCART. Officials were seen as traitors if they abandoned traditional dress and wore Chinese uniforms instead. Khunchung first came to Norbulingka for the morning tea ceremony, wearing traditional Tibetan monk's attire. Later, however, he returned to watch the crowd outside the palace, having changed to a white shirt, dark trousers and a Chinese cap with a white face mask of the sort the Chinese often used to keep out dust. This simple act seems to have enraged the public, who attacked him and beat him to death.[38] The angry crowd dragged his body all round the Barkhor, the centre of Lhasa.

The mob could easily have attacked Chinese establishments or cadres watching the demonstration and it was only on the following day that the people's anger began to turn against the Chinese. The attacks on

Khunchung Sonam Gyatso and Sampho confirm that the masses held the Tibetan élite responsible for what they saw as the 'betrayal' of the Dalai Lama and their faith. Liushar remembers that the crowd shouted abuse to Kashag members when they came out of the Norbulingka and their cars were searched by the people who feared that the Dalai Lama might be hidden in the vehicles. Liushar says that he felt that the populace had no trust in them.

When Barshi and others decided to mobilise the people in order to prevent the Dalai Lama leaving for the Chinese camp, they could not have envisaged the anger of the crowd or predicted the outcome, nor did they want an open revolt. Once the crowd had been prompted by the rumour that their leader was in danger, there was no way that the Kashag or any Tibetan leader could influence the people.

The question remained as to whether the Chinese ever had any intention of abducting the Dalai Lama. They have always maintained that it was the Dalai Lama who 'took the initiative'[39] and asked Deng Shaodong to arrange the show at the military camp. It seems unlikely that the Chinese ever had any plans for abducting the Dalai Lama to Beijing.[40] Despite the Khampa rebellion and the setbacks in eastern Tibet, they knew that they had secured control of the country and that their military supremacy assured them of eventual victory. They were also aware that the relationship between Lhasa and Kham was at best uneasy, and at worst hostile. Phala commented later that had the 10th March Uprising not taken place, there was every likelihood that civil war would have broken out between the Lhasa regime and the Khampas. Nevertheless, we cannot dismiss Tibetan apprehensions lightly, and it must be recognised that the people genuinely believed that the Dalai Lama would have been abducted and kept as a prisoner in Beijing if he had entered the camp. As it turned out, this assumption was confirmed, in the eyes of Tibetans, by the detention in Beijing of the Panchen Rinpoche in the late 1960s.

In retrospect, the immediate cause of the revolt seems to have been a trivial issue of courtly etiquette which could have been easily averted. The Chinese accused the Kashag of organising the demonstrations, but all the evidence shows that the members of the Kashag were surprised by the subsequent developments and tried to minimize their effect. On the morning of 10 March, Kalon Surkhang Wangchen Gelek tried to persuade the crowd gathered outside the Norbulingka to disperse. He addressed the demonstrators using a megaphone, but the crowd demanded to see the Dalai Lama in person.[41] Once ordinary men and women had been mobilised, the question of the Dalai Lama's visit to the show was no longer important and the crowd defiantly marched towards Lhasa dragging Khunchung's body.[42] His killing showed both public defiance of the Chinese (whose loyal supporter he was considered to be) and the extent to which the masses had taken control of the political agenda from the Tibetan ruling classes. Many people who took part in the demonstration told me that their initial anger was against the aristocracy and this is clear from the slogans they used. When Tibetan officials drove or rode past the crowd outside the Norbulingka, the demonstrators shouted, 'Do not sell the Dalai Lama for Da Yuan,' and, 'The Dalai Lama is more precious than a sack full of Da Yuan.'[43]

On the morning of 10 March, the Kashag members went hurriedly to the military camp to calm the Chinese officials in case they decided to deploy troops to guard the palace. For their part, the Chinese seem to have underestimated the seriousness of the demonstration. When the Kashag officials reached the military headquarters, they found schoolchildren holding khatas and flowers lined up along the path leading to the camp: the Chinese had no idea that the Dalai Lama might not come. Ngabo was already at the camp, chairing a study session for the officials of the PCART,[44] at which almost all the members of the Kashag were present. Surkhang told Tan Guansan that the Dalai Lama was unable to come because of the demonstration. Khatshab Shasur tried to assuage the Chinese by describing the demonstration as the work of 'uneducated masses'. He advised them to be tolerant (*bzod-pa sgom*) of the actions of a few uneducated people, but these attempts to placate the Chinese were in vain. Although the initial attitude of the Chinese is unclear, one thing is certain: they were unprepared for such a demonstration. Not only were their leading officials absent from Lhasa but, despite the fact that a massive crowd had gathered outside the Norbulingka, the Chinese were going ahead with their preparations for the show as though nothing had happened.

It was not only the Chinese who were unprepared. The Tibetan ruling classes also seem to have been unaware of the significance of the demonstration. On the afternoon of 10 March the entire Tibetan hierarchy dutifully turned up at the military camp to enjoy the show. They certainly would have known or seen the demonstration taking place in Lhasa that morning and yet they seem to have been unperturbed by the incident. The Dalai Lama's two tutors, members of his family, the entire religious hierarchy and members of the Tibetan aristocracy were at the military camp that afternoon.[45] It is ironic that although the Communists claim that the 'upper class reactionaries' had staged the demonstration, the Tibetan élite were in fact enjoying lavish entertainment provided for them by the PLA, while the Tibetan peasantry demonstrated elsewhere. As they waited for the Dalai Lama, the Tibetan guests were entertained by the senior Chinese cadres; the religious figures were ushered into a film show; mah-jong tables were laid out for the lay aristocrats, while the more fashionable and younger officials took to Western-style ballroom dancing.[46]

The demonstration thus displayed the gulf between the people and aristocracy in Tibet. It also marked the irreparable breakdown of the relationship between the Chinese and the Tibetan masses. It was the point at which either the Chinese would have had to make a major concession to public demands, or the Tibetan Government would have had to give in to the Chinese. The Chinese could no longer assume that the rebellion was confined mainly to a small minority of 'counter revolutionaries' or avoid admitting that it was supported by the Tibetan masses and cut across social and class divisions.[47] The uprising wrested the political agenda from the élite. The question was no longer what type of reforms would be acceptable to the Kashag; the political debate had now shifted to a different domain and brought into question the whole status of the Sino-Tibetan relationship.

Khatshab Liushar remembers that when the public outside the Norbulingka demanded to see the Dalai Lama, Surkhang Wangchen Gelek and other Kalons told the public that it would be impossible to allow all of them to enter the palace and that it would be a gross breach of security. He said that they should select a group of representatives who could come into the palace.[48] This later became the basis for the group 'the People's Representative'. Despite its title, the group was no more than an *ad hoc* committee of people who were selected from the crowd outside the palace. Later, it was amalgamated into another group calling itself 'The People's Assembly'. This gave the impression of cohesion but in fact the group remained disorganised and lacked unified leadership.

Although the group did not have formal approval from the Kashag, many officials in the Norbulingka encouraged the crowd to vent their anger against the Chinese. Barshi claims to have declared that they needed to eradicate the danger to the Dalai Lama permanently: 'The danger comes from the presence of the Communists. The Chinese and Tibetans cannot live together. The only lasting solution is if the Chinese are forced out of the country. As long as the Chinese remained in Tibet, the danger to the Dalai Lama would always be there.' Later, when the representatives of the demonstrators entered the palace, Barshi advised that they should leave a small group to guard the palace while the rest proceeded towards Lhasa. He also told them to put up posters declaring Tibetan independence and telling the Chinese to leave Tibet. Intentionally or not, the Tibetan officials managed to shift the focus of activity from the Norbulingka, where they were under siege. Once the demonstrators moved towards Lhasa, the arena of the confrontation was changed and the public wrath directed at the Tibetan officials was removed.

At first the Kashag's policy was to curb the demonstration in order to prevent the Chinese from deploying the PLA. They believed that the crowd would heed their appeal to disperse. But the Kashag's ability to exercise any authority over the demonstrators had been diminished and they were aware that they could not deploy the small Tibetan army to suppress the demonstration, in case it led to civil war.[49] Moreover, many Tibetan officials openly supported the uprising, which they saw as the last chance to oust the Chinese and restore the power of the Dalai Lama. The demonstration had now developed into a national uprising and the Tibetan masses were no longer prepared to listen to what they saw as the Kashag's appeasement policy. Members of the Kashag like Liushar, Surkhang and Shasur who were staying in the Norbulingka found themselves unable to convince the Chinese that they were not involved in the demonstration; and the Chinese refusal to listen to the Kashag further eroded its authority. Unable to appease the Chinese or suppress the uprising, the Kashag had ceased to be an effective body. The Kashag and officials in Norbulingka began to address the question of the Dalai Lama's security.

The Last Attempts to Win Over the Dalai Lama

The only person who could have exercised any influence over the populace was the Dalai Lama. He felt as if he was 'standing between two volcanoes, each likely to erupt at any moment'.[50] He was dismayed by the uprising, which he saw as suicidal, but the outcome depended on him denouncing or supporting it. The Chinese realised that they had to win him over. Gyatsoling Rinpoche, as one of the debating partners of the Dalai Lama, was still able to move freely in the Norbulingka and that afternoon was summoned to the office of the United Front Department and was given a letter for the Dalai Lama, in which Tan Guansan advised him not to attend the show.[51]

There was no need for Tan to write to the Dalai Lama since it was clear that a decision had been made not to leave the Norbulingka. Perhaps Tan wanted to make it seem that the Chinese were taking the initiative rather than let it appear that the Dalai Lama was being prevented from attending the show by the demonstration. Whatever Tan's motive might have been, his letter initiated a series of private letters. On 11 March, unbeknown to the Kashag and other officials in the Norbulingka, the Dalai Lama wrote to Tan Guansan saying that he would have liked to have attended the show but was prevented by 'reactionary' elements in the palace. Ngabo brought the Dalai Lama a second letter, to which he replied by saying that he was 'taking measures to calm things down'.[52] He implied that he was opposed to the uprising and that control was in the hands of a belligerent group of Tibetan officials in the Norbulingka who refused to heed his advice. In his autobiography the Dalai Lama said the letters were written 'to gain time' and to prevent the Chinese from launching an attack on the palace.[53] Whatever the Dalai Lama's motives might have been, the Chinese became convinced that the Tibetan leader was being held under duress in the palace.

These letters were later published by Xinhua as proof that the Dalai Lama had been abducted against his will by 'reactionaries'.

The Dalai Lama wrote in his memoirs that neither he nor the Kashag was able to influence the crowd, which had by now constructed barricades on the roads leading to the palace.[54] By the evening of 10 March there was still no sign of the demonstration in Lhasa waning. The public began to strengthen the barricades on the road leading to the Norbulingka and the remaining Tibetan soldiers were recalled to the palace for guard duty. The next day Tibetan officials flocked to the Norbulingka seeking guidance from the Dalai Lama. 'I did my best to dissuade them from their action,' he was to write later. He told them that he was not compelled to visit the Chinese military camp and that he 'was not in any fear of personal danger from the Chinese and so they must not create a situation which could have [such] serious consequences for the people.'[55]

Barshi recalls that the officials who had gathered in the Norbulingka on the afternoon of 10 March met to discuss the situation. A clear division emerged between those who supported the demonstration and those who felt that it had endangered the Dalai Lama's security. A monk official, Ta Lama Chokteng, made a brief speech advocating that they follow the Dalai Lama's advice. Many officials felt that the Dalai Lama was compelled to advise caution because of his religious position, (which required him to oppose violence at all times) and because of the fear of the Chinese. If the Chinese thought that the Dalai Lama supported the uprising, they would have no option but to adopt military means to gain control of the situation. As long as they believed there was a chance they could win over the Dalai Lama, they would not launch an attack on the Norbulingka.

The Kashag was concerned that the Norbulingka should not become the centre of revolt. On the morning of 12 March, the Kashag summoned those officials who had supported the rebellion and told them that they could not hold any further meetings in the palace; it also warned that their activities would endanger the safety of the Dalai Lama.[56] Barshi remembers that later meetings were held in Shol, a village below the Potala. Here nearly fifty government officials gathered, and it was apparent that they were all in support of the revolt. They decided to dispatch messages to different monasteries and mutual aid societies (*skyid-sdug*) asking them to send representatives. This once again marked the setting up of a new group, which called itself 'the People's Assembly'. Next day thousands of people turned up in Shol, perhaps the largest ever public demonstration in Lhasa. Some of the government officials took charge while speaker after speaker denounced the Chinese and demanded the restoration of Tibet's independence. The crowd renounced the 17-Point Agreement, saying that the Chinese had betrayed the Agreement by undermining the authority of the Dalai Lama. The repudiation of the Agreement was made by the unofficial body, the People's Assembly; neither the public declaration of independence nor the repudiation of the 17-Point Agreement was made by a member of the Kashag or any other influential figure. As long as the public denunciation was not made at the Norbulingka or by a member of the Kashag, the Tibetan Government could always disassociate itself from the declaration and argue that these declarations were unofficial.

The notion that government officials should not be seen as actively participating in the uprising was not just confined to the members of the Kashag. Even members of institutions established by the Chinese felt that they should not be seen as part of the demonstration. On the third day, the city was taken over by women demonstrators; the influential women of Lhasa were asked to lead the demonstration. One of them, Rinchen Dolma Taring, wrote in her autobiography that the committee members of the Women's Association (which included the Dalai Lama's sister and other leading aristocratic ladies) felt this was not appropriate.[57] In the beginning the Kashag also refused to allow the small Tibetan army to support the protesters, who had appealed to the Kashag for the government's arsenal to be opened and the arms to be distributed to the public. Some of the monasteries around Lhasa had a few weapons of their own, which were distributed among the monks who were guarding the monasteries, but most of the demonstrators remained unarmed.

Three Kashag members, Surkhang, Liushar and Shasur, now sought refuge in the Norbulingka. Of the other two members of the Kashag: Sampho was recovering from the attack earlier in the morning, while Ngabo remained outside the summer palace, which led Tibetans to believe that he was siding with the Chinese. Ngabo's and Sampho's houses were guarded by PLA troops. Ngabo knew that the public saw him as the arch-collaborator and on the second day the demonstrators marched towards his house, but were halted by a strong contingent of PLA troops. In the meantime Ngabo tried to mediate between the officials in Norbulingka and the Chinese; he was, in fact, the only person in a position to do so. Although seen by the public as a collaborator, he remained quite popular among the Tibetan aristocracy and for several days was able to visit the Norbulingka freely, which allowed unrestricted communication between the Dalai Lama and the Chinese.

Within the Norbulingka, the Kashag and the Dalai Lama's advisers were genuinely baffled by the events outside and becoming increasingly isolated as these moved beyond their control. Their main concern was the safety of the Dalai Lama and making sure that they did not lose control of the palace either to the Chinese or to the demonstrators. Their policy of aloofness did not endear them to either side. It left the Tibetan masses leaderless and fending for themselves, while the Chinese continued to believe that the Kashag had instigated the uprising. The city was in chaos, with sounds of demonstrators mingling with Chinese appeals blaring out of the loud-speakers telling the people not to listen to the rumours of the 'reactionaries'. Although the demonstrators lacked a leader and cohesive organisation, in the midst of the chaos there emerged a collective organisation based on the traditional artisans' guilds and on mutual aid societies, which were urged to send representatives to various *ad hoc* meetings held around Lhasa. Langdun Gyatso, a carpenter from Lhasa, described how the Mutual Aid Society of Masons, Carpenters and Builders held a meeting and joined the uprising as an organised group.[58]

On the third day the crowd marched towards the only two foreign missions in Lhasa, the Indian and Nepalese missions. They called for the Indians and Nepalese to support their demands for an independent Tibet. There was nothing that either country could do. Later Nehru told the Indian Parliament that he had instructed the Indian Consul to 'stick to your business and do not get entangled'.[59] The Chinese fortified their offices and barracks. For several days they did nothing to reclaim the city, clinging to their hopes of winning over the Dalai Lama. It is also likely that, having reported the incident to Beijing, the regional military commission was awaiting further instructions from higher authorities. The Chinese must have calculated that there was no way that the uprising could succeed in ousting them from Tibet – their military supremacy assured them of victory.

In the Norbulingka, the Kashag had reached the decision that they would not be able to hold the palace. At the same time they were under increasing pressure from the public to make a declaration supporting the uprising, which we know the Kashag was reluctant to do. They hoped instead to relieve the pressure by moving the Dalai Lama out of the city. Phala was given the task of organising the move with a cryptic instruction involving the Tibetan proverb 'Snatch the egg without frightening the hen.'[60] There is no doubt that the Kashag recognised the Dalai Lama's importance as the only person who would have any influence over the masses. If the Dalai Lama were to fall into Chinese hands, it would effectively mark the end of Tibetan resistance.

For this reason the Kashag wanted to create political and spatial distance between themselves and the Chinese. Phala says that the original intention was to seek a safe area, a sort of buffer zone, from which they could negotiate with the Chinese.[61] It was clear that if they were to stay in the Norbulingka, they could not remain detached from the events and demands of the public. It is also possible that some officials and members of the Kashag felt that the Dalai Lama might concede to the Chinese.

We know that there was correspondence between the Dalai Lama and Tan Guansan.[62] In the last letter, dated 16 March (the day before he fled) the Dalai Lama wrote: 'I shall make my way in secret to the military Area

Command.'[63] Two days earlier, at a meeting of government officials in the Norbulingka the Dalai Lama had reiterated the need to calm the situation. The Dalai Lama's letter to Tan Guansan said that he was able to sway some officials, many of whom could see four days of mass action had not made a dent on the Chinese. They had neither responded by offering compromise nor sought to gain control of Lhasa and may have hoped that the agitation would soon die down.

Phala was given full power by the Kashag to do whatever he thought necessary to arrange the evacuation from the palace. He was assisted by Phuntsog Tashi Takla, the Dalai Lama's brother-in-law. It was decided that the Dalai Lama would be accompanied by his two tutors, his immediate family and members of the Kashag, who were already in the Norbulingka. Phala made two important decisions. First, he dispatched a messenger to summon Athar and Lotse, the two CIA operatives, who were south-east of Lhasa, near Lhuntse Dzong.[64] Second, Phala sent a monk official to the Indian Consulate to inform them that the Dalai Lama might have to seek refuge in India. The Indian Consul, Major Chiba, responded by asking for details of the Tibetans' intentions and enquiring where along the border they intended to enter India. Phala told the Indians that no decision had been reached as to whether the Dalai Lama and his entourage would cross the border or not. He had merely taken the wise precaution of alerting the Indians, since once they left Lhasa, it would not be possible to contact the Indians.[65] Indeed, two days after the Dalai Lama's flight, on 19 March, the Indian foreign secretary sent a telegram to the Consul-General, informing him that the GOI would grant asylum to the Dalai Lama, but the Indian officials were unable to pass the message to the party.[66]

The situation in Lhasa was rapidly deteriorating. For nearly a week, the Chinese had not taken any action to regain control of the city and there was no sign that the uprising would fizzle out. In fact, there was a danger of the revolt spreading into the surrounding area. Already disturbances had occurred in Gyantse and Phari, on the main trade route to India, and news of the revolt was filtering to the outside world. It appears that on the morning of 17 March, the Chinese began to shell some areas to intimidate the Tibetans. In Lhasa there were rumours that the PLA was moving artillery into Lhasa and that it was being aimed at the Potala and the Norbulingka.

Escape of the Dalai Lama

On the morning of 17 March two shells landed near the Norbulingka. This seems to have led the officials in the Norbulingka to think that the Chinese would make their final move and try to gain control of the city. Both the

Kashag and the Dalai Lama consulted the Nechung oracle, who pronounced that it was no longer safe to remain in the palace. That evening, the Dalai Lama (dressed in the traditional gown of a layman) and his entourage crossed the Kyichu river and headed out of Lhasa. It appears that the Chinese were caught by surprise. No detailed accounts have been published of their position during that evening. Why did they not take preventative measures? Once the Dalai Lama stepped out of the palace, the Chinese could only have prevented the escape by force. But it appears that the Chinese officials were not aware of the flight for at least a day or two.

As mentioned earlier, Phala had summoned Athar and Lotse to Lhasa. When they received Phala's message, Athar and Lotse were worried because it required changes to their plan. Since Phala's refusal to allow them to meet the Dalai Lama, they had been instructed by the CIA to work with the main Khampa resistance movement, Four Rivers, Six Ranges. They had been operating independently of Lhasa for nearly a year, and had had no contact with Tibetan Government officials. In fact they were unaware of events in Lhasa and had been concentrating on building up the Khampa resistance movement. A month before the Lhasa revolt, on 22 February, Athar and Lotse had received the second consignment of arms from the CIA. It consisted of ammunition, automatic rifles and new radio sets. Some of the arms were distributed to a few trusted Khampas and the rest of the supply had been hidden. The arms and other supplies were intended for a group of fifteen newly trained Khampas that were about to be parachuted into Tibet. The CIA instructed Athar and Lotse to look for a safe dropping zone.

Before the final drop was arranged, they were recalled to Lhasa. Athar recalls that when he read the message he was worried because it had taken six days to reach him (Athar and Lotse were under orders never to stay in one area for more than three days, and the messenger from Lhasa had taken some time to locate them). Since Phala had not mentioned on what date they intended to leave Lhasa, Athar had no idea whether the Dalai Lama was still in Lhasa. He immediately radioed the Americans and informed them that he had been recalled to Lhasa by Phala and that the Dalai Lama was planning to leave Lhasa to seek refuge near the Indian border. The CIA instructed him to proceed to Lhasa and to report on the meeting. Taking twenty Khampa troops with him as an escort, he rode towards Lhasa. It is clear that the CIA was not involved in organising the Dalai Lama's escape as alleged by the Chinese and some Western writers.[67] But the news of the Dalai Lama's flight once again renewed American interests. When the CIA received Athar's message, they immediately postponed the dropping of the fifteen Khampas into Tibet, presumably awaiting the outcome of the meeting between Phala and their agents.

In reality, neither the CIA nor the *émigré* groups in Kalimpong accused by the Chinese of instigating the revolt were involved in organising either the revolt or the Dalai Lama's flight from Lhasa. The documents captured by the Chinese in Kundeling monastery, on which the Kalimpong allegation was based, show that the People's Assembly only contacted Shakabpa in Kalimpong on 17 March, seven days after the demonstrations started in Lhasa.[68] These documents merely urged them to seek international support rather than launch a revolt. The *émigré* group, with CIA support, was planning a very different strategy. The CIA had advised them to think in terms of a long-term guerrilla war – Athar remembers that the Americans told them that they could never hope to oust the Chinese from Tibet and that the best strategy would be for them to try to disrupt Chinese rule. The CIA was accordingly planning to establish a number of guerrilla cells in various parts of Tibet and was therefore opposed to a nationwide revolt, which they felt would jeopardise their plan.

This plan had been in effect since the winter of 1958, soon after Athar returned from the meeting in Calcutta where Gyalo Dhundup had said that the Americans were going to make arms drops inside Tibet,[69] and therefore advised encouraged a number of Khampas living in India to return, including Lo Nyendrak, an influential and wealthy trader from the Sadhutshang family who had a substantial following among the Khampas. Lo Nyendrak led about a hundred Khampas back into Tibet. They were followed by Baba Lekshe and a young man from Amdo called Jangchub Jinpa, who had been given a 16mm movie camera and told to film the arms drops and the resistance movement. At the time the activities of the main resistance group, Four Rivers, Six Ranges, were above all concentrated in southern Tibet. They were beginning to achieve some success: two arms drops had been made without the Chinese detecting them and increasing numbers of people were able to infiltrate Tibet from India. However, the revolt in Lhasa meant that the CIA had to abort its plan.

The revolt took the leadership of the Four Rivers, Six Ranges by surprise. Gonbo Tashi and the main contingent of Khampa resistance fighters were in the east and did not find out about the Dalai Lama's flight from Lhasa and arrival in India until the beginning of April 1959.[70] It was clear that when the revolt happened, neither the CIA nor the main Tibetan resistance group was prepared.

The revolt was mainly concentrated in Lhasa, where the main task for the Chinese was to disarm the Tibetan army, which numbered about 1,500. In Lhasa the army consisted of the bodyguard regiment and a small Tibetan police unit. There were also a number of soldiers stationed in other areas, notably in Shigatse and Dingri where the Chinese had already taken steps to disarm the Tibetan regiments. In Shigatse, there were about 500 soldiers making up the Panchen Rinpoche's guard. They were disarmed by the PLA without much resistance. The inhabitants of Shigatse – who had always seen themselves as separate from Lhasa and loyal to the Panchen Rinpoche – remained detached from the uprising in Lhasa, and most of the areas under the influence of Tashilhunpo refused to participate in the revolt. But it must also be pointed out that the Chinese, forewarned by the events in Lhasa, had time to deploy large numbers of troops in Shigatse to prevent the uprising spreading there from the capital.

Similarly, the Chinese had started to disarm small groups of Tibetan soldiers in Dingri, and in Shelkar Dzong the PLA troops surrounded the monastery and demanded that arms stored there by the Tibetan Government be handed over to them. At first the monks resisted, but the Chinese brought in one of the commanders of the Tibetan Government regiment captured in Shigatse and he was able to persuade the monks to hand over the weapons.[71] This was the first time the local people had any inkling of the troubles in Lhasa. In other areas the local people only found out about the events in Lhasa on 20 March when Radio Lhasa stopped broadcasting[72] and PLA troops turned up to arrest leading local officials. Some remote areas in western Tibet remained unaffected by events in Lhasa and were not aware of the Dalai Lama's escape until they heard about it on All India Radio.[73]

In Lhasa, the Chinese were caught by surprise. The Kashag began to authorise the distribution of arms from the government arsenals on the third day of the uprising. Liushar himself took charge of releasing large numbers of old Enfield rifles from the Potala. However, many civilians remained unarmed. On 20 March, after more than a week of demonstrations in Lhasa, the PLA was ordered to retake the city. Loudspeakers urged the public to disarm; those who surrendered would be treated leniently. For two days there was fierce fighting while the PLA captured the Norbulingka and the Potala, causing many Tibetan casualties. The Chinese got Ngabo to make an appeal, and his voice could be heard through the loudspeakers asking the people to surrender and warning that otherwise the fighting would reduce Lhasa to rubble. On 23 March, the Chinese hoisted the five-star Red flag over the Potala Palace. It was the first time the Chinese had been able to fly the flag over this most historic and sacred building. 'The Chinese national flag, symbol of light and happiness, flutters in the breeze over Lhasa, greeting the rebirth of this ancient city.'[74] Together with the loudspeakers blaring out the announcement that the PLA had captured the Potala and the Norbulingka, this signalled the end of the revolt. Many feared that the Dalai Lama had been captured by the Chinese and that any further resistance was futile. People began to climb onto the rooftops and hoist white flags. Others emerged gradually from their houses with khatas tied to sticks. Some stood in front of their doors with khatas hanging from their raised arms. The PLA soldiers, in groups of four or five, and sometimes accompanied by Tibetan translators, began to search each house. The houses of influential Tibetans like Lhalu, the former Governor of Kham, were targeted and the occupants were arrested and taken for interrogation. The streets were littered with corpses, some of which had been there for several days and had been mauled by stray dogs. People rushed out to identify the bodies and look for relatives who had failed to return home.

According to Chinese sources, 4,000 people were arrested and 8,000 small arms, 81 light and heavy machine-guns, 27 mortar launchers and ten million rounds of ammunition were captured.[75] This disparity between the number of weapons and prisoners suggests the capture of the Tibetan Government arsenals rather than the detritus of an uprising. It is true that the Tibetan army, which was described by the Chinese as 'rotten to the core, utterly useless in fighting',[76] joined in the revolt and actively fought the PLA. Despite the disparaging Chinese remarks, they were at first able to resist PLA attacks. But they were numerically disadvantaged and they did not possess armoured vehicles and other modern weapons. The Tibetan Government had distributed arms to some people, but the overwhelming number of civilians who took part in the uprising remained unarmed. Langdun Gyatso remembers that 500 people in his Carpenters' and Masons' Association had two rifles and about 25 pistols between them. 'The only thing we could do was to arm ourselves for hand-to-hand combat and so we prepared knives, swords and an assortment of fierce but, as it turned out later, perfectly useless weapons.'[77] On 23 March the Chinese announced the setting up of a special Military Control Committee in the towns and villages which would be responsible for organising local administrative and 'self-defence forces'. It is interesting to note that it was felt that there was no need to set up this committee in Shigatse.[78]

When the Dalai Lama's party reached Rame monastery south-west of Lhasa, they heard the news that the Chinese had launched a full-scale attack on Lhasa. This caused great alarm among the party and they decided to move further south, along the Tsangpo river. Before leaving Rame, the Dalai Lama wrote letters to the two remaining Kalons in Lhasa, Ngabo and Sampho.[79] Another letter was sent to Lobsang Tashi, the former Prime Minister. Since his dismissal in 1952 he had been living quietly in his monastery, and had shown no interest in subsequent political developments. He was appointed as regent in the absence of the Dalai Lama[80] and asked to negotiate with the Chinese. The Dalai Lama also wrote to the Panchen Rinpoche.[81] It is not clear whether these letters ever reached their intended destinations.[82]

The Dalai Lama's escape route was not accessible to vehicles and lay in an area under the control of Khampa resistance fighters, so it was fairly free of PLA incursions. Local people soon learned of the Dalai Lama's escape and flocked to the area to seek blessings from him, presenting an enormous problem for the party in their attempts to keep the escape route secret. Luishar says that he had to ask the Khampas and others to disperse. Far from providing protection for the Dalai Lama, they presented a major security risk.

The Dalai Lama's party proceeded southwards towards Lhunste Dzong, one of the largest settlements in the area and only sixty miles from the Indian border. Four days after leaving Lhasa, the party reached Chongye Riwodechen, where there was a small monastery whose head lama was the Dalai Lama's senior tutor, Ling Rinpoche. At Chongye the party was also met by resistance fighters of Four Rivers, Six Ranges; among them Athar. Later in the afternoon, Athar met with Phala. He once again asked for a meeting with the Dalai Lama. This time Phala said that he would arrange the meeting as soon as the party had settled at the monastery. Phala went on to ask about the strength of the resistance group and whether they would be able to provide protection for the Dalai Lama. Athar gave details of the activities of Four Rivers, Six Ranges and a glowing account of Gonbo Tashi's exploits. He also informed Phala for the first time that the Americans were supplying weapons and that more people had gone for training abroad. Phala looked elated and said that he would inform the Dalai Lama. Next morning, 22 March, Athar was taken to see the Dalai Lama and he told him of the Americans' willingness to provide aid but added that they needed to know what his intentions were. The Dalai Lama told Athar that at that point, neither he nor the Kashag had reached a decision, but he went on to say that he intended to set up a temporary government based in Lhuntse Dzong. Athar radioed the Americans informing them that the party would be setting up a base in Lhuntse Dzong.

The Americans congratulated Athar on a successful meeting. Finally the Americans had made official contact with the Dalai Lama and had established a link between their agents and the escape party. This gave them some of the legitimacy that they had been seeking before. However, even at this late stage neither the Dalai Lama nor the Kashag made any direct appeal to the Americans. Nevertheless, the Americans were confident and told Athar to expect further arms drops. The third drop was to be the largest. There were two plane loads, with enough arms for 2,000 people. The plane was standing by in East Pakistan (Bangladesh), waiting for a signal from Athar and Lotse. Athar wanted the supply to be dropped in Tsethang, near the main base of Four Rivers, Six Ranges in Driguthang, which would avoid the problem of transporting such large quantities of arms. But Athar learned that PLA troops were moving rapidly into the area and that other safe zones had also fallen. He radioed the Americans to cancel the drop for the time being.

Athar and Lotse travelled with the Dalai Lama until they reached Lhuntse Dzong.[83] The area was totally free of Chinese control and home to many more Khampas and Tibetan soldiers. Overnight, this remote part of Tibet, usually administrated by a lowly dzongpon, became the Centre of

Tibetan Government from which the Kashag intended to carry out its plan to conduct negotiations with the Chinese. Meanwhile the Dalai Lama and the Kashag decided to incorporate the Khampa resistance groups into the traditional Tibetan Government structure, awarding Andrug Gonbo Tashi the title of Magchi Dzasag.[84] It was hoped that Four Rivers, Six Ranges and the remaining Tibetan army would form a defence force and that the area would be declared independent of Chinese rule. After reaching Lhunste Dzong, the Dalai Lama and the Kashag issued a proclamation setting up the new temporary Government of Tibet. The Dalai Lama wrote that he felt 'positive' about the future of Tibet.[85]

Next day, Athar and Lotse were summoned by Phala. For the first time they were introduced to the other members of the Kashag and asked whether the Americans would provide political support. Athar told them that the USA had already made two arms drops and that more people were being trained. He also described the strength of the Four Rivers, Six Ranges organisation. The previous night Athar had radioed the Americans and told them about the establishment of the new government and of the intention to resist the Chinese. Athar says that the Americans were delighted with the news and instructed him to congratulate the new government.

The Tibetan Government's intentions suited the CIA's plans. This would provide the CIA with a base and a legal and moral legitimacy for their involvement and would further their plans to establish a network of guerrilla cells in Tibet. Athar was told to look for secure drop zones and advised that, if the Dalai Lama requested it, the Americans were willing to take charge of his security. Athar says this was discussed at the meeting with the Kashag, where he advised them that they should hand over security to the Americans. It is not clear what form this would have taken, but Athar was convinced that, if the Tibetans had requested it, the Americans would have parachuted American soldiers into Tibet.[86] The Kashag told Athar that they would reply after they had discussed it further with the Dalai Lama.

That day a number of officials arrived from Lhasa. They brought news of the fall of Lhasa and descriptions of how the Chinese had destroyed the Potala and Norbulingka, stories that later were found to be untrue. There were also rumours that the Chinese army was marching towards Lhuntse Dzong, which prompted fear and panic among the officials. There was no way that the Khampas or the few Tibetan soldiers would have been able to hold out against the PLA. Already a steady stream of people was crossing the border into India. Later reports arrived saying that the Chinese were trying to cut off the escape route to India. The Dalai Lama had to admit the 'unwelcome truth' that they could no longer remain in Tibetan territory.[87] Athar remembers being woken about midnight by Phala who told him that the Dalai Lama could no longer remain in Lhuntse Dzong as Chinese troops were rapidly advancing towards the area. He was asked to radio the

Americans to tell them about this new development. He was also told to advise the Americans to aproach the GOI for asylum for the Dalai Lama and his party. And Athar was asked to select two people to proceed to the border to contact Indian officials. The next morning Jangchub Jinpa and Baba Lekshe were sent to the border while Athar radioed the Americans.

On 28 March, the Chinese issued a statement signed by Zhou Enlai announcing that the rebellion had effectively 'torn up' the 17-Point Agreement and declaring that the 'local government' had been dissolved and that its duties would be taken over by the PCART. It also said that, in the absence of the Dalai Lama, the Panchen Rinpoche would assume the position of the Chairman of PCART and that Ngabo would be appointed Vice-Chairman. More important, the order named eighteen people, including Phala, Surkhang, Shasur and Liushar, as key leaders of the rebellion and dismissed them from the posts they held on PCART. The order declared that they would be punished.[88] All the named persons were in the Dalai Lama's party and faced execution or life imprisonment if they were captured.

As the Chinese announced that they had gained total control ofi Lhasa, the Dalai Lama and his party moved near to the Indian border. They were still reluctant to cross as they were uncertain about the Indian reaction. When they reached Mangmang, one of the last Tibetan settlements, they were met by Baba Lekshe and Jangchub Jinpa, who were able to confirm that the Indians were prepared to welcome the party. The Indian officials at the border had already been instructed by their government to expect the Dalai Lama. At about the same time Athar received a radio message confirming that the GOI was prepared to grant asylum. The Tibetan party was totally unprepared and did not have any financial resources to support themselves in India, having brought with them sackloads of virtually worthless Tibetan currency. Athar remembered that he and Lotse were authorised by the CIA to hand over to the party two hundred thousand Indian rupees from their fund. In return Phala handed Athar all the Tibetan money they had brought with them. On 30 March 1959, the Dalai Lama, the political and spiritual leader of Tibet, crossed the border into exile.

As the news of the Dalai Lama's escape to India was broadcast on All India Radio, thousands of people crossed the border. Between April and May 1959 more than 7,000 Tibetans entered India and sought asylum.[89] Athar and Lotse turned round at the border and went back into Tibet. But they found that many people had simply given up and saw no point in fighting: many Tibetan soldiers and Khampa fighters were surrendering their weapons at the border and wanted to settle in India. The PLA rapidly advanced into the region. Andrug Gonbo Tashi and his men heard on All India Radio that the Dalai Lama had escaped. They fought fiercely, but gradually all Tibetan territory fell to the advancing PLA troops. By the end of April the morale of the remaining Khampa resistance groups had fallen, and they were pushed further towards the Indian border. They knew there was very little chance of securing a safe base inside Tibet. On 28 April Gonbo Tashi crossed the border. This marked the end of the active campaign inside Tibet. However, pockets of resistance in various parts of eastern and central Tibet continued, and it was not until 1960 that the PLA was able to secure complete control of Tibet.

The 1959 revolt marked the end of the attempt to forge a co-existence between Communist China and Buddhist Tibet. The flight of the Dalai Lama symbolised the final demise of Tibet as an autonomous entity within the People's Republic of China. Whatever the weaknesses of the 17-Point Agreement, it did provide scope for the Chinese and Tibetans to work together. As noted earlier, it was felt by the Tibetans that the Agreement gave a measure of protection to their traditional way of life and the Chinese saw it as giving legitimacy to their entry into Tibet. Once the Agreement had been signed, the PLA met little resistance from the Tibetan masses, and the ruling orders had co-operated with them (although the passivity of the masses should not be viewed as either acceptance or – as claimed by the Chinese – a sign that the masses welcomed them).

Once the Chinese had gained control of Tibet, they faced the problem of how to defend it. The external threat to Chinese rule was negligible. In fact, China rapidly secured international recognition of Tibet as a 'region of China'. American interest was no more than a nuisance, since there was very little the USA could do without a direct appeal from the Dalai Lama, which was never made at the time. In the end, internal problems were to cause most trouble for the Chinese. Despite the geographical proximity of Tibet and China, the values and world views of a Communist China and a Buddhist Tibet were oceans apart. The gap between the Tibetans and the Chinese was described by the Tibetans as being as wide as 'earth and sky'. But the Chinese Communists were motivated by the zeal to transform a society which they saw as governed by superstitions and marred by economic backwardness, and they had been realistic enough to adopt a more gradualist policy of reform and to refrain from radical polices which would impair their relationship with the indigenous ruling classes. By offering the ruling order positions and monetary rewards in the new society, the Communists were able within a short period to make new structures to solidify their rule in Tibet.

Despite their achievements, the revolt was a clear indication that the Chinese had failed. Why had the 17-Point Agreement not worked? Once in exile, the Dalai Lama was to denounce the Agreement as a treaty signed under duress, a refutation which fails to explain why the Tibetans had made no protest for nearly ten years. For the failure of the Agreement, we need to look at the treaty itself.

For the Tibetans, the Agreement promised autonomy and that the 'existing status of the Dalai Lama would not be altered'. They thought that 'autonomy' meant independence in all but name. The term 'autonomy' was translated as '*rang-skyong ljongs*', which literally meant 'self-rule'. But for the Chinese 'autonomy' meant that the Tibetans had accepted Beijing as the ultimate authority. A Tibetan official told me that the Chinese cadres would always emphasise that the decision had been approved by the State Council and they would add that Chairman Mao himself had approved it. This was to imply that the decision was reached at the highest level and was irreversible. For the Tibetans, the ultimate authority always resided with the Dalai Lama. Each party saw what they wanted in the Agreement and it was in many ways doomed to fail from the start.

For the Tibetan masses, the central issue was the question of the Dalai Lama's power and status, which the Tibetans commonly referred to as '*go-gnas*'. The PCART, for example, was achieved with the compliance of the ruling order but was seen by ordinary men and women as undermining the power of the Dalai Lama. This was for many Tibetans the crux of their resentment. The Dalai Lama was the pivot of Tibetan society. He was the incarnation of Avalokitesvara, the Buddha of compassion and the patron deity of Tibet. For ordinary men and women, any tampering with the role of the Dalai Lama and his position as the supreme ruler of the land of snow was unacceptable. The decline in the Dalai Lama's authority was more complex than a mere loss of political power in the Western sense; it was equated with the degeneration of Buddhist Tibet. The Chinese, therefore, were seen not only as political foes but essentially as 'enemies of the faith'. This to some degree provided the ideological basis of the Sino-Tibetan conflict, rather than class or regional differences. The Tibetans' identity as 'the insiders' (*nang pa*), and their identification of others as 'outsiders' (*phyi pa*) overrode internal divisions and gave Tibetans the focus of their ethnicity. The essential weakness of the Chinese was their failure to see the homogeneous nature of Tibetan culture. Tibet was not only a political entity, it was foremost a civilization, covering the whole of the Tibetan-speaking world.

To some extent, the Communists inherited the faults of the Guomindang. Central Tibet under the Dalai Lama's rule was treated as a *de facto* independent state, while the areas the Tibetans called Kham and Amdo had been under nominal Chinese rule, albeit through local warlords who owed nominal allegiance to the Central Government. Since the early part of this century, most of Kham was incorporated into the province of Xikang, and much of Amdo was incorporated into Qinghai. In fact, in the Amdo region, the Lhasa regime never exercised any political authority and the Communists found it easy to regard Kham and Amdo as falling within 'China Proper' and thus subject to the same reforms (which from 1954 onwards became more radical and assimilationist). The implementation of reforms and the subsequent failure of the Great Leap Forward caused a universal resistance to the reforms, and it was not until after the uprising that the Communists were able to coerce the people into accepting them.

The attacks on religion and on their religious institutions led many Tibetans to an apocalyptic perception of events, which was then confirmed by various supernatural signs. In early 1950, the people of Lhasa were amazed by water dripping from a gilded gutter in the Tsuglakhang. The government appointed a team to investigate this mysterious sign. It was followed by earthquakes and floods which were universally accepted as signs marking the beginning of the degeneration of Buddhism. Later in exile the Dalai Lama was to describe the situation as a product of the past accumulation of bad merit by the Tibetans as a people. The religious community, the monks and lamas, simply wanted the PLA exorcised from Tibet.

So, why did the 1959 revolt occur? It was not only a political act in defence of Tibet's independent status, which had been lost with the signing of the 17-Point Agreement. There was no realistic chance of Tibetans being able to drive the PLA out of the country. What impelled people into action was not any narrow class or regional interest, nor the greater international politics of the Cold War. The revolt was essentially in defence of the value system of the ordinary men and women, to which the Dalai Lama was central. The catalyst for the revolt came from the thousands of refugees from eastern Tibet. The Chinese reforms and their ruthless suppression of the Khampa revolt drove thousands of people to seek protection in central Tibet, thus bringing the area into the theatre of conflict and making other Tibetans distrustful of Chinese promises. The Khampas in turn tried to appeal to Tibetans' shared religious and cultural values for support. In a letter to the Tibetan newspaper, *The Mirror*, one appeal was even addressed to '*tsampa* eaters'.[90] *Tsampa* was the staple diet of all Tibetans, transcending class, gender, sect and regionalism, and differentiating them from the Chinese.

After the dismissal of Lukhangwa and Lobsang Tashi, Tibet had lacked a leadership that could stand up to the Chinese. The Dalai Lama was young and inexperienced. His advisers became increasingly insular and their interest had become primarily the safety of the Dalai Lama. When the revolt started, the Tibetan leadership was still trying to appease the Chinese, to the point of being apologetic. No Tibetan leader tried to negotiate with the Chinese when their rule was seriously challenged by the masses. Although the Kashag saw the revolt as leverage on the Chinese, as far as we know they never made any concrete demands. The Kashag and other leaders lingered on in the palace, with no clear idea of how to respond to the revolt. The revolt scattered the Tibetan leadership, whose reaction was to abandon the country and seek safety in a foreign land. In their defence, they claim that they had neither the freedom nor the power to protest. In the circumstances, the only solution was to rescue 'the most precious jewel', the Dalai Lama, from the faithless Red Chinese.

EIGHT

The International Response and Tibet at the UN

The revolt and the subsequent dramatic flight of the Dalai Lama once again drew international attention to Tibet. In 1959, the international situation, although still very much under the influence of the Cold War, was uneventful. Tibet therefore stole the world's headlines. Coming so soon after the Hungarian revolt, the Tibetan conflict was quickly identified by the press as 'another Hungary'. International reactions predictably fell into the Cold War divisions, with the Communist bloc supporting the Chinese claims and the Western bloc much more sympathetic to the Tibetans.

However, although Tibet was treated as a *cause célèbre* in the media, there was a disparity between public support and official restraint. The anti-Communist countries, while deploring the Chinese actions, were nevertheless careful not to provoke the Chinese. The gap between public and attitudes was most glaring in Asia. Some south-east Asian countries were alarmed by the irredentist policies of the PRC: South Vietnamese volunteers registered to go and fight in Tibet; in Ceylon and other Buddhist countries people protested to the Chinese Embassy. The Communist bloc argued that events in Tibet were an internal matter for China. The only Communist country to voice criticism of China was Yugoslavia, where the media carried unprecedented reports of events in Tibet and argued that the Chinese had misread the feelings of Tibetans and that the revolt was caused by misapplication of Marxist nationality policy. They went on to say that the Chinese should have allowed the Tibetans to express their culture and traditions, and that this would have prevented international reactionary forces from rousing the population. However, the Yugoslavs conceded that Tibet was an internal affair of China. China, for its part, remained unconcerned by the international criticism. They steadfastly argued that they would not tolerate interference in domestic affairs.

Most other countries, although sympathetic to the Tibetans' plight, conceded that Tibet was an internal matter for China and that legally the Tibetan issue could not be compared to the revolt in Hungary which, they argued, was a sovereign country with representation at the UN, unlike Tibet which had never received *de jure* recognition of its independence. The international response was, therefore, circumscribed by Tibet's legal status. Even the Americans, who had clandestine relations with the Tibetans, were reluctant either to support Tibetan independence or recognise the Dalai Lama as the head of a government-in-exile. On 28 March the State Department issued a statement expressing 'profound sympathy with the people of Tibet in face of the barbarous intervention of the Chinese Communist imperialists to deprive a proud and brave people of their cherished religion and political autonomy, and to pervert their institutions to communists ends.'[1] The US was trying to avoid any statement on the legal status of Tibet, preferring to speak of 'political autonomy', a term with very little meaning.

Nehru and Tibet

The main burden naturally fell on India. Nehru had no hesitation in granting asylum to the Dalai Lama. Nehru had earlier noted in a letter to the British Prime Minister, Harold MacMillan, that when he visited China in 1954 he raised the issue of asylum granted by the Chinese to K. P. Singh, a Nepalese Communist. Zhou Enlai had told Nehru that India should not mind since this was only international protocol. He had also said that in 1950, when the Dalai Lama had nearly sought asylum in India, China would have considered it as accepted international behaviour, if the GOI had granted asylum.[2] Nehru was therefore of the opinion that the Chinese would accept the Indian position as conforming to international protocol and would not view it as an unfriendly act.[3] Not all Indian officials agreed. Krishna Menon, the influential Defence Minister who had always seen Tibet as a backward region resisting progress, advised Nehru to refuse political asylum for the Dalai Lama[4] and later compared the Tibetan situation to the problems faced by the GOI in Nagaland. But it was clear that Nehru's assistance to Tibet would not extend beyond offering asylum to the Dalai Lama.

At the beginning of April 1959, as the international media was learning of the Dalai Lama's escape, a delegation of Tibetan *émigrés* led by the former Prime Minister, Lukhangwa (who had been living in India since 1955), met Nehru in Delhi. The Tibetans presented a four-point memorandum requesting that (1) GOI should seek some form of guarantee from China for the personal safety of the Dalai Lama; (2) refugees should be allowed to enter India freely; (3) India should send a mercy mission with medical supplies and (4) India should sponsor the Tibetan case at the United Nations.[5] Nehru's response came through an official statement issued to the press. It announced 'the hope that the present difficulties in Tibet would end peacefully' and that Nehru wished to make it clear 'that India was not in a position to intervene and in fact would not like to take any steps which might aggravate the situation there [in Tibet]'.[6] Thus, Nehru made his intentions clear before he had a chance to meet with the Dalai Lama. Whatever case he may have had to present, India was not going to intervene.

Nehru chose to adopt a cautious policy and saw the relationship with China as still of the utmost importance to India. He naïvely announced in the Lok Sabha (the Lower House of the Indian Parliament) that he had 'deliberately suppressed' his criticism of Chinese action 'to avoid adding heat to the Cold War'. Furthermore, in his view India's relation to Tibet was governed by the Sino–Indian trade agreement of 1954, the preamble of which explicitly recognised Tibet as 'a region of China' and thus obliged India to accept events in Tibet as the internal affair of China. Nehru, who was also against India having to accommodate large numbers of refugees, wrote to MacMillan that attempts to provide aid by Western governments would not be 'helpful' and 'might serve to encourage Tibetans to leave their country'.[7] Nehru's policy of sitting on the fence earned him neither the respect of the opposition parties nor understanding from the Chinese.

Apart from the Communists, the opposition parties in the Indian Parliament were united in their criticism of what they saw as Nehru's weakness.[8] Nehru seriously misjudged the Indian public's reaction to the Tibetan issue. Right-wing Hindu parties like the Jan Sangh and Hindu Mahasaba organised demonstrations in major Indian cities and the Praja Socialist Party declared 29 March as 'Tibet Day'. Even Nehru's own Congress Party joined in condemning Chinese actions in Tibet, while the Indian press, even more critical of their government, accused China of the 'rape of Tibet'. Critical reaction in India to events in Tibet did not go unnoticed in Beijing, where the Chinese were quick to adopt a more aggressive attitude towards India.

It would be wrong to dismiss Nehru's position as short-sighted and ill-conceived. Having discarded the previous British Government position on Tibet as a relic of imperialism, and having conceded unconditional recognition of Chinese sovereignty in Tibet, Nehru was naturally constrained by the *de jure* position, by which events in Tibet were essentially an internal affair of China. Later he told Parliament, where the opposition parties relentlessly accused him of selling Tibet to the Chinese, that the GOI's policy towards Tibet was governed by three conflicting considerations: '(1) the preservation of the security and integrity of India; (2) our desire to maintain friendly relations with China; (3) our deep sympathy for the people of Tibet'.[9] On one occasion he added that 'it was patent from the strictly practical point of view, even apart from sentiment, that we could not do anything in Tibet either in law, constitutionally or practically.'[10] Nehru's realism did not appease the Chinese, who were cynical of his motives and policy. At the time Chinese policy was based on simplistic bi-polar division of socialist countries on the one hand and the imperialists and their lackeys on the other. Beijing was quick to lump India with the latter. Beijing's criticism of the Indian position rapidly degenerated into the language of the Cold War.

Nehru's caution was governed by his fear of India being dragged into the Cold War. He would have known that the Dalai Lama and the Tibetans were in touch with the Americans; after all, the Tibetans had asked the Americans to approach the GOI for asylum. This was a serious misjudgement on the part of the Tibetans and Americans. The Indians were not aware of American activities in Tibet and they were inclined to believe that the air drops were from the Guomindang.[11] The approach from the Americans must have alarmed the Indians, who had consistently opposed American involvement in Tibet.[12] Nehru had always believed that any US involvement would slide the Himalayan region into the Cold War and he therefore had to balance his sympathy for the Tibetans with the need to prevent the Americans gaining influence in the Himalayan region. He believed that any active political support from India for Tibet would encourage the Americans. One of the requests made by the Dalai Lama on meeting P. N. Menon, an official from the External Affairs Ministry in charge of publicity, was to petition the GOI to allow Gyalo Dhundup, his elder brother, to meet him in Tezpur. The Indians suspected that Gyalo Dhundup was working for the Guomindang and were reluctant to allow him to proceed to the border region before they had had time to ascertain the Dalai Lama's intentions. On 12 April, P. N. Menon informed the Dalai Lama that the GOI would not give him any active political support and advised that he should not do or say anything that might embarrass the GOI. Menon also told the Dalai Lama that Prime Minister Nehru had advised that he should not make any public statement which would be likely to obstruct his eventual return to Lhasa.[13] Even at this late stage Nehru seems to have felt that a reasonable settlement could be reached between the Tibetans and the Chinese. The Tibetans had no choice but to accept the constraints imposed by the host government.

The GOI was reluctant to give the Dalai Lama and the Tibetan refugees unrestrained freedom in India. The international press was not allowed to proceed to the border area to meet with the Dalai Lama and it was not until 16 April 1959 that the Dalai Lama was able to issue his now famous Tezpur statement (worded in the third person). This was a carefully written text, the main point of which was to counter the Chinese accusation that the Dalai Lama was being held under duress. This was important for the Indians, whom the Chinese were accusing of complicity in the 'abduction of the Dalai Lama'. In the statement, the Dalai Lama made it clear that he was in India of 'his own free will'[14]. The statement went on to give an account of Sino–Tibetan relations since 1950, and implied that the Chinese had broken the terms of the 17-Point Agreement by interfering in the internal affairs of Tibet.

The most revealing aspect of the statement was that for the first time it gave the Tibetans' interpretation of the Agreement. It made clear that 'in that agreement, the suzerainty of China was accepted as there was no alternative left to the Tibetans. But even in the agreement it was stated that Tibet would enjoy full autonomy. Though the control of external events was to be in the hands of the Chinese Government it was agreed that there would be no interference by the Chinese Government in the Tibetan religion and customs and in her internal administration. In fact, after the occupation of Tibet by Chinese armies, the Tibetan Government did not enjoy any measure of autonomy, even in internal matters; the Chinese Government exercised full powers in Tibetan affairs.'[15] Although the Dalai Lama argued that the Chinese broke the Agreement, he did not announce the outright refutation of the Agreement.

The Chinese response came swiftly, through a commentary from Xinhua on 20 April. It gave an interesting and well-argued analysis of the Dalai Lama's statement, arguing that its style and content showed that it was not issued by the Dalai Lama and adding that 'one has reason to suspect that the statement was not made by the Dalai Lama himself but was imposed on him by some person or persons'.[16] It went on to say that some of the concepts and phrases reflected foreign origins, objecting to the use of such terms as 'Chinese suzerainty' as a legacy of British aggression. This was intended to imply that Indian officials had drafted the statement. The Chinese were not wrong in assuming that the statement had been written by the GOI. A highly placed source told me that in fact the statement was written by Nehru himself. The Chinese also rejected the allegation that they had interfered in the internal affairs of Tibet and argued that the suppression of the Khampa revolt was beyond the jurisdiction of the 17-Point Agreement. The terms of the Agreement, they said, only applied to areas under the authority of the Dalai Lama and since Xikang (Kham) was not part of Tibet, their actions there were legitimate.[17]

The Dalai Lama's statement was issued and distributed through the Indian External Ministry. This convinced China that India was involved in some kind of machination. The widespread publicity given to the statement in the international press was seen as an attempt by India to influence international opinion. The Indians asserted they 'did not do anything special except to provide mechanical facilities'. They argued that since none of the Tibetans who crossed the border could speak English or had experience in dealing with the international press, Indian officials naturally had to provide assistance. At the same time Indian officials were coming under increasing criticism from the press corps for refusing to allow them to interview the Dalai Lama. Nehru was anxious to prevent the international press from holding such a meeting, suspecting them of searching only for a sensational story. From Tezpur the Dalai Lama and his entourage were moved to Mussorrie, a hill station in the foothills of the Himalayas where, later, at his first international press conference, the Dalai Lama issued a statement refuting Chinese charges that the previous statement was not compatible with his views. This statement was read in Tibetan and translated into English. Interestingly, the new statement was in the first person, apparently in response to Chinese criticism. 'I wish to make it clear that the earlier statement was issued under my authority and indicated my view, and I stand by it.'[18]

This did not convince the Chinese. Their criticism of India became even stronger. Xinhua released a number of statements attacking 'Indian expansionism' and a resolution was passed at the Second National People's Congress condemning India for interfering in the internal affairs of China.[19] All available evidence shows that the Chinese had seriously misinterpreted India's policy towards the Tibetans. India was anxious to prevent the international media from employing what Nehru saw as sensationalism in its reporting of the great escape story, leading the press to charge that the Dalai Lama was being kept as a prisoner. Even the Indian opposition socialist leader, Ashok Mehta, accused the government of reducing the Dalai Lama's status to that of a 'pampered pensioner'.[20] The quarantine was supposedly to protect the Dalai Lama from press harassment, but in fact prevented the Tibetans from making any statements which might be construed in Beijing as Indian-inspired anti-Chinese propaganda.

The architect of Indian policy was Nehru, who was inclined to view India's relationship with Tibet as merely one of 'history and sentiment'.[21] He failed to see the political and strategic implications of the developments. Not only did he prevent the Tibetans from appealing to foreign governments and the United Nations, but he delayed the Indian Parliament from debating the Tibet issue. It was not until 4 May that the Rajya Sabha (Upper House) had the chance to discuss the Tibetan issue, while the Lok Sabha had to wait another four days for its opportunity. Until then, the opposition had only been able to raise the matter through questions to the Prime Minister. Nehru continued to advocate restraint and viewed any further discussion as likely to provoke the Chinese. He was not immune to criticisms from his own party and it was reported that some of his closest ministerial colleagues threatened to resign. Pandit Pant, the Home Minister, accused Nehru of being 'unnecessarily afraid of China'.[22]

Nehru's policy did not appease the Chinese, who continued to launch attacks about Indian expansionism. The Indian Ambassador in Beijing wrote to Nehru that there was no meeting ground between the two countries on Tibet. Nehru never made any formal approach to Beijing on the subject, but 'contented himself with public expression of India's concern and of her hope that Tibet would enjoy autonomy'.[23] Nehru was disinclined to believe that Sino–Indian relations would be damaged beyond repair, while the Chinese were increasingly annoyed by what they saw as Nehru's unwillingness to curb growing anti-Chinese agitation. The opposition parties and leading Indian politicians like Jaya Prakash Narayan and Acharya Kripalani continued to campaign outside parliament, arguing that the Dalai Lama should be given unrestricted freedom to appeal to foreign countries and that the GOI should bring the Tibetan issue to the United Nations.

The Dalai Lama and important Tibetan officials were now virtually confined to Mussorrie and prevented from contacting any foreign governments. The Tibetans were growing anxious and began discreetly to voice their frustrations. It had been their intention that on arrival in India they would make an appeal to the United Nations and declare a 'government-in-exile', but the GOI was opposed to both of these points on legal grounds. On 24 April Nehru travelled to Mussorrie and met the Dalai Lama for the first time since his arrival in India. Nehru was accompanied by Subimal Dutt, the Foreign Secretary, and the meeting lasted for four hours.[24] It appears that the meeting was not a success. When the Dalai Lama told Nehru that he wanted to set up a government-in-exile, Nehru emphatically replied that the GOI could never recognise it. The Dalai Lama later wrote of 'a profound feeling of disappointment'.[25] For him Nehru's irritation was a 'sign of [a] guilty conscience' for having advised him to return to Tibet in 1956.[26]

Nehru gave a lengthy account of the meeting to Malcolm Macdonald, the British High Commissioner in Delhi, which was also circulated to some Commonwealth leaders. Some parts of the account are completely contradictory. Nehru claimed that 'the Dalai Lama is not thinking of setting up a Government-in-exile in India' and went on to say to the British High Commissioner: 'nor is the Dalai Lama thinking of appealing to the United Nations'.[27] Both of these points were central aims of the Tibetans. So was Nehru misleading other governments? It was clear that Nehru did not want other foreign governments to encourage the Tibetans to think that their aims would be supported. The Dalai Lama was not wrong when he wrote: 'Nehru thought of me as a young person who needed to be scolded from time to time.'[28] Nehru was most condescending about the Dalai Lama, telling the British High Commissioner that 'he felt great sympathy for the Tibetans, but that they were rather difficult people to help, for they were so ignorant of the modern world and its ways.' He went on say that 'the Dalai Lama was probably the best of them, and a charming, intelligent and good young man by any standard; but even he was naïve and incalculable.'[29] However sympathetic he might have been, Nehru made it plain that India would not sacrifice its relations with China for Tibet. S. Gopal quotes another account of a meeting between the Dalai Lama and Nehru, where

Nehru supposedly told the Dalai Lama, 'Let us face facts. One cannot bring heaven to the people in India even if I wish it. The whole world cannot bring freedom to Tibet unless the whole fabric of the Chinese state is destroyed. Only a world war, an atomic war, could perhaps make that possible.'[30]

Nehru summed up his position in a letter to chief ministers: 'It is our policy not to interfere in other countries, and indeed we are not in a position to interfere. But Tibet has been a country with which India has had emotional ties for a long time past. Therefore, occurrences in Tibet had led to emotional responses in our people. This situation thus created is a difficult and delicate one for us as for others. It is not much good for us to give expression to our wishes in strong language. We have to act so as to help in easing the situation and, as far as possible, in helping the Tibetans to have a square deal.'[31]

It appears Nehru had in mind a rather vague notion of autonomy for Tibet. He told Malcolm Macdonald, 'The proper aim of our policy should be to try to ensure that the Tibetans will enjoy autonomy under Chinese suzerainty.' He reportedly told the Dalai Lama that independence for Tibet was an 'impractical aim'.[32] If the Tibetans were to argue for 'autonomy', not only would the Chinese be more amiable but world opinion would be in favour of the Tibetans.[33] But how Tibet was to achieve this, since India was not willing to raise the issue formally with the Chinese, was not clear.

The Tibetans had placed their hope in Nehru and they were inclined to see India as partly responsible for the events in Tibet. The Tibetans argued that if India had stood up for Tibet, it would have prevented the worst excesses of the Chinese. The news of Nehru's refusal to provide political backing left the Tibetans despondent. There were more and more refugees arriving in India and it was apparent that the Chinese were spreading their 'mop up' operations to all parts of Tibet. Sakya Trizin and the Karmapa, two of the leading religious figures in Tibet, had crossed the border into Bhutan.

Had it not been for the continuing attack on India in the Chinese press, it appears that the Tibetan issue would have faded into oblivion. Subimal Dutt made it clear that on legal grounds the GOI could not support Tibet's appeal to the UN, nor would they recognise the Tibetan Government-in-exile. He pointed out that it was unlikely that the Dalai Lama could appeal to the UN 'since Tibet was not recognised as an independent state but only as being an autonomous area under China'. The Indians were also inclined to believe that for practical reasons such an appeal would 'not help the Tibetans at all since it would prejudice further rather than assist their relations with the Chinese Government.'[34] On the question of a government-in-exile, the Indians were equally negative, with Dutt questioning the legal validity of such a proclamation. He noted that 'the Tibetan

Government in Lhasa was not an independent Government but only an administration enjoying local autonomy'. As far as he was concerned, 'the position is different from that of the government of territories conquered by the enemy during the last war since those governments represented peoples who had been independent nations.' In short, Dutt remarked, the Dalai Lama's 'spiritual authority is one thing and his temporal authority is another'.[35] The failure to obtain recognition for the government had serious legal implications.

Without active support from the Indians, there was very little the Tibetans could do. The American involvement still remained covert and they were unwilling to declare any formal contact with the Dalai Lama and so could not bring the Tibetan issue to the UN. Any evidence of American involvement would have immediately led to accusations of turning Tibet into a Cold War issue. As already noted, US relations with India were strained, and the US could not hope to gain any influence or to persuade India to take more interest in the Tibetan issue. However, they had quietly mooted that the US would like to see the Tibetan issue debated in the UN. Britain could have made a decisive contribution to Tibet's case, and could have exercised influence over the Commonwealth countries and European allies, but chose to follow the Indian lead and hide under the legal camouflage.

Support for Tibet

At the beginning of April 1959, Richard Casey (Australian Minister of External Affairs) told a press conference during a visit to South Korea that he thought that the Tibetan question should be raised before the United Nations and that it should be sponsored by one of the great powers. The Australian Ministry decided to ask for British advice on the subject, and the Foreign Office ruled out any idea of the question being brought before the General Assembly.

> (1) A number of countries, including ourselves, were on record as recognising Chinese suzerainty, or even something more, over Tibet and it might be difficult for such countries to formulate their position in a debate in the UN. It would not help if, for example, we were unable to take a common line with the Americans and our other allies. The case was not the same as that of Hungary where Hungary was acknowledged by all to be an independent country.
>
> (2) If taken to UN, the question is likely to be bedevilled by that of Chinese representation. The communists would no doubt be quick to try to divert the debate away from the subject of Chinese behaviour in Tibet

and on to that of Chinese representation and there might be many among neutral and uncommitted countries who, despite their sympathy with the Tibetans, might take the line that the whole problem could have been dealt with much more satisfactorily if only the Peking Government were represented in the UN.

(3) Both [the] above might make difficulties particularly for the Indians. (India was now in the process of rethinking her attitude towards the Chinese and Mr Nehru was threading a delicate path between natural condemnation of the Chinese actions in Tibet and his wish not to make matters worse either for the Tibetans themselves or for Indian–Chinese relations.) The Indian reaction towards events in Tibet was in fact progressing quite well from our point of view and we did not wish to do anything to upset it or to turn Mr Nehru's irritation against the West by instigating actions, e.g. in the UN, which the Indians might find particularly embarrassing.

(4) In view of the indeterminate status of Tibet and the possible parallels that might be drawn between that territory and certain territories under our protection or that of other Western powers, we might be creating a dangerous precedent for ourselves by trying to have the Tibetan question discussed at the United Nations.

(5) In any case the Chinese would take no notice of any resolutions passed in the United Nations and there was in practice nothing that the latter could do to help the Tibetans.[36]

The Australian External Ministry concurred with British views and advised their minister that they could not raise the issue at the United Nations. The objections set out by the British conformed to the view of other Western countries, who also feared that if Tibet were to appeal to the UN it would set a precedent which could lead to their own colonies approaching the UN in the future. On 5 May 1959, the British Government instructed its ambassadors actively to discourage any country from referring the Tibetan question to the UN.[37] Even the Nationalist Chinese let it be known that they were opposed to the question being raised at the UN. Dr Tsiang, the Nationalist representative, told the press that the issue was a domestic matter for China.[38] There were also practical considerations: the Chinese Nationalists were worried that the Tibetan issue would lead the Communist bloc to raise the question of UN membership for China.

Despite the lack of interest from international governments, it was evident that there was growing public criticism that the UN had neglected the Tibetan issue. Press reports were full of condemnation of the UN. This did not go unnoticed in New York, where Dag Hammarskjold, the Secretary-General of the UN, told the British that he wanted to 'create the impression that some thought was being given to Tibet at the UN' and register that the UN was not 'in a state of innocence'[39] about Tibet. The Secretary-General went on to say that he felt no political action could be taken and that he was only willing to provide humanitarian assistance to the Tibetan refugees.

By the end of April, it was apparent that the growing rift between China and India was unbridgeable. Nehru was coming under increasing pressure from the Indian public and the opposition parties to develop a stronger policy towards China. Moreover, his policy had not won him Chinese friendship. On 30 April the *People's Daily* published a full text of Nehru's speech in the Lok Sabha on 27 April and the paper carried an editorial which instructed that all factories, communes and institutions should study Nehru's statement, as it 'revealed the Indian Government's attitude'.[40] Again on 6 May the *People's Daily* carried two pages of editorial, rumoured to have been written by Zhou Enlai himself.[41] India was accused of 'interference in China's internal affairs'. The articles were an implicit attack on Nehru himself. They questioned whether his sympathies lay with reactionary rebels or with progressive China and accused Nehru of a 'deplorable error'.[42] This confirmed the deterioration of the relationship between India and China. It was clear that China saw the granting of asylum to the Dalai Lama as an 'unfriendly act' and as an abrogation of the *Panch Sheela*.[43] According to Dutt's notes of a meeting with the Chinese ambassador in Delhi on 16 May, the ambassador read to him a long statement which ended with a thinly veiled threat to India: 'you cannot have two fronts. Is it not so?' This was clearly a warning that India could not afford to be enemies with both China and Pakistan. When it was shown to Nehru, he became irritated at the tone of the letter and dictated a reply to the effect that GOI would not be pressured into altering its policy.[44]

Nehru was beginning to realise that he could not balance his sympathy for the Tibetans with his friendship for China. Whatever course of action India was to adopt, it was not going to appease China and there was no way that Nehru could silence the growing support for Tibet in India. (The question of the border dispute will be dealt with in the next chapter.) The opposition leader of the Praja Socialist Party, Jaya Prakash Narayan, continued to call for the government to allow unrestricted freedom for the Dalai Lama to campaign. Since the GOI was not going to allow the Dalai Lama to approach foreign governments, Indian opposition leaders took the task upon themselves and lobbied other countries to support Tibet's appeal to the United Nations. They were met with diplomatic rebuffs and told that they 'could do nothing that would embarrass the GOI'.[45] By June 1959, there were murmurs among Tibetan officials to the effect that they were not happy with the constraints imposed by the GOI. There were also rumours that the Dalai Lama might leave India, as well as a report that he had received an invitation from U Nu in Burma and from Ceylonese Buddhists. The Dalai Lama was also anxious to make some public declaration of his future intentions. For the past few months he had observed Nehru's request not to make any political statements which might cause difficulties for the GOI. This had left the public and the international community bewildered about what the Tibetans wanted. The Dalai Lama told Narayan that he could not remain silent about the situation in Tibet as 'he felt that further silence would be a betrayal of his people'.[46]

On 5 June the International Commission of Jurists,[47] under the chairmanship of Purshottam Trikamdas (one of India's leading lawyers and a senior advocate at the Supreme Court of India) published an interim report on *The Question of Tibet and the Rule of Law.* Its findings concluded that 'there is [also] a *prima facie* case that on the part of the Chinese, there has been an attempt to destroy the national, ethnical, racial and religious group of Tibetans by killing members of the group and causing serious bodily harm to members of the group'. The most serious allegation of the report was that 'these acts constitute the crime of genocide under the Genocide Convention of the United Nations of 1948'.[48] On the question of Tibet's legal status the commission came to the conclusion that Tibet was an independent country[49] and that what happened in Tibet did not fall within the internal affairs of China.[50] The report was unashamedly pro-Tibetan and accepted the Tibetans' account without question. Whatever the merits and accuracy of the report, in the anti-Communist climate, the content of the report was accepted and used as the main body of evidence during the debate at the UN General Assembly. The report was a major publicity boost and ensured that the Tibetan issue remained in the media.

Facing increasing public criticism, the GOI decided to allow the press to meet with the Dalai Lama. On 20 June 1959 he was allowed to hold his first press conference since his arrival in India. In response to questions the Dalai Lama replied that 'wherever I am, accompanied by my Government, the Tibetan people recognise us as the government of Tibet'.[51] This claim was widely reported and regarded as tantamount to a declaration of a government-in-exile. Nehru was irritated by the Dalai Lama's statement and instructed the External Ministry to issue a rebuke: 'The GOI want to make it clear that they do not recognise any separate government of Tibet and there is, therefore, no question of a Tibetan government under the Dalai Lama functioning in India.' It was also during this press conference that the Dalai Lama issued his refutation of the 17-Point Agreement: 'the Sino-Tibetan Agreement was imposed by the Chinese in accordance with their own desires and has been violated by the Chinese themselves, thus giving rise to a contradiction. Therefore we cannot abide by this.'[52] The denunciation did not have any immediate implications.

It was dawning on the Tibetans that they would not be able to achieve recognition of their government-in-exile. Nehru had made it clear that he could not recognise such a government. Legally, India was still bound by the terms of the Sino–Indian agreement of 1954. The Dalai Lama's declaration that he and the Kashag-in-exile constituted the legal government of Tibet caused embarrassment for India. Although the GOI made it clear that it could never recognise the Dalai Lama's claim, in Beijing things were seen very differently: for them, it was enough that India had allowed the Dalai Lama to make such a declaration. Beijing did not believe that the Dalai Lama could have made the statement without the assent of the GOI.

There was no realistic hope that the Dalai Lama could achieve recognition from foreign governments for his government-in-exile. Such a recognition was dependent on whether Tibet was ever recognised as a sovereign state. Tibet had never received *de jure* recognition from any state; in any case such recognition would be disputed not only by Beijing but also by the nationalist regime in Taiwan. The Tibetans had always maintained the misguided hope that Britain, the only country which had extensive contact with Tibet, would look on the issue more favourably. But this was not to be. The Foreign Office denied that the Dalai Lama had the right to make such a declaration.[53] Publicly the Foreign Office prevaricated by stating that India had refused to acknowledge such a government and that they could not embarrass the host country. This was an important point, since a prerequisite of recognition of a government-in-exile was explicit recognition from the host country. Without the GOI's acceptance, there was no possibility of other governments extending recognition. Even the Americans remained silent on this issue, despite their covert relations with the Tibetans. Although publicly willing to condemn Chinese actions in Tibet, on the political front they were reluctant to spearhead a campaign for the Tibetans. Instead they cajoled Chiang Kai-shek into issuing a declaration that, under the Guomindang regime, Tibet would enjoy self-determination.

However, the question of an appeal to the UN was entirely different and here the Tibetans were able to score a major success. In August, Gyalo Dhundup travelled to the Philippines to accept the Magsaysay award on behalf of his brother. It appears that while in Manila he received assurances from the Philippine Government that it would be willing to co-sponsor a resolution on Tibet at the UN.[54] On 30 August, Gyalo Dhundup, now acting as 'special envoy of the Dalai Lama', convened a press conference in Delhi and read a statement from him. It announced the Tibetans' intention to appeal to the United Nations. In Delhi on 2 September, when the Dalai Lama met with Nehru for the second time, he told Nehru that he intended to appeal to the UN. It was reported that Nehru tried to dissuade the Dalai Lama, warning that however sympathetic other countries might be, there was no chance that any country would go to war with China, and pointing out that despite the universal condemnation of Russia's action in Hungary, there was nothing that could be done to save them. Nehru went on to say that so far the Russians had kept completely aloof from the Tibetan issue, but if it were raised at the UN the Soviet bloc would unite in defence of China. Lastly, Nehru warned that a discussion in the UN might bring greater repression to Tibet.[55] When the Dalai Lama pressed Nehru on whether India would give its support to a resolution, Nehru made it clear that India could not support any resolution based on the legal and territorial status of Tibet. Nor could they give an unqualified assurance that they would support a resolution based on human rights. The Dalai Lama stuck to his view and insisted that he would go ahead and try to find a sponsor. Later, a resolution was moved in the Lok Sabha urging India to support the Tibetan case at the UN. Nehru restated that it was fruitless to bring the issue before the UN. He told parliament, 'All that will happen is an expression of strong opinions by some, other countries denying it and the matter being raised to the level of the Cold War and probably producing reactions on the Chinese Government which may be more adverse to Tibet and the Tibetan people than even now. So the ultimate result is no relief to the Tibetan people but something the reverse of it.'[56]

Either because of the growing rift with China or because of pressure from the press and other Indian politicians, the GOI had relaxed their control over the Dalai Lama. It was also apparent to the Indians that they could not impose restraints on the Dalai Lama indefinitely. Despite his age and inexperience, the Dalai Lama had shown himself to be a quite determined and able leader, who could exercise moderation and fend for himself. The Dalai Lama was allowed to meet ambassadors from Japan, Ceylon, the Philippines and Thailand, and they were urged to bring the Tibetan case to the UN. The ambassadors merely gave assurances that they would forward the request to their governments.

As noted earlier, the Tibetan issue had been debated in the UN in November 1950. No resolution was passed because the GOI advised that a peaceful settlement could be reached between Tibet and China. It appeared to the Tibetans that, since the General Assembly at the time adopted a technical procedure and postponed *sine die* voting on the resolution, they should now try to revive the debate at the UN. On 9 September the Dalai Lama wrote a direct appeal to the Secretary-General, Dag Hammarskjold. He drew attention to the fact that in November 1950 the debate on Tibet had been adjourned to allow a peaceful settlement between China and Tibet, and continued:

> It is with deepest regret that I am informing you that the act of aggression by Chinese forces has not terminated. On the contrary the area of aggression has been substantially extended with the result that practically

> the whole of Tibet is under the occupation of the Chinese forces. I and my Government have made several appeals for peaceful and friendly settlement but so far these appeals have been completely ignored. In these circumstances and in view of the inhuman treatment and crimes against humanity and religion to which the people of Tibet are being subjected, I solicit immediate intervention of the United Nations.[57]

The appeal went on to list alleged Chinese violations of human rights in Tibet. The Secretary-General's office distributed the Dalai Lama's appeal to member countries and to the press. This was the only action that they could take, as the Secretary-General's office could not move a resolution or encourage member states to sponsor one. At about the same time a Tibetan delegation headed by Gyalo Dhundup, Shakabpa and Sangdu Rinchen arrived in New York to lobby for the Dalai Lama's appeal. The delegation was accompanied by Hugh Richardson, the last British representative in Lhasa, and Mr Sen, an Indian lawyer who was acting as a legal adviser to the Dalai Lama.

In the event of none of the member states taking up the issue, the Tibetan case would have disappeared. In 1950 the UN had been occupied with Korea and the major powers had wanted to use the time to debate the Korean issue, so the Tibetan resolution had been quickly relegated to a secondary concern. At the end of 1959 the UN General Assembly was relatively free and no major international incidents were absorbing the UN's attention. The Tibetan appeal had arrived at an opportune time. When the Dalai Lama wrote to the Secretary-General, he had not received assurance from any country that it would raise the question at the UN.

On 4 September, the Dalai Lama met with the American chargé d'affaires Winthrop Brown, who told the Dalai Lama that he did not think it would be a good idea for a non-Asian country to sponsor the resolution. If the Americans were to raise the issue, they would be accused of Cold War machinations and would face opposition from many neutral countries. However, Brown assured the Dalai Lama that the US was keen to support the hearing of the Tibetan issue in the UN and that 'his government were prepared to use their influence with other countries in an effort to elicit their support'.[58] It also appears that the Americans were prepared to accept the Dalai Lama's making a personal appearance at the General Assembly in New York, but this depended on India's attitude. The Dalai Lama was aware of the difficulties this would impose on India, and he told Brown that his appearance depended on whether he could obtain an assurance from the GOI that he would be allowed to return to India.[59] In the end, the Dalai Lama did not go to New York. Did India threaten to revoke his asylum? Of course, there was the practical problem that if the Dalai Lama were allowed to appear, the UN would also have to extend an invitation to the Chinese.

The Americans told the Indians that they gave their fullest support to the Tibetans' appeal and requested that if they were unable to sponsor the resolution, they should refrain from opposing it. Dutt made it clear that the Indian view depended on the wording and that they would oppose a strongly worded resolution. He added that the people of India would have 'to be friends with a country with whom they have a border of 2,680 miles'.[60] On 13 September, the Dalai Lama wrote to the British asking for their support for his appeal to the UN. In his letter, the Dalai Lama stressed that the UK had recognised 'the sovereign status of Tibet'. The British stance had always been that she would follow India's wishes on the question of Tibet and many of the Commonwealth countries were worried that if they were to vote in favour of the Tibetan issue being discussed at the UN, while the GOI voted against, it would be seen as opposition to India. The Commonwealth countries therefore first sought Indian opinion and reaffirmed that they were willing to follow the advice of GOI. Although India was not willing to sponsor a resolution herself, Dutt told the British and Australians that India would neither oppose or lobby against other countries bringing the issue to the UN and went on to affirm that India would not consider it as an unfriendly act against India if other countries were to vote in favour of a resolution on Tibet.[61] This was taken to mean that India was in fact keen to see the Tibetan issue being debated in the United Nations. As already noted, India was confronted with a very delicate situation, having accepted Tibet as 'a region of China' in the 1954 agreement, and it would therefore be contravening Article 2 (7) of the UN Charter. India feared that it would be setting a precedent which would make it unable to prevent countries from bringing Nagaland and other domestic problems to the UN in the future.

India's signal that she would not lobby against the question being raised at the United Nations gave more freedom to many Western and Commonwealth countries who were sympathetic to the Tibetans but had not been willing to jeopardise their relationship with New Delhi. On 18 September a meeting took place between the US Secretary of State, Christian Herter, the French Minister for Foreign Affairs, Couve de Murville, and the British representative at the UN, Sir Pierce Dixon. Herter told them that the US was keen to have a debate in the General Assembly but they were pinning their hopes on the issue being raised by an Asian country. Herter also told them that most had declined because of fear of China. He reported that the Irish were prepared to bring up the question and that Malaya and the Philippines might support the Irish. The Irish foreign secretary told Herter that he would make his final decision only after he had spoken to the Chinese Nationalist representatives.[62] The Americans tried to persuade the British and the French to vote in favour. However, both these countries made it clear that they could not support any resolution to debate the Tibetan issue at the General Assembly, citing the legal grounds that the discussion would be contrary to Article 2 (7) of the UN charter. The British also pointed out that if the issue was discussed, it would set a precedent allowing issues like Northern Ireland and even segregation in the United States to be brought before the General Assembly. The French too conceded that there were parallels with Algeria and so they could not support the resolution.[63] Three members of the Security Council were opposed to the question being debated in the General Assembly. This left the Americans doubtful whether they could obtain the necessary two-thirds majority to get the issue put on the agenda. They nevertheless told the British and other Western countries that they had given an assurance to the Dalai Lama that they would do their best to get the case before the UN and they therefore just wanted to see a passing reference made at the General Assembly. At the end of September, Gyalo Dhundup, Shakapba and Sangdu Rinchen, (who was a member of the Tibetan delegation that had signed the 17-Point Agreement) arrived in London to lobby the British. On 30 September, they were met by Lord Lansdowne, the Foreign Office Minister.[64] He pointed out that meeting with the Tibetan delegation was simply a courtesy to the Dalai Lama, while the Foreign Office stressed that the meeting did not imply any recognition of the Dalai Lama's government-in-exile, nor guarantee that they would support Tibet's appeal to the United Nations. Gyalo Dhundup tried unsuccessfully to point out that Britain was one of the very few countries who had engaged in treaty relations with Tibet and that the Tibetans were seeking political support and not merely humanitarian aid. Lord Lansdowne was not prepared to make any commitment, and he added that the Tibetans should 'not entertain any exaggerated hopes of what we [Britain] might be able to do.'[65]

UN Debates

Ultimately, support for Tibet came from Malaya and Ireland. On 28 September, the two countries wrote jointly to the Secretary-General proposing the inclusion of 'The question of Tibet' on the agenda of the 14th session of the UN General Assembly. The explanatory memorandum stated that, after studying available material, 'there exists *prima facie* evidence of an attempt to destroy the traditional way of life of the Tibetan people and the religious and cultural autonomy long recognised to belong to them, as well as systematic disregard for the human rights and fundamental freedoms, set out in the Universal Declaration of Human Rights.' It went on to say that 'in such circumstances, the UN has both a moral obligation and a legal duty to discuss the situation'. The Irish made it clear in their opening statement that their proposal was based purely on the issue of the 'violation of human rights in Tibet, and that issue alone'. The Malayan delegate said that his country was concerned only with the issue of the violation of the human rights and freedoms in Tibet, and it did not want to turn the matter into a controversial political question. The joint memorandum and the later resolution refrained from mentioning Communist China.

When the debate opened, the Communist bloc insisted that Tibet was an internal affair of China and that Article 2 (7) forbade the UN from taking action in the domestic affairs of a country. It was interesting that the Chinese Nationalists insisted that Tibet was a part of China but nevertheless voted in favour of the issue being discussed at the General Assembly. The South Africans said that since the status of Tibet was uncertain and it has thus unclear whether Article 2 (7) applied in the case, they would abstain. The British voted for the inclusion of the issue on the agenda but they proposed it should be discussed at the plenary session, which would have reduced the significance of the debate. When the vote was called, eleven countries voted in favour of inclusion of the item on the agenda of the 14th session of the UN General Assembly. Five countries voted against and four abstained. After the vote was cast, the Czechoslovakians moved to support the British proposal that the item should be discussed at plenary session, and this motion was carried by twelve votes.

Although it was clear that the overwhelming majority were in favour of a discussion, there was considerable argument over what form it should take. The Swedish delegation had earlier proposed that no resolution should be passed and that the General Assembly should merely take cognisance of events in Tibet. This argument was supported by the British. The Foreign Secretary, Selwyn Lloyd, told the General Assembly that since the status of Tibet was unclear and there was also uncertainty as to whether Article 2 (7) applied, 'the Assembly's opinion of the events in Tibet might be more firmly and effectively expressed through a consensus of speeches from this rostrum than through a resolution'. The British went on to state that a distinction should be made between the UN 'taking cognisance and taking action.'[66] The British were of the opinion that the vote for inscription of the issue on the agenda and a general discussion would not contravene Article 2 (7), while a resolution would constitute an intervention in the internal affairs of a state. The Soviet bloc advocated that even a discussion was a contravention of Article 2 (7).

The Americans urged that because of the serious violation of human rights involved, Articles 10 and 55 were applicable in the case of Tibet and a resolution therefore did not infringe Article 2 (7), making the General Assembly competent to deal with Tibet's case. The British proposal did not succeed and, on 13 October, the Malayan and Irish delegations tabled a resolution on human rights in Tibet. The resolution asked the UN to condemn the Chinese for increasing international tensions and to:

(1) affirm its belief that respect for the principles of the Charter and of the Universal Declaration of Human Rights is essential for the evolution of a peaceful world order based on the rule of law:

(2) call for the respect for the fundamental human rights of the Tibetan people and for their distinctive cultural and religious life.[67]

Predictably, the general debate fell into acrimonious Cold War accusations. The Communist bloc argued that Tibet was being used to increase international tension and that no proper debate could ever take place without the proper representation of Communist China. Palph Enckell of Finland said his delegation shared the doubts expressed about the competence of the UN in this case. They also felt that a discussion in the absence of the PRC would be 'one-sided and purposeless'. Finland would therefore abstain in the vote on the draft resolution.

The supporters of the resolution argued that the situation in Tibet warranted the attention and condemnation of the United Nations. While most Western countries expressed their support and sympathy for the Tibetans, they voted against the resolution or abstained on judicial grounds. Walter Loridan of Belgium said that, while it seemed there was authentic information to back up charges that human rights had been violated in Tibet, Article 2 (7) of the UN Charter, 'couched in mandatory terms', had to be kept in mind. This article, Loridan declared, took precedence over the human rights provisions of the charter. Armand Bérard of France stressed that events in Tibet had provoked 'deep emotion' in France. However, the provision of Article 2 (7) of the Charter was of paramount importance and could not be violated without weakening the very foundations of the UN. Therefore, France would also abstain. The reservations expressed by Western countries were motivated by the desire to prevent a precedent being set. The French were sensitive about UN intervention in Algeria. Belgium was sensitive to criticism of its policies in the Congo and it also announced that it would abstain. The Irish Foreign Minister, Frank Aiken, made a desperate appeal to the Assembly. The draft resolution represented, he said, 'the minimum assertion of international morality which the Assembly cannot fall below without being untrue to the principles to which we are pledged'. Foss Shanahan of New Zealand supported the joint draft resolution. It would be 'an abdication of responsibility' for the General Assembly to decline to take action on the Tibetan question 'on illusory arguments of expediency'.

When the vote was called, the resolution was approved by 45 countries, 9 against and 26 abstentions. The resolution received the two-thirds majority needed for its effective adoption. The Indian delegation did not vote, because it felt that their voting might influence other countries. If India had voted against the resolution, it was most likely the resolution would not have received the necessary majority.

The adoption of the resolution was a major propaganda victory for the Tibetans. It ensured that the Tibetan question remained in the forefront of international politics of the day. There have been questions as to why Malaya and Ireland decided to sponsor the resolution. Malaya's motivation was governed by the complex internal and external political situation in south-east Asia. In the 1950s Malaya was confronted with the twin problems of Communist revolt and ethnic clashes between the Malays and the Chinese. The Malays were convinced both these problems were fuelled by Communist China.[68] The Irish may have been genuinely concerned at what they saw as the defence of a smaller nation. There is no doubt the Americans had lobbied for support and, without tacit backing from the US, many of the South American countries would not have voted in favour of the resolution.

It was apparent to everyone that the resolution would not have any effect on the Chinese. Nehru might well have been right that the immediate effect was to harden the Chinese resolve not to give in to international pressure. Moreover, as long as the neighbouring countries who were most directly affected by the situation remained unmoved by the resolution, there was very little the UN could do. The resolution was couched in mild diplomatic terms merely condemning the abuse of human rights. It called neither for the Chinese to withdraw nor to negotiate with the Dalai Lama.

In New York, the Tibetan delegation had a meeting with officials from the State Department. The US had so far maintained a dual policy towards Tibet. While the CIA spearheaded covert support, at the official level the US was reluctant to speak on the status of Tibet. The US was constrained by its friendship with the Nationalist Chinese, who had always argued that Tibet was a part of China. The Nationalists had been under pressure from the Americans to modify their stance on Tibet. Earlier, in March 1959, Chiang Kai-shek declared that 'as soon as the puppet Communist regime on the mainland is overthrown and the people of Tibet are again free to express their will, the Government will assist them to realise their aspirations in accordance with the principles of self-determination'. Chiang's speech had been drafted by the Chinese Nationalist Ambassador to Washington, George Yeh. The Americans, without mentioning the Nationalist statement, told Gyalo Dhundup that US policy would be based on the principle of the right to self-determination and went on to say they would be making a public declaration after they had delivered a formal statement to the Dalai Lama.[69]

The US Embassy in London informed the British Foreign Office of their decision, but added that their statement would be carefully drafted to avoid implicit recognition of the Dalai Lama's government-in-exile. The British were inclined to view this as a 'moral encouragement to offset the disappointment caused (presumably) by the inability of the UN to take any practical steps to help Tibet'. They told the Americans that the statement would not alter the British position, and that they would continue their traditional policy of recognising Chinese suzerainty, on the condition that Tibet enjoyed autonomy. The Americans wanted to encourage other Western countries to make a similar declaration in favour of Tibetan self-determination. While this did not present any internal problems for Washington, for other Western countries, faced with their colonies' demands for independence, it presented a major threat. If they were to adhere to the principal of self-determination, they would have to grant self-determination to their own colonies. This was noted by the legal department of the Foreign Office, who feared an American statement would lead to public and parliamentary pressure for the UK to follow suit.[70] The British therefore were keen to influence the Americans in the wording of their statement so that it would avoid any comparison between Tibet and Western colonies. Despite objections from some Western countries, the Americans made public their correspondence with the Dalai Lama, confirming what they had already told Gyalo Dhundup.

At the end of February 1960 the Americans decided to release a letter from Secretary of State Hector to the Dalai Lama, which made public for the first time the declared position of the US towards Tibet. The American statement was released on the pretext of a response to a letter from the Dalai Lama to the Secretary of State, thanking the US for their support at the UN. Hector in his response declared, 'As you know, while it has been the historical position of the US to consider Tibet as an autonomous country under the suzerainty of China, the American people have also traditionally stood for the principle of self-determination. It is the belief of the United States Government that this principle should apply to the people of Tibet and that they should have the determining voice in their own political destiny.'

In many ways, the American statement had an adverse effect on the Tibetan situation. Many countries concluded that the US was trying to use Tibet for Cold War propaganda. The US announcement was not only rebuffed by the Communists; the Nationalists also issued a statement that Tibet was part of the Republic of China. Beijing accused the Americans of attempting to 'sever Tibet from other parts of China' under the pretext of self-determination.[71] The Indians also did not welcome the US announcement, saying that it misled the Tibetans without any practical results.

India was finding itself on an inextricable collision course with China over the border issue and therefore did not want the added complication of the question of the status of Tibet. They warned the British not to establish any formal contact with the Dalai Lama, and advised the Foreign Office not to respond to any approach from the Tibetans in writing. The Indians argued that any contacts with foreign governments would increase the Tibetans' illusion that something could be done to help Tibet. The British were inclined to follow India's advice on the grounds that it would do neither the Dalai Lama nor his cause any good to upset the Indians[72] and so not only refused to support the Tibetans' appeal but also wanted to terminate any formal contact with the Dalai Lama.[73] They declined to provide any written replies to Tibetan letters of appeal but gave only an oral response, as suggested by India, to deter Tibetans from approaching the British Government in the future.[74]

The Tibetan question was again raised at the UN in July 1960, this time sponsored by Thailand and Malaya. The Tibetans had been lobbying for a more substantive resolution, the previous resolution having merely condemned the Chinese. Encouraged by the large majority who voted in favour of the Malay/Irish resolution, the Tibetans now campaigned for a resolution that would have more practical results. The Tibetans wrote to the governments who had supported the earlier resolution, recommending:

> (1) That the United Nations should adopt a resolution recommending conciliation and mediation by a body appointed for the purpose by the General Assembly.
>
> (2) That the Tibetan problem might more easily be resolved if the United Nations were prepared to endorse the declaration made by the Government of the United States recognising the fundamental right of the people of Tibet to self-determination and to recommend specific measures for its early implementation.[75]

The Tibetans' recommendations did not receive support from governments. The first suggestion was unlikely to achieve any success: Communist China was not represented at the UN and it would naturally reject any third-party mediation, especially under the auspices of the UN. The question of self-determination was even more problematic: almost all Western countries would oppose any resolution based on the right of self-determination. The British Foreign Office noted that 'it would [also] be a very bad precedent in relation to UK's dependent territories, and would encourage either the Soviet bloc or the neutrals to promote a resolution on self-determination in respect to those territories'.[76] This view would have been shared by other European colonial powers, who no doubt would have opposed any resolution along these lines at the General Assembly.

Malaya and Thailand wanted to propose a resolution that would gain a large number of affirmative votes. On 19 August 1960, Thai and Malay representatives requested the inclusion of the 'Question of Tibet' on the agenda of the 15th Session of the United Nations' General Assembly. In September, the Dalai Lama wrote a detailed letter to the Secretary General which was clearly intended to bring the question of the international status of Tibet to the forefront of the debate. He stressed that Tibet had been an independent country and gave a lengthy account of Tibet's history.[77] On 10 October, at the pre-agenda meeting, there was once again a discussion as to whether or not the question of Tibet should be included on the agenda. At previous talks, objections had been raised to the UN discussing the issue at all, with the Indonesian representative arguing that the presence of the legitimate Government of China was indispensable for consideration of the question of Tibet. The supporters of the motion argued that the UN was under a moral obligation to consider the grave abuse of human rights in Tibet. When the vote was cast, 49 countries voted in favour of a discussion 13 were against the resolution, and 35 abstained. Despite the large majority in favour, the issue was not discussed. Nineteen sixty was the high-point of the Cold War. In May the American U2 spy plane had been shot down by the Russians, a major propaganda victory for the Communist bloc. The Eisenhower administration was involved in an election campaign, making the Americans keen to reduce international confrontation with the Soviet Union. The Russian Ambassador at the UN made it known that he was in favour of cancelling the debate on Tibet, implying that its continuance would prompt the Soviet Union to raise other issues against the Americans. It was discreetly agreed that in the interests of reducing international tension the discussion on Tibet should be dropped.

When in 1961 J. F. Kennedy came to power with the avowed aim of challenging Communism, the Tibetans received a new impetus. In September 1961, Malaya and Thailand moved to include Tibet on the agenda of the 16th session of the General Assembly, this time with the support of Ireland and El Salvador. The move was approved by 48 votes to 14 with 35 abstentions. Thailand and Malaya proposed a critical resolution, which made specific reference to the rights of self-determination. The preamble to the resolution stated that the continuing events in Tibet constituted a violation of fundamental human rights, including the right of self-determination. The wording was much stronger than the previous resolution adopted by the UN; however, it also avoided mentioning Communist China. The Thai and Malay draft resolution made no concession to the pressure from Western countries that wanted to avoid mention of self-determination. The resolution closely followed the Tibetans' argument that it should be based on the principle of self-determination. The draft resolution:

(1) Reaffirms its conviction that respect for the principles of the Charter and of the Universal Declaration of Human Rights is essential for the evolution of a peaceful world order based on the rule of law;

(2) Solemnly renews its call for the cessation of practices which deprive

the Tibetan people of their fundamental human rights and freedoms including their rights to self-determination;

(3) Expresses the hope that member States will make all possible efforts as appropriate towards achieving the purpose of the present resolution.[78]

The motion was naturally opposed by the Soviet bloc on the grounds that it violated Article 2 (7) of the Charter. The resolution was clearly a great victory for the Tibetans, but in practice it had no effect and has remained dormant ever since. Meanwhile the Tibetans' relationship with the GOI was getting steadily worse. The resolutions at the UN and the growing international support for Tibet had placed India in a delicate situation. Her decision to abstain at the UN had baffled the Indian public and, most importantly, failed to appease the Chinese, who were convinced that the Tibet issue had deliberately been internationalised by India. The growing tension over the border made India even more cautious about the activities of the Tibetans. In reality the GOI did its utmost to avoid any association between the question of asylum for the Dalai Lama and the border dispute and constructed obstacles to deter the Tibetans from gaining any foreign support. In early 1960 the GOI was reluctant to provide travel documents for Gyalo Dhundup, Shakabpa and Sandhu Rinchen for their journey to England and the US,[79] although Shakabpa had now been appointed the Dalai Lama's representative in Delhi. The GOI had also taken steps to prevent foreign governments from communicating directly with the Dalai Lama. In March 1960, Dutt wrote from the Ministry of External Affairs to the Australian High Commissioner, informing him that communication with the Dalai Lama had to be considered as purely private and personal.[80] Later the Indians informed the British and Americans that their offices in Delhi should not be used to maintain contact with the Dalai Lama and his advisers.[81] This presented a major blow to the Tibetans and hampered their international campaign to obtain recognition for their government-in-exile.

Indian attitudes towards the Dalai Lama and his government were to change drastically after the Sino–Indian War. Although the Indians could never acknowledge the Dalai Lama's administration as the legitimate government, they relaxed their restrictions over the activities of the Tibetans and allowed the Dalai Lama to set up a complex administrative system which had total control over the affairs of the refugees. By the mid-sixties the Tibetan issue was beginning to fade from the international arena despite an attempt in 1965 to revive it at the UN. By then, however, the international community had accepted the Tibetan situation as a *fait accompli*. This time India would have liked to have seen the Tibetan issue debated at the UN but it had neither the influence to muster enough support, nor would it have been able to defend itself against the accusation of being anti-Chinese.[82] With the rift between China and the Soviet Union, the Americans were not willing to antagonise China further by bringing up the Tibetan question at the UN. The growing international stature of Communist China and eventual rapprochement between China and America in the early 1970s eclipsed Tibet's international significance and its propaganda value for the West. The Tibetan issue was swiftly abandoned.

NINE

Reform and Repression

The Tibetan revolt occurred at a particularly difficult period in China's history, turning it into a symbol of a much wider malaise affecting China. In the spring of 1959, Mao had been personally attacked for his decision to launch the Great Leap Forward in the drive to transform China overnight into a giant industrialised nation. The failure of the Great Leap Forward and the subsequent shortage of grain caused great hardship in Chinese society, and brought into question Mao's own position as the Chairman of the CCP. The internal economic problems were further compounded by the growing rift with the Soviet Union. Although the Russians defended China's actions in Tibet at the UN, they remained uncommitted to much larger issues, culminating in Khrushchev's refusal to provide China with a prototype of the atom bomb. The Soviet leaders chose to remain neutral over the border dispute with India, describing it as 'sad' and 'stupid'[1] and increasing Soviet aid to India. From Beijing's point of view the failure of one socialist country to support another amounted to a stab in the back.[2]

These much larger issues confronting the leadership in Beijing were to impinge on Chinese policy decisions in Tibet. Both for domestic and international reasons the Chinese knew they could not be seen to be weakened or perturbed by the revolt. Marshal Peng Dehuai, who was visiting Eastern Europe in April 1959, said that the leaders of the Communist bloc were 'keenly following the events in Tibet'.[3] As a result Beijing's ability to handle the revolt was becoming a crucial test for the regime. The Chinese leadership was coming under fire from its allies in Eastern Europe on ideological grounds for the failure to understand and implement Marxist-Leninist principles on nationalities. The emerging ideological and border disputes between the Soviet Union and China meant that the treatment of minority nationalities was becoming a major issue.

The Tibetan revolt was one of the first major set-backs experienced by the new government of the People's Republic of China. However, the Chinese leadership did not show that they were unduly worried by it. The subject was not even discussed at the 7th Plenum of the Central Committee and the issue was relegated to the NPC, where Tibet was the main subject of discussion.[4] The NPC is a symbolic institution, which merely endorses decisions made by the CCP. This shows that there was a unanimous agreement among the higher leadership that the rebellion had to be suppressed by force. It is also interesting to note that none of the Chinese leadership in Tibet was purged. This implied that either Beijing had accepted that the revolt was inevitable and that the Communist officials in Tibet were not to be blamed, or Chinese leaders feared a purge would be seen as an admission of failure of their policy. There was dissension among some Chinese officials stationed in Tibet, where cadres from the North-West Military Region, like Fan Ming, had always been critical of Zhang Guohua and Zhang Jingwu, who were from the South-West Military Region. The officials from the North-West Military Region were more closely connected with the Panchen Rinpoche and, as mentioned earlier, there had been little or no disturbance in areas under the control of Tashilhunpo, which was attributed to the correct handling of the situation by the cadres from the North-West Military Region. But the leadership in Beijing had no time for such internal squabbling. They were aware of the need to present a united front when confronted with a major challenge[5] and both Zhang Guohua and Zhang Jingwu returned to Tibet and continued to occupy important positions. Beijing stood firm, refusing to admit that the revolt was a challenge to their right to rule Tibet.

The failure of the revolt and the subsequent flight of the Dalai Lama left a vacuum in Tibetan society. While the absence of the Dalai Lama and the Kashag meant the extinction of leadership at national level, the flight of other lamas, like the Karmapa and Sakya Trizin, meant that even at a local level the traditional secular and religious leadership had vanished. This allowed the Chinese to establish their authority with relative ease. The absence of national and local leadership also meant that the Chinese could impose their reforms without any collective opposition. Despite the Tibetans' lack of united opposition, the Chinese ability to secure total control of Tibet was largely due to their military superiority: there was never any doubt that the PLA would be able to gain military control of Tibet. Nevertheless, reinforcements had to be brought into Tibet from other military areas: a cavalry regiment had to be sent from Inner Mongolia – where it had been specially trained for the rough terrain of the Tibetan plateau – and military control was passed to General Ding Sheng, who was described as one of the rising stars of the PLA. To some extent, the appointment of Ding Sheng and the deployment of battle-hardened troops from the Korean war reflected the seriousness with which the Chinese authorities saw the revolt.

The Chinese told those who were captured that the revolt was futile and the Tibetans were like a monkey fighting an elephant or an egg being thrown at a cliff face.[6] Chinese propaganda boldly announced that one could not escape from the Communist Party and PLA any more than one could avoid death.[7] But there were more complex social and political problems that the Communists had to confront in Tibet. They had always recognised Tibet's unique position and from the start had followed a policy which made concessions to the prevailing social, economic and political conditions there. However, they had tolerated Tibet's distinctiveness as a strategic necessity. Now they had established full power and the traditional ruling class had been destroyed, it was no longer necessary to promise 'non-interference in internal affairs'. The difficult question still facing the Chinese was, however, whether they should continue to give special consideration to the 'local conditions', or whether the region should be subjected to the same reforms that had already been introduced in China. Some argued that if the reforms were not implemented in the region, Tibet would lag behind China in terms of social progress and in time the gap would become unbridgeable. However, there were moderate cadres who felt that, despite the revolt, Tibet should not be subjected to the full onslaught of socialist transformation. They felt that the Tibetans needed to be convinced of the desirability of democratic reforms.

Smash the Reactionaries!

The immediate practical problem faced by the Chinese was to find a replacement for the Dalai Lama. This was not easy to solve: as Tibet's supreme leader, the Dalai Lama's authority is absolute and no Tibetan would think of accepting a post which undermined that authority. Moreover, the Chinese genuinely believed that he had been abducted. When he was told that the Dalai Lama had escaped, Mao responded perceptively, saying, 'We have lost.'[8] He had always understood the practical importance of the Dalai Lama, and had tried to give the appearance of self-rule by appointing the Dalai Lama Chairman of PCART and obtaining the Dalai Lama's approval for changes. With the flight of the Dalai Lama to India, the Communists were faced with the critical dilemma of how to legitimise their policies. There was also the problem of how to explain the flight of the Dalai Lama to the Tibetan populace. Soon after the Dalai Lama reached India, the *Beijing Review* published the last correspondence between the Dalai Lama and Tan Guansan. As noted earlier, the letters appear to show that the Dalai Lama had no intention of leaving Tibet. The correspondence was widely circulated in Tibet and elsewhere to show that the Dalai Lama was abducted.

As to how to legitimise their authority, the Chinese had two alternatives: either to abandon any pretence of self-government and enforce the reforms regardless of 'local conditions', or to continue with the past policy of winning over the traditional élite. Since 1950 the Chinese had claimed their legitimacy by virtue of the 17-Point Agreement and their relationship with the traditional ruling classes – the aristocracy, the religious leaders and Lhasa Government officials. Now that the agreement had been denounced by both sides and the Dalai Lama was missing, they needed to seek a mandate for their rule by other means. The post-revolt policy can be viewed as an attempt to achieve a degree of acceptance from the Tibetan people, which would enable them to carry out more integrationist policies. The Chinese, knowing that their authority could not be achieved purely by the use of coercion, sought to legitimise the new relationship by promoting reform and going directly to the Tibetan masses. The Communists naïvely believed that in the long run Tibet would be fully integrated into China and that the spectacular material progress brought by them would naturally encourage the masses to look towards Beijing as the source of all power and progress.

The strategy adopted by the Chinese necessitated the introduction of a new political culture. The first decade (1950–9) had seen the Communists essentially engaged in dialogue and negotiation with the traditional ruling class. This had conformed to the Tibetans' assumption that politics was the prerogative of the élite, with the Tibetan masses not participating in the affairs of the state. The second phase (1959–64) could be described as China's attempts to win over the masses. A new ideology and a new style of politics were introduced, whereby the masses were actively encouraged to involve themselves in every aspect of political life. They were subjected to countless meetings and rallies, used by the Chinese mainly to communicate their policies. The Tibetans could never express their demands through these meetings: it was one-way traffic. Supposed to bring the Chinese and the Tibetan masses closer together, in reality the meetings helped to widen the gap between them. The Tibetans believed that the Chinese showed the 'true face' of their rule during these meetings, which left no doubt that the Chinese were in full power. They were always led by the Chinese cadres, who initiated the condemnation of the evils of 'Chitsog Nyinpa' (the old society) and promised a new and happier society under the guidance of the Communist Party, which was to the Tibetans synonymous with Chinese rule.

The Communists did not immediately discard the support of the remnants of the traditional élite. Those who had not participated in the revolt were retained and promoted. Beside Ngabo, who had opposed the uprising and remained a loyal supporter of the Chinese, the only other Kashag member who had not fled was Sampho, who had been injured outside the Norbulingka. He was promoted to Deputy Director of the Military Control Committee and on 15 April he was brought out to condemn the rebellion and to urge the people to work under the leadership of the Communist Party. He and Ngabo continued to play a leading part as figureheads who were especially important to the Chinese because they had been signatories to the 17-Point Agreement. The Chinese continued to believe that the Tibetan ruling class had a useful purpose to serve in legitimising Chinese rule in Tibet. Moreover, the aristocracy and the high lamas had always assumed the role of the bureaucracy and had the advantages of literacy and general knowhow. The Communists had always used the United Front strategy, 'to develop the progressive forces, to win over the middle-of-the-road forces, and to isolate the die-hards',[9] as a cornerstone of their Tibet policy, where it meant winning over what they called the 'patriotic' and 'progressive' forces among the bourgeois class. This meant that those members of the ruling class who had not participated in the revolt would continue to enjoy the support and the protection of the Chinese and would continue to form the main source of Tibetan cadres.

The introduction of a new political culture also marked the first phase of the integration of Tibet into the greater polity of China. In practical terms this was symbolised by making the Renminbi the legal tender of Tibet. Until the revolt the Tibetans had continued to use the old Tibetan currency, despite the fact that its value had decreased with the introduction of the Chinese silver dollar. The new integrationist approach was marked more significantly by the announcement that the traditional locus of power, the Tibetan Government, would be abolished, and that in its place the PCART would 'exercise the function and power of the local Government'.[10] The abolition of what the Chinese called the Tibetan 'local government' erased the last residue of Tibetan self-rule. Naturally, the rudimentary local governing structure based on Dzongs also came to an end. Despite its failings and anachronistic nature, the indigenous polity had given Tibet her identity and marked her separateness from China.

The PCART had never been a powerful institution, and its renewed importance did not mean that it became more powerful. It was a body on which Tibetans were represented and which projected a semblance of Tibetan involvement in decision-making. Those Tibetan officials who had not participated in the revolt and remained in the country were given new posts in PCART.[11] However, PCART remained mainly of symbolic importance. It was clear that *de facto* power would rest with the newly established PLA Military Control Committee. Since 1950 the PLA had played a prominent role in the integration of Tibet and, having successfully suppressed the revolt, it was natural that the army assumed a greater role in the running of Tibet. Nevertheless, the Chinese knew that both for external propaganda reasons and for internal legitimacy they needed a Tibetan figurehead to represent the authority in Tibet.

The Panchen Rinpoche

The most important figure after the Dalai Lama was the Panchen Rinpoche. The areas under the jurisdiction of Tashilhunpo remained unaffected by the events in Lhasa and, on 30 March 1959, *Xinhua* released a telegram reportedly from the Panchen Rinpoche's office to Mao, declaring that all the people under the jurisdiction of the Panchen Rinpoche would 'take an oath that from now on we will, under the leadership of the CCP, always work to further unity, firmly insist on the anti-imperialist and patriotic stand, give energetic support to the PLA, resolutely put down the rebellion and struggle to preserve national unification, carry out reform early, take the socialist road and build a new Tibet'.[12] The Tashilhunpo officials, realising the Chinese would put down the rebellion at all costs, may have decided to dispatch the telegram to placate Beijing and to declare their non-involvement in the uprising. By sending the telegram directly to Beijing addressed to Zhou Enlai and Mao, they made sure that the local officials would not have the chance to accuse them of working with rebels. This allowed the Panchen Rinpoche to assume a new importance. It was announced that, in the absence of the Dalai Lama, the Panchen Rinpoche would be promoted to the position of acting Chairman of the PCART. His new importance was reflected in the welcome he was given when he arrived in Lhasa on 5 April to attend the first meeting of PCART since the revolt.

When the meeting opened in Lhasa the next day, it was clear that it was very important both for domestic and external reasons. The inauguration of the meeting was attended by a large number of Tibetan participants, to show that the rebellion had been brought under control and that the revolt had been confined to a small faction in Tibetan society. It was announced that members of PCART who had fled to India or taken part in the uprising were dismissed and new Tibetan officials had been appointed.[13] The new appointees were still drawn from the traditional ruling class, thus signalling that the Communists would continue with their previous policy of working with the traditional leaders. Tibetan officials had only reluctantly participated in the PCART meetings and since the March rebellion those who had remained in Tibet were compelled to attend, knowing that any opposition would be seen by the Chinese as hidden sympathy for the rebels.

The main purpose of the PCART meeting was to condemn the uprising and endorse the State Council's order of 28 March, which instructed the PLA to suppress the rebellion. All the participants dutifully condemned the revolt and pledged their support to the new Military Commission. The only significant speech was made by Zhang Guohua, who had returned from Beijing to take charge of the situation. He announced that the reforms in Tibet would be 'decided in accordance with the specific conditions' and would be introduced 'through peaceful consultation among the Tibetan people and the public leaders'.[14] This implied that the Chinese would continue with the previous policy and that no major social reforms would be enforced. However, the Chinese leadership was also keen to point out that the 'no reform' decision was merely a temporary honeymoon. Zhang Guohua told the PCART meeting that 'all the nationalities of our country must carry out social reforms and take the road of socialism'.[15]

Although the Chinese had gained firm control of the country, they could not take it for granted that they had eliminated all opposition to the reforms. Opposition to the reforms was not confined to the ruling class but shared by a large section of the Tibetan population. In the early 1950s, the Tibetans had agreed that the reforms would be initiated only after the people demanded them. In fact, the wording of the 17-Point Agreement stated that the Central Government would not compel the Tibetans to carry out reforms and that the changes would be made only after consultation with the people. The Tibetans had accepted that wording because they could not envisage the people ever demanding radical changes. For the Tibetans the reforms not only meant the redistribution of land owned by aristocratic estates: they also meant the dismantling of the economic foundations of the religious institutions and redistribution of the estates belonging to high lamas. There was nothing to indicate that the Tibetan peasantry was dissatisfied with the system and wanted to see its dismantling; on the contrary, the majority of the Tibetans remained very much attached to their religious institutions and the Chinese realised that they would have difficulties in implementing the reforms. The Tibetan people would still need to be cajoled into accepting the reforms and the changes.

Therefore, the decision to introduce the reforms more slowly was a concession to pragmatism and to the need to show a continuity in order to gain the confidence of the Tibetan people. The Chinese also knew they still needed to win over the members of the ruling class who had remained in Tibet, which meant not threatening their positions. The masses were to be won over by the promise of reward. In his speech to the Second NPC meeting Zhou Enlai endorsed the ideas already postulated by Zhang Guohua at the PCART meeting. Zhou restated that the 'Central Government will conduct full consultation with the patriotic people of the upper and middle social strata and the masses to decide the time, steps and measures for their institution. In any case, the reforms will be carried out step by step with full regard for the specific conditions in Tibet and, in the course of the reforms, the religious beliefs and customs and habits of the Tibetan people will be fully respected.'[16] Zhou's announcement showed that the policy of gradual transition had been approved at the highest level of the CCP.

There were also other factors which prevented the Chinese from launching rapid economic changes. It has to be remembered that the communisation and economic reforms in China itself had come under criticism, and had then been slowed down. In Tibet, the Communists never had the chance to prepare the people or the administrative infrastructure necessary to implement the reforms. There were factions that argued that the revolt had been a decisive juncture in the integration of Tibet which had separated the 'revolutionaries' and the 'counter-revolutionaries' and this presented an opportune time to introduce the reforms. Since the rebellion had been defeated and the reactionary clique had torn up the 17-Point Agreement, there were now no obstacles inhibiting Tibet from undergoing socialist transformation. But the set-backs facing the extreme leftist groups in China meant that they were unable to instigate their programme of rapid reform in Tibet.

The Chinese gave two reasons for adopting moderate reforms, one economic, the other political. Because of the fragile economic conditions in Tibet a violent and rapid reform would cause serious economic dislocation and damage agricultural production for many years. We shall see later that this is exactly what happened when the Tibetans were subjected to communisation. In the early phase of the reforms the Communists were realistic enough to recognise that indiscriminate application of reforms would lead to catastrophe. They saw that this was particularly true of nomadic areas. Once the animals had been slaughtered or the number of animals decreased, it would not be possible to bring the number of animals back up to productive levels. It therefore was announced that there would be 'no redistribution of cattle' and no class distinction imposed in pastoral areas.[17] In practical terms, the main Chinese aim was to avoid major economic disruption. Moreover, the Communists argued that the traditional élite – the monks, aristocrats and wealthy traders – still exercised influence over the people and therefore should not be alienated. It was important to win their confidence and their co-operation in implementing the reforms.

Despite the victorious atmosphere of the PCART meetings, there were still pockets of resistance in different parts of the country and the Chinese had yet to win the support of the Tibetan masses. The urgent problems confronting the Chinese in Tibet were now political rather than economic. Until they had gained total political control of the country, they could not begin to address the economic and social problems. The Communists resorted to strategies that had been applied successfully in China during the war against the Nationalists in the early stages of reform. They began to mobilise the people into condemning the revolt, organising public rallies and meetings in towns and villages to show that the Tibetans supported the suppression of the revolt. Hundreds of people were herded to these meetings, no doubt the same people who were engaged only a few weeks before in demonstrations against the Chinese. On 15 April what was officially described as a mammoth public rally was held in Lhasa 'demanding the thorough quelling of the rebellion'.[18] The Chinese had made it clear that non-participation in the rally would be viewed as sympathy for the reactionaries. This strategy marked a shift in approach: for the first time the Chinese were trying to involve the Tibetan masses in their political campaigns. The mass mobilisation strategy was an implicit coercive means of controlling the Tibetan populace. It was said that 'only through the complete mobilisation and organisation of the masses, raising their awareness, transforming the revolutionary movement into mass activity . . . can the revolution in Tibet achieve a great victory'.[19]

Chinese policy was designed to achieve control by isolating and destroying the political influence of the *Log-chopa* (rebels) and the Chinese were selective in the use of force. While they continued to use it to root out scattered resistance groups, the PLA refrained from employing military means in areas where they had gained control. Here they used tactics of mass mobilisation to integrate the people into their political objectives. In Lhasa and other areas where they had established secure control, the Chinese began to divide Tibetans into those who took part in the revolt (*Zhing-yod*) and those who had not been involved (*Zhing-med*). At the second meeting of the PCART, it was announced by the Panchen Rinpoche that 'different treatment will be given to those who joined the rebellion and those who did not'.[20] This was the first labelling exercise that the Chinese authorities had carried out in Tibet; later there was to be much more labelling of people into different classes and political categories. This exercise had far-reaching political consequences. The differentiation of the Tibetan ruling élite on the basis of their involvement in the uprising prevented them from forming a united opposition group and Tibetan officials who were known to have refrained from joining the rebellion remained immune to persecution, despite their reactionary class origin.

Those Tibetan aristocratic leaders who took an active part in the revolt, like Lhalu, the former Governor of Kham, were arrested and immediately subjected to *thumzing* (struggle sessions), and paraded through Lhasa. Almost the entire Tibetan army and many monks were arrested and dispatched to labour camps in various parts of Tibet or to camps in other provinces of China. Even here the Chinese tactic was 'thought reform' rather then outright terror. However, the prisoners were kept in very poor conditions and hundreds died in the camps.[21] The Chinese campaign was to re-orient Tibetans' thinking to ensure their eventual acceptance of Tibet as 'an inseparable part of the motherland'. It was only later that the Chinese began ideological indoctrination in the camps. All the prisoners who had been arrested for taking part in the uprising were treated as counter-revolutionaries and many were not released until 1979, after the death of Mao. The labour camps were not merely centres of re-education but a source of cheap labour. Two of the largest labour camps were Nachenbag, where the prisoners were forced to work in the construction of a hydro-electricity plant, and Jang Tsala Karpo, where, as the name suggests, the Chinese had built a borax mine.[22] The Chinese could only achieve these projects with the extensive use of prison labour. In southern Tibet in the Kongpo region, the Chinese developed a timber industry using prisoners. There are no exact figures for the number of people who died in these labour camps; many who were taken prisoner never returned home and simply disappeared.

While the Chinese were trying to maintain control in Tibet, the international focus shifted to Beijing, where the Second Session of the National People's Conference was being held. At the time there was considerable international press attention focused on Tibet and the NPC provided the Chinese with an opportunity to publicise their policy in Tibet and to refute claims made by the Tibetan leaders in exile. The meeting was supposed to discuss the economy and the progress of the Great Leap Forward campaign, but because of the Tibetan uprising and particularly because of international reaction to the revolt, the meeting was dominated by the Tibetan issue. The speeches at the NPC concentrated on denouncing 'foreign interventionists' and clearly the whole focus of the meeting was directed against the international reaction to the Tibetan crisis. Ngabo's speech was entirely concerned with refuting the Dalai Lama's Tezpur statement. The only other noteworthy speech was made by the Panchen Rinpoche – now being promoted by the Chinese as a 'national leader' – who in his speech admitted that 'the primary task in the Tibet region is to weed out the remnant rebels thoroughly . . . at present, although the rebellion is, in the main, put down, there are still some odd numbers of remnant rebels engaged in harassing activities in some remote areas'.[23] The Chinese continued to suffer attacks from Tibetan rebels in many remote areas and later the PLA had to deal with the resistance groups based in Nepal. The Panchen Rinpoche's speech was also remarkable because it urged that 'the Tibetan people must respect Han-Tibetan friendship as they do the Buddhist Trinity (*skon-mchogs gsum*)'.[24] This reflected a shift in the Chinese viewpoint, for whereas previously they had stressed that Tibet was an inseparable part of China, now they began to advocate the idea that the development of Tibet would be unthinkable without the presence of the Chinese.

The revolt had totally changed the relationship between the Tibetans and the Chinese, leaving the Chinese in a much stronger position than ever before. However powerless the Dalai Lama and the Tibetan Government may have been during the intervening period, they had served as a restraining influence on the Chinese. With the collapse of the resistance and the absence of the Dalai Lama's authority, the Chinese could operate without hindrance, and despite the promise that no reforms would be initiated in Tibet before 1962, it was announced that a moderate phase of reform would be implemented shortly after the suppression of the revolt. A resolution adopted at the 2nd NPC declared that 'the PCART should prepare a constitution according to the hopes of most Tibetans and in line with the social, economic, and cultural characteristics of Tibet; they should effect democratic reforms step by step, plucking the Tibetans up [from] the worst [excess of feudalism] and establishing foundations of prosperous socialism in the New Tibet.'[25]

The Tibetan and Chinese leaders returned to Lhasa in June 1959 with approval from Beijing to carry out preliminary reforms. High-ranking Communist leader Wang Feng, the Vice-Chairman of the Nationalities Affairs Commission and second in charge of the United Front section of the CCP, travelled to Lhasa to inaugurate the reforms. On his return to Lhasa, the Panchen Rinpoche announced that 'the urgent task now confronting us Tibetans is to carry out democratic reforms quickly on the basis of the thorough suppression of the rebellion, to bury the system of feudal serfdom and establish the people's democratic system'.[26] The programme for reform was discussed at the second meeting of PCART in June 1959. Interestingly, it was left to two Tibetans, Ngabo and Panchen Rinpoche, to announce the decision to implement the reforms. The Chinese media gave extensive publicity to their speeches; no doubt the prominence given to the Tibetans was meant to show that they had themselves demanded reform. At the PCART meeting Ngabo announced that 'conditions were now ripe for carrying out democratic reform in Tibet', and went on to stress that reforms would be revolutionary, but peaceful. Ngabo summarised that the reforms would be carried out in two stages; the first stage would involve a campaign to suppress the remnants of the rebellion, followed by the abolition of obligatory labour service (*ulag*) and the reduction in rent. The second stage would involve redistribution of land.[27]

The Chinese began to implement reforms the same month in areas where they had established firm control. While they had had time to educate and prepare people for the reforms in China, in Tibet, because of the urgency of the situation, reform was implemented in haste. According to official statements both stages of the reform were completed by February 1960, meaning that the first phase of the 'democratic reform' lasted only nine months. The reform was preceded by a campaign aimed at 'heightening the class and political consciousness' of the Tibetan masses but the Communists could not assume that the reforms would be popular and voluntarily accepted by the people. It has to be acknowledged that, contrary to Communist propaganda, the reforms were not 'demanded by the people'. For most Tibetans the reforms were imposed from outside by outsiders. The Communists were cautious and knew that the reforms could not be implemented overnight. The key to the success of the reform was 'the mobilisation of the masses',[28] Zhang Guohua told the PCART meeting.

The Communists were also aware that material incentives were in themselves not sufficient to sustain the revolution. For the reforms to take a firm root in Tibetan society there had to be an ideological conversion on the part of the Tibetan masses. For this purpose, the Chinese launched a radical ideological campaign overtly designed to denigrate the old society. Thus began the depiction of the old Tibetan society as a hell on earth, and of the Chinese as liberators or saviours of the Tibetan masses. A system of confronting past grievances was devised in villages, neighbourhood groups, nomadic and labour camps. People were ushered into meetings night after night to hear people recounting their past grievances. The Communists believed that 'only through recall of past miseries can the broad masses [always] remember the past miseries and only through comparison of the present with the past can they appreciate deeply the precious[ness of the] happiness in which they live today'.[29] The development of 'class consciousness' would not only sustain the revolution internally but, armed with the correct ideology and class stand, they would be able to defeat the reactionary forces abroad.

Whatever the theoretical intention might have been, the meetings quickly became so theatrical that they degenerated into false accusations and the settling of old scores. It was not that the people had no grievances about the old society, but the Chinese wanted the Tibetans to trot out their complaints like a sociological thesis. At first the Tibetans were bewildered and did not know what was expected of them. When the meetings failed to produce appropriate responses, the Chinese adopted well-rehearsed routines, whereby local Tibetan cadres, with all the enthusiasm of new converts, would ask rhetorical questions and the people were expected to give the correct formulaic answers in unison. The three evils of the old society were: the Tibetan Government, aristocratic estate holders, and monasteries; the road to salvation was the Communist Party. On 4 March 1960, *Tibet Daily* carried an interesting story intended to show how Communist cadres had successfully raised the class consciousness of the peasantry. It was reported that when cadres visited Medro Gonkar xiang (county), the people did not 'have any complaints to make' about the old society. The article went on to say that, on hearing this, the Party immediately called a meeting of the village and 'many typical examples were cited to them and the villagers were able to recognise the evils of the old society'.[30]

The Chinese announced that these meetings were successful and had heightened the revolutionary fervour of the Tibetan masses. According to Tibetan reports the reality was very different. The Tibetans had learned how to respond with the correct answers and condemned or praised whoever the Chinese wanted. Soon they could recite the correct answers like Buddhists recite mantras.[31]

The reforms were initiated not only on ideological grounds but also to elicit support from the poorest sections of Tibetan society. The Communists were now, for the first time, attempting to widen the basis of their support in Tibet. It was no longer possible for the Chinese to rely on the intercession of the traditional élite to legitimise their rule as they had done before the revolt. The mass mobilisation campaign advertised for the first time the ideological nature of Chinese rule and thrust a new political culture onto Tibet, in effect re-negotiating the relationship between the ruled (Tibetans) and the ruler (Chinese). According to official claims, the campaigns united the people and the Party and achieved victory over the reactionary forces.

It is interesting and ironic that at the 2nd PCART meeting held in Lhasa on 28–30 June 1959, all the participants made a vociferous denunciation of the 'upper-strata reactionaries' for staging the revolt and keeping the Tibetan masses under cruel feudal enslavement. All the Tibetan participants and speakers were either aristocrats or high lamas, the very class they were denouncing and accusing of various crimes. The Tibetan officials who were regarded as 'patriotic' and 'progressive' were treated favourably and did not suffer economically or politically, receiving jobs and positions in local committees and in the Political Consultative Conference. This 'creative application of the Marxist-Leninist principle',[32] as Zhang Jingwu called it, debilitated the opposition to the reforms.

The reforms, summarised in one of the numeric formulae so favoured by the Communists as the 'Three Antis and Two Reductions', were launched throughout Tibet in July 1959. Even in areas where there was little or no resistance to the Chinese, people were not spared the campaign. In nomadic communities in western Tibet the revolt in Lhasa made no impact and the people had not been in any way involved in the uprising, yet they were still subjected to the Anti-Rebellion campaign on the grounds that some had given food to pilgrims who had later fled to India. This simple act of generosity became evidence of helping the rebels and these nomads too were subjected to struggle sessions.

The Anti-Rebellion campaign, coming so soon after the flight of the Dalai Lama, was intended to create fear and instability throughout the country. It cannot be stressed enough that in many areas this was the first real contact between the Tibetans and the Chinese. In the past, Chinese cadres and PLA troops had merely visited remote Tibetan communities and had not asked the people to be involved in political campaigns. Now the Chinese were forcing the local people to attend meetings and accusing those suspected of involvement in the revolt of betraying 'the motherland'. Such meetings and accusations took place in all villages and nomadic communities. In Sakya,

Dawa Norbu recalls, 'no layman or lama was directly involved with the Tibetan revolt; nevertheless, all the ecclesiastics and aristocrats (except for two families) were found guilty of the highest treason: "reactionary rebellion to separate Tibet from the Motherland".'[33] The arbitrary and often ruthless retribution meted out to those suspected of involvement in the revolt did not endear the Chinese to the Tibetans. Most Tibetans who fled to India, particularly those in the border regions in western Tibet, did so after the Chinese campaign. Even in Shigatse, where no rebellion took place, many of the Panchen Rinpoche's personal staff were accused of involvement in the revolt. We will see later that this was to become the main complaint of the Panchen Rinpoche against the Chinese.

The campaign did more damage to Chinese–Tibetan relations than the actual uprising. In China the mass mobilisation and other political campaigns that were adopted to subdue anti-Communist factions had had some success, partly because the campaigns were associated with the concrete concerns of the Chinese masses. But in Tibet there was no meeting point between the Chinese and the Tibetan masses. What the Chinese saw as the most traitorous crime, 'betraying the Motherland', was an empty slogan to the majority of Tibetans who had never looked towards China as a 'Motherland' and to whom the Chinese were foreigners as much as the British or the Indians, with an ideology as alien as Christianity. To the Tibetans the revolt was never seen as a betrayal. Obliged to attend the meetings or participating simply out of indifference, they would return home afterwards to pray for the speedy return of the Dalai Lama. If the Anti-Rebellion campaign was meant to coerce co-operation and compliance, it was successful. It showed clearly who were the new rulers of Tibet.

There was no doubt that land reforms were long overdue in Tibet and it was hoped that the moderate reforms would entice the masses to embrace the new 'Motherland'. However, the first stage of the reform – the abolition of corvée labour and the reduction in rent – was, in fact, purely symbolic, since the revolt had already shattered the traditional system: because the Tibetan Government had been destroyed there was no way that taxes or other services could be enforced. The reduction in rent and interest on loans was a moderate reform which did benefit many farmers who were in serious debt with manorial lords or the monasteries. But the reforms were only applied to those manorial estates owned by aristocrats who had taken part in the revolt, and abolition of debts only applied to those incurred before the end of 1958. It was announced that landlords who had not participated in the uprising would continue to enjoy the revenue from their estates, although the tenant would only have to pay 1 per cent interest per month.

Most Tibetans viewed the reforms with apprehension. Dhondup Choedon, a Tibetan woman from Nyethang Dzong in southern Tibet, wrote: 'the Chinese came to my place in 1959 and declared that henceforth there will no longer be people who are rich or poor. They said all would be equal and everyone would have equal share of wealth. Near our district there were many rich and aristocratic families. So we, the wulagpas [sic], who were the most unfortunate in Tibet, were happy. But hope of a happier future was mixed with a certain fear. We had never seen a Chinese before. We wondered whether they really spoke the truth, whether they could be trusted and how many soldiers they had. Above all, we wondered about their real aims in coming to our land and hoped that they would not stay too long.'[34]

At first the main effect of the reforms was not economic but social: a new style of politics, mass meetings, public struggle sessions and a new message. This new style of political participation made a great impact on the Tibetans. New ideas meant new relationships, between the ruler and the governed, between monks and laity, man and woman, between classes – all of which were experiencing profound transformation. There were some major structural alterations in traditional relations, but they were confined mainly to settled agricultural communities: the nomadic groups were exempted from the original reforms. Ngabo announced at the PCART meeting that in the nomad areas policy would concentrate on implementing the Anti-Rebellion campaign. Reforms would be restricted to abolishing grazing rights granted to manorial lords and redistributing the rights and livestock belonging to those who took part in the revolt.

If the explicit aim of the reforms was to solicit support from the Tibetan masses, the implicit objective was to punish those who had taken part in the revolt. The message was clear: as long as the ruling class continued to co-operate with the Communists, they could still enjoy their positions. The Panchen Rinpoche announced that 'all members of the upper strata who support and agree to actively take part in the reform will have their livelihood secured and their political status guaranteed.'[35] The abolition of corvée labour and the reduction of rent did not cripple the economic status of the lay ruling classes. In fact, leading aristocratic families had recognised the inevitability of reforms and had already begun to redistribute and disband their manorial estates; the Dalai Lama's own family had begun to disband their estates and distribute their lands to the peasants in the early 1950s. Since the 1950s many of the aristocrats had been appointed to various posts in the government and were receiving wages so they no longer depended on revenue from their subjects.

The reforms were to have a very dramatic effect on the religious institutions. What the Tibetans called *chod zhi* (religious estates), provided the income for the monasteries and for the lamas. While the lay manorial estates were concerned with individual families, who could easily look for other economic means, thousands of monks depended on the monastery and on contributions from lay followers. Any reduction in monastic income would undoubtedly have major repercussions on the ability of these monastic establishments to support large numbers of monks. The monasteries would not voluntarily accept any changes in their economic basis, nor would the Tibetans challenge their status and privileges: without these the monasteries and other religious institutions could not function. In Tibet, land was divided between three groups: aristocrats, government and the religious estates. In Lhokha in southern Tibet, for example, 29.6 per cent of the land was owned by the lay aristocracy, 30.9 by the government, while the largest owners were the monasteries with 39.5 per cent.[36] Apart from land, the monasteries were also involved in trade and were the largest source of loans. People would deposit money and receive interest on their savings, and traders would raise capital from the monastic treasury, in many ways similar to a bank.

The Tibetan masses may have resented the wealth and privilege of the lay aristocracy, but the question of the economic power enjoyed by the religious institutions was viewed differently. For non-Tibetans, the economic power of the monastery was simply exploitation and the position of the lamas and the monks parasitic. But for the Tibetans such thoughts were irrelevant: they were willing to accept the special position enjoyed by the religious institutions and in fact much of the wealth of the monasteries was accumulated over centuries from voluntary contributions from the masses. Most of all, almost every Tibetan had a personal connection with a monastery, with either a close relative or a son living in a monastery. Deeply attached to their monasteries, the Tibetans were reluctant to accept the changes proposed by the Chinese. The Chinese realised that the key to the success of the reforms lay in their ability to persuade the monasteries to relinquish their traditional privileges. 'If we do not abolish the evils of the Tibetan Lamaseries, it will directly affect the progress and the growth of the Tibetan[s]', commented one Chinese writer.[37] The reform of the religious establishment was seen as a pre-condition for the successful implementation of the general reform programme. In his speech to the second meeting of PCART the Panchen Rinpoche said that 'we cannot conduct reforms in society and retain the temples' feudal exploitation and oppression'.[38]

Although the changes were couched in the language of social reform, there is no doubt that the monks and the religious hierarchy saw them as an attempt to undermine their status and power. When the monasteries were told that they would have to give up their lands, the monks immediately asked how they were to survive without the revenues from their estates. If the monasteries were to be deprived of their economic basis, they would not be able to support thousands of monks or carry out important religious ceremonies. While there are no reliable figures on the number of monks and nuns in Tibet, it is estimated that there were over 25,000 monks in the three largest monasteries near Lhasa, Sera, Drepung and Gaden. The Chinese say there were 2,469 monasteries and 110,000 monks and nuns in Tibet.[39] This represented 9.3 per cent of the total population of Tibet.[40]

The type of reforms envisaged by the Communists were totally incompatible with the traditional status of the monks. The Communists argued that the position of the majority of the monks was similar to that of 'serfs' belonging to manorial estates. The Communists therefore hoped that they would welcome the reforms. In his speech at the PCART meeting Zhang Guohua announced that the campaign among the religious groups would be based upon opposition to the rebellion, privileges and exploitation and that the cadres would differentiate between those lamas and monasteries that took part in the rebellion and those that did not. Monks from the three largest monasteries had been active in the Lhasa uprising, and many smaller monasteries were accused of having harboured Khampa rebels – monks from eastern Tibet who had sought refuge in monasteries in central Tibet. Therefore, there was hardly a monastery that was not implicated in the revolt.

The second stage of the reforms, the re-distribution of the land, was put into motion shortly after 1960. The estates belonging to Tibetan officials who had fled or had been arrested were distributed to the peasants. Newly established Peasants' Associations were given the initial task of administrating the redistribution of land. Some villagers from Nyemo remembered that Chinese cadres accompanied by Tibetan interpreters came and told them that land would be redistributed to the landless. Although at this stage the Communists had not launched the rigid class-labelling system, the villagers were told that a Peasant's Association should be set up, composed of the poorest section of the village, to form the vanguard of the reforms and to take responsibility for administrating the reforms. The Chinese cadres would identify those whom they regarded as wealthy landowners or reactionaries whose lands were to be redistributed. The manorial estates belonging to aristocrats like Surkhang and Phala who had fled to India were disbanded and redistributed to their subjects. According to a notice issued by PCART in October 1960, 2.8 million *ke* (186,667 hectares) of land had by then been redistributed to former subjects of manorial estates.

The redistribution of the land was carried out with great ceremony. First, the confiscated wealth of the 'reactionary upper classes' was exhibited as the fruits of centuries of extortion and exploitation of the masses. People were made to witness the lavish lifestyles enjoyed by their masters in the hope that when the poorest section of society realised the unequal distribution of wealth, they would be spurred into revolutionary fervour and would demand the eradication of the three exploitative classes – the local government, the monasteries and the manorial estates. In late 1960, the Chinese began to issue land deeds to the peasants, calling villagers to meetings to be told that the control of the land had now passed to the serfs.

In a ceremony befitting a great colonial power, the land deeds were issued to the people. The message was clear: the land was a gift from the Communist Party. This was symbolised by the iconography of the new title deeds: the top of each certificate was adorned with a portrait of Chairman Mao with the flag of the People's Republic of China on each side.

There is no doubt that many poorer sections of Tibetan society welcomed the land redistribution. Some may have regarded it as just, seeing the loss of power and privilege by the aristocrats as karmic retribution. But while the Tibetan masses did not question their right to the land, they doubted whether the Chinese had the right to dispense it. This was particularly true of land owned by the monasteries, where the confiscation of the land was seen in traditional terms. In the past, the Tibetan Government would confiscate land rights of aristocrats, lamas or monasteries because they were involved in conflicts with the government; the monks accordingly saw the Chinese action as punishment for their involvement in the uprising. Some monks tried to plead with the Chinese to spare their estates and others told the Chinese that they had no authority to disband the estates without permission from their head lama, who had left the country. But there was no question of the Chinese giving special treatment to the monasteries. Most had been accused of taking part in the uprising and so could not escape the reforms. In the end the monasteries had no choice but to agree to disband their estates, destroying their economic foundations. For centuries the monasteries and religious institutions had enjoyed the protection of the state and they could in turn exercise considerable influence on politics and society. The new rulers of Tibet had seen the monasteries and the monks as the main obstacle to change and aimed at the eventual eradication of the religious dominance in Tibetan society. The dissolution of the economic power base of the monasteries was the most significant social and political event in the history of Tibet since the introduction of Buddhism. It is unlikely that the monasteries will ever recover their dominant position in Tibetan society.

The reforms were accompanied by the introduction of new social and political organisations. In the process of mass mobilisation, a number of voluntary associations were set up in villages, like the Peasants' Associations, which acted as the arm of the CCP at local level. The two main problems now facing the Chinese were the need to create a strong organisational structure and cadres to manage the system. While in China the Communists could rely on local CCP members and, to some extent, former Nationalist officials. In Tibet the situation was entirely different. As noted earlier, the Communists had not come to power in Tibet through revolution but had seized power by military means. Neither the traditional governing structure nor the indigenous élite in Tibet had adequate knowledge or skills for the task envisaged by the Communists. Even though they may have chosen to work with the new regime, they could not be relied on to carry out the reforms.

The Communists were therefore now concerned with building a party structure at local level which would recruit Tibetan members. When the Chinese first entered Tibet, there were 877 Communist Party Members, of whom only a few were Tibetan. By 1959 the total Party membership had reached 5,846[41] but minorities made up only 875 of the total membership.[42] The Communists now saw an urgent need to expand Party structure and membership. Zhang Jingwu identified the primary function of the Party as being the mobilisation of the masses.[43] Between 1960 and 1963, there was a rapid increase in both Tibetan and Chinese Party membership in Tibet with the regional CCP's membership rising to 14,523 by 1963, of whom 5,711 were from the minorities.[44]

The Chinese were also concerned with creating an administrative structure which would form the basis for the regional government. The few Tibetan recruits to the CCP in Tibet were mainly from the urban areas of Lhasa and Shigatse. The CCP had to extend its domain into rural areas, and the rapid expansion of Peasants' Associations in rural areas provided fertile ground for recruiting Party members. In the beginning the Chinese were reluctant to recruit Party members and often the Peasants' Associations acted as the arm of the Party in remote areas. Most of the recruits were drawn from the Peasant Association. Particular attention was paid to nursing the Young Communist Leagues in various villages where they became the main source of Party membership, so that by 1964, 50 per cent of junior cadres and of officials in charge of mutual aid organisations were directly recruited from the Young Communist League.[45]

The abolition of the traditional government meant that the administrative district based on the Dzong was disbanded. Tibet was instead redivided into eight zones: Lhasa Municipality, Chamdo, Nyingtri, Lhokha, Shigatse, Gyantse, Nagchu and Ngari. These zones were further divided into *xians*.[46] By the beginning of 1960, ceremonies were held in the different localities to inaugurate the administrative bodies at a local level. It was announced that Peoples' Government at *xian* and *qu* (area) levels would be established by the end of 1960,[47] although in fact basic administrative structures in rural and remote areas did not come into practice until much later. On the whole, the question of an administrative structure was relatively simple to solve compared to the problem of recruitment of Tibetan cadres to manage the system. As noted earlier, the traditional Tibetan Government official had been drawn exclusively from the ranks of the Tibetan aristocracy, constituting a small group on which, for practical reasons, the Chinese were forced to rely as a source of future cadres. At the higher and middle levels of the administration the Chinese also continued to rely on the traditional aristocracy, so that all the Tibetan members of the PCART were former government officials or high lamas. But their importance was largely symbolic, designed to show continuity and to achieve compliance from an important section of Tibetan society. The Chinese saw the PCART and the positions granted to the traditional élite as temporary measures, which would continue only until the autonomous region of Tibet was established. They were fully aware of the need for cadres who could be relied upon to be both ideologically and politically loyal to China.

The rapid imposition of reforms made the need to recruit Tibetan cadres even more urgent. While in other minority areas demobilised soldiers and Chinese settlers were used to build a core group of cadres, in Tibet this was not possible, as the soldiers were still needed for military and security purposes and there were no Chinese settlers to speak of.[48] Moreover, the Chinese soon realised that the usual source of cadres – students, progressive peasants and former officials – were in short supply in Tibet. Nevertheless, they were able to develop a small pool of loyal Tibetan cadres, who were initially recruited as Tibetan language teachers, many of whom came from eastern Tibet, Kham and Amdo. Since 1951 hundreds of Tibetan students had been sent to China to study. They were now quickly sent back to Tibet before they had completed their courses to take up posts in the government. In December 1959, *Xinhua* reported that 1,000 students had returned to Tibet. Tibetan cadres were needed, not because the Chinese wanted to practise genuine autonomy and hand over power to the Tibetans but because they were wanted a mediating force between the Tibetan masses and the Chinese. The cadres were described as 'the propagandists of the Party' who would 'become a backbone of strength in carrying out' the Party's policies.[49]

It has to be stressed again that the Chinese were not merely interested in maintaining power and administration in Tibet. The long-term objective of the Communists had always been the total revolution of Tibetan society. This could only be achieved if they had sufficient Tibetans involved in the revolution and they therefore had to recruit and train a large enough number of indigenous cadres.[50] Their main target of recruitment was naturally people from the poorest sections of Tibetan society but they could not escape from the fact that the Tibetan peasantry were uneducated and predominantly illiterate, with neither the educational skills nor the necessary experience for leadership. Moreover, from a Marxist point of view, the Tibetan peasantry were not 'conscious of their class', nor of the exploitative nature of their existence. The Communist education and mass mobilisation campaigns were therefore aimed at raising the 'class consciousness' of the Tibetan masses.

The attempt to raise the social and political consciousness of the Tibetan peasantry thus became the primary task: without raising class consciousness, the Communists believed, the revolution and reforms could not be sustained. For the Tibetans, this was deeply disturbing. There was a large element of subversion in the Chinese campaigns. They published anti-religious pamphlets and stories about the bad old days. People who had for centuries believed in the sacred nature of their temples and shrines were told that their sacred statues were simply made of mud. The campaigns were carried out with a hint of intimidation, and non-compliance was naturally taken to mean secret sympathy for the 'reactionaries'. Sometimes, the meetings were held in monastery courtyards, with armed soldiers posted on the rooftops, no doubt to remind the masses who was in power. Even when Chinese cadres went to carry out education in villages they were always accompanied by lightly armed PLA soldiers. The Communist campaign caused deep psychological and social trauma in Tibetan society, and people saw the whole thing as simple Sinicisation of Tibetan culture and values.

The recruiting of peasants as cadres was based on the hope that their class background and their assumed hatred of the old society would make them loyal models who would implement the reforms. Although there was no shortage of Tibetans willing to join the ranks of Chinese cadres, the Chinese were faced with the problem of where and how to train the newly recruited Tibetan cadres beyond the basic political education which they received, which could last anything from a few weeks to several months.[51] The Chinese claimed that 'over 5,000 Tibetan cadres had been recruited and they are imbued with class consciousness'[52] but it is clear that the majority of the Tibetan cadres received little or no training. When in May 1960 a formal Tibetan Cadre School was opened in Lhasa, the *Tibet Daily* noted that 'students of the training class were mainly persons of the middle and upper strata';[53] the same trend is evident from the names of the officials appointed to various national bodies. Beijing faced an additional problem in Tibet: it needed to find cadres who would 'love the motherland' as well as be 'red' and 'expert', as Schurmann puts it.[54] The training the Tibetan cadres received accordingly included a brief history of Tibet which stressed how Tibet was part of China. But the question of finding and training suitable indigenous cadres was to confront the Chinese for many years and still remains a problematic issue.

Between 1959 and 1964 there was moderate progress in agricultural production, mainly due to the improvements in irrigation, pest control and the increased use of fertilisers. But the increase in production reported in numerous government reports exaggerated the achievements in an attempt to prove the 'superiority of socialist production'. In 1964 the Chinese announced that total grain production had been increased by 52 per cent and the number of livestock had increased by 40 per cent.[55] Today, the Chinese authorities acknowledge that these claims were motivated by the eagerness of local cadres to report higher levels of production to regional/central leaders.[56] The misreporting applied equally to nomadic areas, where the Chinese claimed a massive increase in herds but in fact there were no major innovations, with herding patterns being left very much as before. It was more likely the disruption caused by the revolt might even have led to a decline in the number of animals.

To demonstrate the final incorporation of the region into the mainstream of Chinese affairs, the Chinese began to enact various legislative measures to bring Tibet into line with the rest of China. The first law passed during the 34th Session of the Standing Committee of PCART was the 'Collection of Patriotic Grain Tax'.[57] These laws were a symbolic as well as a practical assertion of Chinese sovereignty over the region. It was announced that the new law was enacted on the basis of Article 102 of the Chinese Constitution, which stipulated that 'a citizen of the PRC has an obligation to pay tax in accordance with the law'.[58] Other laws passed at the same time concerned the regulations governing import and export duties, and the registration of foreign businesses. It was not coincidental that the first set of laws that were passed were concerned with revenue. These were introduced at a time when China was facing serious economic difficulties which had damaged the Central Government's ability to subsidise the region and which were further compounded by the Russian withdrawal of aid.

The integration of Tibet into the main structure of the PRC through introduction of new legislation, the end of the separate development strategy for Tibet and the increasing involvement of the centre, brought more complex problems to the surface, notably the question of who would be responsible for the administration of Tibet. For instance, the establishment of the customs offices and the regulations about import and export duties opened the question of who should benefit from the revenue that was generated: the Central Government or the regional authority?[59]

The 'Patriotic Grain Tax' was meant to replace the traditional taxes and to alleviate the heavy taxes formerly paid by the Tibetan peasants.[60] It was based upon the grain produced by a household. The households were divided into 23 groups according to average yearly grain harvests per capita, with those producing less than 180 *jin* per capita exempted from the tax. The next lowest group, producing 181 to 240 *jin* of grain per capita, were subjected to 3 per cent tax, while the highest group, those who were producing over 1,861 *jin*, were levied at 25 per cent.[61]

Naturally, the taxes were unpopular. Although Chinese propaganda claimed that the Tibetan masses rushed to pay their taxes as a sign of their 'love for the Motherland', in reality the authorities were faced with difficulties in implementing the taxes, with some areas lacking the administrative structure to levy the taxes. There were also difficulties in conveying the grain to the officials despite legislation requiring farmers to transport grain to the nearest collection points. It was announced that district governments would administer the assessment and collection of

1 (*Above*) Lukhangwa Tsewang Repten, the last Prime Minister of Tibet.
2 (*Right*) A group of Tibetans who joined the Long March and were sent to the Party School in Yan'an in 1937. *From left to right*: Tashi Wangchuk, Sangye Yeshi, Sherab Dhondrup, unknown, and Sha Nai.

3 (*Below*) Chinese soldiers arrive in Lhasa in 1951.

4 The Tibetan delegation, led by Ngabo Ngawang Jigme, signs the 17-Point Agreement in Beijing, 23 May 1951.

5 The first task facing the Chinese was to build roads. Within three years they had connected China with Tibet by two major highways.

6 (*Left*) The Dalai Lama and the Panchen Rinpoche attend the National People's Congress, Beijing 1954. *From left to right:* the Panchen Rinpoche, Mao Zedong and the Dalai Lama.

7 (*Above*) In 1956 the Dalai Lama and the Panchen Rinpoche visit India to celebrate Buddha Jayanti, the 2500th Anniversary of Buddha's Birth. *From right to left*: Zhou Enlai, Jawaharlal Nehru, the Dalai Lama and the Panchen Rinpoche in New Delhi.

8 In 1957 the first group of Khampas were flown to the Pacific island of Saipan for training by the CIA. *From left to right*: Athar, Wandgu, Lotsi and Dharlo.

9 Members of Four Rivers and Six Ranges, Lhoka, 1958.

10 A Chinese propaganda photograph shows the Tibetan surrender after the Lhasa uprising.

11 A Chinese propaganda picture shows the 'masses' of Shol (the village below Potala palace) gathering to denounce the revolt.

12 The Dalai Lama (*third from right*) and the escape party. The horseman behind the Dalai Lama is Phala Thupten Woden.

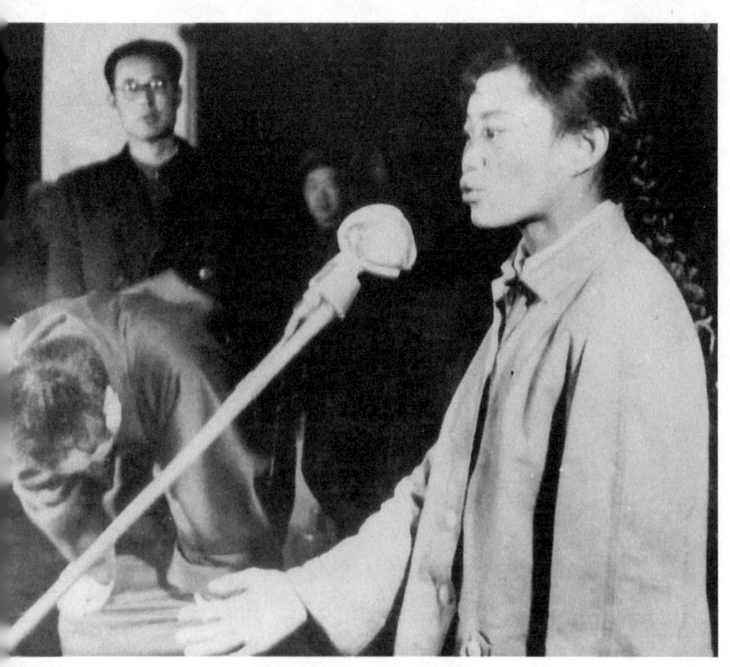

13 The Panchen Rinpoche undergoes a struggle session in Lhasa in 1964.

14 Photographs from an exhibition in Nyemo showing two members of the Nyemo rebellion of 1969. The captions say 'Execute Rindron' and 'Execute Dorji'; the crosses on the two names indicate that the executions were carried out.

15 The destroyed Gaden Monastery, founded in 1409. In 1959, before its destruction during the Cultural Revolution, it housed over three thousand monks.

16 The Dalai Lama receives the Nobel Peace Prize in 1989.

17 (*Below*) Redevelopment in Lhasa: new housing in the Lhalu area, behind the Potala palace, 1996.

taxes, but once again the Chinese authorities were confronted with a shortage of trained and experienced cadres who could act as revenue collectors. It was becoming clear that the few cadres who had been sent out into the rural areas were having to perform a wide range of duties, with the work in remote districts being managed by the Peasants' Associations together with a few Chinese cadres who had been dispatched as advisers and guides. It has to be stressed that, in practice, the imposition of the taxes was a more symbolic than effective means of raising revenue. The Chinese ability to obtain and utilise the potential revenue could not be realised until all the administrative and political difficulties had been surmounted.

Despite the problems faced by the Chinese, they were determined to forge ahead with the implementation of the reforms. In August 1962 PCART announced that an election committee had been set up headed by the Panchen Rinpoche and Zhang Guohua. The Chinese were planning to hold a nationwide election for district- and village-level representatives. The election, said to have 'signified that the Tibetan people were genuinely enjoying the right to run their own affairs and that Tibet had entered a new historical era',[62] was no doubt meant to legitimise the new reforms and represent an affirmation of the people's faith in Chinese rule. The procedure applied in Tibet was an adaption of the 1953 electoral law adopted in China. The voting was strictly controlled, with Chinese cadres visiting villages to supervise the elections, which meant that only those who were approved by the authorities were allowed to stand for election. The electoral law prevented 'counter-revolutionaries' and others who were classified as *Zhing yod* (those who had taken part in the revolt) from participating. The electorate were advised that people with the correct political and class standing should be elected.

The election was held over several years. In April 1964 it was announced that 1,003 villages and 48 per cent of *xian* (counties) had held elections, which meant that the majority of districts were yet to hold the proposed elections. The Chinese claimed that the election had consolidated the people's 'democratic dictatorship'. The elections were held with great fanfare and ceremony. It was clear that most of the people who were elected at village or *xian* level were the same people who headed Rogre (Mutual Aid Groups) and Peasants' Associations and were said to possess the correct political and class backgrounds. The process of election and conferring authority on these new individuals marked the creation of a new ruling élite at the local level. The newly elected officials were given ideological education and were told that they would form the vanguard of the creation of a new socialist Tibet. The elections, however, proved to be a shortlived exercise: by the end of 1964 the Chinese authorities were making few references to the election, which was replaced by the Socialist Education Campaign.

By the beginning of 1960 the Chinese were experiencing some opposition to the reforms from a surprising quarter. The Panchen Rinpoche, regarded by many as a loyal supporter of the Chinese, was to make a damning criticism of the reform policy and of the Anti-Rebellion Campaign. Ever since his arrival in Shigatse in 1951 the Panchen Rinpoche had been dismissed by some Tibetans as a Chinese 'puppet'. While the Lhasa regime sought to make sure that the Panchen Rinpoche's authority was never extended beyond the confines of Tashilhunpo, his followers aimed to restore the power and influence of Tashilhunpo over the whole Tsang region, which they had always seen as his fiefdom. Between 1951 and 1961 the Panchen Rinpoche and his estate were supportive of and co-operated with the Chinese, managing to regain much of the prestige and influence that Tashilhunpo had enjoyed in the early years of the century. Before 1928, under the leadership of the previous Panchen Rinpoche, there had been a governing structure that was in many ways similar to the polity that existed in Lhasa. Shigatse had its own Kalons and other officials, with a local ruling élite that was independent of Lhasa and whose first loyalty was to the Panchen Rinpoche. With the arrival of the Communists, Shigatse's ruling élite was able to restore its power and authority so that once again Tashilhunpo existed as a semi-independent faction within the Tibetan polity. By 1957, Tashilhunpo had managed to re-establish a system in Shigatse closely resembling the pre-1928 arrangement, an achievement only possible through the patronage of the Communists and the strong support given to the Panchen Rinpoche by the officials of the North-West Military Region. Shigatse viewed Lhasa as the main threat to its autonomy rather than the Chinese, who as we noted earlier, afforded the Panchen Rinpoche and his followers the same status as the Lhasa regime through the establishment of PCART.

The historical feud between Lhasa and Shigatse reflected the conflict within the Chinese forces in Tibet. While Lhasa was seen as the domain of the South-West Military Region, with the personnel who ran Tibet at regional level essentially coming from that Military Region and in close association with the Lhasa Government, Shigatse and Ngari in western Tibet, bordering Xinjiang, remained an enclave dominated by the North-West Military Region. This was to have more significant repercussions in the early 1960s. After the crushing of the Lhasa revolt, the Chinese were faced with the problem of what to do with the regime in Shigatse. They were willing to promote the Panchen Rinpoche to the position of acting Chairman of the PCART, but this was a largely symbolic gesture. Given his religious prominence, and the absence of the Dalai Lama, it was natural that he should assume this position.

However, it was not possible to allow Tashilhunpo to function and exercise privileges as it had done in the past. The PCART was originally seen as a body composed of three factions, Lhasa, Shigatse and Chamdo, but after the revolt the Chinese saw no reason why they should continue the system. As noted earlier, immediately after the Lhasa revolt they had abolished the traditional Tibetan Government, thus eliminating the Lhasa faction completely, necessitating changes in the composition of PCART so that it became not a three-way organisation but a unitary body with individual members.

The feud between Shigatse and Lhasa had been used by the Chinese to draw maximum concession from the Lhasa regime, and now that the traditional Tibetan Government in Lhasa had been effectively eliminated, it was no longer necessary for the Chinese either to prop up or to continue making concession to Tashilhunpo. Naturally, it meant that the Panchen Rinpoche and his officials' ability to influence the Chinese or to obtain preferential treatment was greatly diminished. Nevertheless, the Panchen Rinpoche's personal status as the second highest incarnate lama in Tibet afforded him a certain importance, which the Chinese could not dispense with for the time being.

After the revolt, the Chinese introduced a more unified administrative and political structure, further integrating Tibet within the Chinese system. As mentioned earlier, the traditional district boundaries based on the Dzongs had been quickly abolished and a centralised administration similar to that existing in the Chinese provinces set up. The new administrative structure made little or no concession to the traditional division of power in Tibetan society, with the result that the autonomy or separate identity enjoyed by Shigatse was no longer viable. The Panchen Rinpoche's followers did not at first realise that they would have to relinquish much of their power, since the Chinese had promised that the reforms and other related changes would only affect those individuals, areas and organisations that were involved in the revolt. Since neither the officials in Tashilhunpo nor the populace in Shigatse had taken part, they felt they were safe from the dramatic changes that were being instigated in the rest of Tibet. Yet it soon became apparent that although the Chinese were willing to accommodate many of the officials within the new administrative structure, they would not accept Tashilhunpo as having a separate identity.

Another problem that arose between the Chinese and Tashilhunpo concerned the many monks and lay people who had fled from Amdo and Kham after 1956 and had sought the protection of the Panchen Rinpoche, among them the Panchen Rinpoche's religious tutor and other influential incarnate lamas who were particularly close to him. They were arrested despite the Panchen Rinpoche's plea that the lamas had not taken any part in the revolt. For the Chinese, the fact that they had fled from their homes in Amdo and Kham was sufficient evidence of their reactionary sympathies.

While the Chinese were willing to implement moderate economic reforms, they adopted radical means to achieve this, such as subjecting individuals to struggle sessions and transporting those who were labelled as reactionaries to labour camps. The initial promise of not prosecuting those members of the 'upper strata' who had not participated in the reforms was ignored after the Lushan Conference, when Mao launched an Anti-Rightist Opportunist Campaign and the second phase of the Great Leap Forward (GLF). Between April 1959 and 1962 the Panchen Rinpoche appeared to be supportive of the reform policies in public; his speeches at the PCART and the NPC meetings dutifully endorsed the Chinese policy. Behind the scenes, however, the Panchen Rinpoche was perturbed by the harshness of the Anti-Rebellion Campaign and by the indiscriminate application of the reforms. In Tibet, his attempts to curb the excesses of the local cadres were met with indifference.

The 70,000 Character Petition

Unlike other Tibetan officials, the Panchen Rinpoche had access to the leadership in Beijing. The Chinese had always promoted him as a 'national leader' and his importance had spread beyond the Autonomous Region of Tibet. He was required to spend nearly half of the year, from September to April, in Beijing; it was obligatory for him to take part in the National Day ceremonies in October, and to attend the NPC as one of the Vice-Chairmen in April. His position in the NPC placed him in especially close touch with the leaders and it is reported that he got on well Li Weihan, the head of the United Front and the Nationalities Affairs Bureau, to whom he spoke in 1960 while attending the eleventh anniversary of the founding of the PRC.

In the early 1960s China was undergoing a major crisis of confidence. Internationally, the split with the Soviet Union was occupying much of the leadership's attention, while on the domestic front, the collapse of the GLF resulted in serious conflict within the CCP. Between 1960 and 1962 there was a dramatic decline in industrial and agricultural production,[63] leading to a decrease in food production and 'a famine of proportions unprecedented in the 20th Century',[64] which resulted in the deaths of an estimated 40 million people in the three years between 1959 and 1962.[65] The Chinese leadership was therefore mainly concerned with repairing the damage caused by the failure of the GLF, but at the same time was more open to criticism. It was noticeable that the Party was adopting more relaxed policies towards the minority question, recognising that the problems faced in minority regions could only be solved by a long-term process. The cadres began to adopt the slogan 'slower is faster'.[66]

The Panchen Rinpoche's criticism of Chinese policy has to be seen within this context. Given the seriousness of the domestic and international problems besetting the leadership, the problems raised by the Panchen Rinpoche seemed to be minor. He raised them first with Li Weihan, who as the head of the United Front and signatory to the 17-Point Agreement, was one of the few senior leaders in Beijing with direct responsibility for Tibet. (During the Cultural Revolution he would be accused of adopting 'capitulationist policy towards the question of nationalities'.)[67] Li was the Party's United Front strategist and had advocated a more moderate policy, taking into account the social and economic conditions of minority peoples. Under his leadership between 1960 and 1962 there was an attempt to rectify some of the excesses of earlier campaigns among the minority groups[68] and the Panchen Rinpoche's criticisms therefore came at an opportune moment.

The Party was also adopting a more moderate policy towards those members of the bourgeoisie who had opted to work with the Communists. Li Weihan encouraged officials in the United Front to follow Mao's directive and organise themselves into study groups, to investigate and discuss the shortcomings of the CCP's policies. At the time the main topic of discussion was the principle of 'the three selfs' and the 'three nots': raise the question by oneself, analyse by oneself and solve the problem by oneself; not seizing on others' faults, not putting labels on people, and not using big sticks.[69] And in August 1960 Li Weihan had instigated a moderate form of the Hundred Flowers Movement when he encouraged intellectuals to engage in 'gentle breeze and mild rain'.[70] Unlike other campaigns in China, this was not based on mass participation but on the United Front's organised group discussions, known as 'fairy sessions', which were described as a sort of 'liberal forum' in which the bourgeoisie freely discussed the Party's policies and their shortcomings.[71]

These campaigns did not make much impact on the Chinese cadres in Tibet or among the Tibetans, where the primary task was still seen as the fight against the 'reactionary rebels'. Their importance lay in the fact that the Panchen Rinpoche's visit to Beijing coincided with the campaigns and the leadership in Beijing actively encouraged him to express his views about the situation in Tibet. The Panchen Rinpoche was sent on an extensive tour of China, accompanied by Li Weihan and Wang Feng (the deputy director of the United Front Work Committee and a vice chairman of the Nationalities Affairs Commission), during which he made detailed criticisms of the CCP's work in Tibet. Both Li Weihan and Wang Feng were impressed with the criticisms and took them seriously. When Wang Feng was recalled to Beijing, where a special meeting of provincial leaders and secretaries of various departments had been convened, he reported his conversations with the Panchen Rinpoche directly to Mao and other leaders, who were paying particular attention to the Tibet issue because of the international focus and moves at the UN.

At the end of their tour, Li Weihan showed the Panchen Rinpoche the detailed notes he had made and said that the Panchen Rinpoche should make whatever emendations and additions he wished.[72] Later, this became the foundation of the famous Seventy Thousand Character Petition submitted by the Panchen Rinpoche to the Chinese Government at the beginning of June 1962. It was clear that the Panchen Rinpoche's criticism was now reaching the highest level of the CCP. With the reversal of the Great Leap Forward campaign and a more moderate economic policy in ascendancy, the mood of change was soon to prevail in Tibet. At first the Communist Party seemed to welcome the Panchen Rinpoche's forthright comments on the shortcomings of their policy in Tibet. The Central Committee appointed Yang Jingren, the deputy chief of the Nationalities Committee, to head an investigation team to visit Tibet. On 5 January 1961, Yang Jingren returned to Beijing with findings that confirmed the criticisms made by the Panchen Rinpoche. The report concluded that in the campaign against the reactionary rebels, many 'patriotic figures' had been wrongly labelled and that reforms had been carried out without due attention to the local conditions. Finally, Yang said, in typical Communist jargon, that there had been a 'leftist deviation' in carrying out policy in Tibet.[73] His findings were reported to the Party Secretary, Deng Xiaoping, another senior Party leader closely associated with the Tibet policy. At the time of the invasion of Chamdo in 1950, Deng had been the political Commissar of the South-Western Military Region and directly responsible for devising the CCP's Tibet policy, and so he knew the senior cadres and military officials serving there. Deng also accepted Yang's findings and agreed that many people who were not involved in the revolt had been unjustly treated and that the phase of the reforms in Tibet had been carried out in haste.

The same month, the Party's Central Committee summoned Zhang Guohua and Zhang Jingwu to Beijing. While in the capital they had meetings with senior Party leaders Zhou Enlai, Li Weihan and Deng Xiaoping to discuss the issues raised by the Panchen Rinpoche and Yang Jingren's report. Zhang Guohua was told by Deng that the leftist deviation must be rectified and that the reforms should be slowed down; the Tibetans should not be forced into setting up agricultural co-operatives. Zhang, sensing that the national leaders had already accepted the points raised by the Panchen Rinpoche, did not try to defend the situation in Tibet. In fact, it is more likely that veteran cadres, who had been in Tibet since the early fifties, shared some of the criticisms made by the Panchen Rinpoche: as noted earlier, there had developed a rift among the Chinese officials in Tibet. Although there was no disagreement among Chinese cadres over the central issue of eradicating reactionaries, there was, nevertheless, growing tension between the Chinese cadres and the military in Tibet. There was also a conflict between the military personnel who had been rushed into Tibet to crush the revolt and those who had entered Tibet in the early

1950s: it was thought that the newly transferred troops and officials who had fought in the Korean War dismissed the Eighth Route Army as rustic,[74] and accused it of lacking the correct class stand and pampering to the Tibetan ruling élite. The veteran Chinese officials in Tibet argued that mistakes were created by the excessive enthusiasm of the new cadres and PLA troops who lacked sufficient knowledge of the local conditions.

On 23 January the Panchen Rinpoche talked to Mao at a meeting attended by most of the senior leaders of the Party, including Liu Shaoqi, Deng Xiaoping and Li Weihan. Zhang Jingwu, the first secretary of the Tibet Work Committee, was also present. Mao seemed to have accepted Yang Jingren's findings and agreed to redress the 'leftist deviation' in Tibet.[75] He issued a new six-point directive on the CCP's work in Tibet, which incorporated some of the points raised by the Panchen Rinpoche. The first point was that the Tibetan peasantry would not be forced to set up co-operatives, and that the agriculture production should be organised by 'mutual aid' groups. The second point was that members of the Tibetan élite who had not participated in the revolt would not be subjected to ideological education and appropriate jobs should be found for them, with those who had lost property being given compensation. Third, some monasteries would be retained where the monks could continue traditional practices and would not be forced to do manual labour. Mao also advised that the cadres be familiarised with the teachings of various Buddhist schools so that they would be better equipped to carry out work among the masses. Fourth, Mao admitted that it was wrong to have confiscated the property belonging to many of the Panchen Rinpoche's associates, including his parents and Chen Jigme, who had collaborated with the Chinese since the founding of the PRC. Fifth, the Dalai Lama would not be denounced and he would retain his position on the PCART and the NPC. It was also announced that the proposed elections would be held only at district level; national elections would only take place once the Autonomous Region had been established. Finally, Mao gave instructions that a closer working relationship should be established between the Tibet Work Committee and the Panchen Rinpoche. He encouraged the Panchen Rinpoche to express his opinions freely and to advise the cadres working in Tibet.

Further public demonstration of the Party's support for the Panchen Rinpoche came when he left for Tibet after spending over six months in China. A special banquet was held in Beijing hosted by the Deputy Premier, Chen Yi. It was apparent to Chinese officials in Lhasa that the Panchen Rinpoche now enjoyed the backing of the senior leaders of the Party. The Panchen Rinpoche himself must have felt that he had obtained the approval of the Chinese leaders and that they had given him greater authority to express his doubts concerning the reforms in Tibet. More importantly, there were signs that the Panchen Rinpoche had reached maturity and was taking seriously his duties as a leader of the Tibetan people. He realised that, in the absence of the Dalai Lama, the people would naturally look towards him for leadership. On 27 January the Panchen Rinpoche and his entourage left Beijing; on 13 February he finally arrived back in Lhasa after an absence of six months.

The Panchen Rinpoche was given a lavish welcome and the Chinese officials began to revise some of the draconian measures that had been used to implement the reforms. Some prisoners who had been arrested after the revolt were released, on the grounds that they had admitted their mistakes and were now willing to work in the new Tibet. It was announced that more radical socialist reforms would not be implemented and, during the Fifth Plenum of the PCART, held in Lhasa between 2 and 5 April 1961, Zhang Jingwu declared a period of relaxation (*srid-jus gu-yangs*). The Chinese seemed to have recognised that the economic disruption and harsh Anti-Rebellion Campaign were alienating the Tibetans. Moreover, there were still a large number of Tibetans fleeing the country, and the Chinese wanted to put a halt to this. Zhang Jingwu announced that the main task in Tibet was to 'consolidate' the Party's achievements and therefore the socialist transformation of Tibet would be deferred for another five years.[76] He admitted that the time was not right for the socialist transformation of Tibet; but a temporary postponement of reform would 'allow the creation of favourable conditions'.[77] The revision of strategy was in part forced by Tibetan resistance, but mainly due to the disastrous economic performance in China.

However, the Panchen Rinpoche found there were still many outstanding problems. The question of the status of the monasteries and the monks was the most difficult one. Much of the monastic property had been confiscated and the disruption of the traditional economic system meant that the monasteries were not able to function as before. For example, the funding for the Monlam festival had in the past been provided by the Tibetan Government and individual donors. Now the usual sources of revenue for the monasteries no longer existed and individual patronage was limited by restrictions on movement. Traditionally, hundreds of people from all parts of the Tibetan world flocked to Lhasa, dispensing alms to the monks and monasteries. The festival was a major source of income for the monks. In the past, the Communists had recognised the significance of the Monlam festival and had provided funding since 1951; even after 1959 the Chinese realised that they could not prevent it – both for external and internal reasons it was important that the Monlam ceremony should continue. But the ceremony would cease to have its traditional political importance, whereby during the Monlam festival control was passed briefly from the secular authorities to the religious community. This was unthinkable for the

Communists. The Monlam festival could continue as long as it remained a purely religious ceremony.

The whole question of what to do with the monks during this transitional period was a major problem for the Chinese. The long-term aim remained the eradication of the monkhood as a social group (the Chinese saw the monks as mostly occupied with full-time religious study or ceremonies 'economically unproductive') but for the time being the Communists had to tolerate them. The monastic system in Tibet was unique and differed greatly from other Buddhist societies because it relied on the mass recruitment of monks. It was not possible simply to disband the monasteries. How were the thousands of monks to be employed? The problem was similar to that faced by an industrial society after a war, when thousands of soldiers are disbanded. But in an industrial society the demobbed soldiers could be absorbed into the labour force. The sheer number of monks was to present a major problem for the Chinese. The Panchen Rinpoche opposed the disbanding of the monasteries and objected to monks being sent to work in the fields. He complained to the leaders in Beijing that many monks were being held in labour camps. For the Communists it was as difficult to compromise on these issues as it was impossible to introduce land reforms without tempering the position of the monastic establishment.

As far as the Tibetans were concerned, the relaxed policy did not go far enough. On his way back from Beijing, the Panchen Rinpoche made a tour of Tibetan-dominated areas in Qinghai, Gansu and Sichuan, the traditional Kham and Amdo. At the time, the Party had also encouraged leaders to carry out 'on the spot investigations' of factories and communes. The Panchen Rinpoche was appalled by the deterioration in living standards and of the economy caused by ill-conceived communisation programmes and ruthless suppression by the PLA. He learned that many villagers were facing starvation, and he was shocked to find his birthplace had been destroyed.[78] It became clear that most Tibetan autonomous prefectures and *qus* had suffered a decrease in production and a decline in population.[79] The Panchen Rinpoche was disturbed by what he saw and feared that central Tibet would undergo similarly disastrous economic and social changes. He rightly recognised that Tibet could only avoid such a catastrophe if the radical reforms were shelved indefinitely.

The Chinese also recognised that there was a need to diffuse the people's apprehensions about the reforms and were willing to concede on some of the points made by the Panchen Rinpoche. They realised the need to adopt a more conducive policy of winning over the traditional élite through education and persuasion and in many ways could afford to suspend the more radical policies for the time being. Despite problems faced in China, in Tibet the Communists had made substantial gains. Although sporadic resistance continued, the Tibetans could not present a serious challenge to the supremacy of the PLA and the Tibetan economy did not suffer the setbacks experienced in China, enjoying a moderate increase in production. Moreover, by 1962 Tibetan society had already undergone major changes and the Chinese were able to build the rudimentary structure for the eventual launch of a more radical transformation of Tibet. Zhang Jingwu announced that over 90 per cent of Tibet's peasants had been organised into mutual aid groups and that over one hundred Party branches had been set up in various parts of Tibet.[80] All these factors must have suggested it was an opportune time for the Chinese to accommodate some measure of liberal policy and relax the pressure on the Tibetan masses.

On 25 May 1962, Zhang Jingwu wrote an article in *Jen-min Jih-pao* (the *People's Daily*), saying that in 'the course of the reform, the overwhelming majority of cadres were able to understand fully and carried out seriously the Party policy, but there were also a minority of cadres who did not properly understand the Party's "buying out" policy in Tibet.'[81] This of course referred specifically to the policy adopted towards the traditional Tibetan ruling class. Once again the Communists were willing to create conditions that would entice the Tibetan élite to work with the Party. As we have noted before, there was nothing new in the shift in policy: the Communists were prepared to tolerate a period of relaxed policy as long as it did not seriously challenge the supremacy of the Party. Zhang Jingwu went on to reveal a five-point policy towards the monasteries: (1) the monasteries must give up their privileges; (2) they must implement democratic administration; (3) they must implement the constitution of China into the monasteries; (4) the monks must engage in production, and (5) the government would be responsible for old and young lamas and monks. Zhang Jingwu said that these proposals were made by the Panchen Rinpoche.[82] This shows that although the Chinese were prepared to concede on minor points, they were not willing to compromise on the issue of the economic position of the monks and monasteries. The new policy did not cause a dramatic shift in the overall policy, and was mainly a device to placate the Tibetans. It was true that the Panchen Rinpoche had demanded more liberal treatment of the monks and other religious bodies, but the initiatives announced by Zhang Jingwu were probably a compromise thought up in Beijing. The proposals did not satisfy the Tibetans, who wanted the monasteries and monks to retain the position they had held before 1959. But for the Chinese, both for ideological and practical reasons, the key to the reforms lay in the dismantling of the privileges of the religious institutions. Since the monasteries and lamas constituted the largest landowners, there was no possibility that the Communists would agree to the continuation of the status quo. The Panchen Rinpoche had agreed that the number of monks needed to be reduced, but had suggested that the few remaining monks in the monasteries should receive stipends from the state and that they should be exempt from manual labour. A similar suggestion had been made earlier in 1956 by Geshe Sherab Gyatso in Amdo.

The Tibetans wanted fundamental changes in the policy, but when religious institutions were concerned, it was difficult to reconcile the Tibetan desire for greater autonomy with the Communists' abhorrence of anything to do with religion. However, the Communists have always adopted a pragmatic approach, depending on the strength of the Party. In the early 1960s they were willing to tolerate a number of the Tibetan demands.

In April 1962 the Panchen Rinpoche was back in Beijing to attend the NPC meeting. He was determined to demand further concessions from the Party leaders. His tours of eastern Tibet had led him to believe that the situation in Tibet and other Tibetan areas had not been accurately reported to the senior leaders in Beijing. While in Sichuan he had reprimanded Chinese cadres who painted a glowing picture of the situation in eastern Tibet, saying that their reports did not correspond with what he had witnessed in Ngaba and Kanze TAPs. He went on to tell Li Jingquan, the First Secretary of the Sichuan Communist Party and the Political Commissar of the Chengdu Military Area Command, that the main problem was that the channel between the people and the Central Government had been obstructed: the Chinese cadres, he said, had created 'a wall' between the Party and the people.[83] He bluntly referred to senior Party secretaries as 'propitiating secretaries', meaning that they were frightened to report the truth to Chairman Mao, propitiating the leaders like lamas appeasing wrathful deities.

This was unthinkable criticism of the Party and it marked the Panchen Rinpoche as the only figure who would dare to criticise the failure of the CCP's policy. The rest of officialdom participated in the concealment of the disastrous consequences of Mao's policies. The Panchen Rinpoche frankly told the Party officials that they had bent and distorted the truth.[84] Unsurprisingly, this displeased the cadres. Li Jingquan had been one of Mao's bodyguards during the Long March. He was an ultra-leftist follower of the Chairman and regarded by many as one of the most influential figures in the CCP. As brother-in-law of Marshal He Long he also had important connections in the army and must have taken the Panchen Rinpoche's attacks as personal criticism of his work in the region. He and others were later to accuse the Panchen Rinpoche of siding with the rebels. The Panchen Rinpoche felt that he should form what he called a 'golden bridge' between the Party and the Tibetan people, concluding that the problem was that the senior leaders in Beijing were unaware of the true conditions in the regions.[85]

Between 21 April and 29 May the Communist Party held a month-long meeting to discuss its nationalities policy. Originally, the meeting was planned to last only a few days but Li Weihan announced that he had talked over matters with Chairman Mao and Premier Zhou Enlai and they had agreed to elevate the discussions to a review of the entire nationality policy of the CCP and its work in minority regions. The importance of the meeting was reflected in the attendance of senior Party leaders like Deng Xioaping, Zhou Enlai and Zhu De. It was clear to the Chinese that once again the question of national minorities was having serious repercussions on China's national security. While the meeting was in progress in Beijing, there was an exodus of Kazakhs and Uighurs from Xinjiang to Soviet Central Asia, forcing the Chinese to close the border on 26 May. While most Chinese did not rise up in a revolt against the harrowing conditions during the GLF, in almost all minority areas there was widespread unrest. It was a clear signal that the Communists had failed to win them over and the Party therefore needed to adopt more persuasive means to gain acceptance from the minority groups.

The meeting was meant to allow these minority groups to air their grievances. Li Weihan invited non-Party members to participate fully and express their criticisms without fear. This was particularly important for the Tibetans as most prominent Tibetan delegates were not Party members. Because of the recent uprisings in central and eastern Tibet, and because Tibetan delegates were drawn from five different regions, they constituted the largest group at the conference. These two factors meant that the Tibetan issue began to dominate the meeting. The most outspoken person at the meeting was Geshe Sherab Gyatso, the Chairman of the Chinese Buddhist Association, who said that people were reluctant to talk freely at such gatherings despite the Party's encouragement because they feared it was a device to 'lure the snake out of its hole'.[86] He pointed to what had happened during the Anti-Rightist Campaign, carried out after the Hundred Flowers Movement. Nevertheless he launched an attack on the CCP's policy on nationalities and religion. Economic and social conditions among the people were worse than during the period of Ma Bufang and Chiang Kai-shek, he said; the crimes committed by some zealous cadres were worse than the acts carried out by the followers of those leaders. Hundreds of monks had been transported to labour camps from his own monastery of Labrang in Gansu and, as a religious leader, he was particularly concerned about the destruction of the monasteries and the treatment of monks.[87]

Geshe Sherab Gyatso supported the suppression of the rebellion, which he agreed was trying to split the country, but argued that the campaign against the rebels was indiscriminate and had led to many innocent people being punished. The reform campaign, he said, had put too much pressure on the masses and had been carried out without proper consultation. The

Communists had tried to achieve in a few years what would normally take centuries, a feat he compared to trying to attain Buddhahood in a single lifetime. He demanded that the Party rectify the damage caused by leftist mistakes. The Geshe repeated his criticisms in private meetings with Li Weihan, who at the time seemed to accept many of the criticisms. Li assured Gyatso that the meeting would not be used to lure a snake out of the hole.[88]

The meeting once again reiterated the policy of tolerance towards minority culture and the adoption of a gradualist policy towards the promotion of socialist reforms in minority regions. The Party affirmed this in a lengthy article in the *People's Daily* on 3 June 1962, which stressed that the differences of culture and social and economic conditions between China proper and the regions would persist during the transitional period. The Panchen Rinpoche refrained from making a major speech at the conference, but he was encouraged by the atmosphere of openness and must have concluded that the authorities were willing to listen to criticism. Recalling that in Beijing the previous year Li Weihan had solicited him to write down his thoughts on where the Party had gone wrong in dealing with the Tibetans and the minority question, he decided to submit a report to the Central Committee.

While the meeting was in progress the Panchen Rinpoche began writing his famous 'Seventy Thousand Character Petition' to the Party's Central Committee. The report was never published and what we know of the content derives from Red Guard publications during the Cultural Revolution and a biography of the Panchen Rinpoche published after his death in 1989. The latter provides detailed information, for the first time, about the events leading to the writing and the submission of the petition.[89] A Red Guard pamphlet entitled 'The Capitulationist Line of Zhang Jingwu and Zhang Guohua in United Front Work'[90] also gives some details of the content of the document.

The petition is damning in its assessment of Chinese policy in Tibet and other Tibetan regions. It argued that the rapid social and economic changes were endangering the Tibetan people as a nationality: the Tibetan population had dwindled[91] and Buddhism virtually annihilated, so that at this rate the Tibetan nationality would cease to exist or would become unrecognisable through assimilation into other groups. The report gave details of areas where all able young men had been arrested and imprisoned, leaving the villages inhabited only by old people and women.[92]

The report also outlined some suggestions for correcting past mistakes. According to a Red Guard pamphlet, the Panchen Rinpoche demanded that Tashilhunpo monastery should be allowed to function as before; that there should not be any reduction in the number of monks residing in the monastery, and that the traditional structure of the monastery should be kept intact.[93] This referred to Chinese attempts to set up a new body called a

'Democratic Management Committee', theoretically to be composed of an elected group of monks who would have the task of running the monastery. The election would be scrutinised by the CCP's Religious Affairs Bureau. Many monasteries in Tibet had no choice but to agree to these changes, since large numbers of monks had either fled the country or were languishing in labour camps, so that it was not possible for the monasteries to function as before. In Tashilhunpo the monastery structure had remained intact and it had continued unaltered.

The Panchen Rinpoche demanded that innocent people, who had been arrested after the Lhasa revolt, should be released immediately and that the Chinese authorities should apologise to them. Moreover, he wanted those Chinese cadres who had acted wrongly to be punished. While the former demand was acceptable, the latter was not: it would have caused a major upheaval among the Chinese cadres. As noted earlier, despite the revolt and the setback experienced by the Chinese, the Communists had not carried out a purge among the cadres: the Party had no compunction about instigating purges among cadres in China – during the same period the leadership in Beijing had removed many important provincial Party secretaries from their post[94] – but in Tibet the Communists could not afford to destabilise the morale of the Chinese working there. The Panchen Rinpoche's insistence on guilty cadres being punished earned him many enemies among Chinese cadres working in Tibet.[95]

On 18 May 1962, while the United Front Meeting was taking place, the Panchen Rinpoche formally submitted the petition to Premier Zhou Enlai. He was about to embark on a tour of the north-east regions of China. and had no time to go through the report, but he agreed to listen to a verbal submission. In the afternoon, the Panchen Rinpoche went through the report at a meeting attended by Zhou and other Chinese leaders, like Ulanfu (a Mongolian member of the Communist Party), Li Weihan and Xi Zhongxun. The main Chinese figures in Tibet, Zhang Jingwu, Zhang Guohua and Wang Qimei, were also present. Among the Tibetans present were Ngabo and Phagpa Gelek Namgyal, a young incarnate lama from Chamdo, who had been selected as the Chairman of the Chamdo Liberation Committee. The Panchen Rinpoche had earlier shown the report to a number of leading Tibetans including Ngabo, who had advised that the report should begin in a more complimentary tone by stressing the concrete achievements made by the Chinese in Tibet. Both the Panchen Rinpoche's spiritual teacher, Ngulchu Rinpoche, and Chen Jigme, his personal confidant, pleaded with him not to submit the report.[96] Zhou Enlai did not make any serious comment, but merely agreed to look into the report when he returned from his tour.

When the petition was discussed with Zhou Enlai, both Zhang Guohua and Zhang Jingwu vehemently protested that the report exaggerated the mistakes in Tibet. Naturally, they felt that the PLA and the cadres had made tremendous strides in bringing Tibet into the fold of the Motherland and that the reforms had transformed Tibet from a feudal into a socialist society. The meeting resulted in an acrid debate between the Panchen Rinpoche and Chinese cadres from Tibet.[97] In June the report was printed and circulated to leading members of the Party's Central Committee, including Peng Zhen, the mayor of Beijing, who was a powerful figure at the national level, and said to exercise considerable influence in the propaganda division of the party. This time the Panchen Rinpoche was met by Chairman Mao himself.

No senior Chinese leaders were prepared to accept all the criticism; in fact, some of the words used by the Panchen Rinpoche infuriated them. Zhou Enlai said that while it was true that mistakes had been made, the Panchen Rinpoche's use of phrases such as 'death of Tibetan nationality' was inappropriate. Zhou instructed the United Front and senior Chinese cadres from Tibet to review their work in Tibet and come up with a new work programme for the future. By the end of July, they had produced four draft documents. The first one dealt with achieving co-operation between the traditional Tibetan leaders and the Chinese cadres. The second promised to implement the Party's policy on freedom of religion. The third dealt with the question of senior Tibetans who had been accused of involvement in the Uprising. The final document devised plans for the education and recruitment of cadres.[98]

The documents went some way to appeasing the Tibetans. The Chinese made a number of concessions and agreed that senior Tibetans who had co-operated with the Chinese should be given a 'position of power and responsibility' and would be consulted by the Tibet Work Committee. The Panchen Rinpoche had demanded that there should be no reduction in the number of monks at Tashilhunpo. The Chinese agreed that the monastery could maintain up to 2,000 monks. The authorities also agreed that a total of 3,000 monks would be allowed to continue to live in monasteries in other parts of Tibet and that they would be given a stipend by the state. They would not be required to undertake manual labour. On the question of the treatment of former senior Tibetan officials and religious figures accused of participation in the revolt, the Chinese agreed that Tibetans should be involved in sentencing them. The Chinese appointed Ngabo and Chen Jigme to head a 'cases review panel'[99] and on the return of the Panchen Rinpoche and Ngabo to Lhasa, a number of Tibetan officials imprisoned since 1959 were released.[100]

The petition did have some effect on relieving the pressure in Tibet. Zhang Guohua and Zhang Jingwu were unhappy about the extent of support given to the Panchen Rinpoche, fearing that their position would be undermined in Tibet if the Tibetans thought that they could appeal to

Beijing every time there were difficulties. The Chinese cadres knew that once the leadership in Beijing supported the Tibetans there was very little the cadres could do to convince Beijing that what they were doing in Tibet was correct. The extent of their resentment against the Panchen Rinpoche would become clear only later, when they sought to keep him permanently out of Tibet. The leadership in Beijing gave their support to the Panchen Rinpoche not because they concurred with his views or had a real desire to wipe out the excesses of the leftist cadres in Tibet but most likely because they knew that for domestic and international reasons they could ill afford to antagonise the Panchen Rinpoche in case he too fled the country and joined the Dalai Lama in India, which would have been a disaster for the Chinese. They knew they had to retain a Tibetan figurehead whom the Tibetan populace would respect. Moreover, as noted earlier, the Panchen Rinpoche's criticisms came at a time when China was facing a crisis in its internal and external affairs which led to a swing towards a more tolerant policy nationwide. Tibet merely followed this trend. In his biography of the Panchen Rinpoche, Jamphel Gyatso notes that when we look at the array of the problems besetting China at the time, the Tibetan issue represented only a minor concession for the Chinese leaders.

This is not to belittle the significance of the Panchen Rinpoche's petition. Later the Chinese authorities placed its importance equal to Peng Dehuai's criticism of the Party; indeed, it was said that the Panchen Rinpoche's petition exceeded Peng's letter in its 'anti-party and socialist principal'.[101] The importance of the document can also be gauged by the savagery of the attacks by the Chinese authorities a few months later. In Tibet, it established that the Panchen Rinpoche, then only twenty-four years old, could not be dismissed as an immature young lama. The Chinese cadres in Tibet realised that he was not going to be shut up in a monastery, and the Tibetans felt that he was a leader to whom the Chinese would listen.

But this was not to last. The political situation in China was changing rapidly and policy began to swing further left. Faced with the reality of economic failure in the countryside and the total mismanagement of its industrial programmes, the Chinese leadership found that agricultural and industrial projects had degenerated through corruption, and that the revolutionary fervour which had enticed the peasantry into the Party was fading, with cadres becoming involved in racketeering. Mao and other hard-liners were convinced that the revolutionary enthusiasm which had placed the Communists in power needed to be revitalised with a new campaign: the Party's ideology had to be purified by returning to the basic socialist principal. While the shift in ideological slant had serious implications for Tibet, it was the growing border tension between China and India along the Himalayan belt which was to force the Chinese to abandon their attempts to win over the Tibetans by persuasion and to seek a more rapid integration of Tibet.

TEN

War in the Himalayas

The reforms in Tibet had to be shelved temporarily as Beijing's attention shifted to the question of the border dispute with India. The Chinese also found that although Tibetan resistance in central Tibet had been checked by the PLA, the Khampas' activities had shifted to western Tibet, near the Nepal border. The PLA had not established any firm foothold in this sparsely populated territory through which ran an important road linking Tibet and Xinjiang. Now the CIA got deeply involved with the Tibetan resistance movement by increasing the supply of weapons and providing training.

For China, the growing rift with India was the most serious consequence of the Lhasa uprising. For the Indians, the revolt in Tibet had brought home the instability of the Himalayan plateau and the dangers that represented. Nehru's policy on Tibet remained, at best, confused. For many years he had been convinced that confrontation between the two giants of Asia could be avoided.[1] Now, however, he began to accept that the widespread resistance in Tibet had irrevocably altered the course of Sino–Indian relations. The United Nations debate and America's support for Tibet pointed to the severity of the situation for India, and the extent to which Asian politics were inextricably linked to the Cold War.

It was in this milieu that the Sino–Indian border war erupted. Its legacy lasts to this day. Since 1950 the question of the line of demarcation between China and India had been lurking in the background, but neither country had referred to the issue since the establishment of diplomatic relationships. As noted earlier, the Sino–Indian agreement of 1954 made no reference to the border, but in 1962 the treaty of friendship had lapsed and the revolt in Tibet meant it was virtually impossible for India and China to maintain the status quo.

For China, the border issue had to wait until internal economic and security interests were firmly under control. Between 1950 and 1960, China was consolidating its position in Tibet and hence conducted its diplomacy with India and neighbouring countries with extreme caution and skill. The Chinese clearly did not want to complicate relations with India by raising the potentially explosive issue of the border. During this critical period Zhou Enlai assured Nehru that Tibet would continue to enjoy autonomy, and that there were no obstacles to a friendly relationship between India and China. Zhou's charm and diplomatic skills allayed any fears Nehru might have had about the Chinese presence in Tibet. Nehru continued to believe that the border between Tibet and India was firmly defined and that the 1954 agreement had settled all problems with China.

But the crisis in Tibet and the growing numbers of PLA troops on the Himalayan plateau were an increasing cause of concern in New Delhi. While China saw the crushing of the Tibetan revolt and the increase in PLA in the region as internal measures to counter the revolt, India saw things differently. The presence of the Chinese troops required a counter-move from India. Soon after the uprising in Lhasa, diplomatic exchange between China and India on border alignment reached fever-pitch. It was apparent that despite Nehru's initial reluctance to take up this issue, the border question could now not be ignored. Diplomatic dispatches of the time show an unbridgeable chasm between the Indian and Chinese viewpoints.

The crisis was intensified by what Beijing saw as India's active collusion with the Tibetans and anti-Chinese forces – even though India had given no concrete support to the Tibetans and had tried to dissuade the Dalai Lama from turning the Tibetan cause into an international issue. The Chinese preferred to interpret the emotional and popular support for Tibet by the Indian people as interference in the internal affairs of China. The preceding chapters have shown that India was not involved in the Tibetan revolt nor did India actively promote Tibet internationally – internal events in Tibet were beyond the influence of Nehru. However, the presence of the Dalai Lama was putting a strain on Sino–Indian relations. The Chinese even began to fear that the Indians would use the Tibetan issue to counter China's territorial claims. China and India were on a collision course, and some form of confrontation suddenly seemed inevitable.

The Indians had begun to send 'police patrols' and set up checkposts. This was no doubt an attempt to 'show the flag' and exhibit 'symbols of Indian sovereignty'.[2] Since 1958, India and China's relations had deteriorated into open animosity. Indian public opinion, which had once resounded to the sound of *Hindi-Chinee Bhai-Bhai* (Indian–Chinese Brotherhood), had given way to open hatred of China.[3] At governmental level in New Delhi there was a recognition that the arrival of the PLA in Tibet required the strengthening of India's logistical and military capabilities on its northern frontiers, extending from Kashmir in the north-west along the Himalayan belt towards the eastern Himalayas. China saw this as a deliberate attempt to take advantage of Chinese weakness in the region. China also had to watch with concern what they saw as India's slow expansion along the Himalayan border. The border dispute came into the open in October 1958 when the Indians sent a note protesting that they had discovered a road running through a 'part of Ladakh, a region of India for centuries'. The Chinese replied by accusing India of intrusion into Chinese territory.[4]

A Legacy of Empire

The origin of the border dispute stems from unshakeable beliefs held by Delhi and Beijing. The Indians were firmly convinced that they had inherited from the British a clearly defined and demarcated northern border with Tibet,[5] while the Chinese were equally convinced that the border separating India and Tibet had never been formally demarcated. To fully appreciate the depth of the controversy and the genesis of the border dispute is beyond the scope of this book,[6] and I do not intend to deal with the minutiae of the Sino–Indian negotiations. The disputed areas were identified as the Western, Middle and Eastern Sectors. The Western Sector is located in areas where Kashmir, Xinjiang and Tibet meet it, extending over 1,000 miles from the Karakoram Pass in the north of Ladakh to Spiti, in the Indian state of Himachal. The main disputed territory is the locality known as Aksai Chin, which has no direct geographical link with Tibet[7] but, because it borders the Chinese region of Xinjiang, is of strategic and economic importance to Tibet. Between 1950 and 1960 the Chinese constructed the Xinjiang–Tibet highway, which passed right through the disputed territories; in 1950 the PLA entered western Tibet by this road, which the Indians claimed ran through part of the Indian state of Kashmir.[8] Since the area does not directly touch on Tibetan territory, I do not wish to deal at any length with the historical claims and counter-claims made by India and China.

The area which had most significance to Tibet was the five-hundred-mile border extending from Ladakh in the north-west to the Middle Sector, which although the least important of the territories under question, was where conflict first became prominent. Here the disputed area is located where the Sutlej river cuts south into India and eastwards along the Himalayan ridge at Shipki Pass.[9] The eastern Sector lies between Bhutan and Burma. The Indians claim that the entire length of the border was defined by the MacMahon line, the subject of notes exchanged between the British representative, Sir Henry MacMahon, (after whose name the alignment is known today), and the Tibetan representative, Lochen Shatra, at the Simla Conference of 1914.[10] The notes, kept secret from the Nationalist Chinese,[11] defined the alignment of Tibet's southern boundary touching the present-day Indian state of Assam. The region, known by the Tibetans as Monyul, was sparsely populated by indigenous tribes[12] who had loyalty neither to Lhasa nor to Indian princely states, apart from the Tawang tract, which was culturally and politically a part of Tibet. This had been clearly recognised prior to 1914 by the British, who had proposed that the new border alignment should follow the crest of the Himalayas, extending from Bhutan in the west towards the Burmese border. This pushed Tibetan jurisdiction away from the foothills of the Himalayas. Lochen Shatra conceded several hundred square miles of Tibetan territory to the British, including the whole of Tawang, so that even the main monastery at Tawang now came under the British.

Lochen Shatra's acceptance of the new border alignment in 1914 was not without conditions. The British records show that the Tibetans would concede to the new border on the condition that the British would secure Chinese acceptance of the Simla Convention, which would have in turn secured for Tibet a clearly defined border with China.[13] More importantly, it would have obtained an acknowledgment of Tibet's separateness from China. Since the British were not able to obtain such an acceptance, the Tibetans considered the line proposed by MacMahon invalid.[14] The British Government too seem to have accepted that the agreement was not in force[15] and the MacMahon line was never shown on official British maps of the period.[16] However, Tibetan acceptance of the MacMahon line was crucial to British imperial interests, as it would push the border between Tibet and India north from the foothills of the Himalayas, giving easy access to the plains of Assam. As noted earlier, the MacMahon line drew the new border along the crest of the Himalayas, which gave the British a strategic advantage and imperial ambition was such that the British never quite gave up the idea of making the MacMahon line the *de jure* border between Tibet and India. After the Second World War, the British intensified their penetration into the region, seeking to establish permanent check-posts and evicting Tibetan officials who had entered the area to collect taxes. This met with Tibetan protests. In 1945 the Tibetans presented a memorandum, passed by the National Assembly, which stated that 'the British Government have occupied indisputable Tibetan territory by posting British officers and troops'. British action was described as 'a big insect eating up a small one, and the bad name of the British Government will spread like the wind'.[17]

The Chinese Communists knew that the Tibetans also did not accept the boundary alignment shown by Indian maps. As mentioned in an earlier chapter, after the Communists had reached Lhasa they took over the Tibetan Foreign Bureau, which had been largely responsible for negotiating with the British about the border. The Chinese began to debrief important Tibetan officials about their past dealings with Nepal, with the British and later with the new Government of India.[18] As far as the MacMahon line was concerned, the Chinese learned that their views were identical to those of the Tibetans.[19] It was clear that the Chinese had gone through the correspondence between the Tibetans and the Indians and had discovered that when India became independent the Tibetans had asked the new GOI for the 'return of Tibetan territories gradually annexed by the British'. On 16 October 1947, two months after Indian Independence, the Tibetan Foreign Bureau had written to the new GOI demanding the return of Tibetan territories 'such as Zayul [Sayul] and Walong and in Pemakoe, Lonag, Lopa, Mon, Bhutan, Sikkim, Darjeeling and other areas on this side of the river Ganges and Lawo [Lahul], Ladakha'.[20] Nehru dismissed this as a fantastical demand. Although the Tibetan claim was totally unrealistic, the GOI should have inferred that the Tibetans did not accept that the border was clearly delineated.[21] This was what Zhou Enlai understood when he referred to the Tibetan demands in his letter to Nehru. This is not to say that the Chinese disputes with India were merely a continuation of Tibetan demands, whatever the Tibetans might have thought: the Communists would not have based their views purely on Tibetan claims. But, while this does not mean that these claims are right, it has to be accepted that there has been a consistent Chinese view of what they regard as the limits of their frontier in the Himalayas.

The Chinese Communists followed the Nationalists in their rejection of both the Simla Convention and the notes exchanged between McMahon and Lochen Shatra, arguing that whatever was conspired between Lochen Shatra and McMahon was 'illegal, null and void'.[22] The Chinese also believed that Tibet had had no authority to sign an agreement in its own right. (This was important detail for the Chinese: if they had accepted Tibet's right to sign, it would have implied that Tibet was an independent country. And that, in turn, would have rendered the Chinese action in 1950 an invasion of an independent country. No Chinese government was going to accept this.) In many ways the actual geographical line of control – whether drawn in the snow-capped peaks of the Himalayas or not – was unimportant. The Chinese saw the legal implications of the contradictions in the Indian statement, which declared that the notes exchanged between Lochen Shatra and McMahon constituted a valid agreement (implying that Tibet was an independent country) but nevertheless refused to recognise Tibetan independence.[23] This was not missed by the Tibetan *émigrés* in India: in an interview with the press in 1959 the Dalai Lama said, 'if you deny sovereign status to Tibet, you deny the validity of the Simla Convention and therefore deny the validity of the McMahon line'.[24]

It was precisely this contradiction which was at the heart of the Sino-Indian dispute. India had made a major diplomatic blunder in 1954 by legitimising Chinese territorial claims over Tibet without securing any concession vis-à-vis Chinese acceptance of the McMahon line. The issue of the greatest importance to China at the time was the legal status of Tibet. China had, after all, been prepared to reach agreement with Burma in 1960, even though the border alignment was almost identical with the McMahon line. Later, the Sino–Pakistan agreement also followed the line established under British colonial rule. In both of these cases the complexities of Tibet were not an issue, which made speedy settlement possible. This indicated that the actual line of demarcation *per se* was not the most contentious issue: what China objected to most was India's insistence that the McMahon line was the legal border between the two countries.

The untidy legacy left by the British and independent India's misapprehension that its northern border was secured 'by tradition, treaties and custom', along with the Chinese fear of having newly acquired territory with dangerously ill-defined boundaries, made the question of the border very complex. Negotiations between India and China quickly became entrenched, with both sides unwilling to compromise. In 1960, when Zhou Enlai came to Delhi to meet Nehru, he proposed a compromise: if India agreed to accept Aksai Chin as a part of China, in return China would agree to India's claims in the east, thus accepting the McMahon line as the *de jure* boundary between the two countries.[25]

India's moves to strengthen its control in the disputed areas were seen in Beijing as an international move against China, which had the Aksai Chin under effective control which it would never relinquish. It was inevitable that Indian attempts to regain control of the region would be met with a counter-attack in the Eastern Sector.

Moreover, the pressure on China was mounting due to the rift with the Soviet Union, which also led to border clashes. There was also increasing American animosity towards China. Since 1960 CIA involvement with the Tibetans had intensified: earlier attempts to establish small bases inside Tibet had been replaced by the maintenance of a substantial garrison of Tibetan resistance groups along the Himalayan border. China could not accept that these events were unrelated – its view of India shifted from one based on practical considerations to one of ideological interpretation of India's standing in the world.[26] This cast India as a 'lackey' of reactionary forces. Nehru, on the other hand, felt that greater international developments would not touch on Sino–Indian disputes and so tried to isolate the Tibetan issue from the border conflicts.

If it had not been for the Tibetan revolt, the border dispute would have been confined to diplomatic exchanges of notes. The Chinese saw the resistance in Tibet and the border issue as linked aspects of their political security in the region, with all events pointing to the development of an anti-Chinese movement in the Himalayas: not only were the Americans actively supporting the Tibetans, but the Indians too were drawing closer to the Americans.[27] Nehru had done his best to dissuade the Dalai Lama from raising the Tibetan issue at the UN or contacting foreign powers. Despite opposition in India, he was advising the Tibetans to accept the situation as a *fait accompli*. It is most likely that Nehru had his suspicions of the American connection with the Tibetans, but neither he nor Indian intelligence knew of the extent of the CIA activity until the Sino–Indian War.[28]

Tibetan Resistance

CIA involvement with the Tibetans was not supported by everyone. The American Ambassador to India, Kenneth Galbraith, and H. Rositzke, the CIA station chief in India, were opposed to any commitment in the Himalayas and wrote a memorandum advising the State Department to terminate CIA aid to the Tibetans.[29] They felt that American involvement in the region would jeopardise the USA's relationship with India, and Galbraith writes that 'our relations with India would have been poisonous'.[30] If the Indians had known of the extent of CIA involvement, they would have objected to it.[31]

The Chinese could not believe that the Indians were not involved with the American aid to the Tibetans, and the American aid to the groups must have played a significant part in Chinese thinking. The main Tibetan resistance group, 'Four Rivers, Six Ranges', was facing difficulties, with many of its members beginning to drift away, seeing their fighting days as over. The promise of CIA funding meant that the group could now afford to pay its men and obtain other necessary provisions; previously individuals had been responsible for their own food and transport. The group now came under more direct influence from Gyalo Dhundup, who had become the main political figure among the Tibetans in India, acting as 'special envoy' of the Dalai Lama and dealing with the appeal to the UN. The Tibetans did not want the Dalai Lama associated with the resistance movement; it was imperative they keep resistance activities separate from those of the Dalai Lama's government. In reality both were under the influence of Gyalo Dhundup, and the Americans regarded him as the main political mover. It is interesting to note that, two days after they arrived at the CIA training base, all recruits were given a lecture during which the CIA officials showed slides of Andrug Gonbo Tashi, who was referred to as 'the Commander', and of Gyalo Dhundup, referred to as 'Your Prime Minister'.[32]

In mid-1960 Gonbo Tashi arranged a meeting in Darjeeling to discuss the logistics of setting up a permanent base. (Gyalo Dhundup had already informed the CIA that the Tibetans were unable to maintain a base inside Tibet. He had asked his friend Lhamo Tsering to oversee these meetings and form the main link between the resistance group and himself. From that time Lhamo Tsering became the main person in charge of the Mustang guerrilla base and all clandestine activities inside Tibet.) It was attended by Lhamo Tsering and thirty other Khampa leaders.[33] Gonbo Tashi also had first his personal interview with CIA officials – a China specialist named

Mac and a CIA officer stationed in Delhi who used the codename John.[34] The meeting was ostensibly to debrief Gonbo Tashi on his activities in Tibet, but it is likely that the officers also wanted to know his intentions for the future.

Andrug Gonbo Tashi knew well the pilgrim route from Lhasa to Mount Kailash in western Tibet, which is one of the most revered religious sites for Buddhists and Hindus. He had been on a pilgrimage there years before and had stayed for a brief period in Mustang, an area which was politically a part of Nepal but which shared a common religion and language with Tibetans, whose name for the area is Monthang. In the 1960s, Nepalese control in the region was minimal and Gonbo Tashi's suggestion of Mustang as a base was readily agreed to by the Tibetans and CIA officers. The location was ideal for secret military operations because it lay south of the main road connecting Tibet and Xinjiang, one of the two routes linking Tibet with China. The main road in the east from Kham into central Tibet was too far into PLA-controlled territory and it would have been impossible for the Tibetans to secure a permanent base near it. The situation in western Tibet was very different, for the Chinese had been unable to establish firm military control and it was unlikely that the Chinese would cross into Nepalese territory, since they had signed a border agreement and would not want to antagonise the Nepalese.

Caution characterised Chinese dealings with Nepal. On 28 June 1960 PLA troops fired on a party of Nepalese police. One policeman was killed and another seventeen arrested. The Chinese said they had mistaken the Nepalese for Tibetan resistance fighters. At first the Chinese claimed the incident had taken place on Tibetan territory but they later conceded the area was part of Nepal. The Chinese agreed to pay compensation to Nepal: they had far more to gain by keeping Nepal out of the regional conflict than by pushing it further towards India or the West. Nevertheless, in the early 1960s the relationship between Nepal and China was uneasy. The border between the two countries covering the world's highest mountains stretched over 500 miles, and had never been fixed in modern cartographic tradition. There was conflict about Mount Everest, which at one time Beijing claimed was part of China, setting off the first anti-Chinese demonstration in Kathmandu. It was only after Zhou Enlai's public announcement that China would agree to a division along the peak of the mountain that Nepalese fears about Chinese territorial claims were allayed.[35] At the beginning of 1960, the Chinese and Nepalese began to meet to discuss the border issue. There were originally seven points of dispute but by the end the Chinese side had conceded to Nepal all areas claimed by them. Chinese willingness could be seen as a diplomatic tactic: an attempt to contrast China's reasonableness over border disputes with Delhi's intransigence.[36]

While on the surface Nepal was on friendly diplomatic terms with

Beijing, the King who had ousted the elected government and assumed political control was not averse to Tibetan ventures in his territory.[37] Although he could not be seen as actively supporting the Tibetans, in the 1960s King Mahendra visited the Tibetan camp twice and Baba Yeshi, leader of the Tibetan guerrillas, presented the King with Tibetan ponies. The King also made a speech urging the Tibetans to resist Communism, which he described as the common aim of Nepal and Tibet.[38] It has to be remembered that the Chinese had given asylum in Tibet to the Nepalese Communist leader Dr Singh and there was all likelihood that the Nepalese Communists would welcome aid from the Chinese, who, at least in public, had always advocated exporting the revolution to the neighbouring countries. This no doubt meant that the Nepalese leaders were aware of Communist infiltration into the kingdom, and so hoped that any Tibetan resistance in their border areas would ensure the Chinese were occupied with their own security concerns. It would have been clear to the King what the Tibetans were up to. Later the Nepalese Government asked the Tibetans to help them in clearing a landing strip at Jomsom, which is now the main airport linking these remote regions with Kathmandu. The small detachment of Nepalese police in the region were often treated as chief guests at the Tibetan camp, and they no doubt would have reported to their superiors in Kathmandu the activities of the Khampas. Between 1960 and 1971 the Nepalese Government turned a blind eye to Tibetan activities in Mustang and publicly claimed ignorance of the base on their territory. It is also likely that after 1962 the Nepalese Government was under considerable pressure from the Indians to allow the Tibetans to operate from Mustang. The Chinese did not in any case put pressure on the Nepalese to take action against the Tibetans.

Between 1960 and 1962 over 150 Tibetans were sent to America for training. The new recruits were selected from the Four Rivers, Six Ranges group and from Tibetan soldiers who had escaped to India. They were sent across the Indian and East Pakistan border, where they were met by Pakistani officials and then flown to one of the Pacific Islands. Later Americans set up a training centre in Colorado, presumably thinking that the rocky mountains would be a suitable training ground for Tibet. Gonbo Tashi appointed a young man from Bathang in eastern Tibet, called Baba Yeshi, to head the operation in Mustang. He was regarded as a great fighter and had a substantial following among the Khampas from Bathang. His men had been engaged in fighting the PLA since the early fifties. Through the 1960s the camp matured into an efficiently organised military campaign base. The CIA made its first arms drop for the group in early 1960, using Tibetan territory as a landing zone. Over the next few years, thirty CIA-trained personnel were sent into Mustang, including three radio operators, who were essential to long-term plans.

The CIA-trained Tibetans were not parachuted back into Tibet; they usually returned by land from East Pakistan and had to make their way on foot to Mustang. There groups were organised into cells of fifteen, each with a CIA-trained leader. Each cell acted independently of others and carried out raids into Tibet. Some were sent deep into PLA-held territories, from where they maintained radio communication with their controller. The Tibetan resistance activities had forced the PLA to deploy large numbers of PLA soldiers to guard the Tibet–Xinjiang Highway. The Chinese came under constant attack, and throughout the 1960s there were skirmishes.

The Clash of India and China

By the beginning of 1962 the border negotiations between India and China had more or less come to a halt. Both sides refused to accept the other's claims and the joint meetings of experts were unable to agree the exact alignment of their claims. Throughout the early 1960s, the Chinese deployed large numbers of PLA troops, partly to suppress the revolt, only to find that the border regions were still inadequately guarded. The ease with which the Dalai Lama and thousands of Tibetans were able to escape into India meant logically that saboteurs could enter the country from the same areas. The Chinese began to recruit hundreds of Tibetans to work for the PLA, employing them in carrying supplies to the troops and clearing feeder roads in southern Tibet near the disputed areas of Tawang and north of the McMahon line; this manpower was later to provide a major strategic advantage for the PLA.[39] As the border negotiations dragged on, the Indians occupied areas marked by the McMahon line, and by 1962 they had established twenty-four new posts.[40] At the same time, the Chinese established over thirty new posts in the Western Sector.[41]

By late September 1962, the first skirmishes between the two armies had taken place. It was inevitable that, unless both countries withdrew their armies from disputed areas, war would break out. The Indians began to talk of 'evicting' the Chinese from their territories and Indian attempts to push back the PLA were naturally seen by the Chinese as an act of provocation and aggression. On 20 October 1962, China decided to make a decisive move across the McMahon line, attacking Indian army posts across the Western Sector. Coinciding as it did with the Cuban missile crisis, the Chinese timing was very significant. International attention was focused on the apocalyptic confrontation between the two superpowers, and there was little risk of either the Soviets or the Americans becoming embroiled in a Himalayan venture. This left India isolated. The Indian defensive posts collapsed within two days and the Indian army – poorly equipped and inexperienced – was defeated. The terrain in the Himalayas favoured the

PLA, many of whom had long experience of combat in the Korean War. The fighting lasted a month and on 21 November the Chinese declared a unilateral ceasefire and began to withdraw across the McMahon line.[42]

It was a humiliating defeat for India, forcing Nehru to abandon his non-alignment policy. He wrote to President Kennedy requesting US military aid, and the Americans now informed the Indians of their aid to the Tibetans and of the existence of the base in Mustang. In early 1963, a few dozen Tibetans who had been trained in Colorado returned to India. This time they did not have to enter the country clandestinely via East Pakistan, but were flown directly to an Indian airforce base where they were welcomed by the Indian army.[43] The Indian policy towards the Dalai Lama and the Tibetans underwent a dramatic change as India came to realise the potential benefit of the presence of Tibetans in their country. They began to adopt a more supportive policy and encouraged the Tibetans to organise themselves, eventually leading to the Dalai Lama's setting up of a *de facto* 'government-in-exile' based in Himachal Pradesh in Dharamsala. The Indian Government began to allocate substantial aid for the rehabilitation of refugees and, as Indian public sympathy naturally moved towards the Tibetans, the different state governments began to allocate land for the resettlement of Tibetan refugees. The Indian army began to recruit large numbers of Tibetans to work on road construction along its north frontier and also recruited a special reserve of Tibetans, who were trained in modern warfare at a base near Dhera Dun. Many of the CIA-trained Tibetans later joined this regiment. The Mustang venture became a joint operation between the Indians and Americans and a new headquarters was established in Delhi.[44] However, the Tibetans wanted to keep the Mustang operation separate from the Indian–Tibetan regiment which had just been formed.

The Chinese victory was celebrated in Lhasa with a display of captured weapons and Indian prisoners, who were paraded in the Barkhor. They were dressed in flimsy clothes and their defeat on the battlefield made them look dishevelled and dejected. Chinese propaganda blared out the superiority of the PLA and, to the Tibetans, the Chinese appeared invincible. Lhasa radio broadcast stories about Tibetan refugees in India living in abject poverty and forced to beg in Indian cities. The victory also meant that Chinese doubts about their policy in Tibet had vanished. Zhang Guohua and Zhang Jingwu, who had earlier come under criticism, were now seen as heroes of the PLA. They had played an important role during the war and their regiments from the South-West Military Region had fought with great success. The leadership in Beijing no longer needed to worry about external threats to their position in Tibet.

ELEVEN

Socialist Transformation of Tibet

After the Sino–Indian War, the Chinese began to abandon their gradualist approach in favour of a new policy which veered towards bringing Tibet into line with the rest of China. The victory had given China renewed confidence, and the Communist cadres could now boast of their achievements in defending the motherland from foreign aggression. The Chinese leadership in Tibet was still drawn from the military and this naturally meant that victory not only established the PLA's supremacy in Tibet but also insulated the leadership there from further criticism. This also coincided with the general strengthening of the power and prestige of the PLA under the tutelage of Lin Biao. From now on, Beijing would find it difficult to criticise the Chinese leaders and cadres in Tibet, especially since it was believed that there was a real danger of further war on the Chinese frontier. The two most prominent Chinese leaders in Tibet, with their positions secure, Zhang Guohua and Zhang Jingwu felt that they could push ahead with reforms without Beijing's interference.

By the early 1960s there had been many changes in Tibetan society. Chinese propaganda presents these as a move towards modernity and progress but in reality the changes were neither a technological leap nor the advancement of science over superstition.[1] First and foremost, there was an altered relationship between the state and the Tibetan masses. The new state began to penetrate every aspect of Tibetan life. Traditional economic structures based on manorial estates were replaced by mutual aid groups, and taxes paid to estate owners were now extracted by the state. In 1963 the Chinese announced that there were 25,200 agricultural and pastoral mutual aid groups in Tibet, representing 82.3 per cent of all households in Tibet.[2] Nevertheless, during this period the individual household remained the main production unit in agricultural and nomadic areas.

Chinese propaganda boasted about the increase in agricultural production, but it is difficult to establish the accuracy of these figures. There were attempts to cultivate some areas of former grazing land but the produce was of poor quality. Contrary to Chinese claims, many Tibetan refugees say that during the period 1959–65 there was a shortage of food and that a sizeable amount of the produce was extracted in taxes. In the areas of Dromo and Phari, crops failed in the years 1959, 1962 and 1966.[3] There were cultural changes too: one of the most noticeable being the reform of the written and spoken language.[4] Since the early 1950s the Communists had recruited a number of Tibetan scholars to work on translations into Tibetan of Marxist literature and a huge number of bureaucratic memoranda and directives. All these led to the invention of a new style of literary language, and a new Marxist terminology was introduced to general usage. The new literary style was meant to appeal to the masses and to conform to normal spoken Tibetan, making it easier to understand.[5] There were also a number of grammatical changes. For example, in written Tibetan five genitive particles (*'brel sgra*) – *gi, kyi, gyi, yi* and *'i* – are used distinctly according to the preceding suffix or syllable. But in spoken Tibetan no differentiation is made and the particle *gi* is used. Accordingly, from the 1960s only '*gi*' was used in written Tibetan.[6] New lexicons were developed, with Chinese Marxist terms, such as '*gral rim 'thob rtsod*' (class struggle), '*bzo bcos ring lugs pa*' (revisionist), and *bkas bkod rgyun 'zhin gi sa bdags* (feudal landlord) coming into common usage.[7]

During the early 1960s the Communists did not attempt to prohibit the individual practice of religion. However, the central aspects of Tibetan society – the monasteries, the incarnate Lamas and hundreds of monks who were the pillar of Tibetan Buddhism – came under attack and the Communists were successful in dismantling the privileges and power exercised by the monasteries. As noted in the last chapter, the main point of contention between the Tibetans and the Chinese was their irreconcilable views on the place of religion, with the Chinese aim during this period being to reduce Buddhism to a domestic ritual and to deny its centrality in Tibetan life and society. For Tibetans the incarnate lamas and the monasteries had been the centre of their world, but all this was about to change, and Tibet was to be swept into the turbulence of Chinese politics. It mattered very little to the Chinese leaders what the Tibetans thought of their society or what type of reforms they wanted: the logic of Chinese politics dictated that Tibet should be subjected to class struggle.

Just before the Sino–Indian War Mao had been forced to withdraw from the centre of Chinese politics but by the end of 1962 he had regained his position. It was apparent, despite the brief period of leniency, that Mao had not abandoned his radical roots and had returned with an even more ambitious plan to transform Chinese society. This marked the ascendancy of a more hard-line policy. Mao was alarmed by what he saw as the subversion of socialism by international and domestic revisionists. He viewed the developments in the Soviet Union since the 20th Soviet Congress as the restoration of revisionism.[8] On the domestic front he was unhappy about the deterioration of collectivism in farming and the emergence of pockets of market economy in the rural areas – developments which he regarded as deliberate attempts by 'capitalist roaders' in the Party to restore capitalism.

At the 10th Plenum of the Central Committee in September 1962, Mao warned that:

> In our country, the system of man exploiting man has already been abolished as has the economic basis of landlords and bourgeoisie. Since the reactionary classes are not so terrible as hitherto, we speak of them as remnants. Yet on no account must we treat these remnants lightly. We must continue to engage in struggle with them [for] they are still planning a comeback. In a socialist society [moreover] new bourgeois elements may still be produced. Classes and class struggle remain throughout the entire socialist stage and the struggle is protracted, complex and sometimes even violent.[9]

Although no individual was identified, it was a clear sign that Chinese politics was about to experience one of the many campaigns to purge and purify the Party. Every twist and turn in Beijing was to have serious ramifications in Tibet. Mao's theoretical shift in the definition of the antagonisms and contradictions emerging in socialist China meant that the Party's United Front Department had to apply the new theory in their nationality work, a development that was reflected in the thinking of Liu Chun, the Vice Chairman of the Nationality Affairs Commission, when he set out the revised policy on minority groups in a lengthy article in *Hongqi (Red Flag)*, the CCP's theoretical journal.[10] Liu Chun argued that it was an error to have maintained that the nationality problem could be solved by working with the traditional ruling class. This he called 'reformism' and 'relying on the charity of the reactionary ruling class'.[11] He believed that the ruling order would always equate their class interest with the interest of the nationality and that, in terms of the main problem facing China – which was the 'struggle between the two roads of socialism and capitalism' – the ruling class among the minority would always try to push towards the restoration of the feudal system by inciting national and religious sentiments. It was evident that the Party was preparing to abandon its past policy of implementing changes from the top and soliciting the co-operation of the traditional ruling class.

At least on a theoretical level, this provided a pretext for the attack on the Panchen Rinpoche as a 'capitalist roader'. He should perhaps have recognised the signs that things were about to change: when Mao sanctioned the Party to purge reactionary elements in the Party and government, the Tibet Work Committee and many other Party officials in Qinghai, Sichuan and Gansu were quick to identify the Panchen Rinpoche as an easy target to label as a 'reactionary and revisionist' who wanted to hold on to his feudal privileges.

The Purge of the Panchen Rinpoche

While all these changes were taking place in Beijing, the Panchen Rinpoche was in Lhasa. He had returned from China in August 1963 to attend the 6th enlarged meeting of the Tibetan Work Committee (TWC), pleased that he had got the leadership in Beijing to issue four major documents on the CCP's work in Tibet. The Chinese leadership too seemed to have accepted that mistakes had been made and the Panchen Rinpoche felt that, in some ways, he had managed to prevent the more radical reforms from being implemented in Tibet. He had still, it seems, no inkling of how the changes in Beijing would affect him. It is interesting to note that while the Panchen Rinpoche flew back to Lhasa to announce the new work programme, both Zhang Jingwu and Zhang Guohua remained in Beijing, where they would have realised that the Party was about to harden its policy towards the question of minorities. Zhang Jingwu was in a good position to gauge the change: apart from his post in Tibet, he had always held concurrent positions both in the Party and in government in Beijing. From July 1955 he had served in the Chief of Staff Office of the PRC, an important administrative office directly under the control of Mao (and after 1959 under Liu Shaoqi); from the Party Congress of 1956, he had also been an alternate member of the Central Committee.

When the Panchen Rinpoche returned to Lhasa to unveil the new work programme issued from Beijing, he had no reason to suspect that the Chinese leadership would renege on their promises. The new directive was not a simple document produced by a few bureaucrats, but had been drawn up in consultation with some of the most senior leaders of the Party. Mao himself had approved the new work programme. The Panchen Rinpoche's absence from Beijing during the crucial month of September 1963 was unfortunate. Had he been there, he would have learned of Mao's pronouncement about the 'reactionaries' obstructing the revolution. In China, cadres were saying openly that the Panchen had become too 'cocky and sticking his tail as high as a U2 [the US spy plane].'[12] Zhang Guohua and Zhang Jingwu had stayed in Beijing to lobby against the Panchen Rinpoche. They returned to Lhasa at the end of September 1964 reassured by what they had learned and in the knowledge that four directives issued in June would be rescinded.

Although Zhang Guohua and Zhang Jingwu knew that the Panchen Rinpoche was now isolated from the leadership in Beijing and that they had the backing of the senior leaders, they were careful not to remove the Panchen Rinpoche from his post immediately. The first sign that the Chinese leadership had changed their policy towards the Panchen Rinpoche came in October 1963, when custom usually dictated that he attended the National Day celebration in Beijing. That year the Panchen Rinpoche was not invited and he quickly realised that something had gone wrong. Zhang Jingwu explained to the Panchen Rinpoche that he had made serious mistakes and was under investigation. The Panchen Rinpoche was incredulous, and argued with Zhang and other Chinese members of the Tibet Work Committee. Zhang, knowing fully the situation in Beijing, could now feel secure in attacking the Panchen Rinpoche.

Li Weihan, one of the most senior Party officials, was also absent from the National Day celebrations. His downfall had disastrous implications for Tibet. He had been the architect of the CCP's nationality policy and was responsible for Tibetan affairs and, although he did not tolerate demands for Tibetan independence, he was nevertheless a moderate in his dealings. Li once jokingly remarked that he had the most unfortunate name, made up of two Chinese characters: 'Wei', meaning 'to protect', and 'Han', meaning 'ethnic Chinese'. His liberal attitude was despised by Chinese cadres working in the minority regions who felt that the concessions he had made towards traditional minority leaders were undermining their work. When Mao launched one of his witch-hunts against 'reactionary revisionists' in the Party, Li Weihan became one of the first victims. Mao himself identified Li as being 'soft' on nationality issues and as having adopted revisionist tendencies in United Front work.[13] Li was stripped of his important Party positions.

It is not clear why Li Weiham fell. The official view stressed his ideological deficiency but this in itself was not sufficient reason for his dismissal: after all, Li and his wife were veterans of the Long March; he had been a comrade of Deng Xiaoping and Zhou Enlai in France during the embryonic period of the CCP, and had been in charge of the United Front Department since 1944. It is most likely that personal differences accounted for his loss of power. However, the Party, clearly recognising his historical importance, rehabilitated him shortly afterwards. It was announced that Li had corrected his mistakes and earned the trust of the Party. However, he never regained his power and influence, occupying only a minor ceremonial post in the government. He was succeeded as the head of the United Front Department by Xu Bing, whose first task was to investigate the erroneous ideological practices of his predecessor. This led to further allegations against Li. On the ideological front he was accused of being a 'revisionist' who neither practised revolution nor allowed others to do so. On practical grounds he was charged with allowing the Panchen Rinpoche and Geshe Sherab Gyatso to carry out unrestrained attacks on the Party and with having encouraged the criticisms made by the Panchen Rinpoche.[14]

As Li Weihan fell from power, the Panchen Rinpoche's own position came under fire. It was a matter of 'guilt by association'. At the national level the charges brought against Li Weihan became linked with those the Panchen Rinpoche faced in Tibet. It was clear that the power struggle within the upper levels of the leadership was paralleled in Tibet, with the Panchen Rinpoche too being accused of following the revisionist path and obstructing the implementation of socialist reforms. The lofty ideological reasons given for the dismissal of the Tibetan leader coincided with Mao's attack on Soviet revisionism and with the subsequent identification of 'revisionism' as one of the cardinal sins in revolutionary China.

Mao had warned that the advent of revisionism within the Party would lead to the ascendancy of bourgeois rule and the resurrection of capitalism in China and feudalism in Tibet. With their convoluted logic officials used this pronouncement to attack the Panchen Rinpoche, although in fact his only crime had been to describe the consequences of ill-conceived policies in Tibet. Initially, the Panchen Rinpoche remained defiant and refused to admit that he had made any mistakes. He told the Tibet Work Committee that, whatever he had done, he had always consulted Mao and the other leaders of the Party. As noted earlier, the Panchen Rinpoche had been encouraged to express his criticisms by some of the highest-ranking leaders of the CCP and between 1960 and early 1962 Mao himself had urged the Communists to adopt more openness both inside and outside the Party.[15] The Panchen Rinpoche regarded the accusations against him as preposterous.

The 10th Plenum marked the return to power of the radical faction within the CCP after the crisis years of 1958–62. Until 1960 the Tibetans had not been exposed to the volatile political culture of Beijing and, since he was not a member of the Communist Party, the Panchen Rinpoche himself had no idea of the changes that were taking place in Beijing. In Lhasa, although the public were not told of his demotion, they noted his absence from many of the ceremonial functions and soon realised that he was no longer used to promote campaigns. Buddhist teachings and sermons by him now virtually ceased.

At the end of 1962, Mao launched his Socialist Education Movement, (SEM). The campaign once again sought to encourage the masses to immerse themselves in an ideological purification. Also known as the 'Four Clean Ups',[16] the campaign was meant to purify the Party and its cadres politically, economically, organisationally and ideologically. They were largely irrelevant to Tibet. For example, since communes had not yet been introduced, the issue of work-point assessment was redundant. However, the issue of corruption and the accumulation of private wealth by cadres was to become an important question in Tibet. Later, Zhang Jingwu admitted that he had accepted a gift from Panchen Rinpoche of a gold Rolex watch. During the Cultural Revolution Zhang Guohua would be accused of furnishing his house with furniture valued at more than 20,000 yuan.[17]

The extension of the SEM to Tibet marked another turning point. Until then, Tibet had been exempt from campaigns that were being carried out in

China. When in the late fifties the Party carried out the Anti-Rightist Campaign, it was aimed mainly at the Party and at Chinese cadres working in Tibet. Such campaigns had no serious impact on Tibetan society, unlike the Anti-Rebellion Campaign and the land reforms, which were directly targeted at Tibet. The SEM was different in that it implied the Party regarded the situation in Tibet as similar to China. The only concession the Chinese made was to devise for Tibetans a concurrent campaign called 'The Three Big Educations': class consciousness, increasing patriotism and socialist education. The aim was to steer the Tibetan masses into overthrowing the old society and embracing the new society led by the Party, a society which, in Tibet, was synonymous with the Chinese.

In January 1964 Zhang Jingwu called on the cadres and masses in Tibet to increase their class consciousness and maintain vigilance against class enemies, a term which undoubtedly referred to people who would later be identified as revisionists. Zhang's speech was a signal that the SEM was being launched in Tibet. Throughout 1964 the Chinese intensified their political campaigning in Tibet, this time with a more direct ideological orientation. In the past, the Chinese had used material and economic benefits brought about by the land reforms as an incentive, particularly among the poorer sections of the community. The SEM stressed the ideological nature of Chinese rule and presented equality and socialism as the principal objective in Tibet. Nothing had happened in Tibet to provoke such a campaign: the Party's motive in carrying out the SEM lay deep in the political intrigues of the Chinese leadership. It was a signal that the leadership would no longer make concessions to the distinctive characteristics of Tibet. There were practical political forces which prompted the Chinese to apply a universal solution to the problems, irrespective of the local situation. The admonishing of the Panchen Rinpoche marked the suspension of the CCP's attempt to achieve some degree of consensus between the Tibetan ruling élite and the Party. The Communists had courted the traditional Tibetan leaders only to be castigated. When Communist rule in the country was weak, the Party needed the support of rinpoches, lamas and other traditional leaders, but now that the Party had achieved total control, they had become redundant.[18]

However, the Communists knew that they could not simply dismiss the Panchen Rinpoche and hope that he would be forgotten by the Tibetan people. While in China a purged leader could simply be written out of Communist history, in Tibet the religious importance of the Panchen Rinpoche could not be disregarded. Instead he had to discredited in the hope that the Tibetans' faith in him would be diminished. As the SEM intensified, the Panchen Rinpoche became the main target of the campaign. In the press and at conferences there were numerous references to a new bourgeoisie who had not reconciled themselves to their defeat and who were ever looking for an opportunity to resurrect the zombie of feudalism. Mao's theory about the resurgence of a new bourgeois element in Chinese society became the pretext for attacking the Panchen Rinpoche. It was clear that the ideological shifts in Beijing served as a convenient tool for Zhang Guohua and Zhang Jingwu. If there were genuine ideological reasons for the campaign against feudal lords or new bourgeoisie in Tibet, why was it that people like Ngabo, Sampho, Tsego and other former aristocrats who occupied important posts in the PCART were not purged?

The attack on the Panchen Rinpoche naturally led to charges against close followers like Chen Jigme and Ngulchu Rinpoche, who had co-operated fully with the Chinese authorities. Between 1963 and 1964 the Panchen Rinpoche was excluded from various meetings of the PCART and the TWC. While in China the initial phase of SEM saw the purging of Party officials, in Tibet the campaign was directed against traditional Tibetan leaders, particularly the Tashilhunpo faction which had survived the Anti-Rebellion Campaign. During the first phase of the movement the Panchen Rinpoche was singled out 'as the biggest capitalist serf owner', but as the campaign intensified, it became a movement against 'the Panchen clique'. Thus the campaign moved outside the Party and official circles.

As the SEM and the Three Big Educations Campaign were gaining momentum, the Chinese authorities went ahead with preparations for turning Tibet into an Autonomous Region and for the election of the People's Congress in Tibet, which would form the basis for the regional government. The building of the administration went hand in hand with the growing expansion of the bases for the Party through the establishment and recruiting of members for quasi-governmental and party organisations at village level. Often, membership of these organisations was determined by the class labels that were assigned to individuals and families. By 1963 the Chinese had an elaborate system of class groups based on ownership of land and livestock among the nomads.[19] The CCP began to adopt more rigid attitudes towards class groups and established more precise divisions. In the agricultural area, those families or individuals who did not own any land and worked as hired hands for other farmers, together with those people who worked as Nangzen (household servants) to manorial lords, were classed as 'poor farmer'. This group naturally became the target of Communist recruitment; the poor farmers were said to be the basis of the Party and became the target of affirmative policies. Even those poor farmers who had earlier been classed as taking part in the revolt were said to be misguided and not anti-Party. Farmers who owned land but did not hire any farm workers were classed as 'middle farmer', a category that faced greater scrutiny of economic status. This was because the group occupied the territory where the Communists drew the line between good class background – deserving the support of the Party – and the exploitative class.

The criteria for middle farmers was that they should be self-supporting, self-sufficient and without any exploitative relations with the poor farmers. The category of 'middle farmers' was further divided into three sub-groups: upper middle farmers; intermediate middle farmers, and lower middle farmers. The main feature differentiating these subgroups was whether they had hired a farm worker or not. Those middle farmers who regularly hired outside farm workers were said to have formed exploitative relationships and were classified as upper middle farmers. The nomads were similarly subjected to further class divisions with the equivalent of landlord labelled as 'herd owner'. An individual's class group was measured by the number of animals owned and by whether the individual family had hired others to look after its animals.

The Communists also used surplus produce from the land as a means of classifying a family class background. Families that enjoyed over 50 per cent surplus were labelled 'landlords', and those who had 25 per cent surplus 'middle farmers'.[20] Naturally, because of Tibet's social and economic conditions, the categories imposed on nomads and farmers included the majority of the population. In 1964, the Chinese sources showed that the urban population – who were classed as 'Jormed dralrim',[21] – amounted to only 20,000.[22] The urban workers, of course, were only located in Lhasa, Shigatse and Chamdo, where in fact their status as 'worker' had been acquired only through recent changes, mostly through employment in construction, transport and motor repair trades established after 1950. In urban areas, while class categories remained an important aspect of labelling, political labels (such as 'reactionary' and 'revisionist') resulting from specific campaigns carried out by the Party became increasingly important. The monks, who constituted a substantial percentage of Tibetan society, could not evade these classifications. Although the Communists regarded all monks as parasites, they argued that the position of most monks was no better than that of a serf and that they would therefore be classed with other exploited groups. In classifying the monks, the Communists disregarded their family origins and used their ecclesiastic status to determine their class position. Those monks and lamas who occupied high status in the monasteries were said to have exploited the ordinary monks and the populace. According to Chinese sources there were only 4,000 upper-class lamas with economic power, leaving 95 per cent of the clergy as poor. Like the serfs, the poor monks 'suffered heavy political oppression, economic exploitation and spiritual enslavement'.[23] This naturally cast all the trulkus or lamas as exploiters in the same position as landlords. While it was relatively simple for the Communists to portray the landlords as the enemy of the people, it was a different matter with religious figures. The Tibetans shared a common belief in the divinity of the trulkus and found it extremely stressful to denounce the trulkus and other religious figures as class enemies.

A class was thus no longer an abstract sociological term but a real political label assigned by the authorities. An individual's class status and other labels were described in ration and household registration books and it was therefore impossible for an individual to evade categorisation. The class-labelling inevitably led to the identification of class enemies, notably the rich farmers and landlords. The Communists began to advocate that the poor peasants should oppose their enemies, an instruction which was taken to mean that former landlords and rich farmers should be subjected to 'struggle sessions'. Throughout the 1960s the Chinese organised such sessions in villages where important religious figures, rich farmers and landlords were forced to confess to having exploited the poor.

The increasing regimentation of Tibetan society allowed the Chinese to carry out social campaigns with relative ease. The mass mobilisation was now no longer a new phenomenon to the Tibetans and class struggle became the main political issue. In the past the enemy had been clearly identified as those who had taken part in the revolt, but with the advent of class struggle, even land owners and rich nomads who had co-operated with the Chinese found that they were now cast as the enemy, with class exploitation as their crime. In this way the Tibetans were divided between those with a good class background and those with a bad class background: the exploiters and the exploited.

During the SEM another important element intended to raise proletarian consciousness among the Tibetan masses was the mobilisation of the Tibetan youth. The Chinese recognised that young people in Tibet had to be cultivated and won over and in this the Communists can boast some major successes. Many young Tibetans flocked to join the Party's youth organisation in the hope of a new and better life, and many of them were sent to other parts of China to undertake further study. The Tibetan youth became the target of the Socialist Education Movement's drive to 'establish the revolutionary outlook on life'.[24] Bao Yishan, the Secretary of the Communist Youth League in Tibet, announced that by 1964, 50 per cent of his members constituted 'the backbone element of basic level government and in mutual aid groups'.[25]

The Communists claimed that the introduction into the heart of Tibetan politics of class struggle and the Three Big Educations was meant to empower the Tibetan 'serfs'. In reality the Three Big Educations and the consciousness-raising that came with it were aimed at changing the Tibetan world view and persuading the masses to embrace Communism. More importantly, they were aimed at making sure that the Tibetans saw themselves as part of the Chinese nation. This was also done through the manipulation of the language. As noted earlier, the Tibetan word for China, '*rgya nag*', was eliminated from everyday usage. A newly coined term for

Motherland, '*mes rgyal*', came into common usage in the press and in official publications, and this was understood to imply a China that included Tibet.[26] At the same time, those students and cadres who went to study in China were said to have travelled to the 'interior' (*rgyal nang*). Also, there were no longer Tibetans and Chinese: instead there were Tibetans and Han, all of whom were Chinese.

These attempts to change the Tibetans' perception of themselves were hugely ambitious, but, outwardly at least, they met with some success and the Tibetans dutifully began to speak and write about the 'Motherland'. At the same time the Chinese realised that visible symbols of Tibetan power and authority had to be destroyed. The Anti-Revisionists' Campaign accordingly began to focus on the Panchen Rinpoche and from now on he was demonized. On 18 September 1964, the Seventh Enlarged Meeting of the PCART was convened, and instead of the usual discussion of the past year's work and programmes for the coming year, Zhang Guohua announced that as a result of democratic reform the ownership of production had been transferred from the feudal lords to the masses. However, he added, the feudal lords had not been eliminated, were resentful of their defeat and were attempting to regain power by all possible means.[27] A witness who attended the PCART meeting as a reporter for the *Tibet Daily* recalls Zhang Guohua making a rhetorical statement to the effect that a big rock was obstructing the path of socialism and asking the specially invited audience what was to be done with the rock,[28] no doubt a thinly disguised attack on the Panchen Rinpoche. The meeting quickly turned into the trial of the Panchen Rinpoche, who was now described as the 'most dangerous enemy' in all of Tibet.[29] From the middle of September to the end of November 1964 the Chinese staged a meeting which set out to 'reveal' the crimes committed by the Panchen and his clique, who were accused of rebelling against 'the Motherland, the Party, the people and socialism'. In retrospect, it was clear that the evidence brought against the Panchen Rinpoche was exaggerated or fabricated. The Chinese accused him of raising 'fighting dogs',[30] and training cavalry to stage an armed counter-revolution.[31] The Chinese also brought former 'serfs' to reveal the Panchen Rinpoche's exploitation of the masses.

One of the most damning charges brought against the Panchen Rinpoche came from one of his closest followers, Chape Lhamo Sonam, who was then his Tibetan secretary. Chape came from a family that had served all the previous Panchen Rinpoches. The family was also renowned for its scholarship and respected as a leading literary family in Tibet. Chape's father had escaped to China with the 9th Panchen Rinpoche. Chape Lhamo Sonam became the main witness for the Chinese authorities.[32] During the trial the Chinese also exhibited a number of documents which were meant to prove that the Panchen Rinpoche was planning to stage a revolt. The documents are what the Tibetans call tra-yig, which is a method of divination; the Panchen Rinpoche had also kept a written record of prophecies that came to him in dreams. During the time when he was under investigation, the Panchen Rinpoche was not allowed to communicate with the leaders in Beijing and he was virtually kept under house arrest. He resorted to consulting diviners and oracles to find answers to his predicament. At the trial, Chape revealed that the Panchen Rinpoche had harboured counter-revolutionary sentiments and was planning to escape to India. His evidence rested on the fact that the Panchen Rinpoche had consulted diviners and oracles, and had asked when the Dalai Lama would return to Tibet and how long Mao would live. It was customary to write down these questions, together with the the diviner's response. By tradition such documents were usually kept secret and only a few trusted followers would have known about their existence.[33] Later when the Chinese searched the Panchen Rinpoche's residence, they found a number of these documents. They became crucial evidence against the Panchen Rinpoche. The Chinese said that 'even in his dreams the Panchen was thinking about rebelling against the Party and the masses and splitting the Motherland'.[34]

At the same time an exhibition was held in Lhasa and Shigatse to show the Tibetan people the crimes of the Panchen and his clique. It was no doubt meant to destroy the Panchen Rinpoche's popular image. A photograph of a jeep, supposedly adapted for military purposes, was on display, labelled as the counter-revolutionary vehicle which would have taken the Panchen Rinpoche to India if the rebellion had failed. A technical school he had set up in Shigatse was said to be the headquarters of the rebel group. On this basis the masses were urged to denounce the Panchen Rinpoche as a counter-revolutionary. The trial quickly degenerated into a struggle session during which the Panchen Rinpoche was subjected to physical abuse, with some of the participants at the meeting hitting him with their fists while others pulled him by the hair and spat on him. Even one of the incarnate lamas began to hit the Panchen Rinpoche. None the less Panchen Rinpoche remained defiant and refused to admit that he had committed any crimes. At one point he lost his temper and banged his fist on the table and tore up documents; this later became the charge that he had 'behaved badly' and had resisted criticism from the masses.[35]

There was no real evidence that the Panchen Rinpoche had planned to instigate armed rebellion. What was true was that he had remained deeply critical of the Chinese policy and had attracted the attention of Tibetans, who naturally turned towards him as their leader. Nevertheless, in Shigatse and Lhasa there were rumblings of resentment. Tibetans were angered by the extravagant lifestyle of some of his coterie, whom the officials called the 'little Panchens'. It was said that his dogs were fed with fresh meat daily, and later, when encouraged to criticise Panchen and his clique, the populace in Shigatse stoned the dogs to death. The Panchen Rinpoche was, in the language of the day, given three hats: anti-Party, anti-people and splitting the motherland.[36] In the final analysis, whatever the public may have thought, if the Chinese leadership had wanted to keep the Panchen Rinpoche in power, they could have done so. But they were not prepared to see his emergence as a popular leader.

In the end Zhang Jingwu and Zhang Guohua succeeded in destroying the Panchen Rinpoche, his family and his followers. It was a brutal and premeditated purge which met the demands of the Maoist theory that during the transition from capitalism to Communism[37] some feudal leaders who cherished the dream of restoring the old system would make an attempt at its restoration. Whatever the animosity felt by Zhang Guohua and Zhang Jingwu, the decision to punish the Panchen Rinpoche must have been taken at the highest level in Beijing. The Chinese officials in Tibet relished carrying out the purge. It was not until 1988 that the Standing Committee of the NPC formally decided to remove the three labels and begin rehabilitation. In December 1964, at the third meeting of the NPC, Zhou Enlai made a formal announcement that the Panchen Rinpoche was to be stripped of his post as acting Chairman and Vice-Chairman of PCART for organising anti-Party, anti-people and anti-socialist counter-revolutionary activities. Zhou Enlai's speech during the NPC warned the traditional leaders that they should make 'an effort to remould themselves' to work in the new society. It was another sharp warning that the Chinese would not tolerate any activities which the Party regarded as harmful to 'the motherland'.

The Chinese attached great significance to the fall of the Panchen Rinpoche. Late in 1965 a speech by Xie Fuchi, a member of the CCP's Central Committee, mentioned that the struggle against the Panchen clique was of 'tremendous importance' in consolidating the people's democratic dictatorship. 'The Panchen's crimes were very serious,' he said. 'But the Party and the people have given him a chance in the hope that he will repent and make a fresh start. The Party and the people have dealt with him leniently and it is entirely up to him whether he will decide to undertake reform.'[38] The Panchen Rinpoche was allowed to remain as a junior member of the PCART and continued to hold ceremonial posts.[39] He told people that he was merely an actor performing the part assigned to him.[40]

On 17 December 1964 the State Council in Beijing announced that the Dalai Lama's position as the Chairman of PCART and Vice-Chairman of NPC (which had been reserved for him since his flight to India) would now be removed. This marked a decisive change in Chinese policy towards him.

The statement blamed him for having staged 'the traitorous armed counter-revolution' and said that his activities abroad had proved that he was a 'stubborn running dog of imperialism and foreign countries'.[41] Although the dismissal of the Dalai Lama did not have any practical consequence, it was an admission on the part of the Chinese that they did not see any hope of a reconciliation with him.

The impeachment of the Panchen Rinpoche was a shock to the Tibetan leaders. His removal from the centre of Tibetan politics meant that the Chinese had managed to eliminate the only effective Tibetan leader in Tibet. The Dalai Lama was in exile, his influence in the day-to-day affairs of Tibet had all but disappeared, and it was unlikely that any independent Tibetan leaders would emerge. The treatment of the Panchen Rinpoche scared any would-be Tibetan leader into submission. The Chinese continued to rely on Ngabo, the last remaining Tibetan whom the Chinese seemed to trust, but he was never popular among Tibetans, most of whom saw him as a traitor for collaborating with the Chinese, while the more radical Tibetans were suspicious of his class background. Ngabo was shrewd enough not to risk the wrath of the Chinese and, even when invited by the Party to voice his criticisms during the relaxed period from 1960 to 1962, he remained cautious and did not deviate from general Chinese policy.

While at higher levels the Chinese continued to rely on the traditional élite, at village level, those who had been designated as *Zhingpa phugpo* (rich farmers) became the target of the SEM. From the outset they had not been allowed to join mutual aid groups, but now they were subject to public criticism. As in China, the SEM, initially confined to the cadres, was gradually extended to include the entire community. Mao's view that China was in danger of turning to revisionism and that the resurrection of capitalism was imminent, was held to apply equally to Tibet. From 1964 onwards Chinese policies in Tibet became increasingly ideologically oriented. Ideological purity and social transformation became the twin imperatives for the Chinese, helping to widen the gap between the Chinese and the Tibetans. The Party began to adhere to Mao's pronouncement that 'in the final analysis, national struggle is a matter of class struggle'.[42] At the 3rd NPC meeting in Beijing, Zhou Enlai stressed that if class struggle was not placed at the Centre of the Party's nationality policy it would only foster separatism.[43] This meant that the Communists had abandoned all of their previous policies of accommodating differences and tolerating the local culture and traditions wherever practical. The Chinese began to attack the most deeply held views of the Tibetan people. Almost all areas of Tibet had their own local oracles and diviners and the Chinese began to subject them to public struggle sessions and criticism. Diviners were paraded at mass meetings and forced to confess to performing conjuring tricks and admit that they did not have any special powers. With the Panchen Rinpoche now unable to protect religious institutions, the Chinese found it easy to attack them. By 1964 there had been a dramatic decline in the number of monks, and many monasteries were forced to close. The Tibetans began to stop sending their sons to the monasteries, partly because the Chinese promised modern education but mainly because Communist propaganda had made it clear that in the new society there was no place for religious pursuits.

In many ways SEM was a prelude to the Cultural Revolution which was to engulf China and Tibet a few years later. The campaign not only initiated the attack on Tibetan traditions and culture, but placed 'class' in the forefront of politics. Those who had been categorized as counter-revolutionaries or reactionaries were subjected to struggle sessions which inevitably ended in beatings. It has to be remembered that public criticism and struggle sessions were introduced in almost all Tibetan villages. This had a profound social and psychological effect on the population. In Tibet the vast majority of the population still lived in villages and the members knew each other intimately and were often linked by kinship ties. The conflict promoted by the Party shattered traditional ties and loyalties.

The SEM and the Three Big Educations coincided with the return of many of the first Tibetans who had been sent to China for studies in preparation for the setting up of the TAR. No sooner had they returned to take up their posts than they were dispatched to remote areas to 'gain revolutionary experience' from the masses by doing manual labour. These young and educated Tibetans were kept in the rural areas doing dead-end jobs until the end of the 1970s. The Chinese could have conferred some measure of power on the newly emerging Tibetan cadres but, by blindly following Beijing's directive, they lost the opportunity to indigenise the Party and their bureaucracy. Many young Tibetans supported the Chinese in the hope that the Communists would help to modernise the country but soon became disillusioned by the fact that the Chinese were concentrating their energy on ideological education and social transformation rather than promoting industrial and economic development. Moreover, while the Communists emphasised class struggle in public, they still relied mainly on recruiting high-ranking former Tibetan officials to serve in the new administration. The removal of the Panchen Rinpoche, for example, meant that the Chinese needed to reconstitute the Tashilhunpo group in the PCART, which as noted earlier, had been divided into three factions. Almost all the members of the Tashilhunpo faction had been purged, including Chen Jigme. Now the Chinese promoted Chape and Sengchen Lobsang Gyaltsen, an incarnate lama from Shigatse, to head the Tashilhunpo group on the PCART. The new appointments were no doubt a reward for denouncing the Panchen Rinpoche.

The Establishment of the Tibet Autonomous Region

By 1965 the Chinese were claiming that they had achieved 'earth shaking' changes in Tibet. Five years after the abortive rebellion of 1959 the Chinese had managed to create a completely new administrative structure and the remnants of the old polity had been totally destroyed. As noted earlier, the Chinese had began to organise elections at *xiang* (village) level for the setting up of the governmental structure. The election was contrived in so far as the candidates and the result had been predetermined by the Chinese officials, who had selected the candidates most likely to be supportive of their rule. But at a symbolic level it was a successful attempt by the Chinese to seek some measure of popular mandate from the Tibetan people. In July 1965, it was announced that elections at the *xiang* level had been completed and that these deputies would in turn select the representatives at the *xian* (county) level.[44] The following month, the State Council, one of the highest legislative bodies in China, announced that, after studying the reports submitted by the PCART, it had agreed that the 1st Session of the People's Congress of the Autonomous Region should be held on 1 September. This was to mark the setting up of the Tibet Autonomous Region. Since the establishment of the PRC, the Communists had agreed to set up Autonomous Regions (AR) in areas where the minority groups constituted a substantial percentage of the population[45]. This was also in keeping with Article Three of the 17-Point Agreement signed in Beijing in 1951, which had promised that 'the Tibetan people have the right to exercise national autonomy under the unified leadership of the Central People's Government'.

Practical and logistical difficulties had prevented the Chinese from turning Tibet into an Autonomous Region and it was only with the elimination of all opposition that the Chinese were able to begin the process. According to a speech by Ngabo, the crushing of the revolt, victory over India and the exposing of 'the treacherous activities of the Panchen clique' had provided 'the most favourable conditions [for] the founding of the TAR'.[46] From the start the Communists announced that the setting up of the TAR did not mean any legal separation of territory and that the TAR was an 'inalienable part of the motherland'.[47] The setting up of the TAR marked the final integration of Tibet.

It was also a sign the Chinese had succeeded in bringing the region under control, a consequence of a mixture of explicit and implicit threats of violence. Nineteen sixty-five was thus an important transition period. From now on China would not tolerate any opposition. Officially, the period of consultation and consolidation had come to an end and now, magically, Tibet had entered the socialist period. To the Communists, who executed their policy like a timetable, the first decade had been a period of consultation and seeking alliance with the 'upper strata'; and the first half of the 1960s had been a transitional period to socialism. During this period those who chose to work for the new society would be cultivated and those who opposed it would be liquidated. This point was stressed by Zhou Enlai in his work report to the NPC in December 1964.[48]

Nineteen sixty-five revealed a China that was once more confident about its position in the world and whose economic conditions were beginning to improve. The period also saw the re-entry of Mao on the centre stage of Chinese politics. China's military power had received a boost in October 1964, when, under the guidance of the PLA, Chinese scientists successfully exploded their first atomic bomb. China had now entered the superpower league. This renewed confidence was reflected in China's policy towards Tibet and the minority issue. Tibetan criticism was brushed aside and socialism was declared to have finally reached the Roof of the World.

In August 1965 Lhasa's first Municipal People's Congress was held with 180 deputies representing Lhasa and the surrounding areas. What was important about this election was that most of the national leaders were drawn from this group. A new mayor of Lhasa was appointed to replace Tsego (Ngabo's assistant in Chamdo in 1950), who had been serving as acting-mayor of Lhasa since the beginning of 1960s. He was succeeded by Kalsang Namgyal, another former aristocrat. At end of August the Chinese announced the completion of the elections at the municipal and county level and the nomination of representatives to the Regional People's Congress. A large delegation from China, led by Xie Fuchi, Vice-Premier of the State Council, and Liu Chun (the hard-line deputy director of the United Front and the Chairman of the Nationality Affairs Commission of the CCP), arrived in Lhasa. On 1 September a formal celebration was held to mark the convening of the first National People's Congress of Tibet. The Congress announced the establishment of the TAR.

Within a day, three of the most important institutions came into being: the TAR, the regional People's Congress and the regional CCP. It was not coincidental that they should have emerged at the same time. However flawed the elections might have been, from the Chinese point of view they were an attempt to secure some measure of moral basis for the new system. On a practical level, the elections made sure that all the members who had served on the PCART maintained their position in the new government. The First People's Congress of the TAR had 301 deputies, of whom 226 were Tibetans. Others were either Chinese or members of other minority groups in Tibet. The Communists had from the start tried to win over the small group of tribal peoples inhabiting southern Tibet on the slopes of the Himalayas, groups like the Monpa and Lopa.[49] They, too, were allowed to elect representatives to the People's Congress, thus marking the integration of these isolated communities into the mainstream of the new polity.[50] The regional People's Congress also included a number of Chinese. The new system now included a cross-section of different groups in Tibet, with the traditional Tibetan leaders such Ngabo and Phagpa Gelek Namgyal continuing to occupy key posts. Ngabo was appointed the first Governor of Tibet and other departmental heads were also drawn from the traditional élite. The appointment to the new government of Ngabo and other former Tibetan officials was important to the Chinese as a symbol of continuity from the past system. This was the chief reason why Ngabo continued to occupy the centre stage in Tibetan politics.

While regional leadership was reserved for those members of the former ruling class who had 'remoulded themselves' and were prepared to work in the new society, the Communists stressed that the establishment of the TAR marked a transfer of power from the aristocracy to the Tibetan peasantry. The traditional polity effectively barred the participation of the peasantry from political affairs. After the Tibetan revolt, the Party was slowly able to extend its rule into every village. The membership drive deliberately targeted the young and the poorest sections of the Tibetan community. Many Tibetans did join the Party and related organisations, since membership guaranteed a job and conferred privileges. According to Chinese propaganda, on the eve of the founding of the TAR, there were 20,000 Tibetan cadres at the township level and 16,000 in higher positions who had been 'serfs or slaves' in the old society.[51] The representative heads at the *xiang* and *xian* level were drawn from the poorest sections of Tibetan society. The Chinese stressed that, of 200 county heads or deputy heads in Ngari region, 98 per cent were either former poor peasants or herdsmen.[52]

In terms of numbers these were the first attempts to bring the Tibetan masses, and particularly the poor, into the political domain. However, the statistics cannot be taken at face value. As noted earlier, during the first decade the Communists had done very little to obtain the support of the Tibetan peasantry and had felt that the main task was to establish an alliance with the 'upper strata'. The Communists had always taken it for granted that the class interest of the Tibetan peasantry would lead to a natural alliance with the labouring masses who would welcome the Party as its leader. It was only after the revolt that the Chinese began to address the Tibetan peasantry and elevate them to the centre of their political strategy in Tibet. The key to this was the formation of the regional CCP and the People's Congress. Needless to say, many of the elected representatives were selected on the basis of their class background and their fidelity to the Chinese. This point was made by Miao Pi, the director of the Organisation Department of the regional CCP, when he wrote: 'In training Tibetan cadres, we firmly and unwaveringly implemented the line of recruiting cadres mainly from among the labouring people and at the same time actively training patriots and intellectuals to be cadres. When appointing and promoting Tibetan cadres, the Party committees at all levels took care first to select youths of the Tibetan nationality from among poor serfs and slaves and other labouring people who had high class consciousness, and were obedient to the Party.'[53] He went on to say that the cadres must assume a revolutionary and Communist character and take the thoughts of Chairman Mao as their guiding principal.[54]

Many of the elected peasants did not have any knowledge of Chinese and were also illiterate in Tibetan. This led to the creation of a whole system of support, whereby Chinese cadres were appointed as advisers, assistants and translators to handle daily affairs. They were known as the Party's work team. The Chinese like to portray the role of these cadres as helping to awaken the 'class consciousness' of the Tibetan masses, a sort of catalyst in bringing about the revolution in Tibet; this is how the Chinese media saw their role. The November 1965 edition of *China Reconstructs* carried a story about Kalwang Norbu [*sic*], a peasant from Lhodrak county, and Tseten Dolma, a woman, both of whom had recently been elected as representative for their areas. The article reported how the 'work team' had helped them to understand the nature of class struggle. It said that Tseten Dolma denounced the 'rebel chief', Ngawang Tashi (who had exploited her family) at a struggle meeting (*'thab 'dzing*). The Party's work team was able to explain to her that the struggle was not a matter of individual hatred between her family and the rebel chief, but that it was a struggle between 'the whole of the serf class' and the 'serf owning class'. This led to an instant raising of their class consciousness and, as they came to understand the class nature of their struggle, they demanded the destruction of the feudal society.[55]

In every locality the Party's work team became in reality the main political force. It was they who decided which individuals would stand for election and who wrote speeches for the newly elected representatives. This support system became, in turn, a controlling mechanism. It allowed the Chinese to manage affairs and dictate the political agenda. However, this is not to say that the Tibetans were mere passive agents who were totally manipulated by the Chinese cadres: the Communists' promise of modernity, progress and economic and social justice did indeed entice many Tibetans to work for the new society. But the Chinese message made clear that these could only be achieved under the guidance of the Party. Chinese propaganda constantly stressed that the expertise and technical skills of Chinese cadres were indispensable for the development of Tibet, comparing the relationship between the Tibetan peasantry and the Chinese cadres to a fish which cannot survive without water.

From 1965 onwards, the notion of class consciousness and class struggle became the key political symbol directing Chinese policy, a factor which allowed the supremacy of the Party in all affairs, since it was the only legitimate representative of the working masses. In the same year that the formal establishment of the regional CCP was declared, Zhang Guohua (Second Secretary of the TWC and the military commander of the region) became the 1st Secretary of the Communist Party of Tibet. It is interesting to note that Zhang Jingwu, the 'Central Government's Representative' in Tibet, was removed from his post just before the founding of the TAR and in May 1966 took up a new post as a deputy director of the United Front Work Department, a reward for his success and long experience in Tibet. Zhang Guohua was chosen to replace Zhang Jingwu and, since 1950, the two had worked closely together, as far as we know getting on well as a team.

Zhang Guohua's position in Tibet was seen differently from that of his predecessor, and this was reflected in a change of title from 'Central Government's Representative' in Tibet, to First Secretary of the CCP in Tibet. The Chinese had been careful not to stress the ascendancy of the Party in Tibet and had made very little effort to recruit Party members until after the Tibetan revolt, when they began to emphasise the role of the Party in bringing about modernity, progress and socialism. Now the Party was placed at the centre, and a new division among the Tibetans began to appear: Party members and non-Party members. Membership was open to those with the right class background and the correct ideological stand. But the Chinese had devised other means of recruiting Tibetans. Inviting certain targeted people to join the Party by issuing invitations, it stressed the exclusivity of the Party. And the fact that they were invited was no doubt meant to flatter the individuals. Membership of the Party was therefore not a natural right of the working masses, but a privilege. Of course, such invitations could not be rejected and non-acceptance would have been seen as 'turning one's face against the Party'. By 1965 Party membership had reached 14,830, of which 48.2 per cent were said to be from a minority background.[56] However, over 54.5 per cent of the Party members were drawn from people who were classed as cadres (government or party officials).[57]

The establishment of the TAR should have led to greater freedom. It was also meant to guarantee Tibet's cultural separateness. In reality, the creation of the TAR brought Tibet even closer to China. It legally buried the 17-Point Agreement, discarded in 1959, by confirming that Tibet was no longer a 'unique area' within the PRC. In short, the degree of autonomy enjoyed by Tibet was determined by what China was willing to allow. The sinologist George Moseley concluded that regional autonomy is the opposite of what it implies, arguing that a better description would be 'regional detention'.[58] Another important factor limiting autonomy was the dominance of the Party over the government. On the eve of the founding of the TAR the ratio of Chinese to Tibetan cadres in Tibet was 7:3, a figure which Zhou Enlai stated should be reversed during the Fourth Five Year Plan (1971–5).[59] The cadres were not seen as passive government servants, but as revolutionary agents of the Party who were fundamental to bringing about the socialist transformation of Tibet. Therefore the political power remained firmly in the hands of the Communist Party, which was in turn dominated by Chinese at the higher levels.

For most Tibetans, the Communist Party and the Chinese were synonymous. Tibetans saw the recent political developments – the election, the founding of TAR and the regional government – as the further consolidation of Chinese rule. In 1965, Chinese cadres began to emphasise that the main task in Tibet was to catch up with the advanced developments in China. The slogan adopted by the Chinese was 'delete the bracket' (or 'take Tibet out of the bracket'). This referred to the fact that during the period 1950–65 Tibet always appeared in official Chinese publications in brackets, either with the editorial comment 'unknown' or 'estimate only'. Similarly government directives would be marked 'except Tibet', since many government and Party directives were not applicable in Tibet. Of course, this implied that Tibet lagged behind China in economic and social development, and suggested the Chinese had failed to unite Tibet and bring about the socialist transformation of the region. According to the prevailing ideology, it was said that Tibet had been denied the fruits of socialist revolution. The campaign to bring Tibet out of the bracket coincided with the general campaign in other areas which aimed to bridge the economic and social gap between minority areas and China. The Chinese saw that the continuing economic and social disparity fostered local nationalism and therefore decided that bridging this gulf was a crucial task.

However, the solution adopted by the Chinese in Tibet meant implementing even more radical economic and social reforms. The explicit assumption was that the nationality problem (the problem of Tibet's separateness) could only be solved if Tibet caught up with the advanced developments in China. Once the economic and social conditions which gave rise to Tibet's special characteristics had been eliminated, the people would naturally identify with the motherland and take to the 'socialist road'. This assumption was further strengthened by Mao's dictum that the nationality problem was essentially a class problem. The Chinese were quick to equate the fact that they had achieved a measure of stability in the region with the theoretical idea that Tibet had now entered a socialist period. This allowed them to disregard any Tibetan fear and opposition as merely a tiny residue of feudal sentimentalism, which would naturally wither away. The Chinese were so certain of their success in Tibet that they believed communes could be set up in Tibet without going through the intervening stage of agricultural co-operative, thus ignoring the three-stage model used in the development of agricultural production in China proper. Chinese propaganda claimed that the people were eager to establish communes.[60]

The economic policy adopted in Tibet was partly precipitated by the local cadres' desire to appease Beijing and partly intended to advertise their accomplishment at a time when bureaucracy was coming under increasing attacks in China for its failure to carry out socialist policy. It was evident that cadres working in minority areas were the main targets of the Anti-Revisionist Campaign.[61] To argue that conditions in Tibet were not ready for communisation would have invited accusations of being a revisionist preventing Tibet from taking the socialist road. This was particularly true of Chinese cadres who were from rich family backgrounds. Later, during the Cultural Revolution, Wang Qimei was accused of advocating direct transition to the socialist revolution to disguise his reactionary class origins.[62] Soon after the founding of the TAR in 1965, the Chinese phased out mutual aid groups and communes were introduced in rural and nomadic areas. The authorities confidently announced that Tibet had reached the highest stage of socialism. According to Communist propaganda, Tibet had 'leapt from a feudal serf society to a socialist society' without undergoing the transitional stages of advanced feudal and capitalist societies.[63]

The Chinese had never hidden their aim of establishing communes in Tibet and, since the late 1950s, Tibetans had been taken to see how communes operated in China. Like the peasants in China, the Tibetans were also encouraged to learn and emulate the success of the commune Dazhai (a model of socialist agricultural production in Shanxi province) and to heed Mao's call to learn from Daqing (an oil field which became the pride of Chinese industrial development). These examples were meant to encourage the Tibetans so that, with the correct socialist principles and mass enthusiasm, a barren desert could be turned into an oasis of socialist development. The Chinese claimed that such a success could be repeated on the Tibetan plateau. For the authorities, communisation was seen as a panacea which would cure all problems.

Foremost among these problems was the pressing question of how to meet the increased demand for food. Since the borders with India had been closed the Chinese had been burdened with importing huge amounts of goods overland, a process which was immensely expensive and limited the sources from which food and other manufactured items could be bought. The problem could have been resolved by the construction of the Golmud–Lhasa railway line, but this project was never realised. Instead, the Chinese had to rely on importing supplies from Nepal.[64] This was also a period when China was becoming increasingly insular and the break with Russia had forced the Party to advocate the economic goal of self-reliance. The introduction of the communes in Tibet was meant to solve Tibet's economic backwardness and realise the ideological goal of self-reliance.

As in China, the commune transformed Tibet's social, economic and political structure. The core of production was shifted from individual households to the commune, and ownership of land and animals was transferred to collective ownership. This marked the beginning of a highly centralised distribution of goods. During the period of mutual aid groups, the peasants were free to exchange goods in the market but under the commune system no goods could be sold directly to the market. What was more shocking for the people was that the commune not only demanded the disbandment of private land holdings and animals but also required households to relinquish all private chattels. More importantly, like the land reform, the commune system was imposed from the top and inevitably led to conflict with any remaining traditional Tibetan values and social structures.

The land reform was genuinely liked by the Tibetan peasantry, as it had established a more equitable system of land ownership. The Party was now advocating that they should abandon their newly acquired properties. At the time there was a humorous saying: 'I would rather rest here, than travel all the way to socialism', (a reference to the Communist use of the metaphor of travelling along a 'path' or 'road'). The Tibetans would sarcastically remark that 'the soles of their shoes are worn out', meaning that they were exhausted from the constant meetings, campaigns and reforms and implying that they did not want the commune system. The Communists feared that any postponement would deepen the gulf between Tibet and the developments in China. Moreover, the authorities claimed that the reforms had been subverted by capitalist roaders. As evidence the authorities said that land reform and mutual aid groups had fostered new inequalities because they allowed individuals to appropriate wealth and encouraged groups to 'drift apart into rich and poor'.[65] Of course such facts were highlighted to serve a given theory and the ideological needs of the CCP and should not be taken seriously.

It was envisaged that the communes would help to develop a socialist mode of production, which would naturally lead to greater productivity and, on the social level, eliminate the disparity between the rich and poor farmers. The advantages of the commune system were described as the 'three vital benefits': it brought advantage to the government, the society and the individual.[66] The salient feature of the commune was the merging of economic, social, administrative and Party structure within a single organisation. In addition, the commune became the most basic unit of government and Party administration, giving rise to problems in China where, on average, a commune consisted of more than 5,500 households[67] and was often unmanageable. In Tibet this was never the case. In fact, in some remote areas like Garze in Ngari, where nomads have always lived in scattered family units distributed over large areas, communes were established with only 100 families, representing about 500 people; membership of the Red Flag commune in Lhokha district consisted of only 728 people.[68] The commune system was also meant to devolve the decision-making process and allow local groups greater economic and political freedom. However, there was a disparity between theory and practice. The communes were imposed by the Chinese against the will of the people. Communist propaganda always tried to stress that the commune came about by popular demand and presented this idea as some sort of mystical revelation received by the Tibetan peasants who, having studied Chairman Mao's teaching, were enabled to see the superiority of the commune system.[69]

The extreme egalitarian ideal promoted by the commune system did not appeal to the people and they could see that it could not be realised. The Party nevertheless could not solve the self-evident gap between the Tibetans and the Chinese. It was clear to the Tibetans that the Chinese cadres still exercised all the power and that the Tibetans were mere recipients of commands. The communes were in fact more like state farms. They had to follow centrally determined targets and were under pressure to meet state targets set by the higher authority, with production decisions being made by government officials: the communes themselves did not even have the authority to decide what crop to plant. This led to pressure to grow wheat rather than traditional barley, in line with the need to minimise the import of wheat from China to feed the military and the Chinese cadres living in Tibet.[70] Despite the autonomy supposedly exercised by Tibet, and despite the devolved power of the commune system, Tibetans were not allowed to bypass or adapt the regulations or orders of the CCP.

The Tibetans complained that the decision-making power rested with the Chinese cadres who had been assigned to the communes. Much of the commune administration rested with these cadres who, in addition to the work points allocated by the commune, received a salary from the government.[71] The communes which were set up after 1968 were assigned new Tibetan cadres but the local people were also suspicious of these cadres. In 1968, when there was a campaign to send young cadres to the rural areas to learn from the peasants, many young qualified Tibetans were dispatched to remote areas. But they saw the assignment as a punishment and so had no real incentive to better the lives of the people.

The initial opposition to communes was simply motivated by a reluctance to relinquish newly acquired private property. The Tibetan peasantry saw no reason to abandon the private system and many now saw Chinese policy as having been an elaborate charade to win them over in order to claim their land. It was admitted that even among the poor farmers there was a divergence of views, and that those who had become wealthy under the mutual aid system did not want to change to the commune system.[72] The Chinese had failed to carry out sufficient preparation work to allay people's apprehensions, and while people could clearly see the benefits of the land reforms, the commune system held no attractions for them and did not entice the populace. This was a failure to learn from experience: a decade earlier the Tibetan population in Amdo and Kham had violently opposed the setting up of communes and this resistance had led to the uprising in eastern Tibet.

Despite popular resistance, the Communists went ahead with the setting up of communes in agricultural and nomadic areas. At the time, Chinese propaganda tried to portray mass enthusiasm for the establishment of the communes, but in fact the economic adjustment demanded by the communisation programme was affecting production and disrupting the normal flow of trade, since everything was now rationed by the centralised bureaucracy. In the communes, individuals were rewarded with work points, which were converted into money. In the early communes, the authorities also used land and animals pooled from individual families to measure the amount of work points an individual earned, but this was discontinued in 1967.[73] Dhondup Choedon, who escaped to India in 1973, wrote a reliable account of her life in the Red Flag commune in Lhokha district. She belonged to what the Chinese regarded as the serf class and was quickly promoted to the position of the commune's leaders, and therefore well-situated to know the general situation. Dhondup Choedon claims that although there was an increase in the overall production, the commune had to sell 50 per cent of the grain produced to the state procurement board.[74] As a result, the size of the individual rations was insufficient and many families incurred debts to the commune.[75] The Red Flag commune was one of the better off than most, but, even here, conditions were poor.

> In our commune the annual allotments of ration per person is 12.5 Khels of grain, that is, 175 kgs per year or about 14.58 kgs per month. Each person, even a baby, gets a permit to buy this allotment, any time, through work points. But from this amount of grain the household essentials like salt, butter and meat have to be procured through barter. So, if you buy meat and butter for only 2 kgs of grain and salt for 1kg, the amount then left is only 11.58 kgs per month or about 0.38 kgs of grains per day.[76]

The general economic situation in the commune declined, due to bad management and lack of enthusiasm. This was particularly true during the turbulent period of the Cultural Revolution when practical economic considerations were neglected. The drop in locally generated revenue which followed the introduction of the commune system in Tibet meant that the entire budget for Tibet had to be met by subsidies from Beijing.[77] The disastrous effect of the commune system was more acutely felt among the nomadic community, many of whom faced programmes to settle the nomads and turn them into agricultural settlements. In 1970 the nomads of Garze were forcibly settled and the fragile pasture grounds were turned into fields. The Chinese, at great expense, supplied enormous quantities of grain for seed. But the crops continually failed because of the extreme temperature fall at night. Similar experiments were carried out among other nomadic groups, also without success.

By the beginning of 1966, butter, one of the essential commodities for the Tibetans, became scarce. Many Tibetans remember that during this period there was also a shortage of cooking oil, which could only be obtained through rations. During the Tibetan new year it was customary for families to make deep fried biscuits called Khabse. This required an enormous quantity of cooking oil, but in 1966 the making of Khabse was labelled a feudal practice; in fact there was no cooking oil to make them anyway.[78] From 1966 onwards, in Lhasa, Shigatse and other small towns, there was a complete shortage of cooking fuel. In the past, villagers from the surrounding areas would bring dung for sale in the town but this practice virtually ceased. Many people in Lhasa recalled that, during the Cultural Revolution, they were forced to travel further each day to obtain dung, which formed the main source of cooking fuel.

The only concession that the Chinese made was that communes were not imposed at the same time all over Tibet. While in some areas they were introduced in 1966, in remote areas such as Ngari in western Tibet the nomads and the farmers were made to form communes only after 1969. In Dingri the communes were not introduced until the early 1970s, mainly because of geographical isolation rather than political considerations. The Chinese met with strong resistance among the nomads: the nomads of Phala in the Changthang area, who were the subjects of the Panchen Rinpoche, had not taken part in the 1959 revolt but ten years later, when the commune system was imposed, they rebelled, forcing the Chinese to deploy the PLA.[79] Their resistance may be explained by the fact that the Panchen Rinpoche was no longer there to persuade them to accept the new Chinese policy. There was also popular opposition to the imposition of the communes among nomad groups in Nagchuka.

The communes allowed the Chinese even greater control of Tibet. The closed nature of the system made it possible for the Party to carry out its policy of transforming the Tibetans' thoughts and way of life and meant that the Chinese were better able to force the people to discard their traditional values and religious beliefs.[80] Meanwhile the Communists deluded themselves by choosing to believe the grossly exaggerated production figures supplied by the local cadres in response to the intense competition between communes to show greater productivity. To have reported a decline or difficulty in production would have been to doubt the superiority of socialist production, and was therefore avoided.

The logistical difficulties created by the communisation of Tibet could have been overcome had it not been for the advent of the Cultural Revolution, which made economic activities subservient to carrying out the demands of the revolution. During this period, the Communists' task of overcoming Tibet's economic backwardness was forgotten. Communisation thus not only disrupted the flow of goods in Tibet but in many ways destroyed the traditional economic system. Tibet's harsh climate meant that it was crucial to have sufficient grain reserves to last through the long winter as well as to guard against possible natural disasters. Such mundane necessities were forgotten in the fervour of revolutionising.

TWELVE

The Cultural Revolution

From 1966 onwards, Tibet, like China, was caught up in the politics of the Cultural Revolution. Its origin lay in the high levels of the Communist Party, and neither the Tibetan nor the Chinese cadres in Tibet had any involvement in the germination of the movement. Whatever may have been the cause of the Cultural Revolution, the repercussions in Tibet were devastating. It was beyond the control of the leadership in Tibet to exert any influence on the course of events and, to a large extent, the Chinese and the Tibetan masses were victims of a struggle waged in Beijing. Earlier works on origins of the Cultural Revolution tend to concentrate on the struggle in the top leadership in Beijing and see the phenomenon as a result of élite conflict; later writers tend to stress the social forces that motivated the masses who took part.[1] To some degree it is true, particularly after 1965, that events in Tibet were a mere reflection of larger events in Chinese politics. Therefore, the cause and developments of the Cultural Revolution in Tibet are enmeshed with every twist and turn of politics in Beijing.

The official explanation for the Cultural Revolution was given by the 6th plenary session of the 11th Central Committee on 29 June 1981[2] which adopted the resolution on 'the Historical Questions of the Party'. The resolution largely dealt with overall issues and did not mention Tibet specifically but noted in a section on minorities that, 'in the past, particularly during the Cultural Revolution, we committed, on the question of nationalities, the grave mistake of widening the scope of class struggle and wronged a large number of cadres and masses of the minority nationalities. In our work among them, we did not show due respect for their right to autonomy. We must not forget this lesson.'[3] A meek admission on the part of the Chinese hardly provides an adequate explanation for the ten years of trauma and chaos that prevailed in Tibet. The official view that the Cultural Revolution was a 'grave mistake' orchestrated by the Gang of Four, who literally hoodwinked the nation, seems to be ingenuous at best and at worst deceitful.[4] The present Chinese leadership would like to see the Cultural Revolution as an aberration and claims that the mistakes of the past have been rectified.

At the time of the Cultural Revolution, the Chinese asserted that some of the social conditions that made Mao launch the SEM and the Cultural

Revolution were prevalent in Tibet, namely the appearance of rich peasants who had benefited from the land reforms and who were now pushing towards restoring capitalism or at least towards maintaining the status quo.[5] This may be seen as a convenient justification and also mechanical implementation of Beijing's order to stamp out spontaneous capitalist tendencies; the existence of revisionism in Tibet was a polemical statement and not an objective condition or description of the situation. Whether the conditions in Tibet in 1966 were or were not similar to the situation that existed in China is irrelevant, since issues that were debated in China tended to be automatically reiterated in Tibet. There were other conditions which led to the Cultural Revolution, such as the apparent liberal tendencies emerging in artistic and literary circles in China, which Mao feared were undermining the authority of the Party and the revolution. This was certainly absent in Tibet where neither the Chinese cadres nor any Tibetan intellectuals were involved in any such movement. In fact the Chinese had managed to persuade the intellectuals to co-operate with the translation into Tibetan of Mao's works, and many of them had been supportive of the Communists. The problem in Tibet has never been over liberal tendencies, but rather over the question of religious freedom. However, after the fall of the Panchen Rinpoche the Tibetan opposition even on this issue was effectively silenced.

The Communists regarded opposition towards the communisation as coming from those who had benefited from the land reforms and, as mentioned before, this was true to some extent. This resistance was taken as evidence of revisionism in Tibet, adding to the supposed resurgence of revisionism invented earlier primarily as a weapon to admonish the Panchen Rinpoche. Once the Chinese had admitted the existence of the problem, it was not easy for Zhang Guohua to claim it no longer existed. In the long run, it would have been better had the Chinese leadership in Tibet followed a course which argued that the question of revisionism was not an issue in Tibet; this would have allowed them to defend Tibet's unique position, by maintaining that the main issue was the fight against the separatist elements in Tibetan society. There was little the leadership in Tibet could do to prevent the encroachment of the Red Guards. Whatever the political conditions in Tibet may have been on the eve of the Cultural Revolution, the existence of revisionists was not sufficient reason in itself to explain the spread of the Cultural Revolution in Tibet.

Destruction of the 'Four Olds'

Once the Cultural Revolution got under way in China, it became the only issue dominating the Party and the country as a whole. It was inevitable that it would spread to Tibet. Since the founding of the TAR, the argument that the region was unique within the PRC had lost much of its ground. Tibet was now treated on a par with any other province of China, with some minor concessions to its strategic position. The launch of the SEM, albeit with some variations, had set a precedent of involving Tibet in national political campaigns. And, as pointed out earlier, to have argued that Tibet was unique would have implied that the Party had somehow failed in its twin political objectives of socialist transformation and unification of the region.

While there is no doubt that the Cultural Revolution was imported from China, and that the Tibetans played no part in the Communist revolution, during the Cultural Revolution the Tibetan population ceased to be passive, although they still had no power either to determine the course of events or to affect the issues debated at the time. In the day-to-day fighting that ensued for the next three years, the Tibetans who participated were divided by their loyalty to one or other of the two main factions that emerged all over China.

Mao had always recognised that there were two aspects to socialist transformation; the changes in institutions and the radical redirection of the people. In Tibet most of the institutional changes had been accomplished and by 1965 the traditional symbols of power and authority had all been destroyed. However, the Chinese knew that mass compliance had been obtained by means of coercive persuasion rather than by the voluntary expression of shared values. The Cultural Revolution was aimed at the latter: it sought to create a socialist man. At a popular level this was expressed almost in terms of transplanting a new brain (*klad-pa*) – those who held on to old values and traditions were said to possess a 'green brain' (*klad-pa ljang-khu*), while the progressive man had a normal 'white brain' (*klad-pa dkar-po*).[6] The new brain would be filled with the teachings of Chairman Mao. As food provided nourishment to the body, so the teachings of Mao would bring ideological transformation. It was said that without studying the *Thoughts of the Chairman Mao,* the brain would be empty.[7] The assault on Tibetan culture and values was seen as creating a new brain, which would transform the Tibetans into socialists. In China this question was reduced to the dichotomy between the old and new, tradition and modernity, capitalist and socialist cultural outlooks. In Tibet, however, there was the further complication of the natural and insurmountable division between the Tibetans and the Chinese. To the majority of Tibetans, 'the new' was associated with the Chinese. The authorities were aware of this contradiction: they emphasised that the issue was no longer one of China and Tibet and stressed that the question in Tibet was between the old and the new. The recently coined terms 'Chitsog Serpa' (the new society) and 'Chitsog Nyinpa' (the old society) became key words of Chinese rule. The

Cultural Revolution was then seen as the final battle before the coming of the new society.

The official account of the Cultural Revolution passed by the CCP in 1981 gives the beginning of the Cultural Revolution as May 1966 when the May 16th Circular drafted by Mao was adopted by the Politburo.[8] However, for most ordinary Tibetans the beginning of the Cultural Revolution can be traced back to February 1966, when the Chinese authorities for the first time banned the celebration of the Monlam ceremony in Lhasa. For the Tibetans this was an important transitional point. Between 1960 and 1965 the Chinese had allowed the Tibetans to mark this important ceremony, despite the fact that it had in the past served as a focal point for Tibetan solidarity. This concession by the Party was offered as proof that it was willing to tolerate a modicum of religious freedom. In 1966, however, the Chinese began to organise neighbourhood meetings to criticise and ridicule the remnants of feudal traditions, describing the Monlam ceremony as a waste of resources. The banning of the ceremony had a significant effect not only on the few remaining monks but also on Tibetan society. From now on religious devotion could not be publicly expressed and anyone who did so was seen as favouring the old society. A few months after the banning of the Monlam came the campaign against the 'Four Olds'. In June, *Xinhua* reported that in the previous two months 100,000 Tibetans had been mobilised to destroy the mythical rats and rodents which infested the region. This campaign allowed young students to enter the Tsuglakhang, which contained the shrine of Palden Lhamo which was infested with hundreds of rats and mice, said to have some important religious symbolism. At the same time there was a massive campaign to study the recently published Tibetan edition of *Quotations from Chairman Mao Tsetung*. Meetings were held in every village to study Mao's Thoughts, which would guide Tibet into a new socialist paradise.

When Mao first launched the Cultural Revolution, the Chinese leadership in Lhasa had no idea what course it would take and how long it was going to last. Their immediate reaction was to treat it as another directive from Beijing to which they responded obediently and followed diligently. At the end of May 1966, the Regional Party set up the Cultural Revolution committee in Lhasa, headed by Wang Qimei, who had been in Tibet since 1951. He was a leading army officer who had negotiated with Ngabo in Chamdo and had been the head of the Chamdo Liberation Committee. Wang was assisted by Zhang Caiwang, another army official and head of the regional Party propaganda section. May–December 1966 was marked by the campaign to eliminate the Four Olds (old ideas, old culture, old customs and old habits)[9] and establish the Four News. Chinese propaganda boldly urged the people to 'create the new by smashing the old'.[10]

The regional Cultural Revolution committee initiated an officially approved attack on Qin Sha, the editor in chief of *Tibet Daily* (*Xizang Ribao*), in which the staff at the paper's office were encouraged to criticise the editor. However, Wang Qimei imposed the restriction that the criticisms must be confined to the paper's office and the staff were not allowed to organise demonstrations in the streets nor place posters denouncing Qin Sha outside the office. Later the issue became uncontainable and the Party had to dispatch work teams to investigate the various grievances. By launching the attack first in the office of *Tibet Daily*, the Central Committee of the regional CCP either intentionally or by coincidence secured control of the media since the Tibetan edition of the paper was more or less a direct translation of the Chinese edition and editorial decisions were made by the Party's Central Committee. There was increasing pressure on the regional CCP to extend the Cultural Revolution into other offices and work units. The regional Party was divided between those who wanted to confine the Cultural Revolution to the Party apparatus and the more radical faction which wanted to 'shoot the arrows wildly' and 'expose everything'. This group was keen to mimic events in Beijing and to allow the indiscriminate spread of the Cultural Revolution into the wider society.[11] At this stage the Tibetans were not involved, since the debate was mainly confined to high-ranking Party cadres. In 1966, although there were many Tibetan party members, they did not occupy any important positions in the Party and were therefore excluded from the key decision-making groups.

On 5 July the Party was forced to hold an enlarged meeting of all the members at Nyingtri, to resolve the question of whether to extend the Cultural Revolution or restrict it to the Party. The meeting lasted for fifteen days, by the end of which the conservative faction seemed to have gained control, forcing through a resolution which endorsed the principle that the Cultural Revolution should be 'confined to academic and literary circles, notably in the educational, journalist, literary and art circles'.[12] The decision showed that the regional CCP had no inclination for the radical shift that was taking place in Beijing. Further evidence that the local leaders were out of step with developments in Beijing came in the summer of 1966. During the summer season the traditional Tibetan Government usually held picnics (*lingka*) and organised lavish parties for government officials and the aristocracy, a tradition which had been adopted by the Chinese, who had been holding similar parties for the Tibetan ruling class. Accordingly, on 2 July 1966 the regional CCP had invited many of the former Tibetan aristocrats to a lavish picnic,[13] revealing how unaware the Party leaders were of the dramatic events that were about to take place. Within a few days many of the Tibetans who had attended the party were purged and subjected to struggle sessions. Their transformation from 'patriotic personage' to 'counter-revolutionary' was abrupt and unexpected. For the next ten years they were to be labelled class enemies.

The 5 July decision was quickly replicated throughout the various work units and offices. The campaign started with group discussions and studies of documents issued from the centre. The cadres from the Lhasa Municipal Committee, for example, were told merely to study party documents and directives.[14] Chi Zemin, the Director of the Public Security Bureau, issued a directive forbidding attacks on the Party Committee in the department.[15] Individuals could be identified and criticised, but neither the Central Committee of the Regional Party nor the Party itself could be criticised. It was announced that any criticism of the Party would be regarded as counter-revolutionary.[16]

The course of action adopted by the regional Party conformed, in many ways, to the general trends in China where, in the early stages, the leadership held differing views on the direction the Cultural Revolution should take. Liu Shaoqi and Deng were trying to keep it within academic and cultural spheres while Mao saw it as a question of the fundamental redirection of the Party.[17] The issue came to the forefront when the question arose as to how to handle events in Beijing University, where Nie Yuanzi, a professor at the university, had written a poster attacking the university's administration. Liu and Deng wanted the more usual method of investigation to be carried out by the Party's work team while Mao wanted the students (who later became the Red Guards) to take the lead in ousting anti-Party and anti-socialist elements. The question of the general trend and the method of the Cultural Revolution was discussed at the 11th Plenum of the 8th Central Committee of the CCP held in Beijing from 1 to 12 August. While the meeting was in progress, on 5 August, the *People's Daily* printed Mao's statement entitled 'Bombard the Headquarters'. This also marked the beginning of the split within the CCP's Central Committee and the official castigation of Liu Shaoqi. Moreover, it rejected Liu's view of the Cultural Revolution as an academic and internal party debate; he was now condemned as the leader of the capitalist roaders in the Party.[18] Mao had endorsed the idea that the Cultural Revolution was to be a mass movement, and that anyone in the Party who took the capitalist road should be targeted. The 11th Plenum also saw the re-ascendancy of Mao, and Lin Biao became the second most important figure.

The debate about the aims and methods of the Cultural Revolution was replicated in Tibet. It was, however, in the interests of the regional Party to avoid upheaval by preventing the Cultural Revolution from spreading into Tibet. Their efforts proved fruitless. As the Cultural Revolution gained momentum in Beijing, it was inevitable that the Chinese leaders in Lhasa would themselves become a target for criticism. The debate in Beijing shifted to the question of two lines: those in the Party taking the bourgeois reactionary line and the true followers of Mao. Events escalated and on 8 August Mao issued the 16-Point Directive, which formulated the course of the Cultural Revolution defining it as a struggle against those in the Party who were taking the 'capitalist road' and affirming that the masses should take the lead in expunging reactionaries from the Party. Mao thus unleashed a frenzied political campaign which was to create disorder and confusion.

The CCP in Tibet had no alternative but to follow the directive from the Centre. The main target of the Cultural Revolution had now shifted to personality issues among the Chinese élite in Tibet, but there was at the same time a renewed attack on Tibetan culture. On 18 August the regional CCP convened a special meeting to discuss the 16-Point Directive. It dutifully endorsed the new directive but the leaders carried on very much as they had done in the previous few months.[19] Later the radical faction accused the Party Committee of merely pretending to carry out Mao's 16-Point Directive. The regional leadership's ability to maintain control over the events was to some extent dependent on what limits the radical faction in Beijing was going to set.

The Red Guard movement spread in China, either with the direct connivance of the regional Party or spontaneously, and on 24 August the Lhasa Middle School and the Tibet Teacher Training College established the first local Red Guard movement. It is most likely these groups were created by the regional Party to counteract the possible intrusion of Red Guards from China. They were told to study the 16-Point Directives and to prepare themselves to debate with the Red Guards from China.[20] It was also interesting to note that on 27 August 1966, Red Guards from the TAR teacher training college put up posters and distributed leaflets in Lhasa demanding the eradication of *Zhing tren lamlug* (feudal culture).

(1) Bowing and sticking tongue out as a sign of respect should be abolished, as these are signs of feudal oppression of the proletariat.

(2) All observance of religious festivals should be abolished.

(3) All feudal names of parks and streets should be changed (for example the Norbu Linga [Norbulingka] should be named the Peoples' Park).

(4) All large and small chotens must be destroyed.

(5) All books praising the idealism and feudalism should be prohibited.

(6) All mani walls, prayers flags and incense burners should be destroyed.

(7) No one should recite prayers, circumambulate, prostrate. People should not consult oracles and diviners.

(8) People should destroy all photographs of the Dalai and the Panchen.

(9) All photos praising revisionists, feudalism or reactionaries should be destroyed.

(10) All monasteries and temples apart from those that are protected by the government should be converted for general public use.

(11) The *Tibet Daily* and Lhasa radio must use the language of the proletariat (*ngal-rtsal mi-dmangs kyi skad-cha*) and expunge the language of aristocracy (*sku-drag sku-ngo tsho'i skad-cha*). Accordingly, Tibetan grammar should be reformed.

(12) All Muslims should also embrace the new society and destroy the old traditions.

(13) The People's Park, formerly the Norbu Linga, should be opened to the public for recreation.

(14) There should be greater political and ideological education among the monks and nuns. They should be allowed to abandon their religious duties and vows without pressure from the monasteries.

(15) Monks and nuns should be allowed to marry and they must engage in productive labour.

(16) The exploiting class should be subjected to labour education and a close watch should be kept on their conduct.

(17) Feudal practices, such as giving parties, exchanging presents and kha-ta should be stopped.[21]

(18) Feudal marriage practices, such as one man having two wives, one woman having two husbands, father and son sharing a wife, two sisters sharing one husband and two brothers sharing a wife should be eradicated.

(19) Scientific education should be propagated among the people. Films which teach scientific education should be shown.

(20) All stray dogs in Lhasa must be destroyed and people should not keep dogs and cats in the house.[22]

It is surprising that the pamphlet omits any reference to the struggle between the two lines (capitalism and socialism), and it also makes no mention of the regional Party. It appears that they saw the Cultural Revolution as essentially a struggle against feudal traditions. This is an indication that the home-grown Red Guard movement was fomented by the local Party in a deliberate attempt to divert the Red Guard's anger away from the Party to a general attack on Tibetan society. Even after the autumn of 1966 the campaign in Tibet largely remained a movement against the Four Olds. This was to have a devastating effect on Tibetan culture. In every village, the people were mobilised to destroy religious and cultural artefacts. Families were forced to throw out all religious objects from their homes. Lamas, trulkus, diviners and other religious figures came under renewed attack, forced to wear a dunce's hat and paraded through the streets by young activists. There was a feverish effort to rename. The Norbulingka was renamed Mimang Lingka, the 'People's Park', and some people even changed their names to show their revolutionary vigour. Tibet's greatest monuments – the three monasteries of Sera, Drepung and Gaden, which formed the repository of Tibetan learning – were not spared. Centuries-old religious objects were smashed and all copper, bronze, silver and gold items were carefully labelled, removed and transported to China. The most sacred statue, the Jo Atisha in Tsuglakhang temple in Lhasa, was destroyed.[23] The scars left by the campaign against the Four Olds is still evident today from the ruins of monasteries and temples that litter Tibet.[24]

The effect was to destroy Tibet's separate identity. The Chinese now propagated a policy of total assimilation and Tibetan identity was reduced to the language alone, although, as noted above, even this had come under attack. While the intensity of the factional fighting continually varied between 1966 to 1976, this policy towards Tibetan culture remained constant, with the new egalitarian culture emphasised most vividly in the uniformity of dress. The Cultural Revolution quickly spread into rural and nomadic areas, where the Party's work teams were moving in to initiate it. In January 1967 the cadres from Meldrogongkar *xian* wrote an appeal to the Party Committee of the Lhasa Municipality about the decision to launch an indiscriminate and violent campaign the previous September in the village of Pa-lo.

> In the course of the struggle extremely barbarous methods of fascism were adopted to treat the poverty stricken peasants and labouring people who had been branded as demons and monsters. Apart from the general forms of ill-treatment, such as beating with fists, kicking, hair-plucking and ear twisting, other terrifying forms of punishment and torture were also used. These included, for example, detention in a private prison, the wearing of handcuffs and fetters, scorching the body and head with fire, feeding human excreta and cattle and horse dung, muzzling the mouth with a horse bit, etc. The forms of torture are really too numerous to mention one by one.
>
> According to initial statistics in Pa-lo alone 24 persons were seriously injured during the struggle and confined to their beds for one and half months. Today some of them have still not fully recovered. Nine people were crippled. Several had most of their hair pulled out. Apart from an agent, the dead included an expectant mother of working class background. Two miscarriages were caused. The whereabouts of a teacher of a poor peasants school, who tried to escape, is still not known. Three people have lost their mental bearing after being beaten up. And many class brothers had at one time thought of committing suicide.[25]

The appeal also stressed that 61.8 per cent of the victims were classed as 'extremely poor peasants and well-to-do peasants'. As long as it remained a campaign against traditional beliefs and practices, the local leadership would be able to control the movement and they themselves would be free from any direct attack. It was therefore crucial that the Party maintain control and make sure that it did not degenerate into a popular uprising against the leadership. To do this the Party had to initiate the campaigns in the rural areas, and Dhondup Choedon recalls that the Party's work team, composed of two Chinese and six Tibetan cadres, came to the Red Flag commune and selected thirty young people who belonged to the poorest class[26] and urged them to commit themselves to the struggle against the Four Olds.

The regional Party was not able to insulate themselves from criticism indefinitely, especially when the campaign in Beijing turned against Liu and Deng's bourgeois line. Deng Xiaoping had been an important figure in determining Chinese policy towards minorities in general and in particular towards Tibet: as noted before, in 1950 Deng had been the Political Commissar of the South-West Military Region which led the invasion of Tibet. The attack on Deng intensified, and his policy was criticised as pandering to reactionaries.[27] The infiltration of bourgeois ideas into Tibet was ascribed to his early influence. Mao's call to root out followers of Liu and Deng therefore had a special significance for Tibet.

The antagonism towards the local Party apparatus was prompted by the convergence of several factors. At a higher level there was the attack on the CCP's United Front and its nationalities policies over the preceding two decades; earlier policies were criticised as 'capitulationist' and involving excessive compromises with minority leaders. This prompted an investigation by the Red Guards of the CCP's work in Tibet. In Tibet, too, there was growing resentment against the local Party leadership. The Tibetans were angered by the Party's decision to launch indiscriminate campaigns mainly aimed at smashing the Four Olds, while low-ranking cadres were alienated by what they saw as the leadership's attempts to direct the Cultural Revolution downwards. The appeal from the cadres of Meldrogongkar *xian* makes it clear that they had risen in revolt because of the campaign that was carried out in their area. They seemed to feel that they were made victims of the Cultural Revolution, while leading officials were protected from criticism. The regional leadership's attempt to deflect the campaign was cited as evidence that the Central Committee of the regional CCP was a bastion of 'capitalist-roaders'.

The Red Guards who came to Tibet saw the region as an anathema to the socialist revolution. The concessions granted to Tibet were proof that the revolution had been subverted. They felt that Tibet and Tibetans needed to be revolutionised and saw themselves as advanced revolutionaries who had come to the aid of the backward students in this retarded region. These young Chinese were indoctrinated with the image of Tibet as a hell on earth. When the authorities had taken Tibetan peasants who had suffered in the old society to visit schools in various parts of China they had been made to recount terrible stories about mutilations and beatings before liberation, stories which were no doubt meant to justify the Chinese claim that they had liberated Tibet from serfdom.[28] More importantly, this had made a deep impression on the young Chinese students who felt they were now bringing socialist revolution to Tibet.

Smash the Power-holders

The first challenge to the local Party occurred when Yue Zongming, a cadre working in the Cultural Administrative Committee of TAR, wrote a poster entitled 'Bombard the Headquarters, Set Fire to the Leadership of the Regional Party Committee'.[29] Although the poster was identified as originating from a single author, it was most likely produced by a group of people within the regional CCP who had good knowledge of events in China. It was also possible that the attack on the regional Party was sanctioned by the centre: without tacit approval from the top it is unlikely that such an attack could have been launched. The poster was distributed with a number of leaflets to various work units in the region to initiate the attack against the Central Committee of the regional CCP. They accused the Regional Party Committee of following Liu and Deng's bourgeois reactionary line and said that the Central Committee and a handful of capitalistroaders were impeding the progress of the Cultural Revolution and had become 'a stumbling block to the mass movement'. At this stage, no individual was identified as the leader of the Liu and Deng line in Tibet.

The counter-attack against Yue Zongming was decisive and immediate. Within a few days the Party denounced the poster as 'counter-revolutionary' and called on the masses to defend the Party. The Party's education and propaganda department organised a mass letter-writing campaign to refute Yue Zongming's charges. He was accused of being a counter-revolutionary and made to write a self-criticism.[30] The Party issued a 20,000-character booklet in its defence drafted by Wang Qimei, Zhang Caiwang and Chen Wei, the Director of the Culture and Education Department of TAR. Later, these three were christened the 'three antis' and became one of the main targets of the radicals. They claimed that the Party's Central Committee was the true defender of the proletariat and that it had not wavered from the teaching of Mao.

This was the beginning of the formation of factional groups in Tibet, with the radicals arguing that the leadership of the regional CCP were followers of Liu and Deng who had adopted a capitulationist line. The Party was faced with a serious challenge, not only in terms of personality, but also in terms of legitimacy. The conflict had reached a new intensity and was becoming a fight for power. Even at this stage, the local struggle could not be waged independently of events in China. Both factions had to observe diligently the developments in Beijing.

In October 1966, Zhang Guohua and Ngabo were in Beijing to attend the National Day celebration. It is interesting that at the beginning of the Cultural Revolution, Zhang and Ngabo's names were not mentioned in any of the criticisms directed at the Party. They seemed to stand aloof from the violent campaign that was being fomented in Lhasa. This is particularly surprising in the case of Ngabo, since the first victims of the Cultural Revolution were the former Tibetan aristocrats and lamas who had co-operated with the Chinese, many of whom had been recently elected to new posts after the founding of the TAR. At the advent of the Cultural Revolution they were the first to be brought out in public for struggle sessions.[31] In theory their class origin meant they could not be trusted but in fact the traditional Tibetan élite had outlived their usefulness. When the Party turned against them and allowed people to subject them to the most horrendous *thamzing*, Ngabo was the single exception. In September 1966, Ngabo moved to Beijing and, a month later, when Mao inspected a gigantic gathering of Red Guards at the Tiananmen gate, Ngabo was incongruously given the privileged position of standing with other Chinese leaders. This was presumably an affirmation of Chinese support for him and an indication that he should not be subjected to public criticism. It was therefore expected that neither the Party nor the radicals in Tibet would make any damaging attack on him. It was this timely intervention of Beijing which saved Ngabo and his family from certain public criticism[32]. When the Red Guards from Beijing had entered Tibet, one of the first issues they had brought up was the question of Ngabo's membership of the CCP. They had demanded to know how the local Party could have admitted someone of Ngabo's background into the Communist Party. Moreover, it became apparent that Ngabo's membership had been kept secret.[33] The Red Guards demanded the expulsion of Ngabo but, although Ngabo's class origins were criticised as unsuitable for membership of the Party, he himself was never labelled a 'capitalist-roader'. The attack was essentially aimed at Zhang Guohua and Zhang Jingwu for having allowed Ngabo to join the Party.[34]

By autumn 1966 the Regional Party found it was unable to suppress the growing criticism directed at it. The Party's attempt to silence Yue Zongming by labelling him anti-Party and counter-revolutionary had back-fired. While in Beijing Zhang Guohua must have discussed the growing criticism levelled at the Party and his apprehensions about the possible chaos that factional politics would cause in Tibet. It appears that Zhang discovered the Central leadership in Beijing would not support him, and he would have been able to see that the radicals had secured power in the capital. He telephoned Lhasa and commanded the regional Central Committee to rescind its opposition to Yue's poster and to argue that the general content of the poster was correct.[35] On 21 October, the Tibetan branch of *Xinhua* broke ranks and, openly supporting Yue, convened a meeting of 10,000 cadres to demand vindication of 19 September, the date on which a poster had appeared in Lhasa for the first time. The main support for Yue came from the Combat Team, a Red Guard team from the Xinhua group.[36]

In November the opposition groups in Tibet received further backing when the first groups of Red Guards from China arrived. This allowed and encouraged the formation of Red Guards in various work units, who openly opposed the regional Party leadership. The first week of November was a hectic period in Lhasa, with hundreds of Red Guards carrying out frenzied activity, putting up posters denouncing their work leaders, teachers and anyone in authority. They also initiated debate about whether the Regional Party had followed a reactionary bourgeois line or not, leading to the first open clash between the two opposing groups in Lhasa. At this stage the radical groups who accused the Party of following the Liu and Deng line were in the minority, while those who supported the Party as true defenders of the revolutionary line of Chairman Mao were in the majority. They set up a loosely organised group calling itself 'Defence Headquarters' and argued that the Party should be credited for its achievements over the past two decades in Tibet. They went on to argue that the Central Committee of the Party was the true headquarters of the proletarian revolution.

There was no way the debate about the nature of the Party could easily be resolved. The protagonists plunged further into internecine confrontation, leaving Tibet in chaos. At the start of the Cultural Revolution, from May to December 1966, it remained unclear how the situation in Tibet was going to unfold and the Party leadership was unable to resist the incursion of Red Guards from China who radicalised the local opposition groups. At first Zhang Guohua tried to distance himself from day to day events, leaving Wang Qimei and the Cultural Revolution committee of the regional CCP to meet most of the challenges posed by the radicals. It seems that Zhang was floundering about what to do, having apparently adopted the dangerous tactic of trying to balance both sides. While in Beijing he had told the radical leaders in the capital not to dispatch the Red Guards to Tibet because of the region's strategic position, and it was reported that Zhou Enlai supported his request. But they were rebuked by no less a person than Mao's wife, Jiang Qing, who had become the patron of the radical Red Guards.[37] Later, when Red Guards confronted Zhang, he told them that he had personally requested that the Red Guards should be sent to Tibet to start the 'destruction' as there were so few students in Tibet.[38] From the beginning the regional CCP realised that they would have to rely on middle- and low-ranking cadres to initiate the Cultural Revolution, thus making it difficult to attack the Party because of ingrained loyalty and fear of reprisals.

The main contingent of radicals from China was the Metropolitan Red Guard. They were supported by a few cadres who had spoken out against the regional Party. They discovered that in the previous few months the regional Party committee had been systematically carrying out a purge of radical cadres, whom they had accused of being reactionaries. Under the instigation of Wang Qimei, the party had compiled dossiers on individual cadres; this came to be known as the 'black material'. There was therefore growing resentment against the Party leadership for their handling of the Cultural Revolution and their treatment of individual cadres. It came to light that in September 1966 the Party had subjected 127 cadres from the Forestry Department to public struggle sessions, some 25 per cent of the work-force in the department. They were branded 'capitalist-roaders' and counter-revolutionaries.[39] Their cases were taken up by the Red Guards, who demanded that cadres who had been branded as capitalist roaders in the early stages of the Cultural Revolution must be vindicated and the person responsible for the purge of these cadres handed to the masses. This forced the Party to convene a meeting, at which the Party leaders once again adopted their tactic of asking individuals to confess to mistakes and shortcomings.[40] On 19 December Zhang Guohua himself was forced to give an explanation of the failure of the Cultural Revolution committee to intensify the revolution; he had no alternative but to agree that the 19 September poster was revolutionary and generally correct.[41] Zhang also agreed that in the case of the forestry department, the local Party had followed 'the bourgeois reactionary line and created the white terror'.[42]

The radical groups were clearly dissatisfied with Zhang's admission, and posters and pamphlets denouncing him appeared in Lhasa. The radicals were also dissatisfied with the Central Committee's procrastination and with what they regarded as 'piercing the spear downwards', meaning the leadership's continuing attempts to deflect criticism towards the lower echelons of the Party. The Red Guards now began to target Zhang Guohua himself, labelling him and other conservatives in the Party 'royalist dogs'. On 22 December over fifty-six groups, with a total membership of no more than 1,000 people (mainly red guard groups from China) joined together and inaugurated the 'Lhasa Revolutionary Rebel Central Headquarters'.[43] The word 'rebel' was clearly meant to signify radicalism and opposition to the existing power-holders. The group came to be known in Tibetan as Gyenlog, literally meaning 'over throw' the power-holders. The inauguration pamphlet declared:

We will rebel against the handful of persons in authority in the Party

> taking the capitalist road! We will rebel against persons stubbornly persisting in the bourgeois reactionary line! We will rebel against all the monsters and freaks! We will rebel against the bourgeois Royalists! We, a group of lawless revolutionary rebels, will wield the iron sweepers and swing the mighty cudgel to sweep the old world into a mess, and bash people into complete confusion. We will fear no gales and storms, nor flying sand and moving rocks.[44]

The Gyenlog group also established investigation teams to examine the cases of the cadres who had been purged at the onset of the Cultural Revolution. A sub-group calling itself the 'Comfort Group for Joint Investigation into the Forestry Company Incident' demanded as before the reinstatement and vindication of those cadres who had been branded 'capitalist roaders'. Internal assessment made by the Tibet Military Region Party Committee remarked that the Gyenlog lacked organisational discipline and was 'imbued with anarchist ideas'.[45]

Two Factions

A few days after the founding of the Gyenlog, the Party leadership was forced to set up its own group – the 'Lhasa Combat Headquarters for the Defence of Mao Tse-tung Thought'. At the beginning of 1967, a number of other organisations merged with the Defence Headquarters to form the 'Great Alliance Rebel Headquarters of the Lhasa Proletarian Revolution'. The group was known in Tibetan as Nyamdrel, meaning 'together' or 'alliance'. The main objective of Nyamdrel, the more powerful of the two factions and the one with the backing of the regional Party leadership, was to defend the leadership of the regional Party and to assert that it was the legitimate purveyor of Mao's revolution and the sole representative of the proletariat. The same claim was made by Gyenlog.

From the various publications put out by the groups it is difficult to discern any differences in ideology between them. Both make assertions about their revolutionary credentials and claim to be the legitimate exponents of Mao's teachings (later the CCP was itself to acknowledge that there were no ideological differences between the two factions and that their rivalry was simply to gain power).[46] It is true that there was no real ideological divide, but in terms of interest, each faction represented a particular class of people, a fact which the official explanation avoids, failing to acknowledge the split between the senior Party leadership and the low-ranking cadres. It is hard for the CCP to accept that the rebel faction, to some degree, did represent the working class and the interests at least of the lower-ranking cadres.

The Nyamdrel faction was, in the main, composed of senior cadres and those who had benefited during the past decade. It was in their interest to protect the status quo. While the Gyenlog drew its support mainly from Red Guards who had arrived from China and those cadres who were disaffected with the existing Party leadership, its support was strongest among the lower- and middle-ranking cadres who had been purged at the beginning of the Cultural Revolution. It was their support that gave the Gyenlog real impetus. The only section of the Tibetan population who were not allowed to join either faction were people who had been categorised by the authorities as originating from a 'bad class' background, namely the former aristocrats and landlords. They were subjected to struggle sessions from both sides and became the target of abuse. Both sides claimed to be the true representatives of the proletarians and the poor peasants, but an official military report on the two factions describes Nyamdrel more as representative of the poor peasants and says that it took class background into consideration, while the Gyenlog was less discriminatory about the class origins of its supporters.[47] In December 1967, Gyenlog had 7,000 supporters and Nyamdrel 38,000.[48]

For the Chinese and the Tibetans the question of the ethnic composition of the two factions remains controversial and sensitive.[49] The Chinese authorities then, and now, argue that the two factions did not represent an ethnic divide. To some degree the official position is correct: however, there was a greater number of Tibetans supporting the Nyamdrel faction.[50] In fact among the Tibetans there was division between urban and rural areas. In Lhasa, one the strongholds of the Gyenlog, the majority of Tibetans supported the rebel group, while rural areas remained under the control of the Nyamdrel faction. Nagchu area was dominated by the Nyamdrel faction. It is not clear whether the Tibetans' support for one or other faction was based on a conscious decision or whether they were merely following the Chinese leaders in their area; the second is most likely. The Nyamdrel leaders were able to portray the Gyenlog as unruly rebels from outside the region and it would therefore have appeared natural for the Tibetans to support the side of the old cadres and the existing leadership, whom they had known for years. Nyamdrel was also able to draw on those Tibetans who had benefited in the land reform which had made the greatest impact in the rural areas.

One of the largest contingents of Red Guards was the 'Serf Spear'. It was composed mainly of children of poor peasants who had returned from China and who had undoubtedly benefited from the affirmative policy applied by the regional party. At the behest of the leaders of Nyamdrel, the Serf Spear attacked the headquarters of the Gyenlog. Since the Nyamdrel had the support of the existing Party establishment, they had the advantage of being able to draw on the Party resources to mobilise the people. The Gyenlog accused the Nyamdrel group of bringing peasants from outside Lhasa to bolster their strength; the rebels had to rely on setting up a new network to attract people to their side.

Between January and February 1967 changes occurred rapidly. The factions emerged in every village and work unit. There was repeated violent factional fighting as the two groups attempted to wrest power. The Nyamdrel, although it had the backing of the regional Party, acted as though it was an independent group. Each faction fought to establish its supporters as heads of various Party committees, work units and communes and both sides claimed to have discovered 'capitalist roaders' in the regional Party who became their targets. The Gyenlog organisation was not without supporters in the Party. Many cadres who were disaffected or held grudges against the Party leaders were supportive of them. The Red Guard pamphlet identifies Fan Ming and his wife, Liang Fang, as supporters of Gyenlog. Fan Ming, who had entered Tibet with the Panchen Rinpoche in 1951 and belonged to the North-West Military Region group, had been critical of Zhang Guohua and the party leadership in Lhasa and had been criticised as a revisionist when the Panchen Rinpoche was deposed. The disappearance of the Panchen Rinpoche and the role of Shigatse as a separate faction in the Tibetan polity meant that Fan Ming had also lost his political power base.

In January 1967, developments in China spurred the Red Guards to frantic attempts to seize power in Tibet. On the evening of 10 January, the Red News Rebel Regiment, composed mainly of Red Guards from the *Tibet Daily* offices, seized power. Gao Ying, the chief editor, and other senior staff were dismissed, accused of being stooges of the regional Party Committee and of failing to expose the bourgeois reactionary line of the 'capitalist roaders' in the Party. Gao Ying was detained by the Gyenlog faction and made to work under their supervision at the paper's office. However, the faction was able to bring out only one edition of the *Tibet Daily* (11 January):[51] the Nyamdrel faction mobilised their supporters and ousted the Gyenlog group from the office the next day. Both factions recognised the importance of the *Tibet Daily*: the paper was the main organ of propaganda, and moreover, control of the paper would have given them unrestricted access to the printing press. It was therefore natural that the paper was one of the main targets in the power struggle and in fact the Gyenlog faction made a number of attempts to seize power and take control of the news media.

Between January and March 1967 there were numerous attempts to seize power from the incumbent group. The Gyenlog's ultimate aim was to overturn the power structure in the regional CCP and to assume leadership of the Party. In order to target Zhang Guohua and the Party's Central Committee, the Gyenlog organised a group known as the 'special attack task force', which sought to wrest power from the Party's Central Committee. On 3 February, the Gyenlog announced the formation of the 'Preparatory Committee for the Tibet Autonomous Revolutionary Rebel General Command Post', a coalition of eighteen Red Guard organisations. The group declared that it had seized power from the regional Party Central Committee and demanded that all cadres, Party Secretaries at branch level, Standing Committee members and other Party members must now report to the newly established Preparatory Committee.[52]

Once again, these attempts to seize power were not events isolated to Tibet. The Red Guards and the Gyenlog faction were following the precedent set in Shanghai and elsewhere in China, activities fully endorsed by the radical leadership in Beijing. There was no doubt that the attempts to seize power were welcomed by the radicals and low-ranking cadres in Tibet, who saw this as an opportunity to bring to the surface long-held grievances about working conditions in Tibet. Many low-ranking Chinese cadres in Tibet resented the fact that they were stranded there and that in the past, the authorities had deliberately prevented them from returning to China. When the Chinese workers at Nyingtri textile mill seized power, one of the first demands they made was to reclaim the right to return to their homes in China.[53] The truck drivers, for example, complained about unrealistic targets imposed on them by the Party and having to work sixteen hours a day.[54] The restrictions imposed on family reunions were stringent: workers who wished to apply for entry of their families into Tibet were required to have ten years' working experience in Tibet and had to be over thirty-five years of age, while senior cadres could bring their dependants and families 'as they pleased'.[55] The Leftists, for their part, complained that while class background was meant to be all-important in considering promotion, in Tibet the Party leaders had ignored cadres' class origins.[56] A case in point was Wang Qimei, who was a member of the regional Party Central Committee and one of the leaders of the Nyamdrel faction. A contingent of Red Guards arrived in Lhasa to investigate Wang after the Red Guards in Beijing subjected his family to a struggle session and denounced them as members of the landlord class.[57] In Tibet very few people knew about Wang's class background and he had been allowed to emerge as a leader of the regional CCP. This was unacceptable to the Leftists, who argued that the negation of class background was destroying the 'Party's prestige in the minds of the masses'.[58] Since the Gyenlog faction was a coalition of Red Guards from China and lower-ranking cadres, the seizure of power was seen as a legitimate means of overthrowing 'the entrenched power holders' in Tibet.[59]

The authorities recognised that this presented a serious problem going beyond the ideological battles between left and right. The grievances of the lower-ranking cadres – truck drivers, electricians and other skilled workers –

had the potential to undermine Chinese rule in Tibet. The Nyamdrel faction was, however, able to resist the challenge from Gyenlog, mainly through its numerical superiority and its ability to mobilise the Tibetans. The Party leaders were able to induce the Tibetan Red Guards to support them – in one case a large group of Tibetan students who were returning to Tibet to participate in the Cultural Revolution were provided with extra clothing by the local Party leaders and given leave to visit their families, thus immediately wooing them on to the Nyamdrel side.[60] The Nyamdrel faction was also able to prevent the Gyenlog from bringing in reinforcements by using local people in Nagchu and other entry points from China,[61] who in some cases beat up and detained Red Guards entering Tibet. Despite the general difficulties of travelling and the harassment by local people, many Red Guards were able to reach Lhasa but with great skill the Nyamdrel faction was able to portray the radicals as outsiders. The Gyenlog faction, to some extent, did represent outside interest groups, as noted earlier. The real impetus for the Gyenlog group came from Red Guards from outside Tibet who, as outsiders, lacked local support and resources to mobilise the masses to overthrow the Party leadership in Tibet. This is not to say that there was no support for the radicals, but it centred on the small, urban, largely Chinese community in Tibet.

Despite the havoc created by the factional fighting, Beijing was able to maintain a vigilant eye on events in Tibet. The strategic position of the region and the acrimonious relationship with India meant that Chinese leaders had recognised the need to maintain stability in Tibet and were therefore careful not to allow the chaotic politics of factional fighting to intrude into the sensitive border areas. From the start of the Cultural Revolution, it was emphasised that stability in the border region must be maintained and the Chinese made sure that the areas near the border did not succumb to the factional political struggle. Since the early 1960s, the Ngari region had been ruled by the army because of the Tibetan guerrilla base in Mustang, which made sporadic raids into the territory. The Cultural Revolution in the area was mainly confined to the campaign against the Four Olds and the castigation of those who had been classed as rich farmers or nomads. They were subjected to violent struggle sessions and abuse. Neither the Chinese cadres nor the Tibetans were allowed to engage in factional politics. In the rest of Tibet, Gyenlog and Nyamdrel were to dominate the course of the Cultural Revolution, but in the border areas the Red Guards were refused entry and any cadres who tried to catalyse factional politics and control were dealt with severely by the army.

In the district headquarters the Chinese cadres were allowed to criticise the existing leadership. One informant mentions that at the district headquarters in Purang, in Ngari, the cadres held ten days of meetings at the beginning of 1967 to criticise senior officials, but no action was taken to oust the leading district cadres. The senior cadres made the usual admission of mistakes and expressed their desire to improve. The main victims of the Cultural Revolution in these areas were, therefore, the Tibetans, in particular the peasants and nomads, who had to suffer a full-scale attack on Tibetan culture and identity.

As in China, the ensuing fight between the two factions created virtual anarchy in Tibet. Normal economic activities came to a halt, agricultural and industrial production fell. Schools had to be closed because the students were too busy revolutionising and the teachers were paralysed by fear. The PLA represented the only group that was supposedly free from factional politics. The army was referred to by both factions as the 'pillar' of the revolution; both factions recognised the need to get the army onto their side. The Gyenlog put out a circular advising its supporters not to confront any commanders and fighters of the PLA.[62] Both sides advocated that the seizure of power must be based on the 'three-way alliance'. This referred to the alliance of the army, cadres and the workers. Initially, the army showed no sign of wanting to get involved in the factional disputes. The Red Guards were forbidden to exchange or propagate revolution among the soldiers and it was also announced that attacks on the military leadership were not allowed.[63]

However, at the end of January 1967 Mao ordered the army to disband all 'counter-revolutionary organisations'. In Tibet, this provided the pretext for the army and regional Party leadership to crack down on the Gyenlog faction. On 6 February, Zhang Guohua called a meeting of the PLA leadership in Tibet and was able to obtain their support. He was also allowed to bring into Tibet three additional divisions as reinforcements. There had always been a close affinity between the army and senior cadres in Tibet and Zhang had earlier used the army as the basis for his power. It must be noted that Zhang may have had the patronage of Lin Biao himself, with whom he had often worked in the past.[64]

Four days later the army intervened on the side of the Nyamdrel faction. The army was under the command of Zeng Yongya, who came to Tibet in 1962 at the start of the Sino–Indian war. He commanded the 46th Regiment of the Fourth Field Army. Another military official who came to the forefront was Ren Rong, the political commissar of the 46th Army and deputy political commissar of the Tibet Military Region. The Fourth Field Army was increasingly becoming the single most dominant political force in Tibet; officers from this group occupied 38 per cent of the key posts.[65] Their support for the Nyamdrel faction was declared in an open letter distributed all over Tibet which set out to publicise the achievements of the leadership in Tibet over the previous seventeen years and insisted that the Party's accomplishments in Tibet far outweighed its mistakes. More importantly, the letter was also used to declare martial law in Tibet to 'ensure the stability of the regional leadership'.[66]

The army's suppression of the Gyenlog faction was ruthless and swift. The faction was accused of being counter-revolutionary and of colluding with the landlords and 'rightists'. The army arrested thirteen leaders of the Gyenlog and recaptured the Party offices in Lhasa. On 17 February the Gyenlog organised a mass meeting to protest against the army, denouncing the 'fascist atrocities of the revisionists within the CCP and Tibet Military Region'.[67] The Gyenlog was certainly facing a crushing defeat and had no alternative but to appeal to the Central Cultural Revolution Group in Beijing which was under the influence of Jiang Qing, who was more supportive of the radical rebel groups. On 24 February the Committee sent a telegram supporting the Gyenlog faction but, according to the rebel leaders, the regional Party did not make this public.[68] The Gyenlog also tried to set the ordinary soldiers against the officers by broadcasting messages urging the soldiers to give their support to 'the proletarian revolutionary rebels'.[69] The support of the radical leaders in Beijing did have some effect in halting the onslaught on the Gyenlog faction. The army and the Nyamdrel began to make it clear that no further action would be taken if the radicals were to renounce their membership of the Gyenlog.

The radicals remained unwilling to surrender to the army and opposed the declaration of martial law in Tibet,[70] accusing the army of being a 'royalist dog', meaning that they were stooges of Zhang Guohua. Zhang himself was labelled a 'local emperor' seeking to create an 'independent kingdom'.[71] The rebel faction appealed to Beijing, requesting that 'black data' from Zhang Guohua's personal file should be made available so the Red Guards could expose him, but this attack on Zhang did not succeed in bringing him down and he remained the most powerful figure in Tibet. He managed to obtain a written statement from Beijing urging the rebel groups to work with him and describing him as a faithful follower of Chairman Mao.[72]

The army not only began to restore some semblance of law and order, but also advocated a committed policy supporting Zhang and protecting the Party leadership in Lhasa. You Chihuan, the deputy commander of the Tibet Military Region, forbade the Red Guards to make personal attacks on Zhang[73] and it was announced that no one was allowed to topple the regional Party Central Committee on the grounds that such an attack would destroy the 'centre of leadership' and leave the region without the guidance of the Party. The army nearly succeeded in obliterating the Gyenlog: by the end of March a report by the military stated that the rebel faction was reduced to little more than a thousand people, while the membership of Nyamdrel had swelled to over 38,000.[74]

By March the Nyamdrel faction was, with the support of the army, in full power in Tibet, reflecting the pre-eminent position of the PLA. The *Tibet Daily* and other mass media were placed under the army's control and began to accuse the Gyenlog of being agents of capitalists and counter-revolutionaries. On 5 March the army organised a mass rally in Lhasa to celebrate the suppression of the Gyenlog faction; it announced that all units who had supported the rebels would be declared counter-revolutionaries. The leadership in Beijing also seemed to have accepted the victory of the Nyamdrel as a *fait accompli* and ordered the Red Guards to return to China. On 8 March, when a parade was held to send the Red Guards to China, the Nyamdrel faction spat and threw stones at them and shouted 'Farewell to the god of plague'.[75] This was a humiliating defeat for the radicals. Tibet's remoteness from Beijing meant that there was very little that radicals in the capital could do to bolster their power in the region.

The Party leaders were not satisfied with simply restoring their own position. Between March and April 1967 they carried out a purge of cadres who had supported the Gyenlog faction. Reportedly as many as 75 per cent of the cadres in Lhasa were removed from their offices. The leaders of Gyenlog, about 100 people in total, were subjected to struggle sessions and branded as counter-revolutionaries.[76] For a while the army and the Party leaders were able to maintain joint power in Tibet and the region returned to some degree of normality. Zhang Guohua felt that it was safe to leave Tibet, and in middle of March went to Beijing to receive his new appointment, where he was fêted at a special reception held for him and attended by Zhou Enlai and other senior leaders. This was clearly a signal that the central leadership welcomed Zhang's restoration of order in Tibet, as was their request that he take control of the turbulent politics in Sichuan province.[77]

In May it was announced that Zhang was to be transferred to Sichuan as First Political Commissar of the Chengdu Military Region and concurrently 1st Secretary of the South-West Bureau. The turmoil in the province was greater than in Tibet, and his new appointment was more prestigious, since Sichuan was one of the key military areas in China. From Chengdu, where the headquarters of the South-West Military Region was based, Zhang could continue to exercise his influence in Tibet, as we will see later.

Although his elevation left a power vacuum in Tibet, there was no real difficulty in filling the post. The army's intervention had established its supremacy and it was therefore out of the question that the leaders in Beijing could appoint an outsider to fill Zhang Guohua's post. However, because of the continuing factional fighting, the Party structure had virtually disintegrated. The Nyamdrel, with the support of the army, had tried to restore some degree of Party apparatus to Tibet, and in May Zhou Renshan was appointed as Acting First Secretary of the regional Party committee. Zhou had come to Tibet in December 1956 from Amdo (Qinghai), where he had served as the head of the United Front Work Department.[78] In Lhasa he was one of the leaders of the Nyamdrel faction at the beginning of the Cultural Revolution. But his appointment as acting Party Secretary did not mean that the authority of the Party had been restored. We will see that during this period the regional Party was engulfed in factional fighting and that it was not able to reassert itself as the unified authority in the region. In fact, it appears that Zhou's promotion was not acceptable to other senior members of the Party.

During this period the army remained firmly in power, under Zeng Yongya, who was promoted to acting commander of the PLA in Tibet. Another army officer who received promotion was Ren Rong, who was appointed the Political Commissar of the Tibet Military Region. It is likely that their elevation reflected their loyalty to Zhang Guohua. The appointment of Zeng and Ren Rong shows that officials who had entered Tibet in the wake of the Sino–Indian War had secured political control of the region, while veteran civilian and army officials who had entered Tibet in the early 1950s were to occupy lower positions.

The group that emerged as victors in Tibet after February 1967 was an alliance of the senior Party cadres and the army. Despite their claims of being revolutionary, the group's outlook was essentially conservative and they wanted to restore the traditional Party structure. It stressed economic development and discipline among its members. But the struggle with the radicals was not yet over. Mao, who had unleashed the Cultural Revolution to oust the conservatives in the Party, had paradoxically triggered off the 'restoration of the old' – the same people who held power before the Cultural Revolution had managed to retain their positions, and, in many instances, had strengthened their position. Mao therefore decided to unleash another wave of revolutionary masses to root out capitalist roaders still concealed in the Party and the army. Mao and the Central Cultural Revolution Group were also worried about the extent of the army's involvement in the crushing of the 'revolutionary masses'. On 1 April 1967 the Central Committee of the CCP announced that the army or the regional Party leaders could not brand mass organisations as 'counter-revolutionary' at will and declared that the final judgment on whether an organisation was or was not counter-revolutionary would be made by the Centre. A few days later, on 6 April, the Military Affairs Committee issued a ten-point directive which stressed that the army should restrict themselves to 'political work' and that all important decisions must be referred back to the Centre and the PLA's Cultural Revolution Groups.

This seems to have encouraged the radical groups in Tibet to resurrect themselves. Although the Gyenlog faction had been defeated during the 'February Adverse', it soon became apparent that the authorities had not been able to subdue the radicals totally. The Gyenlog was left smouldering with resentment against the Party leaders and the army for their suppression of the revolt. As early as April it was trying to regroup. The repressive measures unleashed by the army did not deter die-hard radical Red Guards, who provocatively set up a group known as 'Ready to Be Arrested' and later established in Lhasa a more formal group calling itself the 'Provisional Command Post of Rebel General Headquarters'. At the end of May some of the Red Guards from China returned to Tibet and declared that they would stay in Tibet and carry out the Great Proletarian Cultural Revolution 'to the very end'.[79]

In the summer of 1967 the Tibet Military Region Party Committee submitted a report on the conditions in Tibet to the Cultural Revolution Group in Beijing. It concluded that both factions in Tibet were 'revolutionary mass organisations' and that their 'general orientation was correct'.[80] The statement had great significance for the Gyenlog, on the one hand vindicating them, and on the other hand signalling that the army was adopting a more balanced policy towards the two factions. The report went on to say that the army was willing to open itself up to self-examination and to rectify its past mistakes. Although vindicated, the Gyenlog felt that the army had been 'falsifying history'. The Metropolitan Red Guards who released the report warned its followers not to think that the army had changed and urged its supporters to 'cast away illusions' and to prepare for struggle against the army leaders.[81]

The hostility against the army developed during that summer. As noted earlier, at the start of the Cultural Revolution, both factions had refrained from directly attacking the army, but during this new phase the Gyenlog was quickly able to build up its strength as new groups of Red Guards arrived in Tibet. They aimed at a total vindication of the charges that were made against them in February, which they described as the restoration of counter-revolutionaries. The Nyamdrel faction was described as a 'conservative' organisation composed of 'faithful henchmen' of the Regional Party Committee.[82]

The Gyenlog had also realised that without the support of the army they were doomed to fail. While criticising the 'handful of people' in the military who supported the capitalist roaders in the Party, the Gyenlog once more tried to woo the army to their side. It was stressed that the seizure of power would be carried out on a 'three-in-one combination' and the group pamphlets began to emphasise that they would strengthen their relations with the army 'like those between fish and water'. The Gyenlog's efforts were timely and had some success: the army was not only divided but, by the middle of 1967, in China itself there was growing anti-army feeling among the people. This became evident when the masses in Wuhan, one of China's major industrial cities, turned against the army. Noticing this trend, the army in Tibet began to distance itself from the Nyamdrel faction.

There were army officers who felt that the active support given to the Nyamdrel had destroyed the PLA's standing as a neutral group. At the same time, there was growing rivalry among the top army officers. Between May and September, there were numerous armed clashes between the two factions in Tibet. The fighting was more violent and ruthless than at the beginning of the Cultural Revolution. On 29 May, in Chamdo, one of the strategic areas in Tibet, the Nyamdrel made an armed attack on the headquarters of the Gyenlog, and in July there was a series of violent armed clashes between the two factions in Lhasa.[83] The Nyamdrel tried to capture the Gyenlog headquarters in the Jokhang temple in the centre of Lhasa, an initiative that resulted in heavy casualties on both sides. The fighting intensified in all parts of Tibet, except the areas close to the border, which remained under military control. It appears that the renewed conflict was not only the result of the radical faction's desire for revenge, but also the result of the recent transfer of Zhang Guohua, which had left senior cadres coveting his position. This was to split both the army and the Party leaders, and the army leaders themselves.

The main cause of the fighting was still the question of who would control the regional Party, also called 'the two lines'. The rhetoric of the campaign remained the same, with each side claiming to be revolutionary and the true followers of Chairman Mao. Both sides went on to claim that they had exposed 'capitalist-roaders' in the Party and agents of Liu and Deng in Tibet. The renewed fighting had meant that Nyamdrel was not able to reconstitute the Party infrastructure at all levels, particularly in work units and communes, where the majority of the workers and cadres had supported the Gyenlog. The Nyamdrel faction's hold on power had suffered a serious setback with the transfer of Zhang Guohua, who had skilfully obtained the military backing and support of his immediate subordinates. That the jockeying for power resulting from Zhang Guohua's promotion had split the Party became apparent when the Nyamdrel faction turned against the acting Party Secretary, Zhou Renshan, denouncing him as the biggest 'capitalist-roader' and an agent of Liu and Deng in Tibet. The accusation seemed rather vague and was shrouded in the usual florid language of the Cultural Revolution questioning his class and political background. It is interesting to note that Zhang Guohua himself seemed to question Zhou's right to membership of the CCP and endorsed the campaign to expose his own successor.[84] The Gyenlog faction claimed that the anti-Zhou Renshan campaign was masterminded by Ren Rong, the influential Political Commissar of the PLA in Tibet. The Nyamdrel faction was given Zhou's personal files, kept by the Party; it was more than likely that they were deliberately leaked by some high-ranking official opposed to Zhou. The files, which contained details of Zhou's early connections with the Guomindang, enabled Nyamdrel to accuse him of hiding his past membership of the Nationalist Party. On the ideological level, he was accused of having advocated the priority of production over politics.

Paradoxically, support for Zhou Renshan came from a surprising quarter. He had been one of the Party leaders responsible for the suppression of the rebel groups in February but in the summer of 1967 the Gyenlog faction began championing Zhou as a true follower of Chairman Mao.[85] The Gyenlog targeted their campaign against Wang Qimei, but he still maintained great influence in the Nyamdrel faction and had the support of many veteran cadres. While at the beginning of the Cultural Revolution, there was a clear divide between senior Party officials and workers, by the summer of 1967 this distinction had somewhat faded, with the result that no one faction was in overall control of the administration of the region. Interestingly, the army showed no inclination to defend Zhou. However, this did not mean that the army refrained from factional fighting.[86]

But during the second phase of the Cultural Revolution the army's position was not clear; it appears to have been divided over what course of action to take. Some officials felt that the total support of the army in February for the Nyamdrel faction was a mistake which damaged the army's standing.[87] While there was no unqualified support from the army for a particular faction, the summer of 1967 saw individual officers and regiments allying themselves either with the Nyamdrel or the Gyenlog faction. This was evident from the fact that, clandestinely, the army was providing arms to the Red Guards of both groups. The troops of the 7894 unit of the PLA openly declared their support for the Nyamdrel and occupied the Potala; the commander of the Lhasa garrison was attacked and beaten by the supporters of the Gyenlog. The divisions which arose in the army were the result of the rivalry for power between Zeng Yongya, who had succeeded Zhang Guohua as the commander of the Tibet Military Region, and Ren Rong, the chief Political Commissar of the armed forces in Tibet. Zeng declared his support for the Gyenlog faction, while Ren Rong supported the Nyamdrel. From May the situation in Tibet degenerated into violent armed clashes between the two opposing groups, resulting in thousands of people being killed or wounded.

The Nyamdrel faction started their campaign with the aim of toppling Zhou Renshan and promoting Wang Qimei as a true revolutionary and follower of Chairman Mao. Wang remained head of the Cultural Revolutionary Committee in Tibet and was opposed by the Gyenlog faction, who now labelled him as 'the renegade' who was seeking to restore capitalism to Tibet. The other problem dominating the latter half of 1967 was the demand by the Gyenlog faction that the Tibet Military Region and Party officials accept that they had made mistakes during the February suppression of the radicals. The Gyenlog wanted, in particular, vindication of the 'Specially Targeting the Local Emperor' group which had been labelled as a 'counter-revolutionary' organisation. The Nyamdrel faction still exerted some influence in the army and, refusing to admit that mistakes had been made during the February suppression, they continued to maintain that the 'Special Targeting' was a counter-revolutionary group.

By August there was no sign that the fighting between the two factions was abating. The army leaders and representatives of both groups went to Chengdu to seek mediation from Zhang Guohua, who seems to have still exercised a great deal of influence in Tibet. Zhang, however, had shifted his position and showed himself to be more supportive of the Gyenlog faction that had originally tried to overthrow him: he described Nyamdrel as lacking 'revolutionary spirit', said that Wang Qimei should be 'overthrown', and agreed that the Gyenlog members who had been denounced as counter-revolutionaries should be rehabilitated.[88] This was naturally unacceptable to the Nyamdrel leaders and to Ren Rong. It became apparent that neither Zhang Guohua nor the army could reconcile the entrenched conflict and the fighting between the two factions continued unabated.

It was already clear that no one faction in Tibet could seize power without the total backing of the army, which meant that the continuing divisions within the military added to the problem. There were, moreover, constant shifts in loyalty among the senior cadres, which meant that the divide between the two factions was becoming confused. Only the direct intervention of the central leadership in Beijing could restore order, and in the end it was Beijing who demanded that the factional fighting be brought to an end. On 18 September, Zhou Enlai, Chen Boda and other senior leaders of the CCP's Central Committee issued a five-point directive for the cessation of factional fighting in Tibet. It declared that (1) both factions are legitimate mass movements; (2) all fighting must be stopped and farmers and nomads must return to their production units and should 'stimulate production'; (3) all people should guard against internal and external enemies of the Party; (4) newspapers should only publish the works of Chairman Mao and directives from the Centre and, finally (5) everyone should concentrate on carrying out their task well.[89]

The immediate response from the factional leaders was to claim that they could not make peace with the enemy and to say that it was necessary 'to have one faction eliminate the other'. The Nyamdrel went on to list six major points of difference between themselves and the Gyenlog but the groups had to cave in to the pressure from the Centre. On 24 September, an eight-point agreement was signed by representatives from the Nyamdrel and the Gyenlog. It stipulated that: (1) both sides would adhere to the directive from the Centre; (2) all persons would be sent back to their work units and anyone violating this should be punished; (3) once having returned to their work place, individuals should not be discriminated against because they had supported one faction or the other; (4) all weapons would be surrendered to the military authorities by 26 September; (5) both factions would hold consultative meetings to step up production; (6) both sides would carry out political and ideological education and agree to inspection by the Military Control Committee; (7) armed struggle would be forbidden, and (8) the army would ensure that both sides would adhere to the agreement.[90]

In the following month, a 'Preparatory Group for Great Alliances of the TAR' was set up. It failed immediately. The day after the inauguration of the organisation, the Gyenlog faction pulled out, declaring that they had fallen into a trap set by the enemy. But in Beijing, Mao had announced that he wanted the Cultural Revolution in Tibet to come to an end by the end of the year (1967) and Zhou Enlai, even more optimistic, had suggested this could be accomplished earlier,[91] placing the Gyenlog under great pressure to agree to form a joint administration. On 26 October the Gyenlog once again agreed to join the preparatory group but the two factions almost immediately started to accuse each other of being 'capitalist-roaders' and agents of Liu and Deng in Tibet. Four days later the Nyamdrel faction organised a meeting in Lhasa to denounce Zhou Renshan which provoked an inevitable response from their opponents, who came to Zhou's defence.[92]

It had been hoped that the army would play a neutral role as mediator, but since it was by now intimately involved in the fighting, it was no longer well placed to bring about rapprochement between the two factions and it became evident that neither side would yield easily to the army's supervision. By the beginning of October, it was apparent that the agreement had failed and a new burst of fighting plunged Tibet further into factional conflict. The beginning of 1968 saw the waning of factional fighting in China, with the formation of Revolutionary Committees all over China (described as 'a temporary supreme organ of power')[93] to represent what was known as the 'three-way alliance' of army, cadres and workers. These organisations were able to restore some degree of order in China, but in Tibet, conflict was even more entrenched than in China and the factional fighting continued unabated, with even Beijing apparently unable to impose order. It took nearly twenty months to set up a Revolutionary Committee in Tibet.

The split in the army was the real impediment to the reconciliation of the two factions and it became necessary to send two new divisions of troops to Tibet to overcome the factional fighting within the ranks of the PLA.[94] It appears that both the army and the leadership had realised that without eliminating some of the main personalities it was unlikely that the two factions would agree to form an alliance. Eventually, it became necessary to denounce Wang Qimei and Zhou Renshan, and both were accused of being agents of Liu Shaoqi in Tibet. A statement issued in the *People's Daily* on 7 September said that the struggle against the two should be continued.[95]

Shortly afterwards it was announced that Zhou Renshan had committed suicide. The removal of Zhou and Wang made it easier for the two factions to submit to the army's command; interestingly, no army officers were denounced.[96] On 5 September 1968 the Revolutionary Committee was finally established in Tibet at a formal gathering of 50,000 people in Lhasa. There was a temporary abeyance in the factional fighting as the Revolutionary Committee took over the running of the Party and the government in Tibet. Given the paramount importance of the army, it was natural that Zeng Yongya, as the head of the army, would assume the leadership of the committee. This allowed the Chinese to start to revive the Party and the general administrative structure in Tibet, which had ceased to function since the middle of 1966.

Ren Rong, who had played a leading role in the factional fighting, was named as one of the 13 Vice-Chairmen, suggesting that Ren had lost his position to Zeng, a position that was later reversed. There were twenty-seven committee members appointed to the Revolutionary Committee, 12 of whom were leaders of mass organisations, 10 from the army and 5 representing the cadres. Only 4 were Tibetan.[97]

With the establishment of the Revolutionary Committee Ngabo resurfaced as one of the leading Tibetan figures. He had been living in Beijing, cocooned by the Chinese, and he continued to reside there even after his new appointment, an indication that his position on the Committee was merely symbolic. During the Cultural Revolution all the factions had been instructed by Beijing not to criticise Ngabo or his family members or subject them to struggle sessions. Ngabo's position as the chief Tibetan negotiator during the 17-Point Agreement made him immune to any criticism from the Chinese. No other Tibetan had been afforded such privileges: even the Panchen Rinpoche had not been granted immunity during the Cultural Revolution. At first the Red Guards from the Minority Institute in Beijing had forced him to undergo a struggle session. Later, Red Guards from Tibet went to Beijing to investigate the 'crimes' of the Panchen Rinpoche and once again subjected him to brutal struggle sessions.[98] All other former Tibetan leaders had either been sent to prison or labelled as 'reactionaries'. The Cultural Revolution saw the destruction of the former Tibetan ruling élite: their class background made them enemies of the people whether they had supported the Chinese or not. Except for Ngabo, Tibetan aristocrats who had obtained high-ranking posts in the government were dismissed and sent to labour camps.

The Chinese always recognised that they could never hope to rule Tibet effectively without some measure of Tibetan support, and after the Cultural Revolution they began to promote Tibetan peasantry to the centre of leadership. Three Tibetans who were appointed to the Revolutionary Committee were said to be former 'serfs'. Notable among them was Pasang.

According to official reports she was born in 1938 and at the age of eighteen she ran away from home to join the PLA. The army sent her to study at the Minority Institute in China and the Party admitted her as a member in 1959. We know very little of what she did prior to her appointment to the Revolutionary Committee. All publications refer to her as 'Pasang'; no other names are given, and we don't even know if Pasang is her first name or her last.[99] Her appointment was significant because she was the first Tibetan from an ordinary background to occupy a leading position. There was no mention of Pasang's affiliation during the Cultural Revolution and her promotion was meant to signify that power had been transferred from the Tibetan aristocracy to the peasantry. The new Tibetan members of the committee represented a safe choice, because their class background as serfs in the old society ensured their fidelity to the Chinese and because they did not present any threat to either faction. As noted before, at a higher level, the Cultural Revolution remained a purely Chinese affair. It is worth noting that of the hundreds of pamphlets produced by the Red Guards not a single Tibetan name was mentioned in them as a power-holder: the power struggle was confined to the Chinese élite. No Tibetan had reached a position where he or she could think of competing for power with the Chinese cadres.

The formation of the Revolutionary Committee marked the official ending of the factional fighting. However, as far as the Tibetans were concerned, the end of the factional fighting did not lessen the official attack on Tibetan culture and identity. Chinese hostility towards Tibetan culture continued, as did officially condoned violence against people with bad class labels. Although Tibetans participated in the violence and factional politics, their participation was due to a high level of coercive persuasion by the Chinese authorities. For the Tibetans there was no question of whether to participate or not in the Cultural Revolution: an individual was faced with pressure from his or her work unit or commune to declare a position and to take part in the fighting.

The Nyemo Revolt

The ongoing attack on Tibetan culture had a devastating effect on all aspects of Tibetan society and inter-personal relations. After all, whatever its impact on élite politics, the Cultural Revolution was intended to be a conscious effort to transform every aspect of Tibetan life. For the radical Red Guards, the onslaught on Tibetan culture was induced by their impatience with what they saw as the slow pace of social change. At the time, it appeared as though the Chinese had succeeded in remoulding Tibetan society: Tibetans were driven with revolutionary fervour and took part in the destruction of temples and monasteries. There was extreme use of violence both by the

Tibetans and Chinese during the Cultural Revolution. The Chinese power to consign labels and extend patronage goes some way towards explaining this violence which allowed people who had bad class and political labels, and even their children, to be subjected to beatings, abuse or constant humiliation. Those who attacked people with a bad label could do so without any consequence because the violence was sanctioned by the Chinese authorities.

The Chinese began to rebuild the governing structure but the ensuing fighting made it almost impossible to restore order. Many local Chinese cadres were reluctant to yield to the new authority and remained loyal to their factional leaders, giving the authorities no choice but to allow local groups to forge a new order. By 1969 the Chinese had managed to achieve some degree of order and the authorities once again began to address the economic problems. In many areas the introduction of communes was resumed. These new economic and social policies further antagonised the Tibetans and, in 1969, the Chinese had to face a major revolt by the Tibetans.

It occurred in different parts of Tibet and there was no single leader or organisation. Its significance lay in its timing. This was in many ways the demarcation between the officially condoned revolt of the Cultural Revolution and the grass-roots uprising of the Tibetan people. The Cultural Revolution was a revolt of the Chinese, with the Tibetans coerced into taking part. But it may have raised the question, if the Chinese were allowed to rebel and demand better conditions, why shouldn't the Tibetans do likewise? In some areas the revolt was prompted by the Chinese attempt to resume introduction of the commune system. While in agricultural settlements it was relatively easy to set up communes, in the nomadic areas the Chinese had to round up individual families and force them to form new groups. The nomads could in turn refuse to co-operate by simply moving to a new camp.

While the revolt in Phala and other nomadic areas could be explained by the refusal to accept the commune system, at almost the same time a revolt started in an area west of Lhasa called Nyemo, less than a hundred kilometres from the city. The area had had its share of political upheavals during the Anti-Rebellion Campaign and the Cultural Revolution. It was, in fact, rural areas that had had to bear the brunt of the contemptuous attitude of the Chinese towards Tibetan culture. The revolt in Nyemo was led by a young nun called Thrinley Choedron. She was an unlikely leader. At the start of the revolt both the Chinese and the Tibetans found it difficult to distinguish what Thrinley Choedron was doing from the violent power seizure by Red Guards. Thrinley Choedron and her followers were identified as members of the Gyenlog faction on the grounds that they targeted senior cadres at the *xian* headquarters. It is interesting to note that while almost all rural areas had remained supporters of the Nyamdrel faction, Nyemo had supported the Gyenlog faction and throughout the Cultural Revolution there was fierce factional fighting in Nyemo *xian*. In fact the fighting continued there for three months after the founding of the Revolutionary Committee in Lhasa. In November 1968 there was a violent attempt to seize power by the Gyenlog faction. According to Chinese propaganda, the revolt in Nyemo broke out on 13 June, when Thrinley Choedron and her followers slaughtered fourteen cadres and soldiers of the PLA Propaganda team stationed in the Barkhor.

The initial Chinese response to the revolt was to treat it as a part of the ongoing factional fighting. There was very little attempt to intervene; however, soon it became apparent that the revolt was characterised less by revolutionary ideology than by the re-assertion of certain aspect of Tibetan culture. The Chinese soon realised that the symbolism and demands articulated by Thrinley Choedron were very different from the language of the Cultural Revolution.

At first, Thrinley Choedron and her followers targeted Chinese cadres and Tibetans who worked for them. This on the surface appeared to be attacking 'power-holders' in the *xian*. However, for Thrinley Choedron it wasn't a question of getting rid of capitalist roaders in the Party. She and her followers identified their target as 'the enemies of the faith' and, for them, the two-line struggle was reduced to the question of Tibetans and Chinese. Thrinley Choedron and her gang marched to the *xian* headquarters in Nyemo, armed with swords and spears, and proceeded to slaughter almost all of the Chinese there, along with their Tibetan workers.[100] The Tibetans who had supported the Chinese had their hands cut off. The uprising in Nyemo was characterised by extreme brutality. It was reported that some of the Chinese victims were set on fire while others had their arms and legs amputated. Today it is difficult to separate the facts from the myths, but a small museum to the 'martyrs' built in Nyemo by the Chinese displayed a number of horrific photographs showing the victims who were killed by Tibetans. The photographs show decomposed bodies and people who had had their limbs amputated by Thrinley Choedron and her gang.

Her fame spread quickly and attracted hundreds of followers. She had brought to the surface the latent anger of the Tibetans. Immediately, there were rumours that she was possessed by a local deity and that she had acquired supernatural and magical powers. It was said that she could not be overpowered by even fifteen men and that bullets did not harm her, not unexpected claims for a society always dominated by a belief in magic and supernatural power. The uprising quickly spread to other parts of Tibet until in the end more than eighteen counties were involved. The revolt attracted popular support from the local people and took the form of a millenarian movement.

The revolt of 1969 was inspired by the Tibetans' desire to regain some measure of social, psychological and cultural freedom. It was not, however, a conscious nationalistic uprising, but a cultural response to the chaos of the Cultural Revolution. The constant attack on Tibetan culture by the Chinese had eroded the Tibetans' confidence in their own value system. The Communist cadres had set about transforming every aspect of Tibetan behaviour but what they saw as social education was seen by the people as an attack on their way of life. One farmer told me that the Chinese had even criticised the Tibetan method of using a spade. This seemingly absurd behaviour illustrates the point that the people were forced to validate every action on ideological grounds. In the past, Tibetan farmers would tie a rope to a spade, so that while one person struck the spade into the ground, another person would pull the rope from the front.[101] A zealous cadre saw this as a waste of two people's energy and told them to stop using the spade in this way. More interesting still was the Chinese explanation: the cadre told the farmers that in the past they had invented this method because they wanted to conserve their energy since the fruits of their labour were expropriated by the manorial lords. Now, under socialism, as they were masters of their own labour, they should use all their vigour and energy in their work. Thus the mundane act of using a spade had been reduced to an ideological issue which the Tibetans naturally saw as another attack on their traditions. In this way every act and social relationship was judged in terms of either the socialist way of doing things – which was scientific and modern – or the traditional Tibetan way, which was seen as irrational and backward. The total negation of traditional Tibetan cultural and religious authority elicited an extreme response from the Tibetans. In some areas, the leaders of the revolt claimed to be possessed by Ling Gesar Gyalpo, Tibet's mythical hero, who in old tales restores order and righteousness in the Land of Snow.

The Chinese had to deploy the PLA in Nyemo and other areas to suppress the revolt. Thrinley Choedron and her followers fled into the mountains from where they waged a guerrilla war, but they were no match for the PLA, who eventually succeeded in capturing them. Thrinley Choedron and fifteen of her followers were brought to Lhasa and publicly executed, allowing the Chinese once again to reassert their absolute power in Tibet and reinforcing their claim that 'under the sun there was no escape from the Party'. The public execution was naturally meant to show that the Party's power was all-pervasive and invincible but the suppression of the Tibetan revolt also served to remind Tibetans that the chaos of the Cultural Revolution was in many ways a carefully orchestrated affair which had been initiated by the Party. In this respect the Cultural Revolution in Tibet was a Chinese affair in which Tibetans were merely instruments of a power struggle among the Chinese élite.

A nationalistic interpretation of the events in Nyemo tends to stress the

Tibetanness of the revolt and view it as an anti-Chinese uprising.[102] However, at this stage we do not know how far the events in Nyemo and other areas can be separated from the turmoil of the Cultural Revolution, and it has to be remembered that it was the Chinese authorities who highlighted the revolt as a nationalist and a separatist movement. This does not necessarily indicate that the rebellion led by Thrinley Choedron was a serious challenge to Chinese rule or that it was, in fact, a separatist revolt. On the contrary, if it had been a nationalist uprising, as claimed by official propaganda, it would have been unlikely that the Chinese gave it as much publicity as they did. There was, after all, a general agreement in China at the time that the Cultural Revolution had got out of control and that the army was now being urged to use its power to put an end to the disorder and that it was publicised all over China that there were reactionaries who were bent on subverting socialism under the guise of the Cultural Revolution. In this context, the army and the leadership emerging in Tibet may have used a localised millenarian movement created by the extreme psychological and physical brutality of the Cultural Revolution as a pretext to suppress factional groups and to urge the people to put aside their differences and oppose Tibetan separatism. It is, as we will see in the next chapter, not inconceivable that in order to unify different factions, the Chinese leaders may have begun to emphasise external danger and the enemies of the revolution. In this context it was natural that the Chinese authorities would use the threat of Tibetan separatists and reactionaries as a rallying point.

For the majority of Tibetans the high politics of China was remote and irrelevant. For them the trauma of the Cultural Revolution would linger in their minds, and evidence of the appalling destruction of Tibet's cultural heritage would haunt the Tibetan landscape. The people who lived through the period still express their incomprehension and describe it as the time 'the sky fell to the earth'.[103]

THIRTEEN

Revolution Postponed?

Tibet emerged from the Cultural Revolution bewildered by three years of chaos. Its people had survived by appearing to comply with every twist and turn in Chinese politics. On the surface it seemed that the Chinese had succeeded in assimilating the Tibetans: all expression of Tibetan identity and culture was forbidden with the single exception of the language, now the only marker of Tibet's separateness from China. This too, had undergone changes to suit the egalitarian ideology. Words such as '*ga ra*' (blacksmith) were expunged because of connotations of class exploitation and replaced by more neutral terms, such as '*lag shes pa*' (craftsman).[1] Even names were affected by the Cultural Revolution: people gave their children names that showed their revolutionary credentials and love of the new motherland, in the hope that this would provide some kind of buttress against charges of being counter-revolutionary.[2]

The formation of the Revolutionary Committee, and Chinese attempts to impose some measure of order, did not decrease their hostility towards Tibetan culture and tradition. For the Communists, everything associated with Tibet was regarded as a remnant of the feudal past and had to be destroyed. For the Tibetans, the question of cultural rights was more real than the superficially imposed struggle between the 'two lines'. But they were in no position to challenge the Chinese, as any opposition would have provoked further repression. By the beginning of 1970, all the monasteries and temples had been vandalised by the Red Guards and left to ruin.[3] The monks who had once dominated Tibetan society disappeared and religious practice of any kind was forbidden; even clandestine worship was not possible. All available time was taken up by endless rounds of revolutionary meetings. It seemed as though the Communists had succeeded in remoulding the Tibetans, who now supposedly held the same values as peasants in China. Most of all, the cult and worship of Mao appeared to have replaced that of the Buddhist deities. His portrait adorned every house and work place. *Om Mani Pad Ma Hum*, the mantra of the Buddha of Compassion, the patron deity of Tibet, was supplanted by *Mao Tsetung wan sui*.[4]

The Tibetans and the Chinese all wore standard uniforms and showed their proletarian consciousness and lifestyle by deliberately sewing patches onto their suits. To all intents and purposes, Tibet had by 1970 ceased to have any distinctive characteristics. It was surmised that socialism would automatically cause all national identities and traditional loyalties to vanish. The Communists believed they had managed to level all cultural differences between the Tibetans and the Chinese, and had succeeded in establishing a unitary proletarian culture. They assumed that the issue of cultural difference was therefore no longer a problem.

The establishment of the Revolutionary Committee soon led to a lull in the factional fighting, but this did not mean that the factions had disappeared. The Revolutionary Committee, now the supreme organ of government in Tibet, was composed of members of the two factions and the army. It became apparent that, in reality, the latter had succeeded in capturing power at all levels. It had more or less forced the two factions to stop fighting, and, as in all parts of China, it was the only body which had the organisation and discipline to start rebuilding the Party and governing structure.

Reconstruction of the Political System

The Chinese began to organise Revolutionary Committees at the local level, in a way which reflected the trends at the regional level where the army maintained the leading role, as the chairman of the Regional Committee. What was most interesting about the Regional Committee was that it allowed the Chinese to appoint some Tibetan activists, such as Pasang, Ragdi and Thupten Nyima, to leading posts. Ragdi, who became a member of the Revolutionary Committee in Nagchu-ka, was later to become one of the most important Tibetan Party members. Pasang was simultaneously a member of the TAR Revolutionary Committee and of the local Revolutionary Committee in Nang county. These two appear to have been able to prove their ideological commitment to the Party and to the 'motherland', and their underprivileged class background enabled the Chinese to proclaim that former serfs had been fully liberated and had taken control of the running of Tibet. It was clear that the Cultural Revolution had boosted the careers of these men as indigenous leaders, bringing them into the national political arena for the first time. As we will see they were later to occupy increasingly important roles, creating a semblance of Tibetan participation at the highest level of the regional CCP. There was no doubt that they achieved their position entirely because the Chinese needed their support and the Party had groomed them for their new rank. The Tibetans disparagingly referred to them as '*hortsun chen*', literally meaning 'those who carried out their task diligently'.

The Chinese slowly began to rebuild the Party and the governing structures at all levels and by the end of 1970 were able to announce that all seventy counties of Tibet had set up a Revolutionary Committee. Although the new governing body was supposed to be composed of an alliance of all factions, the dominance of the army inevitably led to an increasing assertion of the military's role in civil affairs and administration. Areas close to the Indian border had in fact been under the control of the army for a long time but even in those areas there was a new emphasis on the role of the army as well as on the campaign for restoring order. The army was thus not only projected as the unifying element, but more importantly, it gained status as a bulwark against the renewed fear of external threats, which was heightened in part to divert public attention away from domestic factional fighting. The army's significance was further strengthened at the 9th Party Congress by the designation of Lin Biao as the chosen successor to Mao.

During this time China did in fact fear a pre-emptive attack by the Soviet Union. While China had been preoccupied with the Cultural Revolution, the Russians had built up massive military strength and had deployed an army of more than a million soldiers along the border with China. By 1969 this had led to military clashes between the two countries. Tibet was not directly connected with the Sino-Russian border conflict but was still regarded by the Chinese as a vulnerable frontier region. But it was the ethnic conflict developing in Xinjiang which had serious implications in Tibet. Although the Cultural Revolution had shown that the Chinese had total control in Tibet, the Chinese were nevertheless well aware of the potential for a crisis to develop, and of the problems still posed by the Dalai Lama and his followers in exile. The suppression of the Tibetan revolt in 1969 and the public execution of Thrinley Choedron provided the Chinese with a scapegoat and an issue on which all the Chinese in Tibet could unite.

The gradual death of the factional schism at the end of 1969 did not bring an end to the power struggle among the Chinese élite in Tibet, and it soon became evident that factionalism was still a problem. During the first few years of the fighting, both sides had accused the other of being Liu Shaoqi's agent in the region but now the official authorities identified Wang Qimei and Zhou Renshan as the chief agents of Liu and as the 'capitalist roaders' in Tibet. The selection of two main leaders of each faction must have been designed to placate both sides, with Wang and Zhang being most likely used as scapegoats. As long as the situation in Beijing remained in the doldrums and the army was in control, it was unlikely that factional fighting would flare up in Tibet. It was therefore a good opportunity for the army to maintain a check on both sides.

The dominance of the army was marked by the virtual hand-over of civil administration to the PLA. Its paramount power became clear when, in February 1970, the army organised a small rally in Lhasa at which they announced that the dependants of the PLA would receive preferential treatment over cadres.[5] The principal aim of the Cultural Revolution had been to get rid of this sort of privilege, enjoyed by senior cadres. The army justified its claims for special status on the grounds that only it could restore order and deal with the external threat posed by Tibet's strategic position. It therefore became the principal arbiter of ideological and practical issues. When in January 1970 there was a dispute among the staff at the *Tibet Daily* regarding 'ideological erring' by the deputy director, the staff wanted him to be subjected to a struggle session and overthrown. Since renewed fighting in such an important centre would have ramifications beyond the confines of the paper's office, the army propaganda team moved into the office and took on the role of disinterested mediator.[6] In this way, the army was able to portray itself as the only group capable of maintaining order in the region. The army leaders knew that they would still need to carry out propaganda campaigns to elicit further support from the people. Under the guise of a campaign known as 'support the Government and cherish the people' the army was able to intrude into all activities, thus ensuring its dominance in all spheres of activity.

The leadership in Beijing was happy to leave the direction of the new policy in military hands as they began to carry out reforms and reinstate policies that had been abandoned during the Cultural Revolution, and to recreate the rudimentary administration that had been set up during the first few years of the 1960s. Most importantly, the Chinese realised that education and training programmes that had been in the early stages of implementation before the start of the Cultural Revolution had to be revived. Tibetan students who had been sent to China for further education had returned to Tibet without having completed their training, their time and energy taken up with revolutionising. After the formation of the Revolutionary Committee, the authorities had dispersed many of the young Red Guards into rural areas, ostensibly to learn from the masses but in reality to remove to remote areas the radical youth who had been encouraged to rebel and question the party, so that they could not foment any further problems. This resulted in some of the ablest young people being dispatched to rural areas to do manual work. While this did not have serious implications in China, in Tibet one of the main problems confronting the Chinese was the lack of educated and literate Tibetans to work as administrators. Young Tibetans who were sent to rural areas felt isolated and disillusioned. Moreover, because of their literacy in Chinese and Tibetan, they often ended up assisting peasant leaders who had been promoted to high-ranking posts because of their correct class background and who in most cases did not know Chinese and were often illiterate in Tibetan, and thus unable to carry out effective administration in the communes and production brigades.

But during the 1970s the Chinese were not particularly worried about these issues. They had advocated a policy of total assimilation and the Party had ruled out any concessions to the local population. They had given up all pretence of ruling the region with some measure of support from the local population. Their principle was that Tibetans and Chinese alike must move in unison, and what was good for China was good for Tibet. Although on paper Tibet was continually referred to as an 'Autonomous Region', this was a constitutional fiction. Tibet was treated as though it was a suburb of Beijing.

The main concern in the early 1970s was building and strengthening agricultural production. This was achieved by the rapid introduction of the commune system throughout Tibet. As mentioned in an earlier chapter, the Chinese had started to set up communes in 1966, but this had been interrupted by the Cultural Revolution, at the height of which (1967–9) agriculture had been neglected, resulting in severe setbacks in its development. In some areas, the arable land had been left untouched for years and because there was no one to tend the cattle, they grazed in the fields at will. By the early 1970s it had become imperative that there should be an all-out effort to develop agriculture and increase production. With the communes came the extreme egalitarian social structure desired by the Communists.

In August 1971 the 1st session of the Tibetan Autonomous CPC deputy congress was held in Lhasa. This marked the new policy of rebuilding the Party and governing structure. The meeting announced the dismissal of Zhou Renshan and Wang Qimei from the Party committee.[7] This marked a triumph for Ren Rong, who emerged as the 1st General Secretary of the regional CPC.

But new policy did not put an end to ideological campaigning. In fact, the Tibetans were to experience an extremely vigorous campaign focused narrowly on studying the teachings of Chairman Mao, and energetically promoting the cult of Mao. On the theoretical level, the Party stressed the recognition of what was called the 'four existences' during the socialist period: the existence of class contradiction, the struggle between the two lines (between socialism and capitalism); the danger of capitalist restoration, and the danger of the invasion of imperialism and modern revisionism.[8] This meant that the Party could not countenance any idea of peace, either within the party or within society in general. It therefore held frequent 'struggle meetings' in communes and work units, with the main targets among the Tibetans being those who had bad class and political labels, this time accused of obstructing socialist development. The ongoing subjection of individuals to struggle sessions and purges kept the people under control, and allowed the authorities also to carry out periodic purges within the Party.

The attempt to rebuild the Party and other organisations was accompanied by another campaign known as 'struggle, criticism and transformation'. The army was not prepared to countenance any of the free debate and lawlessness of the previous years and saw that the campaign was carried out in an orderly and disciplined manner, under its command and direction. In many ways it was contrived to give the army a leading role, as was evident from the fact that the army's propaganda team became the main vanguard of the new movement, and that it stressed the role of the army as the pillar of the Proletarian Dictatorship.[9]

The campaign once more brought class struggle to the forefront of politics, and the need for a reconciliation among the Chinese élite in Tibet led to further attacks on the Tibetans. The renewed emphasis on class struggle meant that Tibetans who had bad class and political labels were once again dragged out for struggle sessions and made the targets of the new campaign. The Chinese still maintained a policy of cultural assimilation, which meant that they were unrelenting in their hostility towards Tibetan tradition and culture. They found in the commune system an even more effective method of assimilation. The highly organised life in a commune allowed the Chinese to reshape every aspect of the Tibetan way of life.

The importance of the army was appreciated partly because of external considerations. Chinese leaders had realised that the chief threat for China came from the Soviet Union and with it the question not only of ideological rivalry, but also of unsettled border disputes. Any war with the Soviet Union would have dire consequences for China. The Sino–Soviet border was populated by minority groups who had been held in check by the threat of force, and already many Uygurs and Kazakhs living close to the border had migrated to the other side before the start of the Cultural Revolution. Moreover, the Russians had adopted a much more liberal attitude than the Chinese policy towards minorities who, according to official figures, constituted only 6 per cent of China's total population, but 90 per cent of the people in the border areas.[10] All these problems influenced Chinese consideration of its strategic position in Tibet. The concern for security was therefore paramount in the minds of the Chinese leaders.

Tibet had no direct territorial or ethnic connection with Russia,[11] but it did have strategic importance in the context of the general improvement in Indo–Soviet relations since the early 1960s, which the Chinese viewed with increasing alarm. The relationship between India and China had reached a nadir and showed no signs of improvement. Since 1962, India had undergone a massive military modernisation programme, and its army was no longer ill prepared. The Indians had carried out extensive road construction in the foothills of the Himalayas and had reorganised their logistical apparatus. From its position in Beijing, the leadership saw China under siege, with the Russians in the north and the Indians in the south. Its fears were compounded by the troublesome minorities – who could easily turn anti-Chinese – living close to land borders. Given this strategic challenge, it was natural that the leadership in Beijing should allow the military dominance of Tibet.

The Lin Biao Affair and a New Party Secretary

In late 1971 Tibet, like the whole of China, awoke to the shocking news of an attempted *coup d'état* by Lin Biao. The actual political events surrounding the incident did not have any connection with Tibet, but the fact that the army had acquired its influence in Tibet due to the patronage of Lin Biao meant that his death could have serious implications there. Nevertheless, it was in the interest of the Chinese leaders to minimise the effects and the subsequent purge was carried out quietly and secretly, without attracting public attention.

The Lin Biao affair could not have come at a worst time. The fact that Lin made a dash for Russia seemed to point to the fact that the Soviet Union was a real danger to China. In Tibet the only visible consequence of the attempted coup was the removal of Zeng Yongya from the chairmanship of the Revolutionary Committee. (Zeng was closely associated with Lin Biao's 4th Field Army, but even so, his removal may in fact have been a result of manoeuvres by his opponent Ren Rong, who succeeded him as the leading political figure in Tibet.)[12] Zeng had not been given the job of 1st Secretary of the regional CCP because at the time Party organisation was in disarray, and the CCP devoted the whole of 1970 to rebuilding its organisation. He was now transferred to a low-profile job in China and never regained any power in the Party or government. The demise of Zeng marked a new phase in Tibet and was an indication that order had finally been restored.

By the middle of 1971 the Chinese had succeeded in restructuring much of the Party apparatus in Tibet. The regional CCP, formed in 1965, was finally able to hold its first Party Congress – a sign of the end of the factional divide. At the same time it was announced that Tibet would be reduced from the status of Military Region to that of Military Area, which placed it further under the direct control of Chengdu. The change may not even have been noticed by the Tibetan people, but no one could have failed to notice the appointment in August 1971 of Ren Rong – secretary of the Revolutionary Committee; former political commissar of the Tibet Military Region, and long-term opponent of Zeng Yongya – as the 1st Secretary of the regional CCP.

Although the choice of Ren Rong once again confirmed the supremacy of the army, it also marked the beginnings of a move towards civilian rule. Ren, who had come to Tibet during the Sino–Indian War, was not contaminated with the accusation of having compromised with reactionary groups, unlike many of the other high-ranking cadres who had entered Tibet in the early 1950s. Before his arrival in Tibet, he had served as the director of the Political Department of the Chinese People's Volunteers in Korea; his credentials were therefore impeccable. However, unlike his predecessor Zhang Guohua, he had not occupied the post of Commander of the Tibet District nor that of 1st Political Commissar to the armed forces in Tibet, posts which would have given him some degree of power in the army. However, his long association with the army ensured him a measure of their support, and just a few years later, in 1975, Ren was able to acquire the post of 1st Political Commissar of the Tibet Military Area, further consolidating his position in Tibet.

Despite the change in personalities, there was no drastic shift in policy. There was no attempt to bring back either the Political Consultative Committee or the Regional People's Congress, the two institutions on which the Tibetans were mostly strongly represented. The Revolutionary Committee still remained the supreme organ of power and authority. However, there was no doubt that once the Party structure was restored, everyone would look to it as the locus of power in the region. The one significant change took place in the regional CCP. When it was first established in 1965 there were no Tibetans occupying any important posts in the Party. But in 1971, of the seven deputy secretaries, two were Tibetans: Pasang (who was also the only woman holding a high post in the Party) and Tian Bao. As one of the few Tibetans who had joined the Long March, Tian Bao was a person of great symbolic importance for the Chinese, and in October 1976 he was also appointed 2nd Political Commissar of the Tibet Military District, thus becoming one of the few Tibetans to hold both military and civilian posts. Nevertheless, coming as he did from Kham, outside the TAR, Tian Bao was regarded by many as an outsider. Tibetans such as Ragdi and Pasang were labelled as '*Yerlang Zhingtren*', literally meaning 'peasant[s] who had stood up' – people who were committed to the new society and who could therefore be relied on.

The appointment of three Tibetans, Tian Bao, Ragdi and Pasang, to a senior level did not mean that the Chinese had decided to confer any degree of authority on them. Their importance lay in their symbolism rather than in any political power. Pasang, orphaned at the age of thirteen, was proclaimed to be the daughter of a 'slave',[13] while Tian Biao, the pioneer Tibetan communist, represented the new Tibet. But in the final analysis it did not matter who was appointed leader in Tibet: in the 1970s, the regional Party diligently carried out directives from the Centre and saw itself as the Centre's representative in the region. This left no room for local initiative, particularly in the field of economics.

Economically the communes remained the cornerstone of production. In June 1970, Xinhua announced that 34 per cent of Tibetan villages had been formed into communes and a year later this figure was increased to 60 per cent.[14] By 1975 the Chinese were claiming that the communisation of the whole of Tibet had been achieved.[15] Communes had been in existence in China for over fifteen years and had undergone many changes. The push towards a rapid communisation programme in Tibet was impelled not only by the desire to increase economic productivity, but also because, as noted earlier, the commune system provided a unitary administrative and production organisation which suited the Party's objective of achieving order and control. The communes in Tibet were small, less than a thousand people on average, the equivalent of a single production brigade in China.[16] Thus with the introduction of the communes the Chinese were able to realise the twin objectives of restoring order among the masses and meeting their economic and ideological objectives.

The authorities urged the people to hold meetings in the fields so that they could devote more time to production. The new emphasis on increasing production was prompted by the fear of war, and this led to the campaign known as 'Be prepared for war and natural disasters'. The campaign had two effects on the Tibetans. First, throughout the 1970s much time was spent on physical labour, mobilised by campaigns to 'dig tunnels and store grain'.[17] Massive work groups built tunnels and air raid shelters – in Lhasa, hundreds of people were forced to dig in the nearby hills, and in the rural areas the Chinese began to recruit and train Tibetan militia. Second, great emphasis was placed on grain production, in line with campaigns to learn from the model Dazhai commune. This was to have serious repercussions for Tibet.

These decisions were enacted entirely by Beijing: there was a uniformity of agricultural policy throughout China and no exception was made in the case of Tibet. Therefore, the local Party officials had no choice but to implement the policies as dictated from above and the cadres were fearful of questioning their feasibility. A case in point was the demand for grain production, which was naturally taken to mean that wheat should be grown, rather than barley. Although there was no attempt to abandon barley production, the Tibetans, who preferred to eat Tsamba produced from barley, saw the new emphasis on wheat cultivation as a sinister plot by the Chinese. The policy was disastrous. The wheat that was produced was of such poor quality that it could not be consumed by the people, while the disruption and initial difficulties in the commune system meant that the Tibetan peasantry faced their own economic setbacks. Many accounts given by refugees attest to the fact that, although there was a general increase in production, it did not bring about any improvement in people's living standards because most of the surplus was expropriated by the government.

While the Tibetans were encouraged to learn from the agricultural example of Dazhai, on the industrial front they were urged to emulate the success of the Daqing oil field. This led the Chinese to claim that they had introduced modern industries to the roof of the world. The industrial development was in fact limited to small-scale motor and other machinery repair shops, with the largest industrial project being the development of a power plant for electricity. This was not only a basic necessity, but also provided the Chinese with one of their chief propaganda weapons: the claim that they had electrified Tibet. However, the Chinese realised that the electrification of the whole of Tibet would require a massive technological and economic investment, which in the 1970s they could ill afford. And since they could not afford investment the industrialisation of the roof of the world remained a myth.

While the Chinese authorities were able to defuse the factional alliances among the Tibetans, it was more difficult to eradicate the conflicts between the Chinese cadres, who were in competition for power. While no Tibetan could be said to be allied to any particular group in Beijing, this was not the case with the Chinese. Both military and civilian cadres were closely linked with different groupings in Beijing, so any changes in the composition of the leadership in Beijing had ramifications in Tibet. But it was difficult to gauge how far factional politics was influencing events. During the Cultural Revolution political divisions within the CCP had been discussed overtly; as a result, not only outsiders but people in Tibet and China had been able to see the depth of the factional divide within the CCP. But after 1969 the Party became highly secretive again and internal affairs were discussed behind closed doors.

By the early 1970s, it appeared on the surface as if factional politics had been held in check. There was a new emphasis on Party unity, and the new slogan was 'unity is the life of the Party'.[18] In 1973 the Chinese launched another Anti-Revisionist Campaign and the cadres were told to 'rectify the style of work'. This suggested that the campaign was not directed at the masses, who were told to concentrate on economic production, but at the CCP members and cadres. Although the reasons for the new campaign were concealed in the florid language of anti-revisionism, it was clear that the main aim was to prevent the formation of the sort of factions that had recently besieged Chinese politics. The cadres and Party members were warned against 'organising mountain strongholds' and 'attempting to split the Party and the army'.[19] It was pointed out that in carrying out the campaign, the Party 'must not get entangled in old [accounts of] history'.[20] There could be no doubt that the Party would succeed in unifying its members. Yet the Revolutionary Committee was not abolished until 1979.

In Tibet, it was relatively easy for the Chinese to make the adjustment from the chaotic situation of the Cultural Revolution to a more orderly society. In 1972 a few of the former Tibetan leaders who had been denounced as reactionaries or class enemies resurfaced and the Party also revived some of the institutions that had been ignored during the Cultural Revolution. Phagpa Gelek Namgyal was reinstated as Vice-Chairman of the 4th CPPCC, and the Tibetan Women's Association was also resurrected, with Ngabo's wife, Tseten Dolkar, as its Vice-President.[21] That same year the people of Lhasa witnessed something remarkable: a few Chinese and Tibetan workmen moved into the Tsuglhakhang, and started to repair the damage inflicted during the Cultural Revolution. A month later Prince Norodom Sihanouk of Cambodia came to Lhasa, the first foreign leader to visit Tibet.[22] Since he was a devout Buddhist, the Chinese authorities had wanted to show him that the Tibetans were free to practise their religion.

In 1974 Zhou Enlai told Ngabo that the Panchen Rinpoche should be released from prison, but before this could be put into effect[23] Zhou himself became a target of criticism under the guise of an anti-Confucius campaign. We will see later that the Panchen also became a victim of this new campaign.

Sino–US Rapprochement

After the Cultural Revolution China's chief concern in Tibet was its strategic position. The Chinese watched developments in South Asia with concern. Ever since the Sino–Indian war, China and India's arch-enemy, Pakistan, had become China's strongest ally. Because of this, America decided to use Pakistan as the conduit for its clandestine diplomacy with China. In July 1971 Henry Kissenger made his secret visit to Beijing via Pakistan. This was followed by President Nixon's historic visit to China in July of the following year. The visit led to the normalization of relations between the two countries. The Sino–American rapprochement had repercussions worldwide, but the implications for India were dramatic. It was now India's turn to feel that she was under siege, surrounded by Pakistan to the west and east, the Chinese to the north and the Americans in the Indian Ocean. India's response was to formalise its ties with the Soviet Union. In August 1972, just a few weeks after Nixon's visit to Beijing, the Soviet foreign minister Andrei Gromyko travelled to New Delhi and a treaty of peace, friendship and co-operation was signed between the two countries. The agreement actually sounded like a mutual defence pact, with one of the clauses stating, 'in the event of either being subjected to an attack or a threat thereof, the High Contracting Parties shall immediately enter into mutual consultations in order to remove such threat and to take appropriate effective measures to ensure peace and the security of their countries.'[24] Thus, by the beginning of the 1970s, the problems between

China and India were becoming entangled in the global strategic triangle of the great powers, the United States, the Soviet Union and China.

This new Sino–American alliance had serious implications in Tibet and for the political activities of the exile community. The Americans had maintained their clandestine aid to the Tibetans in India, and the guerrilla base in Mustang had been financed by the CIA. Since its inception there had been a strong lobby among American officials opposed to involvement with the exiled Tibetans. In the early 1960s, many in the State Department and the CIA had favoured supporting India rather than giving separate aid to the Tibetans. For this reason, almost all the Tibetans who had been trained at Camp Hale in Colorado were transferred to join a Tibetan group working for the Indian army. The Indians had established a secret Tibetan army base near Dehra Dun at Chakrata, more commonly known to the Tibetans as Unit Twenty-Two.

Since 1963 the Americans and the Indians had maintained joint control of the exiled Tibetans' clandestine activities inside Tibet, but this became increasingly difficult. There were serious disagreements between India and the USA about the best strategy for the Tibetan unit, disagreements which represented the divergent needs of the Indians and the CIA. For India, the long-term value of a Tibetan force lay in its potential combat behind the Chinese line, with the Tibetans engaged in active fighting. The Americans, however, no longer saw China as the main threat to their interests in Asia and therefore told the Tibetans to reduce the number of men in Mustang. The Tibetans were reluctant to agree, because they felt that Mustang allowed them freedom of operation, whereas the group in India was firmly under the command of the Indian army. Both the CIA and the Indians wanted to maintain a comfortable distance from the daily operations of the Mustang base.[25] This suited the Tibetans.

Since the middle of the 1960s many of the trained personnel from Mustang had been transferred to work with the Indian army and the last arms drop was made in the early 1960s.[26] The Tibetans were also facing pressure from the Nepalese Government, but as long as King Mahendra was still in power, they were relatively safe. Nevertheless, the Nepalese Government was under pressure from the Chinese to curb the activities in Mustang. In 1964, the Nepalese Government dispatched a three-man commission to investigate the situation there, and demanded that the Tibetans surrender their arms. The Tibetans denied that they had any arms and the Nepalese accepted the surrender of twelve rifles. The Nepalese knew this was just a charade for the benefit of the Chinese and they duly informed the Chinese that they were satisfied with the situation in Mustang and that the Tibetans were bona fide refugees. In 1969 Crown Prince Birendra visited the Tibetan camps and met the new leader, Gyatho Wangdu.

By the middle 1960s, the CIA was meeting only a fraction of the cost of maintaining the base in Mustang. In fact, in 1965, the CIA told the Tibetans that they would gradually reduce funding, with the aim of stopping it altogether in 1968.[27] A decision to terminate CIA aid to the Tibetans was made long before Kissinger's secret mission to China, prompted by disagreements within the CIA about the value of the Tibetans in American global objectives. Also, once the Sino–Soviet rift became open confrontation, the USA no longer saw China as the main threat to its interest in Asia. The CIA had anyway never envisaged the Mustang group as an active fighting unit, and had told the Tibetans to stop attacking inside Tibet. America had lost much of its anti-Chinese fervour, and its strategic requirements had also changed. Western Tibet was guarded by the soldiers from the North-West Military Region of China, the same group that was primarily responsible for resisting any possible Soviet threat on China's northern border. In discouraging the Tibetans in Mustang from attacking the Chinese, the Americans were trying to ensure that the PLA was free to concentrate on the border with the Soviet Union. The CIA wanted to use the Tibetans as an intelligence-gathering group, and saw their role during the 1960s as long-term information-gathering, whereas the Tibetans saw themselves engaged in active raids into Tibet. The CIA's decision to wind down the operation in Mustang was a serious blow for the Tibetans, who had told the CIA that they wanted to increase the number of men operating there.

By the time the CIA aid came to an end, the group in Mustang was riddled with regional and sectarian feud, as well as with accusations of financial mismanagement. These problems were tearing the group apart. The Tibetan government-in-exile had maintained limited control over the group and had tried to defuse some of the problems, but to no effect. In 1967 Dharamsala sent Phuntsog Tashi Takla and Lhamo Tsering to Mustang to investigate and solve the problems there, but their trip did not put an end to the internal fighting. Baba Yeshi and his followers refused to co-operate with them. In fact they made counter-accusations against the Dalai Lama's brother, Gyalo Dhundup, claiming that he had misappropriated funds destined for Mustang. At the end of the 1960s, Gyalo Dhundup and Dharamsala tried to replace the ageing Baba Yeshi as the head of the Mustang base and summoned him to Dharamsala under a false pretence. When he arrived, he was told that he was not to return to Mustang but as an inducement he was offered the post of Deputy Chief of Security in the Dharamsala government. Baba Yeshi, who could barely read or write, was not prepared to accept a desk job in Dharamsala; popular myth holds that he remarked, 'I never held a pen and paper in my hands.' He and his bodyguards quietly escaped from Dharamsala, pursued by the Indian secret service, and by sheer cunning managed to reach Mustang. However, even before Yeshi's return the Mustang group had been thrown into confusion by rumours that Yeshi had been detained in Dharamsala. This caused immediate factional fighting. Gyalo Dhundup had not prepared the men in Mustang for the change, as he had thought the group was like a modern army, and that the commander could be replaced without much consequence. The men in Mustang, however, were held together not by discipline but by ties of traditional loyalties and when it was announced that Baba Yeshi had been replaced, all the men from his home region of Bathang decided to follow him. When Yeshi arrived in Mustang, Lhamo Tsering and others refused to recognise him as the leader. They told him that as far as they were concerned his presence in Mustang was illegal.[28] This led to Baba Yeshi forming a breakaway group.

The main Mustang group was now under the command of Gyatho Wangdu. He was a charismatic leader from Lithang in Kham. He had received training from the CIA and was the only one from his group to have survived parachuting into Kham in 1959. The CIA was not happy with the choice of Wangdu because they had not viewed him as a potential leader, but they agreed to accept Gyalo Dhundup's choice.[29] Under Gyatho Wangdu's leadership, the internal schism continued. He had the difficult task of uniting the group, and he did not succeed. Without financial aid from the CIA it was impossible for the Mustang group to carry on. The Tibetan leaders had decided to cover up the fact that the Americans had withdrawn their support, as they feared that it would be a severe blow to the morale of the men. But they had to accept that they had to wind down their activities and send men to India. The Indians were not willing to support the Tibetan operation in Mustang but they agreed to take the majority of the men into the Tibetan–Indian army. The Tibetans had hoped that they would be allowed to keep the group as a single unit under Tibetan command, but the Indians wanted the men to merge with the existing Tibetan army unit under Indian command.[30]

One of the main problems facing the CIA was that the relationship between India and the United States had reached a new low point. Mrs Gandhi and President Nixon held a deep personal animosity towards each other.[31] The Americans had based their policy for South Asia on support for Pakistan, and they were suspicious of India's attitude towards them. This made it impossible for India and the Americans to co-operate over Tibet. After Bangladesh gained its independence, it was very difficult for the Americans to aid the Tibetans. In 1971 the struggle for independence by the Bengalis in East Pakistan had reached a crisis point. Both the Americans and the Chinese shared an identical policy and supported the despotic military rulers of Pakistan, with the Chinese accusing India of creating a 'puppet Bangladesh'. There was a real danger that, were India to intervene in Bangladesh, China would support Pakistan. During Kissinger's meeting with Zhou Enlai, the Chinese made it known that they 'would not be indifferent if India attacked Pakistan'.[32]

During the Bangladesh war, the Indian Government deployed the secret contingent of Tibetan soldiers, which numbered between 7,000 and 10,000 men.[33] They were very successful and in many cases bore the brunt of the fighting in Bangladesh.[34] India's success in liberating Bangladesh confirmed China's fears about the potential of an increased Indian military presence in the Himalayas. China told the Americans that if India was allowed to 'dismember' Pakistan, it would set a precedent by which 'other countries might be dismembered by Indian–Soviet collusion'.[35] This statement undoubtedly contained a resonance of the situation in Tibet.[36] The Chinese saw the existence of the Tibetan resistance group in Mustang as a potential danger and were determined that the group should be destroyed. It is not known whether the question of aid to the Tibetans featured in any of the early secret talks between the Americans and Chinese, but it is likely that both sides would have assumed that the normalization of relations between the two countries would lead naturally to a termination of the CIA's support for the Tibetans.

Events in Nepal also became unfavourable for the Tibetans. In 1972 King Mahendra died and was succeeded by Prince Birendra. The former king had been sympathetic to the Tibetans and turned a blind eye to their activities, but his son wanted to move Nepal closer to China and was not willing to tolerate the Tibetans. Moreover, the relationship between India and Nepal was at a low point, and the new Nepali king tried to play off India against China. The Chinese had also encouraged Nepal to look towards Beijing, and in February 1970, Birendra made an official visit there. In his welcoming speech Zhou Enlai referred to Nepal's problem with India when he announced that China would 'firmly support' Nepal's struggle against 'foreign interference', in defence of her 'national independence'.[37] China's attempts to woo Nepal are clear from the records of foreign aid received. In 1960 Chinese aid to Nepal represented only 3.3 per cent of the total foreign aid received by the kingdom, but ten years later this figure had reached 19.3 per cent. In 1973 the Chinese agreed to build both a major ring road around Kathmandu and the Kathmandu–Bhaktapur trolley bus service.[38] The first demand the Chinese made on Nepal was to rationalise the situation in the Nepalese consulate in Lhasa. The consulate, the only foreign representation in Tibet, was situated in the centre of Lhasa and employed a large staff of ethnic Tibetans who held Nepalese citizenship. Many of them were sympathetic to the Tibetans and, having been recruited by Gyalo Dhundup and the Tibetan resistance group in India, had turned the consulate into a spy centre for the Tibetans. The Nepalese agreed to dismiss almost all the ethnic Tibetans employed, and to move the consulate to the outskirts of the city.[39]

In 1973 the Nepalese started to demand that the Tibetans surrender their arms and disband the Mustang base. This was another severe blow to the Tibetans. The Indians were reluctant to provide any assistance and had refused to allow the Tibetans to maintain their own army. The Tibetans therefore quickly hatched a plan to hide a substantial amount of the arms in the mountains and disband the men or send them to join the Indian army.[40] Before this could be realised, the Nepalese stepped up the pressure and demanded an immediate surrender. They offered to resettle all the men and provide one million dollars in aid.[41] Baba Yeshi and his followers were isolated from the main group, and had no means of financial support. They therefore had no choice but to surrender. The main group under the leadership of Gyatho Wangdu were determined not to lose the weapons to the Nepalese. In an attempt to stall them, Gyatho Wangdu promised that the arms would be surrendered on an annual basis, within three years, but this was considered unacceptable.

For the Dalai Lama, Mustang was turning out to be an international embarrassment. For years the Dalai Lama and the Tibetans had maintained the image of a non-violent and peaceful movement, and the Mustang incident could damage their international reputation. The Dalai Lama readily agreed to urge the men to surrender. A recorded message from him was taken to Mustang by Phuntsog Tashi Takla and played to the men in different camps. Gyatho Wangdu and the other leaders had no choice but to surrender, and by the middle of 1974 most of the men had surrendered to the Nepalese army. Gyatho Wangdu knew that his position as leader meant the Nepalese would not allow him to go free, and in fact the Nepalese army had already arrested Lhamo Tsering and other leaders a few months earlier and were in effect holding them as a hostages. This had led to further disintegration and loss of morale among the men. Wangdu, probably out of fear that he too would be arrested and sent to prison, decided to escape with his men to India – a decision that proved fatal. For some weeks Wangdu and his men managed to evade the army, but on 15 September it was announced in the Rastriya Panchayat (Nepalese Parliament) that the army had intercepted Wangdu and his men at Tinker, in the district of Jumla. Skirmishes broke out, and Wangdu and almost all his men were killed.

The Nepalese Government invited the international press to an exhibition of the captured weapons in a park in Kathmandu and accused the Tibetans of creating a reign of terror in Mustang and oppressing the local people. It was conspicuous that Nepal refused to name any third-party involvement in the Mustang affair, and neither the Indians nor the Americans were accused of aiding the Tibetans. The loss of Mustang effectively put an end to the Tibetans' clandestine resistance to the Chinese. India continued to recruit and train Tibetans for its army, but the unit remained firmly under the army's control. Care was taken to avoid deployment anywhere near the

Tibetan border, as this would undoubtedly have been seen by the Chinese as provocation. The Indian army became one of the largest sources of employment for the refugees. The Dalai Lama's government in Dharamsala continued to maintain a loose connection with the army, and many students graduating from the Tibetan refugee schools were sent there for military training.

The Dalai Lama continued to assert that he represented the government-in-exile. However, international political support for the Tibetans had virtually come to an end: as far as the international community was concerned, the question of Tibet had become redundant. Even countries like Ireland, Thailand, Malaysia and El Salvador, which had supported Tibet's appeal to the United Nations, lost interest in the issue. In 1973, however, the Dalai Lama made his first visit to the West. This was ostensibly for religious purposes, but media attention on the visit could not be avoided. To the great annoyance of the Chinese, Tibet began to receive renewed interest in the Western press.

Anti-Confucius, Anti-Dalai and Anti-Panchen Campaigns

In China, meanwhile, following the 10th Party Congress in August 1973, the Chinese leaders launched the 'Anti-Lin Biao and anti-Confucius' movement. This marked the return of the radical leaders of the Cultural Revolution. In Tibet the campaign was translated into the 'Anti-Dalai and anti-Panchen clique' movement. It was said that 'Confucius, Lin Biao and the Dalai are three lamas from the same monastery'.[42] This led to further attacks on Tibetan culture and traditions, with the Chinese stressing that remnants of old ideas were still prevalent among the people and that the new movement would emancipate the people's minds and create a 'materialist world outlook'.[43] The authorities claimed that Tibetan customs and traditions were hindering economic development, arguing that 'when the masses hack[ed] through the mountains', class enemies had misled the people by saying that 'divine mountains' should not be touched.[44] It was true that Tibetan traditional beliefs had prevented planned mining projects from taking place in certain areas but by the early 1970s no one would have dared articulate such statements, as everyone was aware of the consequences. The Chinese decision to launch the campaign in Tibet had nothing to do with ideological resistance from the Tibetans. By the time the movement was carried into Tibet, the Tibetans had been subdued and there was no possibility of any Tibetan overtly advocating resistance to the Chinese. Like all other campaigns, it was imported from China and implemented dutifully by the local cadres according to Party instructions.

The Chinese cited many traditional Tibetan literary works, such as the

Sakya Legshed (Elegant Sayings of the Sakya Lama), as examples of 'Confucian ideology' prevalent in the region. Less likely sources, such as the Western-style constitution promulgated in 1963 by the Dalai Lama, were used by the Communists to illustrate the reactionary or Confucian views of 'the Dalai clique'. The Dalai Lama was denounced as a 'jackal' whose 'hands are stained with the blood of the million former serfs in Tibet'.[45] There was also a renewed attack on the Panchen Rinpoche and his 70,000 character Petition was given as an example of a work influenced by Confucian ideology. People went through the pretence of denouncing such ideology, but for most it was just another attack on Tibetan values and traditions. In the anti-Lin Biao and anti-Confucius movement – which was essentially confined to meetings and sloganising – the street brawls which had characterised campaigning during the Cultural Revolution gave way to organised meetings and study sessions, which were held with tedious regularity. People had no choice but to sit obediently through these countless meetings.

The authorities had accepted the primary importance of economic development, and the Chinese continued to rely on the commune system in nomadic and agricultural areas. They began to address the main social problems confronting Tibet, such as the lack of a good education system and the total absence of any higher education institution in the region – much of the system that had been set up in the late 1950s and early 1960s had been destroyed in the Cultural Revolution. In 1970 schools in China resumed normal educational activities. The minorities institutes, which had become important centres of learning for the Tibetans, were reopened and once again students started to enrol. The Chinese began to recruit large numbers of teachers from China to work in Tibet. Groups from urban areas such as Shanghai were sent in a blaze of publicity. Many of these young Chinese were assigned to work in Tibet as part of the general dispersal of young people into the rural areas. In July 1975 a Tibet Teacher Training College was opened, the first college of further education in the region, but it did not signify a return to a formal educational system. The Party saw education as crucial to the 'ideological transformation' of the Tibetans and to the production of 'successors to the proletarian revolutionaries' and continued to rely heavily on the poor and lower middle-class peasants.[46] Class background therefore became the main criterion for selection.

On the economic front the authorities continued to extol the virtues of Dazhai and Daqing and encouraged each county to build one commune in the style of Dazhai. There was a great deal of pressure on the local Chinese cadres to succeed, with the result that, intentionally or not, fierce competition existed between different communes. The cadres were tempted to insist on their own greater productivity and thus to make false claims about the achievements of their communes. In reality the communes failed to bring economic development, and did not bring about any noticeable improvement in the material circumstances of the people. In fact, throughout this period, many families experienced food shortages. Chinese propaganda, however, continued to extol the great achievements that had taken place in Tibet and stressed that 'Chairman Mao's revolutionary line had become deep rooted in the minds of the people'.

By the middle of the 1970s, events in Tibet had become a mere appendage to the greater political developments in Beijing, and the political situation there remained in the doldrums, with Ren Rong continuing to hold power. In November 1974 Beijing sent a delegation to inspect the situation in the region. It was led by Zhen Yonggui, a member of the Party's Central Committee. He described the situation in Tibet as 'excellent' and a *Tibet Daily* editorial boasted that 'socialism [was] progressing triumphantly'.[47] A year later the Chinese celebrated the tenth anniversary of the founding of the TAR and a large delegation arrived in Lhasa led by the relatively unknown Party bureaucrat Hua Guofeng (then the Vice-Premier of the State Council), who was later to emerge as one of the main contenders for Mao's position. This celebration took place with much fanfare and extolling of the great achievements made over the previous ten years.

The celebration did not mark any change in Chinese policy towards Tibet. Although cadres were urged to carry out the Party's nationality policies, it was apparent that the Party continued to discard special provisions regarding nationalities that had been made earlier. When the new revised constitution was adopted in January 1975 there were only a few references to the minority groups and Article 24 specifically mentioned that regional autonomy could only be exercised 'within the limits of their authority as prescribed by law'.[48] Emphasis was also placed on combating 'local nationalism' and 'big nation chauvinism'. The general assumption was that regional autonomy was contrary to the principle of the dictatorship of the proletariat, and it was argued that the problem of national differences had been solved.[49] The goal advocated was the total assimilation of national minorities.

The Party continued to adhere to the principle of the primacy of class and stressed that it was a 'fallacy' to advocate the idea that there were special circumstances in Tibet.[50] The Tibetans were urged to discard any vestige of old ideas and customs. They were still allowed to use both their written and spoken language, but this was mainly because of their utilitarian value to the Chinese for transmitting revolutionary propaganda. Despite the efforts made to teach Chinese, the majority of Tibetans could not speak, read or write it. Yet Chinese had clearly become the primary language of education and administration. At a cultural level, the Chinese began to advocate a policy of 'nationality in form' and 'socialist in content'. This meant that the identity of the Tibetans (as well as that of other groups) could only be defined through the clearly prescribed guidelines set by the Party. This was best illustrated by the new songs and dances that were devised, supposedly showing Tibetan traditional performing arts, a reflection of the great importance attached by the Chinese to the performing arts as a vehicle of propaganda. The new emphasis reduced Tibetan culture and identity to the semblance of happy natives performing exotic songs and dances. The new style, in which dancers wore colourful Tibetan garb and sang in Tibetan, in words that could only convey the messages of socialism and materialism, was best epitomised by the singing of Tseten Dolma, who was promoted as one of the great artistic figures of Tibet.

The Death of Mao

Yet it was not a shift in Chinese policy or a change in the government's perception of Tibet, but the death of Mao which marked a dramatic change in Tibet. Nineteen seventy-six saw the death not only of Mao but of two other leading figures, Zhu De and Zhou Enlai. Zhou's death did not have any serious repercussions in Tibet – popular myth claimed it was Zhou's restraining hand that had saved the Potala from the Red Guard vandals although in fact as early as the 1950s Zhou was advising Tibetan students in Beijing to emulate the Manchus and assimilate with the Chinese. On 9 September 1976, nine months after Zhou's death, Chairman Mao died after a long illness. His cult had been vigorously promoted in Tibet over the years, as it had been in China, and there was not a single household which did not have his poster. Every meeting began and ended with a eulogy for Mao, and the following popular idiom 'your parents are gracious but Chairman Mao is more gracious'[51] was promoted by the Chinese. The news of his death left everyone shocked. At the official mourning ceremony people grieved openly, but the public display of grief was to some extent a mandatory ritual. In retrospect, some people claimed that they were elated by the news. In reality, however, the reaction was ambivalent and most people were fearful of what would happen next.

Less than a month after the death of Mao, his widow Jiang Qing and her allies, who had presided over the funeral ceremony, were arrested. The term 'Gang of Four' was used for the first time.[52] They became the scapegoats for all of China's maladies. In terms of a change in politics or personalities, neither the death of Mao nor the arrest of the Gang of Four made any immediate impact on Tibet. However, no one could fail to notice that important changes were taking place. On the day that Mao's funeral ceremony was held in Beijing, the American Defence Secretary James Schlesinger arrived for a three-day tour of Tibet.[53] The Chinese were aware that Tibet was a sensitive issue internationally due to the presence of the

Dalai Lama in India, and in the past, foreign visits had been confined to leaders of friendly third-world countries. Schlesinger was perhaps the most important political figure to have visited Tibet, and the visit was no doubt intended to confirm China's willingness to open up even its most sensitive regions to the outside world.[54] Shortly after Schlesinger's visit, the Chinese allowed two Western journalists, Neville Maxwell[55] and Felix Greene, into Tibet; and Greene was allowed to make a documentary film there. It was no accident that both men were sympathetic to the Chinese Communists. On their return, Maxwell and Greene wrote glowing accounts of Chinese rule in Tibet. They were followed by Han Suyin, the well-known novelist, who claimed that Tibet had been transformed into a socialist paradise.[56] The start of foreign visits did not signal any change in Chinese policy towards Tibet. The visits were allowed merely to prove Chinese sincerity in opening the country to the outside world, as the situation in Tibet had attracted unfavourable press coverage in the West and was causing problems for the Chinese.[57]

In Tibet the only noticeable repercussion of the arrest of the Gang of Four was that the ensuing struggle in Beijing created uncertainty and removed some of the pressure in the region. On 8 October Hua Guofeng was officially named Mao's successor as Chairman of the Central Committee of the CCP. As a result of the delegation he had led from Beijing to Lhasa to mark the tenth anniversary of the founding of the TAR, Hua Guofeng was better known in Tibet than in China. The Tibetan people were genuinely grateful to him for doing away with the endless and demanding meetings and study sessions, and after nearly a decade of repression the people could now breathe a sigh of relief at the gradual relaxation of political control. However, despite the fact that the Gang of Four were accused of sabotaging all spheres of activity, in the early stages of Hua Guofeng's rule there was a conspicuous absence of any mention of them sabotaging the work on nationalities. Hua Guofeng continued to adhere to the principle that 'class was the key link' in the policy towards nationalities. On the economic front the Tibetans were still told to emulate the success of Dazhai, which implied that the commune system would continue. There were also attempts to boost developments in Tibet, and the army was instructed to carry out a survey of the Tibet–Qinghai plateau for the construction of the Golmud to Lhasa railway link.

Tibet had neither the economic importance nor the political clout to affect the struggle for the leadership that was being fought in Beijing and the regional CCP endorsed Hua Guofeng as the successor of Mao. It is unclear whether this was a conscious decision, revealing a deliberate preference over Deng Xiaoping, or if they were following the general trend in the country. Hua was well known to the local leadership, whereas Deng was denounced in Tibet as a 'rightist deviationist' with close personal connections with the earlier generation of local Chinese leadership. However, this negative perception of Deng was quickly reversed once he managed to secure his position in the Centre. Meanwhile all was not well in Tibet. Ren Rong repeatedly stressed the message 'unite and don't split' at meetings, and cadres were advised 'don't intrigue and conspire'.[58] Yet after the arrest of the Gang of Four, the authorities in Tibet made moves to purge the supporters of Jiang Qing. Gou Xilan, a deputy secretary of the regional CCP, announced that a campaign had been initiated in Tibet to expose and criticise 'the henchmen of the Gang of Four'.[59] The authorities found that exposing 'the agents' of Jiang Qing was not an easy matter. With memories of the Cultural Revolution still lingering in their minds, the local cadres were reluctant to plunge themselves into another round of purges and counter-purges. Moreover, the cadres were uncertain as to who was to be labelled an agent of the Gang of Four. Gou Xilan mentions that the campaign was hampered by the fact that there were no 'typical examples' of an agent, which meant that the local cadres were unwilling to identify other cadres. By the end of 1978, it was announced that the campaign had come to an end and the authorities acknowledged that it had not been taken seriously in Tibet.[60] The campaign to root out the ultra-leftist faction from the regional CCP was not carried out earnestly until the middle of the 1980s. In reality Ren Rong had more in common with Hua Guofeng than with the reformers, and, like Hua, he had prospered during the Cultural Revolution and overseen the implementation of many of the most radical policies in Tibet. Beijing was only later to realise that Ren Rong's stewardship of the regional CCP was an impediment to implementing the new reforms. However, it must be acknowledged that Ren Rong was in the difficult position of having to weigh the demand for change imposed from Beijing with the need to appease the conservative cadres in Tibet.

Although many Tibetans did emerge during the Cultural Revolution as supporters of the radical faction, none of them had any direct connections with the radical leaders in Beijing and they were therefore spared accusations of association with the Gang of Four. Many of the Tibetan cadres should have been discarded according to the principle of the 'three types of people'[61] to be opposed, but the radical Tibetan Party leaders continued to enjoy high positions in the regional CCP.

There was a popular saying among the Tibetans that change reached Tibet last, in the way that a ripple from the centre of a pool of water finally reaches the edge. It may have taken longer to filter in new policies, but it was inevitable that the change at the Centre would eventually have a profound impact. The first noticeable effect was the revival of the Party's United Front Department, whose work had been neglected during the Cultural Revolution. Its revival had important ramifications for Tibetans. The fundamental principle of the United Front strategy was to seek common ground with those who were not members of the CCP and the United Front Department had played a crucial role in early CCP policies towards Tibet, with its first director, Li Weihan, who led negotiations with Ngabo in 1951. (As noted in an earlier chapter, he was purged in 1963 and disappeared during the Cultural Revolution.) In July 1977, Ulanfu, the only member of a minority group who held an important senior post in the CCP, was chosen as the new director of the United Front. During the Cultural Revolution he had been accused of creating an independent kingdom in Mongolia and had been dismissed from all offices.[62] His appointment signified the revival of more tolerant attitudes towards national minorities. Ulanfu also announced that the Party's Central Committee had removed 'the cap of shame' put on the United Front Department (when they were branded 'followers of defeatism and religionism').[63] The new leaders had noted the CCP 'must take the time to improve ethnic relations and dispel misunderstanding; otherwise we will end up with serious losses'.[64] The consensus that emerged under the reformist leadership was that the nationalities question could not be solved in the immediate future. This naturally led to the abandonment of the policy of instant assimilation. The new policy was concerned with managing diversity rather than with attempting to solve the problem once and for all.[65] However, this did not mean that the Party had rejected the long-term goal of assimilation of all minority groups.

According to the new leaders, what had marred the relationship between Tibet and China were the mistakes made by the Gang of Four in executing the Party's policy on nationality.[66] They therefore saw the challenge in Tibet as being simply a question of finding an appropriate 'work style', rather than of dealing with the deep-seated grievances of the Tibetans. The key to managing the Tibetan affair, in their view, was the Dalai Lama. If China could achieve a reconciliation with him, the Party would be able to recover its position in Tibet. Therefore, the Chinese began to signal that the Dalai Lama would be welcomed back in Tibet. In May 1977 Reuters reported that, in a meeting with a visiting Japanese delegation, Ngabo had announced that the Dalai Lama could return as long as 'he stands on the side of the people'.[67] This did not elicit any direct response from the Tibetans in India where the Dalai Lama adopted a policy of 'wait and see'. In an interview with the *Tibetan Review* he said, 'we'll have to wait a little longer and see how long the apparent liberalisations continue and what other changes are introduced. We are naturally suspicious of these changes in policy, but only time will tell.'[68]

In fact, it was not until the Third Plenum of the Eleventh Central Committee of the CCP, held in December 1978, that a more important policy change came about, rejecting the principles of the Cultural Revolution and mass mobilisation as a means of achieving political and economic objectives. This also marked the end of the ambiguous policies of Hua Guofeng, and more importantly it showed the ascendancy of Deng Xiaoping as the prime initiator of a more liberal policy. His Four Modernisations were enshrined as the political and economic objectives of the CCP. These sweeping and far-reaching reforms were to have a dramatic effect in China and as the reformers strengthened their position in the Party, it was inevitable that Tibet too would fall in line and dutifully carry out the new policies.

The First Phase of Liberalisation

The ascendancy of Deng also marked a shift in the Party's ideological stance from rigid Maoist orthodoxy to a more flexible and pragmatic policy of winning over the minority groups. The new leaders rejected Mao's maxim that the nationalities problem was in essence a class problem. In Tibet, however, Ren Rong announced that while there was no longer any 'need for masses to wage turbulent class struggle', the view that class struggle had died out was at variance with reality.[69] This showed how far Tibet was lagging behind the developments in China. Despite his apparent uncertainties about the policy changes, Ren Rong had to adopt at least some of them because he knew that, in order to secure his own position, he must not only advocate reforms but also see that the masses were experiencing the benefits of such reforms. As we shall see later, the reformist leaders saw Ren Rong as a member of the conservative faction who had to be removed.

On a practical level, the Party's abandonment of a policy of forced assimilation of minority groups was replaced by a view that assimilation would be achieved by natural 'acculturation', whereby the minority groups would choose to absorb the Chinese way of life. Therefore, the Party's task was to create an environment conducive to the eventual assimilation of the minorities.[70] Under the new United Front policy, the Chinese authorities began to revive many of the principles that had been applied in the early 1950s to entice minority leaders into co-operating with the CCP. These changes in nationality areas were not merely a concession to the demands of the people, but the result of the realisation that the past two decades had resulted in the economic stagnation of China, in which in many ways the minority regions had fared the worst. The disparity in economic and social development between the areas inhabited by the minorities in the west and the Chinese in the east had not been bridged; in fact it had widened. The glaring disparity was proved by the third census carried out in 1979. All social indices showed that Tibet lagged behind even the other minority regions.[71] The twin policies of class struggle and of the emphasis on wheat production had left Tibet in abject poverty. In addition to this, there was a further reason why new Chinese leaders wanted to see rapid development in Tibet and the other minority regions in the west: these areas were seen by the planners as primary sources of raw materials for the new economic development of China. Yang Jingren, recently appointed as the Minister of the State Nationalities Affairs Commission, emphasized that the territories inhabited by the minority groups were rich in natural resources; Tibet alone contained 40 per cent of China's mineral resources.[72] Therefore, Tibet and the other minority areas would be utilized in pursuit of the goal of economic modernisation.

The Chinese had realised that they could not hope to achieve economic modernisation without making concessions to the minority groups. The Chinese decided therefore to promise modernisation and economic development, and the minority people would in turn be expected to support the Four Modernisations and the CCP.[73] As had been the case in China, the Four Modernisations would be achieved by adopting some of the features of capitalism and by opening the territories to outside investment.[74] But this could only be achieved by loosening the control exercised by the Party and the bureaucracy, which naturally meant that the Party had to adopt a more tolerant policy towards the aspirations of the people. The regions had to be allowed to exercise cultural and religious freedom.

In March 1978, the Panchen Rinpoche appeared in public for the first time since his purge in 1964. Immediately upon his release he was made a member of the standing committee of the Chinese People's Political Consultative Committee (CPPCC), a body which had ceased to meet during the Cultural Revolution and many of whose members had been imprisoned.[75] The CPPCC was never an important political body; its functions were merely to rubber-stamp decisions made by the Party. However, the resurrection of the CPPCC was a signal that the Party's policy towards non-Communists and traditional minority leaders had changed.

The programme of rehabilitation that was being carried out in China was soon repeated in Tibet. In late 1978 the Chinese began to release many of the former Tibetan Government officials who had been imprisoned during the Cultural Revolution.[76] The Party announced that anyone who had been wrongly accused during the Cultural Revolution would be reinstated. The authorities also decided to release a number of people who had been involved in the March 1959 uprising. Before they were released, the prisoners were taken on a tour of communes, factories and schools.

In January 1979 the Central Committee in Beijing announced the end of discrimination against the children of rich landlords. The Party was now moving away from using class as the sole criteria for selecting cadres and students. It was also announced that it would reinstate the old policy of 'buying out' landlords and aristocrats whose properties had been confiscated during the Cultural Revolution. However, compensation was only given to those who were wrongly accused during the Cultural Revolution, and nothing was given to those who were involved in the 1959 revolt. Over 2,300 people in Tibet were paid compensation, totalling well over 7 million yuan.[77] Within a very short space of time the former Tibetan aristocrats were able to enjoy more or less the same lifestyle as in the past.

In the early phase of the reforms the Tibetans remained sceptical of the changes, tending to see the new policy as a residual benefit of the power struggle being waged by the higher echelon of the Chinese leadership. When Ulanfu called a meeting to discuss the nationalities policy, the Panchen Rinpoche told him bluntly that the changes should not be judged by the leniency shown towards a few leaders: there should be a general rehabilitation of the thousands of ordinary people who had been wrongly labelled and persecuted.[78] The years of imprisonment had not dented the Panchen Rinpoche's courage.

Rehabilitation was not confined to the Tibetans. Many Chinese cadres felt they too had been wrongly accused during the Cultural Revolution and wanted their cases to be reviewed. This was more problematic. The cases of former Tibetan officials could be changed at a stroke of the pen, but the question of the Chinese cadres and Tibetan Party members was more complex as it contained the inherent danger of dividing the Party, for if those who were rehabilitated were innocent then their accusers must be guilty. The innocent could be reinstated, but it would be difficult for the Party to punish the guilty without opening old wounds. However, the authorities did carry out the posthumous rehabilitation of some high-profile leaders such as Zhou Renshan, the leader of the Nyamdrel faction.[79]

The Central Party leadership demanded the dismissal of the Chinese cadres who had been associated with the ultra-leftists, but it was clear that they could not afford to antagonize the few Tibetan members of the Party, as they were desperately needed. As a result, the Tibetan Party members were treated more favourably than the Chinese, despite the fact that many of them had been prominent during the Cultural Revolution. It was apparent that Beijing was faced with a serious problem in implementing the changes in Tibet, as many of the Chinese cadres had vested interests in obstructing the reforms. In an article in *Red Flag*, Yang Jingren accused the local leaders of not carrying out Beijing's directives and of failing to rectify the 'leftist deviation' and to purge leftists from the Party. He said that there were people in power in Tibet who opposed the spirit of the Third Plenum.[80]

Early on the Party imposed two strategies to overcome resistance. The first of these was internal Party reform, which was carried out by expanding the membership base of the regional CCP. Tibetans who had been excluded from joining the Party because of their class origin were now encouraged to join.[81] In the past the Party had relied on mass membership and selection had been based purely on class background, so that many of the existing members lacked educational skills and were illiterate. As a result, their ability to assert themselves effectively within the Party was limited. The second change was the transferral of several thousand Chinese cadres to work in Tibet. These new cadres were supposed to be free from factional affiliation in the region and moreover they had received advance training in new 'work styles' and their presence was intended to enable Party leaders in Tibet to carry out the purge of the radicals without splitting the Party. However, the changes failed to move the old cadres, who were reluctant to surrender their positions. For the first few years of the reforms, Tibet lagged behind China in carrying out the changes.

Beijing–Dharamsala Dialogue

As Deng strengthened the control of the Party, he began to adopt a bold policy towards the problems of Taiwan and Hong Kong under the slogan 'One Country, Two Systems'. Deng accepted that Taiwan could be unified with the mainland while maintaining existing capitalistic economic and social systems. This suggested considerable flexibility on the part of the new leadership in Beijing, and it was welcome news for the Dalai Lama, who saw it as a possible solution to the Tibetan problem. Deng had a long association with the Tibet question and in the early 1950s, as the political commissar of the South-West Military Region, he had been responsible for the region, and there was some resemblance between Chinese policy in the early 1950s and the new policy. During the Cultural Revolution one of the accusations against Deng was that he had advocated a policy of appeasement with the Tibetan ruling élite. It was therefore not surprising that he took up the Tibetan question. Although later, in 1993, Deng referred to Tibet as one of his 'unresolved problems', this was not due merely to sentimental attachment: there were also practical reasons for his interest in the Tibetan question. The Dalai Lama's decision to remain in India was a blemish on China's international image, and this was of great concern to the new leaders. In addition to this, there was another more urgent reason for the Chinese wanting to achieve a reconciliation with the Dalai Lama.

Despite radical reforms, there was no change in China's policy towards the Soviet Union and it had not gone unnoticed in Beijing that the Russian attitude towards the Tibetan question had undergone a dramatic shift[82] nor that the Dalai Lama was making tentative moves towards the Russians. In the late 1970s, he made a number of statements to the effect that the Tibetan issue was not a problem of ideology and there was some compatibility between Buddhism and Communism, comments which were essentially aimed at winning over the Russians.[83] In June 1979, he made his first visit to the Soviet Union and Mongolia, to attend the Asian Buddhist

Conference for Peace, organised by a Russian-inspired Buddhist NGO. For the Chinese this was an unwelcome development in Tibetan affairs and was seen as a Russian attempt to snare the Tibetan leader. For these reasons China had an urgent compulsion to find a *modus vivendi* with the Dalai Lama.

The Dalai Lama compensated for his flirtation with Russia by scaling down his demands. The signals emanating from Dharamsala suggested that the Dalai Lama was willing to dispense with the demand for total independence and that he might be prepared to accept some form of federation with China. The Dalai Lama told the Indian Press that if the 'choice before him was independence (or federation) he would choose that which was more beneficial for the Tibetans'.[84] He began to redefine the essence of the Tibetan question. Whereas throughout the 1960s and early 1970s, he had called for a plebiscite to determine the status of Tibet, in his annual statement issued during the commemoration of the 10 March Uprising in 1978, he seemed to imply that the issue rested on the welfare of the six million Tibetans.[85] Two year later he said that the 'core of the Tibetan issue is the welfare and ultimate happiness [of the six million Tibetans in Tibet]'.[86] The Dalai Lama had thus reduced the question to the issue of social and economic welfare. This was also the basis for Deng's new China, where the reforms were meant to bring prosperity and happiness to the Chinese people. Therefore, it appears that there was some degree of conformity between Deng and the Dalai Lama on the fundamental issue for discussion.

In fact, the Chinese had already taken the initiative and made a series of conciliatory moves. After twenty years they had allowed Tibetans to travel to India to visit their relatives, a dispensation applied particularly to former aristocrats, whose relatives in exile the Chinese believed still exercised power and influence over the Dalai Lama. Before leaving Tibet, they were told to urge their relatives to return and were instructed to report on the progress in Tibet.[87] The Chinese also invited Tibetans living abroad to open businesses in Tibet. As noted before, a number of officials, including Ngabo, made announcements that the Dalai Lama would be welcome to return, but no specific conditions were offered. The invitation was accompanied by an implicit warning that if the relationship between Beijing and New Delhi improved, the Dalai Lama might no longer be welcome in India.[88] The same report warned India that the continuing presence of the Dalai Lama was 'detrimental to good neighbourly relations'.[89]

At the end of 1978 the Xinhua representative in Hong Kong, Li Juisin, contacted Gyalo Dhundup, who had withdrawn from diaspora politics and was living in Hong Kong. We will see later that the choice of Gyalo Dhundup as an intermediary was a significant strategy on the part of the Chinese. The meeting marked the beginning of the serious dialogue between the Dalai Lama and the new Chinese leaders. Li Juisin told Gyalo Dhundup that the Chinese leader was prepared to meet with him in Beijing to discuss the problem of Tibet. The Dalai Lama approved Gyalo Dhundup's trip to Beijing and on 1 March 1979 Gyalo Dhundup met with Ulanfu, the director of the United Front, the department in charge of handling the Tibetan issue. Ulanfu made the usual speech about the past mistakes under the Gang of Four and the new leadership's desire to improve the situation in Tibet. Eleven days later Ulanfu took Gyalo Dhundup to see Deng Xiaoping. The fact that Gyalo Dhundup was taken to see China's paramount leader emphasized the seriousness of the Chinese approach. Deng told Gyalo Dhundup that as long as the Tibetans did not demand independence and separation from China, he was prepared to discuss all the Tibetan grievances. Deng also assured him that the recent alterations were not temporary measures and that he and the new leadership were committed to promoting fundamental changes. He went on to say that if the Dalai Lama had doubts about the sincerity of the reforms, he should send people to investigate the situation in Tibet: it is better to see with one's own eyes than to hear something a hundred times from other people. Deng went even further, suggesting that the Tibetans could put up wall posters to express their views.[90]

Deng's initial proposal was acceptable to the Dalai Lama, who saw it as a reasonable starting point for dialogue. In any case the Dalai Lama could not afford to reject Deng's conciliatory gesture. China under Deng was widely praised by Western countries, and he had become the West's favourite Communist leader, making his first visit to America to an enthusiastic welcome in 1979 and becoming *Time* magazine's 'Man of the Year' in 1980. Deng's growing stature in the West meant that the Tibetans were under pressure to respond to the recent changes in China. The Dalai Lama reciprocated by agreeing to send a fact-finding delegation to Tibet. In fact Deng's invitation to the Dalai Lama to send people to investigate the situation in Tibet later proved to be a fatal mistake. Even so the Tibetan 'government in exile' was unsure of the reaction of the Tibetan people inside Tibet. Over the years the message from Tibet had been that the Dalai Lama should not return, partly because the Tibetans were suspicious of the Chinese reforms, but also because many had reported that the Communists had succeeded in indoctrinating the people. This applied particularly to the younger generation, who were said to have been brainwashed by the Communists. Refugees recounted how Tibetan Red Guards had taken part enthusiastically in the destruction of monasteries and temples. Although the Dharamsala leadership would not publicly admit to having any doubts as to how they would be received in Tibet, they did regard the visit as an opportunity to assess the situation. It transpired that the Chinese had misjudged the mood of the Tibetan people. The Communists had swallowed their own propaganda and believed that after nearly twenty years of rule they had made great progress which would impress the Tibetans in exile. Moreover, they believed that they had won over the people.

In August 1979 the first five-man delegation from Dharamsala left Delhi for Beijing. It was led by Kalon Juchen Thupten, and the other members were Phuntsog Tashi Takla, Lobsang Samten, the Dalai Lama's immediate elder brother, Tashi Topgyal and Lobsang Thargay. The delegation left Delhi secretly – other Dharamsala officials were not told of the news until the eve of its departure.[91] It was left to Xinhua to inform the international press of a visit to Tibet by the Dharamsala delegation. Before the delegation left India, the Chinese had conceded to the Tibetans' demands that they be allowed to visit all Tibetan inhabited areas, not just the TAR, and that they would not travel under 'overseas Chinese passports'. The delegation were to travel using Indian travel documents and they would be admitted into China from Hong Kong without observing immigration formalities.

The two concessions were important for the Tibetans. If they had travelled on overseas Chinese passports,[92] it would have implied that they accepted the Chinese position regarding the status of Tibet. More importantly, the right to tour Tibetan-speaking areas in Qinghai, Sichuan, Gansu and Yunnan implied that Dharamsala spoke for all of Tibet. The Chinese concessions led Dharamsala to believe that this provided a geographical definition of the basis for discussion. As far as China was concerned, the concessions did not amount to an agreement as to the content of the subsequent discussions, but they indicated their openness and sincerity in seeking a reconciliation with the Dalai Lama. However, the fact that Beijing accepted Dharamsala's right to visit the Tibetan areas outside the TAR seemed to place these areas on the agenda for later discussions.

As the Dharamsala delegation entered the Tibetan areas in Sichuan and Qinghai, they were overwhelmed by the welcome they received. Thousands of people mobbed them and recounted the terrible tragedies that they had suffered. The Chinese officials accompanying the delegation were embarrassed and did not know how to respond.[93] They telephoned Ren Rong in Lhasa to suggest that the visit to the TAR should be cancelled. Ren confidently announced that the people in Amdo and Kham were simple nomads and lacked class consciousness. He was sure that the people in the TAR had a better understanding of class and that there was no danger of people there not welcoming the delegation.[94] He had badly misjudged the situation. The first delegation toured for nearly six months, and wherever they went they had the same enthusiastic welcome. Later, when the delegation arrived in Lhasa, the response surpassed anything they had received before. In May 1980 the second delegation led by Tenzin Tethong, the Dalai Lama's representative in New York, left for Tibet. A month later they were followed by the third delegation led by the Dalai Lama's sister, Jetsun Pema, whose group was specifically instructed to investigate educational conditions. All the delegations received the same welcome in all parts of Tibet. In Lhasa each visit became a major anti-Chinese demonstration with people openly shouting slogans demanding Tibetan independence.[95] When the second delegation reached Lhasa, the Chinese found it impossible to control the people's enthusiasm.

On 26 July 1980, while the second delegation was in Lhasa, the Chinese Foreign Ministry brought the international press corps from Beijing to the Tibetan capital. The press knew that earlier in the day the Dharamsala delegation had been besieged by the Tibetans and they made attempts to interview the delegation. Worried by the press interest, the Chinese decided to expel the second delegation on the pretext that it had broken the condition of not contacting the press. The Tibetans protested that it was the Chinese themselves who had brought the journalists to Lhasa. The Chinese realised that the exercise had gone terribly wrong, and that the only way to save even greater embarrassment was to cancel all further visits. Had the visit of the fourth delegation – which consisted of high-ranking lamas – taken place the reception would have surpassed even that of the previous delegations.

The enthusiastic reception had a profound effect on Dharamsala. Any doubts were wiped away; they could now confidently rebuff any Chinese claims about social progress in Tibet. The visits had shown that there was popular support for the Dalai Lama and that the people's religious faith remained uncontaminated by twenty years of Communism. Later, Hu Yaobang said that the people preferred to report their grievances to the Dalai Lama, the symbol of old Tibet, rather than to complain to the Party. This was a direct challenge to Chinese rule and questioned its legitimacy. There was no doubt that, in the hearts and minds of the people, the Dalai Lama still represented their hopes for freedom and everywhere the delegation went the people passionately appealed for a speedy deliverance from their suffering, complaining that the economic situation had worsened since the arrival of the Communists. The delegation had filmed their visit, some of which was later broadcast on Western television,[96] publicity that helped to offset some of the positive images of China that had taken hold in the West through the visits of Western Communists and sympathisers.

When the first delegation returned to Beijing, they protested to China's leaders about what they had witnessed. The reports of the Tibetans' impassioned welcome to the Dalai Lama's delegation had already reached the highest levels of the Chinese leadership and the Communist Party was forced to look seriously into the situation in Tibet. The Party also knew that their policy towards Tibet was keenly observed by the people of Hong Kong and Taiwan and that reconciliation with the Dalai Lama was a prerequisite for any eventual Sino–Indian rapprochement. While two of the Dharamsala delegations were still travelling in Tibet, the Party leadership began to consider its options. By the beginning of 1980, Deng was in a much stronger position to tackle the problem. He had succeeded in taking power away from Hua Guofeng and the conservatives within the Party by placing his supporters in key posts in the Party and the State. In February, at the Fifth Plenum of the CCP, Deng achieved an important victory when a new Party Secretariat was established. This was headed by one of his ardent supporters, Hu Yaobang, who began to engineer farsighted reforms. The new Party Secretariat took over the policy-making decisions which had previously rested with the Politburo, under Hua Guofeng's chairmanship. The first task of the Party Secretariat was to convene a five-man working committee on Tibet, which Hu Yaobang himself chaired. The other Chinese members were Wan Li, from the CCP's Central Committee; Yang Jingren, the director of the Nationalities Affairs Commission; and Zhengqing, the head of the Organisation Department of the CCP. Ngabo Jigme (Vice-Chairman of the NPC) was the only Tibetan member of the group and did not have an important post within the CCP. The committee also co-opted some cadres who had long experience of working in Tibet. Among them was one of China's leading Tibetologists, Wang Yao. Since the working group was convened by the Party, the Panchen Rinpoche was not included because he was not a Party member. The only other likely Tibetan candidate would have been Baba Phuntsog Wangyal, but his views were seen as too radical and unacceptable even for Hu Yaobang.

The first task facing the working group was how to assess the reactions of the Tibetans to the Dalai Lama's delegation. Hu Yaobang and other senior leaders viewed the welcome given to the Dharamsala delegation as an aberration rather than symptomatic of deep-seated resentment against China. They did not think it raised any fundamental questions about the Sino–Tibetan relationship, viewing it not as a rejection of China or of the Communist Party but as a visible sign of the mistakes made by the Gang of Four and their extreme leftist ideology. On this level they were prepared to sympathize with the Tibetan people. A Chinese leader told the Tibetan delegation that they should forget the past and look towards the future.[97] The new leaders in Beijing readily accepted that mistakes had been made, but blamed these on the Gang of Four. With a certain degree of honesty, they too could claim that they had suffered under the Gang of Four. The problem in Tibet seemed to the new leaders to be merely one of redressing the mistakes made during the Cultural Revolution. It boiled down to two issues: the need to alleviate poverty, and the need to relax the restrictions on the cultural and religious practices of the Tibetan people.

The First Tibet Work Forum

By setting up the working group on Tibet, the CCP's Central Committee had in effect authorised the suspension of the regional Party and had taken over the running of Tibet. The working group met in Beijing for several months and took evidence from many Chinese and Tibetan cadres who had worked in Tibet. They also invited the Panchen Rinpoche to submit his suggestions. Once again, he found himself in a similar situation to that which had got him into trouble in 1962, when Li Weihan and Zhou Enlai had invited him to write his famous 70,000 Character Petition. Panchen Rinpoche told the committee that he still stood by the report he had submitted in the early 1960s.[98] The working group soon learned that the regional Party had failed to implement many of the changes that had already been carried out in China. Entrenched leftist influence was identified as the main cause of the failure, and the continuing leadership of Ren Rong was now seen as an impediment to change. It was decided that he should be removed and a new Party Secretary appointed to push through the new reform policy in Tibet. Before the working party left for Lhasa, the Central Committee of the CCP agreed to remove Ren Rong and appointed Yin Fatang as the acting Party Secretary. Yin Fatang was not Hu Yaobang's first choice; it was rumoured that he had wanted to appoint a Tibetan. But there were real difficulties in finding a suitable candidate, as the existing Tibetan leadership was composed of ultra-leftists, who had risen through the ranks during the Cultural Revolution. The only Tibetan eligible to take up the post was Baba Phuntsog Wangyal. It was reported that he was offered the position of the First Secretary but his appointment did not take place. There is evidence to suggest that the some senior members of the Party were reluctant to accept Phuntsog Wangyal's appointment. The Panchen Rinpoche had openly criticised the Party's decision that the Anti-Rightist Campaign was 'basically correct' and 'completely necessary', a judgement which had allowed the Party to defer the rehabilitation of cadres who were still considered to be dangerous.[99] Here, it was likely that the Panchen Rinpoche was thinking of Phuntsog Wangyal, who continued to reject the Party's nationalities policy on ideological grounds and who was still not formally rehabilitated. As noted in an earlier chapter, Phuntsog Wangyal had been purged during the anti-Rightist Campaign for advocating a Soviet type of federal arrangement for minority groups. This was still unacceptable to the Chinese leaders, who saw a republic as the slippery slope towards separatism.

Yin Fatang had entered Tibet in 1950 and worked there for over twenty years, developing a good knowledge of the Tibetan language and familiarity with the country's problems. Moreover, from the outset, it was known that Yin was a close associate of Deng Xiaoping; as far back as the early 1950s he had been known as Deng's man in Tibet and had reported directly to him in Beijing. Therefore, it was not surprising that when Deng returned to power, he appointed one of his own men to preside over a troublesome area.

At the beginning of the Cultural Revolution Yin was the director of the Political Department of the Tibet Military Region but it appears that he did not play a prominent role during the Cultural Revolution: his name hardly appeared in the hundreds of pamphlets that were produced denouncing the senior cadres. Nor was he subjected to struggle sessions. His close association with Deng did not seem to have hindered his position in Tibet. In the early 1970s he was working as the director of the Political Department of the Jinan Military Region, and prior to this new appointment he had risen to become the political commissar of the region. No doubt Yin, who concurrently held the post of the First Political Commissar of the Tibet Military District, was chosen because of his long association with Tibet, and his strong military connections in the region would have made him more acceptable. He was familiar with many of the Chinese and Tibetan cadres, some of whom had served under him.[100] On the morning of 22 May 1980 Yin Fatang was at Gongkar airport to welcome Hu Yaobang, Ngabo and Wan Li. The dismissal of Ren Rong and the visit of Hu Yaobang were clear statements that the reform was not transitory.

Hu Yaobang had chosen the date of his arrival in Lhasa very carefully. The next day was the twenty-ninth anniversary of the signing of the 17-Point Agreement. Hu saw his visit as being on the same historic level. He had summoned the Tibetan signatories of the 1951 Agreement, Sampho and Lhawutara, who had spent nearly twenty years in labour camps, to meet him. Wan Li, holding Sampho's hand, reminded the welcoming party of the significance of the date.[101] It was as if Hu Yaobang was asking the people to induce amnesia and dismiss the past thirty years as though they had never happened. This was to be a new beginning, the intervening years simply a horrible nightmare. Hu Yaobang promised that past mistakes would not be repeated. Sampho clearly did not have any faith in the Chinese leader's promise of better times to come and shortly afterwards left for India.

On 29 May Hu Yaobang convened a meeting of over 4,500 leading regional Communist Party members and Tibetan members of the CPPCC. Hu acknowledged that the Communist Party had failed in Tibet. Far from eradicating poverty, in many areas the people's living standards had declined. Hua went on to say: 'We feel that our party has let the Tibetan people down. We feel bad! The sole purpose of our Communist Party is to work for the happiness of the people, to do good things for them. We have worked nearly thirty years, but the life of the Tibetan people has not notably improved. Are we [the Party] not to blame?'[102] The harshest words were reserved for the Chinese cadres working in Tibet. He asked what had they done with the millions of yuan in grants that the Central Government had made to the TAR, and wondered if they had thrown the money into the Tsangpo river for all the good it had done. He further angered the conservative members of the Party by comparing the situation in Tibet with colonialism.[103] Hu Yaobang's harsh criticisms were deeply resented by Chinese cadres at all levels. They had in the past been prized as pioneers who had unified the motherland and made great sacrifices to serve in hostile lands but now saw their thirty years of work in Tibet described as an utter failure. The old cadres wrote petitions to the Central Committee complaining about Hu's speech.[104]

Finally, Hu Yaobang announced a six-point policy that was meant to solve many of the problems faced in Tibet. On the face of it, the new policies were timely and a wise decision. However, as we shall see, it was one thing to make liberal commitments and another to implement them. The six points were:

(1) Tibet must be given full rights to exercise regional autonomy.

(2) There would be a period of recuperation during the first three years of which people in Tibet would be exempt from paying taxes and meeting state purchase quotas.

(3) A flexible economic policy suited to Tibet's special conditions should be adopted.

(4) A greater part of the state subsidy should be used for the development of agriculture and animal husbandry.

(5) Tibetan culture, language and education should be developed following socialist orientation.

(6) The Party's policy on minority cadres should be implemented and should promote unity between Chinese and Tibetan cadres.[105]

On the surface Hu's new policy did not look very radical, and it did not meet the demands of the Tibetans. However, given the fact that for the previous two decades Tibet had been subjected to rigorous leftist policies, which took little or no account of conditions in the region, Hu's promise to adapt policy to suit the region was welcomed by the Tibetans. The Chinese leader designated the next few years as a period of 'recuperation', and his decision to exempt Tibetan farmers and nomads from all taxes and compulsory state purchase quotas was to have the greatest impact on Tibetan society, genuinely freeing the Tibetan peasantry from the shackles of the communes and the state bureaucracy. The communes, which had controlled every aspect of social and economic life, were to be disbanded, with the communal properties and animals divided equally among members. The farmers could now make their own production decisions but there was no immediate rush to disband the communes, and in some remote areas they continued to function for several years. This was not because of a lack of enthusiasm for the new reform, but rather due to inefficiency in carrying out the changes.

One of the main problems of putting the new reforms into practice was that they were instigated by the leadership, rather than by popular demand from either the local cadres or the regional leaders. Cadres at all levels opposed the reforms for a variety of reasons. On the personal level, the changes threatened their authority and privileges, while on the general level they were seen as a negation of their work in Tibet over the past three decades. To compound the problem, Hu declared in his speech that there were 'unhealthy tendencies among the Chinese cadres'. These were identified as (1) violating the CCP's nationality policy and impairing national unity; (2) taking advantage of their position and power to assign jobs to their own men; (3) practising factionalism; (4) wasting state and collective property; (5) maintaining special privileges by giving gifts and banquets.[106] He implied that the Chinese cadres should be prepared to relinquish their hold over Tibet, saying that the Chinese cadres should 'be glad to see the maturity' of Tibetan cadres. Hu proposed that the Tibetan cadres should make up more than two-thirds of all government functionaries within two or three years. His strategy was to withdraw thousands of Chinese cadres from Tibet, and he intended to achieve this by retiring, dismissing or transferring them to China. Of all the recommendations, this would have had the most impact on the Tibetan society Coupled with a general reduction of Chinese in Tibet, there would be an equal emphasis on the Tibetanisation of cadres. The Chinese cadres under the age of fifty would be required to learn Tibetan and to be able to read papers and documents written in Tibetan.[107] While the PLA was excluded from general criticism and Hu made no specific mention of its future role, the new directives applied equally to the army.

The Chinese recognized that the army was one of the problems. Not only was it the last power base of the Chinese cadres, but, as Yang Jingren noted, since the army was composed mainly of Chinese, the Tibetans regarded the difference between themselves and the army as one of 'ethnic relations'.[108] This was a diplomatic way of saying that the Tibetans viewed the PLA as a foreign army. The need to strengthen relations between Tibetans and the PLA was therefore stressed. The Party's propaganda department would carry out extensive education among Chinese cadres and the PLA on the Party's nationalities policies and would encourage the Chinese to adopt a more flexible policy towards the issue of religion and Tibetan culture.

If these changes could have been realised, there is no doubt that they would have made a great impact on Tibetan society, meeting many of the Tibetans' demands. In fact Hu Yaobang's gesture of appeasement was not only welcomed by the people in Tibet, but also by the Dalai Lama himself.

In March 1981, he wrote a most conciliatory letter to Deng Xiaoping which opened with the words, 'I agree with and believe in the Communist ideology'. He emphasised that he was 'pleased and applaud[ed] Comrade Hu Yaobang's efforts to make every possible attempt to right the wrongs by frankly admitting the past mistakes'.[109] The Dalai Lama believed that there was a realistic chance of coming to terms with the new Chinese leadership. His personal admiration for Hu Yaobang was evident. When Hu was re-elected as Party Secretary in September 1982, he received an unexpected telegram from the Dalai Lama, congratulating him on the election and declaring the hope that he would 'one day to be able to meet him'.[110] The Dalai Lama had earlier asked for a meeting with Hu Yaobang during one of his visits abroad, but this had been refused by the Chinese.

Hu Yaobang and Wan Li left Lhasa on 30 May 1980. Back in Beijing Hu went on to deal with the other main question of Tibet, namely that of the Dalai Lama himself. A year after his trip to Tibet, Hu Yaobang met Gyalo Dhundup in Beijing. The initial contact between Gyalo Dhundup and Deng Xiaoping had not yielded any favourable results for the Chinese. For the Chinese the visit of the Dharamsala delegation was a débâcle which had measurably strengthened the Dalai Lama's negotiating hand, but one from which they could recover by adopting a more liberal policy. In the words of Yang Jingren, the policy in Tibet would be 'leniency, leniency, leniency and more leniency'.[111] The Chinese also recognized that the Dalai Lama was cautious, watching carefully how the new policy would develop. They therefore waited exactly a year before they made their first proposal to the Dalai Lama. On 28 July 1981, at his meeting with Gyalo Dhundup, Hu Yaobang handed over a five-point proposal for the Dalai Lama. The Chinese had invested high hopes in the new policy. It was meant not only to remedy many of the grievances of the Tibetans, but also to counter any criticism from the Dalai Lama about conditions that his delegation had witnessed, and thus to entice the Dalai Lama to return to Tibet. The five points were:

(1) The Dalai Lama should recognise that China has now entered a new period of stability and economic change. If he doubts the reforms, he should observe the changes for the next few years.

(2) The Dalai Lama should not raise the history of repression that followed the suppression of the 1959 rebellion.

(3) The Chinese Government 'sincerely welcomes' the Dalai Lama and his followers to return to the motherland. China hopes that the Dalai Lama would contribute to upholding China's unity and promote solidarity between Han and Tibetan nationalities.

(4) The Dalai Lama would have the same status as he had enjoyed before

> 1959. He may be appointed Vice-Chairman of the NPC. But *it would be necessary that he should not live in Tibet or hold any position in Tibet* as there are younger Tibetans who have taken office and are doing their jobs well. He may visit Tibet as often as he likes.
>
> (5) When the Dalai Lama returns he may make press statements, and arrangements would be made to receive him by a suitable minister.[112]

The five-point proposal clearly showed that Beijing was prepared to make only minor concessions on the personal status of the Dalai Lama. Implicit in the first two conditions were the principles that the Dalai Lama should accept the new regime under Deng and acknowledge that the new leaders were not responsible for the repression in Tibet. This was not a major issue for the Dalai Lama: he was prepared to concede that China had entered a new period, and had faith in the permanency of the reforms. But the fourth point was clearly unacceptable to the Tibetans. The explicit implication was that the Dalai Lama should not play any important political role in the future of Tibet. This was a contentious point, particularly to the Communist Party. The Dalai Lama was the only figure who could present a direct challenge to the Party's authority in Tibet. The Chinese hoped to contain the Dalai Lama's power in the NPC, a position which would be of only symbolic importance and would carry no authority. The Chinese demand that the Dalai Lama should reside in Beijing because of his national position was also an astute attempt to lessen his authority in Tibet, where his presence would automatically create a power block in the region. The regional Party officials could never hope to prevent this repetition of the crisis faced in the late 1950s. The Chinese had refused to allow the Panchen Rinpoche to reside in Tashilhunpo monastery, the traditional abode of all the Panchen Rinpoches, for the same reason, and never bestowed on him any position inside the TAR.

It was evident that there was a wide gap between the Chinese and the Dalai Lama, who immediately rejected the Chinese proposal as attempting to reduce the Tibetan question from that of the status of Tibet and its six million inhabitants to the simple one of the personal status of the Dalai Lama. For the Chinese, the problem was indeed the single issue of the Dalai Lama, whose acquiescence they considered vital for the legitimacy in Tibet, and whose presence in India undermined their growing international stature. This was in fact, a realistic evaluation of the situation: the Chinese knew that the Dalai Lama's complete hold over the Tibetans both inside Tibet and in exile ensured that whatever decision the Dalai Lama made would be acceptable to the Tibetans. Beijing could also see that the support for the Tibetans in the West was largely based on the popularity of the Dalai Lama. If they could win over the Dalai Lama, all other issues would be resolved without much difficulty.

It was hard for Dharamsala politicians to accept this blunt truth. Since the 1960s the political culture that had evolved among the Tibetan refugees meant that the administration in Dharamsala saw itself as an 'exiled government'. This in turn meant that the exiled politicians viewed themselves as the only legitimate representatives of the Tibetan people. This made the negotiations more complex and required major concessions from both sides, which neither was willing to make. Since the start of the Beijing–Dharamsala dialogue, both sides had relied on Gyalo Dhundup as an intermediary. This was particularly important for Beijing, where the decision to use him was a calculated choice. Not only was he seen as a man who could influence the Dalai Lama, but his involvement enhanced the suggestion that the issue was a family matter. The Chinese were not entirely wrong about the significance of the Dalai Lama's family members, who evidently exercised considerable influence in Tibetan diaspora politics: the two delegations sent by the Dalai Lama had included his brother and sister, and several of his family held important positions in the exiled government. There was also another factor influencing the Chinese thinking: they knew that Gyalo Dhundup had in the past had close links with the Indian and American Governments, and they saw him as possibly having the ear of foreign governments as well as of his brother.

As it turned out, the Dalai Lama successfully deflected the Chinese attempt to limit the scope of the dialogue, but as we will see later this was to cost his side dearly. An important part of Dharamsala's strategy was to get the Chinese to meet members of the exiled Kashag. This was significant for the exiled politicians, who felt that their own importance was being reduced and that the Chinese regarded them as unimportant and did not care whether the 80,000 refugees returned to Tibet or not.

In 1982, the Chinese were still eager to entice the Dalai Lama back and had therefore agreed to meet a delegation from Dharamsala. The concession did not indicate any change in policy, but it provided an opportunity for the Dalai Lama to make his own proposals. He sent a team of senior politicians: Kalon Juchen Thubten, Phuntsog Tashi Takla, and Lodro Gyari. The Dalai Lama told the press that, unlike the previous delegation, the new group would 'tackle the real business'.[113]

Central to the Dalai Lama's new proposal were two demands, which would redefine the status of Tibet within China. The first was the unification of all Tibetan-inhabited areas, known as the Cholka-sum (*U-tsang*, Kham and Amdo), as a single political and administrative entity. The second was that Tibet should be given the same special status offered to Taiwan and Hong Kong. Dharamsala had pinned its hopes on persuading Deng to offer the Tibetans the equivalent of his proposal to Taiwan for unification with the mainland.[114] The demand was not unreasonable and in many ways the points granted in the 17-Point Agreement of 1951 looked very similar to the offers made to Hong Kong and Taiwan. The Chinese, however, responded by saying that Tibet had long been liberated and was already unified with the 'motherland'. However, their real reason for rejecting the proposal was more complex: Deng could not afford to be seen to be making excessive compromises. In any case Taiwan and Hong Kong were, from a practical point of view, far more important to China than Tibet. The economic power of the two small islands has given them world importance. We will see later that this demand became even more difficult for Deng to agree to.

The Dalai Lama's demand for unification of the entire Tibetan-speaking area under 'Bod Cholka-sum' has become deeply embedded in the political culture of the Tibetan diaspora, where the core of the refugees' political identity lay in the conception of Tibet as the unity of Kham, Amdo and *U-tsang*.[115] This had been crucial in forging unity among diverse refugee groups. But although the idea enjoys universal support among the exile community, it has no recent historical base and it is difficult to assess the extent of support it might enjoy inside Greater Tibet. Given the Tibetans' experiences under Communism, it is not inconceivable that the people in other Tibetan regions would shift their loyalty to the Dalai Lama: there is no doubt that the Dalai Lama enjoys universal devotion and adoration in all Tibetan-speaking areas and that he is regarded by all Tibetans as their leader (and not merely, as the Chinese claim, in his spiritual capacity). As noted before, the fact that the Chinese allowed the Dharamsala delegations to tour throughout all Tibetan-inhabited areas was an implicit recognition that the Dalai Lama speaks for the territory he claims. Dharamsala was also aware of the fact that historically the Lhasa Government had not exercised political authority in Kham and Amdo (now mostly in Qinghai and Sichuan Provinces), and had carefully arranged that the members of the three-man delegation in 1982 all originated from outside the TAR. This was to stress that the demand for the unification was the 'wish of the people' from Cholka-sum. The symbolism of Dharamsala's diplomacy did not go unnoticed in Beijing.

The Chinese bluntly rejected the Dalai Lama's proposals. They insisted that the only point of negotiation was the five points made by Hu Yaobang. It was apparent that Deng Xiaoping was not prepared to see the Dalai Lama's return at any cost and that the issue would be settled only on Chinese terms. It was more than likely that the Chinese leaders were convinced that they did not need to make any compromise with the Dalai Lama, because they thought the grievances of the Tibetans inside Tibet could be alleviated by the new reforms and that, as economic and social conditions in Tibet improved, the new regime would be accepted there. Not surprisingly, the first round of talks had not produced any firm consensus on the areas of discussion but had allowed both sides to set the parameters of the discussion and their objectives. Neither the Chinese nor the Tibetan side closed avenues of discussion, and for the next few years both sides held firmly to their respective stands.

The Chinese knew that the most important factor in their favour was their ability to manipulate conditions in Tibet. Any improvement in the social and economic conditions in Tibet would bring some measure of legitimacy and eventually force the Dalai Lama to cede to the Chinese terms. The Dalai Lama was aware of his lack of power to negotiate with the Chinese on an equal footing and he could not bring China to the negotiation table either by force or inducement. Although the Tibetans had demonstrated overwhelming support for the Dalai Lama, he had no power to influence day-to-day affairs in Tibet. The lack of power inside the country could only be counterbalanced by bringing international pressure to bear on China, particularly from the Western bloc, and so it was hoped that the growing economic ties between the West and China would make the new Chinese leadership – seen as constructive and pragmatic – susceptible to Western pressure. However, over the next few years there was a lull in the Dharamsala–Beijing dialogue. Having made their respective positions clear, the Chinese and Tibetans were prepared to wait.

Throughout the early 1980s the reformists, led by Deng Xiaoping, Hu Yaobang and Zhao Ziyang, held sway in Beijing. The reforms unleashed by Hu in Tibet had a dramatic effect in meeting the desired economic and social goals and eliminated the maladies of the Cultural Revolution. Initially, many people were suspicious of the changes, having in the past witnessed the Party loosen the noose only to tighten it later. The fact that Hu Yaobang himself came to Lhasa to announce the new reforms helped to dispel people's apprehensions and they began to embrace the reforms with enthusiasm. The decades of economic mismanagement and neglect had left the country in poverty, verging on destitution in some areas. The reforms freed the Tibetan peasantry from the shackles of collectivism and eliminated the bureaucratic hold over economic activities and decision-making. Production decisions reverted to individual households and the income generated became solely for the use of the household, which, as promised by Hu Yaobang, was freed from state taxes and could sell its produce directly to the market. The changes in the management of agriculture production had a major impact on Tibetan society.

The 90 per cent or more of Tibet's population who were engaged in agriculture were the main beneficiaries of the new reforms and by 1981 the per capita income of the Tibetan peasantry had risen sharply: in 1979 the average income was 127 yuan, but within two years it had risen to 220 yuan.[116] While this was an important indication of a marked improvement in living standards, in objective terms the standard of living returned to the level the people had enjoyed before the Chinese 'liberation'. But on the social level the impact was greater. Daily life became more relaxed and there was no longer pressure to attend countless meetings. The Tibetans discarded the drab uniform of socialism and reverted to traditional clothes. Agricultural practices in nomadic and farming areas returned to traditional methods not only because individual households found it expensive to maintain agricultural machinery and purchase fertiliser, but also as part of a categorical rejection by the Tibetans of the Chinese system and a deliberate preference for the Tibetan 'ways of doing things'. In rural areas, traditional social institutions and patterns of marriage quickly re-emerged as the norm. It was evident that the years of propaganda and ideological education had made little or no dent on Tibetan society. Within a short period the Tibetans discarded the veneer of the socialist or proletarian culture imposed by the Chinese, and traditional cultural practices returned with a new vitality.

Just before Hu Yaobang left Lhasa, he invited three young Tibetan cadres, Dorje Tseten, Lobsang Tsultrim and Phuntsog Tashi, for a private meeting. Hu told them that they should become the backbone of Tibet.[117] They were not only Tibetans but committed Party members and were, he said, to become the new generation of Tibetan leaders, who would hold Marxist–Leninist–Mao Zedong thought as their guiding principles. Tibetans had till then constituted less than half of the cadre force in Tibet. The Tibetan cadres were a mixture of early Communists from Kham (such as Tian Biao, who was appointed one of the deputy secretaries of the CCP in Tibet and later became the regional governor) and those who were promoted during the Cultural Revolution because of their class backgrounds. The most powerful Tibetan cadres now belonged to the latter category, exemplified by Ragdi and Pasang. They were indoctrinated with the radical ideology of the period and had very little in common with the new reformists. The leaders of their type were dismissed in the streets as 'thugs' and commanded very little respect from the ordinary people but the Chinese found that they could not afford to dismiss them. There was a third category of Tibetan cadres, whom Hu Yaobang hoped could be relied on to carry out the reforms. They had received their education in China in the 1950s and had been neglected and sent to the countryside during the Cultural Revolution. Many of them had been given bad class labels; some were children of aristocrats, which excluded them from the bureaucracy and the Party. It was this category of Tibetan cadre which the Party now wanted to promote.

The increase in the number of Tibetans in the bureaucracy was mainly achieved by the withdrawal of a large number of Chinese from Tibet, as promised by Hu Yaobang. During 1980–81 thousands of Chinese cadres were transferred to China[118] and the vacancies were rapidly filled by newly recruited Tibetans. In 1981, the percentage of Tibetan cadres exceeded 50 per cent for the first time. The figures below show the numbers and percentage of Tibetan cadres 1965–1981.[119]

Year	Number of Tibetan cadres	%
1965	7,508	32.9
1978	20,023	44.5
1981	29,406	54.4

By 1986 the figure had risen to 60.3 per cent, with an even more marked increase at the lower levels of administration.[120] However, the Chinese found that there were real difficulties in Tibetanising the bureaucracy. The past years of neglect had left Tibet without an educated workforce: many of the Tibetan cadres had no qualifications and 50 per cent of them had only been educated up to junior middle school. This had left them 'barely competent for their work'.[121]

In any case, the surge in the number of Tibetan cadres did not necessarily mean that a transfer of power had taken place. The objective was not to shift the balance of power, but to embellish the Party's 'work style', especially at grass-roots level, where the Tibetan cadres would have a natural advantage over the Chinese, who lacked the linguistic ability to communicate with the masses. More importantly, as the Chinese authorities admitted, the 'left deviation' had damaged and weakened the Party's 'prestige among the people'. The key to recovering the Party's authority was to implement the reforms and the correct work style: 'whether or not the Party's work style could be corrected had become a major issue related to the life or death of the Party', as one Chinese leader put it.[122] The changes in Tibet coincided with the rectification campaign being carried out in the rest of China to restore the Party's legitimacy and prestige; the adjustments in Tibet did not therefore suggest any preferential treatment but rather the new leaders' need to re-establish their authority. This is not to say that the increase in the number of Tibetan cadres, which provided new opportunities for a generation of young educated Tibetans who had suffered during the Cultural Revolution, was not welcomed.[123] However, throughout the 1980s, the changes met stiff resistance from both Tibetan and Chinese cadres, who had a vested interest in keeping the status quo. At all levels the cadres who had gained their positions during the Cultural Revolution were reluctant to surrender their power. They watched with horror the reappearance of all the things that they had earlier denounced.

The Tibetanisation of the cadres was supplemented by a new emphasis on the United Front strategy: the traditional Tibetan élite who had in the past commanded respect from the masses were to be promoted and appointed to positions within the Party and the administration. As noted earlier, soon after the downfall of the Gang of Four the Party had rehabilitated many members of the former Tibetan aristocracy and they were now brought in to play an important role in Tibetanising the bureaucracy. By 1982 the authorities were able to claim that over 600 Tibetan ex-officials were now holding leading posts in the government and the Party. However, as Yin Fatang pointed out, 'the influence of erroneous Leftist ideology remains very deep . . . [it] remains the main obstacle' to change in Tibet.[124] We will see later that both these strategies were to suffer setbacks.

Another important innovation the Party undertook was to introduce legislative measures to institutionalise the reforms.[125] The governmental structure was re-established, the Regional People's Congress and the Political Consultative Committee were reconvened and, as in China, elections were organised for the Regional People's Congress. However, both of these bodies, at national as well as regional level, were seen as cosmetic institutions. In practice they were bodies designed to contain opposition.

In January 1980, at the meeting of the NPC in Beijing, it was announced that a law would be enacted to 'realise the right to autonomy' of the minority nationalities, a concept which, at least since 1967, had been an empty one. The first promise Hu Yaobang made was to respect Tibet's autonomy, which he defined as the 'right to decide for oneself'.[126] When in 1982 China adopted a new constitution, it defined more precisely the right of autonomy.[127] The new constitution remedied the shortcomings of the 1975 constitution, which had discarded the rights granted twenty years earlier to minority groups in China's first constitution.[128]

However, it was not until May 1984 that the NPC passed a law on regional autonomy, based on the relevant articles of the constitution and further clarifying the right of autonomy. On the surface the law on Regional Autonomy granted broad powers to manage internal economic, social and cultural affairs. It allowed the Regional People's Congress to enact specific laws. The Autonomous Region was also granted the right to amend and rectify the laws passed by the NPC in Beijing.[129] However, it was apparent that the wording of the law was too general and that often each of the articles contained limiting clauses. It was also clear that the autonomous areas were required to seek permission from 'higher authority'.

At best, the new law could only be regarded as an aspirational statement rather than a practical policy and Tibetans dismissed it, saying 'Thunder that does not bring rain.'[130] As in the rest of China, no law could moderate the power of the Communist Party which, as the source of all authority, and in the absence of clear-cut separation between the Party and government, exercised final authority in all matters. This situation was even more incontrovertible in Tibet, where the governmental structure remained fragile. Many Tibetans in the government were reluctant to stick their necks out, as they had gained their position only at the 'grace and patronage' of the Chinese and the Party. Everyone knew that the government was subservient to the Party.

There were also other objective factors which prevented Tibet from exercising the freedom granted in the law. The fiscal powers given to an Autonomous Region and the right to keep all the revenue raised, including all foreign exchange earned by Tibet, made very little difference since revenue generated locally made up only a small percentage of the total expenditure in Tibet. Between 1980 and 1982, 98 per cent of the region's budget was met by subsidies from the Centre. In 1983, Tibet generated 500.8 million yuan in revenue but the total disposable revenue was 1,000.5 million yuan. The difference was met by subsides from Beijing.[131] This chronic dependence on Chinese subsidy made the fiscal powers granted in law of little practical value. Moreover, habitual interference from Beijing and other central government offices made 'the provisions requiring special preferences a paper promise only'.[132] Another factor was that Tibet's strategic position meant that the army continued to play a very important role in the region. For these reasons, Tibet could not exercise effectively the autonomy granted in the law. Nevertheless, the situation was clearly better than before and there was a positive aspect to the law: it clearly stipulated that the leading cadres and the governor of Tibet must be of Tibetan nationality.

These changes were welcomed and there was a marked improvement in the daily life of the people though it came neither from the Tibetanisation of the bureaucracy nor the legislative measures. The absence of habitual state and Party interference in daily life in rural areas meant that in the remote areas most aspects of life reverted to the traditional way of life, free from the watchful eyes of Party officials. Religion, which had been denounced in a such a lurid fashion, resurfaced as the centre of Tibetan life. The people were permitted to carry out their religious practices and the cadres were instructed to respect them. However, the Tibetans considered that the changes had only achieved the righting of the wrongs of the past three decades – they were not an end to all grievances.

Despite some minor difficulties during 1980–4, the Chinese were satisfied with the progress in Tibet and in July 1982 allowed the Panchen Rinpoche to visit Tibet for the first time since 1964. It was apparent that the Tibetan people's faith in him had not diminished and he still commanded great devotion and respect. It was reported that the Chinese authorities in Tibet were at first reluctant to acknowledge his importance; the Panchen Rinpoche himself later noted that the Chinese authorities in Tibet had refused his father entry. However, as the Chinese authorities witnessed the warm welcome given to him, they began to change their attitude. For his part, the Panchen Rinpoche was shocked by the amount of destruction to

Tibet's cultural heritage. However, in public speeches the Panchen Rinpoche endorsed the Communist Party's new policy in Tibet.

In February 1983, the Dalai Lama gave a Kalachara teaching at Bodha Gaya in northern India, and the Chinese allowed hundreds of Tibetans to travel to India on pilgrimage to attend. The pilgrims must have given favourable reports on the situation in Tibet, because the Dalai Lama showed that he too was impressed with the course of the reforms and during the sermon unexpectedly announced that he hoped to visit in 1985 'if the present trend of improving the situation in Tibet continues in the right direction'.[133] It was not clear whether a secret invitation from the Chinese existed, or if he took the initiative himself. The choice of the date seems puzzling since the Chinese had already said that 1985 would mark the celebration of the twentieth anniversary of the establishment of the TAR.

The Dalai Lama's statement was an indication that the reform undertaken by Deng and Hu Yaobang had achieved some success in bringing Tibet out of the dark period of Maoism, and that the leaders in China were also confident that a new period of economic and social development could be brought to Tibet. As the momentum of the Deng's 'Four Modernisations' was gathering speed in rest of China, the reformers in the Party realised the pace of development in Tibet would need to be accelerated if it were not to lag behind once more. The period 1979–83 had brought modest economic benefit and the main changes had been gradual relaxation of social and political control. The crucial problem of Tibetan economic development was yet be addressed earnestly.

FOURTEEN

A Road to the New Tibet

The new policy under Deng was received with enthusiasm; whether in Tibet or in exile, Tibetans had high hopes that it would lead to a better future for their country. The Four Modernisations policy was regarded as an attempt to lead China into a new era of 'socialist modernisation'. A programme of agricultural reforms promoting a household-based production system in Tibet was gradually being developed. The Party's official policy in Tibet and China at the time was the propagation of the 'commodity economy' and the 'open door' initiative. These became the new catchword phrases among Party officials in Tibet. The first phase of liberalisation was the relaxation of some of the wide-ranging controls exercised by the party in every sphere of life, with the aim of accelerating the region's stagnant economy. It was envisaged that the new development would shift Tibet's economy from one based on animal husbandry and agriculture to one of small-scale industrial production, exploiting the region's natural resources.

The Second Tibet Work Forum

Between 27 February and 6 March 1984, the CCP Central Secretariat convened the Second Work Forum in Tibet. This time hundreds of cadres and members of the regional CPPCC were flown to Beijing to attend sessions presided over by Hu Yaobang, a sign that the leadership in Beijing had kept a watchful eye on the progress of the reforms in Tibet and that the central leadership was formulating day-to-day policy in Tibet. At the opening of the meeting Hu Yaobang remarked, 'I have no surprises for you.'[1] Clearly he was thinking about his visit to Lhasa four years earlier in 1980. He stressed the continuation of the earlier relaxed policy and the need to allow the region to recover from the ravages of the Cultural Revolution. The meeting went on to initiate a second phase of reforms in Tibet. Although the meeting did not have the same significance as Hu's first visit to Lhasa, it nevertheless became apparent that his new announcements indicated a change of direction and were to have serious repercussions in Tibet. The new direction was officially described as 'the opening of Tibet'.

The key announcement made by Hu Yaobang was the decision to open Tibet up by freeing the restrictions on Chinese from entering Tibet for business and trade. This allowed other provinces, state-owned enterprises and individuals from anywhere in China to open businesses in Tibet. The new open-door policy also meant opening Tibet to the outside world. The Chinese had realised the potential of tourism as a major source of income for the region's economic development and since the early 1980s had noted the growing number of people wanting to visit Tibet. However, between 1980 and 1984, less than 4,000 tourists were allowed entry.[2] To realise the full potential of tourism, the authorities had to improve on and develop a tourist infrastructure, with hotels and communications. One of the key economic projects was aimed precisely at improving these conditions: a joint venture with the leading Western hotel chain Holiday Inn. At first the influx of tourists was not a problem but it eventually caused many difficulties for the Chinese.

The main problem was the opening of the region for migrants from China. At the meeting in Beijing, Dorje Tseten, one of the Tibetan Deputy Party Secretaries, tried to protest that the Tibetans would not be able to compete with the outsiders and that the influx of migrants would create social problems.[3] Others tried to point out potential problems such as antiques smuggling. Hu Yaobang was rather dismissive of these protests, saying they were minor issues which could be handled by laws passed by the regional government. Hu explained that the national policy of opening up China was meant to apply to both external and internal openness and stressed that it was the only possible way to improve the local economy in Tibet. It would be 'suicidal', he told the meeting, for the region to be kept closed any longer.[4] It is interesting to note that the move to open up Tibet was contrary to Hu Yaobang's earlier policy, which suggests either that he had changed his views on the nature of the problem, or that Deng Xiaoping, the only person who could have persuaded Hu Yaobang to reverse his policy, had demanded the opening of Tibet, as he had already done in China. The large numbers of Chinese entering Tibet were to cause major resentment against the authorities.

Another interesting issue discussed by Hu Yaobang at the Second Tibet Work Forum was the question of Leftist opposition to the new policies in Tibet. Between 1983 and 1984 there was renewed emphasis in China on removing those cadres who had made serious political mistakes during the Cultural Revolution and continued to resist change. Hu Yaobang remarked that there were both Tibetans and Chinese who should have been weeded out of the Party, but remained prominent in Tibet. He added that he had received reports identifying Ragdi as one of the 'three categories' of people who should have been expelled from the Party. However, Hu Yaobang went on to defend Ragdi, whom he had met in 1975, when both of them were attending the Party cadre school. During their time together he had come to know Ragdi well and Hu went on to list three of Ragdi's qualities, namely his class origin, his faith in Mao's teaching and his loyalty to the Communist Party.[5] It was clear that even the most liberal leader was not prepared to carry out a purge of Tibetan Leftists, perhaps because – as the qualities Hu mentioned in Ragdi imply – only those Tibetans who had gained most under the Communists could be relied upon to support Beijing.

Ideologically, however, Leftist Tibetans were inclined to support more radical policies. They despised many aspects of Tibetan culture which they saw as 'backward' or 'superstitious' and supported Chinese attempts to reduce the dominance of religion in Tibetan society. This was very useful for the Chinese as they could use the Leftist Tibetans to counter other Tibetan Party members who were more nationalistic in their views. Either intentionally or by chance, the Chinese had managed to divide Tibetan Party members along ideological lines, rather than on ethnic grounds, which would have presented Beijing with serious difficulties. This ensured that Tibetan Party members did not represent a homogeneous group even in the regional CCP.

When the TAR officials returned to Lhasa after attending the third regional Party congress, which merely reiterated the announcement made by Hu Yaobang in Beijing, most of the members were whispering about how 'Hu Yaobang had saved Ragdi'.[6] The decision not to remove Leftists from the regional Party had created a negative impression among the new Tibetan party officials. They interpreted it to mean that the Party would continue to rely on people such as Ragdi, who retained his position as one of the deputy secretaries in the regional CCP. This was contrary to the general trend in the Party, which had decreed that one of the major tasks of the Party's rectification was to weed out the 'three categories of people', who were described in China as 'time bombs hidden within the Party'.[7]

When Hu Yaobang had visited Lhasa in 1980, his private meeting with Dorje Tseten and other Tibetan Party members had implied support for the more liberal faction among the Tibetans, a policy characterised in Tibet as 'repenting for the past mistakes and willing to change'.[8] Now, however, it was felt that as long as Tibetan Leftists mended their ways they could continue to play an important role in the region. However, during the Party Rectification Campaign, the need to 'thoroughly eliminate the impact of Leftist thoughts' was stressed.[9] Yin Fatang claimed that the Leftist influence in Tibet was very serious and that only by breaking away from 'this obsolete thinking' could economic progress be realised.[10] Later the Panchen Rinpoche was to complain that many cadres had 'not got over their leftist hangover' and that despite their crimes during the Cultural Revolution, the Party had given them new positions.[11]

The key element of the new policy was promoted as ' to get rich as soon as possible'. Yin Fatang outlined a five-point objective in the second phase of the reforms:

(1) The main effort must be the economic development of the region.

(2) The region must take a leap from subsistence to commodity economy, and the region should move from a closed to an open door policy.

(3) The reliance on agriculture as the main basis of production should be changed. There should be a move to create a commodity production.

(4) There should be further relaxation of administrative control over the economy.

(5) There should be a change in leadership methods and work styles.[12]

The policy also endorsed the continuation of the 'responsibility' system in rural areas, which was to be extended until 1990, and contracted leases for livestock and land were to be extended to thirty years. While it officially advocated a non-interventionist policy and encouraged the development of a free market, the Party found it increasingly difficult to allow complete freedom. In nomadic areas the wool trade became so lucrative that the nomads were forced to sell a quota to the government at a lower price than they could obtain in an open market.[13] In some remote areas the communes were not completely disbanded and the separation of the government from commune administration did not take place. There were still major administrative reforms that needed to be carried out in Tibet.

The Party's new policy of opening Tibet, and its elevation of economic development as the primary objective, had dire consequences for the Tibetans. The Chinese saw that the main weakness of the Tibetan economy was that the region somehow existed outside the new economic developments in China, and that it was becoming ever more dependent on state subsidies. Chinese economists described the situation as 'blood transfusion', whereby the central government was forever forced to bail out the region because of its inability to generate its own revenue to meet expenditure.[14] Tibet was caught in a spiral of dependency. Moreover, the region produced almost nothing that could be sold in significant quantities in the wider market. The recent reforms had merely strengthened the 'natural economy' of the region, which was tending to move towards self-sufficiency rather than to create a market-oriented economy. Chinese economists noted that although the Tibetan herdsmen produced large quantities of butter, they consumed 90 per cent of it themselves[15] and expended the surplus on non-productive activities such as temple-building. In the Chinese view, the Tibetan peasantry made little or no effort to convert the surplus into marketable goods or profit.[16]

This was naturally seen as a hindrance to the long-term goal of economic development in Tibet. The key to future development was seen as the economic integration of Tibet within the emerging market economies of China and neighbouring countries. The objective, which was to transform the Tibetan peasantry into consumers and producers of modern goods, necessarily entailed the construction of an infrastructure that would push the region towards greater integration with the rest of China. Chinese economists noted that there were many natural barriers preventing the development of a commodity economy in Tibet, such as the difficulties in transport, power supply, and the poor educational level of the people.[17] These objective difficulties would require massive state investment and, without a promise of quick profit, it was highly unlikely there would be any significant amount of private or foreign capital poured into the region, leaving Beijing alone to supply the necessary capital investment. The authorities announced forty-three major projects in Tibet, ranging from the construction of a sports stadium in Lhasa to the upgrading of the Qinghai–Tibet highway, the expansion of the Yangbachen geothermal power station and the building of the Lhasa Hotel. All these projects were designed partly to address the need to create a better infrastructure.

Since Hu Yaobang had first visited Tibet, the Party had instituted a practice of having a senior Party leader regularly inspect the region as a means of keeping the reforms on the right course. In August 1984 Beijing dispatched to Lhasa a high-level delegation led by Hu Quli, a member of the Central Committee, to 'conduct a thorough investigation' of the situation in Tibet. He endorsed the policy of opening up Tibet and allowing its people greater freedom in economic activity, but the visit once again confirmed that the Central Committee intended to keep a tight control on the running of the region. The Chinese leaders were pleased with the progress of the reforms in Tibet and both the leadership in Beijing and the local leadership felt confident that they had basically solved the main problems affecting the region and had gained the approval of the people.

Beijing Hardens Its Policy Towards the Dalai Lama

Meanwhile, it was also becoming apparent that the Chinese attitude towards the Dalai Lama had toughened. During the Second Tibet Work Forum, Hu Yaobang mentioned that if they were successful in improving economic conditions in Tibet, the Dalai Lama's ability to agitate for greater freedom would be blunted. He also confirmed that Beijing would not shift from the five-point proposal for the return of the Dalai Lama. At the 4th Regional People's Congress held in May 1984, Yin Fatang attacked the Dalai Lama in public for the first time since Deng came to power. He declared that the

Dalai Lama's 'greatest mistake was treason' but as long as 'he was willing to admit his mistakes', the authorities would welcome him back.[18] The statement did not go unnoticed in Dharamsala, where the government-in-exile immediately asked the Chinese authorities for clarification, but Beijing refused to respond. For Dharamsala, the statement seemed to be a clear rebuff to the Dalai Lama's announcement that he would like to visit Tibet in 1985. Yin Fatang's speech may have been a deliberate signal of a shift in Beijing policy towards the Dalai Lama but it seems more likely that it was an *ad hoc* speech made without authorisation from Beijing.

Nevertheless, the speech startled the government-in-exile, which had had no contact with the Chinese for three years. There were now worries that the Chinese might break off the dialogue that had begun in 1979. In October 1984, the Dalai Lama once again sent a three-man delegation to Beijing. They were met by Yang Jingren, the director of the United Front, and Jiang Ping, the deputy director. The Tibetan delegation repeated the points they had made earlier but went further in spelling out their demands, which still centred on the unification of the three provinces of Tibet. This time the Tibetans also made a proposal for the de-militarising of Tibet and declaring it a 'zone of peace'.[19]

The Chinese side rejected any discussion of the larger issues. Both in private meetings and in public they held a position of no compromise. Later, through an article in *Beijing Review*, China restated the five-point proposal made by Hu Yaobang in 1981 and made it known that these points were non-negotiable. It was clear that the Chinese had adopted a 'take it or leave it' attitude. In the early stages of the dialogue, Beijing's commitment had underlined the involvement of Deng Xiaoping, China's paramount leader, and of Hu Yaobang, the most senior Party official. Once the Chinese leaders lost interest in the issue and it was delegated to the United Front, any possibility of reaching a compromise was effectively ended. Although the United Front Department was an important part of the CCP, its leaders, such as Yang Jingren, were not in a position to deviate from the guidelines set by Deng Xiaoping and Hu Yaobang.

In retrospect, it appears that Dharamsala had badly misjudged the situation in China and failed to grasp the original opportunity provided by the Chinese leader. One of the main problems was that, for Dharamsala, the developments in China came so swiftly that when Beijing initiated the talks, they had found themselves ill-prepared. Instead of meeting the Chinese offer headlong, they went on to demand petty concessions, which were unrelated to the larger issue. The Dalai Lama's request for a meeting with Ngabo and Phuntsog Wangyal (a former Tibetan communist official), even though neither them was in any position to influence the final outcome, is an example of this. The move suggested to the Chinese that either the Dalai Lama had doubts about the Chinese leaders or he wanted time to formulate his demands. Hence Beijing's warning that the Dalai Lama should not try to 'beat around the bush or look for a bargain'.[20] The Chinese continued to dismiss the fact that there was a 'question of Tibet' to be settled, seeing the problem only in terms of whether or not the Dalai Lama would return. They rejected the Dalai Lama's offer to visit Tibet in 1985, on the shallow pretext that Tibet would be preoccupied with preparations for the celebration of the twentieth anniversary of the TAR. The message was clear that a return could only take place on Chinese terms and the Tibetan delegation returned to India without any sign of success. They were unable to persuade the Chinese either to broaden the scope of the discussion, or to compromise on their initial stand.

China's renewed confidence was undoubtedly based on their success in dealing with some of the problems in Tibet. By 1985, many people in Tibet were saying that they had never had it so good. The Chinese could feel confident about their hold on Tibet: not only had the economy greatly improved but externally they had had some success in obtaining international approval. Since the early 1980s the Chinese authorities had allowed small numbers of Western tourists to enter Tibet, in line with plans to develop tourism as a major industry in the region. The number of tourists increased rapidly, and the influx of Tibetan pilgrims and traders mingling with them added to the relaxed atmosphere in the mid-eighties. This was symbolised for the Chinese by celebration of the twentieth anniversary of the founding of TAR.

A New Party Secretary

The celebration also marked the end of Yin Fatang's tenure as the First Party Secretary. Having successfully brought Tibet through the difficult period of adjustment, he was awarded with a senior post in China. His successor was Wu Jinghua, an Yi national from Southern China. Wu had joined the Communist Party in 1949 and risen rapidly through the ranks of the Party bureaucracy. Under the new regime of 1979 he had become a vice-minister of the newly revived State Nationalities Affairs Commission, and played an important part in the formulation of the liberal policy. All his predecessors as Party Secretary – Zhang Guohua, Ren Rong and Yin Fatang – had had long experience of working in Tibet and had come from the ranks of the PLA. Wu Jinghua had not worked in Tibet nor in the army, nor did he have a network of personal ties in the region. He had to strengthen his position quickly to secure his standing as First Secretary.

Wu Jinghua's appointment was in line with Hu Yaobang's new policy in Tibet. His lack of experience in the area was compensated for by the fact that he himself was from a minority background. Hu must have believed that this would provide a basis for empathy with the problems in Tibet. He also had long experience of working with minority affairs. Between 1981 and 1983 he had presided over the Society for the Modernisation of Agriculture in Sichuan (with particular reference to minority areas in the province), work which had placed him directly in contact with Tibetans outside the TAR. Although Wu Jinghua lacked a base in the army, this was balanced by his strong connections with the leadership in Beijing, where he held the post of First Deputy Minister of the State Nationalities Affairs Commission.

One of the issues that came bubbling to the surface with the appointment of Wu Jinghua was the Tibetans' resentment at Beijing's failure to appoint a Tibetan to head the region, which implied that no Tibetans were ready to take up such a responsible job. The Chinese claimed that there were objective reasons for the failure. Even the most senior Tibetan Party leaders lacked experience outside the region and for years had occupied only decorative positions in the Party. Another minor point was that many of the Tibetan leaders were relatively young; Hu Yaobang pointed out that people like Ragdi would reach only sixty in the year 2000, a remark which seemed to imply that these people would be assuming top leadership positions in that period. However, these were not very convincing arguments. The real reason was a mixture of Beijing's lack of trust of Tibetans and the absence of clearly identifiable candidates. The Chinese authorities tended to stress the difference between the Tibetan and Chinese Party members in terms of objective factors such as the level of education, work experience and ideological knowledge. The many Tibetans who were joining the Party were mostly thought to be doing so for opportunistic reasons. It was noted that many of the Tibetan members lacked a basic knowledge of the Party, and that at a lower level many Tibetan members were not only ignorant of Chinese but also illiterate in Tibetan. Such discoveries led in January 1983 to a series of education classes for Party members arranged by the Party's organisational and propaganda department to familiarise them with the Party's new constitution and socialist ideology. However, the Chinese admitted that there 'existed the nationality and religious problem'.[21] This indicated that there was a gulf between Tibetan and Chinese Party members which went beyond differences of education and experience. The question of Tibetan Party members who continued to believe in religion was a difficult issue for the Communists, as we will see later.

It was apparent that the Tibetan party leaders occupied a precarious position in the CCP. They were faced with the ever-present danger of accusations of showing 'local nationalism' and of putting ethnic interests over the wider concerns of the Party and the motherland. This was clearly illustrated by the removal of one leading Tibetan Party official, Yanling Dorje, who served as one of the deputy Party Secretaries in the early 1980s. In 1985 he was transferred to Sichuan Province and three years later he was appointed vice-chairman of the Sichuan branch of the CPPCC. It was widely believed that Yanling antagonised the Chinese officials, who accused him of 'local nationalism'. Therefore, many senior Tibetan party leaders found it difficult to balance their concern for the region with the need to show loyalty to Beijing. However, we know little about the extent of ethnic conflicts within the Party at this stage. The Chinese authorities have effectively concealed inner Party conflict and continue to paint a rosy picture of the situation.

Any initial reservations the Tibetans may have had over the appointment of Wu Jinghua were quickly dispelled and he won popular support. During the Tibetan New Year ceremony in February 1986, Wu attended the religious ceremony in the Tsuglakhang wearing Tibetan dress, a simple gesture which won the approval of the Tibetans, but alienated many Chinese cadres, who labelled him the 'lama secretary'. The Panchen Rinpoche described him as 'one of the best officials in Tibet'.[22] Wu's liberal attitude towards religion seemed to win the support of the Tibetans, but the Communist Party viewed such actions unfavourably, saying they raised expectations and encouraged the development of unhealthy nationalistic trends. The question of religion was once again revived as the central issue in Tibet. This was to mark the divergence of officially promoted reforms from the changes that were taking place in the society, which were beyond the control of the Party.

It was only after Wu Jinghua came to Tibet that the regional Party began to address the Tibetans' demands for greater religious freedom. Having called for 'a fresh understanding' of Tibet,[23] Wu argued that the Party had to accept the fact that there was a 'universal belief in Buddhism among the Tibetan people.'[24] He was also willing to accept the fact that religion dominated every aspect of life in Tibet and that any attempt to undermine the centrality of Buddhism would be met with resistance.

In February 1986, the Party allowed the celebration of the Monlam ceremony for the first time since it was banned in 1967. This had a major social and psychological impact among Tibetan people, not only in the TAR but throughout the ethnic Tibetan areas. When the news was released that the authorities would allow the monks to hold the ceremony, thousands of pilgrims flocked to Lhasa from every corner of the country. More than anything that the Party had done over the past five years, the decision to allow the Monlam ceremony convinced the Tibetans that the Chinese were prepared to allow the Tibetans to define what type of reforms they wanted.

The Tibetans took full advantage of Wu Jinghua's liberal policy towards religion. For the first time they began publicly to display photos of the Dalai Lama and to defy Chinese laws restricting the rebuilding of monasteries and temples. The state laws forbade anyone under eighteen years of age to become a monk, but no one paid any attention to the restriction and hundreds of young boys were sent to monasteries. In some remote areas like Dagyab there were more students entering monasteries than local schools.[25] The Chinese authorities wanted to restrict the numbers of monasteries and temples rebuilt, and the local people were supposed to seek permission from the Religious Affairs Bureau for such projects, but since the people were able to raise funds privately, there was very little the Chinese could do to prevent increasing construction. The new phase of reform also served to heighten the Tibetans' political awareness and awaken deep-seated grievances. This pushed the reforms in a direction over which the Chinese authorities had no control.

The Communists had hoped to promote a limited but controlled revival of Tibetan culture and tradition. But people were simply not prepared to accept officially defined limits to the new freedom of religion. The Communists had always known that there was an inherent danger in arousing the Tibetans' latent aspirations, which were naturally linked to the question of religion. While the Chinese had granted some privileges to the former secular élite, namely the aristocracy, they hesitated in promoting many of the Tibetan lamas and Rinpoches and tried to draw a clear distinction between what they regarded as the legitimate expression of religion and its illegal use. It was stressed that the authorities would not tolerate the use of religion to undermine the 'unity of the motherland' or to impede economic development. Religious institutions approved by the Chinese, such as the Buddhist Association, commanded little or no respect from the Tibetans; neither did officially promoted Rinpoches such as Phagpa Gelek Namgyal, the head lama of the Chamdo region. The Communists were cynical about such high-ranking lamas and Rinpoches, who were used to convey the Party's message of economic progress and modernisation. While in public the Party promoted Phagpa Gelek Namgyal as a prominent religious leader, it was commonly known in Lhasa that an internal Communist Party document had described him as a 'hooligan' and that he was held in contempt. The officially promoted Rinpoches and lamas were consequently not seen by the Tibetans as their natural leaders.

By the middle of 1986 the Chinese were encountering difficulties in limiting the growing number of monks and related religious institutions. As we shall see later, this was to present a major challenge to the authorities. The revival of religion as the centre of Tibetan life was seen by the Chinese as a step backwards both in terms of ideology and of the modernisation of the region. This view was also shared by many Tibetans who saw the revival of monasticism as an obstacle to modernisation. More importantly, the awakening of religious feelings brought to the fore the question of the Dalai Lama's return. It was evident that there was universal devotion and loyalty to the exiled leader. The Chinese tried to separate the Dalai Lama's spiritual and political authority, but in the minds of the Tibetans the two were fused. There was no doubt that the Tibetans saw the Dalai Lama quite simply as their saviour, Kyabgon.

One of the main contradictions that emerged during Wu Jinghua's period was that while the Party was prepared to make limited concessions to local conditions, it was not willing either to endorse social pluralism or to accept the emergence of social institutions independent of the Party. The demand for change stemmed mostly from religious institutions and the central question was whether the Chinese authorities would be able to contain the growing demand for greater religious freedom in Tibet, which it had hoped to satisfy by the readoption of the United Front and the extension of patronage to religious figures. However, it was apparent that the Chinese authorities would do their utmost to resist any demands that advocated independence. This was reflected in the imprisonment of Geshe Lobsang Wangchuk, a scholarly monk who had openly argued that Tibet not only had the right to independence but that she had never been a part of China.[26] In February 1983, when wall posters appeared in Lhasa advocating Tibetan independence, the Chinese authorities quickly arrested a number of monks from Drepung monastery. In August a monk named Palden Gyatso was found guilty of spreading 'counter revolutionary propaganda' and was sentenced to eight years' imprisonment.[27] The Tibetans were painfully aware of the limits of Chinese tolerance and knew that they would have to work within the restrictions imposed by the Chinese.

The growing assertiveness of the Tibetans coincided with an influx of Chinese migrants into Tibet. As noted earlier, this policy was endorsed by Hu Yaobang himself. By the middle of the 1980s the repatriation of Chinese cadres promised by Hu had come to an end. The resettlement of cadres from Tibet into other parts of China had not been a great success, as other provinces had been reluctant to accept them and to provide jobs and social provisions. The new policy of opening up the region and the concentration on economic development now led to further lifting of the restrictions on Chinese entering Tibet. There was an official policy of importing technical and professional expertise from all over China to service the new construction and development projects, many of which had been handed over to state-owned enterprises or companies owned by other provincial governments which had found that almost all the professional labourers had to be imported from China. According to official sources, in the summer of 1984 over 10,000 self-employed workers entered Tibet.[28] They are said to 'have gone deep into pastoral and farming areas to run catering services, sell goods of all types, spreading economic information and making contributions to invigorating the economy'.[29] When in October 1984 Anhui province opened a construction company in Lhasa, it sent more than 3,000 people to Tibet.[30] Other sources claim that in the first three months of 1985, more than 60,000 Chinese workers entered Tibet.[31] The Chinese announced that these mass transfers were only a temporary measure to assist Tibet's development, and that once the projects were completed the Chinese workers would leave.

Another group of Chinese who were encouraged to settle in Tibet were recently demobilised troops. They were said to be ideally suited for resettlement in the region because many were technicians and skilled labourers.[32] In the past these soldiers would have preferred to have returned to their homes in China, but now a growing urban community, coupled with the uncertainty of finding work, made Tibet more attractive than a few years earlier. There was no doubt that initially the Chinese migrants were merely attracted by the higher pay and had no intention of settling in the region. In fact many of them had been sent by their work units in China. However, with the growing number of Chinese in Tibet and improvements in communications and other related facilities, life was made easier for those who settled. This led to a flourishing Chinese community in Tibet. It was not only skilled labourers and entrepreneurs who were attracted to the country; many intellectuals who had been driven out during the 'anti-spiritual pollution campaign' also found a home in the region,[33] where the Chinese authorities treated them more leniently than would have been the case in China proper. Some of these intellectuals founded 'the Snow Sea Poetry Group'.[34] What was most significant about the Chinese migrants was that for the first time many of them had come to Tibet voluntarily to seek their fortune. In the past almost all Chinese in Tibet had been sent by the government and had resented the fact they were stranded there, always looking forward to returning to China one day.

While the Chinese found that the growing number of their compatriots made the place more conducive to establishing a permanent home, for the Tibetans the influx of thousands of Chinese signalled a further threat to their new-found freedom and identity. The Tibetans viewed official motives with extreme suspicion, and on a personal level the Chinese immigrants threatened their economic security. Very quickly, the new migrants were able to dominate the region's fragile economy. Most of the state development projects employed skilled Chinese workers, and private traders moved in to meet the demand for consumer goods, which had to be imported from China. The Tibetans, lacking technical knowledge, linguistic skills and personal ties with China, were disadvantaged and unable to compete with the Chinese entrepreneurs.

However, this did not at first cause major resentment among the Tibetans. Despite the growing number of Chinese, the mid 1980s were the most relaxed period since 1960. As Tibet opened up, large numbers of Western tourists arrived, bringing to Lhasa a more congenial atmosphere and cosmopolitan character. The influx of Chinese into Tibet was in any case compensated for by Wu Jinghua's more liberal policy, which had the backing of senior leaders in Beijing. In August 1985, Beijing announced that the local authorities in Tibet could 'disregard' the central government's instructions and regulations which did not conform to specific conditions in the region,[35] a significant concession which implied that Beijing was prepared to countenance some degree of local autonomy. In August 1985, Li Peng, while in Lhasa to attend the twentieth anniversary of the TAR, stressed that the policy of 'loosening control' and 'increasing flexibility' would remain unchanged for a long time to come.[36] Under Wu's protection, many Tibetan cadres and Party officials felt confident that there was a real possibility of genuine regional autonomy. The Tibetan leaders also had a realistic appreciation of the main problems confronting them in the drive to develop Tibet, namely the lack of technical and skilled manpower in Tibet. This could only be solved in the long term by better standards of education, and throughout the 1980s there was a new emphasis on the development of educational structures, with special schools being opened in other parts of China to facilitate the rapid increase in the number of Tibetan students gaining qualifications. In his 1985 work report Wu Jinghua announced an ambitious plan to boost Tibet's economy, aiming to raise per capita income to 1,200 yuan by the year 2000 and to create a skilled labour force in the region: it was announced that the government would train 15,000 professional and technical personnel to enable the region to dispense with the need to import large numbers of skilled personnel from China. Without a sufficiently large qualified and trained workforce, there was very little the Tibetan leaders could do to counter the influx of Chinese technicians into the region.

In November 1985 the regional Party announced a major reshuffle. For the first time many Tibetans were appointed to top positions within the Party. Wu Jinghua remained the First Secretary, but of the six Deputy Secretaries, five were Tibetans.[37] This was matched by the growing demands for further Tibetanisation of the administration and education. The issue was taken up by other Tibetan Party members, but the most vocal proponents were Ngabo, who resided in Beijing, and the Panchen Rinpoche, who was not in the Party. During his visit to the Chamdo area in September 1986, the Panchen Rinpoche publicly criticised the local education department for not attaching importance to the teaching and use of the Tibetan language.[38] The following year during the fifth session of the fourth Tibet Regional People's Congress, one of the main issues discussed was the question of language. Ngabo said that during the Cultural Revolution use of the Tibetan language had been 'seriously wrecked', and that there had been 'no fundamental change in the use of the Tibetan language'.[39]

The Tibetans' push towards greater use of their language was in part motivated by the desire to keep the region under their control. Given the Chinese determination to maintain control, the only effective and legitimate means of gaining authority open to the Tibetans was the demand for the Tibetanisation of the administration. If Tibetan were to be adopted as the primary language of bureaucracy, this would weaken the long-term dominance of Chinese cadres. There were, however, many difficulties in this. Many of the senior Chinese cadres would have opposed it because of the inherent dangers in the policy. In fact, even many senior Tibetan Party officials found themselves in a very difficult position. During the Second Tibet Work Forum, Hu Yaobang had defended Ragdi as a potential leader, but had then publicly humiliated him by criticising his ignorance of written Tibetan. Many high-ranking Tibetan Party officials who had risen during the Cultural Revolution had a barely adequate knowledge of written Tibetan, so the resistance came not only from Chinese cadres but from the Tibetans who were threatened by the younger and better-educated cadres. The Party was clearly aware of such anxiety, and when regulations were drawn up, it exempted Tibetan cadres over forty-five years of age and other workers over the age of forty; all others who were illiterate in Tibetan had to learn the language and become proficient within the next three years.[40]

On 19 July 1986 the TAR government issued a circular stipulating a wide range of decisions that had been agreed during the fifth session of the fourth TAR People's Congress. It was announced that on 'a trial basis' Tibetan would be adopted as the main language of administration. More importantly, it was agreed that all primary schools would use Tibetan as the primary medium of education.[41] The question of how far the Chinese authorities were intending to go is difficult to gauge, but it was evident that the language question was now quickly becoming one of the major issues. It was recognised that the homogeneity of written Tibetan ensured that the issue would receive wide and popular support among the Tibetans inside and outside the Party, and in Tibetan areas outside the TAR.

While the question of Tibetan independence was central to the exiled community, most Tibetans inside the country were willing to accept the limits imposed by the Chinese. Except for the most fervent nationalists, the question of independence was not an issue for most politically minded people. They saw that the new changes had allowed them to demand greater freedom without engendering Chinese hostility. The political culture in Tibet began to shift towards questions of policy and the needs of the Tibetans. Given the recent legislative changes in China, Tibetan leaders were content to maximise the limited freedom afforded by the reforms. There was a real possibility that a consensus might emerge between Beijing and the Tibetan leadership coalition composed of Party members and traditional leaders.

As long as the Tibetans did not overtly oppose China's claims over Tibet, Beijing was prepared to concede to many of the Tibetans' demands including the adoption of Tibetan as the primary language of administration and education. However, both sides recognised that there would be objective difficulties and that vested interests would oppose any change in the status quo. But in the mid 1980s Beijing did not see the main opposition coming from the Tibetans, whom they believed had been won over, and the Chinese authorities were confidently announcing that the situation was 'the best since the liberation'.[42] The main threat came from Tibetan and Chinese Leftists, who were opposed to the changes and felt that there was an excessive ideological deviation. As we will see later, there was similar conflict emerging in Beijing between the hard-liners who were opposed to rapid reforms, and the liberals who advocated change in the relationship between the Party and the state.

As in the rest of China, where there were moves towards a civil society, in Tibet emphasis was also placed on the establishment of a 'socialist legal system'. At the end of 1986, the regional Party carried out reforms to streamline Party and government structures. Some departments were merged and moves were made to separate the work of the Party and that of government. However the Party would not tolerate any demands that it could not control or that directly threatened its primary position. It needs to be stressed again that in Tibet the Communist Party was seen as an instrument of Chinese rule, despite the fact that it had a large Tibetan membership.

By the end of 1986, the Chinese had managed to redress many of the Tibetans' grievances, but the success of the reforms was generating further problems, which tested the limits of Chinese tolerance. The challenge came from two sources: exiled Tibetans were starting to relaunch their attack to wrest the initiative away from the Chinese; and China's relationship with India was again becoming strained. As noted before, the last meeting between Dharamsala and Beijing had taken place in October 1984, nearly three years previously. Attempts to revive the contact had failed. The Chinese side had in fact lost much of their interest and to some extent had realised that they could rule Tibet without the Dalai Lama. This was proved by the success of the reforms in Tibet and the increasing international recognition. Besides the enthusiasm of Western tourists to visit the area, various international aid agencies had shown an interest in operating in the region. The United Nations Development Programme (UNDP) and the World Food Programme had started to operate major projects in Tibet. Although these were modest by international standards, for China they signified international acceptance.

Sino–Indian Difficulties

However, in the summer of 1986 there was a breakdown in Sino–Indian relations. In June the Government of India lodged a formal protest to the Chinese against an 'intrusion' into Indian territory. The incident was said to have taken place in the Sumdorung Chu, in the Tawang district of the Indian State of Arunachal Pradesh. The Chinese side not only rejected the Indian claims but made a counter accusation. On 16 July, at a weekly press briefing, the Chinese accused Indian troops and aircrafts of crossing 'the actual line of control' and went on to charge India with 'nibbling and expanding into Chinese territory'.[43] Later that month the Indian and Chinese sides met in Beijing for the 7th round of the Sino–Indian border discussions. The Chinese Foreign Minister Wu Xueqian said that the atmosphere at the meeting was 'not as good as it was before [in] the last few rounds'.[44] It ended without resolving any of the problems. In fact, the tension between the two countries had reached such an extent that press reports claimed that actual fighting had taken place. It soon became apparent that both sides were reinforcing their defence forces. It was said that the Chinese had dispatched an extra 20,000 troops from the 3rd Army Corps in Chengdu and the 13th Army in Lanzhou.[45] When the US Secretary of Defence, Caspar Weinberger, visited Beijing, Deng Xiaoping commented that China would have to 'teach India a lesson' if she did not cease 'nibbling' Chinese territory.[46]

When in September 1986 China and Pakistan signed an agreement on nuclear research co-operation, the Indian press and politicians began to complain about a China–Pakistan axis. Indian fear was heightened when Caspar Weinberger visited Islamabad a month later and announced at a press conference the United States' 'unshakeable support to Pakistan (in the event of Soviet attack)'.[47] This was heard in New Delhi with growing alarm. Although there was no formal strategic co-operation between the three countries, many in India believed that there was a *de facto* alliance between Pakistan, China and America. Indian fears of such an alliance were not entirely unfounded. Whereas in 1962 the United States had supported Indian claims regarding the status of the McMahon line as a legal border in the eastern sector, in June 1984 a State Department spokesman was reported as saying 'we have not committed ourselves to any specific demarcation of the McMahon line on the ground'.[48] This seemed to imply that the US did not automatically accept Indian claims in that area and naturally set alarm bells ringing in New Delhi. Moreover, India's traditional ally, the Soviet Union, was not only facing internal problems but also confronted with setbacks in Afghanistan.

It is beyond the scope of this book to deal in detail with the failure in Sino-Indian negotiations in the summer of 1986. Suffice it to say that their break had serious implications for the Tibetan issue. The immediate ramification was the cancellation of the proposed visit of the fifth delegation from Dharamsala to Tibet. Moreover, it appears that the Chinese may have indicated that they were terminating all contacts with the Tibetans. This was an anxious time for Dharamsala, where Tibetans thought the question of Tibet's status was losing its significance, as they realised that the Chinese were prepared to ignore the Dalai Lama altogether. Although there were repeated announcements from Beijing that the Dalai Lama would be welcome to return to China, there was no alteration in the Chinese position. Gyalo Dhundup confirms that Dharamsala was in a desperate situation in late 1986: they had failed to interest the Chinese or the international community in the Tibetan problem. Dharamsala turned to Gyalo Dhundup and asked if he could revive contact with the Chinese.[49]

It appears that Dharamsala had come to the conclusion that it was an opportune time to approach the Chinese. It is most likely that Dharamsala felt that China's difficulties with India might make them more amenable to reviving the negotiations. When Gyalo Dhundup approached the Chinese embassy in Delhi to ask if he could travel to China, the Chinese replied that he was welcome to visit Beijing any time as he was an 'old friend of China'. Later, Dharamsala approached Gyalo Dhundup again to ask if a senior Dharamsala politican could accompany him. The Chinese rejected the suggestion and insisted that only Gyalo Dhundup was welcome. However, throughout the summer of 1987, there were reports in the *émigré* press of the imminent departure of a Tibetan delegation led by Gyalo Dhundup, and the names of four prominent Tibetans were given as members of the group. The Chinese continued to insist that they would not accept a delegation composed of officials from the 'exiled government', an indication that the Chinese had hardened their attitude towards negotiations. In the end Gyalo Dhundup travelled to Beijing accompanied by his two sons, and the visit was treated as private. It was never revealed what transpired during the visit, although upon his return to Dharamsala Gyalo Dhundup held several days of briefing sessions for senior officials. It can be deduced that the Chinese must have categorically rejected any offers of negotiations and made an unequivocal stand that they would not deviate from their initial offer of the five-point proposals.

It was also a period when the liberal leaders in the CCP were losing their power. The conservatives were alarmed by the growing criticism of the Party and the development of liberal trends within the society. Deng had conceded to pressure from them and launched an attack on 'bourgeois liberalisation'. More significantly, in January 1987, Hu Yaobang was removed as secretary-general of the CCP. The official announcement said that he had resigned after 'making a self-criticism about his mistake'. His fall from power had serious repercussions in Tibet. Since 1980 he had personally managed the CCP's work in Tibet and throughout the 1980s had guided the Party's policy towards Tibet. This had given a strong backing to the reforms. There was jubilation among hard-liners in Tibet when they learned about Hu Yaobang's dismissal. They 'set off fire crackers and drank in celebration'.[50] Hu Yaobang's conciliatory speech to the Tibetans in 1980 had deeply angered many veteran cadres and in Tibet there were rumours that Hu's chief mistake had been identified as his lenient policy towards the country. As a result of the shift in power at the centre, there were rumours that Wu Jinghua would also be removed from his position. The Central Committee had received many reports from Leftist cadres criticising Wu's liberal policy and the Party had asked senior Tibetan leaders for their assessment of Wu's work in Tibet (the Panchen Rinpoche described him as one of the best officials in the region).[51] On 28 March 1987 the Panchen Rinpoche made a strong speech to the NPC Standing Committee of the TAR. Despite the fact that Hu Yaobang had been removed from power, he praised his policy towards Tibet, implying that Hu was the only senior leader who had paid any attention to the country. In retrospect the Panchen Rinpoche's speech was a plea to the Chinese leadership not to abandon the liberal course initiated by Hu Yaobang.

The fear that the senior leaders were losing interest in Tibet also had a serious implication for the dialogue with the Dalai Lama initiated by Hu Yaobang in 1980. It was true that the new leadership in Beijing had shown little or no interest in Tibet and it was unlikely that they would have proved to be more open to negotiation. Even Hu had insisted unswervingly that the dialogue could only take place on the basis of the five-point proposal he had made earlier. With his departure there was no single leader in the Central Committee of the CCP who had the power and the imagination to solve the problems in Tibet.

This left the Dalai Lama in a very difficult position. It was clear from the start that the proposals made by the Chinese did not go anywhere near meeting the demands of the exiled Tibetans, who were determined to elevate the talks to the status of Tibet, while the Chinese remained adamant that the only question to discuss was the return of the Dalai Lama. Therefore in the late 1980s the relationship between the Dalai Lama and Beijing had reached deadlock and it required a major initiative to break the stalemate. The Chinese were content to abandon any links with the Dalai Lama as they saw no reason for appeasing the exiled group, a decision which might have succeeded in pushing the Dalai Lama and the exiled group to the periphery of Tibetan politics, effectively ending their political importance. At the same time it had to be acknowledged that the Tibetans' devotion to the Dalai Lama would mean that it would be hard for the Chinese to achieve this. The Dalai Lama and the exiled group, who had always seen themselves as the sole legitimate spokesmen for the Tibetans, were not prepared to acquiesce to this state of affairs.

The Chinese leadership had another reason for wanting to eliminate the importance of the Dalai Lama. As long as he remained in India, India was provided with important leverage. The Dalai Lama and Tibet played a vital part in India's strategic and political considerations regarding China and the Indians were aware that, while China could find many means of meddling in internal Indian affairs in India,[52] for India the only leverage against China was the Dalai Lama and the Tibetans. If China were to succeed in relegating the importance of the Dalai Lama to some minor issue, there would be serious ramifications for India. New Delhi, therefore, also had an interest in seeing that the Dalai Lama's importance was not reduced.

The conclusion reached in Dharamsala was that it was necessary to do everything possible to counter both China's unwillingness to meet with them and its attempts to diminish the significance of the Dalai Lama. The only viable alternative was the internationalisation of the issue and the mustering of international support, which meant the Western countries, including the USA. The Tibetans had been very successful in gaining popular (rather than governmental) support in the West, but, by the middle of the 1980s, Western interest in Tibet was largely confined to an appreciation of Tibetan culture and religion. Numerous Tibetan religious centres had also been established in most European countries and in North America. At a political level, however, the work had been left entirely to small Tibetan communities scattered in Europe and America who had organised vigils and demonstrations outside Chinese embassies.

Internationalisation of the Tibet Issue

The intensification of the Dalai Lama's international campaign coincided with a further deterioration in Sino–Indian relations. It was apparent that both China and India accepted the importance of the United States as the main power-broker. As noted before, Deng had chosen to send a warning to India through the Americans, which must have been a calculated decision to warn the US to distance itself from India. Both sides felt it was necessary to win over the Americans. From the Chinese point of view the Dalai Lama's campaign in Washington was seen as an extension of Indian foreign policy, aiming to place a wedge between the United States and China. Such an interpretation is not entirely inconceivable, but this is not to say that the Dalai Lama was exploited directly by the Indians.[53] It is most likely that there was a merging of interests of the Dalai Lama and the Indians, with the Dalai Lama seeing American involvement as an opportunity to pressure the

Chinese for resumption of dialogue, and the Indians regarded any discord between Washington and Beijing as beneficial.

The Dalai Lama's move to internationalise the Tibetan issue occurred at an opportune moment. In the late 1980s, popular political culture in the West was rapidly changing. The ideological confrontation which had characterised popular politics had given way to concerns about moral issues such as the human rights, environment, ecology, the rights of indigenous people and fear of the proliferation of nuclear weapons. The exiled Tibetans and their supporters perceptively noted these changes and orchestrated their campaigns on these lines. The nationalist demand for independence was de-emphasised and issues of environment, ecology and coercive birth-control policy were highlighted. More importantly the campaign also emphasised the preservation of Tibet's unique cultural tradition. The Dalai Lama and the exiled Tibetans were promoted as the guardians of a 2,000-year-old civilisation, while the Chinese were portrayed as the destroyers of this unique culture. This was not difficult since it was evident that the Chinese had done irreparable damage to Tibet's cultural heritage in earlier decades, though that distinction was often passed over. The Tibetans found a receptive audience in the West, attracting such sympathisers as the charismatic German Green Party leader, Petra Kelly. This Western support was seen as important in bringing China to the negotiating table.

For the first time since the 1960s, the Tibetan issue was discussed in Western Parliaments. In June 1986 Petra Kelly lodged a written question in the Bundestag (Lower House), asking the German Government to clarify its stance on the Tibetan issue.[54] Although this did not bring any change in Germany's position, it indicated that there was growing support for the Tibetans. The Chinese too had noted the intense interest in Tibet, and whenever Chinese leaders travelled abroad there were invariably questions about Tibet at press conferences. The issue received particular interest in America where it brought friction between the USA and China. When, in October 1986, the US Congress endorsed the revised US Export–Import Bank Act of 1945, normally of little interest, Beijing noted with alarm that the revision listed Tibet as a separate country.[55] The Chinese Foreign Ministry made a formal protest to the State Department, who confirmed that the USA regarded Tibet as 'a part of the People's Republic of China' and said that the listing was a 'technical lapse'.[56] It is likely that the listing was a *lapsus calami* and that it neither sought to test Chinese sensitivity nor to show a sudden shift in policy.

However, the incident showed that the Chinese were sensitive and could easily be perturbed by any questioning of the status of Tibet. While the State Department was opposed to any involvement in the Tibetan issue, this was not the case in the US Congress, where the Dalai Lama had gained some measure of support. In 1985 ninety-one members of Congress signed a letter to Chinese President Li Xiannian asking him to hold direct talks with the Dalai Lama. This call for negotiations was renewed on 18 June 1987 when the Congress passed a bill which declared Tibet to be an occupied country and endorsed many of the claims made by exiled Tibetans. It was clear there existed a strong caucus composed both of right-wingers, who were blatantly anti-Communist, and liberal Senators, who were concerned about human rights.[57]

The Chinese were worried about the growing international attention on Tibet and Beijing decided to counter the exiled Tibetans' attempts to internationalise the issue. They saw this as a matter of gaining international approval of their position in Tibet. During the summer of 1987, the Chinese invited former American president Jimmy Carter to visit Lhasa, and a few days later the 30 June edition of the *China Daily* carried a front-page story saying that Carter was satisfied with the situation in Tibet. A month later another prominent international figure was invited to visit Lhasa. On 17 July, Chancellor Helmut Kohl of Germany arrived in Lhasa for a two-day visit. Beijing claimed that Chancellor Kohl was 'highly satisfied'. It was reported that Kohl had raised questions about the human rights situation, but it was evident that the Chinese had gained much by these two visits. The German Government agreed to provide specific aid to Tibet and the Chinese decided to use Chancellor Kohl's visit to reiterate the conditions for the Dalai Lama's return. At a press conference Dorje Tsering, Chairman of the TAR People's Government, repeated the initial five-point proposal made by Hu Yaobang in 1981 and stressed that there was no change in Beijing's policy.[58]

The international campaign reached a new intensity in September 1987, when the Dalai Lama was scheduled to visit the United States. While the Chinese had always viewed the decision by a foreign country to allow a visit by the Dalai Lama as an anti-Chinese political act, the Dalai Lama himself had stated that he did not wish to embarrass the host government. He had therefore refrained from making overtly political statements during his visits abroad. But the visit to the United States was to be different. The Chinese were aware of this visit and two weeks before it, on 1 September 1987, they expressed their concern and warned that the USA should 'take measures to prevent him [the Dalai Lama] from engaging in any political activities in the United States against the interests of China'.[59] The State Department replied that the Dalai Lama was visiting the United States in a 'private capacity' and had not been officially received by the US Government. The Indian Government too seemed to have been aware that the visit was going to be different. In the past, whenever the Dalai Lama travelled abroad, an Indian government official accompanied him. During this visit, however, the GOI withdrew their official, so that they could not be implicated in the eyes of the Chinese. It also indicated that the Indians knew what was about to happen.

On 19 September, the Dalai Lama arrived in the United States and two days later addressed the US Congressional Human Rights Caucus, where he announced his 'five-point peace' proposal. He argued that 'instead of addressing the real issues facing the six million Tibetan people' the Chinese had reduced the question of Tibet to a discussion of his own personal status. He stated that his attempt to negotiate had been rebutted by the Chinese and that he had been forced to appeal to the international community. Then he outlined his five-point proposal: (1) the transformation of the whole of Tibet into a zone of peace; (2) the abandonment of China's population transfer policy; (3) respect for the Tibetan people's fundamental human rights and democratic freedoms; (4) the restoration and protection of Tibet's natural environment and the abandonment of China's use of Tibet for the production of nuclear weapons and the dumping of nuclear waste; (5) the commencement of 'earnest negotiations' on the future status of Tibet and of relations between Tibetan and Chinese peoples.[60]

The Chinese immediately rejected the Dalai Lama's proposal, which was not surprising since they had already made it clear to the exiled Tibetans that they would not accept these conditions.[61] The proposal seems to have been a mixture of a declaration of the Dalai Lama's minimum conditions for negotiation and an endeavour to entice popular Western support by including the fashionable concerns of the day. I will deal at greater length with the details of the Dalai Lama's proposal later, as he went on to make a statement further clarifying his position. What was of significance to the Chinese was the manner in which the Dalai Lama chose to reveal his position. It was clear that the choice of venue and the timing of the Dalai Lama's announcement on Capitol Hill was meant to break the Chinese resistance to negotiate on Dharamsala's terms. While the Chinese could disregard the actual proposal, they could not ignore the important platform and publicity afforded to the Dalai Lama in the United States. A day after the Dalai Lama's speech, eight senators wrote a joint letter addressed to Zhao Ziyang (who had succeeded Hu Yaobang as Party Secretary), urging China to accept the Dalai Lama's proposals for negotiation. It confirmed that there existed strong support for the Dalai Lama among influential circles in the United States.

However, the Dalai Lama's activities in Washington also angered the State Department, which felt it had been unnecessarily brought into dispute with China. From the State Department's point of view, Tibet did not warrant any serious consideration and the issue was at the bottom of their list of foreign policy priorities. The State Department made its position very clear when its spokesman, Stapleton Roy,[62] testified before the Senate Foreign Affairs Committee on 14 October 1987. He implied that the Dalai

Lama had abused US hospitality by engaging 'in activities inconsistent with his status as a respected religious leader', and that the visa had been issued solely on the grounds of that status.[63] Moreover, he warned the committee not to confuse its concerns for human rights with the political claims of the Dalai Lama about the status of Tibet. He highlighted this as an important distinction in understanding why the State Department 'disavows any support for the Dalai Lama's five-point program'.[64] It was also stressed that neither the US nor any member of the UN had recognised Tibetan independence.

Tibet Under Martial Law

Had it not been for the subsequent developments in Lhasa, the events in Washington would have passed as a minor diplomatic discord between Beijing and Washington. The Chinese would simply have ignored the Dalai Lama's proposal. But on 27 September, at 10 a.m., twenty-one monks from Drepung monastery marched to Lhasa and staged the first pro-independence demonstration since the fact-finding delegations of 1981. The monks circled around the Barkor (the centre of Lhasa), carrying the Tibetan national flag, and shouted demands for Tibetan independence.[65] The demonstration was immediately suppressed by the Chinese police, and most of the monks were beaten and arrested. Later they were charged with the offence of being counter-revolutionaries. News of the beatings triggered off further protests. Early on the morning of 1 October, a group of monks from Sera monastery staged a second demonstration. The monks and about thirty lay people were once again beaten by the police in the street, and this was witnessed by many people, including Western tourists.[66] Later, while the monks were detained in the police station in the Barkor, at least 1,000 Tibetans congregated outside the police station demanding their release. This soon developed into a confrontation between the police and the Tibetans. The Chinese police lost control and the demonstrators burnt down the doors of the police station and released the prisoners. One of the Tibetans, badly burned in the fire, was carried on the shoulders of the demonstrators, in front of a crowd of bystanders which had also swelled to several hundred people. The Chinese police fired into the crowd and between eight and ten people were killed. The Chinese claimed that they were killed by ricochets, but this was contradicted by eye-witnesses and photographs taken by tourists, which showed that the police were aiming directly into the crowd from the nearby rooftops.[67]

From the Chinese point of view, the date of the first demonstration confirmed that it was carefully planned to coincide with the Dalai Lama's announcement in Washington. They saw the action as a meticulously co-ordinated attempt to bring both internal and international pressure on China to negotiate, and a signal from the Dalai Lama that could not be ignored. The question of whether the demonstration on 27 September was conspired from outside or not is a perplexing one. It is unlikely that we shall ever know for certain whether there was a direct connection between the demonstrators and the exiled group. It was apparent from subsequent demonstrations that the protesters drew their inspiration from the exiled group and that some leaflets describing the Dalai Lama's US visit had been sent to Tibet by the exiles. The protesters borrowed some of the symbolism of national identity that had been invented in the exiled community, such as the Tibetan flag emblazoned with two snow lions holding three gems, which had become the main symbol of the protesters although it had only been adopted as a national flag-in-exile.[68] Its acceptance inside Tibet does not prove in itself that the demonstrations were prompted from outside. While it was in the interests of the Chinese to accuse the Dalai Lama of engineering the demonstration, the exiled Tibetans also saw some advantage in claiming responsibility since it suggested that they had the ability to organise activities inside Tibet, which undoubtedly enhanced the exiles' standing internationally.

While it cannot be proved whether the demonstration was engineered by the exiled group or not, the timing suggests that there was a link between the Dalai Lama's activities in the United States and the protest in Lhasa. Demonstrators definitely intended to affirm their support for the Dalai Lama's call for negotiation. Immediately after the Dalai Lama's speech at the US Congress, the Chinese launched a massive media campaign in Tibet, denouncing US interference in the internal affairs of China and accusing the Dalai Lama of wanting to 'split the motherland'. Television news broadcasts showed a clip of the Dalai Lama in the US Congress surrounded by applauding congressmen, over which was laid a text denouncing his speech. What struck most Tibetans was the image of the Dalai Lama being enthusiastically received in the parliament of the most powerful nation in the world. It was seen as an indication of American support for Tibet, as for most Tibetans the distinction between the Congress and the Government had no significance. The vehemence of the Chinese denunciations also strengthened the Tibetans' perception that a US commitment to Tibetan independence really existed and this led them to believe that they too must contribute to hastening the withdrawal of the Chinese from Tibet.

At the end of September 1987, Gyalo Dhundup visited Beijing. He had earlier told the United Front that there was no political significance to the Dalai Lama's visit to Washington,[69] and according to Ngabo he was unaware of the Dalai Lama's speech in Washington.[70] This gave the impression to the Chinese that either Gyalo Dhundup had misled them or he did not after all have influence in the exile movement. The incident was damaging to Gyalo

Dhundup's standing. Yan Mingfu, the new director of the United Front, held a meeting with Gyalo Dhundup and confronted him about the Dalai Lama's statement in Washington. He also sent a memorandum to the exiled government, dated 17 October 1987, which blamed the Dalai Lama for instigating the demonstrations in Lhasa. The memorandum did not make any direct comment on the Dalai Lama's five-point proposal, but it stated that the Chinese would resist any foreign pressure. It warned the Dalai Lama not to make a 'mistake by placing his hopes on external support',[71] and reiterating the five points made by Hu Yaobang in 1980. The memorandum declared that the future course of policy in Tibet would depend on the Dalai Lama, and that if the demonstrations did not cease, the Chinese would be forced to adopt sterner measures in Tibet.[72] It was clear that the Chinese saw the demonstration and the internationalisation of the Tibetan issue as a 'pressure tactic' by the Dalai Lama.

Another interesting point revealed by Yan's memorandum was what Gyalo Dhundup had told the Chinese. This led to growing criticism of him in Dharamsala. It appeared that Gyalo Dhundup not only said he did not support the Dalai Lama's five-point proposal but also suggested he was prepared to make far more drastic concessions to the Chinese than Dharamsala could contemplate. Gyalo Dhundup had stated that independence was 'unattainable' and that the objective of the negotiation was the return of the Dalai Lama to the 'motherland'.[73] These views had been taken by the Chinese to represent the position of the Dalai Lama, so that the speech at Washington was seen by Beijing as contrary to what they had been led to believe. It also caused alarm among the hard-liners in the refugee community who felt that Gyalo Dhundup had acted *ultra vires*. Later, Dharamsala had to issue a document stating that these views were the personal views of Gyalo Dhundup and did not represent the position of either the Dalai Lama or the government-in-exile.[74] It was apparent that Gyalo Dhundup was finding it increasingly difficult to mediate between Dharamsala and Beijing,[75] and neither side could have total confidence in his ability to convey the right message. The Tibetans were suspicious that he was not communicating their position correctly, whereas the Chinese now doubted his ability to influence his brother, the Dalai Lama. However, given the predicament faced by both sides, they could not afford to dispense with Gyalo Dhundup as an intermediary. As we have noted before, he played an important part in Beijing's strategy to deny legal validity to any contacts, signifying that the talks were private discussions between the Dalai Lama and the Central Government of China. Since Beijing refused to meet with representatives of the exiled government, it had no alternative but to relay its messages through Gyalo Dhundup.

The immediate problem faced by the Chinese was the continuing protests in Lhasa. Although they had insisted that the demonstrations were instigated by outsiders, they could not obscure the fact that the movement was gaining some measure of popular support there. The Dalai Lama's speech in Washington explained the timing of the demonstrations. The religious community, composed of ordinary monks and nuns, led almost all the demonstrations that took place between September 1987 and 1990. The monks' role in the unrest was in fact a significant depiction of the insoluble predicament faced by the Chinese in Tibet. Despite the fact that the years from 1979 to 1987 had seen a loosening of Chinese control and the Chinese had made a number of far-reaching concessions, the initial tolerance towards religion had led to an increasing number of monks and nuns, and to many temples and monasteries being reopened without permission from the authorities. In Chamdo Prefecture alone it was reported that eighty-six monasteries and 121 smaller temples were restored or newly opened. In some cases the number of monasteries was greater than before the Cultural Revolution.[76]

In the monasteries near Lhasa there were many monks who did not have official permits and were residing illegally, but the authorities were powerless to prevent so many people moving into the monasteries. The Chinese were aware that taking steps to evict the monks without permission would have led to open protest. The only course that was open to the Party was to accept the growing prominence of religion in Tibet, as long as it did not contest the Party's hegemony and oppose the 'unity of the motherland'. Three weeks before the first demonstration in Lhasa, the Party had discussed the United Front policy and affirmed the need to accept the dominance of religion in Tibetan society. Religion itself was not really an issue, but they were aware of the potential danger of allowing the monasteries' unrestricted growth, which the hard-liners feared would inflame separatists' aspirations. The Party saw the key danger as being the development of a Tibetan separatist movement. It was stated that 'the greatest political dividing line'[77] was whether one supported the unity of the motherland. Therefore as long as the monks did not make demands for independence, the Party was prepared to meet some of their grievances.

For the monks, no amount of Chinese concession could restore the authority of the religious community. For them, only an independent Tibet could guarantee the dominance and the centrality of Buddhism in society. Buddhism had always been seen as the core of Tibetan identity, and its clergy the epitome of 'Tibetanness'. The monks perceived the Chinese Communist state as inherently hostile to religion. The Communist Party had addressed this problem in the early 1980s, both on an ideological and practical level. In 1983, the Party formulated guidelines on religious policy,[78] which stated that the long-term aim of the Party's religious policy was to see the 'natural withering of religion'. The Party could not obscure the fact that its ultimate aim was to see the disappearance of religion.[79] Therefore, attacks on religion was seen *ipso facto* as an anti-Tibetan policy of the CCP.

The Chinese had hoped that social and economic changes would inevitably lead to the weakening of religion as a social force. They presumed that the improvement in people's living standards and in secular education would mean that the masses would no longer need the comfort of religion. Although there was nothing novel in this interpretation, it had practical consequences in Tibet, as it implied that the Communist state would eventually tolerate religion. But the religious community remained sceptical of the changes and saw the reforms as a Trojan horse. Modernisation and secularisation were considered ingenious means of undermining Buddhism in Tibet and many were alarmed by what they saw as the erosion of Tibetan cultural and religious values. The Tibetans complained about the corruption and seduction of youth by modern secular culture. While conflict between traditionalists and reformists finds expression in many parts of the world, in Tibet the question was complicated by the fact that many viewed secularisation and reform as synonymous with the Sinicisation of Tibet. The traditionalists feared that secularisation would inevitably lead towards greater integration with China and the dissipation of Tibet's religious and cultural identity.

The Chinese had not anticipated that the protests would come from ordinary monks and nuns. They had deluded themselves in assuming that the renewed importance of religion could be contained by rewarding high lamas and other important religious figures, who would in turn restrain the monks and nuns. Early on the Chinese had used both the Panchen Rinpoche and Ngabo to expound the message that there was a limit to Chinese tolerance. In June 1987, Ngabo announced that religion must not be taken 'as an excuse to interfere with economic development'.[80] The Panchen Rinpoche too spoke about the need to limit the number of monks and explained that not all the monasteries that were destroyed during the Cultural Revolution could be renovated.[81] The Chinese also maintained control of monasteries through the Tibet branch of the Chinese Buddhist Association, and more importantly, the day-to-day affairs of a monastery were supposedly controlled by the Democratic Management Committee which was under the supervision of the Religious Affairs Bureau. These committees commanded little or no respect as they were seen to be working for the Chinese and officials themselves were less than enthusiastic in enforcing Chinese laws.

These wider social and religious issues were at the core of the Tibetans' grievances. For the traditionalists, the only way to preserve Tibet's religious identity was to restore independence and secure the return of the Dalai Lama. For these reasons, the Tibetans who saw the main task as one of 'modernisation' of the country were more sympathetic to the Chinese. They felt that the return of the Dalai Lama and the restoration of the importance of religion would hinder Tibet's progress. This view was held by a small minority of people who shared an ideological loyalty to the Communist Party. For the majority of people the issue was far less complex and had to do with Tibet's recent history. Despite constant Chinese propaganda claiming that 'Tibet had always been part of China' and depicting the old society as brutal and corrupt, most Tibetans still looked towards the old society as a period when there were no Chinese in Tibet. While the Chinese tended to divide recent history into the period before the liberation and after, the Tibetans categorised the period as before and after the arrival of the Chinese.[82] There had always been a strong historical sense that Tibet had been the exclusive territory of the Tibetan people. This was further strengthened by the shared mythical and religious beliefs which regarded certain geographical landmarks as sacred. While the Chinese espoused the message of the 'unity of the motherland', the Tibetans showed no filial regard towards China. The Chinese talked about the cruel feudal past, but for the Tibetans the brutality and savagery of the Cultural Revolution was fresh in their memories. This image was particularly significant since the majority of those who were directly involved in the demonstrations were young people, who had grown up in the new society. Their parents did not narrate stories about old Tibet but about the suffering they had endured during the Cultural Revolution. For many young people, the new period under Deng Xiaoping did not bring an abundance of opportunity. Most importantly, all education – particularly higher education, the only means of social mobility – was closed to them. For many young people the only options seemed to be the traditional routes of joining a monastery or working on family land. The failure of the education system was evident by the fact that between 1982 and 1990 there was an increase in the illiteracy rate (for the 15–19 age group it was as high as 61.8 per cent.[83] Most of the young nuns and monks who took part in the demonstrations were young people who perceived that they were naturally disadvantaged and that the benefits of economic development had been wrested from them.

Once the latent resentment of the Tibetans had been pushed to the surface, the Chinese found it difficult to extinguish. The immediate repressive methods adopted by the Chinese police ensured that the Tibetans' anger smouldered on, waiting for further impetus to ignite. While the Chinese may well have been right in claiming that the number of people who took an active part in the demonstrations was small, nevertheless, the sentiments of the demonstrators were shared by many. The general malaise was felt throughout the Tibetan population. There was no doubt that there existed a near-universal enmity towards the Chinese, and there was little or no social intercourse between Tibetans and Chinese, beyond the officially staged Han–Tibetan unity gatherings.[84] The Tibetans and Chinese rarely fraternised outside the confines of the official workplace.

The demonstrations also had the danger of dividing Tibetan opinion. Many Tibetan intellectuals and those who worked in the government felt that the outright demand for independence was futile and that it would only succeed in pushing the Chinese into adopting more repressive measures. They felt that their own positions were at stake, but more importantly they saw the demonstrations as subverting the course of the reforms, which in many ways met many of their immediate demands. The Tibetan intellectuals and the educated classes had enjoyed unprecedented freedom to write and publish during the relaxed period (1980–87), which had seen a flourishing of publications in Tibetan language and reprints of many of the ancient manuscripts which had been banned during the Cultural Revolution. There were also the beginnings of a secular literary tradition, and some of these writings angered the conservatives and traditionalists in Tibetan society. The new style of writing tended to be less reverential and inclined to question Tibet's religious and historical traditions. The Chinese authorities realised that these writings had offended the sensibilities of the traditionalists and so they curtailed the freedom enjoyed by the Tibetan intellectuals. At another level, the older generation who could recall the ruthlessness of the Anti-Rebellion Campaign in the early 1960s were fearful and apprehensive about the consequences of the unrest.

The Chinese predictably adopted the familiar campaign of mobilising Tibetan Party members and officials of the CPPCC to make mandatory denunciations of the 'handful of splittists for sabotaging the unity of the motherland'. But the Chinese realised that they had to look seriously into the much wider issues affecting the region. Wu Jinghua was willing to accept that the antecedent for the demonstration lay in the past policies of the CCP and said that the 'fundamental reason' had been that 'we had implemented a leftist policy for a long time in the past, and that we divorced ourselves from the masses and harmed them'.[85] But this argument did not sway the Chinese hard-liners, who countered that the reforms had given away too much and had encouraged the unrestricted growth of local nationalism. Wu's assessment could easily be dismissed as an attempt to deflect the blame for his failure. He was under pressure to avert any further demonstrations, which had already propelled Tibet into the world's headlines and embarrassed the senior leaders in Beijing.

The Tibetans were relentless in their campaigns both at the international level and inside the country, and in June 1988 the Dalai Lama was invited to speak at the European Parliament in Strasbourg. The Chinese launched a strong protest and called upon the parliament to cancel the visit, saying that they would be prepared to cancel the forthcoming visit of the EEC President Lord Plumb to China.[86] This in turn generated enormous press interest.

Chinese pressure had forced the European Parliament to rescind its earlier invitation but Lord Plumb was unable to prevent individual members from inviting the Dalai Lama to address a private meeting at the European Parliament.

On 15 June 1988, when visiting the European Parliament, the Dalai Lama distributed a paper outlining his main initiative 'for resolving the issue of Tibet'. The proposal further clarified the five-point proposal he had made in Washington a year earlier, but it also developed it further. The main thrust of the Dalai Lama's new proposal was that Tibet, composed of the 'Cholka Sum', three unified areas, should become 'a self-governing democratic political entity, in association with the People's Republic of China'.[87] The Dalai Lama would in turn relinquish his claim for independence and would seek a 'voluntary association with China'. On the surface this appears to go some way towards meeting Deng Xiaoping's requirement that as long as the Dalai Lama eschewed the demand for independence, anything could be discussed. The Dalai Lama envisaged that this 'self-governing democratic political entity' should be made up of 'a popularly elected chief executive, a bicameral legislative branch, and an independent judicial system'. The new government of Tibet would have the right to decide on all affairs relating to Tibet and the Tibetans. The Dalai Lama's proposal also addressed what might be seen as China's basic security concerns, by declaring that China 'could remain responsible for Tibet's foreign policy'. As far as defence was concerned the region should, through consultation, be declared a 'zone of peace', but China could maintain 'a restricted number of military installations in Tibet' for defensive purposes. The Dalai Lama's offer was in many ways realistic, and historically this had been the position of the Tibetans since 1950, as long as China could guarantee that Tibet would enjoy 'genuine' autonomy.

The Dalai Lama's proposal caused a great deal of controversy among the exiled community. There were accusations of betrayal and foreign involvement in the decision.[88] As for the officials in the Dharamsala administration, they had been presented with it as a *fait accompli*, being told of the content of the Dalai Lama's proposal only a few days before it was announced in Strasbourg. Even then the way in which it was presented to the Tibetan community differed from the actual text of the speech, which existed only in English: in fact there was no Tibetan version of the speech. Even senior Dharamsala politicians were not aware of the full extent of the meaning of 'association with PRC'. This was taken to mean that Tibet would have a similar relationship with China as that between Bhutan and India, or, in former times, between Mongolia and the Soviet Union. Others saw it as meaning that the Dalai Lama was prepared to accept autonomous status within the PRC.

At an official level the Chinese side did not at first make any direct comment on the Strasbourg proposal. For the Chinese the initial problem was not the content of the Dalai Lama's statement but what they saw as the internationalisation of the Tibetan issue. It was evident that the Dalai Lama commanded immense international respect and support. This, in the Chinese mind, did more serious damage to their long-term interests. The Chinese Embassy in Berne, Switzerland, issued the first statement, saying that 'China's sacred sovereignty' over Tibet cannot be denied and that it would not bow to foreign pressure.[89] On 23 June the Chinese foreign ministry told journalists at a weekly press briefing that the Dalai Lama's statement could not form the basis for negotiation, and it was stated that China would not accept 'independence, semi-independence or even independence in a disguised form'. It was true that the Strasbourg statement advocated some form of semi-independent status for Tibet, so the Chinese announcement was refuting the Dalai Lama's proposal.

Although the Dalai Lama had repeatedly said that he was not asking for the 'independence' of Tibet, the Chinese noted that the whole premise of the Dalai Lama's proposal was based on the assumption that Tibet had always been an independent state and that the Chinese action in October 1950 constituted an invasion of a sovereign state. Moreover, the notion of 'association' presupposed that Tibet was an independent state and that the agreement reached between Tibet and China would be similar to an agreement reached between two sovereign nations.[90] This, according to the Chinese, was 'a distortion of history'.[91] Therefore, as far as the Chinese were concerned, the Dalai Lama had not met their first demand which, it transpired, required the Tibetans not only to eschew calls for future independence but also to acknowledge that Tibet had always been part of China. The other points, regarding the creation of a 'zone of peace' and a democratic government in Tibet, were dismissed either as unrealistic or as the advocation of a Western capitalistic political system.[92]

The solution put forward by the Dalai Lama in his Strasbourg proposal was clearly unacceptable to the Chinese and unlikely to receive support from Western countries. The Dalai Lama's proposal for the demilitarisation of Tibet was primarily aimed at rousing China's fears about exposing its western frontier, and it accorded with the Dalai Lama's Buddhist principles. However, Tibet was vital to Chinese strategic calculations, for the simple reason that the Himalayas presented by far the best vantage point for China's defensive or offensive needs. Therefore it was unlikely that the Dalai Lama's offer of a 'zone of peace' would be acceptable to the Chinese. Both Beijing and Washington must have viewed this as an Indian-inspired proposition. As we have seen in an earlier chapter, Nehru in 1950 advised the Tibetans to prevent the deployment of Chinese troops in Tibet. If this had been in the strategic interests of India in 1950, it was even more so in the late 1980s, as India would still have been the main beneficiary of a demilitarised Tibet. This is not to say that China would not reap some benefits (mainly in terms of reduction in defence expenditure), but Beijing would have had to weigh this against its strategic interests. The withdrawal of the PLA from the Himalayas would have given India dominance in South Asia and beyond into the Indian Ocean. Both Washington and Beijing did not want to see this happen. As we have seen, the US and China shared a parallel strategic interest in South Asia.[93] For the West (namely the US), interest in South Asia focused on the strategic equilibrium between India and her neighbours – Mrs Gandhi used to say that the US had maintained a 'tilt against India'; the presence of Chinese troops on the Tibetan plateau restrained India's natural dominance in South Asia.[94] The type of solution envisaged by the Dalai Lama would have required a radical shift in the geo-political makeup of South Asia and the Himalayan region and there would have to be a total breakdown of the system in China, as was to occur in the Soviet Union and Eastern Europe, for the Dalai Lama's proposed solution to be realised.

Although the Dalai Lama received popular support in the West, and from US politicians, this cannot be represented as genuine change in Western interests. Much of the backing has come from members of parliament who have merely been appeasing their constituents. The question of human rights has played an important part in generating public support, but it has always been subservient to the larger foreign policy interests of the Western powers. Only if strategic interests and moral issues were to converge would the Western powers be willing to apply real pressure on China. Given the geopolitical factors, it is unlikely that the Americans would apply any real diplomatic pressure on Beijing. Moreover, China is not without friends in the West who take a pragmatic appreciation of the situation, given China's overwhelming power and control in Tibet, and see support for Tibet as a 'cruel incitement', and encouragement to the Tibetans to demand independence as 'quixotic'.[95]

The Collapse of the Beijing–Dalai Lama Dialogue

For all of the above-mentioned reasons, the Chinese categorically rejected the Dalai Lama's proposal in 1988. However, they did not go as far as to reject the idea of further talks, as they knew that both for internal and external reasons they could not be seen to be closing the door on negotiations. On 23 September 1988, the Chinese Embassy in New Delhi delivered their formal response to the Dalai Lama's proposal. The Chinese were direct and to the point:

> We welcome the Dalai Lama to have talks with the Central Government

at any time. The talks may be held in Beijing, Hong Kong, or any of our embassies or consulates abroad. If the Dalai Lama finds it inconvenient to conduct talks at these places, he may choose any place he wishes. But there is one condition, that is, no foreigners should be involved. We are ready to designate one official with certain rank to have direct dialogue with the Dalai Lama.

There are two points which need to be clarified:

1. We have never recognised 'the Kashag Government' [exiled government] which has all along indulged in the activities of the independence of Tibet. We will not receive any delegation or fact-finding group designated by the Kashag Government.

2. The new proposal put forward by the Dalai Lama in Strasbourg cannot be considered as the basis for talks with the Central Government because it has not at all relinquished the concept of the 'independence of Tibet'.

If the Dalai Lama is sincere in improving relations with the Central Government and really concerned for the happiness of the Tibetan people, for the economic development and prosperity of the Tibetan nationality, he should truly give up the 'idea of independence'. The Dalai Lama should place himself in the great family of the unified motherland and join the Central Government, the People's Government of Tibet and the Tibetan people in discussing the major policies concerning Tibet.[96]

The Chinese memorandum embodied the central tenet of the Chinese stance since 1979. The wording may have differed but it was evident that Beijing had not made any concessions to the guidelines set by Deng Xiaoping and Hu Yaobang in 1981. The Chinese had rejected the Strasbourg statement as a basis for negotiation. It was apparent that when Beijing had announced its desire to hold 'talks with the Dalai Lama', it had literally meant that the meeting would be held between the person of the Dalai Lama and a Chinese representative. The implication was clear that the talks would be concerned solely with the Dalai Lama's return and there would be no question of discussing the issue of the status of Tibet. This was further reinforced by the refusal to acknowledge in any shape or form the existence of the 'exiled government'. This was the clearest Chinese statement on the limits and scope of the discussions.

The Chinese response was to place the exiled government in some difficulty. While they welcomed the Chinese readiness to hold 'talks with the Dalai Lama', the conditions imposed were clearly unacceptable. Taking up the first sentence of the Chinese statement, Dharamsala responded by publicly announcing that the talks would be held in Geneva in January 1989. The announcement also gave the names of Dharamsala's team of negotiators, which would be headed by Tashi Wangdi, who had been the Dalai

Lama's representative in New Delhi and a minister in the government-in-exile. It also mentioned that the Dutch lawyer Michael van Walt van Praag would be one of the advisors to the Tibetan team.[97] The Dalai Lama must have realised that this would be unacceptable to the Chinese, but on 25 October 1988, Ala Jigme, a member of the exiled cabinet, met with Zhao Xingsong, a councillor from the Chinese Embassy in New Delhi, and handed over the formal proposal to hold the talks in Geneva. Zhao Xingsong must have known that the Dalai Lama had already announced the venue of the talks and the names of the Tibetan delegation. However, Zhao sought further confirmation and asked Ala Jigme if the Dalai Lama would be participating in the talks and whether the Dutch lawyer Michael van Walt van Praag would be involved. Ala said that the Dalai Lama would not be personally taking part and confirmed that Michael van Walt van Praag would be one of the aides assisting the negotiation team.[98]

The Tibetans' attempt to evade the conditions they had set infuriated the Chinese. Moreover, in their eyes the Dalai Lama had breached the rules of diplomacy by making a public announcement of the date and venue for the meeting without seeking further confirmation from Beijing. The Chinese offer of talks in the message of 23 September 1988 contained a prerequisite that the Tibetans accepted the two conditions laid down by them. It is more than likely that the Dalai Lama and his advisors were fully aware that if they were to reject the offer of talks on the basis that they were unable to agree to Chinese conditions, it would have damaged their credibility; by making a public statement they gave the impression that the Dalai Lama had been prepared to attend the talks and that now the onus fell on the Chinese to honour their offer to hold talks. The Chinese knew that they had been placed in a difficult situation by having to explain why they could not go to Geneva, and the international media clearly pointed the finger for the failure towards Beijing.

According to Gyalo Dhundup, the Chinese Embassy in Delhi phoned him to say that they were not prepared to continue with the talks. The embassy official accused the Tibetans of not being 'sincere' and seeking 'cheap publicity'.[99] It was pointed out that, as a matter of diplomatic etiquette, the Dalai Lama should have discussed the date and venue with them before making a unilateral announcement to the press.[100] A month later this view was also expressed by Chin Xin, one of the Vice Ministers of the State Nationalities Affairs Commission. He also accused the Dalai Lama of 'insincerity' and affirmed that China had never recognised the government-in-exile headed by the Dalai Lama. He argued that this was why China would only hold talks with the Dalai Lama himself and not with a so-called 'government' delegation sent by him. He also stated that the inclusion of a foreigner among the Tibetan team contravened the principle of not allowing any foreigners to interfere in the internal affairs of China.

No meeting took place in January 1989 in Geneva, and this marked the end of the Dharamsala–Beijing dialogue that had been initiated a decade earlier. It was clear that neither side was prepared to make any further concessions. For China, despite the unrest in Tibet, the price demanded by the Dalai Lama was too high and the consequence of agreeing to the Tibetan demands would set a precedent for other minority regions, notably Xinjiang. Moreover, increasing regional conflict had been generated by the success of the coastal regions and had spurred demands of greater power from the provinces. If Beijing were to agree to the constitutional changes demanded by the Dalai Lama's proposal, there would be no grounds for resisting similar or further changes in Chinese polity.

The Dalai Lama realised that whatever agreement he reached with the Chinese would be final and would seal the question of Tibet permanently. Therefore, he had to obtain from the Chinese maximum concessions, which would not only give Tibet greater autonomy but would also allow some degree of international personality. The Dalai Lama also knew that he could not simply go back to Lhasa, as this would be falling into China's snare. His strength lay in his continued absence from Lhasa, which enabled him to mobilise international opinion against China. Without one side making some fundamental concession, it was not possible to proceed with the dialogue.

For the Tibetans, coming to some form of resolution with the Chinese was a matter of urgency. It was clear that the international focus on the Tibetan issue was largely due to the personal standing of the Dalai Lama and that he was the cohesive element which cemented the diverse groups in Tibetan society. Already, many individuals had drifted back into Tibet. The decision by an important group of Kargyu lamas to reinstate the new reincarnation of the Gyalwa Karmapa in his traditional abode in Tsuripu was an indication that an influential group of Tibetans felt that again there were means of working with the Communists. The Chinese could see also that without the Dalai Lama the Tibetan political movement would lose much of its potency. In the 1990s the Dalai Lama tried to revive the talks by writing directly to the ageing Deng Xiaoping, but the Chinese leader turned a blind eye to his appeal.

In December 1989, the Indian Prime Minister Rajiv Gandhi made a formal five-day visit to China. This was the first visit by an Indian leader since Nehru's in 1954. It is most likely that the resumption of Sino–Indian talks owed much to the crisis in Tibet. Both sides were conscious of the fact that difficulties in Tibet in 1959 had precipitated the Sino–Indian war, and all the factors that had brought them to war in 1962 were present in the late 1980s: unrest in Tibet, deterioration in Sino–Indian relations, and a breakdown in negotiations between the Dalai Lama and the Chinese.

Beijing had been made aware of the fact that Tibet could be used to put foreign pressure on China. Therefore, it was in its interests to assuage India (which Beijing recognised as the main benefactor of the exiled movement) by agreeing to the resumption of talks. The Chinese in return obtained an affirmation from Rajiv Gandhi that India recognised Tibet as a part of China, and that India would not interfere in China's internal affairs, or allow Tibetans in India to conduct political activities.[101] In the late 1980s both sides wanted to avert the repetition of the war of 1962. The improvement in Sino–Indian relations was a warning to the Dalai Lama that he could be isolated and should not think that international pressure could be applied to China, since his staunchest supporter could also be won over.

The situation inside Tibet remained precarious, and the since September 1987 there had been continuing disturbances in Lhasa. Following a demonstration in Lhasa on 10 December 1988, a group of Tibetan students from the Central Institute for Nationalities in Beijing held a demonstration in Tiananmen Square. It was an indication of how far the situation inside Tibet had deteriorated. On 28 January 1989, the Panchen Rinpoche unexpectedly died in Shigatse in his spiritual home of the Tashilhunpo. This was a major blow to the Chinese, as he had played a vital role in restraining Tibetan anger. We do not know what the Panchen Rinpoche thought privately about the demonstrations or about the Dalai Lama's proposal. A few days before his death he told the Chinese press that Tibet had lost more than it had gained in the past thirty years. This was a damning assessment for the Communist Party. It is more than likely that the Panchen Rinpoche was deeply worried that the crisis would drag Tibet further into repression and allow the ascendancy of the Leftist hardliners.

A month before the Panchen Rinpoche's death, Wu Jinghua had been dismissed as the 1st Secretary of the regional CCP. There is no doubt that this was due to his failure to curb the unrest. Even during the period of unrest Wu Jinghua continued to adhere to the more liberal line and believed that the demonstrations were not merely inflamed by outside agitators. In February 1988, Wu organised what he called a 'heart to heart' meeting between himself and representatives of the monks from the three largest monasteries near Lhasa at which he listened to the list of grievances.[102] But for the Chinese the situation in Tibet had become an international embarrassment and they saw an urgent need to quash any further demonstrations.

The Central Committee appointed Hu Jintao as the new Party Secretary in Tibet. He was a graduate of Qinghua University and the Central Party School, regarded as one of the high-flyers among the younger generation of leaders that was emerging in China. While he had served as the deputy head of the Communist Youth League, there was talk of the 'three Hu' (tigers), a reference to Hu Yaobang, Hu Qili and Hu Jintao,[103] all considered potential leaders of China. Beijing had realised that Tibet could no longer be regarded as a backwater where nothing of any importance occurred. The appointment of Hu Jintao was an indication that Beijing now wanted to assert more control and bring stability to Tibet.

On 5 March 1989 Lhasa witnessed the largest anti-Chinese demonstration in the capital since 1959. For three days the Chinese police fought with Tibetans and between 75 and 750 Tibetans were killed as the police fought to regain control of the centre of the city. The Chinese authorities were aware of the symbolism of 10 March, which was celebrated as the Tibetan National Uprising Day throughout the refugee community (because in 1959 the date had marked the beginning of the nationwide revolt). The Chinese clearly did not want a repetition of 1959 and on 8 March they imposed martial law in Tibet.

FIFTEEN

The Postscript

For the Chinese leadership the closing years of the 1980s turned out to be among the worst of times. The regime which had emerged ten years earlier amid great hopes for reform and economic progress now faced internal opposition not only from Tibetans and Uighurs but also from students in China. The wave of unrest which swept across China in June 1989 not only rocked the Communist Party but triggered off protests in the outside world, so that Deng, once the Communist leader most courted by the West, now found himself denounced by much of the international community.

In Tibet, the Chinese leadership were now obliged to reappraise their position. They began to view the problem there not so much as a sign of any failure of policy by Beijing as the result of instigation by the Dalai Lama and Tibetan exile groups. The extent of the involvement of exile groups in the protests that swept Lhasa in the late 1980s remains a controversial question which has still to be answered, but one development was clear: the Dalai Lama had enhanced his stature in the West. That achievement had been encapsulated by the Nobel Peace Prize, an award which had given the Tibetan issue a new wave of publicity. The Tibetans began to see the award as the 'second best thing' after independence and hailed it as a sign of Western support. The Chinese interpreted it as confirmation of a plan by exiled Tibetans to internationalise the Tibetan issue. Coming so soon after the massacre of students in the protests at Tiananmen Square, the award indicated that China had become a pariah. The threat of isolation was not to last, but it served to reinforce the new Chinese view of their predicament in Tibet.

By the beginning of 1990, the political establishment in Beijing had reached a turning point, with the liberal wing of the Communist Party retreating into the shadows and hardliners emerging in the foreground. In Lhasa, where Chinese rule was in a more precarious position then ever before, the demonstrations were no longer seen by the authorities as isolated and localised incidents, but as an aspect of the events in Beijing, within the wider context of the serious challenge posed to the Party and China as a whole by the unrest in China. The Chinese leadership looked to wider ideological and political reasons for the failure of the reforms and to explain the breakdown of civil order in China and Tibet. The conclusion reached by the Party was summed up by Deng Xiaoping's announcement that the central question facing the Party was the great struggle between socialism and bourgeois liberalisation.

Nevertheless, Deng was adamant that this did not mean a return to the narrow ideological regime imposed by the Maoists. He was prudent enough to see that the reforms had to be continued, but in a more refined and controlled manner. For Tibet, this meant that the region would no longer be treated as a special case and that the concessions that had been made to the Tibetans would be reined in. The new policy would emphasise those factors which engendered greater integration of the region with the rest of China, and which would avoid laying any stress on Tibet's separate identity. The monasteries and other institutions would be tamed and made to follow stricter guidelines laid down by Beijing. Where Tibetan culture and distinctiveness were to be highlighted, it was to be done in a way that was exoticised and desensitised.

For the demonstrators in Lhasa there was no change in the demands they expressed: their central aim remained the withdrawal of China from Tibet. There were no specific grievances on which the Chinese could compromise, and it was clear that Tibetans would not be satisfied with small measures or token reforms. This meant that there was no meeting point between the Chinese authorities and the protesters. For Beijing, therefore, the new initiatives in Tibet did not represent an attempt to remedy any local grievances: the only policy issue was how to curb the nationalists' demand for independence. This meant simply intensifying security measures. The new policy was now characterised by the suppression of any sign of dissent and the encouragement of any policy that weakened separatist sentiments or ideology. In the final analysis, the Chinese knew that they could always exercise their military power to control Tibetan protest.

The liberal policy that had sprung from Hu Yaobang's visit to Tibet in 1980 was seen as having directly encouraged Tibetan demands and as having tolerated the growth of separatism. In Beijing the leaders associated with such liberal policies had already lost their positions: following the downfall of Zhao Ziyang, Yan Mingfu (who as the head of the United Front was seen as responsible for negotiations with the Dalai Lama and had met with Gyalo Dhundup) was replaced by Ding Guangen. In the Tibetan CCP the early 1990s saw a similarly rapid reshuffling of personnel. Hu Jintao, who was seen as a trouble shooter, proved to be a high-flyer who was to spend much of his time in Beijing, dealing with Tibet only peripherally – in itself an indication that Tibet was in effect administered from the Chinese capital. Dorje Tseten left Tibet to manage a research centre in Beijing and Dorje Tsering was elevated to a senior post in Beijing, becoming, as Minister for Civil Affairs, one of the few Tibetans to occupy a high-ranking post with the government. These changes were not demotions, making it unclear whether they reflected a factional division between hardliners and the more liberal wing of the regional Party, or some other political shift. What was evident was that in Lhasa Ragdi and Pasang, both regarded as hard-liners who had come to power during the Cultural Revolution, continued to remain in power.

With respect to the rank and file of the Party, a new concern emerged: the loyalty of Tibetan cadres and party members. There were repeated calls for Party members and cadres to demonstrate their loyalty and to eschew nationalistic sentiments. Stricter discipline was enforced within the Party and it was stated that many Party members had openly taken part in religious ceremonies and had displayed photographs of the Dalai Lama in their homes. The previous lax attitude, Party members were informed, would not be tolerated, and adherence to strict Party discipline would be considered a test of their loyalty. A new emphasis was placed on showing loyalty to the principles of the unity of the motherland and the supremacy of the Party.

The new policy was described by Hu Jintao as 'grasping with both hands': on the one hand the authorities would suppress unrest by using the police or the military, and on the other hand they would accelerate the economic development of the region. In many ways this dual strategy for gaining control of the situation was successful. There was, after all, little that Tibetans could do to offset Chinese rule. The military and para-military organisations in Tibet had been strengthened, with a large number of additional soldiers moved into the region following the imposition of martial law in March 1989. In the first three days of military rule in Lhasa some 300 Tibetans were arrested and questioned about involvement in protests, and the Lhasa valley remained under military rule for thirteen months. Closed-circuit cameras were installed overlooking the Jokhang and the Barkor, the sites of most demonstrations, and there was a dramatic increase in the proportion of the annual budget allocated to security.

The other tactic adopted by the Party was reminiscent of earlier decades: old-style campaigning, mass mobilisation and ideological education. But the party found that the Tibetans were no longer docile souls who would jump to the commands of political instructors. The campaigns lacked enthusiasm both on the part of the cadres who were sent out to workplaces and villages, and on the part of the people, who listened more or less impassively to the cadres' routine denunciations of splittism. In the rural areas, apart from isolated cases of unrest, the authorities had nothing to fear: the protests did not penetrate these geographically remote and sparsely populated areas, particularly nomadic zones. The wider Tibetan populace may have felt secret sympathy towards the demonstrators, but they were unwilling to show it in action. Unlike the revolt of 1959, the unrest of the late 1980s was essentially confined to Lhasa.

Western Criticism

The crisis of this period did not seriously damage Chinese rule in Tibet. The main setback experienced by China in the aftermath of martial law was its image abroad, and in particular its relations with Western countries. Here again, the events in Tibet alone would not have induced the Western response that followed. It was the Tiananmen Square massacre that galvanised Western public opinion against Beijing, which now encountered diplomatic condemnation by Western countries. The emergence of human rights as a policy issue in the dealings of Western nations with China led to increasing pressure on Beijing to improve human rights conditions in Tibet.

For the first time since 1965 China was formally censured by a UN body, the Sub-Commission on Human Rights (known more formally as the Sub-Commission on the Prevention of Discrimination and the Protection of Minorities) in Geneva, where the Chinese delegation had to sit through lengthy reports submitted by non-governmental organisations. On this ground the Chinese had to concede to Western pressure, and the authorities were forced to allow Western diplomatic delegations to inspect prison conditions in Tibet. There were repeated calls for the unconditional release of prisoners detained as a result of demonstrations, although these were largely ineffective.

In April 1991 a meeting in Washington between President Bush and the Dalai Lama indicated that Tibet was continuing to receive favourable support from the United States. But perhaps greater impact came from the inauguration in the same year of Tibetan language broadcasts by the US radio station the Voice of America. Items about Tibet and the Dalai Lama were broadcast daily over the airwaves, and the station gained rapid popularity inside Tibet. More than any other statement, the Americans' decision to allow Tibetan language broadcasting was to be seen by the Chinese as a deliberate attempt to undermine their position in Tibet.

However, Western interest in Tibet was not a serious concern for the Chinese, aware that the Western bloc has no strategic or economic interests in Tibet. The issue could be used as an anti-Chinese irritant but would never be likely to become a priority for the Western powers. Both sides, therefore, were acting in the knowledge that the Tibetan issue was only a minor point in their relations and continued to use it as a device in diplomatic bargaining. Despite their protests, the Chinese also saw the human rights issue as no more than an irritant, and recognised Western concerns as an extension of their foreign policy objective, to gain economic concessions from China. A measure of Western pressure was in any case thwarted by pointing to the double standards in Western policy and by stressing the cultural and ideological differences in the concept of human rights. More importantly, China drew support from her neighbours and from other Third World countries. At the regional meeting of Asian countries in Bangkok, convened to prepare an agenda for the UN-sponsored World Conference of Human Rights in Vienna in June 1993, China was able to secure the support of all the Asian countries (except Japan) in endorsing the principle that human rights concerns should be guided by the principles of non-interference in the internal affairs of a state, and that it should stress the priority of collective rights over individual rights. Most Asian countries moved with China and were not prepared to condemn China's crackdown in Tibet.

Regional Solidarity

The rift between China and the West allowed neighbouring countries to move closer to China. India and China adopted a common position in international forums – notably at the Vienna Conference – and the Chinese made additional moves to strengthen their ties with Nepal and Bhutan. Economic links between the Tibet region and neighbouring countries were strengthened, and in late 1990, Ma Lisheng, a Deputy Party Secretary of the TAR, led a high-level trade delegation to Kathmandu. More controversially, China agreed to sell arms to Nepal. Relations with Bhutan proceeded more cautiously and, in August 1990, Qi Huaiyuan, a Chinese Vice Foreign Minister, arrived in Thimpu to round off the final stages of the border negotiations between the two countries. Proposed visits by the Dalai Lama to Nepal, Bhutan and Thailand in this period had to be cancelled as a result of Chinese pressure.

The Chinese recognised that improvement in their relations with India was crucial for stability in Tibet. Despite India's repeated claims that it does not support any demand for Tibetan independence, and that it would not allow the Tibetans to wage anti-Chinese campaigns on Indian territory, Beijing is aware that this is merely diplomatic coyness. The success of the Dalai Lama's campaigns abroad had depended entirely on India's willingness to turn a blind eye to his foreign travels. In fact, hard-nosed Chinese analysts view the Dalai Lama's campaigns abroad as an extension of Indian foreign policy and argue that India used Tibet as a wedge between Beijing and Washington.

Although there was consensus on the need to ease tension between the two countries, both sides nevertheless recognised that the regional strategic balance had not altered sufficiently to induce any major agreement. As long as there was no overall shift in the strategic balance in South Asia, the basic insecurities remained. Throughout the early 1990s the principal issue between the two nations – border demarcation – was not addressed: China still refused to recognise India's annexation of Sikkim, thus making any hope of a border settlement faint. However, China showed no signs of major concern about the issue.

At the international level, India's support for the exile movement remained implicit. Aware of the limits to the usefulness of Tibet as a negotiating pawn with China, India was reluctant to raise the issue openly in the border negotiations. Both sides were attracted by the need to reduce border tensions and to revitalise cross-border economic development, and China showed signs of a willingness to tolerate Indian dominance in South Asia. During the Indo-Nepalese dispute over trade and transit, Beijing adopted a neutral position, prompted partly by India's refusal to join in the chorus of condemnation that followed the Tiananmen Square massacre and the declaration of martial law in Tibet. While the West rebuffed Beijing diplomatically, India actively engaged in diplomacy with China. India's reward came in December 1991 when Li Peng paid a state visit to India and declared that both countries needed a 'peaceful environment' for domestic economic development. The visit, timed to take place just after President Bush's meeting with the Dalai Lama, was followed two years later by a summit meeting in Beijing at which Li and Narasimha Rao signed a five-point accord. For the first time since 1959 a Sino–Indian agreement explicitly mentioned Tibet and promised that neither the issue of Tibet nor that of Pakistan would be used by India or China against each other.

However, the main issue – the Sino–Indian border dispute – remained unresolved. The two sides agreed to abjure the use of force and to respect the line of control. There was mutual agreement to reduce the number of troops deployed along the disputed border, and it was later announced that the two sides would carry out joint military exercises. These were definite signs of a new level of understanding between the two countries. This was crucial for Chinese policy, and was the external dimension required for the achievement of stability in Tibet. The Chinese were thus able to promote the stability in Tibet not only as being a Chinese internal interest, but as a regional concern. It therefore eliminated any danger of the unrest there flaring into a regional conflict.

Economy

By securing the support of the neighbouring countries the Chinese were able to concentrate on their domestic concerns in Tibet and to blunt Western pressure on human rights. In addition, the improvement in political relations with neighbouring countries provided economic dividends in terms of a growth in border trade – by 1994 Tibet's foreign trade was said to have reached $100 million – yielding benefits which far outweighed the negative image of Chinese policy in the West. Here, too, China was able to fend off criticism by Western governments, aware that Tibet is not a sufficiently significant issue for the West to put its economic interests at risk by the promise of trade and economic benefits. As a result Beijing did not allow Western criticism about its human rights record to distract it from its overall policy in Tibet, which remained, as before, the further integration of Tibet with China by means of institutional reform and the accelerated development of a market-oriented economy.

Economic development, however, was now to assume a different shape. The new emphasis was on infrastructure development, with the focus on the energy resources, transport, telecommunications and light industry capable of supplying local needs. The failure to set up local industry was said to have been one of the main reasons for the lack of economic progress in Tibet, which was lagging far behind development in China, remaining largely on the level of a traditional subsistence economy. The authorities announced that 15 per cent of households were living under the poverty line and many more were at subsistence level. The Chinese answer to Tibet's economic under-development was to open the region further.

As China became increasingly oriented towards a market economy, Tibet became a fertile ground for entrepreneurs and there was a renewed influx of Hui Muslim traders. The new economic philosophy emphasised development of the technical and financial sectors and so brought with it a rush of experts and technically skilled Chinese to run the expanding businesses, tending to push Tibetans further down the ladder of competition towards manual and semi-skilled jobs, while Chinese immigrants dominated the lucrative skilled jobs market. This problem was further compounded by the fact that the overwhelming majority of Tibetans remained in rural areas, lacking basic amenities and access to the benefits brought by the new economic policy. In certain rural areas the increase in population, coupled with a lack of economic opportunity, pushed living standards into a downward spiral.

In July 1994 the Third Tibet Work Forum was convened in Beijing, presided over by Li Peng. There it was stressed that a renewed emphasis was be placed on economic development and that the long-term aim was to achieve a 10 per cent annual growth rate. The conference went on to list sixty-two major projects whose total investment was to equal 2.38 billion yuan (approximately US $270 million). At the time, power supply in Tibet was not sufficient even for domestic consumption. Therefore, before any industrial or agricultural development could take place, the establishment of energy resources was essential.

In 1994, in a parallel attempt to push Tibet towards a market economy, the authorities opened Tibet's first stock exchange in Lhasa. This attracted huge amounts of capital into the region, and by the end of the year the daily turnover at the exchange had reached 5 million yuan (US $580,000). This flow of institutional and private capital into Tibet did not, however, bring any immediate benefits to local Tibetans, who looked with suspicion on this capital investment and saw it as an attempt to attract more Chinese settlers to join the Chinese specialists who were overseeing the development, and the petty traders who were catering for the growing Chinese population.

The new development policies propelled Tibet further towards the mainstream trends prevailing in the rest of China, so that Tibet found itself increasingly caught up in the general movement of population from rural areas to urban centres in search of economic opportunity. Irrespective of whether this flow of Chinese migrants into Tibet was the deliberate aim of government policy or a peripheral consequence of the economic changes, in the eyes of many Tibetans the authorities were complicit in the surge in migration. Officials were willing to turn a blind eye to those entering without permits and a number of tax concessions and flexible loan arrangements were made available at this time, so that a newly arrived worker from China stood to gain a five-fold increase in salary.

The fear of an influx of migrants – shared by almost all Tibetans – became therefore the main issue of conflict. Tibetan officials were also relatively active in raising concerns about the dangers of a huge increase in the population, but Beijing and the Party leaders were now less sympathetic to Tibetan complaints. While Hu Yaobang was in power he did allow the Tibetans to voice their grievances, but the unrest had placed Tibetan officials in an extremely difficult position. The Chinese authorities now began to emphasise that loyalty to the motherland and the struggle against splittism was the central issue, an indication that criticism of policy was liable to be labelled a sign of local nationalism or of veiled sympathy for the separatists. This meant that most Tibetan cadres were forced to adhere to the new policy.

The economic policies adopted in Tibet were governed by a narrow vision of material development and did not address the social and political grievances of the Tibetan people. The chief motive of the economic reforms in Tibet was to accelerate its political integration into China and to modernise the agrarian economy of the region. But Tibet's geographical isolation from China's boom areas in the coastal areas and industrial cities makes it likely that Tibet will remain in the margins of the Chinese economy. Sustained economic growth in Tibet will only come about when Tibet's southern border with India is fully open, a step that has not yet been taken by Beijing.

This redirection of policy towards economic integration did not bring with it any hope of lessening the longstanding conflict between the two communities. It represented an implicit rejection of the argument that the core problem in Tibet lay in the wishes and desires of Tibetans who perceived the system as unjust, and thus failed to advance the prospect of any consensus being reached between the Tibetans and Chinese authorities.

This sense of neglect extended to many of those Tibetans who, until then, may have been loyal to the CCP. After forty years of rule, the authorities had failed to create a homogeneous group of Tibetans on whom the Party could rely to administer the region, a failure epitomised by the continuing inability to appoint a Tibetan as Party Secretary. In 1992 that post, the highest in Tibet, was awarded to Chen Kuiyuan, a Chinese official regarded as a hard-liner. Shortly before taking up the post in Lhasa, Chen had penned an article in *Shijian*, the official journal of the Inner Mongolian Regional CCP, advocating that 'ideology and class' should be brought back into the foreground of nationality policy. Once in his new position, he rapidly introduced a number of changes in line with such ideas, removing some Tibetan officials from their posts because they were seen as too nationalistic or as coming from a privileged class background, and promoting in their stead cadres who had a good class background and had shown an ideologically correct standpoint.

Despite measures to strengthen security, on 23 May 1993 about a thousand lay people protested in Lhasa, the first time that such a number had taken to the streets since the lifting of martial law. Unlike previous demonstrations, the protesters contested recent increases in food prices, the introduction of charges for medical prescriptions, and school fees. Although not articulated by the protesters, one of the main causes of the new wave of demonstrations was the renewed flow of Chinese migrants into the capital. The Chinese authorities recognised that the protesters had legitimate grounds for some economic complaints, but saw the danger of the incident quickly developing into a pro-independence demonstration and the central policy objective accordingly shifted to the maintenance of stability and order. Hence, no protest would be allowed in Tibet and the primary policy was to establish social stability, which could only be achieved by intensifying security operations, and throughout the 1990s there was a significant increase in expenditure on both the civil and paramilitary mechanisms of control.

In 1994 the Party's Central Committee convened a third Tibet Work Forum, following on from the First Work Forum convened by Hu Yaobang fourteen years earlier. The forum had meanwhile become an ongoing body operating as a central working group responsible for the formulation of five-year work programmes for Tibet. The Third Work Forum charted a new course which embodied a radical shift both in ideology and in practical terms. It detailed two main programmes; first, the main task for the next five years was to be the promotion of rapid economic development. This would require a massive subsidy from the Centre to improve essential infrastructure and to boost long-term development. However, a new emphasis was placed on development of energy resources and light industry and, for the first time since the 1960s, agricultural development seemed to occupy a secondary position. Where agriculture was stressed it was in order to improve the marketability of agricultural products and the expansion of the market system into the rural areas. It was a plan which did not divert from the general trend throughout China, but which was to have a major impact on Tibetans in the region.

The second thrust of the Third Forum was the decision to identify separatists as the major cause of instability in Tibet and to instigate a campaign to root out Tibetan nationalists. This meant the removal of any cadres in the Party or in the administration who had shown nationalist tendencies. In the Party, accordingly, there were renewed demands on its members in Tibet to adhere strictly to the Party's guidelines on religion.

Another central aspect of the new campaign was directed against the Dalai Lama personally. This reflected the view held by senior leaders in Beijing that the Tibet question was essentially an issue about the Dalai Lama. It yielded a new strategy: to eliminate both his religious and his political influence from the region. Since 1980, the Chinese had largely refrained from attacking the Dalai Lama personally and had allowed homes, temples and monasteries to display photographs of him. The public display of faith in the Dalai Lama was no longer to be tolerated.

The Panchen Rinpoche Controversy

The campaign of the Chinese authorities against the Dalai Lama reached a new intensity in May 1995 when the Dalai Lama announced from his exiled home the recognition of a young boy from Nagchu in north-west Tibet as the reincarnation of the 10th Panchen Rinpoche, who had passed away in 1989. The Chinese denounced the Dalai Lama's announcement as 'illegal and a political plot by the Dalai clique to split the Motherland'. The Dalai Lama described the issue as a purely religious matter and called on the Chinese not to impede the recognition of the child, but Beijing took the announcement as a direct challenge to its authority and regarded the Dalai Lama's unilateral announcement as an attempt to embarrass the government in Beijing.

The announcement had far-reaching repercussions. It was inevitable, given the state of Sino–Tibetan relations, that the question of the recognition of the Panchen Rinpoche would lead to conflict between two main protagonists. The Dalai Lama's unilateral announcement could be seen as an attempt by the exiles to counter China's attack on the Dalai Lama's religious and political influence inside Tibet; in addition, the exiles may have seen the issue as a stick with which to beat China. They had for years been trying unsuccessfully to bring the Chinese to the negotiating table. By bringing the issue of the recognition of the Panchen Rinpoche to the forefront, they may have hoped to bring pressure on the Chinese. The Dalai Lama's statement was worded so as to highlight the 'unreasonableness' of the Chinese, presenting them as impeding a purely religious matter in which the Dalai Lama's authority was beyond dispute.

Even before the announcement from Dharamsala the Chinese were faced with a difficult dilemma. The unexpected death of the 10th Panchen Rinpoche in Tashilhunpo monastery six years earlier had left China without a credible figurehead in Tibet at a time when there were repeated demonstrations in Lhasa and the Chinese were facing a serious, even unprecedented, challenge to their rule by Tibetan nationalists. Beijing had recognised from the outset the inherent complexity of the issue and established its first priority: to minimise the risk of political damage by ensuring that whatever was done did not undermine Chinese authority in Tibet either in principle or in practice. Soon after the funeral ceremonies Premier Li Peng announced that outsiders would not be allowed to 'meddle in the selection procedure', an indication that the Chinese were not intending to accept the involvement of the Dalai Lama in the selection process.

A month after the Panchen Rinpoche's death the United Front Department convened a high-level meeting in Beijing to discuss the issue. One of the main topics under consideration was the question of the Dalai Lama's involvement. There had already been a number of press statements by the Dalai Lama and announcements from various Dharamsala officials that insisted that the recognition of the reincarnation had to come from the Dalai Lama personally; these were to set alarm bells ringing in Beijing. The growing anti-Chinese agitation in Tibet had meant that the relationship between the Dalai Lama and Beijing was at its lowest point since 1979 and, unsurprisingly, the Chinese were therefore adamant that there should be no role for the Dalai Lama in the process. It was agreed that maximum effort would be made to counter any interference from outside.

In August 1989, the Chinese authorities announced a seven-point plan for the search, selection and recognition of the Panchen Rinpoche. The first four points followed traditional religious practices. However, the last three points stated that the selection would be made by lottery, and that the final public confirmation would be given by the Chinese Central Government. Once again any role for the Dalai Lama was ruled out. The Tibetans saw this as an attempt by the Chinese to circumvent the Dalai Lama's authority.

The procedure advocated by the Chinese placed the monks of Tashilhunpo in a difficult position. The last three points clearly marked a departure from traditional religious procedure and Tashilhunpo was anyway hesitant about ruling the Dalai Lama entirely out of the picture: for them the question of the Dalai Lama's recognition was an important matter of prestige and legitimacy. They therefore argued that, whatever happened, the Chinese must make room for the Dalai Lama. The issue became a point of contention between the monastery and the Chinese authorities. If Tashilhunpo were to reject the Chinese requirements, it faced a likelihood of losing its traditional leading role in Tibetan affairs – there were strong factions in the United Front Department and in the Religious Affairs Bureau which argued that, given the 'national' importance of the Panchen Rinpoche, the search and selection should be carried out by a national body rather than by Tashilhunpo.

In the end Tashilhunpo had to accept the procedure drawn up by the Chinese authorities. It was, however, able to obtain a major concession from the Chinese: it was agreed that although the Chinese Buddhist Association would be nominally in charge of the search and selection process, it would not have any authority over the day-to-day running of the search. Both the monks of Tashilhunpo and the Chinese agreed that the search party should be headed by Chatral Rinpoche, a respected lama from Shigatse who in the early 1960s had studied in the China Buddhist Institute in Beijing and who had since 1982 been, by popular vote, the head of Tashilhunpo's Democratic Management Committee, as well as a member of the 8th National Committee of the national CPPCC.

Initially, it appeared that the Chinese had managed to gain complete control of the process. After the candidates had been selected, the Religious Affairs Bureau would supervise the installation of the final candidate by using a lottery system and the final selection would be made amid much publicity designed to demonstrate China's sovereignty and authority over Tibet. However, all was not well behind the scenes. The Tibetans remained unhappy that the Chinese authorities had dispensed with any involvement by the Dalai Lama, and this unease reached the highest levels of the religious establishment.

In April 1991 a meeting (ostensibly convened to hear a report from Chatral Rinpoche on the progress of the search) was held in Tashilhunpo monastery, attended by high lamas from Qinghai, Sichuan, Yunnan, Inner Mongolia and the TAR. During the meeting some of the lamas made it known that the Dalai Lama's approval was essential for recognition and that it could not simply be dismissed. The lamas were careful to qualify their statements by saying that they disapproved of the Dalai Lama's political campaigns but that his religious authority was nevertheless absolute, whether he lived in exile or in Tibet. There were also murmurings of protest from the public, threatening that a new Panchen Rinpoche would not find popular support among the people if he did not carry the blessing of the Dalai Lama. This was an important issue for the Chinese, who recognised that without support from the Tibetans they would have difficulty in enthroning the new candidate.

The decision by the Chinese to exclude the Dalai Lama had been made at a time when relations between the two sides were at their worst, but in 1993, when the shock of demonstrations had somewhat faded, the Chinese invited Gyalo Dhundup and Sonam Topgyal (a high-ranking official in the Dharamsala government) to visit Beijing. Chatral Rinpoche was specially flown to Beijing and on 17 July he met the exile delegation and handed Gyalo Dhundup a letter addressed to his brother, the Dalai Lama. Although the full contents of the letter have remained secret, it is known to have sought the Dalai Lama's help in searching for the new Panchen Rinpoche. According to information released much later by the Dalai Lama's office in India, Chatral Rinpoche's letter also indicated that the new incarnation would be born to the east of Tashilhunpo, an implication that the boy must be selected from inside Tibet.

A few days later Chatral Rinpoche was back in Shigatse, where once again high lamas from all parts of Tibet had gathered to hear his report on the progress of the search. A three-day meeting was held in Tashilhunpo where Chatral Rinpoche and Gaya Rinpoche, who was promoted by the Chinese as having been the previous Panchen Rinpoche's teacher, gave a detailed account of the progress of the search. It was no more than a list of ceremonies and rituals that had been performed over the past years but, more importantly, Chatral Rinpoche announced that contact had been established with the Dalai Lama and that he had been informed of the progress of the search. This allayed many of the doubts and criticisms expressed in the earlier meeting.

The new contact represented by Chatral Rinpoche's letter did not resolve the problem. It opened up a disagreement as to how the Dalai Lama could be involved. The Chinese seemed to accept that the approval of the Dalai Lama was a mandatory religious requirement without which they would have a hard time convincing the Tibetans and the Buddhist world that they had selected the true candidate, but they appear to have seen the Dalai Lama's role as merely to endorse the candidate selected by them. For the Dalai Lama this was not only unacceptable on political grounds, but would have implied that he had accepted the Chinese Government's right to intervene in purely religious affairs. The Chinese authorities had allowed Tashilhunpo to communicate with the Dalai Lama but expected in return no more than a formal and symbolic acknowledgment of acquiescence from him.

The divergence of views between the Chinese and the Dalai Lama became increasingly apparent. The Dalai Lama had responded by inviting Chatral Rinpoche and other members of the search party to visit India for a discussion. The Chinese refused. Later, in his statement of May 1995, the Dalai Lama was to indicate that his attempts to communicate with the Chinese on this subject through diplomatic and private channels had been rebuffed or ignored. The Chinese maintained that there was 'no need for outside intervention', and insisted that any involvement by the Dalai Lama could take place only on their terms.

The essential political issue was not whether the correct religious rituals were carried out or not. On both sides of the fence the key issue was the symbolism of the process and who is said to hold the final authority in Tibet. For Beijing, it did not even matter which child was to be chosen: the main political value of the confirmation and the recognition of the Panchen Lama was to demonstrate past and present claims of China's sovereignty over Tibet. It was not therefore a matter of installing any particular candidate, who would in any case be a child with no immediate influence or authority for at least a decade. From the outset the Chinese recognized the importance of how the recognition of the new Panchen Rinpoche was to be arranged and presented.

For the Dalai Lama, the death of the Panchen Rinpoche offered both opportunity and risk. It presented him with the chance to assert his authority as the highest spiritual leader and, through his actions, to confirm that no recognition could take place without his approval. This was a claim based on sound historical precedents, since all previous Panchen Rinpoche had been formally recognized by the Dalai Lamas, and if he were to succeed in this course of action the Chinese would be forced to acknowledge his authority, at least in the religious sphere. Equally, the situation posed the risk that the Chinese might install the new Panchen Rinpoche themselves and thus set a precedent for dispensing with the religious authority of the Dalai Lama.

The Chinese insistence on using a system established in the eighteenth century by the Qing Emperor, drawing lots from a 'Golden Urn' to select the new Panchen Rinpoche, derived from the symbolically potency of the ceremony in demonstrating Chinese authority over Tibet. For Beijing it was logical that if China exercised sufficient control to have the right to institute the selection of Tibetan leaders in the eighteenth century, then the present Chinese rule in Tibet must be legitimate. Beijing was thus seeking not so much to deny the prerogative of the Dalai Lama in such matters as to stress the continuity of Chinese authority in Tibet. To some extent the Chinese view is, at least at first sight, well-founded and difficult for Tibetans to refute. How can the Tibetans explain the power exercised by the Qing Emperors in the eighteenth century other than by acknowledging that the Tibetans at the time had accepted Chinese imperial authority? For the Chinese authorities, therefore, the correctness of the selection procedure was secondary: what mattered was to show that the final authority in Tibet had always rested in Beijing. This was the point behind a press statement issued by China's Religious Affairs Bureau which said that the Dalai Lama had 'negated the supreme authority of the central government'.

Needless to say, for the Dalai Lama the opposite was true: he needed to demonstrate that his word was the final authority in Tibet. But it was also the manner in which he made his announcement that was keenly noted by Beijing: the fact that it was presented as a *fait accompli*, without having informed the Chinese in advance, was a source of intense irritation to them. For them to have then accepted the boy already announced by the Dalai Lama would of course have entailed a great loss of face, and would have meant that they had been outwitted by the Tibetans.

By August 1993 the Chinese had instituted a ban on any further formal contact between the Dalai Lama and the search party, but this had not prevented the two from establishing a clandestine line of communication; it is widely believed – and indeed the Chinese themselves claim – that the official search party in Tibet had even submitted a list of candidates for the Dalai Lama's approval. If this was the case, then Tashilhunpo had taken an enormous risk by seeking the Dalai Lama's approval in deliberate contravention of Chinese instructions. The Dalai Lama has been careful so far not to implicate either Chatral Rinpoche or Tashilhunpo monastery in any secret involvement with his decision. But if, as seems likely, they were indeed involved, it would appear that the Tibetans had hoodwinked the Chinese.

However, even if the search party in Tibet had submitted a list of candidates to the Dalai Lama, its members may not have expected him to make a public announcement, and would rather have presumed that he would make a selection in secret, which would be conveyed back via Tashilhunpo, allowing the final announcement to follow, at least in public, the procedure laid down by the Chinese. This would have placated both sides, allowing the Chinese to retain their dignity and the Dalai Lama to maintain that it was he who had selected the new lama. To accomplish this, Chatral Rinpoche would have needed to have had absolute confidence that there was a consensus on the need to avoid confrontation. Needless to say, such a consensus did not exist: the two protagonists in the dispute were clearly swayed by their eagerness to use the issue to gain maximum propaganda value.

The Dalai Lama's announcement placed the Chinese in a difficult position. The religious question had become for them the main source of confrontation in Tibet. The demand for religious freedom and the growth of monasteries had led to the re-emergence of the traditional dominance of high lamas. As the most influential group in Tibetan society, looked on by lay followers not only as spiritual leaders but also as heads of their respective regions, this development clearly had serious implications for the Chinese, for whom the primary objective in Tibet remained the establishment of stability. With Buddhist monks and nuns in the forefront of nationalist agitation, the Chinese authorities found themselves on the one hand restricting the number of monks allowed to join monasteries, while on the other recognising that stability could only be achieved by appeasing the religious leaders, in the hope that they would win the Tibetans over to the Chinese point of view. Beijing's concerns about its contradictory dealings with religion were well illustrated by the founding in 1987 of a special Buddhist college in Beijing, run by the Chinese government, to train young lamas from all over Tibet. The authorities announced that the main task of the college was to produce 'patriotic lamas who would cherish the unity of the motherland'. The Tibetans argued that the training of lamas should be left to the monasteries.

Hard-liners in China and Tibet argued that Beijing should go ahead with prescribed selection procedure and enthrone a new Panchen Rinpoche of its choice, without the involvement of the Dalai Lama. For them, the wave of protests that had occurred in Lhasa had been a result of the excessive compromises made during the liberal period, and no concessions should be made to the Dalai Lama, whatever the difficulties. The Chinese leadership was aware that in religious matters the Dalai Lama's authority was universally accepted and that any attempt to challenge his spiritual prestige would risk inviting protest from the Tibetans. Nevertheless, by the beginning of November 1995, the Chinese authorities had come to a decision. With the support of a few senior monks from Tashilhunpo, the leadership announced in Beijing that the Golden Urn ceremony for the selection of a new incarnation of the Panchen Rinpoche would take place shortly, and that it would not include the child named six months earlier by the Dalai Lama. On 29 November, in conditions of great secrecy, the Chinese held a ceremony in the Jokhang in Lhasa and selected a young boy. He was enthroned at Tashilhunpo nine days later as the 11th Panchen Rinpoche.

The dispute over the recognition of the Panchen Rinpoche had created an irreconcilable gulf between the Chinese authorities and the Dalai Lama. The consequences were not purely symbolic: the child selected by the Dalai Lama had disappeared shortly after the announcement in May 1995; even a year later the Chinese authorities were still refusing to give details of his whereabouts. Chatral Rinpoche had been detained by the authorities, and had been dismissed from his positions as the head of the search party and as the acting abbot of Tashilhunpo; his place of arrest was also kept secret. In April 1996 the Chinese authorities once again intensified their campaign against the Dalai Lama and ordered all religious buildings, shops, hotels and even private houses to take down any photographs of the man now described by the Chinese as a 'political fugitive' and 'not a religious leader'.

There is no doubt that the religious question will remain an unbridgeable gap between the Chinese and the Tibetans. But in the future the main impetus of conflict in Tibet is likely to be generated by the growing gulf between the rich and the poor. Throughout the 1990s there was an impressive growth in the regional economy, but the chief beneficiary was the growing urban Chinese population. The official figures show that while the urban areas saw a growth rate of nearly 10 per cent per annum, the rural areas experienced a modest 3 per cent.

Conclusion

This disparity is likely to be accentuated by the ethnic divide that underlies the urban–rural dichotomy – a predominantly rural population made up of Tibetans as opposed to a substantial urban group of recent Chinese migrants, who, with better access to education and other resources, are likely to become socially dominant. There is already a growing perception that the Tibetans are naturally disadvantaged and discriminated against, which, if allowed to continue, is likely to become insurmountable. At the most simple level there is a deeply polarised conflict of views about the relationship between the Chinese and the Tibetans. Leaving aside the question of independence and the status of Tibet, the majority of Tibetans see the presence of the Chinese both as an embodiment of state power and as a malevolent force which ultimately seeks to destroy Buddhism and Tibetans. The Chinese self-image, as presented by the CCP and widely held among Chinese people, is that their presence is benign and is a contribution to the growth and future prosperity of Tibetans.

Beijing's failure in Tibet stemmed in large part from two ideas, both of which had contributed positively in their own way to the shaping of modern China. One of these was Chinese nationalism. Nurtured by resentment at the historical humiliation of China by Western imperialism, it had encouraged the Chinese to interpret the Tibetan demand for independence as an externally generated conspiracy to dismember China, an opinion held by successive Chinese regimes from the Qing to the Guomindang, as well as by the Communists. It was a view which had led all these dynasties to adopt a policy of integrating Tibet within the greater polity of China, a perspective which sees Tibet as a prior part of China and does not, therefore, allow for consideration of the views or wishes of Tibetans.

While the Party may from time to time have expressed maternal concerns towards its Tibetan subjects, it appears rarely to have been the case, however, that the Tibetans felt any filial affection towards the motherland. This is China's dilemma.

The second formative concept in the ideological apparatus with which China approached Tibet was the narrow Marxist economic-determinist view of national identity. This argument holds that nationality is a product of economic disparity. It follows, therefore, that once economic inequality has been removed, there would occur a natural withering of ethnic distinctiveness. The more complex realities of identity and self-image thus found no place within the Communist way of understanding the Tibetan nationality.

The modalities of Chinese rule over Tibet, and the extent to which they have either tightened or loosened their grip at each phase of their rule, are not therefore governed so much by the internal situation in Tibet as by the more complex issues of ideology and power which confront the leadership of the Communist Party. The future of Tibet thus remains inextricably linked with the ebb and flow at the heart of the Party which will shape China as it enters the twenty-first century.

APPENDIX 1

The Agreement of the Central People's Government and the Local Government of Tibet on Measures for the Peaceful Liberation of Tibet

The Tibetan nationality is one of the nationalities with a long history living within the boundaries of China and, like many other nationalities, it has performed its glorious duty in the course of the creation and development of our great motherland. But over the last 100 years or more, imperialist forces penetrated China, and in consequence also penetrated the Tibetan region and carried out all kinds of deceptions and provocations. Like previous reactionary governments, the Kuomintang reactionary government continued to carry out a policy oppressing and sowing dissension among the nationalities, causing division and disunity among the Tibetan people. And the Local Government of Tibet did not oppose the imperialist deceptions and provocations, and adopted an unpatriotic attitude towards our motherland. Under such conditions, the Tibetan nationality and people were plunged into the depths of enslavement and suffering.

In 1949, basic victory was achieved on a nationwide scale in the Chinese People's War of Liberation; the common domestic enemy of all nationalities – the Kuomintang reactionary government – was overthrown; and the common foreign enemy of all nationalities – the aggressive imperialist forces – was driven out. On this basis, the founding of the People's Republic of China and the Central People's Government was announced. In accordance with the *Common Programme* passed by the Chinese People's Political Consultative Conference, the Central People's Government declared that all nationalities within the boundaries of the People's Republic of China are equal, and that they shall establish unity and mutual aid and oppose imperialism and their public enemies, so that the PRC will become one fraternal and co-operative family, composed of all its nationalities; that within the big family of all nationalities of the PRC, national regional autonomy shall be exercised in areas where national minorities shall have the freedom to develop their spoken and written languages and to preserve or reform their customs, habits and religious beliefs, while the Central People's

Government shall assist all national minorities to develop their political, economic, cultural and educational construction work. Since then, all nationalities within the country, with the exception of those in the areas of Tibet and Taiwan, have gained liberation. Under the unified leadership of the Central People's Government and the direct leadership of higher levels of people's government, all national minorities are fully enjoying the right of national equality and have established, or are establishing, national regional autonomy.

In order that the influences of aggressive imperialist forces in Tibet might be successfully eliminated, the unification of the territory and sovereignty of the People's Republic of China accomplished, and national defence safeguarded: in order that the Tibetan nationality and people might be freed and return to the family of the People's Republic of China to enjoy the same rights of national equality as all the other nationalities in the country and develop their political, economic, cultural and educational work, the Central People's Government, when it ordered the People's Liberation Army to march into Tibet, notified the Local Government of Tibet to send delegates to the central authorities to conduct talks for the conclusion of an agreement on measures for the peaceful liberation of Tibet.

In the latter part of April 1951, the delegates with the full powers of the Local Government of Tibet arrived in Beijing. The Central People's Government appointed representatives with full power to conduct talks on a friendly basis with the delegates of the Local Government of Tibet. As a result of these talks, both parties agreed to conclude this agreement and guarantee that it will be carried in effect.

(1) The Tibetan people shall unite and drive out imperialist aggressive forces from Tibet; the Tibetan people shall return to the family of the motherland – the People's Republic of China.

(2) The Local Government of Tibet shall actively assist the People's Liberation Army to enter Tibet and consolidate the national defence.

(3) In accordance with the policy towards nationalities laid down in the *Common Programme of the Chinese Political Consultative Conference*, the Tibetan people have the right to exercise national regional autonomy under the unified leadership of the Central People's Government.

(4) The central authorities will not alter the existing political system in Tibet. The central authorities also will not alter the established status, functions and powers of the Dalai Lama. Officials of various rank shall hold office as usual.

(5) The established status, functions and powers of the Bainqen Erdini shall be maintained.

(6) By the established status, functions and powers of the Dalai Lama

and of the Bainqen Erdini are meant the status, functions and powers of the 13th Dalai Lama and the 9th Bainqen when they were in friendly and amicable relation with each other.

(7) The policy of freedom of religious belief laid down in the *Common Programme of the Chinese Political Consultative Conference* shall be carried out. The religious beliefs, customs and habits of the Tibetan people shall be respected, and lama monasteries shall be protected. The central authorities will not effect a change in the income of the monasteries.

(8) Tibetan troops shall be reorganized by stages into the People's Liberation Army, and become a part of the national defence forces of the People's Republic of China.

(9) The spoken and written language and school education of the Tibetan nationality shall be developed step by step in accordance with the actual conditions in Tibet.

(10) Tibetan agriculture, livestock raising, industry and commerce shall be developed step by step, and the people's livelihood shall be improved step by step in accordance with the actual conditions in Tibet.

(11) In matters related to various reforms in Tibet there will be no compulsion on the part of the central authorities. The Local Government of Tibet should carry out reforms of its own accord, and demands for reform raised by the people shall be settled by means of consultation with the leading personnel of Tibet.

(12) In so far as former pro-imperialist and pro-Kuomintang officials resolutely sever relations with imperialism and the Kuomintang, and do not engage in sabotage or resistance, they may continue to hold office irrespective of their past.

(13) The People's Liberation Army entering Tibet shall abide by all the above mentioned policies and shall also be fair in all buying and selling and shall not arbitrarily take a single needle or thread from the people.

(14) The Central People's Government shall conduct the centralized handling of all external affairs of Tibet and there will be peaceful co-existence with neighbouring countries and the establishment and development of fair commercial and trading relations with them on the basis of equality, mutual benefit and mutual respect for territory and sovereignty.

(15) In order to ensure the implementation of this agreement, the Central People's Government shall set up a military and administrative committee and a military area headquarters in Tibet, and apart from the personnel sent there by the Central People's Government, shall absorb as many local Tibetan personnel as possible to take part in the work.

Local Tibetan personnel taking part in the military and administrative committee may include patriotic elements from the Local Government of Tibet, various districts and leading monasteries; the name-list shall be drawn up after consultation between the representative designated by the Central People's Government and the various quarters concerned, and shall be submitted to the Central People's Government for appointment.

(16) Funds needed by the military and administrative committee, the military area headquarters and the People's Liberation Army entering Tibet shall be provided by the Central People's Government. The Local Government of Tibet will assist the People's Liberation Army in the purchase and transport of food, fodder and other daily necessities.

(17) This agreement shall come into force immediately after signatures and seals are affixed to it.

Signed in Beijing on the 23rd of May 1951.

Chinese Representatives: Li Weihan, Zhang Jingwu, Zhang Guohua and Sun Zhiyuan.

Tibetan Representatives: Ngabo Ngawang Jigme, Khame Sonam Wangdu, Lhawutara Thupten Tenther, Thupten Lekmon and Sampho Tenzin Dhundup.

APPENDIX 2

Tibetan Spelling

Spelling in book	Tibetan translation
Ala 'Jisme	a-lag 'jigs-med
Alo Chonzed Tsering Dorje	a-lo chos-mdzad tshe-ring rdo-rje
Amdo	a-mdo
Andrug Gonbo Tashi	a-'brug mgon-po bkra-shis
Ani	a-ni
Athar Norbu	a-thar nor-bu
Baba Changtra Tashi	'ba'-pa phyang khra bkra shis
Baba Phuntsog Wangyal	'ba'-pa phun tshogs dbang rgyal
Baba Yeshi	'ba'-pa ye shes
Barkor	bar-bskor
Barshi Ngawang Tenkyong	bar gzhis ngag dbang bsten skyong
Bathang	'ba' thang
Beri	be ri
Bumthang Gyaltsen Lobsang	'bum thang rgyal mtshan blo bzang
Chagtrag Sonam Chophel	lchags phrag bsod nams chos-'phel
Chamdo	chab mdo
Chamdo Khenchung	chab mdo mkhan chung
Changlochen	lcang lo can
Changthang	byang thang
Chatreng Sampheling	cha phreng bsam 'phel gling
Chape Lhamo Sonam	chab spyel lha mo bsod nams
Chen Jigme	cen 'jigs-med
Chi gye Lhakung	phyi rgyal las khungs
Chitsog Nyingpa	spyi tshogs rnying pa
Chitsog Sarpa	spyi tshogs gsar pa
cho zhi	chos-gzhis
Chod yon	mchod yon
Chogyal	chos rgyal
Cholka sum	chol kha gsum
Chomphel Thubten	chos-'phel thub bstan
Choten	mchod rten
Chu zhi Gang drung	chu bzhi sgang drug
Chuba	phyu pa
Chushul	chu shul

Chyikhyab Khenpo	spyi-khyab mkhan-po
Dagyab Loden Sherap	brags gyab blo ldan shes rab
Damshung	'dam gzhung
Darmaru	da ma ru
Dawa Norbu	zla wa nor bu
Depa zhung	sde pa gzhung
Dedon Tsogpa	bde-don tshogs-pa
Dekyi Lingka	bde skyid gling kha
Dengo	ldan go
Depon	mda' dpon
Derge Se Ngawang Kalsang	sde dge sras ngag-dbang skal bzang
Derge	sde dge
Dharlo	dar lho
Dhondub Choedon	don drub chos sgron
Dhondup Namgyal	don drub rnam rgyal
Dingri	ding ri
Do zam	rdo-zam
Domed Chikhyab	mdo smad spyi khyab
Drepung	'bras spungs
Drichu	'bri chu
Driguthang	gri gu thang
Dromo	gro mo
Drung ja	drung ja
Drongdra Magmi	grong drag dmag mi
Drungyigchenmo Chogteng	drung yig chen mo lcog steng
Drungyigchenmo	drung yig chen mo
Dumra wa	ldum ra ba
Dzasa	dza sag
Dzongpon	rdzong dpon
Ga ra	mgar ba
Gaden	dga' ldan
Gadong	dga' gdong
Gadrang	dga' brang
Gelug pa	dge lugs pa
Geshe Chodrak	dge bshes chos grags
Geshe Lodro Gyatso	dge bshes blo gros rgya mtsho
Geshe Sherab Gyatso	dge bshes shes rab rgya mtsho
Geta Rinpoche	dge stag
Gya-Bod	rgya bod
Gyakhar Gonpo Namgyal	rgyal-mkhar mgon po rnam rgyal
Gyalo Dhundup	rgya lo don drub
Gyalthang	rgyal thang
Gyaltsen Phuntsog	rgyal mtshan phun tshogs

Gyaltshab	rgyal tshab
Gyalwa Karmapa	rgyal ba karma pa
Gyamda	rgya mda'
Gyantse	rgyal rtse
Gyapon	brgya dpon
Gyadotsang Wangdu	rgya do tshang dbang 'dus
Gyatsoling Rinpoche	rgya tsho gling rin po che
Gyenlog	gyen log
Gyado Wangdu	rgya do dbang 'dus
Gyueme Dratsang	rgyud smad grva tsang
Horkhang	hor khang
Hortsoen Chen	hur brtson chan
Jampa Wangdu	byams pa dbang 'dus
Jampai Yang Gongma	'jam pa'i dbyangs gong ma
Jamphel Gyatso	'jam dpal rgya mtsho
Jamyang Sakya	'jam dbang sa skya
Jamyang Zhepa	'jam dbyang bzhad pa
Jang Tsala Karpo	byang tsha-la dkar-po
Jangchub Jinpa	byang chub sbyin pa
Je Tsongka pa	rje tsong kha pa
Jetsun Pema	rje btsun padma
Jormed dralrim	'byor med gral rim
Juchen Thupten	'ju-chen thub bstan
Jyekundo	skye dgu mdo
Kalon	bka' blon
Kalon Lama Rampa	bka' blon bla ma ram pa
Kapshoba	ka shod pa
Kargyu	bka'-brgyud pa
Karma Kargyu	kar ma bka' brgyud
Kashag	bka' shag
Katsab	bka' tshab
Kha-ta	kha btags
Khabse	kha zas
Kham	khams
Kheme Sonam Wangdu	khe smad bsod nams dbang 'dus
Khenchung Dawa	mkhan chung zla wa
Khenchung Lobsang Gyaltsen	mkhan chung blo bzang rgyal mtshan
Khenchung Lobsang Tsewang	mkhan chung blo bzang tshe dbang
Khenchung	mkhan chung
Khenchung Tara	mkhan chung rta ra
Khenchung Thupten Legmon	mkhan chung thub bstan legs smon
Khenchung Thupten Sangye	mkhan chung thub bstan sangs rgyas
Khyim zhi	khyim gzhis

Khrimgo Rawang Rangtsen	khrim-'go rang-dbang rang-brsan
Kongpo	kong po
krog-ta	dkrogs brda
Kumbum	sku 'bum
Kumbum Jampaling	sku-'bum byams-pa gling
Kunsangtse Dzasa	kun-bzang rtse dza sag
Kusho Driyul	sku-zhab 'bri yul
Kusung Magmi	sku-srung dmag-mi
Kyabgon	skyabs mgon
Labrang Tashikhyil	bla-brang bkra-shis 'khyil
Lachag Taring	bla-phyag phreng-ring
Lachi	bla-spyi
Lag shes pa	lag-shes pa
Legchoe Lakhung	legs-bcos las-khungs
Lekshe	legs-bshad
Lhabchung Dhargpa Trinley	lha phyug grags pa 'phrin las
Lhalu Tsewang Dorji	lha-klu tshe-dbang rdo-rje
Lhamo Tsering	lha mo tshe ring
Lhamon Yeshe Tsultrim	lha-smon ye shes tshul khrims
Lhasa	lha sa
Lhasa mangtsog ruchen	lha sa mang-tshogs ru-chen
Lhawutara Thupten Tendar	lha'u rta ra thub bstan bstan dar
Lhobdrak	lho brag
Lhoka	lho kha
Lhuntse Dzong	lhun rtse rdzong
Lithang	li thang
Liushar Thupten Tharpa	sne'u shar thub bstan thar pa
Lo Nyandrak	blo snyan grags
Lo pa	klo pa
Lobsang Choekyi Gyaltsen	blo bzang chos kyi rgyal mtshan
Lobsang Samten	blo bzang bsam gtan
Lobsang Tashi	blo bzang bkra shis
Lobsang Thargay	blo bzang dar rgyas
Lodro Gyari	blo gros rgya-ri
Logchod pa	log spyod pa
Lonchen Shatra	blon chen bshad sgra
Lotse	blo tshe
Lukhangwa Tsewang Rapten	klu khang ba tshe dbang rab brtan
Magchi Dzasag	dmag spyi dza sag
Mangmang	mang mang
Markham	smar kham
Medro Gonkar	mal-dro gon dkar
Mimang	mi dmangs

Mimang Thutsog	mi dmangs 'thus tshogs
Mimang Lingka	mi dmangs gling kha
Mimang Tsogdu	mi dmangs tshogs 'du
Miser	mi ser
Monpa	mon pa
Monlam	smon lam
Monthang	smon thang
Monyul	mon yul
Muja Depon	mu bya mda' dpon
Nagchuka	Nag chu kha
Namseling	rnam sras gling
Nangzen	nang zan
Nechung	gnas chung
Ngabo Nawang Jigme	nga phod ngag dbang 'jigs med
Ngari	mnga' ris
Ngawang Lekden	ngag dbang legs ldan
Ngawang Namgyal	ngag dbang rnam rgyal
Ngawang Tashi	ngag dbang bkra shis
Ngulchu Rinpoche	dngul chu rin po che
Norbulingka	nor bu gling kha
Nyarong	nyag rong
Nyamdrel	mnyam sbrel
Nyemo	snye-mo
Nyethang	snye thang
Nyingma pa	rnying ma pa
Palden Gyatso	dpal ldan rgya mtsho
Palden Lhamo	dpal ldan lha mo
Panchen Rinpoche	pan chen rin po che
Pasang	pa sangs
Pasang Gyalpo	pa sangs rgyal po
Pembar Dzong	dpal-'bar rdzong
Phagpalha Gelek Namgyal	'phags pa lha dge legs rnam rgyal
Phala Thupten Woden	ph'a lh thub bstan 'od ldan
Phari	pha ri
Phuntsog Tashi Takla	phun tshogs bkra shis stag lha
Pomda Yanphel	spom mda' yar-'phel
Pomdatsang	spom mda' tshang
Pon	dpon
Potala	po ta la
Ragashag Phuntsog Rabgye	ra kha shag phun tshogs rab rgyas
Ragdi	rag sdi
Rame	ra-smad

Reting Rinpoche	rva sgreng-rin po che
Rimshi Dingja	rim bzhi sding bya
Rimshi Rasa Gyagen	rim bzhi ra sa rgya rgan
Riwoche	ri bo che
Rogre	rogs-res
Sakya	sa skya
Samlingpa Phuntsog Dorje	bsam gling pa phun tshogs rdo rje
Sampho Tenzin Dhundup	bsam pho bstan 'dzin don 'grub
Sa nes zhung	sa gnas gzhung
Sandu Lobsang Rinchen	sa 'du blo bzang rin chen
sang	srang
Sangye Yeshi	sang rgyas ye shes
Sera	se ra
Sera Je	se ra byes
Shakabpa Wangchuk Deden	zhva sgab pa dbang phyug bde ldan
Shang Gaden Chokhor	shangs dga' ldan chos 'khor
Shape	zhabs pad
Shasur Gyurmed Dorje	bshad zur 'gyur med rdo rje
Shelkar Dzong	shel dkar rdzong
Sherab Dhundup	shes rab don grub
Shigatse	gzhis kh rtse
Sholkhang Dhondup Dorje	zhol khang don 'grub rdo rje
Sholkhang	zhol khang
Silon	srid blon
Sitsab	srid tshab
Surkhang Lhawang Topgyal	zur khang lha dbang stobs-rgyal
Surkhang Wangchan Gelek	zur khang dbang chen dge legs
Taktra	stag brag
Taring Dzasa	phreng ring dza sag
Tashi Namgyal	bkra shis rnam rgyal
Tashi Topgyal	bkra shis stobs rgyal
Tashi Wangdi	bkra shis dbang 'dus
Tashilhunpo	bkra shis lhun po
Tendra	bstan dgra
Tensung magmi	bstan srung dmag mi
Tenzin Tsultrim	bstan 'dzin tshul khrims
Thamzing	'thab 'dzing
Thrinley Choedron	'phrin las chos sgron
Thubten Norbu	thub bstan nor bu
Thupten Gyalpo	thub bstan rgyal po
Thupten Norbu	thub bstan nor bu
Thupten Nyinche	thub bstan nyin-byed

Thupten Sangye	thub bstan sangs rgyas
Trapchi	grva-phyi
Trijang Lobsang Yeshe	khri byang blo bzang ye shes
Trijang Rinpoche	khri byang rin po che
Tsampa	rtsam pa
Tsang	gtsang
Tsangpo	gtsang po
Tsarong	tsha rong
Tsatrul Rinpoche	tsha sprul rin po che
Tsechag Gyalpo	rtse phyag rgyal po
Tsedron Yeshi Lhundrup	rtse mgron ye shes lhun grub
Tse drung	rtse drung
Tsen gol	brtsan rgol
Tsering Dolma	tshe ring sgrol ma
Tseten Dolkar	tshe bstan sgrol dkar
Tsethang	rtsed thang
Tsetrung Lobsang Nyenda	rtsis drung blo bzang snyan-g drags
Tsewang Dorji	tshe dbang rdo rje
Tsipon	rtsis dpon
Tsongdu Gya zom	tshogs 'du rgyas 'dzoms
Tsogo	mtsho sgo
Tsongdu	tshogs 'du
Tsuklakhang	gtsug lag khang
U lag	'u lag
U zhung	dbus gzhung
Uyon Lhenkhang	u yon lhan khang
Yerlang Zhingtren	yar langs zhing bran
Yig tsang	yig tshang
Yonru-Pon Sonam Wangyal	g'yon ru dpon bsod nam dbang rgyal
Yuthok Tashi Dhondup	g'yu thog bkra shis don grub
zhab ten	zhabs-brtan
Zhing med	zhing med
Zhing tren lamlug	zhing bran lam lugs
Zhing yod	zhing yod
Zhingpa phyugpo	zhing pa phyug po
Zhingpa Ul phong	zhing pa dbul phongs
Zhung zhab	gzhung bzhabs

NOTES

ONE: The Lull Before the Storm

1 Hugh Richardson, 1984, p. 173. Later Nehru hinted his regret and admitted that '. . . in the early days after independence and partition, our hands were full . . . and we had to face very difficult situations in our country. We ignored . . . Tibet. Not being able to find a suitable person to act as our representative at Lhasa, we allowed for some time the existing British representative to continue at Lhasa.' *Foreign Affairs Record,* April (1959): IV, p. 120.
2 The Chinese name for Tibet is *Xizang*, which means literally the 'treasure house' of the Western region.
3 The five races were Han, Manchu, Mongols, Uygurs and Tibetans. The Nationalists did not mention the other ethnic groups that existed in China.
4 *Summary of World Broadcasts, Part V*, 1949, No. 24, p. 22 (hereafter cited as SWB).
5 Common Programme, Article 50: 'All nationalities within the boundaries of the People's Republic of China are equal. Unity and mutual help shall be effected among them to oppose imperialism and the public enemies within these nationalities so that the People's Republic of China will become a big family of fraternity and cooperation of all nationalities. Greater nationalism and chauvinism shall be opposed and acts of discrimination, oppression and splitting the unity of the various nationalities, shall be prohibited.'
6 Jonathan Spence, 1990, p. 551
7 See differing views of General Huang's visit to Lhasa; Hugh Richardson, 1977, *Bulletin of Tibetology*, Vol. 14, No. 2, pp. 31–5 and Tieh-Tseng Li, 1960. pp. 168–72. Li writes: 'Besides taking in the memorial service for the late Dalai Lama, General Huang issued a proclamation emphatically urging the Tibetan people to place their trust and reliance in the National Government.'
8 Tsipon Shakabpa, 1967. p. 277.
9 Tieh-Tseng Li, 1960, pp. 169–70.
10 Shakabpa, 1967, p. 277.
11 Tieh-Tseng Li, 1960, p. 180. Li states that the purpose of Wu Zhongxin's visit to Lhasa was to 'officiate at the installation ceremony of the new Dalai Lama'. Basil Gould, the British representative at the ceremony, reported that the Chinese were not treated more favorably than other foreign representatives. (Basil Gould, *A Report on the Discovery, Recognition and Installation of the 14th Dalai Lama*, India Office (London), L/P&S/12/4179). See also Ngabo Ngawang Jigme's speech to the second plenary session of the 5th Tibet

Autonomous Region Peoples' Congress. At this meeting (31 July 1989) Ngabo accused the Communists of accepting Guomindang propaganda, pointing out that his own research using Guomindang archives in Nanjing and what he had witnessed showed that Wu Zongxin's mission did not preside over the enthronement of the 14th Dalai Lama. Later the Communists accepted Ngabo's claim but Chinese propaganda continues to propagate the idea that Wu Zhongxin had presided over the ceremony. For a recent Chinese statement on this issue see SWB, 1988, FE/0175/B2/2.

12 PRO (London), FO 371–76315: MR, 1 August 1948.

13 Ibid.

14 SWB, 1949, No. 17, p. 21.

15 Ibid, p. 27.

16 Tieh-Tseng Li, 1960, p. 199. Melvyn Goldstein (1989, p. 613) says that the idea originated with Ngabo, but Phuntsog Tashi Takla told me that Ngabo was not involved at all in this episode.

17 Lhawutara, lHa'u rta-ra Thub-bstan bstan-dar, 1982, p. 93.

18 Interview with Phuntsog Tashi Takla (hereafter cited as Takla).

19 Interview with Richardson.

20 FO 371–76315: MR, 1 August 1948.

21 Ibid.

22 Tharchin was interviewed by Dawa Norbu, 'G. Tharchin: Pioneer and Patriot', TR, December 1975, pp.18–20.

23 FO 371–76315: MR, 1 August 1948.

24 Ibid: MR, 14 November 1949.

25 Melvyn Goldstein, 1989, pp.612–13.

26 Rinchen Dolma Taring, 1970, p. 171.

27 The terms Shape (*zhabs-pad*), Sawang Chenmo (*sa-dbang chen-mo*) and Kalon (*dka' blon*) are interchangeable and refer to a member of the Kashag (*bka' shag*).

28 There were four Drungyigchenmo (*drung-yig chen-mo*). They were the heads of the Ecclesiastic Office, the body which constituted one of the most powerful segments of Tibetan bureaucracy. All matters relating to religious and monastic affairs came under the jurisdiction of Drungyigchenmo. They also had a say in secular affairs. All four Drungyigchenmo were always monks.

29 There were four Tsipons (*rtsis-dpon*), who were responsible for government finance. The term is loosely translated as 'finance minster'.

30 FO 371–84453: MR, 15 December 1949.

31 Ibid.

32 SWB, 1950, No 42. p. 43.

33 Notes on a conversation with Mr Reid, FO 371–84449.

34 India Office Records, L/P&S/ 12/2175: Tibet supply of arms by GOI.

35 FO 371–84453: MR, 15 February 1950.

36 The 1914 Simla Convention, which was initialled by three participants, China, Britain and Tibet, but was never signed. China refused to recognise the Convention. However, Tibet and Britain signed a joint declaration, 'which acknowledged the draft Convention to be binding on the two governments'.

37 FO 371–76315: MR 14 November 1949.

38 Heinrich Harrer, 1953. p. 235.

39 FO 371–84453: MR, 16 March 1950.
40 FO 371–84465.
41 FO 371–84469. Britain was opposed to supplying arms to Tibet because 'of the serious risk that such supplies might fall into Communist hands'.
42 Notes on a conversation with Mr Reid, FO 371–84449.
43 FO 371–84453: MR, 15 January 1950.
44 See Alastair Lamb, *The McMahon Line, A study in the Relations between India, China and Tibet, 1904–1914.* (London, Routledge, Kegan and Paul, 1966). The actual boundary between Lhasa-controlled Kham and territories which fell within Chinese jurisdiction is not fully clear. The Tibetan Government claimed jurisdiction over all Tibetan-speaking people in eastern Tibet, which would have established the Sino–Tibetan boundary as far as Tachienlu. The Chinese insisted that the boundary was at Gyamda, 100 miles from Lhasa. See also Amar Kaur Jasbir Singh, *Himalayan Triangle,* (London, The British Library, 1988). It has an excellent reproduction of maps from the Simla Convention on page 76.
45 A communiqué issued by the Chinese stated there were 2,317 men and 2,000 militia. NCNA, 8 November 1960.
46 Robert Ford, 1958, p. 29.
47 Ibid, p. 36.
48 Takla.
49 FO 371–84453: MR, 15 May 1950.
50 Melvyn Goldstein, 1989, p. 687.
51 Interview with Chagtral Sonam Chophel, Oral Archives, LTWA (hereafter cited as Chagtral Sonam Chophel). In Tibetan, *rigs-ngan chan-gyi khri yi gdan 'zin / tha-ma Bod 'di rgGa yi 'oga-du tsud.*
52 FO 371–84453: MR 15 June 1950.
53 Chagtral Sonam Chophel.
54 FO 371–84453: MR 16 March 1950.
55 Ibid.
56 The 1948 Trade Mission first visited China. They travelled to China on Chinese passports. The Chinese Government refused to recognise Tibetan passports. See Tsering Shakya, '1948 Trade Mission to United Kingdom. An Essay in honour of Tsipon Shakabpa', TJ, Vol. 15, No. 4 (1990), pp. 114–115.
57 A monk member of the Kashag is known as Kalon Lama (*bka'-blon bla ma*).
58 FO 371–76315: MR 15 August 1950.
59 Lowell Thomas Jr, 1954, p. 275.
60 FO 371–84460.
61 FO 371–76317.
62 Ibid.
63 Melvyn Goldstein, 1989, pp. 626–7, and R. D. Taring, 1970, p.170.
64 FO 371–84453: MR 15 January 1950.
65 Tsering Shakya, 1990, pp. 97–114.
66 FO 371–76317.
67 FO 371–76314.
68 Ibid.
69 FO 371–84461.

70 FO 371–76314.
71 Ibid.
72 Ibid.
73 FO 371–84469.
74 The Dalai Lama, 1985 (3rd ed), p. 8.
75 FO 371–84465.
76 See *Foreign Relations of the United States* (hereafter cited as FRUS), 1949. Vol. IX, The Far East; China: 1065–1071. Memorandum by Miss Ruth E. Bacon of the Office of Far Eastern Affairs to the Chief of the Division of Chinese Affairs (Sprouse). This memo discusses arguments for and against recognition of Tibetan Independence.
77 FO 371–84453.
78 FRUS, 1949, Vol. IX, p. 1065.
79 Ibid.
80 Ibid., p. 1075.
81 Ibid., p. 1076.
82 Ibid., p. 1078.
83 Ibid.
84 Ibid., p. 1081.
85 Ibid., pp. 1087–8. The text of the letter was similar to one which had been sent to Ernest Bevin.
86 Ibid., p. 1091.
87 Ibid., p. 109.
88 Ibid., p. 1096.
89 FRUS, 1950, Vol. VI, p. 276.
90 Ibid.
91 Ibid.
92 Ibid., p. 284.
93 FO 371–84469.
94 Ibid.
95 FRUS, 1950, Vol. VI, p. 424.
96 Ibid.
97 Stephen Ambrose, 1983, p. 169.
98 FO 371–84469.
99 FRUS, 1950, p. 424.
100 Ibid.
101 Ibid.
102 Ibid.
103 Ibid.
104 Ibid.
105 Ibid.
106 FO 371–84469.
107 FO 371–84463.
108 FO 371–63943.
109 FO 371–84453: MR, 15 December 1949.
110 FO 371–84457.
111 FO 371–75798.

112 K. M. Panikkar, 1955, p. 103.
113 Ibid., p. 106.
114 Ibid.
115 Sarvepalli Gopal, 1979 (Vol. 2), p. 243.
116 FRUS, 1949, Vol. IX, p. 1082.
117 FO 371–76314.
118 Ibid.
119 This refers to a Memorandum given by British Foreign Secretary Anthony Eden to T.V. Soong (who was not only the brother-in-law of Chiang Kai-shek but also in charge of Chinese foreign policy). In 1943 on a visit to London Soong sought clarification of the British position on Tibet. On 28 July 1943 Eden agreed to provide Soong with a written statement. The key wording was that that British Government '*have always been prepared to recognise Chinese suzerainty over Tibet but only on the understanding that Tibet is regarded as autonomous*' (emphasis added). For discussion on the subject see: Alastair Lamb, *Tibet, China & India 1914–1950, A History of Imperial Diplomacy* (Roxford Books, 1989), pp. 320–7.
120 FO 371–76314 (emphasis added). Some officials in the FO and Commonwealth Relations Office suggested that India should make it conditional for recognition of the PRC that the autonomy of Tibet should be guaranteed by the PRC.
121 FO 371–84453: MR, 15 December 1949.
122 FO 371–76317.
123 FO 371–76315: MR, 14 November 1949.
124 Shakabpa, 1967, p. 300.
125 Takla.
126 FO 371–84470.
127 Ibid.
128 FO 371–84468.
129 FO 371–84470.
130 Ibid.
131 FO 371–84470.
132 FO 371–84468.
133 FO 371–84470.
134 Phuntsog Tashi Takla confirmed that they went to the airport and did not suspect that they would be prevented from boarding the plane. They had confirmed tickets and checked in when Indian security officers told them they could not leave.
135 FO 371–84470.
136 Ibid.
137 Ibid.
138 FO 371–84468.
139 FO 371–84470.
140 Here I have used the term 'priest and patron' as used by Shakabpa in his book. Generally the term 'priest and patron' gives a misleading rendering of Tibetan term *mchod yon*. For a discussion on the topic, see D. Seyfort Ruegg, '*MCHOD YON, YON MCHOD and MCHOD GNAS/ YON GNAS: On*

the historiography and Semantic of a Tibetan Religio-social and Religio-political concept', in Ernst Steinkellner (ed.), *Tibetan History and Language* (Wien, 1991), pp. 440–53. For a detailed study of the nature of the Chinese–Tibetan relationship, see Zahiruddin Ahmad, *Sino-Tibetan relations in the 17th Century* (Roma, IMEO, 1970); Luciano Petech, *China and Tibet in the Early 18th Century* (Leiden, 1970). For an interesting theoretical interpretation of Sino-Tibetan relationship, see Dawa Norbu, '*An analysis of Sino-Tibetan relationships 1245–1911: Imperial Power, Non-Coercive regime and Military dependency*', in Babara Aziz and Mathew Kapstein (eds), *Soundings in Tibetan Civilization* (New Delhi, Manohar, 1985), pp. 176–95.

141 Shakabpa writes that he was given a booklet and does not seem to have been aware that it was actually the 'Common Program' and the articles 50–53 were the basis of the Communist Policy toward minority groups. *Zhwa sgab pa*, 1976, p. 419.

142 Zhwa sgab pa, 1976, p. 420.

143 Ibid. In Tibetan, '*Bod ming-tsam gyi rgya-khongs zhal-bzhes gnang-rgyu.*'

144 FO 371–84469.

TWO China Invades

1 Tibet lost control of areas east of Drichu in the early part of the twentieth century. At the Simla Conference of 1914, the Tibetan Government claimed jurisdiction over the whole of Kham and Amdo. The Chinese refused to accept the Tibetan claim. The conference divided Tibet into Inner and Outer Tibet with the Lhasa Government exercising political authority over Outer Tibet and the Chinese maintaining control over 'Inner Tibet', or Kham. The Nationalist Government created the province of Sikang (Xikang) in 1936, which their map showed extending up to Kongpo Gyamda, less than 150 miles from Lhasa. But they did not exercise any control west of the Drichu. Needless to say, the Nationalist regime in Taiwan does not accept any regional administrative reform made by the PRC and maps published in Taiwan continue to show the province of Sikang. (See: S. A. M. Adshead, *Province and Politics in late Imperial China: Viceregal Government in Szechwan, 1898–1911*, pp. 55–9. Curzon Press, 1984).

2 For a detailed account of the Communists' experience in Kham, see Elliot Sperling, 1976, TR, 10:X1, pp. 11–18.

3 Mao told Edgar Snow, 'This is our only foreign debt and some day we must pay the Mantzu and the Tibetans for the provisions we were obliged to take from them'. Edgar Snow, 1938, p. 193.

4 The Red Army was coming under increasing pressure from government troops and they were divided over the direction in which the Red Army should retreat. Zhang Guotao, one of the founder members of the party in 1921, argued that the army should march westward, but this would have led them further into Tibetan territory. Mao wanted the army to move north. It was Zhou Enlai who advised that it would be wiser to move north on the grounds that the western regions were inhabited by non-Chinese and that they might turn against them, as they had done in Sikang.

5 Edgar Snow, 1938, p. 192.
6 It is interesting to note that all those Tibetans who became Communists adopted Chinese names.
7 Israel Epstein, 1983. p. 15. He claims there were 2,000 Tibetan Communists, many of whom were killed during the war with the Nationalists. This seems unlikely, as that number of Communist Party members would have had a major impact on Tibetan society.
8 It is not clear whether Geta Rinpoche went through an ideological conversion or merely desired to be on the winning side. The former seems unlikely.
9 SWB, 1950, No. 42, p. 28.
10 The Tibetans were aware of the anti-religious stance of the Communists through what had happened in Mongolia during the 1920s and 1930s. It is interesting that in the 'Last Testament of the 13th Dalai Lama' he stated: 'this present era is rampant with the five forms of degeneration, in particular the red ideology. In Outer Mongolia, the search for a reincarnation of Jetsun Dampa was banned; the monastic properties and endowments were confiscated; the Lamas and the monks were forced into the army; and the Buddhist religion destroyed, leaving no trace of identity.' And he went on to say: 'In future, this system will certainly be a force either from within or outside this land . . .'
11 SWB, 1950, No. 51, p. 27.
12 The 'Eight-Point Contract' was proclaimed by Mao and Zhu De on 25 April 1949. See *Tibet 1950–1967* (Hong Kong, Union Research Institute, 1968) (URI) pp. 731–4.
13 This office grew out of a Mongol Affairs Office created by the Manchu. When the Nationalists (Guomindang) came to power, they established the Mongolian and Tibetan Affairs Commission, which continues to function in Taiwan (The Republic of China.)
14 FO 371–84453. MR: 15 March 1950.
15 The Panchen Rinpoche is believed to the incarnation of *'od dpag med* (Tib), or *Amitabha* (Skt), 'the Buddha of Boundless Light'. The title Panchen literally means 'Great Scholar'. In much western writing on Tibet, Panchen Rinpoche is referred to as the Panchen Lama or the Tashi Lama, derived from the name of his monastery, Tashilhunpo. I have preferred to use the correct Tibetan title, 'Panchen Rinpoche'.
16 Under current Chinese administration it is referred to as Yushu.
17 Some sources refer to him as the 6th Panchen Lama or the 9th Panchen Lama. This is because the 5th Dalai Lama first gave the title of Panchen to Lobsang Choekyi Gyaltsen (1570–1662) and the title was conferred retrospectively on previous incarnations, so that Lobsang Chokyi Gyaltsen became referred to as either the 4th Panchen or 1st Panchen Lama of Tashilhunpo.
18 In 1910 the thirteenth Dalai Lama went into exile in India and on his return to Tibet he attempted to introduced reforms to modernise Tibet's social and political systems. Tibet's traditional system allowed the Panchen Rinpoche's estates in Tsang to be treated as autonomous with the right to raise own revenue. The thirteenth Dalai Lama wanted greater contributions from the Panchen Rinpoche's estates to help with the costs of modernisation. He also wanted to reduce the autonomy exercised by his estates. The Lhasa

Government wanted the Panchen's estate to meet a quarter of the total expenditure. By 1922, it was reported that the Panchen estate had defaulted and that some officials of the Tashilhunpo monastery had been arrested by the Lhasa Government. The Panchen requested the British Trade Agent in Gyantse to mediate between Lhasa and Shigatse but the British refused to be involved. On 26 December 1923, the Panchen Rinpoche, accompanied by a hundred attendants, left Shigatse for eastern Tibet.

19 *Tibet: Myth vs. Reality* (Beijing Review Publication, 1988), pp. 135–7 (emphasis added).

20 Ibid.

21 FO 371–76315: MR, 15 September 1949.

22 Ibid.

23 FO 371–84453: MR, 15 January 1950.

24 Ibid.

25 SWB, 23 May 1950, No. 58, p. 15.

26 Ibid.

27 Ibid.

28 Robert Ford, 1957, p. 53.

29 Ibid.

30 Ibid.

31 Ibid.

32 *'rGyal mtshan phun tsog* (Gyaltsen Phuntsog) '*Nga mdo-spyi'i las-byar bskyod skabs kyi gnas-tshul 'ga'-zhig*' (An Account of my work in Kham), in: *Bod kyi rig-gnas lo-rgyus dpyad-gzhi'i rgyu-cha bdams bsgrigs* (Sources on Culture and History of Tibet, hereafter cited as SCHT), 1986, Vol. 9, pp.13–29.

33 FO 371–84453: MR, 16 July 1950.

34 Zhwa sgab pa, 1976, p. 430.

35 Ford, 1957, p. 58.

36 Ibid., p. 62.

37 Ibid., p. 64.

38 SWB, 1950, No. 69, p. 36.

39 SWB, 1950, No. 56, p. 24.

40 SWB, 1950, No. 57, p. 49.

41 Ibid.

42 Geoffrey T. Bull, *When Iron Gates Yield* (London, Hodder and Stoughton, no date), p. 100.

43 An account published in Tibet in 1990 by Wang Gui (*dBang Ku'i*) states that Geta Rinpoche had personally volunteered to go to Tibet to advise the Tibetan Government. He was also carrying a letter from the South-West Military Region commander. See dBang Ku'i, 'Bod du dpung bskyod byed-skabs dGe-stag sphrul-sku'i skor thos-rdogs byong-ba'i gnas- tshul phrin-bu, in Bod-kyi lo-rgyus rig-gnas dpyud gzhi'i rgyu cha- bdmas bsgrigs', 1992, Vol. 5, No. 14, pp. 252–72.

44 Robert Ford, 1957, p. 77.

45 Ibid.

46 FO 371–84453: MR, 15 June 1950. A report written by Hugh Richardson states

that the group was led by a former officer of Ma Pu-fang and entered Lhasa disguised as traders. The group was also accompanied by two Khampas from Lithang, one of whom was the real leader of the party.

47 Thupten Jigme Norbu, 1961, p. 230. Norbu wrote that when the Chinese approached him to lead the mission to Lhasa, he insisted that he would like to take twenty high-ranking dignitaries from Kumbum to add weight to the mission. The Chinese authorities vetted the list of names he presented and finally only approved of two people.

48 Interview with Thupten Norbu, in oral archives of the Library of Tibetan Works and Archives, Dharamsala.

49 Ibid. He states that the Chinese wanted the delegation to be accompanied by PLA. Norbu told the Chinese that this would be seen as provocation by the Tibetans.

50 Ibid.

51 When the group eventually arrived at the Tibetan frontier, there were thirty people in Thubten Norbu's party and another 140 people who were on pilgrimage. In all there were 3,000 yaks, 500 horses and mules. See Thubten Norbu, 1961, p. 234.

52 Thubten Norbu, 1961, p. 235.

53 Ibid.

54 Ford, 1957, p. 102.

55 Ibid. It appears from later actions that Ngabo was determined to avoid being captured by the Chinese. He wanted to retreat to Lhokha Dzong, but his party was encircled by the PLA and his escape route cut off (emphasis added).

56 SWB, 1950, No. 70, p. 46.

57 Zhwa sgab pa, 1976, p. 420.

58 Ibid., p. 421.

59 Ibid., p. 422.

60 Ibid. Shakabpa described the situation as 'the water line had reached the brim and was about to cause a flood' (in Tibetan: *da-cha chu rags-gtugs la bslebs-pas*).

61 Ibid.

62 It seems to me that the Chinese invasion of Tibet could at least partly have been prompted by the American involvement in Korea, which led China to believe that the USA had taken the first step towards an invasion of China from three directions: Korea, Vietnam and Taiwan. At the time Tibet was China's Achilles' heel. Therefore if China were to face a showdown with US, it was imperative that its political and military position in Tibet be secured.

63 Account published in Tibet by Khreng tse kri (SCHT, 1982, vol. I, pp. 211–55) who witnessed the invasion, states that the actual invasion began at midnight on 5 October, 1950, whereas Xinhua reported that the PLA attacked on 7 October. I believe that the PLA might have dispatched a reconnaissance party before the actual invasion on the 7th. Depending on the success of the reconnaissance raid, they would have decided to launch the main thrust of the invasion on 7 October. The date was very significant because China announced its military support to the North Koreans on the same day. The decision to deploy Chinese troops in Korea was only taken on 2 October, making the few days between 2

and 6 October a critical period in which the Chinese military prepared the final move both in Korea and Tibet. I believe that the decision to invade was taken in conjunction with their thinking over Korea.

64 During the Sino–Japanese war Liu Bocheng became known as 'one of the best field commanders in the Red Army'. Evans Carlson, an American military official who met Liu in 1938, described him as 'one of the best tacticians and students of military history'. See Robert B. Rigg, *Red China's Fighting Hordes*, Harrisburg, 1951, p. 32.

65 Chang Kuohua [Zhang Guohua] 'Tibet Returns to the Bosom of the Motherland (Revolutionary Reminiscences)', SCMP, No. 2854, 6 November 1962, pp. 1–12.

66 Ibid.

67 Ibid.

68 Ford, 1957, p. 108.

69 Ibid., p. 116. Ford writes that some of Derge Se's troops fled before the Chinese attack. This is also confirmed by Bull who writes that there was very little fighting between the Tibetans and the PLA.

70 Geoffrey Bull, p. 107.

71 Ibid., p. 109.

72 Ibid., p. 110.

73 Ford, 1957, p. 111.

74 Ibid., pp. 111–13.

75 Aristocratic picnics were lavish affairs often lasting for several days. There is a popular belief that at the time of the invasion many high-ranking Tibetan officials were engrossed in playing mah jong.

76 See Melvyn Goldstein, 1989, p. 692 for full text of the conversation between Tsogo and Dumra.

77 Ford, 1957, p. 122.

78 Ibid., p. 123.

79 Ibid., p. 135.

80 Ibid., p. 137.

81 Ibid., p. 138. G. Bull writes that when Derge Se's troops surrendered they were also given a talk and money. This was very effective propaganda. Later the soldiers gave glowing accounts of their treatment by the PLA.

82 Tibet 1950–67, URI, 1968, p. 2. An account written by Chang Kuohua [Zhang Guohua] states that 'altogether 21 large and small scale engagement were fought, and over 5,700 enemy men were destroyed'. See SCMP, No. 2854 (1962), p. 6.

83 SWB, 1950, No. 77. p. 39.

84 One of the major charges against Deng Xioaping during the Cultural Revolution was his failure to adopt a class perspective on the Tibetan problem, instead trying to appease the upper classes.

85 Tibet 1950–67, URI, 1968, pp. 8–9.

86 Zhwa sgab pa, 1976, p. 422.

87 Ibid.

88 Ibid., p. 425.

89 Ibid., p. 425.

90 Zhwa sgab pa, 1976, pp. 246–147.

91 Ibid., p. 226. To describe the Tibetan proposals Shakabpa used a Tibetan saying which is similar to the English proverb about 'Closing the stable door after the horse has bolted.'

92 Zhwa sgab pa, 1976, pp. 246–147.

93 Ha'u rta ra thub bstan bstan dar, 1982.

94 I have used the description of the event written by Lhawutara Thupten Tender, *'Bod zhi-bas bcings-'grol 'byung-thabs skor gyi gros-mthun don-tshan bcu-bdun la ming-rtgas bkod-p'i sngon-rjes su'* (An Account of the Peaceful Liberation of Tibet and the signing of the 17-Point Agreement). SCHT. Vol. 1 (1982), pp. 88–117.

95 The Dalai Lama, 1985, p. 83.

96 Ibid.

97 The Chinese interpret this differently. Yuan Shan writes that 'according to usual practice, the Dalai Lama's assumption of the reins of government would become legally effective only after the approval of China's Central Government. Through the repeated consultation of the principal officials in the local government of Tibet, it was decided that due to the inconvenient transportation conditions between Tibet and the interior, the letter was brought to India by Surkhang.' See Yuan Shan, '*The Dalai Lama and 17 Article Agreement*', Renmin Ribao overseas edition, Beijing, 22 April 1991. As published in SWB, 24 April 1991, B2/1.

98 rGyl-mtshan phun-tsogs, 1986, p. 24.

99 DO 35/3096: MR, 15 December 1950.

100 Ibid.

101 Ibid. See Ngabo, 1989. He confirms that he did send a second set of messengers, Lhodro Kalsang and Chagdrul Chichag, to Lhasa but does not mention what he had told them.

102 Interview with Phuntsog Tashi Takla.

103 lHa'u rta ra thub bstan bstan dar, 1982, pp. 88–117.

104 Ibid. lHa'u rta ra states that the Kashag received a message from Shakabpa in India, which stated that the Americans were going to provide military assistance and that a plane would land in Lhasa to pick up the Dalai Lama. Shakabpa mentions no such message in his book. Nor are there any other archive sources which confirm this. However, it was true that the Tibetans did begin to prepare a landing strip, as indicated by Lhawutara. In an interview Phuntsog Tashi Takla (who was in India with Shakabpa) told me there was an American plan to send a plane to Lhasa and Shakabpa had been meeting separately with CIA officers in India. There is no mention of these meetings in United States Foreign Relations Documents. The Dalai Lama told me that Thupten Gyalpo (one of the members of Shakabpa's delegation to China), who was in then India, later told him that an American individual had offered to fly to Lhasa and rescue him.

105 Ibid.

106 Heinrich Harrer, 1953, p. 274.

107 FRUS, Vol XII, (1951), p. 1507.

THREE Tibet Appeals to the UN and the 17-Point Agreement

1 DO 35/3096.
2 Text of the cablegram from Kashag to UNO; UN document no A/15549. *Tibet in the United Nations, 1950–1961*, published by the Bureau of His Holiness the Dalai Lama, New Delhi.
3 Tsering Shakya, 'Tibet and League of Nations', TJ, X:3 (1985), pp. 48–56.
4 FO 371–84454.
5 Ibid.
6 DO 35/3095.
7 *Foreign Relations of the United States* Vol. VI: East Asia (1950), p. 546. This refers to the question of the legality of the integration of Hyderabad into India. Hyderabad was ruled by a Muslim ruler, with only 11 per cent Muslim population. On the eve of Indian Independence, the Nazim had not acceded either to India or Pakistan. As there was growing tension between India and Pakistan over Kashmir, India feared that the Nazim of Hyderabad might support Pakistan, thus presenting India with a major security problem in South and Central India. In September 1948, India had occupied Hyderabad.
8 Ibid., p. 578.
9 FO 371–84454.
10 Article 35(2) of the UN Charter: 'a state which is not a member of the United Nations may bring to the attention of the Security Council or of the General Assembly any dispute to which it is a party if it accepts in advance, for the purpose of the dispute, the obligations of pacific settlement provided in the present charter'.
11 FO 371–84454.
12 Ibid.
13 Ibid.
14 Ibid.
15 FRUS, Vol. VI, (1950), pp. 550–1.
16 Ibid., p. 577.
17 DO 35/3094.
18 Tibetans knew nothing of El Salvador. Rene von Nebesky-Wojkowitz, an Austrian Tibetologist who was living in Kalimpong, remembers that Surkhang visited Prince Peter of Greece, who was also staying in Kalimpong at the time, to inquire as to the whereabouts of El Salvador. Prince Peter opened an atlas and pointed to the map using a magnifying glass. Surkhang disappointedly exclaimed, 'But this State is hardly as big as Bhutan'. Nebesky writes that Tibetans were 'under the impression that San Salvador was one of the Great Powers'. Rene von Nebesky-Wojkowitz, 1956, p. 102.
19 *Tibet in the United Nations, 1950–1961*, p. 6.
20 This was clearly was not the case. The Foreign Office made an exhaustive study of the legal status of Tibet and had reached the conclusion that Tibet had all the features of a State (emphasis added).
21 *Tibet in the United Nations, 1950–1961*, p. 14.
22 Ibid.
23 Ibid.

24 FO 371–84454 (emphasis added).
25 There was also misunderstanding regarding the Chinese and Indian interpretation of the word autonomy. The Indian and the British understanding of the word is based on what is commonly known as the Eden Memorandum, which recognised Tibet's right to 'internal' and 'external' autonomy. When the Chinese informed the Indians that China would respect Tibet's autonomy, it meant something entirely different. The Chinese used the word in its narrowest sense, and it rejected Tibet's right to maintain external relations.
26 FRUS, Vol. VI, (1950), p. 584. Bajpai also told Henderson that the statement made by Rau was 'his own interpretation' of the Chinese note to Delhi. On 30 November Bajpai told the British High Commissioner (A. Nye) that he had received a report from the Indian Mission in Lhasa, and that 'there is no repeat no truth in the reports that the Tibetans and Chinese are entering into discussion'.
27 FO 371–84455. Bajpai told Nye this was the instruction sent to Rau at the UN.
28 Ibid.
29 Ibid.
30 Ibid. Letter from Sir P. Dixon to Sir Gladwyn Jebb.
31 Ibid. (emphasis added).
32 Ibid.
33 FRUS, Vol. VI (1950), p. 611.
34 Ibid., p. 612.
35 DO 35/3094. The same document is printed in FRUS, Vol. VI (1950), pp. 612–3 (emphasis added).
36 DO 35/3094.
37 FRUS, Vol. VII (1950), p. 1528.
38 Lu'o Yus-hung, '*Bod zhi-bas bcings'-grol skor gyi nyin-tho gnad bshus*' (Diary of Peaceful Liberation of Tibet) SCHT, Vol. 1 (1951), p. 118. This was also confirmed to me by Phuntsog Tashi Takla.
39 Interview with Phuntsog Tashi Takla.
40 Ngabo Ngawang Jigme, *Rang-skyong ljong mi-dmangs 'thus-tshogs rgyun kyi kru'u-rin Nga-phod Ngag-dbang 'jigs-med kyi rang-skyong ljongs kyi skabs lnga-pa'i mi-dmang 'thus-tshog du-thengs gnyis-pa'i thog ngang-ba'i gal che'i gsung-bshad.* (Speech by Ngabo Ngawang Jigme at the 2nd Plenary Session of the 5th Tibet Autonomous People's Congress; hereafter cited as Ngabo 1989).
41 Ibid.
42 The Dalai Lama, 1985, pp. 85–6.
43 lHa'u rta ra thub bstan bstan dar, 1982.
44 Although four members of the delegation have written their account of the meeting, none has listed the original ten-point proposal given by the Kashag. I asked Phuntsog Tashi Takla, who does not recall the ten points. Similarly, M. Goldstein says Sambo also stated that he did not recall the ten points. Lhawutara writes that the Tibetan delegation presented a 'nine-point proposal' but does not mention what the points were.
45 lHa'u rta-ra thub-bstan bstan-dar (1982). His account of the meeting was confirmed by P. T. Takla. Indian records of the meeting differ slightly from the account given by lHa'u rta-ra. The Indian records make no mention of Tibet's

request for GOI to mediate between China and Tibet. Bajpai told A. Nye that the Tibetan delegation told him that they intended resisting any deployment of Chinese troops in Tibet and would seek to maintain the traditional close ties with the GOI whose representative should remain in Lhasa.

46 Sambo in an interview with M. Goldstein states that he was alone at the railway station, but Takla remembers both he and Sandhu Rinchen were there.

47 In Tibetan, *nang khul du rang btsan bdag yin dgos.*

48 Ngabo Ngawang Jigme, 1989.

49 Ibid.

50 Ibid.

51 It is interesting that Ngabo seems to imply that only point worth discussing was the status of Tibet and that if the Kashag was only to accept Tibet as part of China then he felt other issues were of such a minor consequence that it was pointless to press the Chinese, who were willing to agree to minor adjustments.

52 Phuntsog Tashi Takla.

53 lHa'u rta ra, 1982.

54 Phuntsog Tashi Takla.

55 A writer with long experience of negotiating with the Chinese noted: 'It can be argued that limiting the agenda in one's favour is a common tactic of international negotiations and no monopoly of the Chinese. Yet the Chinese seem to attach a special importance to the agenda, and the intensity with which they insist on the inclusion or exclusion of certain subjects surprises many international negotiators. Agreement to put a subject on the agenda seems to imply to the Chinese a certain concession on the matter. The Chinese do not share the view widely held in western countries that agreement on the agenda does not necessarily prejudice the nature of a negotiation.' (Oguru Kazuo, 'How the "Inscrutable" Negotiate with the "Inscrutables": Chinese Negotiating Tactics *Vis-À Vis* the Japanese'. CQ, 79 [1979], pp. 528–52.) The Tibetans' experience seems to confirm Oguru Kazuo's statement.

56 Words such as 'the People' and 'Liberation' caused particular difficulties (see Huang Mingxin, 'The Tibetan Version of the 17-Article Agreement', *China's Tibet* [Autumn 1992], pp. 12–15). It is interesting to note that author writes, 'in the Tibetan language, there was no word which meant 'China'. When the Tibetans use the word '*rGya nag* ', this excludes the Tibetans, and explicitly recognises Tibetan separateness from China.

57 lHa'u rta-ra, (1982), pp. 106–7. His account published in Tibet does not mention the incident. However, he writes that, as instructed by the Kashag, he objected to the deployment of the PLA in Tibet and therefore the meeting broke down for several days during which time he was worried that the PLA troops might have resumed their advance in Tibet. Accounts published in India by members of the delegation agree that the meeting broke down because of lHa'u rta-ra's questioning and Li Weihan's statement. See Sambo's autobiography, *'mi-tshe' rba-rlabs 'khrug-po*, (1987), p. 109. A biography of lHa'u rta-ra published in India by his former secretary, Tenzin Gyaltsen, and entitled simply 'lHa'u rta ra', (1988) also confirms the threat made by Li Weihan (pp. 20–1). P. T. Takla also confirmed this account.

58 lHa'u rta ra (1982), pp. 106–7.

59 SWB, No. 111, 5 June 1951.
60 Jiang Ping, 'Great Victory for the Cause of National Unity and Progress', *China's Tibet,* Spring (1991), p.8.
61 Ngabo Ngawang Jigme, 1989.
62 Ibid.
63 Ibid.
64 Jiang Ping (1991), p. 8.
65 Ngabo Ngawang Jigme, 1989.
66 Ibid.
67 Jiang Ping, 1991.
68 Ngabo Ngawang Jigme, 1989.
69 Ibid.
70 Ibid.
71 lH'u rta ra, 1982, p. 108.
72 SWB, No. 111, 5 June 1951, p. 9.
73 Takla Phuntsog Tashi.
74 Ngabo Ngawang Jigme, 1989.
75 Phala Thupten Woden, Oral Archives of LTWA, Dharamsala.
76 The exiled Tibetans and their supporters usually claim that the Agreement is invalid because the seals were forged, an argument which is disingenuous and which does not take account of subsequent developments. This also implies that the Chinese had surreptitiously affixed the seals to the document, which was not the case. The delegation was fully aware that the Chinese had the seals newly made.

In 1992 the Chinese held a press conference in Beijing to mark the thirtieth anniversary of the Agreement. At the conference Ngabo was asked by a journalist whether the seals were forged or not. He simply replied that they were made in Beijing.
77 lHa'u rta-ra, 1982, p. 108.
78 The Dalai Lama 1985, p. 88.
79 Ibid.
80 lHa'u rta-ra, 1982, pp. 108–9.
81 Phuntsog Tashi Takla.
82 This of course depended on India's approval.
83 FRUS, Vol. VII, Part 2 (1951), p. 1609.
84 Ibid. p. 1611.
85 Ibid. pp. 1612–13.
86 FRUS, Vol. VII, Part 2 (1951), pp. 1687–9.
87 Ibid.
88 US documents refer to Thubten Norbu by the formal title, Takster. I have used his personal name.
89 FRUS, Vol. VII, Part 2 (1951), pp. 1689–91.
90 Ibid., p. 1692.
91 Ibid., p. 1696.
92 FO 371 84469.
93 Interview with George Patterson. Also a number of former Indian Intelligence officers working in Kalimpong (commonly known as 'Watchers') told me that

they kept surveillance on American visitors to Kalimpong and were aware that Tibetan officials were meeting with the Americans.

94 FRUS, 1951, Vol. VII, Part 2, pp. 1694–5.

95 Ibid.

96 Ibid., pp. 1707–10.

97 Ibid.

98 DO 35/2931.

99 Ibid.

100 DO 35/3097.

101 FRUS, Vol. VI, Part 2 (1951), p. 1719.

102 Ibid., p. 1717.

103 FRUS, Vol. VII, Part 2 (1951), p. 1718.

104 Ibid., p. 1726.

105 Ibid.

106 DO 35/3097.

107 Ibid.

108 Ibid.

109 DO 35/3097. It is difficult to argue that the individual members of the Tibetan delegation were coerced. However, the second argument could be applied to this case. Though Ngabo himself had written that he was instructed to consult Dromo before signing any agreement, clearly he did not do so.

110 FRUS, Vol. VII (1951), p. 1722.

111 The full title of the paper was *Mirror of News from all sides of the World*. The paper was founded in 1925 and was published and edited by Tharchin himself. Originally the paper was funded by a Scottish Missionary group, but later when Tharchin fell out with the group he decided to raise the finance himself and became the sole owner of the paper. During the Second World War many local papers had to close because of shortage of paper, but the British Political officer in Sikkim, Basil Gould, allowed the paper to continue and moreover secured government funding for the paper. Gould argued that since this was the only Tibetan newspaper, it should be considered as a part of the war propaganda effort. After the war the funding was withdrawn and Tharchin had to rely on the patronage of wealthy friends. It ceased publication in 1964, but by this time the Tibetan Exile Government had founded a new Tibetan paper called *Rang-dbang ser-shog* (Freedom Press). It was reported that Tharchin commented: '*Rang-dbang yod-dus, Rang dbang-med / Rang-dbang med-dus, Rang-dbang shar-song*' ('When there was freedom, there was no Freedom. When there is no freedom, the Freedom has appeared').

112 Unpublished manuscript of a biography of Tharchin, in possession of his son Sherab Tharchin, who kindly allowed me to read the manuscript. Phuntsog Tashi Takla remembers Tharchin making the speech, but does not recall him being carried on people's shoulders.

113 Ibid.

114 FRUS, Vol. VII (1951), pp. 1728–9.

115 Ibid.

116 Ibid., p. 1733.

117 The letter was supposed to be untraceable and not identifiable with the US

Government. However, in this paragraph, it mentions that Thubten Norbu (Taktse Rinpoche) would be going to 'our country'. His arrival in New York was splashed all over the newspapers in the States and Europe. Therefore, the Chinese would surely have guessed the origin of the letter.

118 FRUS, Vol. VII. Part 2 (1951) pp. 1744–5.
119 For an account of Thubten Norbu's escape to US, see George Patterson, *Requiem for Tibet* (London, Aurum Press, 1990), pp. 125–31.
120 Ibid.
121 lHa'u rta ra, 1982, p. 110–11.
122 Ibid.
123 Ibid.
124 Zhol khang bsod rnams dar rgyas, '*krung-dbang sku-tshab Bod-du phebs-par phebs-bsu zhus pa'i dzin-tho*', in *krung go'i bod-ljongs*, 1991, pp. 17–25. (See English translation of the article in *China's Tibet* [Spring 1990], p. 12.)
125 The Dalai Lama, 1985, pp. 89–90.
126 lHa'u rta ra, 1982, p. 112.
127 FRUS, Vol. VII, Part 2 (1951), p. 1747.
128 Ibid., p. 1745.
129 FRUS, Vol. VII, Part 2 (1951), p. 1751.
130 Ibid., p. 1752.
131 DO 35/3096.
132 DO 35/3097.
133 Ibid.
134 Zhol khang bsod rnams dar rgyas, 1990, p. 14.
135 The name has been deleted from US documents.
136 FRUS, Part 2, Vol. 11 (1951), p. 1754.
137 Ibid., p. 1755.
138 George Patterson, 1990, p. 132.
139 The name had been deleted from the US documents.
140 FRUS, Vol VII, Part 2 (1951), pp. 1776–8.
141 Ibid.
142 Ibid.
143 FRUS, Vol. VII, Part 2 (1951), pp. 1786–7.
144 Ibid., p. 1795.
145 Ibid., p. 1802. Tibetan assets in the US were minimal, not more than 2–3 million US dollars, the majority of which belonged to the Pomdatsang family.
146 FRUS, Vol VII, Part 2 (1951), pp. 1803–4.
147 Phuntsog Tashi Takla.
148 lHa'u rta ra, 1982, p. 113.
149 Ngabo Ngawang Jigme, 1989.
150 Ibid.
151 Lha'u rta-ra, 1982, pp. 114–15.
152 Interview with P. T. Takla. The language of the 17-Point Agreement reflected the changing political status of Tibet. In the course of the discussion, Tibet was referred to as 'Local Government' and a new Tibetan word, '*sanas-zhung*', was invented for the term Local Government. China was referred to as the 'dbus-gzhung' (literally Head Government): the Central Government.

153 *Tibet: Myth vs. Reality* (Beijing Review Publication, 1988), p. 134.
154 SWB, No 133, 6 November 1951, p. 39.
155 Dawa Norbu, 'Tibetan Response to Chinese Liberation', *Asian Affairs*, 62 (1975), pp. 266–78.
156 Parthasarathi, G. *Jawaharlal Nehru; Letters to Chief Minister, Vol. 5. 1958–1964* (University of Oxford Press, India, 1989). pp. 227–9.

FOUR An Uneasy Co-existence

1 These kinds of explanations are very much influenced by Cold War rhetoric in which all Communist actions were interpreted as part of a Communist desire for world domination.
2 During the period of the Ambans, the Chinese resident was allowed to maintain 300 troops. The first expulsion of Chinese troops took place in 1913, when the Amban was expelled from Lhasa. Since then the Chinese had not been able to station any troops in the territories controlled by the Tibetan Government.
3 George Moseley, 'China's fresh approach to the national minority question', CQ, 24 (1965), pp. 16–17. 'In contrast to the Russian Revolution in which peoples other than the Great Russians played a significant role, the revolution in China was purely a Han Chinese affair.'
4 I quote this from Dawa Norbu's 'The 1959 Tibetan Rebellion: An Interpretation', CQ, No. 77 (1979), pp. 77–8.
5 Lu'o Yus-hung, '*Bod-bskyod nyin-tho gnad-bshus*' (*gnyis-pa*), SCHT, Vol. 8 (1985), p. 313.
6 There are no reliable demographic statistics on Tibet for this period, though many writers have given rough figures on the total population of Lhasa and of Tibet.
7 Dronyerchenmo (Chief of Protocol) Palha Thupten Woden, Oral archive of Library of Tibetan Works and Archives (LTWA). This interview was conducted as a group discussion of former leading Tibetan Government officials Phala, Luishar Thupten Tharpa and Phuntsog Tashi Takla, and staff from LTWA. It forms one of the major sources on the period (here after cited as Phala).
8 Ibid. See also R. D Taring, 1970, p. 175.
9 FO 371–99659: MR, 15 December 1951.
10 Tibet 1950–1967, URI, 1968, p. 7.
11 Sylvain Mangeot, *The Adventures of a Manchurian: The story of Lobsang Thondup* (London, The Travel Book Club, 1975), p. 104.
12 FO 371–99659: MR, 15 December 1951.
13 Ibid
14 Ibid.
15 In Tibetan: *dmag bshor-pa las / drod-khog ltogs-pa / dka'-las khag-gyi re*. See lHa-klu tshe-dbang rdo rje (Lhalu Tsewang Dorje), '*mi-dmangs bchings-'grol dmag lha-sar bca'-sdod byas rjes*', (Arrival of PLA in Lhasa). SCHT, Vol. 1 (1982), p. 348.
16 Chang Kuohua [Zhang Guohua], SCMP, No. 2854 (1962), p. 9.

17 Phala.
18 lHa klu tshe dbang rdo rje, 1982, pp. 347–8.
19 Ibid.
20 Phala.
21 lHa klu tshe dbang rdo rje, 1982.
22 Even Mao was concerned about Tibet having its own flag. Later, when the Dalai Lama visited China, he was asked by Mao about the origin of the Tibetan flag.
23 Ibid.
24 Phala.
25 dByin Pha'-thang (Yin Fatang), *Bod-skyod thong-ma'i dus kyi 'tsham-'dri'i byed[snd]sgo zhig dran-gso byas-pa*, SCHT, Vol. 2 (1983), p. 228.
26 Ibid.
27 Broadcast by Zhang Guohua, SWB, No. 255, 3 June 1953, p. 13.
28 FO 371–99659: MR, 15 February 1952.
29 Lhalu writes that originally the Chinese nominated him, but because of his criticism of the two Prime Ministers, the Kashag did not approve of the Chinese nomination.
30 Chang Kuohua, 1962.
31 Lu'o Yus hung, 1985, op. cit.
32 Monlam (*smon lam*) was introduced by Tsong Kha-pa (1357–1475), the founder of the Gelug pa school of Tibetan Buddhism. One of the most interesting features of the ceremony was that during the period of Monlam, monks known as '*zhal ngo*' take over the jurisdiction of Lhasa. They can impose summary judgement on outstanding disputes, impose fines and punish criminals.
33 Lu'o Yus hung, 1985, op. cit.
34 In one of Mao's much-quoted statements on religious belief, he wrote: 'We cannot abolish religion by administrative orders; nor can we force people not to believe in it. We cannot compel people to give up idealism, any more than we can force them to believe in Marxism.' He went on to say that 'in settling matters of an ideological nature or controversial issues among the people, we can only use democratic methods, methods of discussion, of criticism, of persuasion and education, not coercive, high-handed methods.' (Here I have used the translation by Holmes Welch, *Buddhism under Mao*, Harvard University Press, 1972, p. 365.
35 FO 371–99659: MR, 16 May 1952.
36 Lu'o Yus hung, 1985, op. cit.
37 FO 371–184166: MR, 15 March 1952.
38 Ibid.
39 Phala.
40 Yang dbyi-kran, *Bod-dmag khul-khang thog- mar 'dzugas skabs dang mi-dmangs tshogs-'du 'zer-ba rdzus-mar 'thab-rtsod byas-pa' gnas-tshul* (Establishment of Tibet Military Command and Struggle Against the Bogus People's Organisation), SCHT, Vol. 9, 1986, pp. 58–85.
41 Ibid.
42 Ibid.

43 Ibid., p. 68.
44 Ibid.
45 Ibid., p. 80.
46 Ibid.
47 FO 371–99659: MR, 16 April 1952.
48 Phala.
49 Lu'o Yus hung, 1985, op. cit.
50 Tibetan sources merely state that the attack occurred at Ngabo's house and do not give any further details. The incident became one of the main turning points in Chinese attitudes towards the Prime Ministers. It seems unlikely that there was a deliberate attack on Ngabo's house, for, although he was unpopular, there was never an attempt to oust him from power. The Tibetan Government never demoted him or restricted his position. In any case, the majority of the Tibetan élite believed in working with the Chinese at the time.
51 In the early stages, the Chinese were anxious to avoid a direct armed conflict with the Tibetan masses. The growing anti-Chinese agitation in Lhasa meant that the Chinese were worried that they might have to resort to armed confrontation in Lhasa, which would ignite nationwide revolt, as happened later on.
52 On the Policies for Our Work in Tibet, Directive of the Central Committee of the Communist Party of China, from *Selected Works of Mao Tsetung*, Beijing, 1977, (Vol. V), pp. 73–6.
53 Ibid.
54 Phala.
55 The Tibet Bureau was established in 1930 as the representative of Tibetan Government in China.
56 Phala.
57 FO 371–99659: MR, 16 April 11952.
58 The Dalai Lama, 1985, p. 97.
59 Ibid.
60 FO 371–99659: MR, 16 May 1952.
61 Ibid.
62 *Selected Writings of Mao Tsetung*, Beijing, 1977, (Vol. V), pp. 73–6.
63 Takla.
64 FO 371–99659: MR, 15 April 1952.
65 Ibid.
66 Ibid.
67 The Dalai Lama, 1985, p. 98.
68 Lukhangwa died in Delhi on 24 February 1966.
69 Lobsang Tashi remained in Tibet.
70 FO 371–110228.
71 Ibid.
72 Account of Panchen Rinpoche's arrival in Lhasa; see Ya' Han-krang, 1982, pp. 280–341.
73 Ibid., p. 318.
74 Also known as Jigme Dragpa.
75 FO 371–99659: MR, 16 May 1952.

76 Ya Hanzhang, *The Biographies of the Dalai Lama* (Beijing, Foreign Language Press, 1991), p. 438.
77 FO 371–99659: MR, 15 December 1952.
78 Ya' Han-krang, 1982, p. 327.
79 FO 371–99659: MR, 16 June 1952.
80 Ibid.
81 Tibet 1950–1965, URI, 1968, pp. 44–5.
82 Xinhua reported: 'in the past the American and British imperialism had tried to force down its price and increase the import tax on wool, thereby disrupting the economic life of the Tibetans. The interest shown by the Central People's Government offered a new and broad outlet for Tibetan products . . . it has dealt a severe blow to the "economic aggression" of the imperialists and solved the merchant's problem of frozen assets; the contract would have a beneficial effect on improving the people's livelihood.' (SWB, No. 162, 27 May 1952, p. 36.)
83 The largest Chinese import into Tibet was tea and some luxury goods. Even in eastern Tibet, as far as Amdo or Kham, they were trading extensively with India. It is interesting that all the largest trading families in Tibet had established themselves in Kalimpong. Tibet's export was all channelled through India.
84 From the start the Chinese began to restrict the business activities of Nepalese traders. To some extent the Chinese saw the trade privileges enjoyed by the Nepalese and Indian merchants as extra-territorial rights, similar to the privileges enjoyed by Western traders in China.
85 Nepal did not have direct contact with China, where its interests were conducted by India. The Chinese were keen to establish a direct relationship. However, Nepal's relationship with Tibet was governed by the treaty of 1856. In article 1 Tibet promised to send annual tribute, the sum of 10,000 rupees, to Nepal. According to Article 2 Nepal would assist Tibet if a foreign power invaded Tibet.

It is interesting that the Tibetan Government did not request help from Nepal when the Chinese invaded in October 1950. The treaty made it incumbent on Nepal to come to the aid of Tibet and it was still clearly valid. The last Tibetan tribute mission to Nepal arrived in Kathmandu with 10,000 rupees in January 1952. The Nepalese Government informed the GOI and asked them to advise them in the event of Tibet raising the issue resulting from the treaty of 1856. The GOI advised Nepal that they should not volunteer to raise the issue. However, if Tibet were to raise the issue then Nepal should give up extra-territoral rights in Tibet and the right to extract annual tribute from Lhasa. The GOI recommended that Nepal should maintain the right to a Mission in Lhasa.
86 FO 371–99659: MR, 16 June 1952.
87 Interview with Ngawang Dhondup Narkyid. He told me that he himself and a group of young aristocratic officials volunteered to go to China for studies.
88 There has been a protracted debate among Social Anthropologists about the exact translation of the Tibetan term '*mi-ser*'. Melvyn Goldstein prefers to translate the term as a 'serf' and others have suggested that term could best

translated as 'subject'. See Melvyn Goldstein, 'Re-examining Choice, Dependency and Command in the Tibetan Social System: Tax Appendages and Other Landless Serfs'. TJ, 4 (1986), pp. 79–112; Beatrice D. Miller, 'A response to Goldstein's article', TJ, 2 (1987), pp. 65–7; 'Melvyn Goldstein's Rejoinder', TJ, 3 (1988), pp. 61–5; Beatrice D. Miller's Rejoinder, TJ, op. cit., pp. 64–6.

89 tsong kha lha mo tshe ring, 1992, p. 122.

90 FO 371–99659: MR, 16 August 1952.

91 Dawa Norbu, 'Tibetan Response to Chinese Liberation', Asian Affairs, 62 (1975), pp. 266–78.

92 FO 370–110228.

93 K. M. Panikkar, 1955, p. 175.

94 Ibid.

95 'Five Principles of Co-existence' (*Panch Sheela*) are (1) mutual respect for each other's territorial integrity and sovereignty; (2) mutual non-aggression; (3) mutual non-interference in each other's internal affairs; (4) equality and mutual benefit, and (5) peaceful co-existence.

96 The Sino–Indian Agreement stated that facilities would be transferred at a reasonable cost.

97 The 1954 Indo–Chinese Agreement was designed to supersede the Anglo–Chinese Convention of 1906 and Trade Regulation of 1908. It is interesting to note that trade regulation between Tibet and India, and much of the extra-territorial rights exercised by the British and later by the Republic of India were governed by the Anglo-Tibetan Trade Agreement of 1914, which was initialled by the Tibetans' representative Lochen Shatra, the British representative Henry MacMahon and the Chinese representative Ivan Chen, but the Chinese had later refused to ratify the agreement and had made it clear that they would not recognise any bilateral agreement signed between Tibet and Britain. However, between 1914 and 1947 the Trade Agreement was in force and in 1947 the rights obtained by the British were transferred to independent India. When the Sino–Indian Trade Agreement was discussed in 1954, the Communists took the same position as the nationalists and refused to recognise the Anglo–Tibetan Agreement of 1914. Had the Chinese agreed that the antecedent to the 1954 Agreement was the Anglo–Tibetan Agreement of 1914, this would have implied that the Communists recognised Tibet's right to external autonomy. Since India did not make any direct connection between the two agreements, it gave the impression that she was willing to concede that independent India did not recognise the Anglo–Tibetan Agreement of 1914. The implication of this neglect became evident when open dispute occurred over the border issue. This subject will be dealt with in a later chapter.

98 The Agreement made no mention of the boundary between India and Tibet (China). By the fact that, so far, Chinese had made no mention of the boundary, India assumed that the PRC accepted that there were no boundary disputes and that China accepted the status quo. See Gopal, 1979, Vol. 2, p. 181.

99 SWB, No. 362, 15 June 1954.

100 B. N. Mullik, *My Years with Nehru, The Chinese Betrayal* (Bombay, Allied Publishers, 1971), p. 180.

101 Ibid., pp. 181–83.

102 Ibid.
103 FO 371–110647.
104 Ibid.
105 Ibid.
106 Once the Nepalese realised that the Chinese occupation of Tibet was a *fait accompli*, and once India had signed an agreement, Nepal could no longer avoid reaching an agreement with China.
107 Tibet 1950–1967, op. cit.
108 The Chinese liberality with money led to a popular song: 'The Chinese Communist Party is like a kind parent, To whom we owe a great debt of gratitude; They give us silver dollars like showers of rain'.
109 Ka-bshod chos-rgyal nyi ma. *Ngas byas-pa'i don-chung zhig*. SCHT, 3 (1985), pp. 71–81.
110 The Tibetans looked to British India for political and economic support for the simple reason that communication between Tibet and India was far easier. It was far easier and safer for Chinese officials to travel to Tibet via India to reach Lhasa.
111 The Dalai Lama, 1985, p. 99.
112 Ibid., p. 100.
113 Ibid.
114 See Dawa Norbu, 'Chinese Communist View on National Self-determination, 1922–1956: Origins of China's National Minorities Policy', International Studies, 25:4 (1988), pp. 317–42.
115 The Dalai Lama, 1985, p. 117.
116 Ibid.
117 Sylvain Mangeot, 1975, op. cit. p. 117.
118 Rinchen Dolma Taring, 1970, p. 199.
119 It is interesting that the Dalai Lama in his autobiography described how they used the traditional symbol of 'Four Harmonious Brothers' (*mthun-po-spun-bzhi*) on the new year invitation card, which the Dalai Lama wrote 'were meant to emphasise, from our own point of view, the union of the nationalities'. I am sure that the symbolism was much appreciated by the Chinese (see The Dalai Lama, 1985, op. cit., p. 121).
120 SWB. No. 436, 3 March 1955, p. 13.
121 Ibid., p. 14.
122 The Dalai Lama, 1985, op. cit., p. 116.
123 Tibet 1950–1967, op. cit., p. 171.
124 Ibid., p. 112.
125 Ibid., p. 113.
126 The Dalai Lama, 1985, p. 132.
127 PRO, FO 371–122126. Translation of Chen Yi's speech from the *People's Daily*.
128 The Dalai Lama's speech was carefully worded with warnings to the Chinese that if they were to rush into promoting reforms, they would face difficulties. The Dalai Lama also qualified each remark by noting that it had been promised by Mao himself. See *Tibet, 1950–1967*, op. cit. p. 147.
129 *Tibet, 1950–1967*, op. cit., p. 52.

130 This was a clear reference to the growing Chinese agitation in eastern Tibet, (Kham and Amdo). On his way to China, the Dalai Lama was able to hear from Khampas and Amdowa first-hand news of Chinese attempts to introduce reforms.
131 Ibid.
132 The People's Liberation Committee of Chamdo was set up soon after the Chinese had occupied the area. In January 1951, the advancing PLA troops organised a 'People's Conference of all Classes of the Population' in Chamdo, which also marked the founding of the CLC. However, it was not until 1954, that it was defined and given specific task.
133 *Tibet, 1950–1967*, URI, op. cit., pp. 121–4.
134 Ibid., p. 173.
135 The Dalai Lama, 1985, p. 116.
136 The original State Council Resolution issued on 9 March 1955 mentions that there would be 51 members.
137 *Tibet, 1950–1967*, URI, op. cit., p. 173.
138 The Dalai Lama, 1985, p. 133.
139 The 14 Departments were (1) the General Office (2) Economics (3) Religious Affairs (4) Civil Affairs (5) Construction (6) Cultural and Education (7) Public Health (8) Public Security (9) Agriculture and Forestry (10) Animal Husbandry (11) Industry and Commerce (12) Communication (13) Justice Department and (14) Finance.

FIVE The Rift

1 Alo chos mdzad (Alo Chonze), *Bod kyi gnas-lugs bden-dzin sgo phye-ba'i ldi-mig zhes bya-ba.* (privately published, 1983), pp. 158–9.
2 Jamyang Sakya, 1990, p. 243.
3 Ibid., p. 244.
4 Many officials accepted the Chinese salary and at the same time continued to run their estates, which had traditionally been granted in lieu of salary by the Tibetan Government. The Chinese did not initially demand the surrender of estates by Tibetan officials.
5 Dawa Norbu, 1974, p. 132.
6 The Tibetan Buddhist sects are not like sects in the Christian tradition. The sects are not organised in any hierarchical or political structure, with central authority and different councils. As far as laymen were concerned, no distinction was made between the different sects. Many lay people were genuinely perplexed when asked which sect they belonged to.
7 Jamyang Sakya, 1990, p. 259.
8 Chagtral Sonam Chophel, Oral Archive, LTWA.
9 Ibid.
10 *Tibet, 1950–67*, URI, p. 99.
11 Ibid., p. 101.
12 Mao's directive, 6 April 1952.
13 Interview with Pasang Gyalpo.

14 André Migot, 1955, pp. 97–8.
15 The Chinese have always looked down on minorities, but with the advent of Communism, their conviction that minorities were backward was reinforced by crude Marxist notions of evolution of society. The economic system of minorities areas dominated by pure nomadism or pastoralism was considered an earlier stage of socio-economic development.
16 These were the Kantze Tibetan Autonomous Zhou; the Ngaba Tibetan Autonomous Zhou; the Jyekundo Tibetan Autonomous Zhou; the Golok Tibetan Autonomous Zhou; the Haibei Tibetan Autonomous Zhou; the Hainan Tibetan Autonomous Zhou; and the Huangnan Tibetan Autonomous Zhou,
17 June Teufel Dryer, 'Traditional Minorities Elites', in Robert Scalapino's *Elites in the Peoples Republic of China* (University of Washington Press, 1972), pp. 416–50.
18 Ibid., p. 84.
19 Gonbo Tashi, 1973, p. 38.
20 Phala.
21 Interview with Lithang Ather Norbu.
22 Speech by Geshe Sherab Gyatso at the 3rd Session of the 1st National People's Congress in June 1956 (see *Tibet, 1950–67*, URI, p. 181). This refers to the fact that in many Tibetan temples, there is a special chapel dedicated to wrathful deities. It is normal for guns and other weapons to be placed before an image of a wrathful deity.
23 Anna Louise Strong, 1960, pp. 65–6.
24 Interview with Changtrimpa Tenzin Tsultrim.
25 Ibid.
26 Ibid.
27 Interview with Lithang Athar.
28 The Dalai Lama, 1985, p. 158.
29 Phala.
30 Ibid.
31 Ibid.
32 The Dalai Lama, 1985, p. 158.
33 Speech by Geshe Sherab Gyatso in June 1956. See *Tibet, 1950–67*, URI. p. 181.
34 Kuang Haolin, 1991. pp. 123–55.
35 Speech by Geshe Sherab Gyatso in June 1956. See *Tibet, 1950–67*, URI, pp. 180–1.
36 Ibid.
37 *Tibet, 1950–67*, URI, p. 187.
38 Alo chos mdzad, 1983, p. 170.
39 Ibid., p. 139.
40 Ibid., p. 137.
41 Sa-byang Tshe-brten rnam-rgyal, 1984, pp. 245–55.
42 Interview with Pasang Gyalpo.
43 Sa byang Tshe-brten rnam-rgyal, 1984, p. 253.
44 Alo chos mdzad, 1983, p. 136.
45 Ibid., p. 138.
46 Ibid.

47 Ibid., p. 171.
48 Ibid.
49 Ibid.
50 Everyone seems to accept Lhabchug died of natural causes. There was no question of torture or ill treatment during the incarceration.
51 Alo Chonzed worked for several years in the Tibetan government-in-exile in charge of a co-operative in a Tibetan refugee settlement in south India. He felt that his work for the Mimang Tsongdu was never acknowledged by the Tibetan officials. Later, he became a passionate critic of the Dalai Lama's family. He maintained that the Dalai Lama's brother Gyalo Thundup and his brother-in-law, Phuntsog Tashi Takla, were working for the Guomindang. In 1981 he returned to Tibet and was selected as a member of the People's Political Consultative Conference. But in 1990 he came to back to India, where when he visited his daughter in Dharamsala (North India) he was beaten up by a mob of Tibetan women.
52 Nari Rustomji, 1987, p. 47.
53 In a note given by the Chinese Foreign Office to the India Consular authorities in Lhasa dated 10 July 1958, the Chinese raised issues regarding the activities of the Tibetan *émigrés* and Guomindang agents living in Kalimpong. The Chinese also lodged a complaint about the only Tibetan language paper, the *Tibet Mirror*, published by Tharchin in Kalimpong. It was described as 'a reactionary newspaper hostile to the Chinese government and people'. On 3 August 1958, the Chinese again protested about a campaign launched by the Tibetan *émigré* community in Kalimpong. These marked the beginning of the decline in Sino–Indian relations. The notes exchanged between GOI and PRC were published in a White Paper by the Ministry of External Affairs (GOI): *Notes, memoranda and letters exchanged and agreements signed between the GOI and China 1954–1959*, pp. 60–7 (no date of publication cited).
54 B. N. Mullik, 1971, p. 183.
55 The Dalai Lama, 1985, pp. 140–1.
56 Nari Rustomji, 1987, p. 53.
57 *krung-go gung-khreng tang krung-dbyang u-yon lhan-khang skyabs brgyad-pa'i tshang- 'dzam gros-tshogs thengs gnyis-pa'i thog gi gtam bshad. m'o tse-tung-gi gsung rtsom- bsdus*, 1977, Vol. 5, p. 489. Speech by Mao at the Second Plenum of the 8th Central Committee (15 November 1956), hereafter cited as Speech at the Second Plenum. See English translation, John K. Leung & Michael Y. M. Kau, *The Writings of Mao Zedong, 1949–1976, Volume 2*, (M. E. Sharpe, 1984), p. 170. There are several versions of the speech which differ from each other. A version published in the *Selected Works of Mao Zedong*, Vol. 5, pp. 332–49 has a lengthy paragraph dealing with the Dalai Lama's visit to India. A version published in *Wansui*, pp. 112–18, makes no reference to the Dalai Lama and a new section has been inserted dealing with the problem of minority nationalities.
58 The Dalai Lama, 1985, p. 140.
59 Ibid.
60 Speech at the Second Plenum, 1957, op. cit., p. 489.
61 FO 371–121147. In his meeting with the British, Thubten Norbu told them

that in the past the Dalai Lama was inclined to leave Tibet. He had secured US assistance but Tibetans felt US support did not go far enough. There was no mention of the Dalai Lama's visit to India.

62 The Dalai Lama, 1983, p. 142.
63 John K. Leung & Michael Y. M. Kau, 1984, p. 170.
64 Ibid.
65 NCNA, 13.1.57.
66 B. N. Mullik, 1971, p. 160.
67 The Dalai Lama, 1983, p. 148.
68 Ibid.
69 Sarvepalli Gopal, Vol. 3, 1984, p. 36.
70 The Dalai Lama, 1983, p. 148.
71 Anon.
72 Sarvepalli Gopal, 1984, p. 36.
73 Ibid.
74 H. G. Parthasarathi, 1989, pp. 228–9.
75 John K. Leung and Michael Y. M. Kau, 1984, p. 170.
76 Ibid.
77 Thubten Norbu told me that in 1956 the US did not specifically urge the Dalai Lama to remain in India.
78 Thubten Norbu, 1961, p. 254.
79 The Dalai Lama, 1985, p. 149.
80 Thubten Norbu, 1961, p. 254.
81 The Dalai Lama, 1985, p. 150.
82 Phala. (He says that nine people went to see Zhou.)
83 The Dalai Lama, 1985, pp. 148–9.
84 FO 371–127639. In April 1957 the Chogyal of Sikkim was in London, where he told British Foreign Office officials that he was informed by his uncle Ragashag that when the Tibetan delegation met Zhou Enlai in Delhi they presented an ultimatum demanding the withdrawal of Chinese troops from Tibet and the restoration of Tibetan independence, based on the reunion of all Tibetan-inhabited areas including those of the upper Yangtse (Drichu). Ragashag also said that it was Ngabo who led the discussion. Phala confirms that it was Ngabo who was most critical of the Chinese and spoke very bluntly with Zhou.
85 Phala.
86 The Dalai Lama, 1985, p. 151.
87 John K. Leung and Michael Y. M. Kau, 1984, p. 281.
88 Phuntsog Tashi Takla.
89 The Dalai Lama, 1985, p. 151.
90 Ibid., p. 152.
91 As quoted in Sarvepalli Gopal, 1984, p. 36.
92 Phuntsog Tashi Takla.
93 Ibid.
94 *Concerning the Question of Tibet*, Foreign Language Press, Peking, 1950, p. 183.
95 Anon.
96 *Collected Works*, Vol. V, pp. 384–412.
97 The speech was not published in its entirety until much later and was not

available in the West in its original form until 1985. See an interesting comparison of the two versions by Michael Schoenhals, 1986, pp. 99–111.

98 I used the text published in Roderick MacFarquhar, 1989, pp. 131–99.

99 I mean speeches given by Mao at the Second Plenum of the Eighth Central Committee and his address to the Conference of Provincial and Municipal Party Secretaries, 27 January 1957.

100 The Dalai Lama and the Tibetans would not have been aware of the full contents of Mao's speech. However, Xinhua gave extensive coverage to the Mao announcement that the reforms in Tibet would be postponed for five years. The Tibetans in India became aware of the speech through the Indian press.

101 At a press conference in London on 2 December 1991, in response to a question from a Xinhua correspondent, the Dalai Lama said that he returned to Tibet in 1956 because of promises given by Zhou Enlai.

102 The Dalai Lama, 1983, p. 157.

103 SWB, 1957, No. 659, p. 30.

104 Ibid.

105 Ibid.

106 *Tibet, 1950–67*, URI, p. 218.

107 Ibid., p. 261.

108 SWB, 1957, No. 662. pp. 17–18.

109 Literally, 'defender of faith' (The Tibetan army). I am quoting this song as published in Dawa Norbu's 'The 1959 Tibetan Rebellion: An Interpretation', CQ, 77, 1979, p. 74

110 Statement of Gyakhar Gonpo in 'Tibet under the Chinese Communist Rule', A Compilation of Refugee Statements 1958–1975, Information & Publicity Office of HH the Dalai Lama, 1975, pp. 25–6 (Hereafter cited as TUCCR).

111 Ibid.

112 *Tibet, 1950–67*, URI, p. 140.

113 Gonbo Tashi, 1973, p. 48.

SIX The Revolt

1 Michel Peissel, 1972, p. 90. I believe that many Khampas privately share views expressed by Peissel in his book, although they do not personally blame the Dalai Lama: anger was more directed towards the Tibetan aristocracy. In fact in the course of my research I met many people from eastern Tibet who expressed strong resentment against the Lhasa authorities for their failure to support them.

2 Gonbo Tashi, 1973, p. 57.

3 Chodrak, who was studying veterinary science in China, remembered that even those who had not completed their training were told they could return home and continue their education later.

4 Ngawang Dhondup.

5 '*btsan-rgol*' means revolt. It was meant as revolt against the 17-Point Agreement.

Only a few people knew the name, which was used as a code when establishing contact.

6 In Tibetan, *brtan-bzhugs zhabs-brtan.*

7 Gonpo Tashi, 1973, pp. 52–3.

8 It was a measure of the people's sympathy and concern that people from all levels of society contributed enthusiastically. For the details of the ceremony and of the amount of gold and other precious gems that was raised, see Andrug Gonpo Tashi 1973, pp. 52–4. According to Andrug it amounted to 4745 tolas of gold.

9 Ibid., p. 51.

10 Phala.

11 See Ann Louise Strong, 1960, for Chinese account of events leading to the Khampa Revolt.

12 Michel Peissel, 1972, p. 95.

13 Andrug Gonpo Tashi, 1973, p. 55.

14 Another name for the group was 'the National Volunteer Defence Army' (in Tibetan, *bsten-srung dang-blangs dmag-mi*).

15 The four rivers are: 1. the Salween (*rgya mo rngu chu*); 2. the Yangtse (*'bri chu*); 3. the Mekong (*rdza chu*); 4. the Yellow River, (*rma chu*). The six ranges are: 1. Ngul Dza Zhamo Gang (*rngl rdza zal mol sgang*); 2. Por bor Gang (*spor 'bor sgang*); 3. Mi ngya Rawa Gang (*mi nyag 'a ba sgang*); 4. Tshawa Gang (*tsha sgang*); 5. Markham Gang (*smar khams sgang*); 6. Marzha Gang (*dmar rdza sgang*).

16 Mao called for this special meeting to discuss his 'On Contradiction'.

17 For details of the Rectification Campaign among minority groups see June Teufel Dreyer, 1976, pp. 150–8.

18 Tibet 1950–67, URI, pp. 267–70.

19 Ibid., pp. 222–34.

20 Ibid.

21 Ibid.

22 Ibid., pp. 271–83.

23 The Dalai Lama, 1990, p. 122.

24 Anon.

25 *Tibet, 1950–67*, URI, pp. 271–83.

26 Ibid.

27 The Dalai Lama remembers that the Chinese simply told him that Phuntsog Wangyal would not be returning to Tibet as 'he was a dangerous man'. See The Dalai Lama, 1990, p. 122.

28 The Khampas inflicted severe damage on the PLA. Guomindang sources reported that the Communists suffered 65–75,000 casualties in clashes with the Khampas (SWB, 1959, No. 833 p. 35.

29 One of my informants remembers that there were more than thirty different regiments. The Lithangpa group was the largest.

30 I am grateful to Tenzin Sonam and Ritu Sarin for giving me a transcript of their interview with Loden.

31 Baba Lekshe.

32 Stephen E. Ambrose, 1983, p. 206.

33 Ibid., 1984, pp. 284–6.
34 Ibid., pp. 212–13.
35 Popular accounts of CIA activities, such as Willaim Blum's *The CIA: A Forgotten History* (Zed Books Ltd., 1986), grossly exaggerate the CIA's role in the Tibetan revolt and imply that the CIA trained 'many thousands' of Tibetans. See also John Ranelagh, *The Agency, The Rise and Decline of the CIA* (Weidenfeld and Nicolson, 1986), pp. 335–6. There are a number of books written by former CIA agents which give accounts of CIA activities in Tibet, notably L. Fletcher Prouty *The Secret Team, The CIA and its Allies in Control of the United States and the World* (1973), and Victor Marchetti and John D. Marks, *The CIA and the Cult of Intelligence* (1974). These books also tend to give exaggerated accounts of the CIA's role in the Tibetan revolt. Prouty (p. 352) writes that without the help of CIA the Dalai Lama could not have made his escape from Lhasa.
36 CIA document TDCSPD/3639,989.
37 Lithang Athar, one of the first Khampas recruited for training, claims that he first met Thubten Norbu during this visit, and they began to recruit Khampas living in Kalimpong and Darjeeling.
38 Interview with Lithang Athar.
39 Ibid.
40 Ibid.
41 Phala.
42 Phala and Liushar.
43 The dates cited by Athar and Lhamo Tsering require verification from archive sources. However, this is not possible because the CIA files on the subject remain closed to the public.
44 The Dalai Lama, 1990, p. 140.
45 All information on these events comes from Lithang Athar, whom I have known since my childhood. I conducted in-depth interviews with him on three occasions, in Kathmandu, New Delhi and London.
46 Phala.
47 Athar.
48 During our interviews Athar said that he could never forgive the Tibetan Government for their failure to accept the American offer. He argues that if the Tibetan Government had acted then and worked with the Four Rivers, Six Ranges, the Khampas would have succeeded in gaining control of central Tibet. The Khampas failed because they lacked weapons and because American help came much too late.
49 Ibid.
50 Lhamo Tsering has written a detailed account of his first meeting with Gyalo Dhundup. See: Tsong Kha Lha mo tshe ring. *sku'i gchen-po lha-sras rGya-lo don-drub mchog gi thog-ma'i mdzad-phyogs dang gus-gnyis dbar chab-srid 'brel-ba byong-stangs skor*, Amnye Machen Institute, Dhramsala. 1992.
51 I have been asked by my informants not to reveal the identity of the CIA agent.
52 Athar and Lhamo Tsering. Confirmation of the accuracy of the account given by my informants awaits public access to CIA archives.
53 Gonpo Tashi, 1973, p. 66.

54 Interview with Diwa Lang.
55 You can see the extent of movement of the Khampas resistance by looking at the route followed by Andrug Gonpo Tashi and his group. From July 1958 to April 1959, Andrug and his men travelled from Driguthang in Lhokh as far north-east Chungpo Tenchen. (See route map in Gonpo Tashi, 1973, p. 64.)
56 Athar.
57 This was mainly because the previous Panchen Rinpoche had spent a long time in exile in Kham and Amdo.
58 In Tibetan, *krung-dbyangs dgongs-pa dang-ba dang / khams-rigs kyi zing-cha 'jag -tabs.*
59 Lhawutara.
60 Ibid.
61 An account given by Barshi Ngawang Tenkhong, 1984, LTWE (hereafter cited as Barshi).
62 Lhawutara claims that he made this suggestion, but Phala says that it was Lhalu who made it.
63 Barshi.
64 Namseling Paljor Jigme, *rNam gling dpal 'byor 'jigs med*, 1988, p. 94.
65 Ibid.
66 Gonpo Tashi, 1973, p. 69–71.
67 Ibid.
68 Phala.
69 Ibid.
70 Byams pa. *zing-slong jag pas Shang dGa'-ldan chos-'khor dgon nas mthon-cha 'don-'khyer byas skor*, SCHT, 1985, Vol. 5, pp. 222–9.
71 Phala.
72 Gonpo Tashi, 1973, pp.74–5.
73 Byams pa, 1985, p. 227.
74 SWB, 8 January 1959.

SEVEN The Flight of the Dalai Lama

1 The Dalai Lama, 1983, p. 163.
2 This view was expressed by Phala.
3 SWB, 1959, No. 849, p. 18.
4 Barshi.
5 In Tibetan, *nged kyi slob dpon mthong ba don ldna 'di / phyi bskyed med pa'a bskul ma 'debs re ran.*
6 *bsam-khar.*
7 Barshi.
8 Ibid.
9 Ngabo, *On the 1959 Armed Rebellion, in Tibetans of Tibet*, published by China Reconstructs Press (no date cited), pp. 157–67. I have a Tibetan version of this paper, which was broadcast over Lhasa Radio. Ngabo gives an account of the events leading up to the 10th March Uprising in Lhasa. Dharamsala has written a response to this article but has not refuted Ngabo's central claim that it was not the Chinese who invited the Dalai Lama to the military camp for the

performance. It was the Dalai Lama himself who chose the venue and timing of the show.

10 The Dalai Lama (1990, p. 142) has claimed that he received an invitation from General Chiang Chin-wu (*sic*) (Zhang Jianghua) shortly after the new year while he was in the Jokhang. I think he is mistaken as Zhang Jianghua was not in Lhasa at the time. The highest-ranking Chinese officer present in Lhasa was Tan Guansan.

11 The Dalai Lama, 1990, pp. 164–8.

12 Ibid., p. 165–6.

13 In Tibetan, '*da tsar-ba re*'.

14 Ngabo, *On the 1959 Armed Rebellion, in Tibetans of Tibet*, China Reconstructs Press (no date), pp 157–67.

15 Takla.

16 Barshi.

17 Barshi does not say which *bla-spyi* he wrote to. There were generally three *bla-spyi* in Drepung and three in Sera. *bla-spyi* forms the highest administrative body in the monastery. They are generally selected from high rank incarnate lamas (Rinpoche) for three years' service.

18 Barshi.

19 Ibid.

20 Liushar.

21 Ibid., p. 273.

22 The Dalai Lama, 1985, p. 168.

23 Accounts given by Barshi and Phala differ slightly. Phala claims that he went to meet Gadrang with Takla and does not mention the names of the others, while Barshi mentions the names of three other monk officials.

24 Barshi. This was also confirmed by Phala in his interview.

25 Phala.

26 Barshi claims that they decided to mobilise the public immediately after the meeting with Gadrang and that he did not know that the Dalai Lama had refused to accept their appeal. In the accounts given by Takla and Phala, they claim that other officials decided to mobilise the public after they had failed to persuade the Dalai Lama, which seems likely to be more accurate.

27 Barshi. Phala confirms that some officials had gone about spreading the rumour in Lhasa that night.

28 China's White Paper on Tibet, SWB, 24 September, 1992, p. C1/8.

29 Barshi claims that some officials came to see him next morning and told him that Surkhang and Shasur had advised them not to precede with the plan to mobilise the people.

30 Yuthok, 1990, p. 265.

31 Pronounced Khag.

32 The Dalai Lama, 1983, p. 169.

33 Michel Peissel and Noel Barber claim that the people started to gather outside the Norbulingka in the evening of 9 March. They write that nearly 10,000 people had surrounded the Norbulingka and that on that day the people also started to besiege the Nepalese and Indian Consulates. Evidence given by Phala, Barshi and others shows that people came to the Norbulingka only on the

morning of 10 March. See Michel Peissel, 1972, p. 120; Noel Barber, 1969, p. 77.

34 Some popular books on Tibet cite the number of people outside the Norbulingka as 10,000: Noel Barber, *The Flight of the Dalai Lama*, Hodder and Stoughton, 1960, p. 106, and Michel Peissel, 1972, p. 120. John F. Avedon, in his book *In Exile from the Land of Snows*, Wisdom, 1984, p. 71, cites a figure of 30,000 people outside the Norbulingka. A Chinese source claims that there were only 2,000 people involved in the demonstration. See China's White Paper on Tibet, SWB, 24 September 1992. p. C1/8.

35 Sambo himself does not mention this incident in detail in his biography.

36 Liushar.

37 He was more commonly known as 'Chamdo Khenchung'. He is the brother of Chamdo Phagpa Gelek Namgyal, who is a young incarnate lama and the Chairman of the Chamdo Liberation Committee. Since 1950 he has occupied various positions in the Tibetan Government.

38 Some people I spoke to claim that Khunchung Sonam Gyamtso fired a pistol in the air to ward off the crowd, others claim that he was carrying a hand grenade. The crowd immediately accused him of attempting to assassinate the Dalai Lama. See description of the event in Hugh Richardson's biography of Tashi Lhakap, *Adventures of a Tibetan Fighting Monk*, The Tamarind Press, Bangkok, 1986, p. 91.

39 China's White Paper on Tibet, SWB, 24 September 1992, p. C1/8.

40 Dawa Norbu in his article (CQ, 1979, No. 77, p. 89) writes that 'it is clear from my own findings that Tibetan fears and suspicions were unfounded, and that the Chinese had no such intentions'. He cites Luishar Thupten Tharpa as a source.

41 Liushar.

42 One Chinese eyewitness claims that Khunchung was slung over the back of a horse. See Shan Chao, 'Sunshine after Rain', *Peking Review*, 5 May 1950, p. 10.

43 This is also reported by another eye-witness, Langdun Gyatso, see TR, March 1969, pp. 3–5.

44 Michel Peissel and others have implied that Ngabo's presence among the Chinese was sinister. Peissel goes as far as saying that Ngabo might have been 'the principal instigator of the so-called Chinese plot to abduct the Dalai Lama'. See Michel Peissel, 1972, p. 121.

45 See the account of the event written by a leading Tibetan aristocrat who was at the reception: Jamyang Sakya, 1990, pp. 271–3.

46 Ibid.

47 Recent publications from China and Tibet show differences in emphasis concerning the class nature of the revolt. The Communists cannot accept that the Tibetan revolt was supported by the 'lower classes' and have maintained that the revolt was essentially organised by the 'upper class', while Tibetan writers tend to portray the revolt as a popular uprising supported by different social classes. In *Master Panchen*, Jamphel Gyatso goes so far as to say that the revolt in Kham was supported by the 'masses'. It is also interesting to note that the Tibetan edition of Dung-dkar Blo-bzang 'phrin-las's *Bod kyi chos srid zung 'brel skor bshad-pa* (*The Merging of Religious and Secular Rule in Tibet*, Beijing

1983) says that the 1959 revolt was supported by the 'upper classes and the middle class' but the phrase 'middle class' is omitted from the English translation. Although he does say that the masses supported the revolt, given the sensitivity of the subject, the inclusion of 'middle class' is significant. For the Communists, the class composition of the revolt was very important, for if they were to admit that the Tibetan masses supported the uprising, then the Communist Party would lose its legitimacy for claiming that it represented the Tibetan masses.

48 Liushar.

49 Many Tibetan officials I have talked to say that they feared there would be a Civil War either between the people of *U-tsang* and the Khampas or between the army and the Kham rebels.

50 The Dalai Lama, 1985, p. 172.

51 See *Peking Review*, 1959, Vol. XXI. pp.10–11, on how General Tan's first letter was brought to the Dalai Lama.

52 The correspondence between the Dalai Lama and Tan Guansan has been published as *Concerning the Question of Tibet*, Foreign Languages Press, Beijing, 1959, pp. 26–40.

53 The Dalai Lama, 1985, p. 187.

54 Ibid., p. 189.

55 Ibid.

56 Barshi.

57 Rinchen Dolma Taring, 1970, p. 226.

58 TR, March 1969. pp. 3–7.

59 Nehru's speech in the Lok Sabha, on 4 May 1959. (As reproduced in Raja Hutheesing, 1960. p. 41.)

60 In Tibetan, *bya-ma dkrog-par sgo-nga len.*

61 This was also confirmed by Luishar and Takla.

62 The Dalai Lama, 1985, pp. 186–8.

63 Ibid. The Dalai Lama has written in his autobiography that 'my letters to the Chinese general were written to disguise my true intentions'. He says: 'I felt and still feel that they were justified.'

64 Phala.

65 Ibid. The message was taken to the Indian Mission by a monk official, Tralkhang Khenchung. According to Nehru the first the GOI heard about the demonstration in Lhasa was on 11 March. He received a telegram from the Indian Consulate dated 10 March, and a second telegram was received on 14 March. Most probably, Phala's message was sent on the latter date. The reports from the Indian Consular must have been alarming, for the GOI recognised the seriousness of the events in Lhasa. On 14 March Nehru told the Lok Sabha that 'there was a clash of wills in Lhasa'. See Prime Minister's Reply to the debate in the Rajya Sabha on 4 May 1959, as reproduced in Chanakya Sen, *Tibet Disappears*, Asia Publishing House, 1960, pp. 198–9.

66 Sarvepalli Gopal, 1984, p. 88.

67 There have been a number of books and articles written by Westerners arguing that the Dalai Lama's flight was 'engineered' by the CIA. One of the widely quoted articles is by T. D. Allman, 'On the CIA's role in the Tibet: Pawn to

check Peking', which appeared in the *Guardian*, 31 December 1973. He writes: 'According to sources with first hand knowledge, the Dalai Lama's departure was engineered by the CIA.' See also Tom Grunfeld, 1987, pp. 150–1. Quoting George Patterson as a source, he asserts that the CIA was planning to spirit the Dalai Lama out of Tibet long before the March Uprising. L. Fletcher Prouty, 1973, writes that without the CIA's help the Dalai Lama could not have escaped to India, an assumption shared by Grunfeld. They claim that 'the logistics of the operation were too complex' for the Tibetans to have carried out. There is no evidence to support these claims.

68 Tibet, 1950–67, URI, pp. 365–7.

69 Interview with Riga, who was one of the companions of Lo Nyendrak.

70 Michel Peissel, 1972, pp. 131 & 150. He writes that the Khampas were the main instigators of the Lhasa revolt and he even goes so far as to say that the Khampas actually made the decision to abduct the Dalai Lama from Lhasa. But he gives no evidence to support his conclusion. There is no doubt that many Khampa refugees living in Lhasa were active in the revolt but it is an exaggeration to say that they organised it. Peissel and others have painted an overly romantic view of the Khampas' role in the Tibetan revolt.

71 Interview with Gyasto la who was a Thangka painter living in Shelkar.

72 This is also how the international community realised that something was happening in the country. Between 20 and 24 March, Radio Lhasa stopped broadcasting. This was noted by the BBC monitoring service. Xinhua (NCNA) also did not release any stories until 28 March (SWB, No. 859, 1959, p. 2).

73 Some Tibetan refugees living in Ladakh only knew of the events in Lhasa and the subsequent escape of the Dalai Lama to India when they were told by Ladakhi Muslim merchants who heard about it through broadcasts on Pakistani radio.

74 SWB, 1959, No. 859. p. 2.

75 Communiqué on the revolt issued by the NCNA (as reproduced in *Tibet, 1950–67*, URI, pp.348–56).

76 Ibid.

77 TR, March 1969, p. 4.

78 *Tibet, 1950–67*, URI, p. 353.

79 The Dalai Lama, 1985, p. 204.

80 The letter was taken to Lhasa by Thupten Sodpa.

81 The Dalai Lama, 1990, p.154. He says that he wrote to the Panchen Rinpoche asking him to join him in India. This seems to imply that the decision to move to India had already been made. Phala's account says that the decision to cross the border was only made in Lhuntse Dzong, four days later. This is confirmed by Liushar. Athar, who radioed the decision to the CIA, also confirms that the decision was only made in Lhuntse Dzong.

82 Athar says that the two Khampa messengers were killed before they reached Shigatse.

83 In his second autobiography (1990, p. 154), the Dalai Lama claims that a cook assigned to him during the escape was trained by the CIA. He is clearly mistaken on this point. Athar and Lhamo Tsering, two of the main people responsible for running the CIA operation inside Tibet, assured me that at the time there were only two CIA-trained agents – Athar himself and Lotse.

84 Andrug Gonpo Tashi, 1973, p. 106.
85 The Dalai Lama, 1985, p. 212.
86 Interview with Tenzin Sonam/ Ritu Sarin. Athar claims that he discussed with the CIA the possibility of sending a plane to pick up the Dalai Lama and his party.
87 The Dalai Lama, 1985.
88 Order of the State Council of the Chinese People's Republic, Tibet 1950–1967, URI, pp. 357–8.
89 Although the GOI had granted asylum for the Dalai Lama and the party, they were at first ambivalent about the large number of refugees crossing the border.
90 I am grateful to Sherab Tharchin for giving me a number of copies of letters that were sent to his father's newspaper.

EIGHT The International Response and Tibet at the UN

1 Keesing Contemporary Archives (KCA), No. XI, 1959–1960, p. 16802.
2 FO 371–115018, Nehru's letter to Anthony Eden, dated 29 January 1955.
3 According Sarvepalli Gopal, 1984. Vol. 3, p. 89. Zhou also told Panikkar in 1954 that granting asylum to the Dalai Lama would not be considered an 'unfriendly act'.
4 Subimal Dutt, *With Nehru in the Foreign Office*, Minerva, 1977, p. 150. (The author was the Indian Foreign Secretary, 1954–1961.) Dutt does not mention Menon by name, he merely writes about 'A senior colleague of his [Nehrus], one in whom he had great confidence'. Dutt also says that the Soviet Union made it known that they wanted India to refuse asylum for the Dalai Lama (Dutt, op. cit., p. 210).
5 KCA, No. XI, 1959–1960, p. 16800.
6 Ibid.
7 FO 371–141591/ 171758. Nehru's letter to Harold MacMillan 6/4/59. S. Dutt, the Foreign Secretary, told the British High Commissioner that India cannot declare 'open door' for all refugees (FO 371–141592).
8 In 1959, the opposition parties had only a few members in the Parliament. In fact the Communist Party constituted the largest opposition party with 31 MPs; the second largest was the Praja Socialist Party with 19 MPs. Other parties did not have more than 10 MPs each. With Congress domination, it was unlikely that any motion by the opposition would have succeeded in parliament.
9 Nehru's statement in the Lok Sabha on 27 April 1959, as reproduced in Chanakya Sen, *Tibet Disappears*, 1960, p. 188.
10 Nehru's statement in the Lok Sabha on 30 March 1959, as reproduced in Chanakya Sen, 1960, p. 165.
11 According the Nehru's biographer (Sarvepalli Gopal, 1984, Vol. 3, p. 89), 'there is no evidence to suggest that the GOI were aware of the American complicity in the flight of the Dalai Lama'. Nehru's letter to MacMillian says that arms were dropped in Tibet by the Guomindang.
12 Apart from a general desire to avoid any involvement in the Cold War, the relationship between India and America was at a low point. In January 1959 a

treaty had been signed between Pakistan and the United States agreeing that the US would supply 'non-conventional' weapons and establish launching sites for missiles. India had objected to these developments.

13 Personal source.
14 I have used the text of the Tezpur Statement as reproduced in *Tibet, 1950–67*, URI, pp. 375–8.
15 Ibid.
16 Ibid., 'Commentary on the So-called Statement of the Dalai Lama,' pp. 379–85.
17 Ibid.
18 As reproduced in Raja Hutheesingh, 1960, pp. 91–2.
19 *Tibet, 1950–67*, URI, pp. 388–93.
20 FO 371–141595. British High Commissioner's report.
21 FO 371 141593. A telegram from the British High Commission, Delhi to CRO. Malcolm Macdonald wrote: 'the PM [Nehru] insisted that India's interest in Tibet was "historical, sentimental, and religious and not essentially political".'
22 Ibid.
23 Sarvepalli Gopal, 1984, p. 90.
24 Subimal Dutt, 1977, p. 152. He writes that 'the Dalai Lama spoke calmly and showed no trace of bitterness against anybody despite the physical and the mental strain through which he had passed,' and adds: 'The talk with the Dalai Lama had a strange effect on Nehru for the rest of the day. He was in a reflective and reminiscent mood.' Dutt omits the detail of the discussion and merely reproduces Nehru's speech in parliament giving his account of the meeting.
25 The Dalai Lama, 1990, p. 162.
26 Ibid.
27 FO 371–141593. Note of a talk with Mr Nehru on Tibet held on 29 April.
28 The Dalai Lama, 1990, p. 161.
29 Ibid.
30 Sarvepalli Gopal, 1984, p. 90.
31 G. Parthsarathi, *Jawaharal Nehru's letters to Chief Ministers*, Vol. 5, 1958–1964, Oxford University Press, India, 1989, p. 227 (my italics).
32 FO 371–141593. According to Nehru, the Dalai Lama concurred with him.
33 Ibid.
34 FO 371–141592.
35 Ibid.
36 FO 371–141593. Notes of a conversation between Mr Davies of Australia House and Messrs Trench and Dalton of CRO.
37 FO 371–141593.
38 *Herald Tribune*, 23 April 59.
39 FO 371–141596.
40 SWB, FE/16/C/6, 2 May 1959.
41 A report from the British Embassy in Beijing to the Foreign Office. F0 371–141594.
42 'The Revolution in Tibet and Nehru's Philosophy', by the editorial department of the *People's Daily*, 6 May 1959. Reproduced in Chanakya Sen, 1960, pp. 330–56.

43 The Chinese accused the Americans of poisoning Sino–Indian friendship. Such a view was also held by left-wing elements in India. According to Karunakar Gupta *(Spotlight on Sino-Indian Frontiers,* New Book Centre, Calcutta, 1982, pp. 14–15), this view was also shared by Sarder Panikkar, the former Indian ambassador to China. He told Gupta that the reasons for deteriorating relationship were (1) a powerful American lobby was operating in India and (2) Apa Pant, the Indian Political officer in Sikkim, who supposedly had influence over leading Indian politicians including Jai Prakash Narayan and President Rajendra Prasad. K. Gupta (pp. 37–8) cites CIA aid to the Khampas as evidence of the US poisoning of Sino–Indian relations. Did the CIA influence Indian politicians like Narayan et al. and were they involved in the massive anti-Chinese reaction that dominated the Indian press? There was no doubt that the CIA was operating on a large scale in India but it is not clear how far they influenced Indian public opinion on Tibet.
44 Subimal Dutt, 1977, pp. 155–6.
45 FO 371–141596. Note of a conversation between Malcolm Macdonald and Jaya Prakash Narayan.
46 Ibid.
47 The International Commission of Jurists is a non-governmental organisation of 35,000 lawyers in 53 countries (mostly Western) with consultative status in the UN Economic and Social Council.
48 Chanakya Sen, 1960, p. 412.
49 The report does not deal with the status of Tibet before 1913, it only deals with the status of Tibet between 1913 and 1950 and concludes that Tibet was *de facto* independent. The Chinese accept that during this period their authority in Tibet was absent but they argue that the absence of authority was the result of foreign aggression (i.e. British machinations) and that therefore, the absence of Chinese authority did not create a legal situation. In October 1959, the Chinese convened a meeting of the International Association of Democratic Lawyers, an organisation of lawyers from the Communist bloc plus some left-wing lawyers from Western countries who concluded that the situation in Tibet between 1913 to 1950 was *ex iniuria ius non critur.*
50 The detailed report was not published until September 1960.
51 The transcript of the press conference was republished in *The Question of Tibet and the Rule of Law. A Preliminary Report*, published by the International Commission of Jurists, 1959, Document 20, pp. 200–3.
52 FO 371–141596.
53 Ibid.
54 He also travelled to Japan at the same time, but I have not been able to find out whether the Japanese gave a similar assurance or not.
55 An account of Nehru's discussion with the Dalai Lama was given to the British High Commissioner by Dutt, the Indian External Minister. FO 371–141597.
56 S. Dutt, 1977, p. 157.
57 Chanakya Sen, 1960, pp. 470–2.
58 FO 371–141600.
59 Ibid.
60 Ibid.

61 Ibid.
62 The Chinese Nationalists would have undoubtedly told the Irish that they would not accept any resolution based on the legal status of Tibet.
63 This is based on the British records of the meeting. F0 371–141600.
64 The Tibetans asked to meet the British Prime Minister but the visit coincided with the 1959 General Election. As a result the Prime Minister and the Foreign Secretary were busy with campaigning.
65 FO 371–141602.
66 Selwyn Lloyd's speech to the UN on 17 September 1959.
67 *Tibet in the United Nations 1950–1960*, p. 230.
68 In 1959 Chinese in Malaya constituted 37 per cent of the population. The ethnic Chinese population in south-east Asia was staunchly pro-PRC and looked with pride at the emergence of the new China. The Communist parties were also dominated by ethnic Chinese and they received support from the PRC. The Malays saw the strong affinity between the PRC and the Chinese population in their country as a potential danger.
69 FO 371–141605.
70 FO 371–150710.
71 SWB, 1960, 7/3/60, p. A1/1.
72 FO 371–150712. The Tibetans wrote several times to the British urging them to support Tibet's appeal to the UN and Shakabpa held meetings with the British High Commissioner in Delhi. The British stressed that these meetings were held only as a courtesy to the Dalai Lama as a respected religious leader.
73 In 1960 the Dalai Lama sent New Year's greetings cards to the British Prime Minister and Foreign Secretary, causing a great deal of confusion and debate in the FO. The FO instructed the High Commissioner in Delhi to inform the Dalai Lama of the receipt of the cards. The High Commissioner, ever mindful of diplomacy, wrote back to the FO saying that he could not reply to the Dalai Lama's card because it would be seen as establishing formal contact with the Tibetan government-in-exile. He advised that the Prime Minister's Office and the FO should send a direct reply by ordinary mail. The FO, mindful of their position, immediately objected to the suggestion, claiming that since the offices of the Prime Minister and FO were higher than the High Commission in Delhi, a direct letter would mean that they had given higher recognition.
74 FO 371–150710.
75 Letter from Gyalo Dhundup to British Foreign Office, FO 371–150713.
76 FO 371–150713.
77 The Dalai Lama's letters to the Secretary General are reproduced in *Tibet in the United Nations, 1950–1960*, pp. 232–8.
78 Ibid., p. 311.
79 FO 371–150712. When the Indians refused to give travel documents, the Tibetans reapplied on the pretext of travelling for medical treatment for the Dalai Lama's mother. The Indians became suspicious when Gyalo Dhundup's, Shakabpa's and Sandu Rinchen's names appeared with those accompanying the Dalai Lama's mother. The Indians were even reluctant to provide travel documents for her and told the Tibetans that the treatment could be obtained in

India. Eventually travel documents were provided for the Dalai Lama's mother and Mrs Taring to travel to London.

80 FO 371–150719. A copy of the letter was given to the British by the Australian High Commission, in Delhi

81 Ibid.

82 The Dalai Lama, 1990, p. 194. He writes that the Indian Prime Minister Shastri was thinking of recognising the Tibetan government-in-exile but died before he made his final decision. If India had recognised the Tibetan government-in-exile it would have been most likely that China would have broken off diplomatic relations.

NINE Reform and Repression

1 CHC, Vol. 14, 1987, p. 513.

2 The Chinese also noted that Russian economic aid to India was increasing. In September 1959 Russia agreed to extend more than $375 million for India's 3rd Five Year Plan, doubling its total previous aid.

3 Peng Dehuai, *Memoirs of a Chinese Marshal, The Autobiographical Notes of Peng Dehuai (1898–1974)*, Foreign Language Press, Beijing, 1984, p. 489.

4 It may be that the Tibetan issue was discussed but without information having been made available. In view of the important role played by the army, the subject would have been most directly dealt with in secret by the Military Affairs Sub-Committee of the Central Committee. Apart from Zhou Enlai's work report to the NPC, no high-ranking Chinese leader made any direct public statement on the subject.

5 There is also the question of the internal struggle within the Communist Party hierarchy. We know that the main opposition to Mao came from Marshal Peng Dehuai, who was the head of the North-West Military Region. In his own account, Peng Dehuai claimed that he had the Tibet issue in mind when the Lushan Conference was convened, but he never had the chance to bring it to discussion. Mao had successfully ousted Peng from power (see Kenneth Lieberthal, 'The Great Leap Forward and the Split in the Yenan Leadership', in CHC, Vol. 14, 1987, p. 11). It may be possible that the ousting of Peng Dehuai made the officials from the North-West Military Region stationed in Tibet reluctant to voice their criticisms.

6 An interesting account of events immediately after the revolt was written in Tibetan by a Ladhaki monk who was captured by the Chinese: Lobsang Jampa, *Escape from Hell*, 1962, p. 4 (published by G. Tharchin, Kalimpong).

7 Another famous slogan was: 'Under the sky there is no escape from the Communist Party and PLA.'

8 This story was told by the Dalai Lama at a hearing of Members of the European Parliament in Brussels, 25 April 1990.

9 Tang Tsou, *The Cultural Revolution and Post-Mao Reforms, A Historical Perspective*, University of Chicago Press, 1988, p. 26.

10 Order of the State Council of the Chinese People's Republic, in *Tibet 1950–1967*, URI, p. 357.
11 Ibid.
12 SWB, 1959, No. 859, p. 2.
13 The Dalai Lama was considered to have been abducted as so retained his position on paper.
14 SWB, 1959, No. 861, p. 4.
15 Ibid.
16 Zhou Enlai's report on the work of the government to the First Session of the Second NPC, SWB, 18 April 1959 (New Series), FE/5/C2/20.
17 Chang Ching-wu, The Victory of Democratic reform in Tibet, SCMP, No. 2218, 1960, pp. 29–36.
18 SWB, 1959, FE/3/C/1.
19 SCMP, 1960, No. 2218, p. 31.
20 Speech by the Panchen Rinpoche at the 2nd Plenary Session of PCART, 28 June 1959 (SWB, 1959, FE/69/C/3).
21 The experiences of one prominent Tibetan, Tenzin Chodrak, the personal physician to the Dalai Lama, is detailed in John. F. Avedon, *In Exile from the Land of Snows*, A Wisdom Book, 1985, pp. 301–28. He was arrested and sent to the notorious Jiuzhen labour camp in Gansu.
22 Life in Jang Tsala Karpo labour camp is described by Tashi Palden, a monk from Dragyab, in 'Tibet Under Chinese Communist Rule, A Compilation of Refugee Statements, 1958–1975', published by the Information Office of the Dalai Lama, Dharamsala, 1976, pp. 37–52.
23 SWB, 1959, FE/9/C/4.
24 Ibid., FE/58/C/2.
25 SWB, 1959, FE/14/C//6–8.
26 Ibid., FE/22/6/59.
27 SWB, 1959, FE/58/C/2.
28 Ibid., FE/69/C/5.
29 SCMM, 1965, No. 388, p. 14.
30 SCMP, 1963, No. 5, p. 45.
31 For details of these meetings see Dawa Norbu, 1987, pp. 186–96, and Tashi Palden's statement in TUCCR, 1976, pp. 38–41.
32 SCMP, 1960, No. 2218, p. 33.
33 Dawa Norbu, 1987, p. 197.
34 Dhondup Choedon, 1985, pp. 301–28.
35 SWB, 1959, FE/69/C/2.
36 SWB, 1959, FE/69/C/4.
37 'Do Away with Feudal Prerogative of and Exploitation by the Tibetan Lamaseries', JPRS, No. 11440, 5 February 1960, p. 24.
38 SWB, 1959, FE/69/C/3.
39 This figure only accounts for the number of monasteries and monks in TAR.
40 According to the NCNA the total population of Tibet in 1959 was 1,180,000. Of course if we look at the percentage of male population it would reach nearly 20 per cent.
41 Zhong guo gong chan tang Xizang zi zhi qu zhu zhi zi liao 1950–1987 (Data for

the History of the CCP Organisation in the TAR), published by the TAR Publishing House, 1993, p. 67 (restricted circulation: hereafter cited as Data on the CCP in the TAR).

42 It is not clear from the sources whether this refers exclusively to Tibetans or to minority groups in general.

43 SCMP, 1960, No. 2218, p. 34.

44 Data on the CCP in the TAR, 1993, p. 128.

45 Pao Yi-shan, 'Hold High the Red Banner of the Thought of Mao Tse-tung and Do Our Work Well as the First Generation of Revolutionary Youth in Tibet', SCMM, 1964, No. 442, pp. 8–11.

46 SCMP, 1960, No. 2, pp. 30–1.

47 Ibid., pp. 28–9. Speech by Wang Ch'i Mei at the inaugural meeting of the Chamdo Administrative District.

48 In Xinjiang the demobilised troops had played an important role in the economy and integration of the region with China. See Donald H. McMillen, *Chinese Communist Power and Policy in Xinjiang, 1949–1977*, Westview/Dawson Replica Edition, 1977, pp. 56–67.

49 SCMP, 1960, No. 2, p. 30.

50 Of course the Communists also found a somewhat similar problem in China. When they came to power, the membership was predominantly drawn from the countryside and in the 1950s the party was unhappy about having to rely on the urban intelligentsia as a source of cadre recruitment. The Party began to establish Party schools to train workers and peasants to form the vanguard of the reforms. However, there remained what Franz Schurmann has called the Red and the Expert contradiction; that is the regime needed urban bourgeois professionals to run the factories, schools and administration, and Red cadres to lead the revolution. See Franz Schurmann, *Ideology and Organization in Communist China*, University of California Press, 2nd edition, 1968, pp. 168–72.

51 Dhondup Choedon, 1985, p. v. She was selected as a cadre from her village and claims that her training lasted for three months.

52 SWB, 1960, FE/318/B/3.

53 SCMP, 1960, No. 14, p. 45.

54 Franz Schurmann, 1968, p. 165.

55 'Tibet Today', PR. 1964, No. 54, pp. 18–20.

56 This kind of misreporting of statistics was widespread in China and the issue of the accuracy of government grain production figures was raised by Marshal Peng Dehuai. The failure of the Great Leap Forward, for example, was concealed by deliberately distorting figures.

57 For details of the new tax, see 'Provisional Measure for the Collection of Patriotic Public Grain Tax'. Adopted at the 34th Meeting of the Standing Committee of the PCART, 4 August 1960, SCMP, 1960, No. 34. pp. 20–5.

58 Ibid.

59 JPRS, 1962, No. 1298, pp. 97–8.

60 Traditionally the Tibetan peasants paid taxes to their manorial lords.

61 *jin* is equal to 0.5 kilograms.

62 *Tibet, 1950–59*, URI, p. 426.

63 Dittmer, 1987, p. 35. According to Dittmer industrial production decreased by 38.2 per cent and agricultural output fell by 26.3 per cent.
64 CHC, Vol. 14, 1987, p. 370.
65 Barbara Barnouin and Yu Changgen, *Ten Years of Turbulence: The Chinese Cultural Revolution.* Kegan Paul International, London, 1993, p. 303.
66 June Teufel Dreyer, 1976, p. 175.
67 SCMM (Supplement), 1967, No. 179, pp. 1–5.
68 During the period other minority leaders were rehabilitated, notably Long Hun and the Hui leader, Ma Sung-t'ing: June Teufel Dreyer, 1976, p. 187.
69 Frederick Teiwes, *Politics and Purges in China: Rectification and the Decline of Party Norms 1950–1965*, M. E. Shrape, inc. Dawson, 1979, p. 483.
70 Ibid., p. 446.
71 Fairy Sessions for Bourgeois Elements. SWB, 1961, FE/ W110/A/5. It was reported in May 1961 that less than one million people were involved in the campaign. This confirms that it was mainly targeted at the so-called 'Bourgeois Elements', former leaders of industry, religious figures, the upper strata of the minority nationalities and members of political parties who had accepted the Communist rule.
72 Jamphel Gyatso, *Master Panchen.* This biography of Panchen Rinpoche was published shortly after his death in 1989 by the Oriental Publishing House in Beijing. However, in the wake of Tiananmen incident in May 1989 and the subsequent shift towards a more hard-line policy, the book was withdrawn from general circulation. The authorities argued that hitherto-unknown facts about the treatment of Panchen Rinpoche during the Cultural Revolution and facts about the Tibetan uprising revealed in the book were too sensitive for discussion during the difficult period. The book certainly bring to light many new accounts of Tibet's recent history. In many ways it was groundbreaking in its frankness and treatment of Tibet's recent past. Even in the original Chinese publication the authorities expunged figures cited of the number of Tibetans killed during the anti-rebellion campaign in eastern Tibetan. I have used a privately translated manuscript of the book; hereafter it will be refered to as Jamphel Gyatso, 1989.
73 Jamphel Gyatso, 1989.
74 Ibid.
75 Ibid.
76 *Current Scene*, 1961, Vol. 1, No. 1, pp. 1–8.
77 Ibid.
78 Jamphel Gyatso, 1989.
79 Ibid.
80 *Tibet, 1950–1970*, URI, pp. 428–9.
81 Ibid.
82 Ibid.
83 Jamphel Gyatso, 1989.
84 Ibid.
85 Ibid.
86 Ibid.

87 Ibid.

88 Geshe Sherab Gyatso's attack on the Party worried his friends, and close advisers told him that he should withdraw his statement. Chen Mo, a Chinese disciple who had acted as interpreter, refused to translate. During Geshe Sherab Gyatso's speech Chen Mo felt so nervous that he had to be replaced by an official interpreter appointed by the United Front. Later Chen Mo asked the officials not to print Geshe Sherab Gyatso's speech in the written report and submitted a revised written statement.

89 According to Jamphel Gyatso the petition was entitled: 'A report on the sufferings of the masses in Tibet and other Tibetan regions and suggestions for future work to the Central Committee through the respected Premier Zhou.'

90 SCMM, 1967, No. 179, pp. 1–5. This pamphlet was produced by a group calling itself 'Headquarters of Lhasa Rebels and Capital's Revolutionary Rebel Headquarters Going to Tibet'. It is said that the Seventy Thousand Character Petition was entitled 'Result, Defect, Analysis and Improvement on the Work of Suppressing Rebellion and Reform in Tibet'.

91 Here the Panchen Rinpoche was mainly concerned with the situation in eastern Tibet, in Tibetan-dominated areas in Qinghai, Gansu and Sichuan. In these areas the Tibetan population came under pressure from the resettlement of large numbers of Chinese into the region. There is no doubt that thousands of Tibetans in the region were either killed in the suppression of the revolt or died as the result of economic disaster. The situation in Tibet proper was different, but it is interesting to note that figures released by the State Statistical Bureau in November 1954 give the total population of Tibet as 1,273,969 while the figure released by NCNA in 1959 is 1,180,000. It seems from the official Chinese statement that there was a 7.4 per cent decline in Tibetan population in Tibet (TAR). It is difficult to explain the discrepancy between the two figures. The decline cannot be attributed to either the reforms or the crushing of the revolt as both events occurred after 1959.

92 Jamphel Gyatso, 1989.

93 SCMM, 1967, No. 179, pp. 1–5.

94 Kao Feng of Qinghai and Zhang Chong Liang of Gansu were dismissed from their posts. Panchen Rinpoche's criticism also related to these two regions.

95 Anon.

96 Jamphel Gyatso, 1989.

97 Anon.

98 SCMM, 1967, No. 179, pp. 1–5.

99 This in some ways relates to the campaign in China proper reversing verdicts, where cadres who suffered during the anti-Rightist campaign were rehabilitated. Deng Xiaoping declared that 80 to 90 per cent of the verdicts passed during the campaign were wrong and issued a notice that punishments levelled against them should be ignored.

100 Ibid. Later, during the Cultural Revolution, Ngabo and other members of the panel were accused of only releasing their relatives.

101 Jamphel Gyatso, 1989.

TEN War in the Himalayas

1 In 1942 Nehru wrote: 'The future of which I dream is inextricably interwoven with close friendship and something almost approaching union with China'. See Krishna Hutheesingh, *Nehru's Letters to His Sister*, Faber & Faber, 1963, p. 95.
2 Sarvepalli Gopal, 1984, p. 127.
3 After the flight of the Dalai Lama, demonstrations were organised in most Indian cities. After demonstrators burned an effigy of Mao, the Chinese protested to the Indians that it was an insult to the Chinese leader.
4 The basic Chinese and Indian claims are put forward in letters exchanged between the two Prime Ministers. Zhou's letter to Nehru, 8 September 1959, sets out China's position (see, *White Paper* II, pp. 27–33) and the Indian stand is made clear in Nehru's response, dated 28 September 1959 (*White Paper* II, pp. 34–52.
5 The critics of Indian claims argued that Nehru was deliberately misled by Indian officials in the Historical Division of the Ministry of External Affairs; see K. Gupta, 'Hidden History of the Sino-Indian Frontier', Part 1, 1947–54, and Part II, 1954–1959, *Economic & Political Weekly*, 11 May 1974, pp. 721–6 and 765–72.
6 There are many books which have outlined the historical origins of the Indo-Tibetan border in great detail. Alastair Lamb is extremely thorough in his two-volume *The McMahon Line: A Study in the Relations between India, China and Tibet, 1904–1914* (Routledge & Kegan Paul, London, 1966). See also *The China–Indian Border. The Origins of the Disputed Boundaries* (Chatham House Essays), Oxford University Press, 1964. The *Report of the Officials of the Government of India and the People's Republic of China on the Boundary Question*, published by the Ministry of External Affairs of the GOI in 1961, is one of the main primary sources on the subject. While there are numerous publications from India, there are few publications from the Chinese side.
7 Such was the confusion of the border alignment between Tibet and India during the British occupation of India, one of the border markings applied by Sir Henry MacMahon showed some part of Aksai Chin as a part of Tibet. Jasbir. K. Singh, 1988, op. cit., p. 80.
8 It has to be noted that Pakistan saw the negotiations between India and China over Ladakh, which they claimed as part of Kashmir, as illegal, and implying Chinese recognition of India's occupation of a disputed territory. If China had signed a border agreement with India, it would naturally have been tantamount to Chinese recognition of Indian sovereignty in Kashmir.
9 The Indians claim that the boundary between Tibet and the Indian states of Punjab, Himachal and Uttar Pradesh was confirmed by the Sino-Indian trade agreement of 1954.
10 The actual exchange of the notes took place in Delhi on 24 and 25 March 1914.
11 Most Tibetan officials also did not know the exact details of the notes exchanged between Lochen Shatra and MacMahon. In a 1960 *Xinhua*, Chensel Khunphel la (*spyan gsal Kun 'phel lags*), one of the closest officials of the 13th Dalai Lama, said that he never heard of the exchange of notes between Lochen Shatra and MacMahon.

12 The Tibetans were aware of the groups inhabiting these areas, known as *blo ba*. The tribes are Akas, Daflas, Miris, Abors and Mishmis.
13 The main objective of the Simla Conference was to define the border between Tibet and China. The Tibetans had participated at the conference in the hope of gaining secure and legal recognition of Tibetan independence.
14 Alastair Lamb, 1989. p. 469.
15 The British clearly recognised that the acceptance of the agreement had serious international implications. The agreement certainly breached the Anglo-Russian agreement of 1907.
16 Alastair Lamb, 1989. p. 415. Lord Harding, the Viceroy of India, had dismissed the exchange of notes between Lochen Shatra and McMahon as outside the mandate of the Simla Convention. He went so far as to say that the notes represented the 'private views' of Sir Henry McMahon.
17 Alastair Lamb, 1989, p. 468.
18 Phuntsog Tashi Takla, who worked in the Foreign Bureau, told me that the Chinese were particularly interested in where the Tibetans thought their border with India, Nepal and Bhutan lay.
19 *Xinhua* carried an interview with Sambo, whose family was a direct descendant of the 7th Dalai Lama. He mentioned that his family had a manorial estate in Tawang district granted by the Tibetan Government.
20 White Paper II, p. 39, Nehru to Zhou Enlai, 28 September 1959; see also Zhou's letter to Nehru, 8 September 1959, pp. 29–30.
21 It is interesting to note that Hugh Richardson was equally dismissive of the territorial demands and advised Delhi not to take seriously the Tibetan claim, which he saw as an 'attempt to test the Indian attitude' (see Richardson, 1984, p. 174).
22 *Report of the Officials of the GOI and the PRC on the Boundary Question*, published by the Ministry of External Affairs, 1961, p. 25.
23 India reaffirmed Tibet as a 'region of China' by signing the Sino-Indian Trade Agreement of 1954.
24 *The Times*, 8 September 1959.
25 There is some conflict as to whether Zhou Enlai ever made such an offer to Nehru. Two of the chief officials in the Indian External Ministry, Subimal Dutt and Krishna P. Menon, give different accounts. In his biography Dutt writes that Zhou never made such a proposal. However, this was the only solution that could be proposed, given the fact that each side was in occupation of the disputed regions. The Chinese had secured complete control of the Aksai Chin and the Indians had moved into the Eastern Sector.
26 Neville Maxwell, *India's China War*, Penguin Books, 1972, p. 277.
27 In December 1959 President Eisenhower visited India.
28 Lhamo Tsering.
29 Kenneth Galbraith, *A life of Our Times, Memoirs*, André Deutsch, London, 1981, pp. 394–7.
30 Ibid. Galbraith claims that with the help of Robert Kennedy, he 'persuaded the President [J. F. Kennedy] to bring these to an end'.
31 One of the reasons for their objections may be explained by internal rivalries in the State Department and the CIA. The CIA's work among the Tibetans was

carried out by the Far East Section, whose objective was to destabilise China. But the objective in India (and South Asia) was very different: to win over the Indians to the Western side. Therefore, it was natural that the ambassador and the CIA station officer felt that aid to the Tibetans would undermine their work.

32 This was told to me by a number of Tibetans who were in training in Colorado.

33 Lhamo Tsering.

34 Ibid.

35 Leo E Rose, *Nepal: Strategy for Survival*, University of California Press, 1971, p. 227.

36 In 1960 China also signed a border agreement with Burma, where they accepted the alignment drawn by the British and which in fact consisted of the continuation of the MacMahon line. During this period China also reached border agreements with Mongolia and Pakistan.

37 On 15 December 1960, King Mahendra ousted the elected Congress Government of B. P. Koirala and assumed political control of the country. It is possible that if Koirala's Government had been in power, the Tibetans may not have been allowed to establish the base in Mustang. The Nepalese Foreign Minister said at a press conference that Nepal would not object to the PLA crossing the Nepalese border in pursuit of Tibetan resistance fighters. The Chinese, however, preferred authoritarian monarchical rule to the Congress Government, which it viewed as an extension of the Indian Congress Party.

38 Lhamo Tsering.

39 In a speech to the TAR People's Congress on 28 March 1987, the Panchen Rinpoche said that the PLA was able to win the war 'because the Tibetans provided the logistic service with their backs and pack animals'.

40 Neville Maxwell, 1972, p. 317.

41 Sarvepalli Gopal, 1984, p. 218.

42 It is beyond the scope of this book to analyse the details of the events which led to the war, a subject which has received a great deal of attention both in India and abroad. Views on the cause of and blame for the war naturally vary according to the writer's support for India or China. Earlier works published in India and the West tended to lean slightly towards India. In 1970, Neville Maxwell, a former *Times* correspondent in India, published *India's China War*, which argued that the failure of the border negotiations and the war lies with India. The book was received favourably by Beijing and serialised in a Chinese newspaper while the Indian Government banned publication. The Indian side of the case is presented in numerous books published in India, notably: B. N. Mullick, *The Chinese Betrayal*, and J. P Dalvi, *Himalayan Blunder*. Sarvepalli Gopal's 3-volume biography of Nehru also provides a defence of India's case.

43 Lhamo Tsering.

44 Of course during the war, CIA became actively involved in advising the Indians. The American Embassy in Delhi was staffed with the top ranking CIA officials like W. Lowrie Campbell, reported to be CIA's authority on mountain warfare and Desmond FitzGerald, the CIA's chief of clandestine operations.

ELEVEN Socialist Transformation of Tibet

1 Many Western apologists for China like to portray the period as a triumph of science over superstition. Edgar Snow, one of the most noted China watchers, wrote that the authority of the lamas was 'undermined by the magic of science' and 'Lamaism and its gods were formally entering the limbo of forgotten folklore'. See *The Long Revolution*, Hutchinson & Co, London, 1973, p. 196.

2 Tibet, 1959–1967, URI, p. 449.

3 See statements in TUCCR by Pema Lhundup, pp. 103–9 and by Wangdu Dorji, pp. 110–14.

4 This is also true of China itself. After coming to power the Communists adopted more simplified characters. In other minority areas a similar language policy was adopted; among the Uygur and the Miao, for example there were attempts to introduce a romanized script. See Henry G. Schwarz, 1962, CQ, No. 12, pp. 170–82.

5 The Lhasa dialect was chosen as the standard for written Tibetan.

6 The changes can be best gleaned by reading the *Collected Works of Mao*, which became required reading for workers, students and cadres.

7 These terms later lost all their original meaning and were used merely as terms of abuse without objective meaning, so that a 'reactionary' or 'revisionist', for example, is anyone the Party happened to identify as an enemy at a given time.

8 Khrushchev argued that in Soviet Union, under the leadership of the Communist Party, class struggle was longer an issue and the Communist Party was a party for all people.

9 Quote from B. Brugger, 1978, p. 25.

10 For translation of the article see SCMM, 1964, No. 428, pp. 8–18.

11 Ibid.

12 Jamphel Gyatso, 1989.

13 Frederick C. Teiwes, 1979, p. 508.

14 Jamphel Gyatso, 1989.

15 Frederick C. Teiwes, 1979, p. 510.

16 The Four Clean Ups referred to attempts to rectify corrupt practices in (1) economic accounting; (2) public granaries; (3) state and collective properties, and (4) assessment of work points.

17 SCMP 1968, No. 223, pp. 20–2.

18 It is interesting to note that in areas where the Chinese were confronted with difficulties they were ready to abandon ideology for practical considerations. For example while 1963 saw more radical policies adopted in Tibet, in Xinjiang where the Communists were faced with the problem of mass exodus of Uygurs and Kazakhs to Russia, the Chinese adopted more liberal policies with the promise of cultural freedom. This was an attempt to counter Soviet propaganda.

19 The Chinese use of the term class does not accord with the strict Marxist interpretation of class: the Chinese tend to use the term to mean a wide range of social groupings, using occupational status as the chief criterion.

20 Dhondup Choedon, 1978, p. 33.

21 Literally, 'wealthless class'.

22 CNA, 1965, No. 548. p. 2.
23 Sui Jia, 1991, p. 5.
24 SCMM, 1964, No. 442, p. 11.
25 Ibid., p. 10.
26 It is interesting to note that in Tibetan it is more common to use the term 'fatherland' (*pha yul*) while it is more common in Chinese to use the term 'motherland' (*zuguo*, which strictly speaking means 'ancestral' land in Chinese).
27 Tibet, 1950–1967, URI, p. 447.
28 Kunsang Paljor, 1977, p. 26.
29 Jamphel Gyatso, 1989.
30 According to his biographer, the Panchen Rinpoche had once mentioned that he liked dogs, especially Alsatians, to Chen Yi, who immediately asked the Kunming Military if they could donate one or two Alsatians. Somehow the authorities in Kunming dispatched twelve Alsatians to Shigatse, which later became the evidence that the Panchen Rinpoche had raised fighting dogs.
31 The horses too were presents, this time given by Ulanfu.
32 It is not clear why Chape turned against the Panchen Rinpoche, his Guru. Did he do it purely to obtain personal gain or was he coerced by the Chinese? I am inclined to believe that the Chinese must have put a great deal of pressure on to him to procure such a denunciation.
33 Mao later told Edgar Snow (1973, p. 196) that 'the Panchen Lama had been keeping company with some bad eggs of the old privileged class who not only obstructed change but had organised a clique. *Certain members of the clique had exposed their plans* [My emphasis].'
34 During the campaign against Lin Biao and Confucius, the CCP produced a pamphlet entitled 'Deeper Refutations of Lin Biao and Confucius while criticising Dalai and Panchen'. The pamphlet contains examples of *tra-yig* and a record of the Panchen Rinpoche's dreams.
35 Jamphel Gyatso, 1989.
36 In Tibetan, *tang la ngo rgol*, *mi dmangs la ngo rgol* and *mes rgyal kha bral tu gtong ba*.
37 In Tibet's case from feudalism to communism.
38 Tibet 1950–1967, URI, 1968, p. 472.
39 *Xinhua*, 31 December 1964.
40 Anon.
41 *Xinhua*, 26 December 1964.
42 This statement was made by Mao in a conversation with an African delegation visiting Beijing in August 1963. However, it was more than likely that the theoretical shift in Mao's thoughts on the nationality question were first discussed at the 10th Plenum of the 8th Central Committee, when Mao made the pronouncement 'never to forget the class struggle'. This had placed the 'class struggle' at the centre of the political campaign.

It is also interesting to note that Mao's dictum about the national problem being essentially class struggle was not meant merely for internal policy consumption. More importantly it was an appeal to the international working classes. Mao drew a direct parallel to events in the United States, where the Civil Rights movement was at its height. Mao saw this as essentially class conflict and was using the idea of class struggle as an extension of China's foreign policy. Later the Chinese were to expound a new concept of the UN based on an alliance of Afro-Asian and Latin American countries.

43 *Xinhua*, 31 December 1964.

44 *Xinhua*, 5 August 1965.

45 The right of Regional Autonomy was enshrined in the PRC Constitution adopted on 20 September 1954. Article 3 says: 'The People's Republic of China is a unitary multinational state. All the nationalities are equal. Discrimination against, or oppression of, any nationality, or any act undermining the unity of the nationalities is prohibited. All the nationalities have freedom to use and foster the growth of their spoken and written languages, and to preserve or reform their own customs or ways. Regional autonomy shall be exercised in areas entirely or largely inhabited by minority nationalities. Such autonomous areas are inalienable parts of the People's Republic of China.'

46 Tibet 1950–67, URI, p. 426.

47 There are four other Autonomous Regions: Inner Mongol AR, set up in May 1947 nearly two years before the Communists took power in China; Xinjiang Uygur AR, founded on October 1955; Guangxi Zhuang AR, established in May 1958, and Ningxia Hui AR, established in October 1958.

48 *Xinhua*, 31 December 1964.

49 In the past they had existed virtually free from any Tibetan Government interference and had very little connection with the Tibetans. Therefore, the Tibetan revolt in 1959 did not have any impact on these groups. Some Tibetans escaped through their territories to India. These people had more in common with the tribal peoples of Assam. There are few anthropological or scholarly researches into the history and culture of these groups. Later Chinese sources often cite conflicting figures for Monpa and Lopa population. *Questions and Answers about China's Minority Nationalities* (compiled by Ma Yin, 1985) gives Lopa population as 2,000 or more and, for Monpas, it gives 6,000 or more. Yet in 1979 the Monpas population was cited as 40,000. See *China Reconstructs*, No. 7, July 1979, p. 54.

50 Article 68 of PRC's 1954 constitution states: 'In all autonomous regions, autonomous prefectures, and autonomous counties where nationalities live together, each nationality is entitled to appropriate representation in the organs of self-government.'

51 Tibet 1950–1967, URI, 1968, p. 493.

52 Ibid., p. 505.

53 SCMM, 1965, No. 498, pp. 17–22.

54 Ibid.

55 China Reconstructs, November 1965.

56 Data on CCP in TAR, Lhasa 1993, p. 128.

57 Ibid.

58 George Moseley, 1965, p. 16.

59 *Peking Review*, 25 May 1978.

60 Israel Epstein, 1977, p. 33.

61 June Dreyer, 1976, p. 202.

62 SCMP 1968, No. 218, p. 6.

63 Qi Yan, 1991, p. 3.
64 In 1961, Nepal accepted the Chinese offer to build a road linking Tibet with Kathmandu, although there was no doubt that the road was of strategic interest to both countries. For Nepal the road connected outlying areas with Kathmandu and for the Chinese it allowed easy access to rice from the Terai and other manufactured goods. The Chinese imported Nepalese jute, cigarettes and sugar. However, severe economic constraints in Nepal meant that its ability to supply was limited.
65 Israel Epstein, 1983, p. 96.
66 TUCCR, 1976, p. 149.
67 CHC, Vol. 14, 1987, p. 365.
68 Dhondup Choedon, 1978, p. 5.
69 Israel Epstein, 1983, p. 97.
70 According to Dhondup Choedon, in the Red Flag commune there was a strict quota for agricultural production. 70–80 per cent of the production was geared towards cereals, with the emphasis on wheat. 20 per cent was devoted to pulses and mustard.
71 Dhondup Choedon, 1978, p. 28. She writes that the cadres received an additional 15 yuan per month.
72 Israel Epstein, 1977, p. 35.
73 *Peking Review*, 7 August 1985, p. 22.
74 Ibid., p. 43.
75 Dhondup Choedon, 1978, p. 8.
76 Ibid., p. 35.
77 Wang Xiaoqing and Bai Nanfeng, 1991, p. 67.
78 Many informants remember that, during the Tibetan New Year, the Chinese used to broadcast a special message to the Tibetans in India, inviting them to return. In 1966, one of the broadcasts began: 'The alleyways in Lhasa are filled with the smell of oil from the frying of Khabse.'
79 Goldstein and Beal, 1989, pp. 622–3.
80 Dhondup Choedon, 1978, p. 27. She remembers being told by a Chinese cadre that the communes should be praised because: '(1) It is easy to advise the people, (2) it is easy to assign work, (3) it is easy to collect news, (4) it is easy to bring reforms, (5) it is of great benefit to the nation, (6) it is easy to organise and hence there is a more effective use of labour of the masses and (7) it is easy to lead the masses.'

TWELVE The Cultural Revolution

1 See the general assessment of the academic writing on the Cultural Revolution, Lucian Pye, 1988, pp. 597–612.
2 See the full text, 'Resolution on CPC History, 1949–1981', Beijing, 1981.
3 Ibid., p. 81.
4 Anita Chen, 1992, writes that the official definition of the CR given by the Party in 1981 was a 'gross distortion of historical reality'. The 1981 document, she

says, 'can be considered the victors' last say on the matter after a protracted feud'.

5 Israel Epstein, 1977, p. 33.
6 It is interesting that the term 'Green Brain' crept into modern usage as a term of abuse.
7 Tibet, 1950–1967. URI, p. 603.
8 The importance of the identification of the beginning of the Cultural Revolution as May 1966 has been noted, see Anita Chen, 1992. Deng Xiaoping is thereby exonerated from involvement in the decision to launch the Cultural Revolution and identified as a victim, because it is known that after May 1966 Deng himself became a target of the Red Guards.
9 In Tibetan, Four Olds, *bsam-blo rnying-pa, rig-gnas rnying-pa, yul-srol rnying-pa, goms-gshis rnying-pa,*.
10 Tibet 1950–1967, URI, p. 604.
11 SCMP, 1968, No. 216, p. 27.
12 Ibid.
13 Ibid., No. 230, pp. 8–9.
14 Ibid., No. 216. p. 27.
15 Ibid., p. 28.
16 Ibid., p. 28.
17 Barnouin and Changgen, 1993, p. 72
18 Ibid.
19 SCMP, 1968, No. 216, p. 29.
20 Ibid.
21 It is interesting to note that while the Red Guards were saying that the *Kha ta* was a remnant of the feudal tradition and it should be forbidden, the adorning of Mao's portrait with *Kha ta* was seen as acceptable. Chinese propaganda at the time stressed how people would use *Kha ta* to wrap Mao's red book to show their love of him. There were many other contradictory and humorous occasions when the Red Guards and staff working at Lhasa Radio debated what constituted proletarian language and what language was appropriate to use when speaking about Chairman Mao. If one used non-honorific language one was liable to attack for not respecting the great leader and if one used honorific language, another Red Guard faction would attack you for going against the teaching of the beloved leader of the people.
22 This is from a four-page pamphlet written in Tibetan that was distributed in Lhasa by the Red Guards from Lhasa teacher training college. I obtained this pamphlet in Kathmandu.
23 *ser smad ri-'bur sprul-sku.*
24 According to figures given by the TAR Vice Chairman in 1987, there were 2,700 monasteries in TAR, 80 per cent of which were destroyed by 1965. The rest, apart from thirteen, were destroyed during the Cultural Revolution.
25 SCMP, 1968, No. 205, pp. 22–3.
26 Dhondup Choedon 1978, p. 64
27 See the detailed denunciation of Deng Xiaoping by Red Guards from Shanghai. Tibet 1950–1968, URI, pp. 689–99.
28 Jung Chang, 1993, p. 343. She says that during her student days in 1964, her

class was taken to see an exhibition about Tibet, where there was a display of 'photos of dungeons crawling with scorpions, and horrific instruments of torture, including a tool for scooping out eyes and knives for cutting the tendons in the ankles. A man in a wheelchair who came to our school to give a talk told us he was a former serf from Tibet who had had his ankle tendons severed for some trivial offence'.

29 SCMP, 1968, No. 15, p. 30.
30 Tibet 1950–1967, URI, p. 631.
31 I have in mind people like Sambo, who was a member of the Tibetan delegation which signed the 17-Point Agreement; Phagpa Gelek Namgyal; the head Lama of Chamdo Kabsopa, a former Khalon who had been supportive of the Chinese; and Tsego, a former mayor of Lhasa. There are too many to mention them all.
32 There is a general belief that Zhou Enlai personally interfered and had Ngabo transferred to Beijing.
33 Interview with Tsering Wangchuk, a former member of staff at the *Tibet Daily*, now living in India.
34 SCMP, 1968, No. 179, pp. 1–5.
35 SCMP, 1968, No. 216, p. 32.
36 Ibid.
37 Stanley Karnow, 1984, pp. 306–7.
38 *Tibet, 1950–1967*, URI, p. 686.
39 SCMP, 1968, No. 216, p. 33.
40 Ibid.
41 *Tibet, 1950–1967*, URI, p. 631.
42 Ibid., p. 630.
43 Here the rebel groups were emulating events in China. The first rebel organisation, the Shanghai Workers' Revolutionary Rebel Headquarters, was set up nearly two months earlier, on 9 November.
44 *Tibet, 1950–1967*, URI, p. 633.
45 SCMP, 1968, No. 215, p. 20.
46 Keith Forster, 1990, p. 5.
47 SCMP, 1986, No. 215, pp. 18–24. This report by the Tibet Military Commission on the situation in Tibet was first made public by the Red Guards from the Gyenlog group. They naturally condemned the report as biased and falsifying the true situation.
48 Ibid., p. 21. The figures are cited in the above mentioned report. A reliable report published by Tibetans in India says that Gyenlog had 20,000 followers and Nyamdrel 50,000.
49 It is interesting to note that the original report mentioned above cites the ethnic composition of each group. However, when it was published by the Red Guards, these figures had been erased. It was most likely that the authorities felt the people would have taken the figures as showing ethnic division between the two factions.
50 *pyi-lo 1965 lor bod rang-skyong ljongs brchugs-pa nas bar bod-nang gi gnas-tsul la zhib 'jug zhus- pa'i pyongs bsthoms snyan zhu*, p. 25.
51 SCMP, 1968, No. 178, pp. 10–13.
52 Ibid., No. 225. p. 42.

53 *Tibet, 1950–67*, URI, p. 665.
54 SCMP, 1968, No. 223, pp. 33–4. The documents mention that many drivers suffered from arthritis, hemoptysis and high-altitude sickness.
55 SCMP, 1968, No. 204, p. 25.
56 One regulation highlighted by the Red Guards was access to medical treatment in China. The Party would pay 50 per cent of medical treatment. The regulation stated that here no class background would be taken into account. SCMP, 1968, No. 201, p. 25.
57 Ibid., No. 213, p. 19.
58 Ibid.
59 Ibid.
60 SCMP, 1967, No. 225, p. 37.
61 Ibid., No. 215, p. 25.
62 Ibid., No. 178, p. 1.
63 Ibid., No. 204, p. 18–21.
64 Before the Communist takeover of power in China, Zhang Guohua had served as a regimental commissar of the Red First Army Corps headed by Lin Biao. During the war against the Japanese, Zhang also served as a battalion commissar of Lin Biao's 115th division.
65 William Whitson, 1973, p. 331.
66 Yang Tsang-hao, 1976, p. 50.
67 SCMP, 1968, No. 228, p. 6.
68 Ibid., p. 16.
69 Yang Tsang-hao, 1967, p. 51.
70 Ibid.
71 Ibid., p. 49.
72 Ibid.
73 Ibid., p. 50.
74 SCMP, 1968. No. 215, p. 21.
75 Ibid., No. 216, p. 41.
76 Ibid.
77 Chien Yu-shen, 1969, pp. 27–9.
78 See the detailed appraisal of Zhou Renshan's work in Qinghai, SCMP, 1968, No. 230, pp. 41–50.
79 Tibet 1950–67, URI, p. 671.
80 SCMP, 1968, No. 215, p. 24.
81 Ibid., p. 16.
82 Tibet 1950–67, URI, pp. 666–9.
83 I have not gone into detail in each of the incidents. There are a number of Red Guard eye-witness accounts of the events published in SCMP.
84 *Facts and Features*, 1968, No. 16, pp. 18–19.
85 See two opposing views on Zhou Renshan, one by the Gyenlog and the other by the Nyamdrel faction in SCMP, 1967, No. 221, pp. 25–9.
86 SCMP, 1968, No. 228, pp. 17–18.
87 Ibid., No. 231, pp. 8–9.
88 See notes of the meeting: *Tibet, 1950–67*, URI, pp. 683–8.
89 *Facts and Features*, 1967, No 1, pp. 21–2.

90 SCMP, 1968, No. 218, pp. 12–14.
91 *Facts and Features*, 1968, Vol. 1, No. 12, pp. 22–3.
92 Ibid.
93 Jurgen Domes, 1970, pp. 122–45.
94 Chien Yu-shen, 1969, p. 24.
95 CNA, 1969, No. 789, p. 1.
96 But Data on Party states that Zhou Renshan and Wang Qimei were dismissed from the Party in August 1971 at the 1st session of the TAR CPC Deputy Congress.
97 Jurgen Domes, 1970, p. 124.
98 Jamphel Gyatso, 1989.
99 This is also the case with another important Tibetan official, Ragti, who became Party Secretary in the 1980s.
100 Interview with Tenzin Chodrak, who was from Nyemo and now lives in India. One of his relatives was executed along with Thrinley Choedron.
101 I have been told that this method is also used in China. The point is not the way a spade was used, but the interpretation made by the Chinese and the farmers who were forced to abandon the practice.
102 See Jigme Ngabo, 1988, pp. 24–5.
103 In Tibetan, '*rnam sa-la zher-pa 'i skyab*'.

THIRTEEN Revolution Postponed?

1 In traditional Tibetan society blacksmiths, butchers and other craftsmen were considered as outcasts and suffered considerable social prejudice.
2 Names such as 'Liberation', 'Red Flag', and 'Modernity'. See Tiley Chodag, 1988, p. 266.
3 Once ransacked, the monasteries and the temples quickly deteriorated, in part because after the Cultural Revolution the local people and the Chinese began to strip the ruins of all their timber for fuel.
4 May Mao Tsetung Live for Ten Thousand Years.
5 SWB, 1970, No. 3298/B11/3.
6 SWB, 1970, No 3275/B11/16.
7 The organisational history of the TAR's Party and government system.
8 SWB, 1970, No. 3533/B11/13.
9 The authorities began to release painstakingly compiled statistics such as the number of free haircuts carried out by the PLA, the number of farm implements that they repaired, and amount of manure the PLA moved to the fields. This was meant to show how much the army was helping the people.
10 Lucian W. Pye, 1975, p. 500.
11 In the past Tibet had very close religious and cultural ties with Kalmyk and Buryat Mongols, who were followers of Tibetan Buddhism. After the Russian Revolution this connection came to an end.
12 Jurgen Domes, 1977, p. 143. He notes that a review of the purge of the PLA after the Lin Biao affair reveals that 65 per cent of the officers who were removed were from the 4th Field Army.

13 Israel Epstein, 1983, p. 162.
14 *Current Scene* 1971, No. 10, p. 14.
15 Israel Epstein, 1983, p. 12.
16 *Current Scene* 1971, No. 10, p. 14.
17 SWB, 1991, No. 4210/B11/10.
18 SWB, 1973, No. 4210/B11/10.
19 Ibid., No. 4228/B11/1.
20 Ibid., No. 4220/B11/14.
21 It is interesting to note that in 1965 she had been nominated President and in 1981 she was reinstated to the same post.
22 On 28 April 1972 in Beijing, Prince Sihanouk proclaimed his Cambodian government-in-exile and the setting up of a liberation army. China espoused his cause.
23 Jamphel Gyatso, 1990.
24 KCA, 1971, Vol. XVIII. p. 24773.
25 The Tibetan operation in Mustang had been kept secret and there had never been any publicity. In 1964 George Patterson and the British film-makers Adrian Cowell and Chris Menges managed to get to Mustang and film the Tibetan guerrillas attacking a Chinese military convoy. When the news of this reached the CIA, an urgent meeting was held. The CIA instructed the Tibetans to confiscate the films at all costs, but Patterson and his friends had managed to leave India. The film was later broadcast in Britain by ITV as 'Raid into Tibet'. However, Patterson and the film-makers were unaware of the connection between the CIA and the Tibetans.
26 Lhamo Tsering.
27 Without archival sources it is difficult to date the exact time when the decision was reached.
28 Ibid.
29 Ibid.
30 It should be noted that the Chinese were active in arming anti-Indian groups. The Chinese supplied and trained the Nagas and Mizo groups, which were demanding independence from India. Throughout the 1970s and early 80s the Chinese continued to support Mizo National Front (MNF) and its military wing, the Mizo National Army. Laldenga, the leader of MNF, was a frequent visitor to Beijing. I met him when he was living in England in the early 1980s, and he told me that some of the soldiers from the MNF may have been trained in Tibet. There were also leaders of Naga National Council (NNC), like Thuingaleng Muivah and Thinoselie Medom Keyho, living in Beijing. Both of them were attending Party school in Beijing and their fighters were being trained in China.
31 Kissinger described talks between Mrs Gandhi and Nixon as 'a dialogue of the deaf', adding that Nixon's comments about Mrs Gandhi 'were not always printable'. See H. Kissinger, 1979, pp. 848–81.
32 Henry Kissinger, 1979, p. 862. Kissinger also noted that Zhou Enlai was so concerned about India that 'he spent most his time talking about India'.
33 In 1970s the Tibetans claimed there were 80,000 refugees in India. This would mean that at the best estimate between 10 and 20 per cent of male Tibetan

refugees were under arms. Also see Avedon, 1984, p. 165. He says there were 10,500 Tibetans serving in the Indian army.

34 After the war, when the Indian Government organised a parade to celebrate victory, the Tibetans were not allowed to participate and no ceremonies were held to award the men their medals. The existence of Unit 22 was kept secret by the GOI but in the 1980s popular Indian papers began to write about the group and the abuse of power by Indian officers.

35 Henry Kissinger, 1979, p. 906.

36 Although Kissinger does not mention Tibet, he would have recognised that this was one of China's main concerns.

37 SWB, 1970, No. FE/3328/A3/1.

38 Girish Pant, 1991, p. 155. It is interesting to note that by the late 1970s Chinese aid had dropped to 2.7 per cent.

39 The Nepalese Government appointed the well-known Nepali anthropologist Dor Bhadur Bista as Consul General in Lhasa.

40 Lhamo Tsering.

41 Ibid.

42 SWB, 1975, No. FE/4812/B11/19.

43 SWB,1974, No. FE/4762/B11/21.

44 Ibid.

45 SWB, 1974, No. FE/4691/B11/15.

46 SWB, 1974, No. FE/4780/B11/14.

47 SWB, 1974, No. FE/4765/B11/6.

48 *Chinese Law and Government*, Vol. 4, 1982, p. 71.

49 Bernard Vincent Olivier, 1993, p. 149.

50 SWB, 1976, No. FE/5154/B11/12.

51 In Tibetan, *'pa-dring ma-dring 'di las M'o-kru'u dring-che'*.

52 The Gang of Four were Jiang Qing; Zhang Chunqiao, the head of Shanghai CCP; Wang Hongwen, who was also a cadre from Shanghai; and Yao Wenyuan, who wrote the article attacking Wu Han's *The Dismissal of Hai Rui from Office*. The article had marked the beginning of the Cultural Revolution.

53 Edward Luttwak, a prominent American academic, accompanied Schlesinger and wrote a number of articles about his trip. Luttwak was clearly not impressed with the situation there. Despite Chinese attempts to impress the visitors, the Americans left with the impression that Tibet had become a Chinese colony. Luttwak's article was reproduced in TR, 1977, Vol. XII, No. 4, pp. 14–17.

54 It is interesting to note that the Chinese authorities refused to allow the visitors to purchase local newspapers. This was confirmed by Charles Benoit, who accompanied Schlesinger as the official interpreter. See TR, 1977, Vol. XII, Nos 1 & pp. 5–6.

55 Maxwell was the author of *India's China War* which blamed India for the 1962 war. The Tibetans were familiar with Maxwell's name as his book had been translated into Chinese and reprinted in the *People's Daily*. It was given such importance that it became required reading for political study sessions.

56 Han Suyin's book was entitled *Lhasa the Open City*, A definite misnomer. She boldly asserted that Tibet had never been so open and cited as evidence the

visits of the King of Nepal, the Shah of Iran's sister and James Schlesinger, none of whom could be regarded as ordinary visitors to Tibet.

57 Visits by Maxwell, Greene and Han Suyin brought extensive positive coverage of Chinese rule in Tibet. Maxwell's articles appeared in all the major Western newspapers, including *The Times* and the *New York Times*; and Greene's film was shown on the BBC and other Western television channels. They managed to create the view among Western liberals and leftists that the Chinese had brought economic and social benefits to Tibet.

58 SWB, 1976, No. FE/5343/B11/7.

59 SWB, 1978, No. FE/5996/B11/17.

60 Ibid.

61 The 'three types' were cadres who during the Cultural Revolution (1) had gained power illegitimately (2) had engaged in factional struggle and (3) had killed and robbed.

62 Paul Hyer, 1969, pp. 24–62.

63 Laszlo Ladany, 1988, p. 285.

64 Yang Jingren, 1981–82, p. 93.

65 An article entitled 'On the protracted nature of the nationalities problem in the Socialist period' appeared in the 6 April edition of the *People's Daily*. Authors Liu Xianzhao and Wei Shiming stressed that 'the final disappearance of the nationalities can be realised progressively only after Communism has been attained in the whole world.' The authors therefore considered it 'utterly absurd and stupid to deny the existence of a nationalities problem in the socialist period'. See English translation of the article, SWB, 1979, No. FE/6099/B11/10–12.

66 Yang Jingren, 1981–2, p. 100.

67 TR, 1977, Vol. XII. No. 5, p. 5.

68 TR, 1979, Vol. XIV, No. 11, p. 19.

69 SWB, 1979, No. FE/6193/C/3.

70 The issue was discussed at length in an article in the *People's Daily*, 6 April 1979. See English translation SWB, 1979, No. FE/6099/B11/10.

71 The Chinese argue that the figures on Tibet cannot be compared with other regions because Tibet began from a lower starting point.

72 *Xinhua*, 21/10/1983. The same report goes on to say that the Bureau of Geology and Mineral Resources had discovered over 60 minerals in the TAR. The region has the largest deposit of lithium in the world and one of the largest reserves of chromite, as well as the second largest reserve of copper in China. The report also lists the following minerals: porphyry copper, tungsten, gold, silver and iron.

73 The Four Modernisations were in the areas of agriculture, economy, military and science and technology.

74 In the case of the Muslim minority, there was the added dimension of wooing the oil-rich Arab countries to invest in China.

75 Jamphel Gyatso, 1989.

76 For a list of prisoners released, see TR, 1978, Vol. XIII, No. 11. pp. 5–6.

77 SWB, 1979, No. FE/6099/B11/12.

78 Jamphel Gyatso, 1989.

79 SWB, 1979, No. FE/6032/B11/10–12.
80 Yang Jingren, 1980, p. 100.
81 SWB, 1979, No FE/6149/B11/12.
82 Israel Epstein, 1983, pp. 517–21.
83 It is interesting to note that in April 1979 the formation of a Tibetan Communist Party-in-exile was announced.
84 TB, 1979, Vol. XI, No. 2, p. 5.
85 *dus-dran thengs bchu-dgu pa'i bka'-slob. chab-srid lam-ston*. Dhramsala, 1982, p. 285.
86 Ibid., p. 326.
87 Because the border between India and Tibet was closed, the Tibetans could only enter via Nepal. The Tibetans only had visas for Nepal and once reaching Kathmandu, they made their way to Dharamsala without valid travel documents. However, the Indians turned a blind eye to the illegal entry of Tibetans.
88 SWB, 1979, No. FE/6020/A3/12–13.
89 Ibid.
90 In 1991 Gyalo Dhundup conducted a lengthy private interview giving an account of his involvement in Tibetan affairs since 1949. The interview was videotaped and was widely circulated in the Tibetan community (hereafter cited as Gyalo Dhundup video).
91 Some members urged the Dalai Lama to cancel the visit while others accused the leaders of failing to inform the Assembly of Tibetan People's Deputies, which had functioned as a parliament in exile. See TR, 1979, Vol. XIV, No. 8, p. 7.
92 In 1951 when the Tibetan delegation went to Beijing they travelled using Chinese passports.
93 Some of the members of the Tibetan delegation told me that the Chinese officials who accompanied them were at a loss for words. They became embarrassed and walked away from the scene.
94 Ngabo Jigme, 1988, p. 25.
95 The Chinese briefly imprisoned a woman called Tsering Dolma, who shouted, 'Bod rang-tsen' (Independence for Tibet). The delegation protested to the Chinese and she was later released and allowed to leave for India.
96 The BBC's *The World About Us* series made a two-part documentary film produced by Simon Normanton on the history of Tibet in the twentieth century. The film was a mixture of nostalgia for the lost Shangri la and the destruction of Tibet's unique cultural heritage by the Chinese. The second part of the documentary made extensive use of the films taken by the Dharamsala delegation.
97 TB, 1980, Vol. XII, No. 2, p. 8.
98 Jamphel Gyatso, 1989.
99 Ibid.
100 It is interesting to note that at same time the Communist Party reappointed another former cadre to head Xinjiang, another sensitive region. Wang Enmao, for a long time Party Secretary in Xinjiang, was purged in 1969 but was sent back in 1981 to take up his old job.

101 Wang Yao, 1994, pp. 385–289.
102 Ibid., p. 288.
103 Ngabo Jigme, 1988, p. 26.
104 Ibid.
105 SWB, 1980, No. FE/6436/B11/1–6.
106 Ibid.
107 SWB, 1980, No. FE/6430/B11/3.
108 Yang Jingren, 1980, p. 93.
109 The letter was released to the press by the Dalai Lama on 4 September 1993. For full version of the letter see TR, 1993. Vol. XXVIII, No. 10, 1993, pp. 9–14.
110 Yang Zhongmei, 1988, p. 143.
111 Yang Jingren, 1981–2.
112 *Xinhua*, 29 November 1984. The proposal was not made public when it was given to Gyalo Dhundup in 1981. (Italics added for emphasis.)
113 FEER, 16 July 1982, p. 29.
114 In September 1981 Marshal Ye Jianying, chairman of the NPC, announced a nine-point proposal for Taiwan's unification with the mainland: (1) talks should be held as soon as possible to realise the 'great cause' of reunification; (2) there would be exchanges of mail, trade and tourism; (3) after reunification Taiwan would be a special administrative zone and Beijing would not interfere with local affairs; (4) Taiwan could keep its socio-economic system, including private property and foreign investment; (5) people in authority would take new jobs but retain their political power; (6) the PRC would give aid to help resolve local financial problems; (7) there would be freedom of entry and exit; (8) Taiwan's investments in China would be guaranteed, and (9) Beijing hoped that the Guomindang would stick to its one-China policy and 'join hands in promoting reunification'.
115 It is interesting to note that the idea of unification of all the Tibetan-speaking population applies only to regions under Chinese control. There was no attempt among the refugees to identify Tibetan-speaking populations of Nepal, India and Bhutan as part of Greater Tibet.
116 Tseten Wangchuk Sharlho, 1992, p. 44.
117 Wang Yao, 1994, p. 289.
118 It is interesting to note that the Chinese never published precise figures on the number of cadres withdrawn from Tibet.
119 'Tibet; Today and Yesterday', *China Today*, 1983, No. 7, p. 16.
120 Data on CCP in Tibet, 1993, p. 296.
121 'Tibet; Today and Yesterday', *China Today*, 1983, No. 7, p. 43.
122 SWB, 1982, No. FE/6959/B11/7. This phrase was used by Chen Yun in an article in *Red Flag*, 1982.
123 It was reported that 83 per cent of the cadres were under forty-five years of age. SWB, 1985, No. FE/7900/B11/11.
124 SWB, 1981, No. FE/6717/C/15.
125 SWB, 1980, No. FE/6335/B11/1.
126 Ibid., No. FE/6436/B11/3.
127 Article 116 empowered the Regional People's Congress to examine and ratify

laws passed by the NPC. Article 117 gave the autonomous regions the right of fiscal management of the region. (This was the right to decide on revenue generated locally). Article 118 gave the regions the right to plan and control economic development. Article 119 gave similar rights over education, culture and science. Article 120 allowed autonomous regions to organise their public security.

128 It is beyond the scope of this book to deal with all the legislative changes made during the 1980s. The most significant new law was the electoral law of the NPC.

129 For example, when in 1981 the NPC passed China's Marriage Laws, the regional NPC in Tibet decided that age of marriage in Tibet should be two years less for men and women than the limit set in China of 22 for a man and 20 for a woman.

130 In Tibetan, *'brug-skad rgyab-nas char-par btang-yar min-'dug.*

131 Wang Xiaoqing and Bai Nanfeng, 1991, p. 68.

132 An Zhiguo, BR, 1987, No. 47, p. 5.

133 TR, 1983, Vol. XVIII, No. 2, p. 6.

FOURTEEN A Road to the New Tibet

1 Hu Yaobang presided over seven meetings, and his speeches were compiled into a single document entitled, '*blo-mthun Hu'u ya'o pang gis bod-ljongs kyi las-dun skor gyi bzhugs-mol tshogs-'du 'i thog gnag-ba' a gsung-bshad*' (hereafter cited as Hu Yaobang, 1984).

2 SWB, 1984, No. FE/7806/B11/5.

3 Hu Yaobang, 1984.

4 Ibid.

5 Ibid.

6 In Tibetan, '*Hu'u ya'o pang gis Rag-'di skyobs-pa red'*.

7 SWB, 1984, No. FE/7642/B11/6.

8 A speech by the Panchen Rinpoche to the TAR Standing Committee meeting of the NPC held in Beijing on 28 March 1987. This document was published in 1991 by the Tibetan government-in-exile in Dharamsala under the title 'The Panchen Lama Speaks' (hereafter cited as the Panchen Lama, 1987).

9 SWB, 1984, No. FE/7641/B11/5.

10 Ibid., No. FE/7688/B11/1.

11 Ibid.

12 SWB, 1984, No. FE/7632/B11/1.

13 M. Goldstein and C. Beall, 1989, p. 634.

14 Wang Xiaoqing and Bai Nanfeng, 1991, p. 30.

15 Ibid.

16 Ibid.

17 bid.

18 SWB, 1984, No. FE/7645/B11/7.

19 TB, 1985, Vol. XV, No. 5, p. 1.

20 *Xinhua*, 29 November 1984

21 SWB, 1983, No. FE/7237/B11/15.
22 The Panchen Lama, 1987, p. 15.
23 SWB, 1985, No. FE/7987/B11/7.
24 Ibid., No. FE/7980/B11/8.
25 It is also interesting to note that almost all young Tibetans who escaped to India and Nepal in the late 1980s gave as chief reason for leaving the country the wish to join monasteries in India.
26 He was released from prison in November 1987 and died not long after at his relatives' home in Lhasa.
27 Interview with Palden Gyatso.
28 SWB, 1985, No. FE/7885/B11/7. This figure was said to be incomplete.
29 Ibid.
30 SWB, 1984, No. FE/7785/B11/3.
31 Tseten Wangchuk Sharlho, 1992, p. 50.
32 SWB, 1985, No. FE/7858/B11/7.
33 Catriona Bass, 1990, p. 50.
34 For the English translation of some of the poetry written by this group, see Barme and Minford, 1989, pp. 432–53.
35 SWB, 1985, No. FE/8043/B11/6.
36 SWB, 1985, No. FE/8047/B11/1.
37 They were Ragdi, Pasang, Gyaltsen Norbu, Tenzin and Dorje Tsering (SWB, 1985, No. FE/8113/B11/7).
38 SWB, 1986, No. FE/8372/B11/16.
39 SWB, 1986, No. FE/8614/B11/7.
40 Ibid., No. FE/8633/B11/15.
41 Ibid.
42 SWB, 1987, No. FE/8667/B11/5.
43 SWB, 1986, No. FE/8314/A3/3.
44 Ibid., No. FE/8317/A3/3.
45 FEER, 4 June 1987, p. 46.
46 Ibid., p. 42.
47 It has to be remembered that in 1986 Soviet troops were still in Afghanistan.
48 FEER, 4 June 1987, p. 4.
49 Gyalo Dhundup video, 1990.
50 The Panchen Rinpoche, 1987, p. 7.
51 Ibid.
52 As noted in an earlier chapter the Chinese had in the past provided military aid to secessionist groups in India. Therefore, there were always Indian fears about Chinese aid to various anti-government movements.
53 In India at the time some senior politicians and the press were calling for India to use 'Tibet as a lever on China'. See article by Rashat Puri in the *Hindustan Times*, reproduced in *India Weekly* (London) 12–18 September 1987. Lt-Gen. E. A. Vas, former commander in charge of Eastern Command, wrote an article in the *Asian Herald* (28 May–3 June 1987), where he urged Indian politicians not to adopt a rushed military means to evict the 'intruders' and went on to say that 'there are more ways of countering China's political aims' than military means.

54 TR, 1986, Vol. 21, No. 8, pp. 8–10.
55 It should be noted that Tibet was listed as a separate country in the 1945 Act. It had gone unnoticed either by the Tibetans or the Nationalist Chinese, who were occupied with the civil war. Had it come to the notice of the Guomindang government at the time, it is most likely that they too would have protested at the inclusion of Tibet as a separate State.
56 TR, 1986, Vol. 21, No. 11, p. 6.
57 For example, Senator Jesse Helms, renowned for his anti-Communist views, and Senator Claiborne Pell, who is regarded as a moderate.
58 SWB, 1987, No. FE/8624/A1/2.
59 *China Daily*, 29 September 1987.
60 Five-Point Peace Plan for Tibet (Information Office, Central Tibetan Secretariat, Dharamsala), pp. 4–5.
61 On 28 September 1987, the State Nationality Affairs Commission issued a detailed rejection of the Dalai Lama's proposal.
62 He was the Deputy Secretary in the Bureau of East Asian and Pacific Affairs.
63 State Department Bulletin, Vol. 87, No. 212a, December 1987.
64 Ibid.
65 An official Chinese account of the demonstration was given in BR, March–April 1989, pp. 27–30.
66 The Chinese said that those present had participated in the demonstration. This was directly contradicted by many Westerners. For the nature of Western tourist involvement during and after the demonstration, see Ronald Schwart, 1991, pp. 588–604.
67 At the 44th Session of the UN Commission on Human Right held in Geneva (Switzerland), on 4 March 1988, the Chinese delegation was forced to admit that the police had shot and killed Tibetans during the demonstration. The Chinese admission came after testimony given to the commission by Robert Barnett, who had witnessed the demonstration in October. He presented ten sworn statements from other eye witnesses who also confirmed that the police had aimed directly into the crowd. Barnett also showed photographs supporting these accounts.
68 Most Tibetans-in-exile believe that origin of the flag lies in great antiquity and accept that it has always been the national flag of Tibet. It was first displayed at the 1947 Inter-Asian Relations Conference.
69 *rGya-nag dbus 'thab-pyods gchig-gyus khang-gi bco-'jin Yin-ming Phu nas sku-zhab rGyal-lo Don-'grub brgyud btsan-byol gzhung-la btang-ba'i chig-tho* (hereafter cited as Yan Mingfu, 1987).
70 Ngabo, 1989. The day after the first demonstration in Lhasa, Ngabo was summoned to Beijing and a few days later met with Gyalo Dhundup. According to Ngabo, Gyalo Dhundup expressed his disbelief that the Dalai Lama had made the speech in Washington.
71 Yan Mingfu, 1987.
72 The last section of the memorandum dealt with Gyalo Dhundup. It stated that he had told them that the Dalai Lama did not advocate independence and that Gyalo Dhundup himself personally regarded independence as an unrealistic

goal. The exiled government published a rebuttal of Yang Mingfu's memorandum. On the last point the exiled government commented that it was Gyalo Dhundup's personal assessment of the Dalai Lama's position. I think this also marked the point when Gyalo Dhundup ceased to be an effective mediator. Firstly, it showed the Chinese that Dhondup was not able to influence the Dalai Lama or the exiled government. Secondly, the Chinese revelation about Gyalo Dhundup's personal views made exiled Tibetans suspicious of him.

73 Yan Mingfu, 1987.

74 *Bod-rGya dbar gyi 'bral-lam* (a document issued by the Kashag in Dharamsala 1988).

75 Gyalo Dhundup video, 1990.

76 Pema Namgyal, 1994, p. 66.

77 SWB, 1987, No. FE/8373/B11/1.

78 This was an important document published in the Party's theoretical journal, *Red Flag*, 16 June 1983. See English translation in *Missiology: An International Review*, 1983, Vol. XI, No. 3, pp. 267–89.

79 The last paragraph of the document states: 'under the socialist conditions, the only correct way to solve the religious problem is that, under the premise of protecting the freedom of religious belief, we greatly develop the socialist economy, culture, science and technology and achieve great progress in developing socialist material and spiritual civilizations so as to gradually eliminate the social and cognitive sources that have given rise to religion and enable it to exist.'

80 *Xinhua*, 9 July 1987.

81 SWB, 1986, No. FE/8373/B11/1.

82 In Tibetan, *rGya-mi ma-yong skyab or rGya-mi med-ba'i skyab* (before the arrival of the Chinese, or, when there were no Chinese) and *rGya-mi slebs-nas* (since the arrival of Chinese).

83 Zhang Tianlu and Zhang Mei, 1994, p. 63.

84 Ma Rong, 1993.

85 SWB, 1988, No. FE/0082/B2/1.

86 While Chinese pressure on Western countries is less effective, this is not the case with Asian and Third World countries, which are dependent on trade and aid from China. Soon after the Dalai Lama's visit to the United States in September 1987, he was scheduled to visit Thailand, which under pressure from China refused to grant him a visa. Similarly, Nepal has constantly refused to allow the Dalai Lama entry.

87 Address to Members of the European Parliament by His Holiness The Dalai Lama, Strasbourg, 15 June 1988.

88 The Dalai Lama's announcement was angrily criticised by hardliners in the exile community. The Dalai Lama's brother, Thubten Norbu, circulated a letter in the exile community asking the people to reject Strasbourg. For other criticisms see Phuntsog Wangyal, 'Giving Up the Struggle', TR, Vol. 23, No. 9, 1988, pp. 9–11; Jamyang Norbu, 'In Deng's Grave New World, An Illusion Dies', TR, Vol. 24, No. 8, 1989, pp.13–17; Tashi Tobgye Jamyangling, 'The Tibetan Challenge. A Political Menopause?', TR, Vol. 24, No. 2, 1989, pp. 14–17.

89 *Daily Telegraph*, 23 June 1988.
90 Sha Zhou, 1990, pp. 3–5. Also published in the *Beijing Review*, it provides in greater detail the Chinese analysis of the content of the Strasbourg proposal and their objections.
91 Ibid.
92 Ibid., p. 4.
93 Winston Lord, 1989, p. 16. (Author served as US Ambassador to China 1985–1989.)
94 The neighbouring states, Pakistan, Bhutan, Nepal and Bangladesh, would have resisted the withdrawal of China from Tibet.
95 Winston Lord, 1989, p. 16.
96 Press Release from the Chinese Embassy in New Delhi, India, 28 September 1988.
97 Some exiled Tibetans have been critical of the role played by Michael van Walt van Praag and accused him of influencing the Dalai Lama to eschew Tibetan independence (See Jamyang Norbu, TR, 1989, Vol. 24, No. 8, pp. 13–17), because they see some similarity between the Strasbourg proposal and the options he had advocated in his book *The Status of Tibet*, Westview Press, 1987, pp. 197–203. In a letter to TR, 1989, Vol. 25, No. 11, pp. 22–3, Michael van Walt van Praag denied that he had influenced the Dalai Lama or the Tibetan government-in-exile. It was unlikely that the Dalai Lama was influenced by a single individual; the ideas he had advocated in his Washington and Strasbourg speeches had been the culmination of many years of discussion within the inner circles of Dharamsala decision-makers. However, the Dalai Lama told me that the actual proposal that was distributed in Strasbourg was written by Michael van Walt van Praag.
98 TR, 1988, Vol. 23, No. 11, p. 4.
99 Gyalo Dhundup video, 1990.
100 Ibid.
101 SWB, 1989, No. FE/0039/A3/2.
102 SWB, 1988, No. FE/0082/B2/1.
103 FBIS-CHI-89-022/ 15 March 1989, pp. 39–42.

Bibliography

Official Publications

China, Violations of Human Rights. Prisoners of Conscience and the Death Penality in the People's Republic of China, Amnesty International Publications, London 1984.

Concerning the Question of Tibet, Foreign Language Press, Peking 1959.

Defying the Dragon. China and Human Rights in Tibet, a report issued by The Law Association for Asia and the Pacific Human Rights Standing Committee (LAWASIA) and the Tibet Information Network (TIN), 1991.

His Holiness the XIV Dalai Lama, Collected Statements, Interviews and Articles, Information Office, Dharamsala, 1986.

Notes, Memoranda and Letters Exchanged and Agreements Signed Between the Governments of India and China; White Paper, 1959–1963, published by Ministry of External Affairs, Government of India.

People's Republic of China, Recent Reports on Political Prisoners and Prisoners of Conscience in Tibet, Amnesty International Publications, London, AI Index ASA 17/62/91.

People's Republic of China, Repression in Tibet, 1987–1992, Amnesty International Publications, London, AI Index ASA 17/19/92.

The Question of Tibet and the Rule of Law, International Commission of Jurists, 1959.

Report of the Officials of the Governments of India and the People's Republic of China on the Boundary Question, published by Ministry of External Affairs, Government of India, 1961.

Resolution on CPC History, (1949–1981), Foreign Language Press, Beijing 1981.

Sino-Indian Boundary Question, (enlarged edition), Foreign Language Press, Peking, 1962.

Tibet, 1950–1967 (1968), Union Research Institute, Hong Kong.

Tibet and the Chinese People's Republic, a report to the International Commission of Jurists by its Legal Inquiry Committee on Tibet, Geneva, 1960.

Tibet in the United Nations, 1950–1961, issued by the Bureau of His Holiness the Dalai Lama, New Dehi.

Tibet: Proving Truth From Fact, Department of Information and International Relations, Central Tibetan Adminstration of H.H. the Dalai Lama, 1993.

Tibet, The Facts, published by Tibetan Young Buddhist Association, Dhramsala, 1990.

Tibet Under Chinese Communist Rule, a compilation of Refugee Statements, 1958–1975, Information Office & Publicity Office of His Holiness the Dalai Lama, Dharamsala, 1976 (TUCCR).

White Paper: Tibet – Its Ownership And Human Rights Situation, issued by the State Council of People's Republic of China, 1993.

English Language Sources

Addy, Premen, *Tibet on the Imperial Chessboard*, New Delhi: Academic Publishers, 1960.

——, 'Historical Problems in Sino-Indian Relations', *International Studies*, Vol. 2, 1987, pp. 18–49.

Ahmad, Zahiruddin, *Sino-Tibetan Relations in the Seventeenth Century*, Roma: Is. M. E. O., 1970.

——, *China and Tibet, 1708–1959; A Resumé of Facts*, Oxford Univeristy Press, 1960.

——, 'The Historical Status of China in Tibet', *TJ*, No. 1, 1975, pp. 24–35.

Ambrose, Stephen E., *Rise to Globalism: American Foreign Policy Since 1938*, London: Penguin Books, 1983.

——, *Eisenhower. The President. Vols. 1 & 2*, London: George Allen & Unwin, 1984.

An Zhiguo, 'Implementing Regional Autonomy Law', *BR*, No. 47, 1987, pp. 4–5.

Andrug, Gonpo Tashi, *Four Rivers, Six Ranges, Reminiscences of the Resistance Movement in Tibet*, Dharamsala: The Information and Publicity Office of H.H. the Dalai Lama, 1973.

Anon, *China's Minority Nationalities. Selected Articles from Chinese Sources*, San Francisco: Red Sun Publishers, 1977.

Anon, 'Communization of Tibet After Purge of the Panchen Lama', *Free China & Asia*, No. 3, 1965, pp. 9–13.

Anon, *Tibet: Myth vs. Reality*, Beijing Review Publication, 1988.

Anon, *Tibetans on Tibet*, China Reconstructs Press, 1988.

Aris, Michael, and Aung San Suu Kyi (eds), *Tibetan Studies in Honour of Hugh Richardson. Proceedings of the International Seminar of Tibetan Studies, 1979*, London: Aris & Phillips, 1980

Avedon, John F., *In Exile from the Land of Snows*, London: Wisdom Publication, 1984.

Barber, Noel, *The Flight of the Dalai Lama*, London: Hodder & Stoughton, 1960.

——, *From the Land of Lost Content*, London: Collins, 1969.

Barme, Geremie, and John Minford (eds), *Seeds of Fire. Chinese Voices of Conscience*, Newcastle upon Tyne: Bloodaxe Books, 1989.

Barnett, Doak A., *China's Far West. Four Decades of Change*, Boulder: Westview Press, 1994.

Barnett, Robert (ed.), *Resistance and Reform in Tibet*, London: Hurst & Company, 1994.

Barnouin, B., and Changgen Yu, *Ten Years of Turbulence: The Chinese Cultural Revolution*, London: Kegan Paul, 1993.

Bass, Catriona, *Inside the Treasure House. A Time in Tibet*, London: Victor Gollancz, 1990.

Bloodworth, Dennis, *The Messiah and the Mandarins: The Paradox of Mao's China*, London: Weidenfeld and Nicolson, 1982.

Blum, Willaim, *The CIA; A Forgotten History*, London: Zed Books Ltd, 1986.

Bogoslovsky, V. 'Tibet and the Cultural Revolution', *Far Eastern Affairs*, Vol. 1, 1976, pp. 116–22.

Bradnock, Robert, *India's Foreign Policy Since 1971*, London: The Royal Institute of International Affairs, 1990.

Branda, H. W., *The Cold Peace, India and the United States*, Boston: Twayne Publishers, 1990.

Bridgham, Philip, 'Mao's Cultural Revolution: The Struggle to Consolidate Power', *CQ*, No. 41, 1970, pp. 1–25.

Brugger, Bill, *Contemporary China*, London: Croom Helm, 1977.

Brugger, Bill (ed.), *China. The Impact of the Cultural Revolution*, London: Croom Helm, 1978.

Bull, Geoffrey, *When Iron Gate Yield*, London: Hodder & Stoughton (no date).

Cannon, Terry, 'National Minorities and the Internal Frontier', in *China's Regional Development*, ed. David Goodman, London: Routledge, 1989, pp. 164–78.

Cassinelli, C. W., and Robert Ekvall, *A Tibetan Principality, the Political System of Sa-Kya*, NY: Cornell University Press, 1969.

Chaliand, Gerard (ed.), *Minority Peoples In the Age of the Nation-State*, London: Pluto Press, 1989.

Chan, Anita, 'Dispelling Misconceptions About the Red Guard Movement', *Journal of Contemporary China*, Vol. 1, No. 1, 1992, pp. 61–85.

Chang, Chingwu, 'The Victory of Democratic Reform in Tibet', *SCMP*, No. 2218, 1960, pp. 29–36.

Chang, Kuo-hua, 'Tibet Returns to the Bosom of the Motherland, Revolutionary Reminiscences', *SCMP*, No. 2854, 1962, pp. 1–12.

Chang, Y. C., *Factional and Coalition Politics in China. The Cultural Revolution and Its Aftermath*, New York: Praeger Publishers, 1976.

Chen, Guangguo, 'A Brief Account of the Legal Regulations in the Tibetan Region Before the Democratic Reform', *Social Sciences in China*, No. 4, 1988, pp. 150–70.

Chesneaux, Jean, *China: The People's Republic, 1949–76*, Harvester Press, 1979.

Chien, Yu-shen, *China's Fading Revolution, Army Dissent and Military Division, 1967–68*, Centre of Contemporary Chinese Studies, Hong Kong, 1969.

Chu, Godwin, and Francis Hsu (eds), *Moving A Mountain. Cultural Change in China*, An East–West Centre Book, The University of Hawaii, 1979.

Choedon, Dhondup, *Life in the Red Flag People's Commune*, Dharamsala: Information Office of H.H. the Dalai Lama, 1978.

Chui, Hungdah, and June Dreyer, *Tibet: Past and Present*, Contemporary Asian Studies, No. 4, School of Law University of Maryland, 1989.

Chu Wen-lin, 'The Tibet Autonomous Region Revolutionary Committee', *Issues & Studies*, Vol. 3, 1968, pp. 18–21.

Cooper, John, *China Diplomacy. The Washington–Taipei–Beijing Triangle*, Boulder: Westview Press, 1992.

The Dalai Lama, *My Land and My People*, NY: Potala Corporation, 1985.

——, *Freedom in Exile*, London: Hodder & Stoughton, 1990.

Dalvi, J. P., *Himalayan Blunder*, Bombay: Orient Paperback, 1969.

Darwin, John, *Britain and Decolonisation. The Retreat From Empire in the Post-War World*, London: MacMillan, 1988.

de Voe, Dorsh Marie, 'The Refugee Problem and Tibetan Refugees', *TJ*, No. 3, 1981, pp. 22–42.

DeGlopper, Donald. R., 'Chinese Nationality Policy and The Tibet Question', *Problems of Communism*, Nov–Dec 1990, pp. 81–9.

Dittmer, Lowell, *China's Continuous Revolution: The Post-liberation Epoch, 1949–81*, University of California Press, 1987.

Domes, Jurgen, *China after the Cultural Revolution*, University of California Press, 1977.

——, 'The Role of the Military in the Formation of the Revolutionary Committees 1967–68', *CQ*, No. 44, 1970, pp. 122–45.

Dorje, Cedan, 'The Present Stage of Tibetology in China', *Asian Research Trends*, No. 4, 1994, pp. 145–56.

Dreyer, June Teufel, *China's Forty Million. Minority Nationalities and National Integration in the People's Republic of China*, Harvard University Press, 1976.

——, 'China's Minority Nationalities in the Cultural Revolution', CQ, No. 35, 1968, pp. 96–109.

——, *China's Political System: Modernization and Tradition*, London: MacMillan Press, 1993.

——, 'Traditional Minorities Elites', in Robert Scalapino (ed.), *Elites in the Peoples Republic of China*, University of Washington Press, 1972, pp. 416–50.

Duara, Prasenjit, 'De-constructing the Chinese Nation', *Australian Journal of Chinese Affairs*, No. 30, 1993, pp. 1–26.

Dutt, Gargi, and V. P. Dutt, *China After Mao*, New Delhi: Vikas Publishing House, 1992.

Dutt, Subimal, *With Nehru in the Foreign Office*, Calcutta: Minerva Association Publications, 1977

Ekvall, Robert, 'Nomads of Tibet: A Chinese Dilemma', *Current Scene*, No. 13, 1961, pp. 1–10.

Epstein, Israel, *Tibet Transformed*, Beijing: New World Press, 1983.

——, 'Serfs and Slaves Rule Khaesum Manor', *Eastern Horizon*, Vol. XV, No. 17, 1977, pp. 21–35.

Fairbank, John King, *The Chinese World Order. Traditional China's Foreign Relations*, Cambridge: Harvard University Press, 1968.

——, *The United States and China*, Cambridge: Harvard University Press, 1976.

——, *Cambridge History of China, 1800–1911*, Vol. 10, Part 1, Cambridge University Press, 1978.

Fan Wenlan, 'Problems of Conflict and Fusion of Nationalities in Chinese History', *Social Sciences in China*, Vol. 1, 1980, pp. 71–93.

Fei Xiaotong, 'Ethnic Identification in China', *Social Sciences in China*, No. 1, 1980, pp. 94–102.

Fisher, Margaret, Leo Rose and Robert Huttenback, *Himalayan Battleground. Sino-Indian Rivalry in Ladakh*, London: Pall Mall Press, 1963.

FitzGerald, C. P., *Mao Tsetung and China*, London: Hodder and Stoughton, 1976.

Fitzgerald, John, 'The Nationless State: The Search for a Nation in Modern Chinese Nationalism', *The Australian Journal of Chinese Affairs*, No. 33, 1995, pp. 75–105.

Fletcher, Joseph, 'The Heyday of the Ch'ing Order in Mongolia, Sinkiang and Tibet', in John King Fairbank (ed.), *CHC, Vol. 10*, Cambridge University Press, 1978. pp. 351–408.

Ford, Robert, *Captured in Tibet*, London: Pan Books Ltd, 1958.

Forster, Keith, *Rebellion and Factionalism in a Chinese Province: Zhejiang, 1966–76*, An East Gate Book: M. E. Sharpe Inc, 1990.

Friedman, Edward, 'Ethnic Identity and the Denationalization and Democratization of Leninist States', in M. Crawford Young, (ed.), *The Rising*

Tide of Cultural Pluralism: The Nation State at Bay? University of Wisconsin Press, 1993, pp. 222–42.

——, 'Reconstructing China's National Identity: A Southern Alternative to Mao-Era Anti-Imperialist Nationalism', *The Journal of Asian Studies*, Vol. 53, No. 1, 1994, pp. 67–91.

——, 'Chinese Nationalism, Taiwan Autonomy and the Prospects of a Larger War', *Journal of Contemporary China*, Vol. 6, No. 14, 1997, pp. 5–32.

Furen, Wang, and Wenqing Suo, *Highlights of Tibetan History*, Beijing: New World Press, 1984.

Galbraith, John Kenneth, *A Life of Our Times, Memoirs*, London: André Deutsch, 1981.

Gao Yuan, *Born Red, A Chronicle of the Cultural Revolution*, Stanford University Press, 1987.

Gellner, Ernest, *Nations and Nationalism*, Oxford: Blackwell, 1992.

Ginsburg, George, and Michael Mathos, *Communist China and Tibet: The First Dozen Years*, The Hague: Martinus Nijhoff, 1964.

Gladney, Dru C., 'The Peoples of the People's Republic: Finally in the Vanguard?', *Fletcher Forum of World Affairs*, Vol. 12, No. 1, 1990, pp. 62–76.

——, *Muslim Chinese: Ethnic Nationalism in the People's Republic*, Cambridge: Harvard University Press, 1991.

——, 'The Muslim Face of China', *Current History*, Vol. 92, No. 575, 1993, pp. 241–5.

——, 'Representing Nationality in China: Refiguring Majority/Minority Identities', *The Journal of Asian Studies*, Vol. 52, No. 1, 1994, pp. 92–123.

Goldstein, Melvyn C., 'The Dragon and the Snow Lion: The Tibet Question in the 20th Century', in Anthony T. Kane (ed.), *China Briefing 1990*, New York: The Asia Society, 1990, pp. 129–67.

——, *A History of Modern Tibet, 1913–1951. The Demise of the Lamaist State*, University of California Press, 1989.

——, 'Re-examining Choice, Dependency and Command in the Tibetan Social System: Tax Appendages and Other Landless Serfs', *TJ*, No. 4, 1986, pp. 79–112.

——, 'Lhasa Street Songs: Political and Social Satire in Traditional Tibet', *TJ*, Nos. 1 & 2, 1982, pp. 56–66.

——, *An Anthropological Study of the Tibetan Political System*, Ph.D. dissertation, University of Washington, 1968.

Goldstein, Melvyn C., and Cynthia M. Beall, 'The Impact of China's Reform Policy on the Nomads of Western Tibet', *Asian Survy*, No. 6, 1989, pp. 619–41.

Goodman, David, *Deng Xiaoping*, London: A Cardinal Book, 1990.

——, 'Li Jingquan and the South-west Region, 1958–66: The Life and "Crimes" of a Local Emperor', *CQ*, No. 81, 1980, pp. 67–96.
Goodman, Michael Harris, *The Last Dalai Lama: A Biography*, London: Sidgwick & Jackson, 1986.
Gopal, Sarvepalli, *Jawaharlal Nehru, A Biography, Vols 1–3*, London: Jonathan Cape, 1976, 1979, 1984.
Grunfeld, Tom, *The Making of Modern Tibet*, London: Zed Press, 1987.
Guangqin Xu, 'The United States and the Tibet Issue', *Asian Survey*, No. 37, 1997, pp. 1062–76.
Gupta, Karunakar, *Spotlight on Sino-Indian Frontiers*, Calcutta: New Book Centre, 1982.
——, 'Hidden History of the Sino-Indian Frontier', *Economic and Politcal Weekly*, Part 1, 4 May 1974; Part 2, 11 May 1974.
Han Suyin, *Lhasa: The Open City*, London: Jonathan Cape, 1977.
Hang Tianlu, 'Population Development and Changes in China's Minority Nationalities', in *A Census of One Billion People*, Hong Kong: Economic Information Agency, 1987, pp. 434–51.
Harding, Harry, *China's Second Revolution. Reform after Mao*, Washington, DC: The Brooking Institution, 1987.
Harrer, Heinrich, *Seven Years in Tibet*, London: Rupert Hart-Davis, 1953.
Havnevik, Hanna, *Tibetan Buddhist Nuns. History, Cultural Norms and Social Reality*, Oslo: Norwegian University Press, 1990.
Hinton, Harold, *An Introduction to Chinese Politics*, London: David & Charles, 1973.
Hobsbawm, E. J., *Nations and Nationalism since 1780*, Cambridge University Press, 1990.
Huang, Mingxin, 'The Tibetan Version of the 17-Article Agreement', *China's Tibet*, No. 3, 1991, pp. 12–14.
Huang, Yasheng, 'China's Cadre Transfer Policy toward Tibet in the 1980s', *Modern China*, Vol. 21, No. 2, pp. 184–204.
Hung-mao Tien, 'Sinicization of National Minorities in China', *Current Scene*, No. 2, 1974, pp. 1–13.
Hutheesing, Raja, *Tibet – Fight For Freedom*, Delhi: Orient Longmans, 1960.
Hutheesingh, Krishna, *Nehru's Letters to His Sister*, London: Faber & Faber, 1963.
Hyer, Paul, 'Ulanfu and Inner Mongolian Autonomy Under the Chinese People's Republic', *The Mongolia Society Bulletin*, No. 8, 1969, pp. 24–62.
Ispahani, Mahnaz, *Roads and Rivals. The Politics of Access in the Borderlands of Asia*, London: I. B. Tauris & Co. Ltd, 1989.
Jenner, W. J. F., *The Tyranny of History. The Roots of China's Crisis*, London: The Penguin Press, 1992.
Jiang Ping, 'Great Victory for the Cause of National Unity and Progress.

Commemorating the 40th anniversary of the peaceful liberation of Tibet', *China's Tibet*, Vol. 2, No. 1, 1991, pp. 5–11.

Jiang Ping, and Huang Zhu, 'Certain Questions in Nationalities Work' (original in *People's Daily*, 3 May 1982), SWB, 1982, FE/7025/B11/1–8.

Jing Wei (ed.), *100 Questions About Tibet*, Beijing Review Press, 1989.

Jung Chang, *Wild Swans, Three Daughters of China*, London: Flamingo, 1993.

Kaldhen, Jampel, 'Interest Rates in Tibet', *TJ*, No. 1, 1975, pp. 109–12.

Karan, Pradyumna, *The Changing Face of Tibet. The Impact of Chinese Communist Ideology on the Landscape*, The University Press of Kentucky, 1976.

Karnow, Stanley, *Mao and China: Inside China's Culture Revolution*, London: Penguin Books, 1984.

Kaul, P. N., *Frontier Callings*, New Delhi: Vikas Publishing, 1976.

Kazuo, Ogura, 'How the "Inscrutable" Negotiate with the "Inscrutable": Chinese Negotiating Tactics Vis-A-Vis the Japanese', *CQ*, No. 79, 1979, pp. 529–52.

Kim, Samuel S., *China, the United Nations, and World Order*, Princeton University Press, 1979.

Kissinger, Henry, *The White House Years*, London: Weidenfeld and Nicolson and Michael Joseph, 1979.

Kuang, Haolin, 'On the Temple Economy of Tibetan Areas in Modern Times', *Social Sciences in China*, Vol. XII, No. 3, 1991, pp. 123–55.

Kux, Dennis, *Estranged Democracies, India and the United States 1941–1991*, New Delhi: Sage Publications, 1994.

Ladany, Laszlo, *The Communist Party of China and Marxism, 1921–1985. A Self-Portrait*, London: C. Hurst & Company, 1988.

Lall, Arthur, *How Communist China Negotiates*, Columbia University Press, 1968.

Lamb, Alastair, *The China–India Border, the Origins of the Disputed Boundaries*, Chatham House Essays, Oxford University Press, 1964.

——, *Tibet, China & India 1914–1950. A History of Imperial Diplomacy*, Roxford Books, 1989.

Lapidus, Gail W., 'Gorbachev's Nationalities Problem', *Foreign Affairs*, No. 68, 1989, pp. 92–108.

Lazzarotto, Angelo S., 'The Chinese Communist Party and Religion', *Missiology. An International Review*, No. 3, 1983, pp. 287–90.

Leung, John K. and Michael Y. M. Kau, *The Writings of Mao Zedong, 1949–1976. Vol. 2*, M. E. Sharpe, 1984.

Leys, Simon, *The Burning Forest. Essays on Culture and Politics in Contemporary China*, London: Grafton Books, 1988.

——, *The Chairman's New Clothes. Mao and the Cultural Revolution*, New York: St Martin's Press, 1977.

Li Qin, and Lu Yun, 'Real Causes of "March 10 Incident" of 1959', *China's Tibet*, Vol. 1, No. 1, 1990, pp. 115–17.

Li, Tieh-Tseng, *Tibet: Today and Yesterday*, New York: Bookman Associates, 1960.

Li, Weihan, 'Regional Autonomy For Nationalities', *Chinese Law and Government. Vol. XIV*, No. 4, 1981–2, pp. 13–19.

Liao, Hollis, 'Communist China's policy towards Tibet', *Issues & Studies*, No. 3, 1981, pp. 23–35.

——, 'Tibet's Economic Reform Since Teng Hsiao-p'ing's South China Tour'. *Issues & Studies*, No. 3, 1994, pp. 15–34.

Lin, Jing, *The Red Guards' Path to Violence: Political, Educational, and Psychological Factors*, New York: Praeger, 1991.

Lindbeck, John M. H. (ed.), *China: Management of Revolutionary Society*, London: George Allen & Unwin, 1972.

Liu Ch'un, 'The Current Nationality Question and Class struggle in our Country', *SCMM*, No. 428, 1964, pp. 8–18.

Long, Jeff, 'Going After Wangdu', *Rocky Mountain Magazine*, No. 33, 1981, pp. 36–42.

Lord, Wiston, 'China and America; Beyond the Big Chill', *Foreign Affairs*, Vol. 68, No. 4, 1989, pp. 1–26.

Lu Daji, 'On the Nature of Religion', *Social Sciences in China*, No. 4, 1988, pp. 90–107.

Lu Yun, 'State Aid to Poor Counties of National Minorities', *BR*, No. 52, 1989, pp. 29–33.

Ma Rong, 'Residential Patterns and their Impact on Han-Tibetan Relations in Lhasa City, the Tibet Autonomous Region', in Greg Guldin and Aidan Southall (eds), *Urban Anthropolopgy in China*, Leiden: E.J. Brill, 1993.

Ma Rong, and Pan Naigu, 'Demographic Changes', *BR*, No. 31, 1987, pp. 21–4.

Ma Yin, *Questions and Answers About China's Minority Nationalities*, Beijing: New World Press, 1985.

MacFarquhar, Roderick, *The Hundred Flowers Campaign and the Chinese Intellectuals*, New York: Praeger, 1960.

——, *The Origin of the Cultural Revolution: 1. Contradictions Among the People, 1956–7*, Oxford University Press, 1974.

——, *The Origin of the Cultural Revolution: 2. The Great Leap Forward 1958–1960*, Oxford University Press, 1983.

MacFarquhar, Roderick (ed.), *The Secret Speeches of Chairman Mao: From the Hundred Flowers to the Great Leap Forward*, Harvard Contemporary China Series, 6. Cambridge, Mass. 1989.

MacFarquhar, Roderick, and John King Fairbank, *Cambridge History of China, Vol. 14. The People's Republic of China, Part 1: The Emergence of Revolutionary China, 1949–1965*, Cambridge University Press, 1987.

MacInnis, Donald, *Religious Policy and Practice in Communist China*, NY: The Macmillan Company, 1972.

Malhortra, Inder, *Indira Gandhi. A Personal and Political Biography*, London: Hodder & Stoughton, 1989.

Mansingh, Surjit, and Steven I. Levine, 'China and India: Moving Beyond Confrontation', *Problems of Communism*, March–June 1989, pp. 30–49.

Marchetti, Victor, and John D. Mark, *The CIA and the Cult of Intelligence*, New York: Alfred A. Knopf, 1974.

Maxwell, Neville, *India's China War*, London: Penguin Books, 1972.

McMillen, Donald H., *Chinese Communist Power and Policy in Xinjiang, 1949–1977*, A Westview/Dawson Replica Edition, 1979.

——, 'Xinjiang and Wang Enmao: New Directions in Power, Policy and Integration?', *CQ*, No. 99, 1984, pp. 569–93.

Mehra, Parshotam, *The North-Eastern Frontier. A Documentary Study of the Internecine Rivalry between India, Tibet and China. Vol. 1, 1906–14 & Vol. 2, 1914–51*, New York: Oxford University Press, 1979.

Michael, Franz, 'Traditional Tibetan Polity and its Potential for Modernization', *TJ*, No. 4, 1986, pp. 70–8.

——, *Rule by Incarnation: Tibetan Buddhism and its Role in Society and State*, Boulder: Westview Press, 1982.

Migot, Andre, *Tibetan Marches*, London: Rupert Hart-Davis, 1955.

Moody, Peter. R., 'The Reappraisal of the Cultural Revolution', *The Journal of Contemporary China*, No. 4, 1993, pp. 58–74.

Moraes, Frank, *The Revolt in Tibet*, New York: The MacMillan Company, 1960.

Moseley, George, *The Consolidation of the South China Frontier*, University of California Press, 1973.

——, 'China's Fresh Approach to the National Minority Question', *CQ*, No. 24, 1965, pp. 14–27.

——, 'The Frontier Regions in China's Recent International Politics', in Jack Gray (ed.), *Modern China's Search for a Political Form*, Oxford University Press, 1979, pp. 299–329.

Moseley, George (ed.), *The Party and the National Question in China*, Cambridge, Mass., 1966.

Mullik, B. N., *My Years with Nehru, the Chinese Betrayal*, New Delhi: Allied Publishers, 1971.

Namgyal, Pama, 'Lamaism in the Tibetan Autonomous Region', *Chinese Sociology & Anthropology*, Spring 1994, pp. 61–72.

Nathan, Andrew, *Chinese Democracy. The Individual and the State in 20th Century China*, London: I. B. Tauris & Co. Ltd, 1985.

——, Human Rights in Chinese Foreign Policy', *CQ*, No. 139, 1994, pp. 622–43.

Ngabo, Jigme, 'Behind the Unrest in Tibet', *China Spring Digest*, January/February 1988, pp. 22–32.

Norbu, Dawa, 'G. Tharchin: Pioneer and Patriot', *TR*, December 1975, pp. 18–20.

——, Tibetan response to Chinese Liberation', *Asian Affairs*, No. 24, 1975, pp. 266–76.

——, 'The 1959 Tibetan Rebellion: An Interpretation', *CQ*, No. 77, 1979, pp. 74–100.

——, 'An analysis of Sino-Tibetan relationships 1245–1911: Imperial Power, Non-Coercive Regime and Military Dependency', in Barbara Aziz and Mathew Eapstein (eds), *Sounding in Tibetan Civilisation*, New Delhi: Manohar, 1985, pp. 176–95.

——, *Red Star Over Tibet*, Oriental University Press, 1987.

——, *Culture and the Politics of Third World Nationalism*, London: Routledge, 1992.

——, 'China's Dialogue with the Dalai Lama 1978–90: Pre-negotiation Stage or Dead End', *Pacific Affairs*, No. 64, Vol. 43, 1993, pp. 351–72.

——, 'Tibet in Sino-Indian Relations: The Centrality of Marginality', *Asian Survey*, No. 11, 1997, pp. 1078–95.

Norbu, Jamyang, *Horseman in the Snow. The story of Aten and the Khampas' Fight for the Freedom of their Country*, London: Wisdom Books, 1987.

Norbu, Thupten, *Tibet is My Country*, London: Dutton & Co, 1961.

Nowak, Margaret, *Tibetan Refugees, Youth and the New Generation of Meaning*, Rutgers University Press, 1984.

Olivier, Bernard Vincent, *The Implementation of China's Nationality Policy in the Northeastern Provinces*, Mullen Research University Press, 1993.

Palakshappa, T. C., *Tibetans in India. A Case Study of Mundgod Tibetans*, New Delhi: Sterling Publishers, 1976.

Palden, Nima, 'The Way Out for Tibetan Education', *Chinese Education and Society*, Vol. 30, No. 4, 1997, pp. 7–20.

Paljor, Kunsang, *Tibet: The Undying Flame*, Dharamsala: Information of Office of H.H. the Dalai Lama, 1977.

Panikkar, K. M., *In Two Chinas, Memoirs of a Diplomat*, London: George Allen & Unwin, 1955.

Pant, Girish. P., *Foreign Aid, Economic Growth and Social Cost-Benefit Analysis*, Kathmandu: Avebury, 1991.

Parthasarathi, G. (ed.), *Jawaharlal Nehru, Letters to Chief Ministers, 1947–1964*, New Delhi: Oxford University Press, 1989.

Patterson, George N., *Tragic Destiny*, London: Faber and Faber, 1959.

——, 'China and Tibet: Background to the Revolt', *CQ*, No. 1, 1960, pp. 87–102.

——, *Requiem for Tibet*, London: Aurum Press, 1990.

Peissel, Michel, *Cavaliers of Kham. The Secret War In Tibet*, London: Heinemann, 1972.

Petech, Luciano, *Aristcracy and Government in Tibet, 1728–1959*, Roma: Instituto Italiano per il Medio ed Estremo Oriente, 1973.

Ping, Jiang, 'Great Victory for the Cause of Nationality Unity and Progress', *China's Tibet*, No. 2, 1990, pp. 8–12.

Prados, John, *President's Secret Wars*, NY: Quill, William Marrow, 1988.

Prouty, Fletcher, *The Secret Team. The CIA and Allies in Control of the United States and the World*, NY: Prentice-Hall, Inc., 1973.

Pye, Lucian W., 'China: Ethnic Minorities and National Security', in Nathan Glazer and Daniel Moynihan (eds), *Ethnicity, Theory and Experience*, Harvard University Press, 1975.

——, 'Reasssessing the Cultural Revolution', *CQ*, No. 108, 1986, pp. 597–612.

Qi Yan, *Tibet – Four Decades of Tremendous Change*, Beijing: New Star Publishers, 1991.

Rato, Khyongla, *My Life and Lives: The Story of a Tibetan Incarnation*, New York: E. R. Button, 1977.

Renelagh, John, *The Agency, the Rise and Decline of the CIA*, London: Weidenfeld & Nicolson, 1986.

Ribhur Trulku, *Search for Jiwo Mikyoe Dorjiee*, Dhramsala: The Office of Information & International Relations, 1988.

Richardson, Hugh, *Tibet and its History*, Boulder: Shambhala, 1984.

——, 'General Huang Mu-sang at Lhasa', *Bulletin of Tibetology*, No. 2, 1977, pp. 31–5.

Richardson, Hugh (ed.), *Adventures of a Tibetan Fighting Monk*, Bangkok: The Tamarind Press, 1986.

Rigg, Robert B., *Red China's Fighting Hordes*, Harrisburg, 1951.

Robinson, Thomas (ed.), *The Cultural Revolution in China*, University of California Press, 1971.

Rose, Leo E., *Nepal: Strategy for Survival*, University of California Press, 1971.

Rose, Leo E., and Eric Gonsalves, *Towards a New World Order; Adjusting India–US Relations*, Institute of East Asian Studies, University of California, 1992.

Rosett, Arthur, 'Legal Structure for Special Treament of Minorities in the People's Republic of China', *Notre Dame Law Review*, No. 66, 1991, pp. 1503–27.

Rositzke, Harry A., *The CIA's Secret Operation*, New York: Reader's Digest Press, 1977.

Rustomji, Nari, *Sikkim. A Himalayan Tragedy*, India: Allied Publishers Ltd, 1987.

Saklani, Girija, *The Uprooted Tibetans in India*, New Delhi: Cosmo Publications, 1984.

Sakya, Jamyang, and Julie Emery, *Princess in the Land of Snow. The Life of Jamyang Sakya in Tibet*, Boston: Shambhala, 1990.

Samuel, Geoffrey, *Civilized Shamans, Buddhism in Tibetan Societies*, Smithsonian Institution Press, 1993.

——, 'Tibet as a Stateless Society and Some Islamic Parallels', *Journal of Asian Studies*, Vol. 41, No. 2, 1982, pp. 215–29.

Scalapino, Robert A. (ed.), *Elites in the People's Republic of China*, University of Washington Press, 1972.

Schoenhals, Michael, 'Original Contradiction: On the unrevised text of Mao Zedong's "On the correct handling of contradictions among the people" ', *Australian Journal of Chinese Affairs*, No. 16, 1986, pp. 99–111.

Schram, Stuart (ed.), *Authority Participation and Cultural Change in China*, Cambridge University Press, 1973.

Schurmann, Franz, *Ideology and Organisation in Communist China*, University of California Press, 1968.

Schwartz, Ronald. D., 'Reform and Repression in Tibet', *Telos*, No. 80, 1989, pp. 7–25.

——, 'Travellers Under Fire: Tourists in the Tibetan Uprising', *Annals of Tourism Research*, No. 18, 1991, pp. 588–604.

Schwarz, Henry G., 'Language Policies towards Ethnic Minorities', *CQ*, No. 12, 1962, pp. 170–82.

Sen, Chanakya, *Tibet Disappears*, New Delhi: Asia Publishing House, 1960.

Seyfort Ruegg, 'MCHOD YON, YON MCHOD and MCHOD GNAS/ YON GNAS: On the Historiography and Semantic of a Tibetan Religio-Social and Religio-Political Concept', in Ernst Steinkellner (ed.), *Tibetan History and Language*, Wein 1991, pp. 440–53.

Sha Zhou, 'What Is the Essence of the Strasbourg "Proposal"?', *China's Tibet*, Vol. 1, No. 1, 1990, pp. 3–5.

Shakabpa, W. D., *Tibet: A Political History*, Yale University Press, 1967.

Shakya, Tsering, 'The Genesis of the 17 Point Agreement: An analysis of the Sino-Tibetan Agreement of 1951', in Per Kvaerne (ed.), *Tibetan Studies, Proceeding of the papers presented at the 6th Seminar of the International Association for Tibetan Studies*, Oslo: The Institute for Comparative Research in Human Culture, 1994, pp. 754–93.

——, 'Whither the Tsampa Eaters', *Himal*, Vol. 6, No. 5, 1993, pp. 8–11.

——, '1948 Trade Mission to United Kingdom. An Essay in honour of Tsipon Shakabpa', *TJ*, Vol. XV, No. 4, 1990, pp. 97–114.

——, 'Tibet and the League of Nations', *TJ*, Vol. X, No. 3, 1985, pp. 48–56.

——, 'China's New Religious Policy', *TR*, Vol. XIV, No. 11, 1983, pp. 9–12.

Shang, Jiali, 'Load-Bearing Capacity of Tibetan Land Resources', *Tibetan Studies*, No. 2, 1990, pp. 124–39.

Shao, Kuo-kang, 'Chou En-lai's Diplomatic Approach to Non-aligned States in Asia: 1953–1960', *CQ*, No. 78, 1977, pp. 324–39.

Sharlho, Tseten Wangchuk, 'China's Reform in Tibet: Issues and Dilemmas', *Journal of Contemporary China*, Vol. 1, No. 1, 1992, pp. 34–60.

Sharma, Troloki Nath, 'The Predicament of Lhasa Muslims in Tibet', *Journal of the Institute of Muslim Minority Affairs*, Vol. 10, No. 1, 1989, pp. 23–7.

Shue, Vivienne, 'The Fate of the Commune', *Modern China*, Vol. 10, No. 3, 1984, pp. 259–83.

Singh, Amar Kaur Jasbir, *Himalayan Triangle. A Historical Survey of British India's Relations with Tibet, Sikkim and Bhutan. 1765–1950*, London: The British Library, 1988.

——, 'How the Tibetan Problem Influenced China's Foreign Relations', *China Report*, Vol. 28, No. 3, 1992, pp. 261–89.

Smith, Warren, 'China's Tibetan Dilemma', *The Fletcher Forum of World Affairs*, Vol. 14, No. 1, 1990, pp. 77–86.

——, *Tibetan Nation, A History of Tibetan Nationalism and Sino-Tibetan Relations*, WestviewPress, 1996.

Snow, Edgar, *Red Star Over China*, NY: Random House, 1938.

——, *The Long Revolution*, London: Hutchinson & Co, 1973.

Solinger, Dorothy, *Regional Government and Political Integration in Southwest China, 1949–54. A Case Study*, University of California Press, 1977.

Spence, Jonathan D., *The Search for Modern China*, London: Hutchinson, 1990.

Sperling, Elliot, 'Red Army's First Encounter with Tibet Experiences on the Long March', *TR*, Vol. XI, No. 10, 1976, pp. 11–18.

Stein, R. A., *Tibetan Civilization*, London: Faber and Faber, 1972.

Stoddard, Heather, 'The long life of rDo-sbis dGe-bses Ses-rab rGya-mcho (1884–1968)', in Helga Uebach and Jampa L. Panglung (eds), *Tibetan Studies, Proceedings of the 4th Seminar of the International Association for Tibetan Studies*, Munich: 1985, pp. 465–71.

Strong, Ann Louise, *When Serfs Stood Up in Tibet*, Peking: New World Press, 1960.

Su Jia, *Freedom of Religious Belief in Tibet*, Beijing: New Star Publishers, 1991.

Subba, Tanka, *Flight and Adaption. Tibetan Refugees in the Darjeeling-Sikkim Himalaya*, Dharamsala: LTWA, 1990.

Subranhmanyam, K., *India's Security. The North and North-East Dimension*, London: The Centre for Security and Conflict Studies, 1988.

Surkhang, Wangchen Gelek, 'Government, Monastic and Private Taxation in Tibet', *TJ*, No. 1, 1982, pp. 21–40.

——, 'The 6th Panchen Lama', *TJ*, No. 1, 1983, pp. 20–9.

——, 'The Discovery of the 14th Dalai Lama', *TJ*, No. 3, 1983, pp. 37–45.

Takla, T. N., 'Notes on Some Early Tibetan Communists', *TR*, Vol. 11, No. 17, 1969, pp. 7–10.

Taring, Rinchen, '*Daughter of Tibet*', London: John Murray, 1970.

Tarling, Nicholas, *China and Its Place in the World*, Auckland: Blackwood & Janet Paul, 1967.

Teiwes, Frederick. C., *Politics & Purges in China: Rectification and the Decline of Party Norms 1950–1965*, M. E. Sharpe, inc., Dawson, 1979.

Terrill, Ross., *Mao, A Biography*, New Delhi: Harper & Row, 1980.

——, *The White Boned Demon: A Biography of Madam Mao Zedong*, William Morrow and Company, Inc. 1984.

Thierry, François, 'Empire and Minority in China', in Gerard Chaliand (ed.), *Minority Peoples in the Age of the Nation-State*, London: Pluto Press, 1989, pp. 76–99.

Thomas Jr., Lowell, *Out of this World: To Forbidden Tibet*, New York: Avon Publications, 1954.

——, *The Silent War in Tibet*, New York: Doubleday & Company, 1959.

Tideman, Sander, 'Tibetans and Other Minorities in China's Legal System', *Review of Socialist Law*, No. 14, 1988, pp. 5–45.

Tiley Chodag, *Tibet: The Land and The People*, Beijing: New World Press, 1988.

Trungpa, Chogyam, *Born in Tibet*, Boulder: Shambhala, 1977.

Tsou, Tang, *The Cultural Revolution and Post Mao Reforms. A Historical Perspective*, The University of Chicago Press, 1988.

Ulanhu, 'Report on the General Program for the Implementation of Regional Autonomy for Nationalities', *Chinese Law and Government*, Vol. XIV, No. 4, 1981–82, pp. 20–7.

Uprety, Prem. R., *Nepal–Tibet Relations 1850–1930*, Kathmandu: Puga Nara, 1980.

van Ginnekan, Jaa P., *The Rise and Fall of Lin Biao*, London: Penguin Books, 1976.

van Walt van Praag, Michael, *The Status of Tibet. History, Rights and Prospects in International Law*, Boulder: Westview Press, 1987.

Wang, Fu-jen, 'Do away with Feudal Prerogatives of the Explitation by the Tibetan Lamaseries', *JPRS*, No. 1140, 5 Febuary 1960, pp. 17–44.

Wang Furen, and Suo Wenqing, *Highlights of Tibetan History*, Beijing: New World Press, 1984.

Wang Xiaoqing, and Bai Nanfeng, *The Poverty of Plenty*, London: MacMillan, 1991.

Wang Yao, 'Hu Yaobang's visit to Tibet, May 22–31, 1980', in Robert Barnett (ed.), *Resistance and Reform in Tibet*, London: Hurst & Company, 1994, pp. 285–9.

Wangyal, Phuntsog, 'The Revolt of 1959', *TR*, July–August 1974, pp. 24–7.

Welch, Holmes, *Buddhism Under Mao*, Harvard University Press, 1972.

Wen-lin, Chu, 'Peiping's Nationality Policy in the Culture Revolution', Part I, *Issues and Studies*, No. 8, 1969, pp. 12-23; Part 2, *Issues and Studies*, No. 9, 1969, pp. 26–41.

White, Lynn T, *Policies of Chaos. The Organizational Causes of Violence in China's Cultural Revolution*, Princeton University Press, 1989.

Whitson, William, *The Chinese High Command. A History of Communist Military Politics, 1927–71*, MacMillan Press, 1973.

Wiley, Thomas, 'Macro Exchanges: Tibetan Economics and the Roles of Politics and Religion', *TJ*, No. 1, 1986, pp. 3–21.

Wilson, Bryan, *Magic and the Millennium*, London: Paladin, 1975.

Wilson, Dick, *Chou. The Story of Zhou Enlai 1898–1976*, London: Hutchinson, 1984.

Wise, David, *The Politics of Lying: Government Deception, Secrecy and Power*, New York: Vintage Books, 1973.

Woodman, Dorothy, *Himalayan Frontiers, A Political Review of British, Chinese, Indian and Russian Rivalries*, London: Cresset Press, 1969.

Wylie, T. V., 'A Standard System of Tibetan Transcription', *Harvard Journal of Asiatic Studies*, No. 22, 1959, pp. 262–7.

Ya Hanzhang, *The Biographies of the Dalai Lamas*, Beijing: Foreign Language Press, 1991.

——, *The Biographies of the Tibetan Spiritual leaders Panchen Erdenis*, Beijing: Foreign Language Press, 1994.

Yang, Jingren, 'Resolutely Carry Out the Party Central Committee's Instructions and Do the Work in Xizang Well', *Chinese Law and Government*, Vol. XIV, No. 4, 1981–82, pp. 88–105.

Yang, Tsang-hao, 'The Reality of the Power Seizer in Tibet', *Chinese Communist Affairs*, No. 4, 1976, pp. 45–52.

Yang, Zhongmei, *Hu Yaobang. A Chinese Biography*, An East Gate Book, M. E. Sharpe, 1988.

Yuan, Shan, 'The Dalai Lama and 17-Article Agreement', *China's Tibet*, No. 1, 1991, pp. 21–6.

Yufan, Hao, and Zhihai, 'China's Decision to Enter the Korean War: History Revisted', *CQ*, No. 121, 1990, pp. 94–115.

Yuthok, Dorje Yudon, *House of the Turquoise Roof*, New York: Snow Lion Publications, 1990.

Zhang Jianghua, and Wu Chongzhong, 'Tibet's Menba Nationality', *China Reconstructs*, No. 7, 1979, pp. 54–5.

Zhang Tianlu, and Zhang Mei, 'The Present Population of the Tibetan Nationality in China', *Social Sciences in China*, Vol. XV, No. 1, 1994, pp. 62–4.

Zhou Enlai, 'Report on the Question of the Boundary Line Between China and Burma', in *Selected Works of Zhou Enlai, Vol. 2*, Beijing: Foreign Language Press, 1989, pp. 245–52.

——, 'Questions Relating to Our Policies Towards China's Nationalities', *Selected Works of Zhou Enlai, Vol. 2*, Beijing: Foreign Language Press, 1989, pp. 253–78.

Ziring, Lawrence (ed.), *The Subcontinent in World Politics. India; its Neighbours, and the Great Powers*, New York: Praeger, 1982.

Tibetan Language Sources

Ka-shod chos-rgyal nyi-ma, 'dam-gzhung gnam-gru 'bab-thang gsar-skrun skabs kyi gnas-tshul rjes-dran byas-pa, SCHT, 1983, Vol. 2, pp. 164–80.

——, ngas byas-pa'i don-chung zhig, SCHT, 1985, Vol. 3, pp. 71–81.

Ke'u-tshang sprul-sku 'Jam dpal ye shes, ma-bltas kun-gyis mthong-ba skyid-sdug gi myong-bya, Sermey Printing Press, Karnataka, India.

Kun-bzang dpal-'byor, bsregs-kyang mi-'tshig-pa'i bod, Tibetan Cultural Printing Press, Dharamsala, 1971.

bKras-mthong Thub-bstan chos-dar, dge-'dun chos-'phel-gyi lo-rgyus (Biography of Gedun Chophel), LWTA, Dharamsala, 1980.

Khe-smad bSod-nams dbang-'dus, rgas-po'i lo-rgyus 'bel-gtam (Old man's story), LTWA, Dharamsala, 1982.

Khren Han-khru'u yi, spyi-tshogs ring-lugs-kyi lo-rgyus mdo-tsam brjod-pa (A Brief History of Socialism), Nationalities Publishing House, Beijing, 1986.

Khreng tse kre, chab-mdo sa-khul bcings-'grol btang-ba'i dmag 'thab, SCHT, Vol. 1, 1982, pp. 211–54.

rGyal-mtshan, rgya'i btson-khang nang Bod-mis sdug-sbyong ji-ltar btang-ba'i don-dngos lo-rgyus, Bod-gzhung snar-thang par-khang, Dharamsala, 1992.

rGyal-mtshan phun-tshogs, nga mdo-spyi'i las-byar bskyod-skabs-kyi gnas-tshul 'ga'-zhig, SCHT, Vol. 9, 1986, pp. 13–29.

Nga-phod Ngag-dbang 'jigs-med (Ngabo Ngawang Jigme), rang-skyong-ljongs mi-dmangs 'thus-tshogs rgyun-las-kyi kru'u-rin nga-phod ngag-dbang 'jigs-med kyi rang-skyong ljongs-kyi skabs lnga-pa'i mi-dmangs 'thus-mi'i tshogs- 'du-thengs gnyis-pa'i-thog gnang-ba'i gal-che'i gsung-bshad, (Speech by Ngabo Ngawang Jigme at the 2nd Plenary Session of the 5th Tibet Autonomous People's Congress) 1989.

Cang Tse-rmin, krung-hva mi-dmangs spyi-mthun rgyal-khab dbu-brnyes-nas lo bzhi-bcu 'khor-bar rten-'brel zhu-ba'i tshogs-chen thog-gi gtam-bshad, Beijing Nationalities Publishing House, 1989.

Chos-dbyangs, mi dmangs bcings-'grol-dmag dang thog mar 'brel-ba byas pa'i myong-tshor 'gai-zhig, SCHT, 1990, Vol. 11, pp. 226–39.

Nyag-rong A-brtan, nga'i mi-tshe'i lo-rgyus, Dharamsala, 1982.

Ta'-la'i bla-ma, ngos-kyi yul-dang ngos-kyi mi-dmangs (Autobiography of 14th Dalai Lama), Dharamsala, 1962.

sTag lha phun tshog bkra shii, mi-tshe'i byung-ba brzhod-pa, bod-kyi dpe-mzhod khang, 1994.

Teng Zha'o-phin (Deng Xiaoping), dus-skabs gsar-pa'i nang-gi 'thab-phyogs gchig-gyur-dang mi-dmangs chab-gros-kyi las-don.

bsTan-'dzin rgyal-mtshan, lha'u rta-ra'i lo-rgyus (Account of Lhawutara), LTWA, Dharamsala, 1988.

Thub-bstan sangs-rgyas, rgya-nag-tu bod-kyi sku-tshab don-gcod skabs-dang-gnyis tshugs-stangs skor-gyi lo-rgyus thabs-bral zur-lan zhes-bya-ba dge'o, LTWA, Dharamsala, 1982.

Dung-dkar Blo-bzang 'phrin-las, Bod-kyi chos-srid zung-'brel-skor bshad-pa. krung-dbyang mi-rigs dpe-skrun-khang, Beijing Nationalities Publishing House, 1983.

rDor-gdan Blo-bzang tshe-ring, gzhis-rtse-nas shel-ding-bar gzhung-lam gsar-bzo byas-pa'i skor, SCHT, 1984, Vol. 4, pp. 208–14.

rNam-gling dpal-'byor 'jigs-med, mi-tshe'i lo-rgyus-dang 'brel-yod sna-tshogs (Autobiography of Namseling), LTWA, Dharamsala, 1988.

Bar-gzhis ngag-dbang bstan-skyong, rang-gzhung dbus sman-rtsis khang-gi 'gan-'dzin phyag-rogs sku-ngo rtse-mgron bar-gzhis ngag-dbang bstan-skyong mchog-nas sman-rtsis slob-phrug rnams-la de-sngon phyi-lo 1959 lor lha-ldan rgyal-sar rgya-dmar-nas drag-shugs btsan-'dzul-gyis zing-'khrung ji-ltar bslangs-stangs-dang rtse-skor gzhung-zhabs-sogs gsang-ba'i sgrig-btsugs thog-nas rgyal-ba'i sku-phyva-dang bstan-srid bde-thabs-skor zhi-drag-gi thabs-byus 'gan-'khur ji-ltar bkyed-bzhes gnang-stangs-sogs lo-rgyus gsung bshad. (A lecture given by Barshi Ngawang Tenkyong to the students from Tibetan Medical Institute [Dhramsala], on his involvement in the 1959 revolt against the Chinese).

Byams-pa, zing-slong jag-pas shang dga'-ldan chos-'khor dgon-nas mtshon-cha 'don-'khyer byas-skor, SCHT, 1985, Vol. 5, pp. 222–9.

dBang Ku'i, bod-du-dpung bskyod byed-skabs dge-stag-sprul-sku'i-skor thos-rtogs-byung-ba'i gnas-tshul phran-bu, In bod-kyi lo-rgyus rig-gnas dpyad-gzhi'i rgyu-cha bdams-bsgrigs, 1992, Vol. 5, No. 14, pp. 252–72.

dByin phā thang (Yin Fantang), bod skyod thog-ma'i dus-kyi 'tsham-'dri'i byed sgo

dByin phā thang, Bod-skyod thog-ma'i dus kyi 'tsham-'dri'i byed-sgo zhig dran-gso byas-pa, SCHT, 1983, Vol. 2, pp. 224–50.

dByang dbyi-kren (Yang Jingren), spyi-tshogs ring-lugs-kyi deng-rabs can-du 'gyur-ba'i 'dzugs-skrun byed-skabs-kyi mi-rigs las-don-gyi las-'gan, Beijing, 1990.

lBang shan ma'i, chab-mdo nas lha-sa bar dpung-skyod byas-pa'i gnas-tshul, SCHT, Vol. 1, 1982, pp. 356–79.

Ma'o Tse-tung (Mao Tsedung), krung-gung krung-dbyang-gi bod-ljongs las-ka'i byed- phyogs skor-gyi mdzub-ston, ma'o tse-tung-gi gsung rtsom- bsdus. 1977, Vol. 5, pp. 85–90.

——, krung-go gung-khreng tang krung-dbyang u-yon lhan-khang skabs brgyad-pa'i tshang- 'dzam gros-tshogs thengs gnyis-pa'i thog gi gtam bshad, ma'o tse-tung-gi gsung rtsom-bsdus. 1977, Vol. 5, pp. 468–94.

Wang Shan ma'e, cham-mdo nas lha-sar dpung-skyod byas-pa'i gnas-tshul. SCHT, 1982, Vol. 1, pp. 352–47.

Tse Chun-krin, mnga'-ris gdong-skyod dpung-sde'i "dpa'- bo'i le'n" yi le'n krang le ti san gyi gnas-tshul bkod-pa. SCHT, Vol. 3, 1984, pp. 292–325.

Tsong-kha lHa-mo tshe-ring, sku'i gcen-po lha-sras rgya-lo don-drub mchog-gi thog-ma'i mdzad-phyogs-dang gus-gnyis-dbar chab-srid 'brel-ba byung-stangs skor, Amnye Machen Institute, Dhramsala, 1992.

Zhva-sgab pa dBang-phyug bde-ldan, bod-kyi srid-don rgyal-rabs. (A Political History of Tibet), Vols. 1 & 2, Kalimpong, 1976.

Zhol-khang bSod-rnams dar-rgyas, krung-dbyang sku-tshab bod-du phebs-par phebs-bsu zhus-pa'i zin-tho, In krung-go'i bod-ljongs, 1991, pp. 17–25.

——, krung-dbang sku-tshab krang cing wu'u bod la thog-mar phebs skabs ngas sne-shan du bskyod-pa'i skor-gyi gnas-tshul 'ga'-zhig, SCHT, 1986, Vol. 9, pp. 133-59.

Ya' Han-krang, pan-chen bod-du phyir-pebs la srungs-skyob zhus-pa'i dran-gso", SCHT, 1982, Vol. 1, pp. 280–341.

Yang dbyi-kran, bod-dmag khul-khang thog-mar 'dzugs skabs dang "mi-dmangs tshogs-'d' zer-ba rdzus-mar 'thab-rtsod byas-pa' gnas-tshul, (Establishment of Tibet Military Command and struggle against the bogus People's Organisation), SCHT, Vol. 9, 1986, pp. 58–85.

Li Wu'e-hen, bod mi-rigs la bcings-'grol 'thob-thabs kyi 'grol lam, SCHT, Vol. 1, 1982, pp. 7–50.

Lu'o Yus-hung, bod zhi-bas bcings-'grol skor-gyi nyin-tho gnad-bshus, (Diary of Peaceful Liberation of Tibet), SCHT, Vol. 1, 1982, p. 120–72.

Sa-byang Tshe-brtan rnam-rgyal, gzhis-rtse sa-khul-gyi "mi-dmangs tshogs-pa" rdzus-ma'i- skor, SCHT, Vol. 4, 1984, pp. 245–55.

Seng-ge dpal-ldan, bkras-mthong ci'i 'jigs-med mchog la dran-gso zhus pa, SCHT, Vol. 9, 1987, pp. 30–1.

Shan-kha-ba 'Gyur-med bsod-nams stobs rgyal, rang-gi lo-rgyus lhad-med rang-byung-zangs (Autobiography of Shankawa Gyurme Sonam Tobgyal), Dharamsala.

bSam-'grub pho-brang bsTan-'dzin don-grub, mi-tshe'i rba-rlabs 'khrags-po, privately published, Rajpur, 1987.

lHa klu Tshe dbang rdo rje, mi-dmangs bcings-'grol dmag lha-sa bca'-sdod byas-rjes, SCHT, Vol. 1, 1982, pp. 342–55.

——, bod kyi lo-rgyus rig-gnas dpyad gzhi'i rgyu cha bdams bsgrigs

(Autobiography of Lhalu Tsewang Dorje), Vol. 7, No. 16, 1993,

lHa'u rta-ra Thub-bstan bstan-dar, bod zhi-bas bcings-'grol 'byung-thabs skor-gyi gros-mthun don-tshan bcu-bdun-la ming-rtgas bkod-pa'i sngon-rjes-su. SCHT, Vol. 1, 1982, pp. 88–117.

——, gros-mthun don-tshan bcu-bdun' la ming-rtags bkod-pa dang lag-len bstar-rgyu'i skor gyi gnas-tshul, SCHT, Vol. 9, 1986, pp. 44–57.

Hu'u Ya'o pang (Hu Yoabang), blo-mthun hu'u ya'o pang-gis bod-ljongs-kyi las-don skor-gyi bzhugs-mol tshogs-'du'i thog gnang-ba'i gsung-bshad (Speech by comrade Hu Yaobang during the 2nd Tibet Work Conference), 1984.

Hren Ha'o Yi, mi-rigs sa-khongs rang-skyong bca'-krims skor-gyi dri-ba dris-lan (Questions and Answers on laws relating to Autonomous regions), Beijing Nationalities Publishing House, 1987.

A-lo chos-mdzad (Alo Chonzed), bod-kyi gnas-lugs bden-rdzun sgo-phye-ba'i lde-mig zhes-bya-ba (The Key that opens the door to truth to the Tibetan situation), privately distributed, 1983.

krug-hva mi-dmangs spyi-mthun rgyal-khab-kyi rtsa-khrims (The Consititution of PRC), Nationalities Publishing House, Beijing, 1954.

rGyal-yongs mi-dmangs 'thus-mi tshogs-chen mi-rigs u-yon lhan khang, mi-rigs sa-skyong-gi bca'-khrims skor-gyi gdam-shad, Nationalities Publishing House, Beijing, 1985.

dus-skabs gsar-pa'i mi-rigs las-don skor-gyi tshad-ldan yig-cha bdams bsgrigs.

mi-rigs sa-khongs ran-skyong bca'-khrims skor-gyi dri-ba dris-lan.

gsar-brje'i dran-tho, 1959–1989, bod-du dmangs-gtso'i bcos-bsgyur byas-nas lo sum-cu 'khor-bar rten-'brel zhu, bod-ljongs mi-dmangs dpe-skrun-khang, 1989.

'od-zer ldan-pa'i 'gro-lam, gzengs-su thon-pa'i grub-'bras, bod zhi-bas bcings-'grol btang-nas lo bzhi-bcu 'khor-bar dran-gso zhu-ba.

dus-skabs gsar-pa'i mi-rigs las-don skor-gyi tshad-ldan yig-cha bdams-bsgigs, rgyal-khab-kyi mi-rigs don-gcod u-yon lhan-khang dang krung-gung krung-dbyang tshad-ldan yig-cha zhib-'jug khang-gis bsgrigs, mi-rigs dpe-skrun-khang, Beijing, 1990.

bod-kyi lo-rgyus rags-rim g'yu-yi phreng-ba, bod-ljongs spyi-tshogs tshan-rig khang-nas sgrig-rtsom byas pa, bod-ljongs bod-yig dpe-rnying dpe-skrun khang-nas bskrun, 1991.

bod-ljongs sphyi-bshad, bod-ljongs mi-dmangs dpe-skrun-khang, Lhasa.

zhing-las-dang grong-gseb-kyi las-don-la gom-gang mdun-spos-kyis shugs-snon rgyag-rgyu'i skor-gyi krung-gung krung-dbyang-gi chod-don, TAR People's Publishing House, 1992.

Index